SOUTHERN BIOGRAPHY S
WILLIAM J. COOPER, JR.

Alexander H. Stephens of Georgia

Alexander H. Stephens

of Georgia

A BIOGRAPHY

THOMAS E. SCHOTT

LOUISIANA STATE UNIVERSITY PRESS
BATON ROUGE AND LONDON

Designer: Diane B. Didier
Typeface: Linotron Sabon
Typesetter: G & S Typesetters, Inc.
Printer: Thomson-Shore, Inc.
Binder: John H. Dekker & Sons

LIBRARY OF CONGRESS CATALOGING-IN-PUBLICATION DATA

Schott, Thomas Edwin, 1943–
    Alexander H. Stephens of Georgia.

    Bibliography: p.
    Includes index.
    1. Stephens, Alexander Hamilton, 1812–1883.
2. Confederate States of America—Vice-Presidents—
Biography.   3. Georgia—Governors—Biography.
4. Legislators—United States—Biography.
5. United States. Congress. House—Biography.
6. Confederate States of America—Politics and
government.   7. Georgia—Politics and government—
1775–1865.   I. Title.
E467.1.S85S36   1987   973.7′13′0924 [B]   87-12487
ISBN 0-8071-1373-5

Several of the illustrations are reproduced courtesy of Robert G. Stephens, Jr., member of Congress, 1961–1977, representing the Tenth District of Georgia, and great great-nephew of Alexander H. Stephens.

Frontispiece: Alexander H. Stephens as a congressman in 1858, at the height of his power. Courtesy Special Collections Division, University of Georgia Libraries.

For Susan, Tanya, Stu, and Ben
and for Vic Galier, who still lives

Contents

Illustrations

Abbreviations

AHS	Alexander Hamilton Stephens
JLS	John Lindsey Stephens
LS	Linton Stephens
DU	Duke University Library, Durham, North Carolina
EU	Emory University Library, Atlanta, Georgia
GDAH	Georgia Department of Archives and History, Atlanta, Georgia
UG	University of Georgia Library, Athens, Georgia
HSP	Historical Society of Pennsylvania, Philadelphia, Pennsylvania
LC	Division of Manuscripts, Library of Congress, Washington, D.C.
MDAH	Mississippi Department of Archives and History, Jackson, Mississippi
MC	Manhattanville College of the Sacred Heart, Purchase, New York
NA	National Archives, Washington, D.C.
SHC/NC	Southern Historical Collection, University of North Carolina Library, Chapel Hill, North Carolina
TU	Tulane University Library, New Orleans, Louisiana

Preface

Little Aleck Stephens became part of my life over thirteen years ago, when on a whim I picked him as a subject for a graduate school paper. Little did I realize that this intense little Georgian, dead more than a hundred years now, would capture me for such a long time and that eventually I would find myself trying to bring him to life again in words. It's an impossible task, of course. "Biographies," Mark Twain reminds us, "are but the clothes and buttons of the man—the biography of the man himself cannot be written."

Nonetheless I have tried, although the "man himself"—that most profound of mysteries—sometimes proved elusive. With our modern tendency to merge the man into the mass, we often lose sight of any one individual's extraordinary complexity. I have tried simply to tell the story of one individual, a basically decent and high-minded man caught up in the great drama of sectional controversy and civil war. Southerner, Whig, Democrat, slaveowner, unionist, Confederate, defender of individual liberties, racist: Stephens was all of these. But labels don't explain him. He always hewed his own course, although he was no more able than most of us to transcend the limits of his time and place.

In many ways Stephens was typical, a representative man in a society being wrenched violently into the modern age. As with all southern politicians of the middle period the defense of slavery constituted the *sine qua non* of Stephens' political existence. Stephens' tragedy as a public man was one he shared with all southern politicians: they were compelled to defend the indefensible. Defending slavery extracted a high price from him. It besmirched his moral vision and blinded him to the demands of prudence. It corrupted his conception of truth and justice. It brought out the worst in him, stifling in its imperious insistence almost all the instincts of his better nature.

In the end his struggle was fruitless, as it had to be. Slavery, a horrifying blotch on the American democratic experiment and an even worse one on the nation's pretensions to equality, was doomed, doomed by forces far stronger than its defenders with all their guile and skill could contain. And in the end, too, Stephens, a man who revered order and the rule of law above all, had to witness secession and war. To him these were excursions into madness, the unleashing of men's dark passions, the very forces of violence and destruction he feared with all his soul—and yet had done so much to abet.

But Stephens' own personal tragedy ran even deeper. Gifted with a fine mind and a sensitive, generous nature, he was also plagued with a freakish appearance and a profusion of physical ailments against which he struggled throughout his life. He was always trying to prove his manhood, hiding his pain and loneliness under a mantle of self-righteous pride. Money meant nothing to him. Nor did fame or power in and of themselves. What Stephens craved was recognition, acknowledgment of his superiority in the only field upon which nature allowed him to compete: the realm of politics. He pursued nothing in life more assiduously than this recognition, and nothing proved more elusive. No honor, no amount of money or fame ever tempered his craving for it. Nothing short of universal adulation for his superior gifts ever would have. People loved and respected him for his essential goodness, not his ideas. But for him, this was never enough.

He was not a brilliant man. His thinking was conventional and unimaginative, not creative or original. Stephens' world was Georgia, a white man's world, a world in which the natural gradations among men, black and white, had been fixed long before his birth. It was an ordered, safe, predictable world, in which honor was the supreme virtue and talent and industry would earn rewards. He never questioned these assumptions; he held to them tenaciously all of his days. They defined his politics, his notion of liberty, and his views of justice.

The law, especially the law embodied in the federal Constitution, stood as the majestic source of all Stephens held dear. The law preserved order; it guaranteed as well as limited liberty; it dispensed justice. The law was grounded in immutable, glittering truth, which—as Stephens never ceased to congratulate himself for—he had discerned very early in life.

But life, the grubby reality, the real truth that he and the rest of mankind experienced, was not orderly or just. It was capricious. It was filled with suffering and death and ugliness. It seemed subject to no law at all. Every day of his own life made a mockery of all of Stephens' glorious abstractions. And yet he endured and, in the end, even came to peace with it.

Acknowledgments

Without doubt, this book would have never been done but for the generous assistance I received from many people. Archivists and librarians at Louisiana State and Duke universities, the University of Georgia, and the Georgia Department of Archives and History were particularly helpful. Evelyn Edwards of Crawfordville, Georgia, not only provided an excellent tour of Liberty Hall and answered many questions but personally escorted me through the woods and brambles to view the Stephens family graveyard.

My uncle Matthew J. Schott of the University of Southwestern Louisiana and his wife, Leah, assisted with the manuscript in its early stages. So did my friends and colleagues at Louisiana State University: Robert A. Becker, an eagle-eyed editor who always asked the right questions, and John L. Loos, long a trusty guide who has delighted me with his wry humor and enlightened me with his wisdom. The late T. Harry Williams of Louisiana State University, my patient, generous, and respected mentor through graduate school, was much more to me than teacher. He was my friend, and his impress is on this work in countless places.

Robert G. Stephens, Jr., of Athens, Georgia, former congressman and great great-nephew of Alexander Stephens, generously allowed me to use several photographs from his private collection to illustrate this book.

Dr. J. Michael Lee of Oklahoma City offered me invaluable assistance in analyzing Stephens' medical history and in evaluating the effect of Stephens' health on his personality. My Air Force history compatriot J. Dillard Hunley generously lent his incisive editorial skills to the reading of the manuscript. His questions and suggestions have improved this study throughout.

Joseph G. Dawson of Texas A&M University and George C. Rable of Anderson College also read the manuscript and offered many, sometimes extensive, critiques of both style and interpretation. Both have been generous in sharing with me the fruits of their own research and experience. Much more valuable, however, was the honor of their friendship and their constant encouragement. My debts to them, which stretch back over years, can never be repaid.

The editor of this series, William J. Cooper, Jr., of Louisiana State University, helped spur my initial interest in Stephens over thirteen years ago. Since then he has been a constant source of help. He read and critiqued every draft of the manuscript, bringing his vast knowledge of the nineteenth-century South to bear on this book in numerous places. Without his enthusiasm for this work and his unflagging faith in its author from that time till now, this book would never have been written.

Trudie Calvert, my editor for the Louisiana State University Press, edited the manuscript with thoroughness and skill. Her diligence improved the manuscript in numberless places.

My friend Vic Galier, who battled cancer with undaunted courage, good humor, and faith while I worked on this book, was a constant source of inspiration to me. Vic died in December, 1986, and it is my honor to remember him in the dedication of this work.

My wife, Susan, daughter, Tanya, and sons, Stu and Ben, not only bore the burden of living with Little Aleck Stephens but also the one of living with me—heavy burdens in either case. Their love has made everything possible.

Alexander H. Stephens of Georgia

I

A Child of Despair

It's just a short drive down an orange-red dirt road. On the right, not far, is an empty, weather-beaten shack of undetermined age, its roof partially caved in. After crossing a couple of rickety plank bridges, the road swings off to the right. A few hundred yards more and you have to stop and go on foot—up a small embankment, through some strands of rusty, sagging barbed wire and into dense, dark woods. After struggling through the vines and thorny brambles, you finally come to a crumbling stone wall, moldy and gray with age. The wall encloses the Stephens family graveyard, an area all but indistinguishable from the surrounding forest but for the tombstones poking out of the undergrowth and fallen trees. Only a few shafts of sunlight have struggled through the trees to reach here.

This is where Alexander Stephens wished to be buried—in this dark and lonely place beside his father and mother, his grandfather, and his brother Aaron. He did not get his wish. His body lies two miles to the south, back down that orange-red road, beside an imposing monument in front of the house he lived in for almost fifty years. And beside him there lies Linton, the brother he dearly loved.

Solitary, sad walks brought Stephens often to this lonely spot in the woods—cleared ground then—to stand at these graves, musing, remembering his boyhood and his father, pondering the mysteries of time and fate and what ravages they made of a man's hopes and fame. And as often as not, here beside these graves, he would weep.

Alexander Stephens never knew the grandfather whose name he bore. He was an infant in 1813 when the old Scot, aged eighty-seven, died. Had he been born earlier, he might have heard the old man's stories of having fought for Charles Edward Stuart, the Young Pretender, in the second Jacobite Rebellion of the mid-1740s—a cause as lost as the one his grandson would fight for—of the flight from England after the battle of Culloden Moor, of life among the Shawnees on the Pennsylvania frontier to which he had fled, and of his colonial militia service in the Great War for Empire and in the Revolution on the patriot side. Perhaps, too, the old man might have told his wide-eyed listeners how he wooed and, in 1766, married Catherine Baskins, a Pennsylvania ferryman's daughter, and how in the early 1790s he and Catherine with their eight children—three sons and five daughters—moved to Georgia, the southernmost state of the new American Union. They came first to Elbert County and then to a plot of rented land on the banks of Kettle Creek in next-door Wilkes County.[1]

Alexander's father, Andrew B. Stephens, was the only son to remain in Georgia. Four of the daughters married and also left, leaving Andrew and his sister Jane alone with their father to tend the farm. (Catherine Baskins Stephens, Alexander's paternal grandmother, died in 1794.) Fortunately for the old warrior, his son Andrew was cut from a different bolt. Guns held little attraction for him. Instead, he liked to farm—and he liked books. Andrew's aptitude for learning prompted his father to spare him from the plow whenever possible and send him to the nearest field-school. Andrew progressed quickly; by the time he was ten years old he had outgrown this frontier hall of learning. So at some sacrifice, Alexander Stephens enrolled his son in Reverend Hope Hull's Methodist Academy at Washington, the county seat—for its time, we are told, a "famous school."[2]

---

1. James Z. Rabun, "Alexander H. Stephens, 1812–1860" (Ph.D. dissertation, University of Chicago, 1948), 1–5; Richard Malcolm Johnston and William Hand Browne, *Life of Alexander H. Stephens* (Philadelphia, 1878), 17–19; Rudolph Von Abele, *Alexander H. Stephens: A Biography* (New York, 1946), 21–23. Family documents are in Lucian Lamar Knight and Mrs. Horace M. Holden, *Alexander H. Stephens, The Sage of Liberty Hall: Georgia's Great Commoner* [Athens, Ga., 1930]; and Martha F. Norwood, *Liberty Hall, Taliaferro County, Georgia: A History of the Structures Known as Liberty Hall and Their Owners from 1827 to the Present* (Atlanta, 1977).
2. Johnston and Browne, *Stephens*, 19.

Young Andrew performed so brilliantly there that when it came time for Hull to recommend a schoolmaster for a proposed school at the far end of the county, he unhesitatingly nominated Andrew for the job. The committee of inquiring gentlemen, not to mention Andrew himself, must have been surprised at Hull's choice. The boy was only fourteen years old. Andrew accepted the job, and with his earnings from his first year's teaching and his bond for the balance, he bought a hundred acres of land near the future site of Crawfordville. In time, he moved his father and sister to the property, and upon his marriage on July 12, 1806, he brought his bride there too.

The bride's name was Margaret Grier, daughter of Aaron Grier, a descendant of a clan that had been in Georgia since the 1760s. Andrew's courtship of Margaret, like everything else he did, was studied and proper. In this, too, he was unlike his father, who, the tale goes, was smitten by Catherine Baskins the minute he saw her on her father's ferry and won her despite her father's opposition and threats of disinheritance. Andrew had a different style. He impressed his future in-laws, if not with his fortune (it was strictly in a state of potency at the time), at least with his probity.[3]

Andrew and Margaret moved into a rude log house about fifteen miles southwest of Washington in the Georgia Piedmont, the wide, fertile belt of red loam soil running from northeast to southwest across the heart of the state. Sandwiched between the rocky, mountainous region to the north and the sandy, flat pine tree barrens to the south, middle Georgia is rolling country. Pretty and inviting in its lush greenness today, it must have also been so to its first settlers, who, pushing down from Virginia or the western Carolinas in the late 1700s, took advantage of the state's generous headright land grants, cleared the land, and laid in crops of grain, tobacco, and Indian corn.

But by the time Andrew Stephens settled down to farm what his celebrated son would call the "old homestead," cotton had permanently altered the economic life of Wilkes County. Eli Whitney's gin had turned green-seed upland cotton into a profitable export crop. The red soil of middle Georgia, like the inexpensive black slave labor soon pouring onto it, was admirably suited to its cultivation. Like a spill of white paint, cotton washed across the countryside—into Oglethorpe, Greene, and Morgan counties and beyond, pausing only

---

3. The preceding paragraphs are based on *ibid.*, 19–20, and Rabun, "Stephens," 7–8.

long enough to enable the whites to vacate the Indian titles. Here and there cotton made a few men rich; some eventually became rich enough to number their acres in thousands and their slaves in hundreds. Rich enough, too, to make a large planter conspicuous, enviable, and politically powerful in a society composed largely of middling yeoman farmers.

These yeomen were, and would remain, the backbone of middle Georgia society, and in 1806, they still set its tone. Most of them owned and farmed their land. Some owned a few slaves; most did not. Few had attended school; fewer still had attained Andrew Stephens' educational heights. Rough-hewn, hardworking people, they most admired the strong among them, those quick with fists or skilled with gun and knife. A man such as Andrew Stephens, the schoolmaster, had strength of a different kind—he was quiet, even-tempered, pious, and upright. Such a man deserved respect.[4]

Stephens earned the respect and admiration of his children, too. Margaret soon presented him with three: Mary, Aaron Grier, and, in the early morning hours of February 11, 1812, Alexander. Little is known of Alexander Stephens' mother. Her son later described her as mild, intelligent, and gentle, but not very strong. He never knew her, for within months of his birth she died. The infant son, like his mother, was frail and sickly. And so he remained for the rest of his life.[5]

With three small children, a farm to work, and a school to teach, the sensible father lost no time in finding another wife. In 1813 Stephens married Matilda Lindsey, daughter of Colonel John Lindsey, a revolutionary war veteran of some means. Young Aleck admitted that "there never did exist much filial affection" between him and his stepmother. Just why, he did not know—or would not say. Perhaps she scolded him, or was strict, or, worse, beat him for reasons he deemed insufficient. But his father was strict too, and on occasion would wield a memorable strap for serious infractions of his exacting standards of conduct. Whatever the cause of the coolness between them, Alexander rarely spoke of his stepmother.[6]

4. The preceding paragraphs are based on Enoch Marvin Banks, *The Economics of Land Tenure in Georgia* (New York, 1905), 15; Robert Preston Brooks, *The Agrarian Revolution in Georgia* (Madison, 1914), 83; Ralph Betts Flanders, *Plantation Slavery in Georgia* (Chapel Hill, 1933), 60ff.

5. AHS to LS, February 9, 1853, in Stephens Papers, MC.

6. AHS MS Diary, April 19, 1834, in Stephens Papers, LC.

It seems clear that Matilda Lindsey exerted a powerful, albeit un-known, effect on her stepson's life. Previous biographers have dis-missed her, being content to characterize Stephens as his father's son. This view is understandable given the plethora of evidence on the father's influence. But even this evidence demonstrates that the young boy was impressionable, and Matilda was an everyday presence in his life for thirteen years. That he *does not* mention her is extremely sug-gestive. This fact, coupled with his prudishness, his puritanical view of sex, his abhorrence of the carnal side of man's nature, his impatience with and condescension toward the innocent diversions of dancing and flirtation—as well as his utterly romanticized view of women, and his peculiar, to say the least, relationships with them ("I never was a ladies man, and I never expect to be," he wrote at the ripe old age of twenty-two)—could indicate something more than the effect of a stern and pious father on a sensitive or even excessively religious son. Matilda's influence on Stephens may at least partially account for his strange distrust of the passions he and the rest of mankind were born with. She may have been a passionate, sensual woman or, conversely, even more upright and pious than her husband. It is certain that as a boy Stephens often felt misunderstood and mistreated. On the death of his aunt Mary in 1851, he remarked that she had been the "only per-son . . . in my boyhood that seemed to *understand* me and to sym-pathize with me. She never *seemed* to me to think I was a bad boy." Apparently Matilda Lindsey often did. The only concrete evidence we have of Stephens' life with his stepmother is his mention of childhood whippings. And he did not remember those fondly.[7]

But he cherished his father's memory. He spoke and wrote of him often, grieved for him on each anniversary of his death, and consciously patterned his own conduct on what he could remember of his father's. "The principles and precepts he taught me have been my guiding-star through life," he wrote. "Even now the thought often occurs to me: I wonder what my father thinks of this?" Long after he was buried,

7. AHS to LS, December 26, 1851, in Stephens Papers, LC; AHS to M. Liddell Bar-ron, May 7, 1834, in Stephens Papers, EU. On sex, passions, weakness of women, and dancing, see AHS MS Diary, May 23, September 7, 1834, in Stephens Papers, LC; on the passions of the young ("a great deal of near *animal* in its composition"), see AHS to LS, April 27, 1850, in Stephens Papers, MC; on his romantic views of love and marriage, see his letters of advice to his niece Mary Stephens, January 30, February 28, 1858, in Ste-phens Papers, DU.

Andrew Stephens remained a spectral presence in his son's life, a model to live by, and yet withal, an eerie and forbidding presence, in Stephens' words, "a ghost of . . . admonition" astride the path of his life.[8]

As a youth, Andrew Stephens had been robust; age had brought white hair, neuralgia in the back, and severe earaches. But even then, gray-eyed and erect, he cut a purposeful appearance as he sharpened his plows or skillfully grafted the trees in his fruit orchards. He took pride in his labor and independence, and he impressed on his children the worthiness of honorable industry to advance one's fortune. (There were plenty of children to impress—eight in all, five by Matilda Lindsey: four sons, John L., Andrew B., Benjamin F., and Linton, and a daughter, Catherine. Two of the boys, Andrew and Benjamin, died at birth.) A humorless man with a serious mien that mirrored the cast of his mind, Andrew Stephens took greatest delight in his farm and work. A skilled craftsman like many of his neighbors, equally adept at carpentry, masonry, tanning, and leatherworking, he would have been content to spend all his time on his farm. For though he loved reading and writing, he did not like teaching. Only the entreaties of his neighbors, who had no one else to call on, induced him to endure the peculiar tortures of attempting to educate a roomful of frontier moppets.[9]

Teaching, he believed, was a duty. And duty he took seriously—duty to God above all. "The thoughts of Death, Immortality, invisibi[lity a]nd Eternity are mostly on my mind," he once wrote. "And above all I hope we'll meet with JESUS." His less devout neighbors soon discovered that swearing or ribald stories within his earshot brought a swift rebuke, and that a friendly Sunday afternoon visit earned them a front row center seat to a sermon reading. It was a foolproof way, Andrew had discovered, of dispersing unwanted Sunday guests and keeping the sabbath holy.[10]

But his neighbors forgave these quirks. In the first place, he often set a far better example of Christian behavior than they did. And he was always available to share with them his skills with the pen: writing their letters, notes, contracts, or deeds. Their children loved him too,

8. AHS to LS, February 9, 1853, in Stephens Papers, MC.

9. "Peter Finkle" [AHS] to "Mr. Giles" [Richard M. Johnston], November 11, 1863, in Johnston and Browne, *Stephens*, 33.

10. A[ndrew] B. Stephens to Mrs. Jane B. Jones, November 10, 1824, in Stephens Papers, LC; "Finkle" to "Giles," November 11, 1863, in Johnston and Browne, *Stephens*, 33.

despite his unusual manner in the classroom. Indeed, his manner was what probably endeared him to them.[11]

Had it been imagined, hazardous duty pay for southern field-school teachers in the early nineteenth century might have been a worthwhile innovation. The practice of "turning out," physically keeping a teacher out of school until he declared a holiday, was a universal prank. And the rule of the rod, however efficacious for the advancement of knowledge, exerted a tenuous and always challengeable discipline, its effectiveness decreasing in direct proportion to the size and belligerence of the recalcitrant scholar. With such working conditions and the generally miserable pay that went with them, the teaching profession rarely attracted high-quality practitioners. It was part-time work, and few children attended school for more than three or four months of the year, two or three years of their lives.

Andrew Stephens was molded differently than most field-school teachers. Unlike "old Nat Day," Alexander's first teacher, a gentleman as quick to quaff a dram as raise the switch, he abhorred drinking. However tried, he rarely lost patience with his raw young pupils, rarely scolded, pulled ears, or employed the rod. Somehow, by the force of his personality alone, he managed to keep order and, no doubt, impart the rudiments of spelling, reading, and manners (this last being his own addition to the usual curriculum) to his students. No less important were the virtues he attempted to instill: "sobriety, morality, industry, energy, and honor." Ever after his students remembered him with fondness.[12]

Alexander Stephens did not sit in his father's class until he was eight years old. But his father's at-home influence was pervasive; we can be sure that by that time the boy had been well instructed in the principles of righteous living. As a farm youngster, he performed the usual chores his feeble strength allowed: hauling water and manure, digging the garden, shooing away the calves at milking time, driving the cattle, and tending sheep. He shepherded the younger children, too, as the human flock in the household grew. Not strong enough to plow until he was eleven, he had long since, he says, become an expert corn-dropper, able to seed a moist, red furrow as fast as any plowman could turn it.[13]

11. AHS to LS, January 1, 1860, in Stephens Papers, MC.
12. "Finkle" to "Giles," November 17, 1863, in Johnston and Browne, *Stephens*, 38.
13. *Ibid.*, April 12[?], 1863, 30–31.

Except for three months at Nat Day's school in 1818, Alexander had no formal education until 1820. In that year and for the next four, he attended his father's schools about three months out of the twelve. At the end of his first term, he memorized and recited an address on charity by Hugh Blair, a Scottish divine, to the crowd at the school "exhibition," a gala affair that gave young scholars a chance to parade their oratorical talents. Blair's address, he wrote later, made a deep impression on him. Evidently, considering the future contours of his thinking. It contained the "sentiments of Job." [14]

Until the summer of 1824, however, Alexander evinced no great interest in learning. A momentous change occurred one bright Sunday morning. With a Bible in one hand and his father's strong grip on the other, he took his place in the Sunday school class at Powder Creek meetinghouse. Young Stephens was entranced. Books had captured a hostage for life. He lay awake reading far into the nights, sprawled beside the pine knot fire, enthralled by the Old Testament stories. His reading improved rapidly, and before his class was out of Genesis he had finished the Old Testament. His astonishing progress in Bible class, a fact much remarked upon by his peers and betters alike, had several important effects on the boy. First, it whetted an appetite for reading and for history. More important, it stirred from slumber an ego heretofore "very timid and self-distrustful, bashful and afraid" of asserting itself. "It gave me reputation," he wrote. And the taste of reputation, startlingly new then, he found exceedingly pleasant. [15]

Two years later came yet a greater turning point in Stephens' life. On May 7, 1826, Andrew Stephens, forty-four years old, contracted pneumonia, lapsed into a coma, and died. Aleck knew his father was sick. Only about a week before, Andrew had told his son he was dying. But the young boy could not comprehend it when, rushing in from the plow at a desperate summons, he arrived breathless beside his father's bed. He stood there for hours, unrecognized, listening to the delirium, the low moans, the labored, rattling breathing. And when that breathing finally stopped, he knew he had seen death, the end. [16]

14. Myrta Lockett Avary (ed.), *Recollections of Alexander H. Stephens: His Diary Kept When a Prisoner at Fort Warren, Boston Harbor, 1865; Giving Incidents and Reflections of His Prison Life and Some Letters and Reminiscences* (New York, 1910), 290–91.

15. "Finkle" to "Giles," [May 1863?], in Johnston and Browne, *Stephens*, 43.

16. AHS to LS, September 22, 1845, in Stephens Papers, MC.

His grief was boundless. Oblivious to a weeping friend who vainly attempted to console him, Stephens threw himself on the grass and rolled over and over. Consolation was impossible. Even tears were impossible. In an image aptly conveying the searing of his mind and soul, he later wrote, "My eyes were as dry as if scorched in the fire." Many times Stephens tried to put into words what had happened to him that day, and he always admitted that words failed him. The copious tears he shed later on remembering the death he had witnessed testified much better to his grief. Words, even his own, were a pitiful substitute: "The heart of my own soul ceased to beat. The light of my life went out. Despair! Despair! Despair!" Fourteen-year-old Stephens had tasted yet another emotion. This one, too, would become part of his nature.[17]

To describe Alexander Stephens as congenitally melancholy is merely to characterize, to label him. His despondency and fits of morbid depression, his preoccupation with death, destruction, and decay were habitual. But they were also a way of defining himself, of putting himself into an awful cosmic scheme, which decreed for him life with constant bodily suffering and death, the inscrutable end, for one after another of those he loved. Because he tried so hard to fathom this mystery and failed, Stephens became a child of despair. He trod the edge of the eternal abyss, sometimes with fear, often with haunting wonder—and sometimes, too, with ill-disguised longing.

Stephens' melancholy is complex—terrifying in intensity, fascinating in expression, and bewildering in texture. Perhaps it is fruitless to search for the source of this despondency. But one cannot but be struck by the centrality of death in his despair—as perhaps it must be in any despair. Stephens' desperation had many layers, but at its heart lay death, his father's death on a springtime morning in 1826. "With that last breath my last hope expired," he wrote. "Everything looked dreary; life seemed not worth living, and I longed to take my peaceful sleep by my father's side."[18]

A week later the Stephens children were orphans. Matilda followed her husband to the grave, a victim of the same disease. "It was the consumation of my woes," said Stephens. Not because his stepmother had died but because now the children would be scattered. Alexander and

17. *Ibid.*, December 31, 1852.
18. AHS MS Diary, April 19, 1834, in Stephens Papers, LC.

Aaron went off to Raytown in Warren County to live with their uncle Aaron Grier and his sister Elizabeth. The children of the second marriage, John, Catherine, and Linton, were parceled out to relatives of their mother.[19]

Andrew Stephens was not rich, but twenty years of assiduous labor on his farm had improved his fortune. His farm encompassed 230 acres, worth about $2,300, and he had acquired nine slaves, appraised at between $1,700 and $1,900. Personal property of the estate brought $934.49 at public auction. The slaves were hired out for three years and then divided by lot among the children. Alexander received Ede, a female valued at $300. Although the share for each eventually amounted to about $627, the children realized immediately only about $186 apiece.[20]

Fortunately, Uncle Aaron and Aunt Betsey allowed the Stephens boys free room and board in exchange for farm work. Later that summer both enrolled in a Roman Catholic school in Locust Grove. Since chores occupied much of their time, they attended sporadically. But during the fall of 1826, the first of Stephens' fortuitous benefactors crossed his path. His name was Williams, a Presbyterian minister come to Raytown to establish a Sunday school. On a social call at the Grier farm, he met Aleck. Both the boy and his aunt thought the Sunday school a fine idea, so Alexander accompanied Williams on his recruiting trips around the neighborhood. The minister soon recognized his young companion as a kindred spirit. Alexander, always serious-minded, had become even more so since his father's death—and increasingly religious. Brooding on the state of his soul occupied much of his time.[21]

The Sunday school soon boasted an excellent scholar, young Stephens. Like his father, he was soon promoted to teacher. Besides excellence in biblical studies, the boy evinced other noteworthy characteristics: piety, gravity, and an inclination toward melancholy—excellent qualifications, his observant elders thought, for a minister.

Stephens, too, had been wondering about his future, and it did not look promising. He liked school but had had to beg his uncle for the time to complete the term. Uncle Aaron now urged him to quit school and hire on at the farm permanently. For Aleck, this was out of the

19. AHS to LS, December 31, 1852, in Stephens Papers, MC.
20. Norwood, *Liberty Hall*, 58. Estate papers are in *ibid.*, Appendix B, 193–200; Rabun, "Stephens," 20n.
21. AHS MS Diary, April 19, 1834, in Stephens Papers, LC.

question. Farm labor was physically impossible for him. Only desk work would suit—perhaps he might get a clerkship in a store, save some money, and then continue his studies, he thought. Meanwhile, it would be wasteful to stay in school without studying for a profession.[22]

Learning that this promising youngster aspired to nothing more than tending store, Charles C. Mills, superintendent of the Sunday school, suggested that Stephens go to the academy at Washington, Georgia, and study Latin. Money would be no problem; he would provide it. Stephens fancied this arrangement, but such a step would require consultation with his guardians. Uncle Aaron was indifferent, content to let Aleck make up his own mind; Aunt Betsey urged him to accept the offer. He did, and on July 28, 1827, arrived at the comfortable home of Alexander Hamilton Webster, minister of the Presbyterian church at Washington. Webster and Mills knew each other well, of course, and though Stephens didn't know it at the time, Webster had suggested Washington Academy for the boy.[23]

Washington, fifty-three miles northwest of Augusta on the road to Nashville, was a pretty, prosperous little town. County seat and home for about eight hundred people, it had a branch of the state bank, a courthouse "with an excellent clock," a jail, three Protestant churches, and several imposing homes. Amid these pleasing surroundings, Stephens began his study of Latin and geography. After only three weeks with Latin grammar, he had progressed enough to be placed in a reading class. *Historiae Sacrae* proved no great obstacle either; his biblical studies had prepared him for it. By the end of September, having led his class, he began a new term with *Caesar's Commentaries*.[24]

By this time the lonely youth had become quite attached to his benefactor. Indeed, upon learning Webster's full name from the cover of a book, he adopted "Hamilton" as his own middle name. Webster reciprocated the boy's feelings. Only a few weeks' observation had convinced him that the reports about Alexander were true: the sad, lonesome, and gifted young man of seemingly irreproachable morality was eminently suitable for the ministry. Webster proposed the idea to him.

Confused by this entirely unexpected turn of events, Stephens could

22. *Ibid.*

23. "Finkle" to "Giles," undated, in Johnston and Browne, *Stephens*, 47–48.

24. Adiel Sherwood, *A Gazetteer of the State of Georgia, Containing a Particular Description of the State, Its Resources, Counties, Towns, and Villages* (Washington, D.C., 1837), 48, 251.

not make up his mind what to do. Alluring as the service of God might be, preparation for it would require still more debts. Embarrassed by conflicting emotions, he let the subject lapse for a time. But at the end of the September term, Webster returned to Raytown with him. Aunt Betsey's urging ended Stephens' indecision. He would continue his studies at the academy and then go to Franklin College at Athens under the auspices of the Georgia Education Society to prepare for the ministry. Stephens required only one proviso: if, upon graduation, he felt no call to preach the gospel, it would not be held against him. In any case, he would repay the society, with interest.[25]

No sooner had he returned to Washington when Webster, his beloved patron, died at the age of twenty-six of "a malignant autumn fever." It was yet another numbing blow: a dear friend and a chance to attend at college both snuffed out at once. Sadly, Stephens prepared to leave school. But he had not reckoned on others in the town. Another patron, Adam L. Alexander, one of Webster's closest friends, pledged to carry out Webster's plans for the boy. Several church elders also promised aid should it be necessary. Boarding with successive families about town, Stephens remained in school till June, 1828, when he was adjudged ready for college.[26]

The term at Franklin College did not begin until August. Stephens spent several weeks at home reviewing for the entrance exam. Then he returned to Washington, and, accompanied by a sponsor's son, made the bumpy stage ride to Athens. Another of Webster's friends, Reverend Alonzo Church, then a professor and later president of the college, provided board for him.

On the bright morning of August 2, 1828, Alexander Stephens, Greek Testament and copy of Virgil in hand, arrived at the college chapel for his entrance examination. The oral examinations consisted of translation and parsing. Twenty-nine other hopefuls were already there; Alexander took his place in the last row. What then happened nearly scared him out of several years' growth, which, considering his skeletal appearance—he weighed seventy-four pounds—no doubt would have been fatal.

He thought his review had been sufficient. He was ready for Virgil, conversant with the Testament. A hush fell as Moses Waddell, the col-

25. "Finkle" to "Giles," undated, in Johnston and Browne, *Stephens*, 50–51.
26. Rabun, "Stephens," 24–25.

lege president, and Church entered and assumed their imposing places before the assembly. The examinations commenced. To his horror, Stephens discovered that he would be quizzed on Cicero. He was not prepared for this. He thought he might bluff through the orations against Catiline, which he knew but had not reviewed, but a hastily borrowed and frantically scanned text convinced him that the passages he was hearing would be impossible. He would fail and be humiliated. As Stephens sweated in agonized suspense, the recitals advanced toward him. Three orations against Catiline were reached and passed before his turn came. "Next!" He stood up. "On the next page," growled Waddell, "beginning with the words *video duas adhuc.*"

Fate had given him a passage about capital punishment, a subject that interested him. He recognized it immediately as the only one in the book he knew perfectly. He read like a Roman. Waddell pushed up his spectacles; everybody else stared. His examiner's half-audible compliment sang in his ears as he sat down in triumph. The afternoon was anticlimactic: he easily disposed of the assigned passage in the Greek Testament. That evening at dinner Stephens answered a smiling question from Professor Church. Yes, he had been scared; he had not expected Cicero. But he kept silent about his fantastic stroke of luck. Indeed. Why, with the unvarnished truth, should he dim the luster on the beginnings of a bright reputation?[27]

Franklin College, twenty-six years old in 1828, had been on the verge of extinction when Moses Waddell arrived in 1818. Waddell, until then master of a well-known academy in South Carolina, was a minister who disciplined with rigor, and under his tutelage the reputation and enrollment of the college improved dramatically. One hundred students attended when Stephens arrived, up from a mere seven ten years before.[28]

The Oconee River murmured peacefully at the bottom of the hill upon which perched the campus buildings: the president's house, two large brick buildings known as the Old and New Colleges, a chapel, a dining hall, and a "two story brick building housing the grammar

27. The preceding paragraphs are based on "Finkle" to "Giles," October 13, 1863, in Johnston and Browne, *Stephens*, 55–56, and Avary (ed.), *Stephens Recollections*, 277–79.

28. A. L. Hull, *A Historical Sketch of the University of Georgia* (Atlanta, 1894), 34–35.

school." Backing up to the campus, its entrance appropriately on Front Street, was the Presbyterian church of Athens, its Doric columns and gothic windows in keeping with the town's many "elegant" dwellings.[29]

The "seat of literature" had grown with the college. Counting the students, Athens was home for 1,100 people, 583 whites, the balance black. "A genuine ease and gentility of manners" characterized these people, even though they did consider themselves a cut above the rest of Georgia in taste and refinement. As well they might, for Athens was home for several prominent Georgia families: the Cobbs, the Lumpkins, the Doughertys, and the Claytons. It was an agreeable little town in which to receive one's education.[30]

The staple of that education was New England classicism: Latin (Virgil, Horace, Cicero, Caesar) and Greek (Xenophon, Homer, and of course the Greek Testament) dispensed in increasingly intoxicating or nauseating doses, according to one's point of view. Courses in moral philosophy, geography, literature, composition, logic, natural philosophy, and Christianity provided variety. But even this variety was mandatory; all students followed the same curriculum. Classes for all but seniors began before breakfast. Students also had to contend with a formidable array of rules and regulations, all enforced by roving professorial patrols. Heinous immoralities like fornication, dueling, robbery, blasphemy, forgery, and striking a professor were, of course, unforgivable; their commission merited expulsion. But the law also provided penalties for innumerable other infractions, from profanity to cockfighting. Moreover, the students' spiritual welfare was strictly monitored. The rules required Sunday church attendance and prayer twice daily.[31]

Stephens found this regimen, if not completely congenial, at least palatable. Consistently at the top of his class throughout his four-year term, he never once received a demerit from either the college or the Phi Kappas, his literary society. He naturally got along well with the faculty, but he was popular with the students too. His room became the "resort" for many of them. There, good-natured bantering alternated with serious conversation and with other treats: "fruit, melons,

---

29. E. Merton Coulter, *College Life in the Old South* (Athens, Ga., 1951), 34; Sherwood, *Gazetteer of Georgia*, 112–13.
30. Coulter, *College Life*, 211.
31. *Ibid.*, 59–64, 80.

and . . . nicknacks of the season," which Stephens thoughtfully provided out of his meager budget. As befitted a student for the ministry,
Stephens allowed no "dissapation" in his room—no cards, liquor, or
dirty jokes. But his rectitude proved to be no obstacle to his association with the "most dissapated" and "ascetically pious" students alike.
Stephens enjoyed his popularity, and he got to know well men who
would later figure prominently in Georgia history—Howell Cobb,
John Lumpkin, Herschel V. Johnson.[32]
Doubtless the most dissipated didn't find membership in either
of the two campus literary societies, the Phi Kappa Society or the
Demosthenians, rewarding. These clubs obviously appealed to the less
frivolous, for at their secret Saturday morning meetings they debated
questions of philosophy, history, logic, literature, current politics, and,
of course, religion and morality. Should a man be forced to marry a
woman he had seduced? Did God display His wisdom or power in
creation? Office in the Phi Kappa Society was the only position of
honor Stephens actively sought. He was twice elected president, a rare
honor.[33]
Oratory, like salt pork and fresh vegetables, was a staple in the
nineteenth-century southerner's diet. Both art and entertainment, it
instructed and exhorted, insulted and defamed. Oratorical displays, in
the grandiloquent and prolix style of the day, were ubiquitous. Any
gathering larger than ten people called for a speech or two, and larger
gatherings, like college commencements or political meetings, occasioned elocutionary orgies. To meet these challenges, the up-and-
coming young men of Franklin College honed their rhetorical skills
every Saturday. The frequent debates and oratorical displays the literary societies staged quickened in Stephens a lasting interest in ar-
gumentative discourse and philosophical disquisition. Here also he
began developing the public speaking skills destined to make him
famous as an orator. And for the first time, he became interested in
politics. The controversial Andrew Jackson occupied the White House,
and his audacious strokes in the capital generated no end of rhetorical
controversy.[34]

32. "Finkle" to "Giles," October 13, 1863, in Johnston and Browne, *Stephens,*
56—57.
33. Rabun, "Stephens," 31.
34. Coulter, *College Life,* 103—33.

But other, more pressing questions required Stephens' examination, questions he later called "skeletons" in his house. Had he really received a call from God? How would it appear to accept charity from the Georgia Education Society only to forego entrance into the ministry at graduation? For two anxious, uncomfortable years Stephens wrestled with these questions. Finally, he decided. He would obtain his two hundred dollars patrimony from his uncle, borrow more from his brother Aaron, and cut free of his obligation to the society. His jealous regard for his reputation as an honest man allowed no other course. His religious feelings remained strong in a quiet, serious way, but the pulpit was not his destiny.[35]

Stephens graduated from Franklin College in August 1832, first in his class. Suddenly he made a disquieting discovery: there was much he did not know, nor did he believe others knew much either. This leap in logical progression no doubt violated several rules he had recently been forced to learn. Nevertheless, he "thought the time opportune to discant a little upon the *ignorance* of the learned," and he delivered the graduation salutatory on "the Imperfection of Science."[36]

Stephens took no joy in graduation. The normally happy event only increased his melancholy because it destroyed the artificial society in which he had occupied a respected, conspicuous position. Many of his close friends were sons of wealthy planters, the scions of southern society. In college, wrote Stephens, "there were no distinctions but of merit." By this measure, to Stephens a perfectly just and natural one, he had accepted as his due his "extensive influence" and "considerable character in the opinion of all." But now all this was ending—the friendships, "the libraries, the gardens, the societies" were memories now, prologues to a cheerless future.[37]

With wretched envy he watched the splendid carriages carry off his friends, "released from all restraints" to vacations at the springs or in the mountains. The last lesson he had learned in college was no abstract one he could "discant a little upon" before a large commencement crowd. It was a private and painful one: "Money . . . regulates human society and appoints each his place."[38]

35. "Finkle" to "Giles," October 13, 1863, in Johnston and Browne, *Stephens,* 57–59.
36. AHS to LS, June 5, 1842, in Stephens Papers, MC.
37. AHS MS Diary, April 19, 1834, in Stephens Papers, LC.
38. *Ibid.*

All the honors, esteem, and respect he had earned at Franklin weighed little on the scale that mattered most in human affairs. He was venturing into the world a poor man, and the thought tortured him. All his fame, his accomplishments, his self-esteem settled like the red dust in the road behind those fine carriages. At age twenty, with his life before him, Alexander Stephens was miserable.

11

Made to Figure in a Storm

The day after graduation, August 2, 1832, Stephens arrived in Madison, a little town twenty-seven miles southwest of Athens in Morgan County. While still in college, he had arranged with Leander A. Lewis, the headmaster of the local academy, to come there and teach. The next four months, said Stephens, were "the most miserable . . . of my life." [1]

Although monotonous, teaching was not what made him miserable. But he *had* to teach to eat, and this rankled. The idea that he had been destined for something other than this insignificant position nagged him continually. Nor was his bitterness mollified by his being a stranger in town, or by realizing that Madison offered nothing approaching the intellectual stimulation of Athens. No one could share his sorrow, so he would rise early (he and Lewis boarded together in an upstairs room at the local lawyer's house) and trudge one or two miles out of town down the Athens road, weeping in solitary wretchedness. [2]

To assuage his grief Stephens threw himself completely into his work, a remedy that soon became habitual. The school's fifty-odd students were a hodgepodge by any description: boys and girls, four years old to "grown-up," at all levels of scholastic attainment. Often the

1. "Finkle" to "Giles," November 4, 1863, in Johnston and Browne, *Stephens*, 66.
2. *Ibid.*, 67.

teachers arrived early and stayed late, taking a two-hour noon break. Like his father, Stephens enjoined a strict moral code upon his students and also enforced rigorous standards of classroom behavior. By an early, judicious application of the rod, he soon secured perfect order in his half of the class.[3]

Despite his scrawniness, Stephens had an abundance of physical courage. His applying the rod to these students—many his superior in size and strength—was the first of many instances in which he seemed compelled to prove it. This was an understandable trait in a man so puny, shaped by a society that put a premium on physical prowess. But Stephens' courage, unfortunately, was more often than not foolhardy. He could not tolerate the idea of being mistaken and would rather fight than admit his limitations.

These, too, he had in abundance. He always viewed the rest of humanity from a lofty perch, a position to which he firmly believed his moral and mental attributes had assigned him. It became easy, therefore, to question everyone's motives but his own, to minimize his shortcomings and exaggerate others', and to strike an irritating pose before his fellow men as a paragon of righteousness. Rooted in his exalted estimation of his own rectitude, Stephens' pride grew to monumental proportions. And yet his pride could not shield him from the judgment of others. His sensitivity to their indifference, to slights real or imagined, was obsessive, corrosive, and painful.

"Oh what have I suffered from a look! . . . from the tone of a remark! . . . from a supposed injury!" he once wrote. Such slights "brought out the latent fires," forcing him to prove his worth, to demonstrate his superiority. They were the wellsprings of his ambition, the source not only of his energy but of much that was execrable in his character. Stephens never sought to hurt or humiliate men, only to compel their recognition of his own value. "To get above them to excel them, to enjoy . . . seeing them feel that they were wrong . . . to command their admiration for my own superior virtues," he explained, "was the extent of my ambition." He never wanted to "trample the *vile crew*" or "to punish them for their follies." Power for its own sake never drove Stephens, nor did position. But he craved, indeed required, the recognition that went with both. Recognition was life's blood to him. And his need for it both drove and blinded him.[4]

---

3. *Ibid.,* 68.
4. AHS to LS, February 3, 1851, in Stephens Papers, MC.

What caused this crippling sensitivity? It was a combination of factors. In the first place, he looked like a freak. His head was small, with protruding, slightly oversized ears. A pair of blazing black eyes, wide-set on either side of a thin, sharp nose, dominated his ashen countenance. Thin, pale lips turned downward at the corners. His long, bony fingers looked like claws attached to the ends of broomstick arms. Early in his public life someone tagged him with the sobriquet "Little Aleck." The nickname stuck, not because of his height—he stood five feet, seven inches—but because he was so emaciated that he resembled a skeleton, "frail and thin to painful meagerness." Well into his life people mistook him for a child, "a boyish invalid escaped from some hospital," one observer wrote. People always remarked the pallor of his skin: like a corpse's "glued to his frame." Rare was the observer not thunderstruck with amazement upon first seeing Stephens. "What a shock I received," exclaimed an Augusta woman, "as his diminutive size and person bearing the stamp of a reall 'Piney Woods Cracker' first dawned upon my sight." [5]

He looked like anything but a leader who deserved unqualified respect and admiration, and Stephens was painfully conscious of it. By his own description he was "a malformed ill-shaped half finished thing." Nor, in a society exquisitely class conscious, could he forget his embarrassing "Cracker" origins. Though they would later become a source of pride (and a political asset unblushingly flaunted), early in life he writhed under the tortures of social inferiority. So he took refuge in pride, nurturing a self-image that canceled considerations of early poverty, constant ill health, and physical ugliness. And he spent the rest of his life projecting this image to the world. [6]

Stephens' health was his own private plague. Sickly from birth, he contended with a host of ailments throughout his life. The most prominent of these was rheumatoid arthritis, a degenerative and chronic inflammation of the joints that caused him severe pain in his hands, arms, and legs. His arthritis probably also spawned cervical disk disease, which caused a pinched nerve in his upper back or neck. Several times during his life Stephens was prostrated by agonizing pain in his

5. William Dallam Armes (ed.), *Autobiography of Joseph LeConte* (New York, 1903), 32; undated MS speech in Justin S. Morrill Papers, LC; Ella Gertrude Thomas Diary, DU.

6. AHS to LS, June 30, 1838, in Stephens Papers, MC; I. W. Avery, *In Memory: The Last Sickness, Death, and Funeral Obsequies of Alexander H. Stephens, Governor of Georgia* (Atlanta, 1883), *passim.*

face, neck, and teeth. He also suffered from colitis, a recurrent inflammation of the mucuous membranes of the large intestine, a condition that caused frequent abdominal pain, diarrhea, and various digestive ailments. The evidence is fairly clear that Stephens contracted pneumoccocal pneumonia two or three times and almost died from it on each occasion. For most of his life he was extremely sensitive to changes in temperature. The bulk of winter wraps he wore was legendary. He also had bladder stones, which caused him excruciating pain on several occasions during his middle and old age. It is also likely that he developed a heart ailment, probably angina, during his later years. Chronic illnesses aside, Stephens suffered on occasion from migraine headaches, pruritis, and toothache and from the effects of miscellaneous accidents—broken bones, sprains, cuts, and contusions. The most serious accident occurred in 1869, when he permanently damaged the sciatic nerve in his hip. This mishap made him an invalid, unable to walk and barely able to fend for himself in the most mundane tasks.

The state of medical science in the nineteenth century was primitive. Stephens did not rely on doctors regularly until his old age, when he submitted himself to a fantastic array of their ministrations. Stephens also aggravated the effects of his illnesses with alcohol and, late in his life, with morphine and other drugs. Stephens used alcohol medicinally for most of his life, not in great quantity—he took it by the tablespoonful—but habitually. His chronically emaciated condition—he never weighed more than a hundred pounds, and his weight typically stayed between seventy and eighty pounds—and his almost constant sickness would have magnified the effects of even a slight amount of alcohol. Alcohol certainly made his colitis worse. It is uncertain but entirely possible that Stephens was an alcoholic. And he may have become addicted to morphine during the last twelve or fifteen years of his life. Evidence for his use of morphine does not appear until after his 1869 accident, but it plainly indicates that Stephens took the drug by hypodermic often during the 1870s and 1880s and in staggering quantities. Thrice daily doses of seven and a half milligrams of morphine were not unusual. By contrast, doctors today consider five milligrams a substantial dose for the most severe pain.[7]

7. The preceding paragraphs are based on an analysis by Dr. J. Michael Lee of Oklahoma City, Thomas Schott, "The Medical History of Alexander H. Stephens, 1812–1883," unpublished MS. in my possession, and on notes taken during my interview with Dr. Lee on March 25, 1985.

Although his chronic pain doubtless contributed to Stephens' depression and morbidity, he was never hateful, spiteful, or even misanthropic. Proud he might be; cruel and cynical he was not. Because he suffered much, he felt intensely the sufferings of others. He always had a special and touching empathy for the poor, the sick, and the unfortunate, and he became famous for his charity and generosity. He was "indiscriminate" in it, according to Richard Johnston, one of his closest friends. Over the course of his life he paid for the education of almost two hundred young people, about fifty or sixty of them women and some of them black. He found it impossible to refuse almost any ragged beggar on the streets or at his door. Although occasionally insensitive and always vain, he had a capacity for love that endeared him to friends, family, and countless strangers.[8]

Moreover, for all his pride, he recognized the futility of his own hubris. For it was tempered by an acute awareness that, whatever his attainments, he shared mankind's fate. Wealth, glory, honor, fame—all were empty. Men were like bubbles in a running brook, he wrote, destined only to burst without leaving a trace. "The only difference between them is that some become more inflated . . . only however to encircle a larger degree of vanity and emptiness." Death constantly whispered in his ear, and the grave's finality tortured him. But to expose this inner misery to others, thought Stephens, would be like exhibiting a sore. A man must put on as cheerful a face to the world as possible. He could share his pain only with his brother Linton, the single person in his life he trusted enough to confide in fully. So along with sorrow, a profound loneliness also stalked his life. He hid "the spirits preying upon my heart," trying to appear as happy as possible to people "so as not to give them pain by sympathy."[9]

Alexander Stephens was rarely happy. He could not accept the world and human beings as they were. Nor could he believe that mankind would ever improve. To him progress was a delusion; mankind's misery and depravity would never change. Out of step in an age of ebullient optimism about the social and moral elevation of men, he saw only pain, never promise. Only sin, never hope.

Despair of the world he might, hate it he could not. His tender and

8. Nashville *Daily American*, October 6, 1888, clipping in Richard M. Johnston Papers, GDAH.

9. AHS to LS, February 2, 1845, December 24, 1854, July 31, 1857, in Stephens Papers, MC.

humane feelings clashed with his view of the world as a harsh, mean, and cold place. Raging contradictions defined his character. The same man who found the mass of mankind "low, groveling, selfish, and mean" could also describe himself as being of "tender mould" and declare that "the only thing approximating happiness I ever *felt was* in seeing other people happy, and in trying to render them happy." Stephens characterized the antithesis in sinister, eerie terms: "Sometimes my *evil genius jeers* and *taunts* my milk of human kindness, bids me turn *cynick*. . . . Oh the fiendish grins of the tempting imp!" [10]

Stephens constantly battled this malevolent ghoul, sometimes losing a skirmish, but never surrendering the field. However he might scorn men's weakness or condescend to their frailties, he could never completely forsake them. He was too conscious of the evil lurking unseen in himself for that. Deep down he knew he was like everyone else.

One event in Madison poignantly underscored Stephens' loneliness. He fell in love with one of his students. The "young girl lovely both in person and character" flits briefly, silently through his story, unknown but for this cryptic reference. She never knew how Stephens felt. Too shy, poor, and proud, Stephens kept silent—neither she nor anyone else, save one or two of his closest friends, ever learned of his private and unrequited love. [11]

Perhaps she was one of the reasons he left the job. There were others. Work at the academy taxed his endurance. And Stephens was ill; he had begun to experience frequent violent headaches. So on a chilly November night in 1832, Stephens climbed into a buggy with his brother Aaron and left Madison. Bumping through the darkness and into his future, Stephens suffered a blinding headache. [12]

With no time for recuperation, he went almost immediately down to Liberty County in the southeastern section of the state, near Sunbury, the so-called Midland District, to serve as tutor to the children of Dr. Louis LeConte. The year Stephens spent at Woodmanston, his patron's plantation, was one of the quietest of his life. Few people lived in this low, sandy country, and the pace of life was languid. Though his health was little better, Stephens' gloom lifted temporarily. He was

10. AHS MS Diary, April 19, 1834, in Stephens Papers, LC; AHS to LS, February 3, 1851, in Stephens Papers, MC.
11. Johnston and Browne, *Stephens*, 69.
12. "Finkle" to "Giles," November 4, 1863, in *ibid*.

paid well, five hundred dollars a year, and he enjoyed his association with the cultivated LeContes and his thirteen students. One of them remembered fondly how Stephens would strip off his coat and laughingly play ball with them. He remembered also his tutor's "utter detestation of lying, deceit, and meaness of every kind" and "the sense of self-respect and honor" he attempted to cultivate.[13]

Teaching, however, failed to serve Stephens' sense of self-respect. Despite the fabulous inducement LeConte offered him to stay—fifteen hundred dollars a year—he decided to give up teaching. "The sedentary life did not suit me," he explained. By now he had saved enough money to begin studying law, so in January, 1834, he returned to middle Georgia. Originally he planned to read law in the office of a well-known Warrenton attorney, but for some unknown reason he became dissatisfied and left. He spent the next two months wandering around western Georgia, visiting relatives of his stepmother, vainly hoping that travel might improve his health. It was during these ramblings that Stephens first took an interest in his half-brother, Linton, who was only three years old when the family broke up in 1826. Something in the mild, studious lad appealed to him, and the boy reciprocated his feelings. The attachment thus begun would last almost forty years.[14]

Stephens finally settled down in familiar territory, Crawfordville, his boyhood home. A county seat, the town was incorporated in 1826, one year after Taliaferro County had been carved from five surrounding counties. It had a tavern, a jail, two churches, and fewer than thirty dwellings. Its courthouse was about all that distinguished Crawfordville from the nearby villages of Greensboro, Powelton, and Lexington. A crude, new place, home for three or four hundred people, its modest boom time—when the Georgia Railroad laid its tracks through the center of town—still lay a few years in the future. Even then its homes would never equal the splendor of those in Washington, twenty miles to the northeast. Little did Stephens realize in April, 1834, that he himself would put this little town on the map. To this day the fact that he lived here is its only claim to attention.[15]

It cost Stephens twenty-five dollars to set up to study law. The town's only lawyer, Swepston C. Jeffries, was giving up his practice in town

---

13. Armes (ed.), *Leconte Autobiography*, 30–32.
14. Johnston and Browne, *Stephens*, 71.
15. Norwood, *Liberty Hall*, 2–7.

and sold the young aspirant copies of a few basic works. By day Stephens studied his books alone in a small room on the second floor of the courthouse, which the county sheriff provided in exchange for legal advice. He also got some practical experience by assisting the court clerk, Quinea O'Neal, with his duties in an adjoining room. At day's end Stephens would walk the few hundred yards to the home of Williamson Bird, his stepmother's brother-in-law. Bird, a Methodist minister, was also a successful planter, farming the land that once belonged to Stephens' father.[16]

The spring and early summer days settled into a pattern: study, home to read the newspapers ("a passionate fondness," he confessed), conversation with the Birds, an entry in his journal, and back in the morning to the courthouse. Life's slow pace left plenty of time for brooding. And brood he did: about his future, about the poor and ignorant specimens of humanity he met in Crawfordville and how they wasted his time by interrupting his studies, about his low station in the social hierarchy and his burning desire to improve it. But even as he criticized others, he doubted himself. His feelings and hopes, he wrote, constantly vibrated "between assurance and despondency."[17]

Crawfordville's sleepy environment did not portend a glorious future. He found it "a dry place." Nor did he find the "common vulgar" of the town congenial company. He was meant for better things. His ambition, "a desire not [to] stop short of the highest places of distinction," gnawed at him daily like a boreworm. "I must be the most restless, miserable, ambitious soul that ever lived," he concluded.[18]

And as usual, he was pathetically lonely. He felt "unlinked to human society." He loved his friends and cherished any kindness shown him. The "warm affection" of his heart easily moved him to sympathy, but he had no "bosom confidant," no "equal" sharing his tastes and interests. With such a one he could "be happy." He knew he was different from the ordinary men he observed, seemingly content with their humdrum, obscure lives. "I have an independence extending to criminality," he wrote fiercely, "and an amb[i]tion towering as thought."[19]

16. Henry Cleveland, *Alexander H. Stephens, in Public and Private: With Letters and Speeches, Before, During, and Since the War* (Philadelphia, 1866), 42.
17. Johnston and Browne, *Stephens*, 72; AHS MS Diary, May 2, 12, June 9, 1834, in Stephens Papers, LC.
18. AHS MS Diary, May 12, June 9, 1834, in Stephens Papers, LC.
19. *Ibid.*, May 12, June 6, 1834.

The height from which he observed the conduct of Crawfordville's simple folk was also towering. The atmosphere of the town was "polluted," he declared, and on the basis of his extremely limited experience in such matters, he pronounced "sensuality and *sexuality*" the "moving principles of Mankind." He longed to associate with a "mind that soars above the infirmities and corruptions of human nature, that lives . . . in the pure element of truth." The diversions of ordinary people he found "revolting." How was it possible, he marveled, that thinking beings should spend their nights "skipping to an old shreaking fiddle like drunken apes—or longing [*sic*] about a grog shop from morning to eve?" But, he observed philosophically, one shouldn't let his feelings run away with him in such matters. The "error is in nature—it must be pitied, not blamed." And then with unintended self-revelation, he added, "Perhaps I may appear as objectionable and odious to others as others to me." [20]

Stephens rarely had such moments of insight. He complained mostly about others, but he sometimes had "a most contemptible contemptuous opinion" of himself too. Stephens feared he would "never be worth anything," a thought that was "death to his soul." Failing to distinguish himself from "dull" Crawfordville and its inhabitants would forever identify him with what he despised. This is why his ambition raged like a "volcano," "an aching aspiring thirst." A Tantalus in his thirst for recognition, Stephens lacked even the consolation of knowing that he had chosen the right line of work to vault him into prominence. Occasionally Little Aleck could prophesy accurately: "I was made to figure in a storm," he once wrote. Argument and discussion delighted him. "I long to be where I will have an argument daily." [21]

Naturally, then, Stephens found himself drawn irresistibly to law and to its especially American adjunct, politics. Until now he had recorded few political opinions. In 1833 he had written disapprovingly of the gubernatorial triumph of Georgia's pro-Jackson Union party, which was only natural in Taliaferro County, where the anti-Jackson Troup party dominated. But in his journal he had expressed at least a qualified approval of Jackson—condemning his force bill but admiring his removal of deposits from the Bank of the United States, "a reptile" deserving strangulation, according to Stephens. On economic issues, he

20. *Ibid.*, May 23, 1834.
21. *Ibid.*, June 7, 9, 1834.

favored expansion of the railroads, a subject much discussed at the time. The possibility of traveling behind steam engines at a safe and rapid fifteen miles an hour was "stupendous," he thought.[22]

Because politics had begun to interest him intensely, he eagerly responded to the prompting of Dr. Thomas Foster, the town physician, and consented to deliver the Fourth of July address in Crawfordville. After three drafts he was satisfied. The speech he delivered the next day contained the usual paeans to the Founding Fathers, republicanism, democracy, and liberty. But Stephens, ever the pedagogue, also used the occasion to deliver a lecture on states' rights and correct constitutional interpretation.[23]

With the approach of his bar examination, scheduled for July 22, Stephens temporarily put politics aside. He had not studied diligently; between sessions with his law books he had frittered away much time. So in the few days he had left, he crammed like crazy. The night before his examination he hardly slept. Anxious and agitated, he arrived at the courthouse promptly at eight the next morning. The eminent examining committee would have quailed the most self-confident aspirant. Presiding over what would be his last candidate's examination was Judge William H. Crawford, former cabinet member and presidential candidate. Three other distinguished attorneys and politicians rounded out the committee: William C. Dawson, Daniel Chandler, and Joseph Henry Lumpkin. Also attending was a crowd of Stephens' former classmates, neighbors and friends of his father, members of the Crawfordville courthouse gang, and a host of strangers—lawyers and litigants in town for the court session.[24]

Stephens need not have worried. He sailed easily through the oral examination, missing only one question. All his examiners, he noted carefully, complimented him, particularly Lumpkin, who said it was the best examination he had ever heard. Once admitted to the bar, twenty-two-year-old Stephens admitted that a "great burthen of an[x]iety" had been lifted from him.[25]

For all his disparaging comments about Crawfordville, Stephens hated the thought of leaving. The familiar childhood haunts proved

22. AHS to A. W. Grier, December 3, 1833, in Stephens Papers, LC; AHS MS Diary, May 8, June 3, 1834, in Stephens Papers, LC.
23. Rabun, "Stephens," 52.
24. Avary (ed.), *Stephens Recollections*, 362–64.
25. *Ibid.*, 364; AHS MS Diary, July 22, 1834, in Stephens Papers, LC.

more attractive than Swepston Jeffries' offer—a full partnership and a guarantee of fifteen hundred dollars a year in Columbus at the other end of the state. Money might mean power, but Crawfordville was home. Even if practice there yielded only one hundred dollars a year, thought Stephens, it would be better than five thousand dollars somewhere else. (Stephens earned a healthy four hundred dollars his first year in Crawfordville, much more later.)[26]

Most legal practice in Georgia in the 1830s, as throughout the South, took place in the circuit courts of agricultural counties. Litigation, with rare exceptions, dealt with land or slaves, estate settlement, or debt collection. The state had ten circuits, each administered by a single-judge superior court. Inferior courts had five judges. (Georgia did not have a supreme court until 1845.) Court sessions, lasting five days twice a year, took place successively in the county seats of each circuit. Stephens practiced in the northern circuit: Wilkes, Greene, Elbert, Franklin, Columbia, and Oglethorpe counties. It was the most illustrious in the state, containing outstanding lawyers and the state's sharpest politicians—men like Howell Cobb, Charles Jenkins, William Dawson, and Robert Toombs. The nature of the work threw these men into close contact. Friendships—and enmities—formed on the circuit endured for years.[27]

Stephens made such a friendship on his first trip to circuit court. He had been a lawyer for a week when he met Robert Toombs in Washington court. Their professional connection soon blossomed into one of Stephens' closest friendships. Toombs, the fifth son of a well-to-do planter of Wilkes County, was two years older than Stephens. Contemptuous of authority, he had been expelled from Franklin College after several serious infractions. He went on to graduate from Union College in Schenectady, New York, and then spent a year at Virginia Law School, leaving before obtaining a degree. He had been practicing law for four years when he met Little Aleck.[28]

Toombs was everything Stephens was not. A big man, strong and healthy, his huge head elegantly topped with great shocks of dark brown hair, Toombs was gregarious, impulsive, passionate, and rich, a man who grabbed life with both hands and roared in its face if it dared

---

26. Johnston and Browne, *Stephens*, 90; Cleveland, *Stephens*, 43–44.
27. Pleasant A. Stovall, *Robert Toombs: Statesman, Speaker, Soldier, Sage: His Career in Congress and on the Hustings—His Work in the Courts—His Work with the Army* (New York, 1892), 15–16.
28. William Y. Thompson, *Robert Toombs of Georgia* (Baton Rouge, 1966), 3–12.

protest. Boisterous and profane, Toombs also had an enduring fondness for alcohol. As skeptical of religion as Stephens was pious, as convivial and hearty as Stephens was introspective, Toombs was about as prone to melancholy as Bacchus himself.

Bob Toombs would seem to have been the last man on earth to be compatible with Stephens. But their characters formed an almost perfect mesh: opposing—yet complementary—life forces. One was imperious, domineering, and outgoing, the other, controlled, introspective, and studious. Their relationship, both political and personal, became a legend. Other than his wife Julia, upon whom Toombs bestowed a solicitous affection that belied his blustery exterior, Stephens was the only person in the world capable of influencing him. Their disagreements over more than forty years could be numbered on one hand. Toombs, wrote a sensitive observer, loved Stephens with an "almost pathetic" tenderness "and, in all matters of importance, Mr. Toombs came up, in the end, on Mr. Stephens' side."[29]

Like his friend Toombs, Stephens was a good lawyer. The operation of the legal system—with no appeal from a superior court judgment—placed a premium on obtaining jury verdicts. This result required eloquence and persuasiveness, qualities Stephens possessed in abundance. Usually he tried to win over juries by logical exposition of the principles involved in a case. But Stephens succeeded so powerfully as an advocate because he knew when to apply the other tools of his trade. He could be fiery and passionate when the occasion demanded, playing to the emotions rather than appealing to reason.

By all accounts Stephens was an arresting and compelling speaker. His high-pitched, almost feminine voice struck a listener first, and when in top form, Stephens could play it like a lyre: now low and soft in a conversational let-us-reason-together tone, now loud and penetrating, with words and phrases propelled at the audience like bullets. But Stephens had an even more effective tool, an uncanny ability to gauge the quality and temper of an audience and to adjust his manner and argument accordingly. Wherever he spoke—on the stump, in a courtroom, or on the floor of Congress—Little Aleck Stephens commanded undivided attention.[30]

29. Varina Howell Davis, *Jefferson Davis, Ex-President of the Confederate States of America: A Memoir by His Wife* (2 vols.; New York, 1890), I, 410–11.

30. The preceding paragraphs are based on Richard Malcolm Johnston, *Autobiography of Col. Richard Malcolm Johnston* (Washington, D.C., 1900), 103, 113, 142–43.

How much income Stephens later derived from his law practice is difficult to ascertain. According to one observer, three or four thousand dollars a year was a large income for a lawyer, and handsome fees were the exception, not the rule. But the legal business was at least steady, not subject to the vicissitudes of the season as was planting. Good lawyers stayed busy, for prominent citizens were almost always involved in one or more suits. Stephens, a superior lawyer and, once he began public life, a famous one, earned much more from his practice than the typical Georgia attorney.[31]

But prosperous days still lay in the future during the hot summer months of 1834. So little business found its way to Stephens' courthouse office that he began to think about moving west to Alabama or Mississippi. The entire month of August netted him one promissory note for the sum of twenty-five dollars. The first hard cash he received for his services—literally, for it was four silver half dollars—did not materialize until early September. Other than drawing up a few legal documents, Stephens had accomplished nothing as a lawyer. Friends in newer portions of the state started receiving inquiries. Was there a future out there for a sharp young lawyer?[32]

Then came a break. On September 10, a man by the name of James Hilsman came to the office and employed his services. Hilsman was a ne'er-do-well, a besotted drifter, but he needed a lawyer and promised to pay twenty dollars. Upon hearing his story, Stephens took the case. Hilsman's wife, née Amanda Askew, had been a widow when he married her. Her first husband, Uriah Battle, had died shortly after the birth of a daughter. Battle's father, a wealthy Hancock County planter, immediately took out letters of guardianship on the infant. Then Hilsman staggered into the picture and married Amanda. On the basis of his letters of guardianship, the horrified grandfather had the child seized from its mother and carried to his home. Hilsman then appealed to the law to recover custody of his wife's child.

The case excited extraordinary interest in Taliaferro and surrounding counties. The Battles were an extended and influential family, and public opinion was overwhelmingly on their side. When it finally went to trial, a large crowd of area citizens, some from twenty or thirty miles off (for that time a full day's journey), jammed the courthouse.

31. Robert Moses Autobiography (typescript), in SHC/NC, 42.
32. AHS to LS, August 20, 1834, in Stephens Papers, MC.; AHS MS Diary, September 7, 1834, James W. Esby to AHS, September 27, 1834, both in Stephens Papers, LC.

Battle's lawyer was none other than Swepston Jeffries, Stephens' benefactor and a highly regarded attorney. But the younger lawyer would
prevail that day. Although unknown to nine-tenths of the courtroom
crowd, the pale, ghastly thin young man with the piping voice soon
transfixed them with his eloquence on the sanctity of motherhood, the
law of nature that required even forest brutes to fight to the death for
the safety of their offspring. By the time he had finished, most of courtroom, we are told, including the five judges, were in tears. Battle's
letters were set aside. The mother regained custody of her child, and
the case made Stephens' reputation.[33]

But his fame didn't grow fast enough to suit him; he continued to
consider moving out of Crawfordville. For a while he toyed with the
idea of going into newspaper work, writing A. B. Longstreet of the
Augusta *State Rights Sentinel* about possible openings. But restless as
he was, by this time Stephens had become too attached to Crawfordville to seriously consider leaving. About this time Jeffries made him
the offer of a full partnership in Columbus. He refused. He had set his
heart not only on staying but also on buying back his father's old property when the opportunity arose. The "hooks of steel," as he later
called them, that bound him to Crawfordville were already firmly
embedded.[34]

By 1835 Stephens was making a living. Clients were not breaking
down his door, but business was slowly improving. Still the young
lawyer was restive. So in March, Stephens and a small party of friends
took a horseback journey to the wild but rapidly developing western
part of the state and across the border into Alabama. There the party
rode through Creek Indian territory. The "sunken and degraded"
Creeks, Stephens decided, actually surpassed the "heterogeneous mass
of irregular and confused material" that made up the white population
of the state. Finding in Alabama "no uniformity of character" and
"all varieties of morals, dispositions, tempers, and conditions of life,"
Stephens decided something he had probably known all along. He
would rather stay in Georgia.[35]

Evidently this trip gave him a taste for travel, for in the spring of
1836 he went off again—this time to the North on the pretext of investi-

33. The preceding paragraphs are based on Johnston and Browne, *Stephens*, 95–97.
34. Rabun, "Stephens," 59; Avary (ed.), *Stephens Recollections*, 139.
35. AHS MS Diary, May 25, 1835, in Stephens Papers, LC.

gating two pension claims. He departed in May by stage from Milledgeville, Georgia's state capital. The Georgia legislature did not fare any better in his opinion than Alabama's confused material had. The gothic statehouse and its denizens left him singularly unimpressed: it was a "Hall of eloquence, corruption, treachery and bribery," he sniffed.[36]

Stephens arrived at Washington on May 28, 1836, eager for his first brush with national politics. By this time the subject fascinated him. His opinions were already of a Whiggish hue, but like the good Jeffersonian he always claimed to be, he categorically condemned the interstate slave trade as an "abominable, inhuman traffic." In 1835 at least, Stephens had not yet discerned the "positive good" of the institution he would later proclaim as the cornerstone of a glorious southern civilization.[37]

He remained painfully self-conscious of his own poverty, or what he interpreted as poverty. For some uncomfortable minutes on the stage trip—until he struck up a pleasant conversation with them—he squirmed under the gaze of a "lordling nabob" and his lady. In the presence of his social betters Stephens found it difficult to remember his own excellencies. Alone with his journal, though, he reverted to form. Not surprisingly, his first glimpse of the white marble of the Capitol in Washington elicited only contempt. It reminded him of "the whited walls of the sepulcher, fair and white without, but within . . . full of rottenness and corruption." The next day, however, the sepulcher provided the first stop on the agenda, and the Georgia tourist was "dazzled" and "astounded" by its magnificence.

Nor did his fear of finding rottenness and corruption keep him from visiting both houses of Congress. The House disappointed him. Neither the oratory nor the decorum much impressed him. "There is too much attention paid to rant & cant in our country in this age." This chamber, he decided, had little real talent. The proceedings in the Senate pleased him much more. The upper chamber was "dignified." Awed by the sight of so many famous men—John C. Calhoun, Martin Van Buren, Hugh Lawson White (only Henry Clay was missing)—Stephens likened them to "lions," lordly and magnificent in their contempt for "the chattering . . . little tribe of monkey[s], apes, [and] baboons around them." Daniel Webster, Stephens decided, was his favorite lion.

Congress inspected, private citizen Stephens paid a visit to the presi-

36. *Ibid.*, May 27, 1836.
37. *Ibid.*, October 27, 1836.

dent of the United States. The way this was done in 1835 strikes the modern American, accustomed to an unapproachable president insulated from the people by layers of functionaries and security agents, as almost unbelievable. Stephens simply went to the White House and asked to speak to Andrew Jackson. After a short wait, he was shown into a large room. The Old Hero, dressed in a "rather dirty" ruffled shirt and loose slippers, sat beside a coal fire at the end of a long table. Motioning his young visitor around to a seat beside him, Jackson inquired of the news from Georgia. Nothing more than a few Indian disturbances on the western frontier, Stephens replied innocently.

Jackson exploded. He knew of these disturbances all right. Mail stages were being robbed and U.S. citizens killed by the vile savages. Now this young Georgian had reminded him of it. The report of unruly Indians kept Jackson going "perhaps twenty minutes." The president's soliloquy, reported an awed and slightly scandalized Stephens, bristled with oaths and profanity. Experiencing Jackson close up impressed the Georgian. He was much better looking than the Whig caricatures portrayed him and, in spite of his profanity, extremely approachable and engaging. And what energy he had for one so old! (To the twenty-three-year-old Stephens, Jackson, aged sixty-eight, appeared ancient.)[38]

After his stay in Washington, Stephens headed north via Baltimore (his first train ride) and Harrisburg to visit New York City. On the way he paid a visit to his Pennsylvania relatives in Perry County, his father's brother James and family, whom he had never met. They were delighted with their unexpected guest—delighted, that is, until in the midst of a convivial dinner Uncle James asked what business Stephens was in. "I am a lawyer," he proudly replied. A horrified silence, broken only by the clattering of Uncle James's knife and fork to the table, immediately descended on the gathering.

"A lawyer?" said Uncle James sadly. "Alexander, don't you have to tell lies?" (Uncle James was obviously a man of some percipience.) An amused Stephens immediately seized the moment to instruct the misinformed. "No, sir," he said. A lawyer's business was "neither to tell lies or defend lies but to protect and maintain right, truth, and justice." It was the noblest calling on earth. With this upright explanation the Perry County Stephenses seemed reassured.[39]

Two days later Stephens went on to Philadelphia and then to New

---

38. The preceding paragraphs are from *ibid.*, January 8, 1837.
39. The preceding paragraphs are from Johnston and Browne, *Stephens*, 104–105.

York, where he spent five days before returning home. He arrived back in Crawfordville in time for the annual Fourth of July festivities at which he read the Declaration of Independence to the crowd. At the barbecue following the speeches, Stephens sounded a decidedly discordant note by offering a toast condemning nominating conventions as "dangerous inroads upon Republican simplicity." Most of the simple republicans attending utterly failed to perceive their peril. One or two objected, and few drank the toast.

"So . . . pass on the unthinking multitude," thought Stephens, never worrying about "their rights," blindly following the dictates of "higher authorities." Just what Stephens meant is difficult to say. But Andrew Jackson's Democrats a few years earlier had adopted nominating conventions as needed innovations to free the candidate-selection process from the trammels of party bosses. And in Taliaferro County, almost anything Democratic aroused suspicion, particularly for a young man who found Whig ideas more intriguing by the day. The Whigs were just beginning to coalesce in opposition to Jackson and his policies, and it would be several years before Georgia would have what could properly be called a Whig party. Likely the toast was the best anti-Democratic rhetoric Stephens could muster at the time.[40]

For the next two years Stephens worked hard, and his business steadily improved. Conscientious and ambitious, he spent many hours over his law books. But law did not occupy all his time. He served as clerk to the town council, for example, and as a member of the Crawfordville Thespian Society. He also joined the county debating society, and for recreation of a different sort he roamed the fields and hollows of the "old homestead" with his brother Aaron, recalling the past and visiting the graves. He never wasted his time lounging about the village.[41]

It was during these busy months that Stephens became friendly with Dr. Foster, the man who had talked him into giving the Fourth of July speech a year earlier. Foster had taken a paternal interest in Stephens. Knowing the value of relaxation, he would pry the young man away from his office for long rides out into the country, sometimes as far as fifteen miles out of town and to the edges of the county in all directions. The doctor, who had a sharp mind and a knowledge of history,

40. The preceding paragraphs are from AHS MS Diary, July 4, 1836, in Stephens Papers, LC.
41. Rabun, "Stephens," 70–71.

art, and science, besides what passed for medicine in those days, had a character that appealed to Stephens. He knew about railroads and politics, too.[42]

Local affairs or national affairs, it didn't matter—Stephens would talk politics with anyone. And as they rode along Foster plied him with arguments for railroad development, painting marvelous vistas of the prosperity steam locomotion would bring to the state. Stephens, though ignorant of it at the time, was being groomed. Foster had a financial interest in railroad development in Georgia and had discovered in Stephens a young man of promise. With Jeffries gone off to Columbus, the Taliaferro County seat in the state assembly stood vacant. Maybe Stephens was the man to fill it.

42. Johnston and Browne, *Stephens,* 107–108.

III

Political Apprenticeship

Politics in early nineteenth century America was the single avenue open to a man of modest means who desired wide recognition, and Alexander Stephens moved as unerringly into politics as a compass needle drawn to magnetic north. Steeped in his own righteousness, he had probably decided that his presence in the Milledgeville statehouse would remedy the corruption he found so conspicuous there. Stephens' entry into politics was fortuitous: Taliaferro's seat in the assembly had been vacant since Jeffries' departure. Moreover, the young lawyer had met many voters on his journeys with Foster. So in the fall of 1836 Stephens became a candidate for representative in the state assembly.[1]

Georgia's political alignments in 1836 were just emerging from a murky flux, their normal condition almost since statehood in 1790. Exasperated observers trying to make sense of the state's tangled political allegiances could easily agree with the editor of *Niles' Register* that it was impossible to understand Georgia politics. Until 1832 and the nullification crisis, Georgians had waged political contests under the banners of state leaders, with little reference to issues or ideology. During the 1820s Stephens' section of the state followed the lead of George

1. Cleveland, *Stephens*, 49.

M. Troup, who opposed John Clark, the champion of the state's newer western counties, where slaves were scarce. Although both groups loved Andrew Jackson, a southern slaveholder and Indian hater, Troup's followers, who called themselves the State Rights party, broke with the president over his proclamation to the people of South Carolina and subsequent force bill. The Union party, Clark's people, supported Jackson and his policies. Over the next two years discernible party lines began to emerge in Georgia.[2]

These solidified in 1836, a presidential election year. Martin Van Buren, Jackson's hand-picked successor, could nowhere near fill the Old Hero's boots in many Georgians' eyes, but the Union party men, soon to begin calling themselves Democrats, loyally supported him— to no avail. The State Rights party succeeded in carrying the state for its own presidential candidate, Hugh Lawson White of Tennessee. Vicious mudslinging by both sides characterized the campaign, with the issues of slavery and race at the forefront. The Clark men charged that White belonged to an abolition society. Troup's forces countered by accusing Van Buren of being a friend of abolitionists, an advocate of black suffrage in New York, and a northerner with no sympathy for the South, among other things. The pattern in Georgia's antebellum politics had been set. Henceforth slavery and its protection would always be the fundamental issue in party politics.[3]

This, then, was the political situation Alexander Stephens thrust himself into in 1836. Taliaferro County, along with neighboring Greene, was the staunchest Troup area in the state. Stephens had cast his first vote there in 1833, for Joel Crawford, the State Rights candidate for governor. In Taliaferro between 1831 and 1835 Troup men captured more than 95 percent of the vote. But the county was hardly monolithic. The factions of two local leaders, Brown and Janes, vied bitterly for control. Stephens attempted, unsuccessfully, to avoid irritating either. But his association with Foster had already identified him with the Brown group, and he made the identification complete when he

2. Ulrich B. Phillips, *Georgia and State Rights: A Study of the Political History of Georgia from the Revolution to the Civil War, with Particular Regard to Federal Relations* (1902; rpr. Yellow Springs, Ohio, 1968), II, 127; Richard P. McCormick, *The Second American Party System: Party Formation in the Jacksonian Era* (New York, 1973), 236–39, 241–42.
3. McCormick, *Second Party System*, 243; Paul K. Murray, *The Whig Party in Georgia* (Chapel Hill, 1948), 74–75; William J. Cooper, Jr., *The South and the Politics of Slavery, 1828–1856* (Baton Rouge, 1978), 5–11, 65–69.

endorsed a friend, also a Brown man, as a candidate for the state senate.[4]

Stephens' first campaign, a savage one, centered on local animosities. Slander dominated the campaign rhetoric. Stephens was accused of defending Jackson and the force bill—charges he angrily denied. He was also accused of being an abolitionist. This absurd but always mortifying and dangerous charge in southern politics stemmed from his role in discouraging the formation of a local vigilance committee. Several counties in Georgia had organized such committees to deal summarily with circulators of northern abolitionist literature. When someone proposed forming a committee in Taliaferro, Stephens, almost alone, opposed it, arguing that punishment of offenders must be by duly constituted authority and not mob rule. He succeeded in preventing formation of the committee, but the Janes faction carried the issue into the campaign. So desperately did they assail him that Stephens, in spite of a raging fever, rose from his sickbed to defend his love of justice. Evidently the voters believed him: he beat his opponent by a two-to-one margin.[5]

Little did the voters of Taliaferro realize that they had launched one of the most celebrated political careers in the nineteenth-century South. They liked this pallid little lawyer and admired him for his spunk and independence. Stephens had revealed in his first campaign a trait that would characterize him for the rest of his life: a fierce devotion to the rule of law, especially law that protected and enshrined individual civil liberties. But there was also a streak of stubborn perverseness in Stephens. He enjoyed bucking popular political opinions, as only one who believed he had a special corner on virtue and the truth could. Never was Little Aleck a more fierce or uncompromising opponent than when he defended an unpopular position, whether he was right—as he was in this campaign—or wrong, a condition he almost always believed impossible.

Stephens spent five years in state House of Representatives. Declining to run in 1840 to pay more attention to his law practice, he ran successfully for a seat in the state senate in 1842. These six years consti-

---

4. Rabun, "Stephens," 86; Avary (ed.), *Stephens Recollections*, 15; AHS to B. O'Bryan, September 27, 1836, in Stephens Papers, LC.
    5. Johnston and Browne, *Stephens*, 125–26.

tuted his political apprenticeship during which he absorbed lessons essential for his future success. He learned how to heed the wishes of his constituents and how to weld them into a solid bloc of support. During this time he also mastered skills in legislative tactics, parliamentary procedure, and party strategy. He learned his lessons well but could claim few tangible accomplishments.

His only real triumph came during his first year in office. The House was in the midst of a great debate on the merits of a state-financed railroad, the Western and Atlantic, a monumental project to connect Atlanta and Chattanooga. It was not a party issue. Some men had no faith in the future of the dangerous, smoky steam engines with their trains of excruciatingly uncomfortable coaches. The proposed "main trunk line" ("a *great snout*," snorted one skeptic) over mountains in north Georgia that even a spider couldn't climb (complained another) was hopelessly visionary. Others opposed any internal improvements at state expense, particularly this frightfully expensive project. Proponents of the line urged its vast importance: it would bring prosperity to the state and especially, it would enable Savannah to compete with Charleston for trade with the growing Northwest.[6]

Stephens had recently been primed for his legislative debut by a visit from Foster. The doctor stopped in Milledgeville on his way back from a railroad convention in Macon, which had been called expressly to urge the legislature to finance construction of the road. Arming himself with a formidable array of figures, Stephens spent days preparing his maiden address.[7]

When his opportunity finally came, the speech produced an "electrical" effect. He argued that an immense increase in Georgia's aggregate wealth would accrue if the line were built. For an expense of $4 million, he said, the state would realize $15 million. And he noted a point previous speakers had overlooked: that property values along the proposed route would appreciate. Once finished, the young man from Taliaferro was unknown no longer. Applause erupted from both the galleries and the floor of the House. The speech, reported Stephens with typical modesty, brought him "great credit," and many thought it helped pass the bill. It may well have done so, but Stephens' hopes for the great railroad would not be realized for almost twenty years. This

6. AHS to Williams Rutherford, March 13, 1857, in Cleveland, *Stephens*, 606–607.
7. Johnston and Browne, *Stephens*, 126–27.

speech was the only oratorical effort Stephens made in the legislature that anyone noticed. His correspondence for the two months of each year he spent at the capital is silent on his political affairs. Legislative journals limn a dutiful lawmaker who introduced few bills but who diligently looked after his constituents.[8]

In his first year Stephens drew an insignificant assignment to the Committee on Engrossing—a place to learn something about bills but little else. Later he received better committee assignments: judiciary four times, state of the republic twice, finance and public education and free schools once each.

The legislature dealt largely with financial issues during Stephens' tenure. Such questions never much interested him; he preferred the more abstruse realms of constitutional theory. But Robert Toombs, who joined his friend in the House in 1837, loved economic issues. Toombs, already rich and destined to get richer, was an unshakable fiscal conservative. In economic and monetary matters Stephens usually followed Toombs's lead.[9]

The onset of the national panic in 1837, which punctured the bloated bubble of land speculation and exposed the wildcat banking practices upon which the boom rested, hit Georgia hard. By May, 1837, only seventeen banks remained open, and only one, the Central Bank of Georgia, was still redeeming its notes in specie. Many of Georgia's hard-pressed citizens looked to this institution for relief, and the majority Democrats were only too happy to use the Central Bank as a hobbyhorse.[10]

Toombs and Stephens, along with the rest of the State Rights minority in the House, futilely opposed authorizing the Central Bank to borrow $150,000 to make relief loans to Georgia citizens. Two years later, however, they managed to defeat a Democratic attempt to increase the bank's capital, another scheme aimed at providing relief. Nonetheless, they had to watch the Democrats pass legislation allowing the bank to issue notes up to twice its amount of capital. Toombs and Stephens

8. Iverson L. Harris to Rutherford, May 10, 1857, AHS to Rutherford, March 13, 1857, both in Cleveland, *Stephens*, 53, 610. Most of the bills and resolutions Stephens introduced dealt with local matters: to establish two academies in Taliaferro County, to define the limits of railroad liability for destruction of livestock, to adjust county lines, and to amend various court procedures (*Georgia House Journal, 1836*, 64–65; *1837*, 58; *1838*, 36–37; *1839*, 38–39; *1840*, 35; *Georgia Senate Journal, 1842*, 41).
9. Rabun, "Stephens," 92–94.
10. Murray, *Whig Party in Georgia*, 69.

joined fifty other indignant protesters in signing a statement declaring use of public credit to relieve private wants "outrageous" and "radically wrong." Such measures would require universal and oppressive taxation to redeem them—taxation that would fall heaviest on the large property owners of middle Georgia. Stephens and Toombs, like others of their party, were more liberal in supporting internal improvements at public expense. Both favored appropriations for river navigation and road building, and they also tried (unsuccessfully) to push state support for further construction of the Western and Atlantic.[11]

Georgia's State Rights party did not move toward amalgamation with a national political party until after 1837. Democrats, building on Jackson's personal popularity and the voters' general approval of his war on the Bank of the United States and the compromise tariff of 1833, had found the process easier. After the panic, however, when the State Rights men shifted to substantive questions such as sound business practices and economy in government, their affiliation with the national Whigs probably became inevitable. Like it or not, Stephens' party had begun to sound like the Whigs throughout the rest of the country, excoriating Jackson and the train of evils his policies had brought upon the nation.[12]

The national Whigs were a curious aggregation, a bewildering hodgepodge of conflicting and contradictory interests and tendencies. To paraphrase John C. Calhoun, one of the party's earliest (and unlikeliest) members, they were brought together under the cohesive power of a common hatred for Jackson and his policies. But from its inception the party was inherently unstable. Like the man-made elements in atomic physics, the Whigs were destined, after a series of short half-lives, to break down into more basic components. No wonder the party could never agree on a platform capable of carrying it to victory in a presidential election. Midwife at the Whig party's birth, political expediency would serve as pallbearer at its funeral.

To combat the Democrats and ensure their own political survival, southerners who entered the Whig party found it essential to embrace principles of the national party that many found distasteful. Few southern Whigs had any great ardor for Henry Clay's American System (a protective tariff, a national bank, and a system of federally financed

11. Rabun, "Stephens," 93, 95; *Georgia House Journal, 1839*, 410–12.
12. Murray, *Whig Party in Georgia*, 87–88.

internal improvements). And unlike the northern wing of the party, the southerners were proslavery and militant exponents of state sovereignty. But the Whigs offered southern anti-Jacksonians a lifeline, so they grabbed it, slippery though it might be.[13]

Georgia's anti-Jacksonians hesitated, however. When national economic issues were carried into the prepresidential campaign in 1839, the State Rights party could not bring itself to endorse national Whiggery's darling, Clay, and instead proposed native son George M. Troup. Clay aroused suspicion because he had engineered the Missouri Compromise of 1820, tacit admission, most thought, of Congress' right to interfere with territorial slavery. Moreover, many believed Clay responsible for the tariff and in its wake the overabundant national treasury with all its attendant corruptions.[14]

Stephens agreed with his State Rights colleagues who found the Whigs' unbounded nationalism disquieting. The Whigs, he said at the July Fourth festivities in 1839, embodied "the reviving spirit of the old Federalists." But he reserved his choicest barbs for the "known enemy," the Democrats. "Judas-like traitors" they were, betraying Jeffersonian republicanism for the spoils of office and increasing public expenditures while promising retrenchment. He would rather see his sister marry a rake than see Georgians rally round one of these parties. Association with either "would be death to our principles."[15]

One wonders what the fate of Stephens' rhetorical sister would have been when the inevitable marriage of the Georgia State Rights party with the Whigs took place the next summer. At the Milledgeville state convention the State Rights party withdrew its nomination of Troup and endorsed William Henry Harrison, the national Whig candidate, for president. Only a few militant Calhoun nullifiers scorned this expedient. Stephens did not join the opposition but was hardly thrilled with the party's nominee, "a choice of evils," in his opinion. But because Georgia Whigs, like Whigs throughout the country, ignored issues in the campaign and concentrated on portraying Harrison as a simple man of the people, Stephens could console himself with the thought that precious principles had little role in this election. Almost without realizing it, Little Aleck had become a Whig—not because he particularly wanted to but because he had no choice.[16]

13. Arthur C. Cole, *The Whig Party in the South* (Washington, D.C., 1914), 1–63.
14. Murray, *Whig Party in Georgia*, 89.
15. Milledgeville *Southern Recorder*, July 4, 1839.
16. Johnston and Browne, *Stephens*, 140.

The years Stephens spent in the state legislature, critically important for his development as politician and parliamentarian, were also personally significant. During these years his close relationship with Linton began. Until 1836 Little Aleck had taken only a mildly fraternal interest in his thirteen-year-old half-brother; but now, Stephens decided, Linton's life needed direction. In 1837, he arranged that the boy's guardianship be transferred to himself, moved him to Crawfordville, and put him in school.[17]

Linton's entrance into college a year later marked the beginning of a prodigious correspondence between the two brothers that would continue unabated for over thirty years. Linton, eleven years Alexander's junior, was mild-mannered, studious, and pliable, and for a time their relationship was like that between father and son. This eventually gave way to an extraordinarily close fraternal attachment marked by mutual respect and deference. Linton filled an unmistakable void in his brother's life. He was the confidant and companion to whom Aleck could reveal his innermost self without fear. Stephens, who once claimed "feeling" as "always my characteristic quality," grew to love Linton with passionate, near possessive intensity. For his part, Linton was tender and sympathetic, understanding and responsive to the strange nuances of his brother's character. For Stephens, Linton embodied all that was good in his life. Indeed, he could not imagine life without him. Stephens' law business thrived, so he decided to assume the responsibility and expense for Linton's education. Nothing but the best would do. Linton spent a year at the Crawfordville academy; Stephens then sent him to Franklin College. Linton graduated in 1843 and then, after reading law in Toombs's office, attended law school at the University of Virginia. After graduating in 1845, he spent some months at Harvard.[18]

Reading the letters from Stephens to Linton during the latter's school years is a numbing experience. Linton was fortunate in having to read them singly, for they contain, at tedious length, a steady barrage of questions and advice, overlaid with cloying solicitousness. No detail of Linton's daily existence—his studies, grades, expenses, handwriting, companions, teachers, spelling, grammar, eating and exercise habits—

17. AHS to "Dear Brothers," September 11, 1836, in Stephens Papers, DU.

18. AHS MS Diary, April 14, 1834, in Stephens Papers, LC; James D. Waddell (ed.), *Biographical Sketch of Linton Stephens Containing a Selection of His Letters, Speeches, State Papers, Etc.* (Atlanta, 1877), 10, 48.

escaped Aleck's attention. But on no subject was he more insistent or interminable than in exhortation to virtue: industry, ambition, honor, moral courage, and independence. Linton's welfare had become the "abode of all that interests me," Stephens confessed in 1838. It was the only thing that brought him any real happiness.[19]

His health certainly didn't. Never really good, it got worse after 1836. In spring, 1837, he contracted pneumonia, then a digestive ailment. A long buggy trip with his brother Aaron seemed to help some, but the next spring his health failed again. On Dr. Foster's advice he took a longer trip, a four-month jaunt north to Washington, Boston, and New England. Not until he bathed in the waters at White Sulphur Springs, Virginia, though, did his health show any improvement.[20]

Separation from Linton pained him more than sickness. "No day passes," he wrote, "but you are in my mind. And you do not escape my dreams by night." Fretting over whether he had counseled Linton sufficiently before his departure, he kept up a steady drumfire of advice by letter. He also recommended a long list of approved authors: Locke, Bacon, Franklin, Milton, Shakespeare ("only his sound maxims," not "his vulgar obscenity"), Virgil, Livy, Cicero, Horace, Burns, Paley, and Cervantes.[21]

The sojourn at the springs revived Stephens; he would not get sick again for some time. This was fortunate because he was entering on busy days. He had caught the attention of a wider constituency in 1839. Prominent enough to be selected delegate to the Charleston Commercial Convention, he delivered there a "brilliant, eloquent, and powerful" speech against the establishment of a southern review, which, he argued, would become a "political engine." In his first brush with nascent southern nationalism Stephens was characteristically cautious. But his speech, like the convention itself—called to advocate direct southern trade with Europe—failed to achieve its purpose. Stephens had to be satisfied only with the enhancement of his reputation.[22]

It was secure enough by 1841 for him to forego running for reelection. His law business demanded much of his time, and even the partner he had taken on in 1839, Robert Burch, failed to relieve the burden. But Stephens was prospering. In March, 1840, he bought a buggy for trav-

19. AHS to LS, August 31, 1839, May 12, 1838, in Stephens Papers, MC.
20. Johnston and Browne, *Stephens*, 129–30.
21. AHS to LS, May 12, June 4, June 30, 1838, in Stephens Papers, MC.
22. Milledgeville *Southern Recorder*, July 18, 1843.

eling the circuit, and when he lost it in a swamp, promptly replaced it with another. In the early 1840s, too, Stephens began acquiring other important trappings of prosperity—land and slaves. In January, 1841, he bought the first of five parcels of land that would constitute his Taliaferro County property (920 acres by 1853), and throughout the decade he augmented this with extensive land speculations in other parts of Georgia and the South. Eventually he owned some five thousand acres.[23]

Still boarding with Williamson Bird, Stephens had no need of house servants. But his land required labor, so he became a slaveholder. Ede, the slave he had inherited, worked in the Bird household. He soon began acquiring others, whom he sent out to work the "old homestead." By 1845, the year he bought the Bird house and its ten-acre lot, Stephens owned ten slaves. On the eve of his career in national politics, then, he had acquired the requisite appurtenances of respectability. He had come a long way since his earlier, less prosperous days, and he would go farther yet.[24]

If he lived, that is. In April, 1842, he got so sick with a serious pulmonary disorder (probably pneumonia) that members of the household feared for his life. Foster had moved to north Georgia, so the patient doctored himself through the dangerous illness. Eating almost nothing, blistering his bony chest with tartar emetic, drinking an extract of liverwort to suppress his cough, and attempting to draw fluid from his sides by suction "cupping," Stephens, by some miracle, managed to survive his own ministrations and recovered.[25]

Not surprisingly, Stephens thought about death during his illness, but the idea did not depress him. Life and death should be regarded "philosophically," he told Linton. For him life was but a preparation for death, and he wasn't sure if taking his "turn in advance" would not be "more agreeable" than lingering on. But linger he did, and after recovering Stephens enjoyed his best health since 1836.[26]

It was a good thing Stephens regarded death philosophically, because in his next campaign he was more than ready to risk it. Heated antebellum political campaigns in the South often generated duels, and

23. Robert Burch to AHS, June 15, 1839, in Ralph E. Wager Papers, EU; Rabun, "Stephens," 165–66.
24. Von Abele, *Stephens*, 73–74.
25. *Ibid.*, 77.
26. AHS to LS, August 15, 1842, in Stephens Papers, MC.

several times Stephens attempted to prove his manhood by getting involved in one. He never did, but his 1842 campaign for the state senate produced the first near miss. Stephens' opponent, a hard-drinking man named Felix Moore, despised him. He once threatened to have Stephens brought to the town tavern for a thrashing. Another time this believer in the direct approach, slightly in his cups, challenged Stephens to a duel. Little Aleck accepted immediately, but the affair blew over without incident the next day, when Moore regained his senses along with his sobriety. The election results must have been even more sobering. It was Moore who got thrashed—by a vote of 295 to 102.[27]

Although the Whigs had won a resounding victory in the national campaign of 1840, they were a minority in Georgia's General Assembly when Stephens took his seat in the senate in 1842. Consequently, Stephens and Toombs, who had been reelected to the House, spent most of their time opposing Democratic schemes to revive the near comatose Central Bank and defending the actions of John M. Berrien, the state's Whig senator in Washington.

By late 1843 Georgia's Whigs were firmly wedded to Henry Clay and his economic program. Their recently adjourned state convention had endorsed him for president in 1844, and Whig editors were already plying the voters with pro-Clay arguments. A revenue tariff was the only kind the Kentuckian ever stood for, they said. A sound national currency would guarantee agricultural stability. Distribution of the federal surplus to the states made sound fiscal sense.[28]

Stephens played a key role in endorsing Whig principles in the minority report of the Senate Committee on the State of the Republic, which he wrote in response to demands by both the Democratic governor and the senate majority that Berrien resign his seat. Stephens defended Berrien and denied, on constitutional grounds, the right of a state legislature to instruct a U.S. senator. Most Georgians opposed neither distribution of the federal surplus nor a national bank, he claimed. Nor did they wish to destroy the president's veto power. He defended Clay's proposed amendment to the Constitution, which would make it easier for Congress to override President John Tyler's vetoes of Whig financial measures. On the tariff Stephens echoed the

27. *Ibid.*, February 6, 1842.
28. Murray, *Whig Party in Georgia*, 104–105.

popular southern Whig straddle: the party favored a tariff for revenue only, he said. If it "incidentally" encouraged or protected domestic industry, so be it.[29]

With this report Stephens ended his service in the state legislature. Political apprentice no longer, he was ready to put the lessons he had learned into practice in a larger arena. In that arena he soon discovered one issue that could not be straddled as could the tariff. That issue was slavery.

29. Johnston and Browne, *Stephens*, 157–67. Stephens was not a member of the committee but was asked to prepare the report. AHS to LS, June 17, 1843, in Stephens Papers, MC.

IV

Riding the Texas "Hobby"

Stephens' talents for public office had become apparent during the years he served in the state asssembly. As early as 1839 the Milledgeville *Georgia Journal* had suggested that he should run for Congress. Foster had recognized Stephens' potential much earlier and in the summer of 1842 reported that people considered him one of the "big men in Georgia." People in western Georgia, near Hamilton, came to the same conclusion even earlier. In 1839 John L. Stephens sounded his brother out on the possibility of his running for Congress in 1840. Stephens answered abruptly: "The world is no judge of a man's business." He refused to run then and again in 1842.[1]

But by 1843 he was ready to seek the seat in the Georgia congressional delegation formerly held by Mark A. Cooper, a State Rights party apostate now running as a Democrat for governor. Stephens, along with Toombs and George W. Crawford, were the Whigs' most dedicated young zealots. Already prominent in the party, he was the obvious choice to run for Cooper's old seat, and the Whigs chose him at their 1843 convention.

1. Milledgeville *Georgia Journal*, December 31, 1839, quoted in Rabun, "Stephens," 111; Thomas Foster to AHS, June 3, 1842, JLS to AHS, August 9, 1839, May 15, 1842, AHS to JLS, September 11, 1839, all in Stephens Papers, DU.

Forced to run on a general or statewide ticket, Stephens canvassed much of the state. Since middle Georgia was less fluid in political loyalties than the northern counties, he and Crawford spent most of their time in the twenty-two mostly mountainous so-called Cherokee counties, which contained about half of the state's population but few slaves or plantations. Cherokee's small farmers generally voted Democratic, but there were enough independent-minded voters to merit attention from anyone, even a Whig, aspiring to statewide office.[2]

Stephens' opponent was James H. Starke, whom he met only once in debate during the campaign. At all the other little towns on the canvass the Democrats trotted out other speakers to joust with Stephens, some of them big guns like Senator Walter T. Colquitt, Congressman William Stiles, and gubernatorial candidate Cooper. None, it seems, much daunted Stephens. At Cassville, for example, he claimed to have completely "*used up*" Stiles, leaving less than a "greasy spot" of him. The campaign had even hotter moments. At Spring Place, whence Cooper had come to correct what he called Stephens' "falsehoods and lies," the meeting broke up in a general row. No doubt Little Aleck's personal attacks on Cooper in the Augusta *Chronicle and Sentinel* helped spur the fracas. There was residual antipathy between the two anyway, dating back to a Crawfordville debate in 1840; and since the Democrats now castigated the Whigs as friends of aristocrats, banks, and corporations, Stephens relished pointing out that Cooper was himself an aristocrat and a bank president to boot.[3]

Generally, though, Stephens avoided personal attacks, preferring to defend the Whig program of tariffs, distribution, and a national bank. He doubted his arguments would sway the north Georgians and expected to lose. But the excitement of the canvass, the controversy he was stirring up, and his triumphs on the stump fired him like an elixir. "I am in perfect spirits," he exulted to Linton, "and enjoying myself well, never better."[4]

He proved to be a poor prophet about his own success; he defeated Starke 38,051 votes to 35,001. Crawford wrested the governorship from the Democrats by a similar margin, and the Whigs won major-

2. Rabun, "Stephens," 112–14.
3. AHS to LS, July 29, August 16, 1843, in Stephens Papers, MC; Cooper quoted in Rabun, "Stephens," 119.
4. Augusta *Chronicle and Sentinel*, August 22, 1843; AHS to LS, August 16, 1843, in Stephens Papers, MC.

ities in both houses of the General Assembly. Although general dissatisfaction with the Democratic record weighed heavily in their victory, the Whigs recognized Stephens' personal contribution. His "laborious efforts" and "lucid explanation," said the Milledgeville *Southern Recorder*, deserved the gratitude of all the state's Whigs. Georgia's leading Whig paper, the *Chronicle and Sentinel*, dubbed Little Aleck "the Hero of Taliaferro."[5]

Whatever joy Stephens may have felt from his triumph soon turned to ashes, for his brother Aaron, a reliable helper and companion, died shortly after the election. Stephens plunged into an unfathomable sorrow. "Oh my brother," he told John, "you cannot imagine my agony." Thoughts of Aaron's death and the mysterious workings of Providence plagued him as he left Charleston in late November on a steamer for Washington. "To live today, to be warm, to move, and think," he had written earlier that year, "and tomorrow to be cold and dead, devoid of mind and sense—fast mouldering into dust—only fit food for worms." Given to such despair even in normal times, Stephens agonized continually whenever a friend or loved one died. Thus obsessed by thoughts of death and decay he traveled to his first term in Congress.[6]

For several weeks after his arrival in Washington, he had yet another reason for gloom; he was sick, unable to get out of bed, much less attend Congress regularly. Finally well again in January, he was still despondent. He had never before passed such a period of "unbroken, unmitigated, and unconsolable melancholly," he wrote, and the future appeared no brighter.[7]

When he had recovered enough to attend Congress, Stephens, a freshman congressman, naturally drew an unimportant committee assignment—claims, a body handling routine monetary claims of citizens against the government. The speeches in the House bored him, and committee work hardly improved his disposition. His colleagues, he thought, were the "grandest set of blockheads" ever gathered, lack-

5. Milledgeville *Southern Recorder*, September 23, 1843; Augusta *Chronicle and Sentinel*, October 14, 1843; election returns in Milledgeville *Federal Union*, November 14, 1843.
6. AHS to JLS, October 8, 1843 [misdated "September" in original], in Stephens Papers, EU; AHS to LS, May 19, 1843, in Stephens Papers, MC.
7. Augusta *Chronicle and Sentinel*, December 8, 28, 1843; AHS to John Bird, January 2, 1844, in Ralph E. Wager Papers, EU. Stephens did attend Congress on December 11, apparently to take the oath (*Congressional Globe*, 28th Cong., 1st Sess., 23).

ing the sense to understand the "true merits of any question." Of course, Stephens was sure *he* understood the true merits of any number of questions, and soon he got himself involved, both in and out of Congress, on two of them—the tariff and his own election.[8]

His long public letter defending the latest Whig tariff had been disingenuous enough, "proving" (by sly selective listing of rates) the new "incidental protection" measure less onerous than the old law. But the other issue, which arose from Stephens' first speech in Congress on February 9, 1844, proved more sensational. He argued that his own election had been unconstitutional because it had contravened an act of Congress requiring the states to elect representatives by district. Stephens based his apparently strange position on his own reading of the Constitution and buttressed his case with an imposing array of authorities.[9]

The power of Congress to require elections by district was clearly constitutional, he said, because "ultimately" Congress possessed whatever regulatory powers over elections that the fundamental law had given "primarily" to states. Congress, however, the sole judge of its members' qualifications, could seat or reject members elected on general tickets as it pleased. He professed indifference about whether Congress allowed him his seat. (There was little danger Congress would not. It declared all the doubtful representatives duly elected the next day.) Finally, he defended the district system as being the most "equal" because it gave state minorities a voice in national government, and its "conservative tendency" tended to balance parties within states and neutralize violent factional clashes.[10]

One Georgia Democrat listening to the speech was William Stiles, whom Stephens had bested on the stump during the campaign. Furious,

8. AHS to George W. Crawford, January 19, 1844, in Stephens Papers, EU.

9. AHS to "A gentleman of Lumpkin," January 25, 1844, in Milledgeville *Southern Recorder*, February 27, 1844.

10. Speech in Cleveland, *Stephens*, 259–79. The Democrats, who controlled the House, 142 to 79, were perfectly content to overlook the fact that Georgia as well as several other states had disregarded the districting law. These states had returned eighteen Democrats to only two Georgia Whigs, Stephens and Absalom Chappell. Over Whig protests, the House Democrats seated all of the newly elected congressmen from the general ticket states and referred the matter to the Committee on Elections. This committee brought in a majority report declaring all the general ticket elections lawful and constitutional, and it took a slap at the Whigs by declaring the section of the act of 1842 requiring states to elect representatives by district unconstitutional. This was the report Stephens attacked in his speech.

he replied in a speech replete with naked innuendos against Stephens' integrity for accepting an "unconstitutional" seat. Little Aleck never allowed such abuse to go unanswered. Waiting until Stiles's speech appeared in the *Congressional Globe*, Stephens, because he would not, he said, profane the halls of the House with a personal quarrel, soon demonstrated that he had no such compunctions about contaminating the columns of Georgia newspapers. In a card widely printed throughout the state, he tried to provoke a duel by labeling Stiles "a knave by nature and a poltroon at heart."[11]

Stiles refused to take the bait, contenting himself with a public letter ridiculing Stephens' "parade of vulgar epithets." But his sally failed to end the unfortunate affair. By lifelong custom Stephens never let an opponent have the last word. In a final blast, in which he likened Stiles to a "cur" and a "viper," the correspondence ended.[12]

Georgia's Whigs, from Governor Crawford on down, loved this tasteless bluster. One Oglethorpe County Whig told Stephens that Stiles had got just what he deserved. But the most objective comment on the affair came from Hope Hull, a Democratic editor and friend of Howell Cobb. Both men, he said, had made themselves "abundantly ridiculous."[13]

Stephens spoke only once more during this session. According to him at least, his speech on May 8 defending the tariff attracted more attention than the first. "I piled it down on them for an hour," he wrote happily. He was beginning to sound a lot like Henry Clay. One of the Constitution's main objects, far from establishing free trade, as the Democrats contended, was to protect the country's industries, he declared. Furthermore, he knew no one in his section of the country who felt "oppressed" by the tariff, as southern Democrats charged. If his words sounded more emphatic than the diluted tariff doctrine the Whigs normally served in the South, it was because 1844 was an election year. And Georgia's Whigs, with Stephens in the vanguard, had been rallying for Clay since the summer of 1842. But this cozy alliance soon took a rude jolt over an issue that until now had lain dormant: Texas.[14]

11. Milledgeville *Federal Union*, February 27, March 19, 1844.
12. *Ibid.*, March 19, 1844; Augusta *Chronicle and Sentinel*, March 14, 1844.
13. George W. Crawford to AHS, March 6, 1844, George F. Plott to AHS, April 30, 1844, both in Stephens Papers, LC; H. Hull to Howell Cobb, March 30, 1844, in Cobb Papers, UG.
14. AHS to LS, May 8, 1844, in Stephens Papers, MC; *Congressional Globe*, 28th Cong., 1st Sess., 592.

President Tyler and his secretary of state, John C. Calhoun, had irretrievably opened the expansion issue by negotiating a treaty of annexation with Texas. Although expansionists could advance several reasons for annexation, Calhoun focused on the most volatile. In letters that leaked to the press, he urged annexation as vital to slavery's security in the South and to southern political power in the Union. To many protesting northerners, slavery appeared to be the controlling factor in the administration's plan. It mattered little that many southerners, particularly Whigs, had good reasons of their own for opposing the annexation of Texas. Once slavery got involved, rational consideration of the issue was impossible. Thus slavery became tangled with Texas and Texas with the presidential election.[15]

Clay took a cautious position on the annexation issue. Five days after Tyler submitted the Texas treaty to the Senate, he came out against annexation in his famous "Raleigh letter." To annex Texas, he said, would compromise the national character, endanger the Union, and provoke war with Mexico. Of course, Clay was aware of the opposition of northern Whigs, and he knew the hated Tyler wanted Texas. But he was also convinced that his southern adherents would support his stand.[16]

This turned out to be a sad miscalculation, but Clay had good reason to expect southern support. His Raleigh letter had come at the end of a triumphal tour of the Deep South. John J. Crittenden, Clay's chief lieutenant, had shown Stephens the letter before publication, and the Georgian had pronounced it "full, clear, and satisfactory." Stephens realized that Clay did not intend to stand against Texas forever, and, like the rest of the party, he expected Martin Van Buren to be the Democratic opponent in the election. Van Buren had also written a public letter opposing annexation; both party leaders, it seemed, wanted to keep the issue out of the campaign.[17]

15. Frederick Merk, *Slavery and the Annexation of Texas* (New York, 1972), 44–82.

16. Washington *National Intelligencer*, April 27, 1844; Henry Clay to Thurlow Weed, May 6, 1844, in Henry Clay Papers, DU.

17. Clay to John J. Crittenden, April 17, 1844, in Crittenden Papers, LC; AHS to LS, April 23, 1844, in Stephens Papers, MC. According to Stephens, he had spoken to Clay during his tour through Georgia and had urged him not to write an anti-Texas letter. But Clay brought him around to his "policy" by assuring him that he favored annexation of Texas when it could be done without danger to the Union (Avary [ed.], *Stephens Recollections*, 17–18). Previous Stephens biographers, Von Abele (*Stephens*, 87n.) and

The Whigs nominated Clay unanimously at their convention on May 1, 1844, and delegate Stephens returned from Baltimore zealous for the cause. The tariff question rather than Texas, he told Linton, monopolized Washington talk. But in Georgia, and especially among Democrats, Texas was the prime topic. "We must have Texas," one Democrat told Cobb. Texas "is our very life blood," echoed another. Van Buren's letter had confounded them, and many spurned him, some even going so far as to suggest forming a third party behind an annexation candidate. Even a few restive Whigs stood ready to bolt for a pro-Texas Democrat, although, as one Democrat conceded, the majority would go for Clay even "if he expressed the opinion that God Almighty was the Devil incarnate." [18]

The Democrats made the most of their opportunity. At their convention in Baltimore on May 27, they rejected Van Buren in favor of James K. Polk of Tennessee, former Speaker of the House, friend of Jackson, and an outspoken expansionist. To appeal to like-minded men North and South, the party platform demanded "the reoccupation of Oregon and the reannexation of Texas at the earliest practicable period." Clearly, the issues would involve something more this time than economics. [19]

Several days before Polk's nomination, while Tyler's treaty still hung fire in the Senate (hopelessly entangled with presidential politics, it was overwhelmingly defeated in early June), Stephens dashed off an angry letter on the Texas question to a friend. It was all "a miserable political humbug," he grumbled, designed to divide the southern Whigs. Tyler was surely devious enough to push Texas for southern support, but Calhoun, he suspected, aimed at dissolution of the Union. The Demo-

---

Rabun ("Stephens," 138n.), point out the inconsistency between this statement and what Stephens told Linton in the letter cited above. Rabun questions whether Stephens actually talked to Clay. Both overlook the possibility that Stephens may have voiced opposition and then changed his mind when Clay explained his reasoning. That Clay chose to let Stephens see the Raleigh letter before its publication is strong evidence that the two had met and discussed the matter. There is no evidence that Clay had met Stephens before this time, and he certainly would not have singled Stephens out by name to Crittenden without some reason. Stephens, after all, was just another freshman congressman.

18. AHS to LS, May 4, 1844, in Stephens Papers, MC; Watkins to Cobb, March 28, 1844, Wm Mitchell to Cobb, May 21, 1844, James Jackson to Cobb, May 7, 1844, all in Cobb Papers, UG.

19. Glyndon Van Deusen, *The Jacksonian Era* (New York, 1959), 185.

crats and their opportunistic plots would fail, though, because Clay's election was "inevitable." [20]

As the political dimensions of the Texas question became clearer, Georgia's Whig editors reacted as angrily as Stephens had. Democrats were steadily attacking their weakest point. Where, they demanded, was safety for the South and slavery's western border if Texas remained out of the Union? Texas was preeminently a *southern* question, on which there could be no division. Whigs did their best to respond. Democrats were simply trying to delude the voters, sneered one editor. Since Democrats knew that any mention of slavery easily "bamboozled" voters, especially southerners, guaranteeing a "storm of passion," they harped on this spurious issue. [21]

But the Whigs still needed the voters, bamboozled or not. At their state convention in June they carefully enacted a resolution (drawn up by Stephens in Washington) favoring annexation of Texas at "the earliest practicable period consistent with the honor and faith of the nation." Daring Democrats to attack the undefinable qualification, the Whigs then tried to turn the campaign toward the more comfortable and familiar economic questions. [22]

In early July Stephens returned to Georgia to campaign, both for his own seat and for Clay. Along the way he gave speeches in Richmond, Petersburg, Wilmington, Savannah, and Milledgeville. Although he praised the Whig leader extravagantly, he could not ignore Texas. He denounced the Texas treaty as the ploy of unscrupulous presidential aspirants who meant to "dismember the Union and form a Southern confederacy." He would not oppose annexation "at the proper time and proper manner," but he was unwilling to endanger the Union over it. The trip exhausted Stephens. Back in Georgia on 5 July, he felt so weak he almost "broke down." [23]

He recovered quickly, though, and was soon heavily involved in the campaign. He and Toombs, now running for Congress himself, led the Whig speakers in the canvass, and everywhere they denounced the Texas "humbug." Characteristically extravagant, Toombs denounced the treaty as "morally indefensible and an attempt to despoil a weak

20. AHS to James Thomas, May 17, 1844, in Stephens Papers, LC.
21. Savannah *Republican*, May 22, 1844.
22. Milledgeville *Southern Recorder*, July 2, 1844.
23. Columbus *Enquirer*, July 2, 1844; AHS to JLS, July 5, 1844, in Stephens Papers, EU.

neighbor." Such intemperate language graphically illustrated the southern Whigs' plight. Texas was a leech on them; they could not pull it off without bleeding, but it steadily sapped the party's lifeblood, the simple dirt-farming voters who cared not a fig for national morality when southern rights, real or imagined, were involved.[24]

Safe in their own districts, Stephens and other party luminaries ventured into enemy territory. Stephens, Berrien, and Toombs, for example, stumped the Sixth District, Cobb's home turf, attempting to offset his steady trumpeting of Texas. And in an effort to blunt Alabama Democrats and revive sagging spirits, Stephens went over to Montgomery. He delivered a "great speech" there, said one observer, to an audience both amazed and delighted by the pale little congressman with the blazing eyes and "shrill but musical" voice.[25]

Most Georgia stump speaking took place before modest crowds, but occasionally both parties sponsored rallies that drew great crowds of voters and their sunbonneted women out for a political circus. These monster affairs were meat and drink to the sweating throngs, who sat in what shade they could find to enjoy endless hours of oratory every bit as blistering as a Georgia summer's sun. Just such a rally occupied four solid days at the end of July in Madison. On the climactic day, July 31, fully twenty-five thousand people attended, according to the ecstatic reporter of the Columbus *Enquirer*. Any number of fascinating sights and sounds regaled the crowd: glee clubs, bands, a booming cannon, and the sixteen-wheel omnibus, drawn by eight yokes of oxen, that conveyed the Clarke County delegation to its place. An "old fashioned barbeque spread on a table *one mile and ten yards long*" provided refreshment; continuous oratory provided entertainment. Stephens delivered the last speech of the rally at the main stand and, said the reporter, "*outdid himself.*"[26]

This magnificent display of Whig solidarity must have heartened Stephens. The campaign hoopla resembled the "Log Cabin and Hard Cider" obfuscation of 1840. But there the resemblance ended. In 1844 it would take more than extravaganzas, the tariff, appeals to national

24. Quoted in Murray, *Whig Party in Georgia*, 109.
25. H. H. Armstrong to AHS, July 28, 1844, in Stephens Papers, LC; Henry W. Hilliard, *Politics and Pen Pictures at Home and Abroad* (New York, 1892), 118. Georgia had finally complied with the 1842 districting law and divided the state into eight congressional districts. The Whig-controlled assembly obligingly carved out safe districts for both Stephens (the Seventh District) and Toombs (the Eighth).
26. Columbus *Enquirer*, August 7, 1844.

honor, or eulogies to the Union, even more than Henry Clay to carry this election for the Whigs. For the Democrats in the South had seized an issue that no amount of Whig enthusiasm could counteract, an issue that spurred a most powerful southern emotion—fear for the safety of slavery. Upon slavery rested the South's economy, its prosperity, and its vital system of race control. If the institution were threatened, so men believed, life itself in the South would be in jeopardy.[27]

It was this fear, finally, that tipped the political balance in 1844. In losing the election to Polk, Clay failed to carry a single Deep South state, including Georgia, although Georgia Whigs managed to win four of the eight congressional seats. Stephens easily won in the Seventh District by almost a thousand votes; Toombs did even better in the Eighth. Meanwhile, in north Georgia's Fifth and Sixth districts, Democrats Cobb and Joseph H. Lumpkin romped to victory by a combined majority of almost five thousand. Georgia Whigs had been sorely thumped—and they knew it. Beaten but not vanquished, the Whigs had been "too sanguine," wrote Stephens. Another observer agreed but added that the Democrats' devastating "charge of coalition with 'abolitionism'" had hurt too. Southern Whigs were fast learning their leson. For voter appeal, no issue, not even the entire Whig economic program, could hold a candle to southern rights. It was a lesson they never forgot.[28]

In early December Alexander Stephens returned to Washington, the "great river of political filth," in a mood no cheerier than his metaphor. The election still rankled. Clay, "the ablest American statesman," had fallen before a coalition of northern Democrats and abolitionists, the same coalition that had finally succeeded in repealing the House's gag rule, which allowed automatic tabling of abolitionist petitions. Now Democrats were concocting another foul scheme to unite behind a tariff and Texas annexation, thus appeasing both the northern and southern wings of the party.[29]

Stephens' scorn for Democratic politicking did not necessarily extend to individual Democrats. Two of his closest associates during this

27. Cooper, *Politics of Slavery*, 189–219.

28. AHS to Crawford, November 18, 1844, in Stephens Papers, DU; James E. Hamby to Thomas Butler King, October 22, 1844, in Thomas Butler King Papers, SHC/NC.

29. AHS to LS, December 2, 1844, Stephens Papers, MC.

session were Cobb and Lumpkin, both rollicking, jovial men. The trio often spent time together, visiting one another's rooms and joking on long walks around the city. Little Aleck had moved to a new boarding-house, Mrs. Carter's, on Capitol Hill. In those days, members of Washington's political community commonly lived together in boarding-houses—"messes," they were called. For twelve dollars a week Stephens was privileged to mess with Chief Justice Roger B. Taney and three associate justices of the Supreme Court, plus several congressmen, among them Milton Brown of Tennessee, Henry Grider of Kentucky, and Jacob Collamer of Vermont.

Stephens' upstairs room was sparsely but adequately furnished: a big four-poster bed, a table for the profusion of papers, a few chairs, a spittoon, a washbasin and ewer. Breakfast was served in the large common dining room at nine, dinner at four, and tea at six. The fare at Mrs. Carter's was more varied than at his previous mess, and Stephens liked it better. A creature of regular habits, he arose promptly at eight-thirty. He spent ten minutes or so beside the fireplace, almost completely swallowed up in the depths of a large, cushioned, calico-covered chair, scanning the morning papers. After breakfast he returned to his room, smoked two or three cigars, finished the papers, and read "miscellaneous matter" until the House session opened at noon. Back shortly after three, he worked on his prodigious correspondence—sometimes twenty or twenty-five letters a day—till seven, taking time out for dinner and tea. Then came more reading before bed at midnight.

A voracious, if not venturesome, reader, Stephens never cared much for light reading. He read little fiction before he reached middle age. He liked Walter Scott and Jonathan Swift, and the English poets Robert Burns, Alexander Pope, and George Byron, all of whom he quoted occasionally in letters. He concentrated mostly on history and constitutional treatises, and he read all the debates on the ratification of the Constitution he could get his hands on. Along with various travel accounts, Stephens read a miscellaneous grab bag of genuine classics: Plato's *Republic*, Adam Smith's *Wealth of Nations*, Boswell's *Johnson*, and Milton's *Paradise Lost*. Not surprisingly, he also found time to read Robert Burton's *Anatomy of Melancholy*.[30]

Melancholy he certainly was this December, although his health was good. As is true of most lonely people, holiday gaiety only aggravated

30. The preceding paragraphs are taken from *ibid.*, December 4, 5, 6, 20, 1844.

his depression. He would spend Christmas, he told Linton, alone in his room by the fire, pondering the past and future—which, naturally, appeared bleak. A year had gone by, he reflected, and he was still in the same place, marveling at changes wrought by the "whirlwind of time" and "its blasting and destroying effects upon man's prospects hopes and ambitions."[31]

The Texas gale continued to blow, fanned now by President Tyler's new scheme to annex the Lone Star Republic. Tyler had awaited the election results after his treaty failed. Now, he decided, the voters favored expansion. So in his December message he proposed that Congress annex Texas by joint resolution, which required only a simple majority of both houses. The message prompted a spate of proposed bills and resolutions, differing from one another only in modes of dealing with the slavery question in Texas.

Like all southern Whigs, Stephens found himself in a severe squeeze. Several sound arguments dictated continued opposition to the annexation of Texas. The question threatened party unity, for almost all northern Whigs opposed annexation as solely a plot to extend slavery. For those who equated a robust Whig party with continued health for the nation, the Texas question imperiled the Union itself. Furthermore, annexation would almost surely spark a war with Mexico. Constitutional difficulties abounded: Senator Berrien, for one, was convinced that Congress could constitutionally annex territory only by a two-thirds vote of the Senate. Finally, annexation was not only a Democratic project but also a Tyler project, both anathema to any orthodox Whig. But a strong public current at home favored annexation. During the campaign, the Democrats had demanded Texas as essential for southern safety, an argument Whigs could ignore only at their peril. And northern antislavery arguments against annexation made opposition to the measure by any southerner extremely difficult. In the end, Stephens would support annexation, but he would not come to this position easily.[32]

He would have preferred to support Clay's position of eventual annexation of Texas, a temporizing stance acceptable to the northern wing of the party. The Democratic blather about southern rights might be "humbug," but the voters in Georgia thought otherwise. Now Tyler

31. *Ibid.*, December 24, 1844.
32. Cooper, *Politics of Slavery*, 219–22.

had forced the issue and there was no time for temporizing. He and his like-minded southern Whig colleagues could not let Democrats at home exploit the Texas issue any longer. It had to be put to rest and in a way that protected the party's interests at home. "Let the Southern Whigs go for annexation immediately if not sooner," advised one Alabama Whig, "for we can never come to power until that question is settled." Stephens agreed. He wanted the matter done with. Annexation was "almost certain," he told Governor Crawford, and "upon proper principles . . . it ought to be done."[33]

Deciding the "proper principles" presented Stephens with a prickly problem. He was certain that the country could not acquire territory by treaty, despite Jefferson's opinion on Louisiana. He was also sure that, despite all the Democratic brouhaha about southern rights, the annexation of Texas offered no advantage to the "material interest" of the South. But on what terms to carry out annexation and how to handle Mexico's claims were vexing questions. Unsure and afraid of appearing foolish, he refused to speak on the question in early January.[34]

From his vantage point in Georgia, Toombs advised his friend to bend to the "popular will" embodied in the plan of Senator Ephraim Foster of Tennessee. Foster's resolutions, introduced on January 13 in the Senate and in the House by his colleague Milton Brown, proposed to admit Texas into the Union as a state, bypassing the territorial stage altogether. The new state would retain both her public debts and her public lands, and, with Texas' consent, new states might be formed out of her territory. The slavery question would be settled by allowing Texas, or any new states formed out of her lying below the Missouri Compromise line of 36°30', to come in "with or without slavery as the people of each State . . . may desire."[35]

Toombs's advice amused Stephens, for the two had been discussing the Texas question through the mail and up until now Toombs had appeared mired in a constitutional quandary. Stephens was ready to accept admission of Texas but insisted that the "shape of the question" would determine his vote. It had become obvious that a handful of

33. H. M. Cunningham to AHS, December 21, 1844, in Stephens Papers, LC; AHS to Crawford, December 23, 1844, in Stephens Papers, DU.

34. AHS to LS, January 5, 1845, in Stephens Papers, MC.

35. Toombs to AHS, January 24, 1845, in Ulrich B. Phillips (ed.), *The Correspondence of Robert Toombs, Alexander H. Stephens, and Howell Cobb* (1913; rpr. New York, 1970), 61. [Hereinafter cited as Phillips (ed.), *TSC Correspondence*.]; *Congressional Globe*, 28th Cong., 2nd Sess., 129–30.

pro-Texas southern Whigs held the balance of power in the House, and Little Aleck had helped his messmate Brown draw up a resolution that shaped the question to their own liking. Admitting Texas as a state was the best way of avoiding the questions of slavery and debt assumption. Meanwhile, one of Mexico's periodic revolutions had for the moment blunted the troublesome concern about that nation's response to annexation. Under these circumstances, not only would the popular will be served but also the interests of the southern Whigs.[36]

Up to now Stephens had held his peace on the House floor during weeks of endless speeches on Texas. Finally, on January 25, 1845, pained by "the constant din of broken processes of rationalization," he decided to add his voice to the din. He spoke for an hour, supporting annexation of Texas if carried out on proper principles. Two issues concerned him: the slavery question and proper settlement of Texas' debts. Unless the slavery issue were settled, he said, continued agitation might endanger the Union. Taking a swipe at Calhoun, he denied that the federal government could act to strengthen slavery in the states. If it could legislate to strengthen, it could also legislate to weaken. On federal assumption of the Texas debt, Stephens stood on typical Whig ground, advocating fiscal responsibility. The government had other outstanding obligations to meet first. Besides, no one knew the size of the Texas debt. Of all the plans proposed so far, only the Brown resolutions met his objections. They not only left the Texas debt in the state but also disposed of the slavery question, shutting the door on "future mischief, discord, and strife from that quarter."[37]

Of the several reasons Stephens gave for supporting annexation the one he offered for home consumption was the most revealing. Acquisition of Texas would increase southern political power in the Union, he said. He would oppose annexation if done solely to extend slavery. "I am no defender of slavery in the abstract," he declared. "Stern necessity," decreed by God Himself, required slavery in Texas as well as the other southern states. Slavery would always be necessary wherever whites and blacks were "blended together in the same proportions."[38]

36. AHS to LS, January 27, 1845, in Stephens Papers, MC; AHS to Crawford, January 14, 1845, in Francis W. Pickens Papers, DU; AHS to John Bird, January 10, 1845, in Stephens Papers, EU; AHS to Robert Sims Burch, June 15, 1854, in *American Historical Review*, VIII (1902), 94; Avary (ed.), *Stephens Recollections*, 18.

37. AHS to LS, January 22, 1845, in Stephens Papers, MC; Stephens' speech in *Congressional Globe*, 28th Cong., 2nd Sess., Appendix, 309–14.

38. *Congressional Globe*, 28th Cong., 2nd Sess., Appendix, 311.

Unwittingly, Stephens had revealed his total commitment to slavery even as he denied defending the institution. Although he condemned the slave trade and did not yet embrace the "positive good" of slavery, his mind was made up about race control: it was essential and would remain so. It was inconceivable to him that any system other than slavery could ensure social stability in the South. "Truth," he had stated in his speech, "is fixed, indelible, immutable, and eternal." Black inferiority and subordination to the white race, albeit regrettable, were "stern necessity" because for Stephens they were eternal truths. Thus he could deny defending slavery in the abstract—whatever that meant— because it existed nowhere. But slavery as a socioeconomic reality in the South—that was another matter. It would not be long before Stephens discerned its connection with southern "rights" just as clearly as any Democrat.[39]

Brown's resolutions passed 122 to 98, with eight southern Whigs joining the Democrats to carry them. Whether Stephens' oratory had affected the outcome or not, he thought he made one of his best speeches. He was particularly pleased at being in the van of the southern Whigs. He and his friends had been decisive, he told his brother John, forcing the Democrats "to take our terms . . . or none at all." Typically, he exaggerated his own importance. Texas would have come into the Union eventually no matter what Stephens did. The Senate passed the resolutions, and on his last day in office Tyler offered annexation to Texas. Incoming president Polk allowed the action to stand. Unfortunately, annexation did little to soothe either a distracted country or some of Georgia's Whigs.[40]

Stephens had taken an advanced and hardly universal position in the state party. Berrien and his supporters immediately interpreted the speech as a play by the "shrewd & wily" Stephens to assume leadership of Georgia's Whigs. Constitutional purists feared the party would be torn in two over the issue. Even Toombs agreed. "I fear nothing now can save us from total wreck on this ill-starred Texas question," he told Berrien.[41]

Stephens had obviously acted on his own, judging from his anxiety

39. *Ibid.*
40. AHS to LS, January 25, 1845, in Stephens Papers, MC; AHS to JLS, January 31, 1845, in Stephens Papers, EU.
41. Charles J. Jenkins to John M. Berrien, February 3, 1845, Toombs to Berrien, February 13, 1845, both in Berrien Papers, SHC/NC.

about Georgia Whig opinion plus expressions of disapproval that began arriving in the mail. Nevertheless, he had accurately gauged Georgia sentiment. What points he lost among Whigs he picked up from Democrats. Some of the latter, like the editor of the Augusta *Constitutionalist*, patronizingly congratulated him for belatedly taking the right course. Others thought he deserved "sincere thanks" and "great credit."[42]

Actually Little Aleck had not misjudged most Whigs. Toombs, despite his concern for party unity, assured him that Whigs "universally" approved his course. Many, including himself, differed with him on the constitutional question, but all endorsed the terms of the annexation because they were "very favourable to the South." In the end, this consideration overrode all others. No split ensued in the Georgia Whig party, although Berrien's supporters remained disgruntled. Stephens had recognized the Texas question for what it was—a sectional issue, one that ultimately outweighed any constitutional quibbles over the means of increasing southern power. It was also patently clear that the Democrats had carried Georgia because the Whigs had lagged on this key issue.[43]

One Georgia Whig, writing to commend Little Aleck's course, had told him: "We want no more political hob[b]ies for the democracy to ride to office on." Stephens didn't need to be reminded. He knew that to survive in Georgia the Whigs had to be right on southern questions. And get right they would, Stephens decided, under his leadership, if necessary—even if Berrien disapproved. He had not plotted his accession to leadership; it came naturally. Alexander Stephens was not cut out to be a follower.[44]

42. Augusta *Constitutionalist*, June 17, 1845; J. W. Burney to Cobb, January 31, 1845, in Phillips (ed.), *TSC Correspondence*, 62.

43. Toombs to AHS, February 16, 1845, in Phillips (ed.), *TSC Correspondence*, 64.

44. Gabriel T. Spearman to AHS, March 4, 1845, in Stephens Papers, MC.

V

A Whole Catalog of Evils

At one o'clock in the morning of February 27, 1845, Stephens stepped off the train at Crawfordville. The crisp, clear night, as still as death, held the little congressman motionless on the station platform for a long while. Death occupied his thoughts. The shimmering pinpricks of light in the cloudless sky were windows to, reminders of, a changeless, stable world beyond time. He was thinking, perhaps, of Aaron, or of Williamson Bird and his wife, with whom he had lived since 1834. Bird had died in 1843, and this past winter his wife had died. People he used to look for on returning home were dead and gone, he mused. An overpowering wave of sadness engulfed him.

In 1839 Stephens had been named executor of Bird's will, and within a week of his return home, he bought the Bird house and ten-acre lot "for $250 credit until Christmas." It would be his home for the rest of his life. Facing south, the house capped a small rise a few hundred yards from where the Georgia Railroad tracks bisected the town. It was simply built, a two-story gable-roofed structure with four chimneys and a four-over-four-room central hall plan. That summer Stephens spent several hundred dollars on fresh paint, new roofing, and wallpaper. At the front door he added a small, one-story portico with white Tuscan columns—his only bow to the contemporary southern mania for

Greek Revival architecture. A magnificent stand of oak, hickory, and locust trees amply shaded the grounds.[1]

John L. Bird, Williamson's son, continued to live at the house, as did prim and proper Quinea "Parson" O'Neal, the clerk of the court of ordinary. Later, in 1845, a young lawyer, George Bristow, whom Stephens had helped through school and educated in the law, moved in. Linton, finally a lawyer himself, joined them the next year. Until 1859 Stephens, logically enough, called his home "Bachelor's Hall." Although his extended family soon included several female relatives who would have relished keeping house for him, he apparently wanted no women around. Only Old Mat, a black slave, who cooked, stocked the pantry, and ran the household, was accorded the privilege. As with her successors, Eliza and Dora, the household domain belonged to her totally.

Stephens never kept more than four or five blacks about the house. And he required strictest probity of them. Drunkenness, for example, meant banishment to the "back lot"—field work. On one occasion, after repeated offenses, Stephens did so banish Bob, the handyman, to the fields. It was strange, he told Linton, how Negroes didn't know when they were well off: "They soon become spoiled and make fools of themselves."[2]

Stephens seldom spoke so negatively of his slaves. Habitually kind and patient with their faults and idiosyncrasies, he "spoiled" them himself in many ways. Once purchased by Stephens, a slave could be sure of a home for life, for Little Aleck did not believe in selling his "people" or in separating families. For all his racist presumptions, not to mention his innate conviction of superiority, Stephens was a benign and indulgent master. He put up with thievery by Pierce, a body servant, for years. And Georgia Parker, one of Stephens' former slaves, tells of a slave named Dave, whom Stephens gave some money and told to disappear because "he got in trouble wid a white woman." By comparative standards, even his field hands led comfortable lives. They had more than enough to eat and could hunt or fish and tend a huge vegetable garden of their own. A white physician promptly tended the sick. No slave was ever whipped or jailed. The task system governed the

1. AHS to LS, February 28, March 6, 1845, in Stephens Papers, MC.
2. *Ibid.*, July 9, 1845.

work routine: when the day's alloted task was done, work ended for the day. Every slave on Stephens' place had a pass to leave the plantation, and slave patrollers were barred from his property. The slaves generally got all day Sunday as well as Thursday and Saturday afternoons off. Christmas week was holiday, and Christmas Day, with a gigantic feast and whiskey in abundance, an occasion of much hilarity. Two singular facts underscore Stephens' benevolence as a master: not one of his slaves ever ran away from home. And in and around Crawfordville Stephens' slaves had a nickname—people called them "Stephens' free niggers." [3]

Melancholy plagued Stephens for most of the year, although sometimes he actually seemed to enjoy it. He would never wish this depression and weariness of life on Linton, he told him, but had to admit they brought him a bittersweet pleasure. Rather than attempt to divert his mind, he cultivated his woe by solitude, taking long walks through the woods and over the fields. Constantly tormented by the transitory nature of being, he fueled his unhappiness by visiting old ramshackle houses and places associated with friends who had died. Ruins, he said, were "congenial to my spirit." In nature's timeless beauties, which have inspired in countless poets thoughts of a reassuring permanence, Stephens found only "the association of age, the lapse of time." Preferring "a hermit's cave grotto or hole to any place on earth," he would sometimes shun visitors and go off by himself the better to savor his misery. The death of yet another Crawfordville friend, Chelsea Bristow, in September brought back the doleful memories of his father's death and Aaron's. "Life to me seems but little of good," he concluded. [4]

Some men he encountered in life didn't seem much good either. His sensitive spirit rebelled against the blatant cruelties of the slavery system. A female runaway slave from town had been recaptured and lashed with a whip three hundred times. Stephens was appalled. The baseness and brutality of men and the suffering they inflicted on others almost tempted him "to turn misanthrope," he said. What was man but a

3. "Narrative of Georgia Parker," in George P. Rawick (ed.), *The American Slave: A Composite Autobiography* (1972; rpr. Westport, Conn., 1977), XII, 38–57. Many letters in the Stephens Papers, LC, from Stephens' former slaves attest to their great devotion to him.
   4. AHS to LS, March 25, April 21, August 24, September 17, 22, 1845, in Stephens Papers, MC.

cruel animal, driving his beasts of burden to death and frequently killing other life for pure amusement? Not content, men had even turned on their own species, making beasts of burden of them. Scarcely a month after this heartfelt outburst, Stephens laid out $650 to buy two slaves—a woman and her eight-year-old son.[5]

Except to attend court, Stephens mostly stayed in Crawfordville between congressional sessions. But he did attend the state Whig convention in Milledgeville, where, much to Berrien's mortification, the delegates selected Duncan Clinch, who had voted with Stephens on Texas, as president of the convention. Nominated for another term as governor, Crawford went on to win the election on a platform pledging rigid economy in state government. Stephens signed a statement defending Whig principles, but he did no speaking.[6]

The legislature assembled in Milledgeville in early November, and Stephens saw Berrien humiliated further. The Whig caucus refused to nominate the senator to succeed himself for the term beginning in 1847, in effect repudiating his alliance with the national Whigs. Berrien immediately resigned his seat, causing what Stephens called "a perfect snarl" in the party. "To keep out of the excitement," Little Aleck left town while the Whigs attempted to regroup by reelecting Berrien to the seat he had just resigned. This little charade at least had the virtue of silencing the crowing Democrats and restoring a semblance of Whig unity. But the lessons of Milledgeville were not lost on younger Whigs. Clearly Berrien had forfeited his power in Georgia by hewing too closely to the party line on Texas.[7]

In December, 1845, Stephens returned to a House securely controlled by the Democrats. Being in the minority, either along party lines or by personal choice, soon became a familiar position for him. Depending on the issue (or "principle," he would say) involved, Stephens could be a tenacious obstructionist. Like many politicians, he was sometimes prone to let personalities influence his stand on an issue. Such was the case with Stephens and James K. Polk. Almost all Whigs loathed the president with fraternal unanimity, but Stephens hated him with special intensity. Polk's policies threatened Stephens politically, but for Little Aleck the president also epitomized what he most despised—an

---

5. *Ibid.*, August 15, 1845.
6. *Ibid.*, July 5, 1845.
7. *Ibid.*, November 10, 17, 1845.

ignorant and amoral adventurer and, far worse, one with the power to enforce his reckless schemes. Stephens naturally reacted to Polk with righteous combativeness.

His first clash with the administration came almost immediately. In his first message to Congress, Polk requested authorization to notify England that joint occupation of Oregon by the two countries would be terminated in one year. The request had raised a storm in Congress, even bringing Calhoun back to the Senate out of a short-lived retirement. What was at stake, Calhoun and many others believed, was war or peace with Great Britain.[8]

Since 1818 settlers from both nations had occupied Oregon jointly. Three times the United States had offered to establish a boundary at the forty-ninth parallel from the Rockies to the Pacific, and each time Britain, because of her lucrative fur trade interests south of the line, had refused. A flood of American settlers into Oregon had now changed the balance of power there, and Polk determined to settle the question for good. After yet another British refusal to agree on 49°, he reacted with characteristic vigor. He asserted a U.S. claim to the entire Oregon country. The president intended to bluster the British into acquiescing to the original U.S. claim. Unfortunately, he had been secretive about his purpose, not only raising extravagant expectations in the Northwest but also alarming the Whigs and Calhounites, who feared war with England unless Polk modified his demands.[9]

Throughout January and February of 1846 Congress debated the Oregon question furiously. Stephens, however, remained silent. For a while he could not decide what effect giving notice to England would have. At first, he thought Polk's "bad management" had made war with England "*inevitable*," but by February he had become convinced that serving notice would probably spur negotiations and compromise. Unless Polk relented on his claim to all of Oregon, however, war *would* be inevitable. Stephens refused to support this claim. By his reckoning, U.S. rights in Oregon to that extent were simply not clear.[10]

8. John C. Calhoun to R. M. T. Hunter, March 26, 1845, in Charles Henry Ambler (ed.), *The Correspondence of Robert M. T. Hunter, 1826–1876*, Vol. II of *Annual Report of the American Historical Association for the Year 1916* (Washington, D.C., 1918), 75–76.

9. Charles Sellers, *James K. Polk: Continentalist, 1843–46* (Princeton, 1966), 244, 249–50, 359.

10. AHS to Crawford, February 3, 1846, in Stephens Papers, LC; AHS to John L. Stephens, January 4, 1846, in Stephens Papers, EU; AHS to "My dear sir," January 28, 1846, in Telamon Cuyler Collection, UG.

Toombs agreed, but he also grasped the sectional implications of the question. Acquisition of any part of Oregon would not help the South. He didn't "care a fig" about Oregon and would gladly give it to anybody but the British. Still, Oregon was free territory, and he did not "want a foot of [it] or . . . any country especially without 'niggers.'"[11]

By the time the question came to a vote, however, both Stephens and Toombs cast their ballots against giving notice to England. State Department documents released by Polk made it appear that, even in the face of warlike preparations in England, the United States would insist on its title to the entire Oregon territory. Neither Georgian could support such a position. To Stephens, Polk's uncompromising truculence meant war, a refusal to compromise on an issue where both parties clearly had rights. Throughout his career Stephens had an almost instinctive disposition to compromise—even, as will be seen, when the "rights" at issue were not so patently questionable as the U.S. claim to all of Oregon. National honor, Stephens told Georgians in a public letter, could be maintained only by demanding what was right, not by submitting to what was wrong.[12]

Polk's leadership may have been debatable, but he knew how to get what he wanted. Britain and the United States eventually signed a treaty dividing Oregon at 49°, but by then the president's expansionist designs in the Southwest had produced a war with the Republic of Mexico. Fighting had broken out in May, before settlement of the Oregon question. No one, however, took the Mexicans seriously. The consequence of such a war, wrote Cobb, "scarcely creates a ripple upon the water."[13]

The Mexican War, destined to create not a ripple but a tidal wave in American history, had its origins in the Texas revolution of the 1830s. Never resigned to Texas' independence, Mexico had sundered diplomatic relations with Washington upon its annexation. Two disputes between the countries existed when Polk took office: damage claims by American citizens against Mexico and Texas' uncertain western boundary. The United States backed Texas' contention that the Rio Grande constituted the state's southern and western boundary. Polk wanted

11. Toombs to Crawford, February 6, 1846, in Toombs Papers, LC.
12. *Congressional Globe*, 29th Cong., 1st Sess., 332–35; AHS to LS, February 8, 1846, in Stephens Papers, MC; AHS to Messers. Grieve & Orme, February 9, 1846, in Augusta *Chronicle and Sentinel*, February 19, 1846.
13. Cobb to his wife, April 28, 1846, in Cobb Papers, UG.

these disputes settled, but he also wanted California and a sizable chunk of coastal territory. And to achieve this objective, he was prepared to pay or fight, whichever was necessary.

Polk first attempted negotiation, sending a minister plenipotentiary, John Slidell, to Mexico with full authority to settle the disputes and buy Mexico's northern territory (New Mexico and California) at the best possible price. As fate would have it, Slidell arrived during one of Mexico's periodic internal convulsions, and neither the first government nor its replacement received him. In early January, when word of this situation reached Washington, Polk ordered General Zachary Taylor and a large detachment of troops to take up a position on the Rio Grande. Committed to war upon the failure of the mission, Polk stayed his hand only because of the delicate state of relations with Britain.[14]

Slidell's return forced him to act. In the midst of preparing a war message to Congress, the president learned of a clash between American and Mexican forces on the Rio Grande. Several American soldiers had been killed. He now claimed in his message that Mexico "invaded our territory and shed American blood upon American soil," that war existed by Mexico's own act. Many congressmen then and later questioned these assertions, but few could deny Polk the means to wage a war already begun. The declaration of war passed both houses of Congress by large majorities.[15]

Polk got his war, but without any help from Stephens. Even before the war message reached the House on May 11, he had criticized Taylor's move to the Rio Grande as provocative. Stephens abstained from voting on the war bill. Democratic strategists had coupled to it a preamble declaring that war existed "by the act of the Republic of Mexico." Whigs faced a bitter choice, for to man the army they were forced to endorse Polk's reading of events on the Rio Grande. In the House, debate was rushed, and when the matter came to a vote few Whigs were willing to hogtie the army. The war bill passed the House, 174 to 14, and the Senate, 40 to 2. In the upper house, Calhoun argued strenuously against the preamble and urged delay, but an implacable Democratic majority would brook none. When the vote was finally taken, Calhoun, Berrien, and George Evans of Maine abstained.[16]

14. The preceding paragraphs are based on Sellers, *Polk*, 213, 398–405.
15. James D. Richardson (ed.), *A Compilation of the Messages and Papers of the Presidents, 1879–1902* (10 vols.; Washington, D.C., 1903), IV, 437–43.
16. AHS to JLS, May 10, 1846, in Stephens Papers, EU; *Congressional Globe*, 29th Cong., 1st Sess., 795–97, 804.

Stephens suddenly found himself in the highly unusual position of agreeing with, even admiring, Calhoun. He applauded his speech and told Linton he would have said the same in the House had he got the chance. He feared war with France and England, both potential allies of Mexico. And there was no doubt about who had caused the crisis: "The whole catalogue of evils is properly and justly chargeable upon Mr. Polk." Toombs concurred with his friend. Marching Taylor to the Rio Grande, he stormed, had been unlawful, a usurpation on the rights of the House, and an aggression against Mexico.[17]

Once the Whigs in Congress began denouncing Polk, any chance of bipartisan support for the war evaporated. Whigs had to accept the war's existence, so they continued to vote supplies. But the war was a political issue from the beginning, one of the most bitterly opposed conflicts in American history. Southern Whigs resisted it violently, particularly after it became apparent that the war was being waged to force territorial concessions, a policy Whigs found not only morally repugnant but politically explosive. Even before Polk's intentions became clear, the Whig press was raising a warning. "We have territory enough," argued one Georgia editor, "especially if every province, like Texas, is to bring in its train war and debt and death."[18]

The Democrats' ruthless zeal in pressing the war disgusted Stephens. He found it difficult to keep silent on the House floor. After studying the correspondence Polk had submitted with his war message, he could hold his peace no more. So on June 16 he consumed his allotted hour on the floor blistering Polk for his "imprudence, indiscretion, and mismanagement." The letters proved the needlessness of Taylor's move to Matamoras, he said. The Mexicans had evinced no hostility, nor had any Texas citizens in the area requested aid. Only the president's *"masked design of provoking Mexico to war"* could explain it. Moreover, Polk had no legal right to order military occupation of disputed territory without congressional approval. Congress had wisely left the boundary question to be negotiated. By ordering Taylor into the disputed area the president had fixed the boundary himself by military means, abrogating congressional warmaking powers to himself.

Stephens made it clear that he would continue to vote supplies, but he wanted it plainly stated why the war was being fought. Was it "to

17. AHS to LS, May 13, 1846, in Stephens Papers, MC; *Congressional Globe*, 29th Cong., 1st Sess., 837.
18. Columbus *Enquirer*, July 22, 1846.

repel invasion, to protect Texas, to establish the Rio Grande as the Boundary"—or for other objects? He would not abide a war for territorial conquest. Republics could never be spread by arms; only voluntary accession could accomplish that end. He expected and welcomed the eventual spread of American institutions over the continent in good time, but only if it were done peacefully. He could not resist a dig at the Democrats. The Whigs were the party of "true progress" in the United States, he said. Others advocated an entirely different kind of progress, one "of party—of excitement—of lust of power—a spirit of war—aggression—violence and licentiousness" that, if allowed, would overturn "all law—all order—and the Constitution itself." [19]

Despite a good deal of partisan cant, Stephens had clearly stated his bedrock reasons for opposing the Mexican War. The war had been brought about by Polk's despicable design; it was being fought to appropriate the territory of a smaller and weaker neighbor. These aspects of the case were clear. But the conflict posed a far more serious threat. It eroded political values Stephens believed elemental in relations between men and nations: law, order, and constitutionalism. Without these, there could be no progress, only anarchy.

The Democrats, of course, did not share his fears, and several rose to dispute him. One of these was another silver-tongued southern orator, William L. Yancey of Alabama. Regrettably, said Yancey, Stephens had joined "the contemptible horde of abolitionists who infest this Hall" in opposing the war. He thought the speech had been a calculated effort to cool the patriotic ardor of the country. Yancey's speech contained nothing particularly offensive—"contemptible abolitionists" was a common enough sobriquet for northern Whigs—but it riled Stephens. Perhaps Yancey's manner bothered the Georgian, for two days later hot words passed between them, and the thin-skinned Stephens, via Toombs, dispatched a challenge. Several days later, though, the *National Intelligencer* announced the restoration of relations between the two men. Apparently, the seconds, Toombs and Armistead Burt, smoothed things over. [20]

Whig reaction to Stephens' speech also soothed the wounds Yancey's barbs had inflicted. Congratulatory messages poured in from all over

19. AHS to JLS, May 29, 1846, in Stephens Papers, EU; speech in Cleveland, *Stephens*, 303–19.
20. *Congressional Globe*, 29th Cong., 1st Sess., Appendix, 952, 961; Washington *National Intelligencer*, June 27, 1846.

the country. Supreme Court Justice John McLean spoke for most Whigs when he agreed with Stephens that the war served "party purposes" and not the national interest. He too feared Polk's expansionist designs. But Democrat Calhoun also admired Stephens' speech and told him so. Self-appointed spokesman for the South, Calhoun foresaw nothing but unmitigated evil for his section in continuing the war. When he could—the unresolved Oregon question had sealed his lips for the moment—Calhoun told Stephens he would take the identical position on Mexico as the Georgian. And he later did.[21]

Georgia's Democrats, however, responded in kind to the Whigs' fierce attacks on the war issue. Following their congressional leaders, the Whigs had become "perfectly rabid" in opposing the war, said one Democrat. To counter them, the Democrats employed an ageless technique: they impugned the patriotism of their opponents. Naturally Stephens presented a conspicuous target. One staunch Democrat who dipped his pen in sulfuric acid to scorch Little Aleck was rotund Milledgeville lawyer Herschel Johnson, an old college chum of Stephens, who wrote a series of articles under the *nom de plume* "Baldwin" in the Milledgeville *Federal Union*. On July 14, he accused Stephens of "vanity," "sophistry," "sophomoric pedantry," and unleashing a "torrent of unmeaning bombast." Though sharp, these insults did not cut to the quick. What did was a sentence appearing a week later: Stephens' Texas annexation vote "stares him in the face," wrote Johnson, thereby branding his recent statements with "unequivocal falsehood."[22]

Stephens could not abide being called a liar. After finding out who "Baldwin" was, he demanded a public retraction of the sentence. (The conventions governing disclosure by newspaper editors of the names of anonymous scribblers were peculiar: the editor could not reveal the name unless a duel were threatened, at which point he was obliged to help the aggrieved party kill his tormentor if he could by revealing the name.) Johnson refused to retract, professing to see nothing offensive in the statement. So Little Aleck followed his usual course; he sent Johnson an immediate challenge. Johnson, as Stiles had earlier, remained unruffled and refused the challenge. With his only "honorable" avenue closed, Stephens felt compelled to release the entire cor-

21. John McLean to AHS, July 15, 1846, in Stephens Papers, MC; Avary (ed.), *Stephens Recollections*, 18–19.

22. John B. Lamar to Cobb, June 24, 1846, in Phillips (ed.), *TSC Correspondence*, 82; Milledgeville *Federal Union*, July 14, 21, 1846.

respondence to the press. Herschel Johnson would eventually become one of Stephens' closest friends, but for the next nine years neither man spoke to the other.[23]

Although the Democrats, according to the *Chronicle*, "exhausted ingenuity" to defeat him in 1846, Stephens easily won reelection in the Seventh District. (Georgia Whigs did well generally, carrying four congressional districts—and in one, the Fifth, they ran no candidate.) Fortified by Whig approbation at home, Stephens returned to Washington more determined than ever to resist what he regarded as an unholy and unconstitutional war.[24]

Polk had come out fighting. In his December message he assailed his critics for giving aid and comfort to the enemy. The Whigs were sensitive to this charge. Recalling the painful experience of the New England Federalists, who had paid for their opposition to the War of 1812 by disappearing as a party, the Whigs did not want to appear unpatriotic. Moreover, the war was proceeding gloriously for American arms. By early 1847 American forces had overrun most of northern Mexico. These vast land seizures represented, paradoxically, both the administration's strongest and weakest points in defending the war. Democrats could claim the territorial conquests as "indemnities" due the United States for Mexican intransigence, but their opponents could legitimately ask if this prize were the real reason for fighting. Was all this land, and who knew how much more, to be annexed? Repeatedly asking such questions allowed the Whigs to shift the moral burden of the war back onto the Democrats, while they themselves avoided the charge of being unpatriotic. Southern Whigs had even more pressing reasons to ask these questions. They knew that territorial aggrandizement by the United States would reopen the slavery question. And raising this issue again they feared like death itself.[25]

Slavery had thrust its noxious presence into the proceedings in late August, 1846. Polk had requested a $2 million appropriation from Congress to dangle before the Mexicans in exchange for boundary adjustments. To this bill, David Wilmot, a Pennsylvania Democrat, had

23. AHS to Herschel Johnson, August 19, 20, 1846, Johnson to AHS, August 20, 1846, all in Stephens Papers, MC; Johnson to AHS, August 29, 1846, in Herschel Johnson Papers, DU.

24. Augusta *Chronicle and Sentinel*, September 28, 1846.

25. Royce C. McCrary, "Georgia Politics and the Mexican War," *Georgia Historical Quarterly*, LX (Fall, 1976), 218.

attached an amendment barring slavery from any territory secured from Mexico by the war—the Wilmot Proviso, it came to be called. When the measure came to a vote in the House, an assortment of northern Democrats, disgruntled with the administration for one reason or another, joined an almost unanimous bloc of northern Whigs in supporting it. Having passed the House by a lopsided sectional vote, the appropriation bill eventually failed because Congress adjourned before the Senate could act on it.[26]

The proviso appeared again in early 1847, grafted onto a new appropriation bill Polk wanted. In August the president had been perplexed: what did slavery have to do with peace? he wondered. But now he was alarmed. He feared slavery agitation could endanger the Union. For the only time in his life, Stephens agreed with Polk. The North intended to stick the proviso onto every bill, he told Linton, forcing southerners to vote against every such measure. A "tremendous struggle" loomed; the future appeared dark.[27]

Stephens spoke as a southerner, not as a Whig. The Wilmot Proviso mortally threatened the South, striking at her political power in the Union, which in turn guarded her social system. But even more, it was a gross personal and collective insult to proud southerners. In their eyes, it branded them as unclean, dishonorable, and unfit to direct their own destinies, unequal members in a Union of supposedly equal states. United southern opposition to the proviso was far less a question of whether southerners desired slavery's expansion (some did, others didn't) than a reaction to perceived insult. This was why southerners saw no practical difference between an abolitionist and a freesoiler. Both were equally execrable; both desecrated the South's image of itself as an honorable and decent society.

But southern politicians could never agree on a practical political way to deal with the proviso. To retain power in their states, most of these politicians—Calhoun and his small cadre excepted—had to operate within the party system. And that highly competitive system only intensified internal southern discord, despite universal southern agreement that the heinous proviso ought to be repudiated.

The southern Whigs moved quickly to avert this grave political dan-

26. Sellers, *Polk*, 477–83.
27. Milo Milton Quaife (ed.), *The Diary of James K. Polk During His Presidency, 1845–49* (4 vols.; Chicago, 1910), II, 75, 305; AHS to LS, January 5, 1847, in Stephens Papers, MC.

ger. The most obvious way was to prevent *any* territorial acquisition from Mexico. So on January 22, 1847, Stephens tried to introduce resolutions in the House declaring that the war was not being fought for conquest of territory and calling for a speedy end to the fighting. By an almost strict party vote, the House refused to suspend its rules to allow their introduction.[28]

His resolutions had failed, but Stephens' reputation with the country's Whigs took a quantum leap. Whig presses North and South congratulated him, and by mid-autumn the "no territory" position had become Whig doctrine. In November, Clay himself endorsed it. But by that time the real question was not whether to devour Mexican territory, but how much of it to swallow. As it turned out, only a few square miles were enough to cause terminal indigestion.[29]

The Democrats bitterly attacked Stephens' resolutions. To label them "absurdities," said the *Constitutionalist*, wasn't strong enough. Refusing territory would be "humiliating," a sacrifice of southern rights to antislavery northern bullies. In a curious, twisted way northern Democrats echoed their southern colleagues. The "cry of no more territory," said the *New Hampshire Patriot*, was simply a slaveholder's ploy to avoid the proviso.[30]

As always, Calhoun saw the trend of events in apocalyptic terms. As a steadily shrinking minority in the Union, the South had to be united to maintain her rights, he believed. On February 19, 1847, he introduced his own set of resolutions on the territorial slavery question. The territories were the common property of all the states, they declared, and Congress could make no law depriving any state of its full rights in the territories without violating the Constitution.[31]

Far from producing southern unity, Calhoun succeeded only in alienating administration supporters. Southern Democrats could hardly endorse a man who had opposed Polk's policies from the beginning. Indeed, most Democratic editors in Georgia had already read him out of the party. Georgia Whigs were more receptive, however. Toombs even

28. *Congressional Globe*, 29th Cong., 2nd Sess., 240.
29. Augusta *Chronicle and Sentinel*, January 30, February 4, 10, 1847; Washington *National Intelligencer*, January 24, 1847.
30. Augusta *Constitutionalist*, January 29, 1847; *New Hampshire Patriot* quoted in Joseph G. Rayback, *Free Soil: The Election of 1848* (Lexington, Ky., 1970), 123.
31. Resolutions in Richard K. Cralle (ed.), *The Works of John C. Calhoun* (6 vols.; New York, 1854–55), IV, 347–48.

endorsed the Carolinian's leadership. The South's policy on the Mexican question "will be in your hands," he told Calhoun.[32]

It is doubtful whether Stephens had any praise for Calhoun. He harbored a deep-seated suspicion of extremism. Although intellectually indebted to Calhoun, he shared neither his disdain for parties nor his taste for confrontation politics. Disposed to compromise if he could, Stephens, unlike Calhoun, always labored to advance the fortunes of his party.

Nevertheless, he just as consistently denied partisan, much less personal, motives. Part of his facade was attempting to appear principled and idealistic, always motivated in politics by the loftiest goals of justice and patriotism. Unfortunately, while trying to convince others that he acted wholly from disinterested motives, he often deceived himself. He was capable of tempestuous passion, yet condemned by physical health, upbringing, and disposition to being sedentary. Moreover, as a philosophical idealist rigorously schooled in the forbidding tenets of fundamentalist Christianity, he instinctively distrusted and despised the passions. To him they were the weakest element in man's tripartite nature of body, mind, and soul, an element to be rigidly controlled, suppressed. He could have never conceived, much less accepted, the idea that they were integral to man's nature. Hence Stephens wore the mask of the principled statesman, a man actuated only by the disembodied ideals of honor, justice, and truth. But every so often the mask would slip.

It was indeed sadly askew when he rose in the House on February 12, 1847, to speak. Although the House was considering a $3 million appropriation bill to advance negotiations with the Mexicans, Stephens preferred raking Polk over the coals in a series of savage denunciations. Little Aleck's speech bristled with aspersions on the president's character. His "unskillfulness" and "faithlessness" had run the country onto the breakers. The war had been "improperly, unwisely, [and] wickedly commenced" solely and unconstitutionally by the president. No one acquainted with Polk's "unparalleled duplicity" could possibly believe his protestations that the war was not being waged for conquest.

---

32. Augusta *Constitutionalist*, February 18, 1847; Augusta *Chronicle and Sentinel*, February 27, 1847; Toombs to Calhoun, April 30, 1847, in Chauncey S. Boucher and Robert P. Brooks (eds.), *Correspondence Addressed to John C. Calhoun, 1837–1849,* in Vol. II of *Annual Report of the American Historical Association for the Year 1929* (Washington, D.C., 1930), 373–74.

Toward the end of the speech Stephens became less strident. He begged his colleagues not to allow expansion by force of arms, a course not only "wrong in itself" but contrary "to the whole spirit of and genius of the liberty we enjoy." No part of Mexico should be seized as indemnity, he urged, for it would cost more to own and protect it than the territory would be worth. This would be reason enough to oppose the appropriation, but the Wilmot Proviso provided far more compelling ones. Was the House willing to risk the harmony of the Union for more territory?

In marked contrast to his remarks on slavery during the Texas crisis, Stephens now felt it necessary to defend the institution outright. Slavery stood on the rock-solid moral foundation of the Bible, he claimed. Until Christianity itself was overthrown, it could never be considered an offense against God's law. As a political question he would not even argue the subject. It was beyond Congress' power to affect. Slavery was a state matter. There the Constitution had placed it, and there Congress, if it were wise, would leave it. As long as sectional feelings stayed quiet, the Union would remain strong and permanent. The administration's policy, to seize Mexican territory at any cost, would, he feared, severely test that permanency.[33]

Whether Stephens' grim warning changed any minds is a moot question. As it turned out, the House approved the "Three Million Bill"—without the proviso—on the last day of the session. Polk got his money, but beyond this, the session did little but further exacerbate sectional animosities. Both Stephens and Toombs missed the final vote on the bill, having left Washington for home and the spring court sessions.

Georgians elected a governor in 1847, a year of politics as usual. The Wilmot Proviso figured in the campaign, but only to the extent that it allowed Georgia parties to extol their own soundness, and their opponents' weakness, in opposing it. Georgians' ingrained habits of partisanship permitted nothing remotely resembling the southern solidarity Calhoun envisioned.

The Whigs' approval of the Carolinian's February resolutions had sadly misled Calhoun. He had hoped that it signaled a union of all southerners regardless of party to confront the North on the slavery question. "With union among ourselves, there is nothing to fear," he

33. Speech in Cleveland, *Stephens*, 321–32.

wrote. But although the Georgia Whig convention thanked Calhoun for his opposition to the war, it did not mention his resolutions. Instead it went serenely about its business of nominating a candidate for governor, Duncan Clinch, a former militia general, and condemning the proviso as unjust and unconstitutional.[34]

The Democrats were more pugnacious on the proviso question, resolving not to support any candidate for president who did not openly repudiate it. They accused the Whigs of vacillating on the issue for fear of offending their northern allies. Their candidate, George W. B. Towns of Talbot County, a spirited fighter, immediately took to the stump and put the Whigs on the defensive. Whig efforts to blame the Democrats for the proviso or turn the discussion to local issues had little effect. Clinch was beaten, but the Whigs managed to retain a slim majority in the General Assembly, which they promptly used to elect Berrien and William C. Dawson to Senate seats.[35]

If Stephens took any active part in this ill-fated campaign, no record of it has survived. He remained at home, enjoying the company of Linton and his other bachelor boarders. Meanwhile, Winfield Scott led a victorious American army into the Mexican capital, and Nicholas Trist, Polk's trusted envoy, negotiated the treaty that would bring vast new territories into the Union. A whole new catalog of evils was about to beset the nation.

34. Calhoun quoted in Richard Harrison Shryock, *Georgia and the Union in 1850* (Durham, N.C., 1926), 142–43.
35. Augusta *Constitutionalist*, July 7, 1847.

VI

Young Indian

"I am very much like a chronometer," Stephens wrote Linton shortly after his return to Washington. "I need something *bearing down* upon me to keep me in motion . . . without it I am disposed to be inert and idle." Who could tell, he wondered, what monsters time's womb would produce in the next year.[1]

Political monsters there already were aplenty. General Scott had occupied Mexico City in September, and Stephens had more reason to oppose territorial acquisition than ever. The Whigs, who had won a small majority in the House in the recent elections, were impressively united in their demand that the United States seize no territorial indemnities from Mexico. And Henry Clay, in a widely heralded speech in November at Lexington, had added his considerable influence to the demand. Georgia's Whig-controlled assembly, over stiff Democratic opposition, had also passed resolutions endorsing Stephens' "no territory" position. But Georgians were united on at least one point. The assembly had unanimously asserted that all parties in the state would maintain southern rights in the territories. Party cleavage in the state was clear. Democrats were willing to court the Wilmot Proviso issue; Whigs shunned it like a leper. The proviso, of course, did not deter Polk. In his annual message he asserted that peace could be obtained

---

1. AHS to LS, December 22, 27, 1847, in Stephens Papers, MC.

only by seizing California and New Mexico, and he hinted that even more Mexican territory might be required.[2]

These developments gave Stephens ample reason to reintroduce his resolutions against seizing Mexican territory on December 21, 1847. These were among a host of similar anti-administration proposals, and his speech on February 2, 1848, was only one of dozens plodding over the much-plowed ground of Polk's responsibility for the war. For vituperation of Polk, this address outdid anything he had delivered before. The war was "a wanton outrage upon the Constitution" commenced by Polk's "most miserable subterfuges." The president's policies were "incredible," "mendacious," "ruinous," "mischievous," "disgraceful," "dishonorable," "reckless," "infamous." Polk, waging war against the Constitution, was a free people's greatest enemy. He, for one, said Stephens, would henceforth refuse to vote a single penny to prosecute the war. If his constituents wanted to continue Polk's "odious and detestable" policy, then they could send someone else to Washington.[3]

Those in his audience who had never heard Stephens speak were impressed. Stephens' "wonderful earnestness" struck young Charles Lanman, Daniel Webster's future biographer, although he remarked to a friend that he had thought the cadaverous speaker might not live to finish the speech. A first-term congressman from Illinois, Abraham Lincoln, thought Stephens' oratory "the very best speech, of an hours length" he had ever heard. "My old, withered eyes are full of tears yet."[4]

Further support for the war soon became a moot question. Even as Stephens spoke, Nicholas Trist was signing the Treaty of Guadalupe Hidalgo with Mexican commissioners. By its terms Mexico yielded the New Mexico and California territories to the United States for the sum of $15 million and recognized the Rio Grande as the boundary of Texas. Polk had got what he wanted; the Senate ratified the treaty on March 10, 1848.

The end of hostilities didn't stop Stephens' personal war on Polk, however. Through resolutions he continued to pepper the president

2. Richardson (ed.), *Messages and Papers of the Presidents*, IV, 533–45.
3. *Congressional Globe*, 30th Cong., 1st Sess., 61, Appendix, 159–63.
4. Charles Lanman, *Haphazard Personalities Chiefly of Noted Americans* (Boston, 1885), 342; Abraham Lincoln to William Herndon, February 2, 1848, in Roy P. Basler (ed.), *The Collected Works of Abraham Lincoln* (New Brunswick, N.J., 1953–55), II, 219.

with requests for documents, maps, and correspondence. Though of little ultimate effect, Stephens' requests formed part of a larger, more momentous battle over the organization of the new territories. Just as Stephens had feared, the slavery issue had so tied up the proceedings in Congress that nothing but the most routine business got done. A solution to the territorial problem seemed so remote, and the consequences of sectional confrontation so fearful, that one Georgia editor hoped the territories would remain unorganized "for yet a long time to come." [5]

This forlorn hope was whistling in the graveyard. Organization of the territories, including Oregon (for two years still without a territorial government because of the slavery issue), would have to be done sooner or later. But how, when both sections of the country implacably insisted on their "rights"? The status of slavery in the territories was a labyrinth of conflicting constitutional passages, which would have required the cunning of Theseus to traverse. And the territorial issue encompassed other problems: the hard economic question of whether slavery could prove profitable in the Southwest, the moral questions surrounding the institution, and ultimately the question of the blacks' place in American society. Politics was the one arena that focused the problem in all its diffused aspects, the one arena forcing a direct confrontation between the sections. Thus in the hands of partisan politicians and editors, slavery, in addition to all its other complexities, became a question of party and sectional power.

By mid-1848 the presidential campaign was in full swing, and both major parties had chosen their candidates. For the Whigs it was General Zachary Taylor, "Old Zack," "Old Rough and Ready," a hero of the Mexican War and a career soldier. His Democratic opponent was sixty-six-year-old Lewis Cass, a grizzled political veteran and U.S. senator from Michigan.

How Taylor, a political novice who had never voted or expressed a political opinion before 1846, obtained the Whig nomination is a long, tangled story. To hear Stephens tell it, one would think Little Aleck accomplished the task almost single-handed. Writing in 1871, Stephens claimed he had urged Taylor on the Whigs and had secured his nomination by the Georgia Whig convention soon after the battles of Resaca and Palo Alto. And in December, 1847, he had been the

5. Milledgeville *Southern Recorder*, March 21, 1848.

prime mover in setting up the pro-Taylor Young Indians club in Congress, who immediately opened an "extensive correspondence" in their candidate's behalf.[6]

With typical modesty and memory dimmed by years, Stephens exaggerated his own role. Many Whigs played a part in the nomination. Both Thurlow Weed, a crafty political operator and kingpin in the New York party, and John J. Crittenden, one of Clay's close Kentucky associates, recognized Old Zack's presidential potential early in the war. Coy at first, by December, 1846, Taylor was hinting that he might accept a popular draft. After the general's brilliant victory at Buena Vista the following February, popular clamor for the hero increased and Crittenden firmly committed himself to Taylor's candidacy. Overnight Taylor had become the most available man in the Union.

Georgia's Whigs got caught up in the popular clamor. Several county conclaves endorsed the general, and the state's Whig press began trumpeting "Taylor for President" at every opportunity. Old Zack's endorsement by the state Whig convention in July followed as a matter of course. But if Stephens had any part in these moves, indeed if he even attended the convention, no evidence of it remains. Interestingly, too, at the height of the Taylor boom in spring, 1847, Little Aleck's Georgia organ, the Augusta *Chronicle*, disapproved hasty endorsements of Taylor and stated its own preference for the more experienced Clay. Moreover, it seems strange that if the correspondence the Young Indians opened for Taylor in December, 1847, was "extensive" no trace of it survives in Stephens' papers. Stephens hardly mentioned Taylor until March, 1848. By then it was clear that he was the favorite.[7]

Clay, encouraged by the reception his Lexington speech had received, made a belated entrance into the nomination arena in April. But his position in the cotton South was hopeless. The Democrats had immediately blasted the speech, with its lamentations over slavery's evils, as an ill-disguised effort to court the votes of abolitionists and Wilmot Proviso men. Ultrasensitive and politically vulnerable on this point, Whigs tended to agree with Democrats on the issue. Georgia's Whigs had long suspected Clay, wrote one of Berrien's friends. Only by

6. AHS to J. Fairfax McLaughlin, March 18, 1871, in Stephens Papers, EU. Other members of the Young Indians were Toombs, Abraham Lincoln of Illinois, Truman Smith of Connecticut, and William Ballard Preston, Thomas Flournoy, and John Pendleton, all of Virginia.

7. Augusta *Chronicle and Sentinel*, April 21, 1847.

an immediate and complete repudiation of the proviso could he possibly garner support in Georgia. Taylor, however, could save the Whigs, he thought: "Nothing *can destroy* the Democracy but Genl. Taylor."[8]

Although aware of sentiment in Georgia, Stephens seems to have believed that Clay might receive the nomination, at least until the beginning of the session. But by January he had changed his mind. Efforts to elect Clay were "useless" because general opinion in Washington said he could not win. The thought was "painful," he said a week later, but true. The pain didn't last long. By March Stephens was supporting Taylor "out and out" because he could be elected and Clay could not. Taylor was "as true a whig as lives in this country," he wrote. "I know it."[9]

Stephens *knew* no such thing, but he *believed* it and spent most of his time with men who agreed. On March 13, Stephens had moved from Mrs. Carter's, taking up new lodgings at the Rush house on Washington Avenue. Toombs had rented the place and was living there with his family and Crittenden, Taylor's manager in the capital. If Stephens needed any convincing about the right man for the Whigs, these two Taylor stalwarts certainly would have provided it. Taylor, a nonpolitical military hero, besides being eminently available, offered one indisputable advantage to the southern Whigs: he was a southerner and a slaveholder. He could, therefore, be counted on to veto the Wilmot Proviso if necessary.[10]

Stephens hardly bothered to question this assumption. A Taylor presidency held out too much glittering promise: not only safety for the South and slavery but political ascendancy at home for the southern Whigs. Characteristically, Toombs had railed bitterly at Clay's treachery for entering the race. Stephens had been kinder. He based his support of Taylor on strictly pragmatic grounds; toward Clay he felt only wistful pity. "I regret Mr. Clay desires to be run again. He cannot be elected."[11]

Unfortunately, Taylor was hardly acting like an electable Whig. In

8. Augusta *Constitutionalist*, December 4, 1847; Iverson L. Harris to Berrien, December 15, 1847, in Berrien Papers, SHC/NC.

9. AHS to LS, January 11, 18, March 22, 1848, in Stephens Papers, MC.

10. *Ibid.*, March 14, 1848; AHS to J. W. Harris, July 11, 1848, in Toombs Papers, LC.

11. Toombs to James Thomas, April 16, May 1, 1848, in Toombs Papers, LC; AHS to JLS, April 19, 1848, in Stephens Papers, EU.

the first place, he accepted the nomination of any local meeting, Whig, Democrat, or otherwise. Worse, his feckless pen had spawned numerous gaffes. In 1847 he had approved free-soil Democratic suggestions that the Ordinance of 1787 (barring slavery) be extended over the new territories. A few weeks later he told a Whig correspondent that he lacked the time to study the constitutionality of a national bank or protective tariff. He was also too busy, he informed Tennessee Democrats, to respond to a set of resolutions damning the entire Whig program. Then in February, 1848, the general announced in yet another public letter that he would not accept a party nomination but only one made independent of party considerations. The shock waves from this proclamation reached every corner of national Whiggery.[12]

Obviously something would have to be done to put Taylor right before the Whigs, and his Washington lieutenants swung into action. Crittenden, after consulting with Toombs and Stephens, drafted a letter for Taylor's signature and dispatched it to Baton Rouge. On April 22, this letter (or the substance of it) appeared in the New Orleans *Daily Picayune*. Known as the "first Allison Letter," it served as the closest thing to a platform the Whigs had during the campaign. Taylor acknowledged being "a Whig but not an ultra Whig," while disavowing party purposes. On specific issues the letter was a masterpiece of ambiguity. The veto power, said Taylor, was "a high conservative power" to be used only "when the Constitution was clearly violated or in cases of manifest Congressional haste." On the tariff, currency, and internal improvements he promised to follow the will of the people as expressed by Congress.[13]

Democrats naturally scoffed at the letter and questioned Taylor's authorship, but it mollified nervous Taylor Whigs. By the time of their convention, congressional Whigs opposed Clay almost to a man. The Young Indians had done their work well. "It was impossible to counteract the movements made by members of Congress," wrote one despondent Clay supporter.[14]

12. Brainerd Dyer, *Zachary Taylor* (Baton Rouge, 1946), 272–73, 277–79.

13. AHS to Mary Butler Coleman, October 13, 1870, in John J. Crittenden Papers, DU; "Allison Letter" in Holman Hamilton, *Zachary Taylor* (2 vols.; Indianapolis, 1941–51), II, 79–81.

14. Milledgeville *Federal Union*, May 2, 1848; James Harlan to Clay, June 15, 1848, quoted in Albert D. Kirwan, *John J. Crittenden: The Struggle for the Union* (Lexington, Ky., 1962), 220.

Alexander and Linton Stephens attended the Philadelphia convention as interested observers. Taylor's organization functioned flawlessly, and on the fourth ballot he secured the nomination. As a sop to the northern Whigs, Millard Fillmore of New York was chosen as his running mate. Following its successful strategy of 1840, trusting another gallant military chieftain to carry the election personally, the party drafted no platform. But in early June, it remained questionable whether northern antislavery Whigs could reconcile themselves to the titular leadership of a Louisiana plantation owner and slaveholder.

Veteran Democratic politician Lewis Cass of Michigan, Taylor's opponent, had won the nomination by being the first prominent Democrat to espouse the "popular sovereignty" formula for solving the problem of slavery in the territories. On its face, popular sovereignty was a plausible idea. The people of a territory would decide for themselves whether slavery would exist there, thus sidestepping the divisive issue of congressional authority on the matter. From a political perspective, the formula had merit: it bought time to solve the problem, possibly avoiding a showdown on territorial slavery forever, while at the same time keeping the party and the country together. Although it never for a moment fooled the Calhounites or militant antislavery people in the party, the popular sovereignty doctrine, or "congressional nonintervention," became Democratic dogma. And for the best of reasons: it allowed Democrats both North and South to construe the formula's hypothetical operation to their own advantage. Like the theory of cosmic ether, popular sovereignty worked perfectly well until it was tested—and then it proved to be an abstraction just as insubstantial.

Stephens had nothing but scorn for Cass's doctrine, and to ensure that Georgia Whigs got properly educated on the matter, he wrote several articles for the *Southern Recorder* assailing the formula. That the "mixed" population of a territory could shut out slavery was inconceivable. How could southern rights depend on the will or caprice of such a people? It was "preposterous," "absurd," "an insult." If a planter with two hundred slaves could not be trusted over Cass of Michigan, said Stephens, then the Whigs should give up. In short, why devise a formula to solve the problem when the election of a slaveholder obviated it? Stephens had sounded the keynote of the Whig campaign in the South.[15]

15. AHS to "Dear Doctor," July 17, 1848, in Miscellaneous File 434, Stephens Letter, GDAH.

Before returning home Stephens still had one more significant role to play in the House. It was mid-July, abysmally hot and muggy in the capital. Legislative tempers had been frayed by months of indecisive wrangling. Oregon, New Mexico, and California territories remained unorganized, and Polk desperately needed a settlement. But the Democratic party was torn by dissension. Van Buren's followers, the Barnburners, solidly antislavery and anti-Polk, had bolted the party in June. (In August these disaffected Democrats would join with various other antislaveryites to form the Free Soil party and run Van Buren for president on a platform demanding restriction of slavery to its present boundaries.)

Several tries at organizing Oregon had been made. Extending the Missouri Compromise line to the area had failed twice. The popular sovereignty formula had been tabled. On every occasion, Calhoun, his sensitive Carolina nose sniffing danger to the South, had led the opposition. Finally, on July 12, John M. Clayton, a Whig senator from Delaware, proposed forming an eight-man committee (equally divided between parties and sections) to hammer out an acceptable compromise on the slavery question in the territories. Six days later the select committee, on which Calhoun sat, reported a palaverous bill, the so-called "Clayton Compromise." On the crucial territorial question the bill recognized the validity of Oregon's antislavery laws but allowed its legislature to change them in the future, prohibited the territorial legislatures in the Mexican cession from passing any laws on slavery, and provided that all constitutional questions on territorial slavery be referred to the Supreme Court. In short, Congress decided to dump the problem into the lap of the Court.[16]

The bill's ambiguity attracted votes on both sides of the Senate. On July 27, after marathon debate, with Calhoun, Berrien, Cass, and Jefferson Davis all voting "aye," the Senate passed the measure 33 to 22. But as soon as the bill reached the House, Stephens moved to table it. The bill simply postponed the question and would not quiet the country, he said. Congress had been in session long enough; it was time to go home. After perfunctory debate and amid utter consternation, Stephens' motion carried by a vote of 112 to 97. Not one of the 73 northern Whigs voted "nay," and not one of 49 southern Democrats voted "aye." Both northern Democrats and southern Whigs had di-

16. David M. Potter, *The Impending Crisis, 1848–1861* (New York, 1976), 63–74.

vided on the test vote, 31 to 21 and 8 to 27 respectively. Obviously, Stephens and his seven southern Whig colleagues had held the balance of power.[17]

Georgia Democrats yowled. "Oh Whiggery! manifold are thy sins! But this is the climax of its iniquities," raged the *Constitutionalist*. "A Georgian . . . took the lead in this act, which stabs the very bosom of his country's peace." The editor foamed like this for weeks. The *Federal Union* immediately established on its front page a black-bordered box headed "Who Killed the Compromise Bill?" followed by a list, en-titled "The Immortal Eight," with Stephens' name in block capitals at the top. Stephens, sneered the Milledgeville editor, had such an exalted opinion of himself "that he will not deign to be guided by the wisdom of the towering intellects around him. . . . If he is Solomon, then Calhoun and Berrien are *ninnies* and fools." [18]

Some Georgia Whigs were similarly outraged. The Augusta *Republic* hoped that the "calculating demagogue" who would hazard the country's safety would "be damned forever." Berrien's friends naturally saw Stephens' action as yet another wily move to control the state party. Most Georgia Whigs, however, were content to await some explanation from Stephens.[19]

As usual, the *Chronicle* defended Stephens. Little in the Clayton bill would have helped the South, it said. The North would get all the "*substance*" and the South but the "*shadow*." Ensuring a "reasonable share" of the territories was far wiser than risking everything on a decision of the Court. Passing the bill, said the *Chronicle*, would have inflamed northern antislavery men and "helped Southern Democrats to defeat the election of a *Southern* President." [20]

Stephens responded to his critics personally in an hour-long speech on August 7, as the House considered two special messages from Polk. His opposition to Clayton's bill typically rested on his own legal interpretations. The so-called "compromise" completely surrendered southern rights in the territories and ought to be entitled the South's "Articles of Capitulation," he said. By well-known principles of international law, all laws of a conquered country remained in force until altered or abol-

17. *Congressional Globe*, 30th Cong., 1st Sess., 1006–1007.

18. Augusta *Constitutionalist*, August 1, 1848; Milledgeville *Federal Union*, September 29, 1848.

19. Augusta *Republic*, August 11, 1848, quoted in Rabun, "Stephens," 208; Harris to Berrien, August 23, 1848, in Berrien Papers, SHC/NC.

20. Augusta *Chronicle and Sentinel*, July 26, August 1, 7, 1848.

ished by the conquering power. Mexico had abolished slavery in 1829; the institution had no legal status there. Hence the Supreme Court could rule only one way on the question. He flatly denied Calhoun's position—that slavery, protected by the Constitution, would automatically follow it and the flag into the new territories. Slavery's existence depended on *local* law. The Constitution surely protected slavery where it existed, but "it establishes it nowhere it is prohibited by law."

Although Stephens hinted that he believed it Congress' duty to protect slavery by positive legislation—a position he later repudiated—he surely knew that such action would be impossible. He would accept a division of the territory along the Missouri Compromise line or some other geographical line. Otherwise he would not vote a single dollar to acquire new territories. If either of these compromises failed, and the North enacted the Wilmot Proviso, then the southern people would have to take the course "their interest and honor demand."

In taking this position Stephens obviously hoped to gain political advantage for the Whigs. But he hardly chose to keep the slavery issue alive simply to aid Taylor in the election. Indeed, he would have been pleased to have the issue "settled" by a geographic division of the territory. But if the issue did get carried into the election, he was anxious that Cass not be allowed to weasel out of having to defend popular sovereignty, "a universally condemned position." The slavery issue had to be met squarely, he said, "sooner or later." And no "shifting of responsibility" or "postponement" to carry the election could change that.[21]

Stephens' reasons for opposing the bill went deeper. He was convinced that he stood on firm legal ground. Several other competent authorities also foresaw an inevitable northern victory should the issue go to the Supreme Court. It is difficult to believe, as one historian has suggested, that the eight "avid Taylor men" in the House opposed the bill to "safeguard Taylor's election and all it promised for southern Whiggery" when so many other avid southern Taylorites supported the measure: Toombs, for example, and fellow Young Indians Henry W. Hilliard, William Ballard Preston, and John Pendleton—not to mention the vast majority of southern Whigs in the House.[22]

21. The speech, as quoted in the preceding paragraphs, is in Cleveland, *Stephens*, 334–52.

22. John A. Campbell to Calhoun, March 1, 1848, in Boucher and Brooks (eds.), *Calhoun Correspondence*, 430–34; Augusta *Chronicle and Sentinel*, June 21, 24, 1848; Cooper, *Politics of Slavery*, 265.

Safeguarding Taylor's election didn't matter nearly as much to Stephens as stubbornly maintaining the correctness of his own ideas. Defying the learned opinions of the "towers of intellect" around him simply made the exercise more enjoyable. In matters of intelligence Stephens always believed himself *primus inter pares*. He had concluded that the Clayton bill offered no "settlement" of the slavery issue, and just as he had insisted on a clear decision when Texas was annexed, he now demanded the same for New Mexico and California.

Unfortunately, the Clayton bill had promised settlement enough to many Georgians, and when Stephens returned home to campaign he found himself as much an issue as the presidential election. Most of the Whig press loyally supported him. The Democrats, of course, were furious; "traitor" was the most common epithet they applied to him. To counter the criticism and allay the confusion among some Whigs, Stephens amplified what he had said in Congress in two long letters to the Milledgeville papers.[23]

Neither Congress nor a territorial legislature had the constitutional right, "either in honor, justice or good faith," to exclude slavery in the territories, he wrote in his letter to the *Federal Union*. But neither could the Constitution prohibit slavery where local law prohibited it, as in California and New Mexico. Nevertheless, despite the Mexican laws, the South's right to equal participation in the territories deserved legal protection by Congress. The Clayton bill surrendered this protection, forcing the South to sue for her rights in the new territories while the North had hers gratis in Oregon. "*Upon the broad principle of justice*" the South had equal rights in the territories, which, after all, were "*the fruit of common blood and treasure.*" If the South demanded this justice in "an unbroken front," Congress would have to recognize her claim. Referring the question to the Court totally abandoned the principle. The Court was not the place to decide political questions, he concluded; Congress was.[24]

If one accepts Stephens' premise that the South had territorial rights that Congress had to recognize, the rest of the argument follows logically. For the moment, slavery was simply a political question to him, not a judicial one. A few years later, he would be only too happy to get

23. Augusta *Chronicle and Sentinel*, August 17, 26, 1848; Milledgeville *Southern Recorder*, September 5, 1848.
24. AHS to the editor, August 30, 1848, in Milledgeville *Federal Union*, September 12, 1848.

a Supreme Court ruling on the question. But for now he was content to trust Congress with the explosive issue, hoping that "justice," almost by some mysterious and supranatural power of its own, would prevail.

Predictably, the *Federal Union* found Stephens' reasoning "vague and unsatisfactory," savoring "more of transcendentalism than sound, practical statesmanship." But evidently transcendentalism satisfied the voters of the Seventh District. Not until the campaign's final month did the Democrats find a sacrificial lamb, one Joseph Day, to oppose Stephens. At one point, Herschel Johnson even solicited Calhoun to write letters for Democrats to use against Little Aleck in the state, a measure of their desperation of ever beating him.[25]

With their own districts safe and Berrien's followers (still Clay men at heart) sulking, Toombs and Stephens had to campaign hard for Taylor. The Democrats were up and furious, marveled Toombs, campaigning "with a determination I never before witnessed." Both parties employed the time-honored strategy of "proving" their opponents less trustworthy in defense of southern rights, linking the candidates to antislavery elements in their party. Each side appealed to the other's malcontents and emphasized divisions in the opponent's ranks. Whigs harped on Calhoun's differences with Polk; Democrats emphasized the Berrien-Stephens split on the Clayton bill and the former's silence during the campaign. In September, however, the Whigs received an unexpected boost. An enraged Democrat almost killed Alexander Stephens, and this event was enough to stimulate the herd instinct among Georgia's Whigs. It even brought Berrien out onto the stump.[26]

Judge Francis Cone, Stephens' assailant, was a jovial giant of a man. Stephens had known Cone for years, having practiced law with him on the northern circuit since the middle 1830s. Like many other Democrats, Cone was furious over Stephens' role in tabling the Clayton bill and had bitterly denounced him as a traitor to the South. Rumors of the charge, which at first he discounted, had already reached Stephens before he and Cone met at a political barbecue in late August in Putnam County. When Little Aleck asked him about it, Cone denied the

25. Milledgeville *Federal Union*, September 12, 1848; Johnson to Calhoun, August 25, 1848, in Boucher and Brooks (eds.), *Calhoun Correspondence*, 470.
26. Toombs to Crittenden, September 27, 1848, in Phillips (ed.), *TSC Correspondence*, 128; Augusta *Constitutionalist*, June 24, 1848; Milledgeville *Southern Recorder*, July 11, 1848.

rumors. Good, Stephens replied, for had they been true, he would have slapped Cone's jaws. And, he continued, in fairness, he should mention that he had told others of his intentions. The judge apparently took this in his usual good spirits.

There the matter might have ended but for Cone's sensitivity and the hundreds of twittings he began to receive. All Georgia was gossiping about the "confrontation" between the two, and for the next few days Cone was mercilessly ribbed. Had Little Aleck slapped his jaws yet? Did he need help if Stephens should assault him? Everyone enjoyed the joke but Cone, who apparently convinced himself that people thought him a coward—and in the antebellum South only a Negro was lower. On August 26, Cone penned a frosty note to Stephens demanding a retraction of the threat. Stephens replied three days later in an infuriatingly mild little letter saying that the threat had been only contingent. Since Cone had denied calling him a traitor, the matter was closed.

Before receiving this reply, Cone encountered Stephens—whether by design or accident is unclear—on the piazza of the Thompson Hotel in Atlanta. Stephens was passing through on the train from Macon, en route to Crawfordville. The dinner bell had rung, and all the passengers save Stephens had gone into the hotel. Cone sat alone on the porch as Stephens walked up from the depot. At the entrance to the hotel the judge stopped him and brusquely demanded a retraction of the threat. Icily Stephens replied that he had already replied in writing and did not intend to discuss the matter further. Accounts vary about what Cone then said. He either called Stephens "a miserable little traitor" or "a damned puppy." Whatever his remark, he was instantly answered with a stinging blow across the face from a thin rattan cane Stephens always carried.

The enraged Cone drew a knife and started slashing. Stephens, his body and arms cut in several places, attempted to fend off the blows with his cane, but as his assailant pressed his full weight on him the bloodied congressman toppled backward to the floor. Cone, atop him in a flash, pinioned Stephens' head to the boards and, brandishing the knife before Stephens' eyes, roared, "Retract or I'll cut your damned throat!"

"Never! Cut!" The knife flashed down and Stephens caught it in his right hand. It sliced between the thumb and forefinger, a two-inch gash clear to the bone. Several bystanders, attracted by the commotion, succeeded in pulling Cone away. Little Aleck staggered to his feet. Disheveled, trembling, and bloody, he was carried into the hotel. Fortunately, three doctors, one an army surgeon, were there to dress Stephens' wounds. There were six: one on each side and each hand and two on the chest, one a puncture near the heart. That night an anxious crowd thronged the Crawfordville depot awaiting news from up the line. First reports had been frightening—Stephens would not live, they said. When the train from Atlanta chugged in and a passenger shouted that his life was not in danger, a roar went up from the crowd.

Cone was arrested and charged with assault with intent to murder. Stephens, who knew the corrosive power of anger as well as anyone, refused to prosecute. And he let it be known, before the election, that he had forgiven the judge. Cone later pleaded guilty to the lesser charge of stabbing and was fined eight hundred dollars.[27]

The Whigs naturally attempted to get as much political mileage out of the incident as possible. All over the country they portrayed the attack as politically motivated, a cowardly assault by desperate Democrats on one of the purest statesmen in the nation. Democrats, of course, expressed regrets, but beyond this they could do little to repair the damage. "Stephens, as the whole country knows is getting a damned sight too insulting for civilized people," wrote one of Cobb's disgusted friends. But, he continued, if only half of what he read in the Washington papers were true, the party would be severely hurt.[28]

Georgia Whigs played Stephens' near martyrdom for all it was worth. At a mammoth rally in Atlanta on the night of September 14, a profusion of banners and transparencies depicting the incident fluttered above the heads of some eight thousand party faithful. Little Aleck himself attended, at the head of a torchlit procession of Whig dignitaries. Much to the revulsion of Democrats, Stephens "was drawn through the streets in an open barouche, by some of his obsequious followers, who for the occasion discharged the duty of horses." (The Whigs explained later that they feared trusting this precious cargo to skittish horses.)[29]

27. The previous paragraphs are based on accounts in Johnston and Browne, *Stephens*, 232–34, Rabun, "Stephens," 224–26, and Savannah *Republican*, September 8, 1848. The Stephens-Cone correspondence is in Milledgeville *Southern Recorder*, September 12, 1848.

28. Thomas D. Harris to Cobb, September 8, 1848, in Cobb Papers, UG.

29. Milledgeville *Federal Union*, September 19, 1848.

How could the Whigs have resisted such an opportunity to exhibit their wounded hero? It had been whispered that Stephens would come, but no one knew for sure. When his frail form hove into view, the sultry air echoed with a continuous cry—"Stephens! Stephens! Stephens!" A Whig reporter found this demonstration of affection so "touching, elo-quent, [and] sublime" that it "caused the manly tear to start in many an eye." After several others spoke, constant cries from the crowd brought Stephens to his feet. And as he tottered to the front of the plat-form, the roar became deafening. He was too weak to speak, he said, but he did relate a little story about a poor Mexican War veteran, who, upon taking leave of a kindly benefactor, had been asked for but one thing in return—"Don't forget to vote for Old Zack." This was all he, too, could ask of his friends, he said. The "wild excitement" attending this little speech impressed even Democratic observers.[30]

Stephens convalesced for a month but carefully kept in touch with party leaders, scribbling in a painful scrawl with his left hand. He couldn't use his right hand for several months. On election day, Oc-tober 2, the parties once again divided the state's eight seats evenly, with Stephens and Toombs carrying their respective districts easily. Democratic margins were noticeably thinner than before, however. "There is more defection in our ranks than . . . anyone supposed a month ago," lamented Alfred Iverson to Cobb.[31]

Whether Stephens' return to the stump in mid-October had any-thing to do with the final poll for president in Georgia is hard to say. But he spent most of his time in small north Georgia communities, areas of traditional Democratic strength. And in these areas, like the state as a whole, Democratic percentages fell from those of 1844. The country voted for president on November 7, and Georgia went for Taylor, 47,527 votes to 44,790 for Cass.[32]

Old Zack did not need Georgia's ten electoral votes. He carried the electoral college, 163 to 127. As usual, neither party in the South had attempted to enlighten voters through candid examination of the issues. But the Whigs had outdone themselves this time. In the South, Taylor

30. Augusta *Chronicle and Sentinel*, September 18, 1848; Augusta *Constitutionalist*, September 17, 1848.
31. AHS to Crittenden, September 26, 1848, in Crittenden Papers, LC; Iverson to Cobb, October 17, 1848, in Phillips (ed.), *TSC Correspondence*, 130.
32. AHS to LS, October 22, 1848, in Stephens Papers, MC.

had been trumpeted because of his geographical origins and because fate had destined him to fight battles against one of the most inept armies in history. What principles Taylor had were as unknown now as they had been before Crittenden sat down back in April to manufacture some for him in the Allison Letter.

An elated Stephens returned to Washington in December and pleaded with Crittenden to join him "to fill the cup of our rejoicing." Stephens' own cup must have been heavily spiked, or he might have been suspicious of the men he saw "very busy making a cabinet for Taylor." But he dismissed these interlopers out of hand as people who did not understand the "Taylor movement." "The real Taylor men are all right," he continued. They were "disinterested," basking in "public deliverence . . . not a *party victory*." Euphoric, Stephens believed Taylor's election would open a new era in the nation's history. Only one cloud marred the glimmering horizon; indeed, it was "the greatest possible danger": the prospect of Henry Clay's reelection to the Senate.[33]

Stephens obviously feared Clay. Without saying so directly, he hoped to wield some influence in the new administration. No doubt he considered his own contribution to Taylor's victory as anything but inconsequential, and he also expected his close association with Crittenden to pay handsome political dividends. Clay—the man whom Taylor had bested in the convention with overwhelming southern Whig support, whom Crittenden had spurned, whom thousands of northern Whigs still fanatically revered—might spoil it all. His possible presence in Washington filled Stephens with foreboding.

For once, though, he didn't dwell on portents of future disasters. Savoring victory was too sweet. "The tone and temper here," he concluded contentedly, "are all right." Such ebullient moods were too rare with Stephens to be spoiled by a glimpse of the future. Such a glimpse would have surely soured him, for disaster lay barely a month away.[34]

33. AHS to Crittenden, December 5, 1848, in Crittenden Papers, DU.
34. *Ibid.*

VII

Out of Party and into the Maelstrom

The southern Whigs had elected "their" president, but the sectional impasse remained. To some embittered Democrats it appeared that the Whigs would support Taylor no matter what he did about the Wilmot Proviso. According to one Columbus Democrat, the Whigs were already preparing excuses for Taylor should he refuse to veto the proviso. Toombs only confirmed such fears when he urged calmness and moderation on the issue. The South, he said, had little practical interest in the Southwest anyway.[1]

Stephens, like his friend, counting on Taylor to protect southern interests in the Southwest, no doubt agreed. On the surface he displayed an arrogant cockiness. Shortly after his arrival in Washington, he publicly abused the voters of Joshua Giddings' Ohio district for reelecting their abolitionist congressman. But privately Stephens wondered about Taylor's reliability on the proviso question. "Will Genl. Taylor veto the Proviso?" he mused to Crittenden. "Can we get the North to let the question rest until the time comes for territories to be formed into state and be admitted . . . according to their own notions?"[2]

1. John Forsyth to Cobb, November 10, 1848, in Phillips (ed.), *TSC Correspondence*, 136.
2. Joshua Giddings to his daughter, December 7, 1848, in Giddings-Julian Papers, LC; AHS to Crittenden, December 8, 1848, in Crittenden Papers, LC.

Stephens was echoing an idea several politicians favored. Clayton of Delaware, for example, suggested that if the people of New Mexico and California formed state constitutions, those areas could be admitted as states at the next session of Congress and "relieve us from the trouble forever." Crittenden, whom Clayton sounded out on the plan, approved, as did Democrat Stephen A. Douglas. On December 11, Douglas introduced a bill organizing the entire Mexican cession into one state, a plan Georgia's Whigs heartily supported. But Douglas' plan and a similar one William Ballard Preston introduced in the House were doomed. When Congress opened in December, 1848, the free-soilers threw down a gauntlet.[3]

On December 13, the House approved a resolution introduced by an Ohio Whig, instructing the Committee on the Territories to report a bill providing territorial governments for New Mexico and California that excluded slavery. Nor was this the only blow the northerners struck. Eight days later, Daniel Gott, a New York Whig, offered a resolution condemning the slave trade in Washington, D.C., which passed by a 98 to 88 vote.[4]

The southerners reacted immediately. With Calhoun leading, they called a caucus for the next night, December 22, in the Senate chamber. Southern Whigs were instantly suspicious. Although greatly upset by Gott's resolution, they were hardly inclined to favor a Calhoun-instigated movement loudly supported by southern Democrats. Stephens and other Whigs refused even to sign the call for the meeting. Toombs suspected a plot to disorganize the southern Whigs and either destroy Taylor or force him into the arms of the Democrats. The Whigs, however, could do nothing by remaining aloof, so they attended the caucus "in order to control and crush it."[5]

Stephens led the opposition, first arguing against action until some overt act against the South was taken, then proposing formation of a fifteen-man committee to consider resolutions and report to the full caucus on January 15, 1849. Originally proposed as chairman of this committee, Stephens yielded to its own choice, John C. Calhoun. Calhoun, as head of a special subcommittee, prepared a paper that be-

3. John M. Clayton to Crittenden, December 13, 1848, Crittenden to Clayton, December 19, 1848, both in Clayton Papers, LC.
4. *Congressional Globe*, 30th Cong., 2nd Sess., 38–39, 55–56, 83–84.
5. Toombs to Crittenden, January 3, 1849, in Phillips (ed.), *TSC Correspondence*, 139.

came famous as the "Southern Address." It was the Carolinian's most determined effort to unite southerners across party lines. Minutely and passionately tracing the course of northern aggressions from the Ordinance of 1787 to the latest outrages, the address argued that all these events, particularly the attempt to exclude the South from the territories, tended toward abolition and Negro domination of the South. The time for temporizing was over, Calhoun said; the South must resist now or be doomed.[6]

Instead of eliciting unity, Calhoun's address produced just the opposite. When the southern caucus met again on January 15, 1849, the Whigs, with Stephens and Clayton in the lead, tried to table the document. When this failed, Little Aleck and three other members of the committee resigned, and the address was referred back to the committee for modification. A week later Calhoun's address reappeared, along with a much milder substitute prepared by Berrien. In a wild session lasting until two in the morning, the caucus rejected Berrien's paper and adopted Calhoun's. Before the final vote, Stephens, Toombs, and most of the Whigs had bolted the meeting. Out of 121 southerners in Congress, only 48, almost all Democrats, signed Calhoun's address. Forty-six Whigs and 27 Democrats (including Cobb and three other Georgians) refused to sign. "We completely foiled Calhoun in his miserable attempt to form a Southern party," Toombs crowed.[7]

Calhoun's plan had failed ultimately because of partisan politics. Whigs and orthodox Democrats alike shared a pervasive distrust of the Carolinian. Calhoun had only one object, said Howell Cobb: destruction of the Democratic party, Union or no Union. Although he hardly excused the southern Whigs—their alliance with their northern brethren had "brought us to the very abys of ruin"—he could not support a statement that made no mention of the South's true northern friends, the Democrats.[8]

Whigs generally trembled at the prospect of disunion, and to thousands Calhoun personified it. The evils of the proviso, said the New Orleans *Bee*, were "a thousandfold more endurable" than the "un-

---

6. Milledgeville *Federal Union*, January 9, 1849; Cralle (ed.), *Works of Calhoun*, VI, 290–313.

7. Milledgeville *Federal Union*, January 22, 1849; Toombs to Crittenden, January 22, 1849, in Crittenden Papers, LC. Herschel Johnson, whom the governor had appointed to the Senate in January, 1848, was the only Georgian to sign the address.

8. Cobb to Lamar, January 16, 24, 1849, in Cobb Papers, UG.

numbered" woes of disunion. "On anything concerning *niggers*," said Whig Senator George E. Badger of North Carolina, Calhoun was "absolutely deranged." He, for one, spurned any movement hazarding the Union simply for the "privilege of carrying slaves to California or keeping up private gaols for slave dealers" in Washington.[9]

Stephens also distrusted Calhoun, but he feared even more an attempt to deprive southern Whigs of the fruits of their recent victory. The southern Whigs "feel *secure* under General Taylor," he told Crittenden, and would "insist upon his controlling the [slavery] Question." Southerners would break with the party if the northern Whigs continued to press against slavery in the capital. Already many of these northern Clay Whigs, not to mention the Democrats, free-soilers, and southern Clay supporters, like Berrien, were hoping "to break [Taylor] down" with the slavery issue. "It will not do for Mr. Clay to come back here if it can be prevented," Stephens concluded grimly.[10]

This was the crux of it: Stephens and most of Taylor's southern supporters envisioned unparalleled treachery, not only at the hands of Calhoun-led Democrats but also from the northern/Clay wing of their own party. Old Zack's southern cohorts trusted the new president to save them. Why should they cooperate with Democrats? Or, more to the point, why should they join a movement that could only play into the hands of their enemies in the Whig party? The Augusta *Chronicle* sounded the dominant note for the southern Taylorites: "wait patiently"—wait for Taylor and all would be well.[11]

But not all southerners were willing to wait. Calhoun's address ignited a powerful resistance movement in the South. Between February and April, 1849, several Deep South and border states took militant stands against the proviso. Georgia's Democrats were also in turmoil. Moderates, like Hopkins Holsey, clearly recognized their predicament. "We will not *follow* Calhoun, but must cooperate with him in resisting encroachment." Cobb's middle-ground position would ultimately become untenable, he predicted.[12]

Georgia's Whigs were much less divided than the Democrats. Only

9. New Orleans *Bee*, undated, January, 1849, quoted in Cole, *Whig Party in the South*, 141–42; George E. Badger to Crittenden, January 13, 1849, in Crittenden Papers, LC.

10. AHS to Crittenden, January 17, 1849, in Crittenden Papers, LC.

11. Augusta *Chronicle and Sentinel*, January 16, 1849.

12. Hopkins Holsey to Cobb, February 24, 1849, in Phillips (ed.), *TSC Correspondence*, 154–55.

Berrien's followers, who could expect little favor from the incoming administration, occupied radical ground. Most viewed Calhoun's movement as aiming at secession and therefore supported Toombs and Stephens' stand, calling for resistance only in case of some overt act. But the furious discussions at home could not be ignored, so southern Whigs in Washington made a final attempt to defuse the territorial issue before Taylor's inauguration. On February 7, 1849, Preston of Virginia introduced a bill to organize the entire Mexican cession into one state, which would be admitted into the Union on October 1, 1849, with no mention of slavery. The Whigs knew perfectly well that the proposed new state would not permit slavery. "We have only the point of honor to save," said Toombs.[13]

One is tempted to speculate what course the country's history might have taken had Preston's proposal been successful. One thing is certain. The bill attracted large bipartisan support among southerners. Toombs claimed that southern Whigs were "unanimous" for it and predicted that the measure would "easily" carry in the House. Well-informed observers in Washington agreed. The Washington correspondent of the Richmond *Whig* estimated that thirty-seven signers of the Southern Address favored the measure.[14]

But it died aborning. On February 27, a New York free-soiler attached an amendment prohibiting slavery in the new state, which carried by a close vote of 91 to 88. Once up for final passage, the bill received not a single aye. Although evidence is sketchy, it indicates that this promising measure failed because extremists of both sections were determined to kill it. Antislavery zealots, intent on extracting concessions from the new administration, wanted to postpone settlement of the slavery question until Taylor took office. Hence the proviso amendment.[15]

But even had the bill passed the House, it faced Calhoun's unremitting hostility in the Senate. Settlement of the slavery question on any reasonable terms—and to most southerners "reasonable" simply meant something they could live with—would doom his movement

13. *Congressional Globe*, 30th Cong., 2nd Sess., 477; Toombs to Crittenden, January 22, 1849, in Phillips (ed.), *TSC Correspondence*, 140–42.

14. Toombs to Crittenden, January 22, 1849, in Phillips (ed.), *TSC Correspondence*, 140–42; Toombs to Crittenden, February 9, 1849 [misdated "January" in original], in Crittenden Papers, LC; A FRIEND to editor of the Richmond *Whig*, quoted in Augusta *Chronicle and Sentinel*, February 16, 1849.

15. *Congressional Globe*, 30th Cong., 2nd Sess., 608.

for militant southern solidarity. Whether Calhoun would have succeeded in scuttling the bill is a moot question. The failure of Preston's
bill underscored the desperate means extremists would resort to for
their own ends. Once again moderates of both parties and sections had
failed to enact a possibly workable compromise. Once the proviso got
attached to the bill, northerners and southerners alike were forced
willy-nilly back into hard-line sectional alignments.

Stephens' correspondence is strangely silent on Preston's bill, but we
can be sure he shared Cobb's fervently expressed wish that the "Heavenly Father" call the "old reprobate" Calhoun home. But if a celestial
homecoming could solve the nation's problems in February, 1849, God
would have had to prepare a fair-sized welcome. Calhoun was hardly
the only implacable sectionalist in the national councils.[16]

For Stephens, the failure of Preston's plan was simply another crime
that could be laid at the feet of the hated Polk. He had been harassing
the president at every opportunity. Obviously, the problem of territorial slavery with all its doleful consequences would never have arisen
without Polk's war. So even now, months after the ratification of the
treaty, Stephens was still trying to block the acquisition of the territory.
In early February he accused the president of flagrant usurpation of
power because he had withheld from the Senate a routine protocol
that had been signed by Mexican and American commissioners incident to the treaty. Nor was the treaty binding, he said, because it obli-
gated the House to appropriate money to carry out its provisions.[17]

When the appropriation bill reached the House floor on February
17, Stephens opposed it bitterly. The House had the constitutional
right to withhold appropriations effecting a treaty if it considered the
treaty unwise or improper, he argued. This appropriation merely continued the policy of aggressive war. Even worse, it sanctioned every aggression Polk had perpetrated on the Constitution. Once again he
begged the House to recognize the monstrous dangers the new territories presented to the tranquillity of the Union. Stephens ended his
speech in familiar fashion—by lambasting the president. In 1846, during an interview with Wilmot urging passage of his "Two Million" bill,

16. Cobb to his wife, February 8, 1849, in R. P. Brooks (ed.), "Howell Cobb
Papers," *Georgia Historical Quarterly*, V (June, 1921), 38.

17. *Congressional Globe*, 30th Cong., 2nd Sess., 348–49, 438, 448–50. Privately
Stephens considered Polk's "suppression" of the protocol "criminal" and an "impeach-
able offense" (AHS to Charles Lanman, June 24, 1849, in Charles Lanman Papers, LC).

he said, Polk had declared himself opposed to extending slavery beyond its present limits. The president had begun his administration by cheating and would end it the same way. He had cheated his party on Oregon, the Mexicans in the treaty, and now the South in his remarks to Wilmot. "Duplicity, hypocrisy, and treachery" characterized the man, and his entire administration had been nothing but "enormities of misrule." [18]

After almost four years of enduring Stephens' barbs, Polk finally noted one his speeches. The Wilmot story stung most. That accusation, Polk confided to his diary, was "wickedly and basely false," the product of "a bitter and partisan Whig." Wilmot, however, confirmed Stephens' report of the conversation on the House floor. Polk, it appears, was not above a little duplicity himself to further his ends. [19]

On March 4, 1849, Zachary Taylor, sixty-five years of age, became president of the United States. Nothing in the appearance or manner of the man inspired confidence. Short, heavy-set, and potbellied, Taylor perfectly fit the description "dumpy-looking." One "thunderstruck" observer, on seeing Taylor for the first time, described him as "old, outrageously ugly, uncultivated, [and] uninformed . . . [a] sure enough mere *military* chieftan," who couldn't even "converse in decent language." [20]

A career soldier, Taylor had spent forty years at various frontier posts on the fringes of developed America. He was in many ways as Whig campaign propaganda had portrayed him: plain, honest, simple, straightforward. Much more than a watchword to him, duty was part of his nature, a wellspring of his life. But he was also a novice in politics, equally inept at choosing advisers as at inspiring others with either his sagacity or oratory. Thrown into a situation requiring the sensitivity and acuity of a Lincoln, Old Zack possessed a mind hopelessly impervious to the nuances and subtleties of democratic politics. Like Andrew Jackson, Taylor had a fierce devotion to the Union; but unlike the Old Hero, he lacked natural political instincts. What the country required in the White House in 1849 was a bonafide statesman—or, at least, a skillful politician. Zachary Taylor was neither.

18. *Congressional Globe*, 30th Cong., 2nd Sess., Appendix, 145–49.
19. Quaife (ed.), *Polk Diary*, IV, 344; Augusta *Chronicle and Sentinel*, February 22, 1849.
20. George W. Julian to "Brother Isaac," January 25, 1850, in Giddings-Julian Papers, LC.

The quality of Taylor's cabinet should have given pause to careful observers. Both Stephens and Toombs, aware of Taylor's lack of experience and severely shaken by the fury of the sectional discord, had strenuously urged Crittenden to accept a cabinet post, but Crittenden had just been elected governor of Kentucky, and there he stayed. But the Kentuckian had exercised a decisive influence on Taylor's cabinet selections.[21]

Georgia got one of the plums: George W. Crawford was selected as secretary of war, only one of several lackluster appointments. Only three posts rated men of stature: John Clayton, secretary of state; Thomas Ewing of Ohio, secretary of the home department (later interior); and Reverdy Johnson of Maryland, attorney general. Treasury Secretary William Meredith of Pennsylvania, Preston at the Navy Department, and Stephens' old messmate Jacob Collamer of Vermont as postmaster general rounded out the cabinet. After his arrival in Washington, Taylor had consulted with Little Aleck about the cabinet. Everyone but Clayton met Stephens' approval.[22]

Because of his inexperience, the new president could be expected to rely heavily for guidance on his official family. Unfortunately, the cabinet lacked a man adroit and strong enough to assume the prime adviser role. Almost by default, then, this role fell to the newly elected senator from New York, William H. Seward, a product of Thurlow Weed's machine. Seward had carefully cultivated potential allies before Taylor's arrival, and he moved quickly into a position of influence.

Having once again won the presidency, the Whigs immediately began planning how to retain it. To succeed in 1852, Seward and his cabinet allies reasoned, the Deep South's influence in the party would have to be curtailed and northern free-soil elements mollified. The plan would be carried out with as little offense to the southern Whigs as possible, but in any case the North would have to receive the substance of the proviso in the territories.

To do this, the Mexican cession would be divided into states and admitted to the Union as swiftly as possible. Crittenden had endorsed the plan when Clayton proposed it early in 1849. Taylor now made it the cornerstone of his territorial policy. The president did not care how

21. AHS to Crittenden, December 5, 1849, in Crittenden Papers, DU; Toombs to Crittenden, January 3, 1849, in Crittenden Papers, LC.
22. AHS to Crittenden, February 6, 1849, in Phillips (ed.), *TSC Correspondence*, 146.

California and New Mexico came into the Union—at Congress' invitation or at the behest of the people themselves—so long as it was done quickly. So in April he dispatched a personal emissary, Thomas B. King of Georgia, to California to urge people there to form a constitution and apply for statehood. King's mission had been Clayton's idea, and during discussions of the plan Seward began attending cabinet meetings. There a bargain was struck. In return for his support of the California statehood scheme, Seward got the New York patronage. Clayton was ecstatic. "Everything is done as you would wish it," he told Crittenden. "The plan I proposed to you last winter will be carried out fully. The States will be admitted—free and Whig!"[23]

Meanwhile, Clayton's Georgia compatriots were far from happy. The administration had shown an alarming reluctance to replace Democratic officeholders. One Georgian reported general discontent on this score from Virginia to Georgia. But these grumblings were almost inconsequential compared to anger over the slavery question. Both Stephens and Toombs had been surprised by the intense feelings they found at home. What made it so dangerous, said Toombs, was not the excitement, but a grim "determination in all classes not to submit to [the proviso]."[24]

Calhounism took its toll on political moderates all over the South, but the Whigs paid most dearly. Rumors that Taylor had succumbed to the antislavery wing of the party floated about all summer, and in August the president seemed to confirm them. During a northern tour, he reportedly said that he "regarded slavery as a great moral and political evil" and, furthermore, that Congress had the right to prevent its extension to the territories. With howls of indignation, Democratic papers gave the report the widest possible circulation.[25]

Even before Taylor's remarks, the Whigs had sustained heavy losses in the congressional elections that erased the party's slim majority in Congress. For the first time in eight years Democrats captured both the

23. The preceding paragraphs are based on Glyndon G. Van Deusen, *William Henry Seward* (New York, 1967), 114; Robert J. Rayback, *Millard Fillmore: Biography of a President* (Buffalo, 1959), 194, 199–201; Crittenden to Clayton, January 7, 1849, in Clayton Papers, LC; Clayton to Crittenden, April 18, 1849, in Crittenden Papers, LC.
24. James E. Harvey to Clayton, May 5, 1849, in Clayton Papers, LC; AHS to William B. Preston, March 21, 1849, in Stephens Papers, EU; Toombs to Preston, May 18, 1849, in Miscellaneous Collections, Autograph Letters, EU.
25. Milledgeville *Federal Union*, September 25, 1849; Augusta *Constitutionalist*, August 19, 1849.

General Assembly and the governorship in Georgia in a campaign dominated by the proviso question. The Whigs had run a sorry campaign. Most of them doubtless would have agreed with Berrien that the proviso was unconstitutional, but the party was not clearly united in this belief. Divisions among Whigs made fine targets for the Democrats, who charged that Whig evasiveness on the proviso cloaked not only a belief in its constitutionality but also a disposition to submit to it. Organs of the Southern Rights Whigs joined the strident chorus. Indeed, Berrien's supporters blamed Stephens, Toombs, and Crawford for the party's troubles. "There must be an end to the unhealthy and selfish domination of these gentlemen," wrote one.[26]

Stephens, Toombs, and their followers lacked Berrien's taste for confrontation, but neither did they fear the senator's influence in the state party. Stephens did not attend the June convention; he spent the summer minding legal business, visiting his brother John in LaGrange, and recovering from an attack of diarrhea at Warm Springs, a fashionable Georgia watering hole. Why Stephens and Toombs remained inactive is unclear. Near the end of the canvass Toombs hinted that he and Stephens disagreed with the party's stand on the slavery question.[27]

It's tempting, especially in view of their later actions, to suppose that the two men had already decided to break with the administration. But the criticism both of them received from the Democrats and the Berrien Whigs indicates that they held a moderate position on slavery. As yet neither of them knew how Taylor intended to deal with the question, and their silence during the summer indicates an implicit trust in Taylor. Despite ominous reports on the president, it would have been stupid of them to forsake the administration without firsthand proof of its unreliability. At this point, neither Stephens nor Toombs believed that Taylor could or would betray them. Others were not so sure. If the party adopted the Stephens-Toombs position, wrote one Southern Rights Whig, "the Whig party as such would have ceased to exist—or been doomed to a hopeless minority for years."[28]

As a bipartisan convention in Mississippi called for a convention of the slave states to meet in Nashville in early June of 1850, Georgians also went on record for resistance. In October the assembly authorized

26. Harris to Berrien, October 6, 1849, in Berrien Papers, SHC/NC.

27. AHS to LS, July 29, 1849, in Stephens Papers, MC; Harris to Berrien, October 6, 1849, in Berrien Papers, SHC/NC.

28. Harris to Berrien, October 6, 1849, in Berrien Papers, SHC/NC.

an election of delegates to the Nashville meeting and called for a state convention if California were admitted as a free state or the Wilmot Proviso were passed in Congress. Both parties had split on the question. Linton Stephens, the new House delegate for Hancock County and spokesman for his brother, registered the lone "nay" vote on a resolution holding out the possibility of secession. He also joined eleven other Whigs in voting against the convention bill.[29]

Charles J. Jenkins, a late convert to Stephens' views, summed up the dilemma confronting moderate Whigs. They were caught in an irresistible tide. The legislature's action had "embarrassed" him, he said. He did not believe that the people would "resort to *extreme* resistance" on the proviso question. But the resistance movement had fierce momentum. "Some action seems inevitable," he sighed. "A contest has been commenced [on] who can . . . thunder most loudly."[30]

Before Stephens returned to Congress in December, 1849, Californians had set the stage for the momentous session to follow by drawing up a free state constitution and petitioning Congress for statehood. It arrived amid the worst sectional crisis yet. The summer's agitation had brought practically every problem connected with slavery to the surface: the fate of slavery and the slave trade in the District of Columbia, organization of the territories (including the related issues of fixing the Texas boundary and adjusting her debt), and the enforcement of the fugitive slave law. In the acrimonious interval between sessions sectional passions had heated to the boiling point. The problems seemed as insoluble as ever.

Stephens and Toombs soon discovered that the worst reports about Taylor were true. As Toombs saw it, the entire cabinet, Crawford excepted, had thrown its patronage into Seward's lap as part of Preston's scheme to cement the North to Taylor in 1852. This antislavery fanatic was forcing northern Whigs to adopt his line on slavery. Worse, Toombs came away from an interview with Taylor convinced that he would sign the proviso if it passed. Diehard southern Taylorites realized the shocking truth: "their" president meant to betray them. An enraged Toombs resolved then and there to oppose the proviso "even to . . . a dissolu-

29. Shryock, *Georgia and the Union*, 217–34.
30. Jenkins to Berrien, [December] 1849, in Berrien Papers, SHC/NC.

tion of the union," and he and Stephens immediately set out to make it a litmus test for the party.[31]

The Whig caucus met on Saturday evening, December 1, to select its candidate for Speaker of the House. Toombs at once offered a resolution: Congress ought not pass any law against slavery in the territories or abolishing the slave trade in the capital. Stephens pleaded passionately for passage of the resolution. Why should northern and western Whigs mortify the South by passing the proviso especially with California applying for statehood? Slavery in the District of Columbia, he said, was a matter of utmost principle to the South. If the northern majority persisted in shoving abolition down the South's throat, the Union would be dissolved, and its best southern friends would be powerless to stop it. Stephens pleaded in vain. The caucus voted to postpone the resolution, and with that, six southern Whigs, Toombs and Stephens at their head, walked out of the room and the party.[32]

Neither man would yet drop the Whig label, but their fealty to the national organization had ended. Indeed, for the next few months both would act and sound like extremists, for all the world like the Southern Rights crowd they professed to despise. The key to Stephens and Toombs's position in the coming weeks lay in the sense of deep personal betrayal both men felt. Disposed personally to compromise on the slavery issue, they discovered that the northern wing of their party was intransigent. "The North is insolent and unyielding," Stephens indignantly told Linton. "My southern blood . . . is up and . . . I am prepared to fight at all hazzards and to the last extremity in vindication of our honor and our rights."[33]

The six bolters now set out to thwart the organization of the House and succeeded gloriously. Electing the Speaker would take three weeks and sixty-three ballots. With the rules requiring a majority vote and the parties closely divided (108 Democrats, 103 Whigs, and 9 or 10 Free-Soilers), the southern bloc and the Free-Soilers could refuse to support a caucus candidate, thereby postponing the start of business almost indefinitely.

31. Toombs to Crittenden, April 23, 1850, in Mrs. Chapman Coleman (ed.), *The Life of John J. Crittenden with Selections from His Correspondence and Speeches* (2 vols.; Philadelphia, 1871), I, 364–66.
32. Washington *National Intelligencer*, December 6, 1849.
33. AHS to LS, December 2, 1849, in Stephens Papers, MC.

Stephens focused all his anger and frustration on the northern Whigs, the architects of the foul betrayal. They were "determined to *yield* nothing," he told Linton. "They intend to carry abolition any-where by the Constitution they can." If the South really intended to resist abolition, he said, it ought to be preparing "men and money arms and munitions &c." "No people who are not fit for the lowest degradation count the cost a hazzard of defending their honor or their rights. . . . I would rather today to see the whole southern race buried in honorable graves than to see them insolently triumphed over by such canting whining ruling hypocrites as are setting themselves up as their rulers." [34]

A long talk with Taylor the next day cooled Stephens down. He came away pleased, convinced that the position of the Whig bolters would be "conformable" to the one Old Zack would take in his forth-coming message to Congress. How Stephens reached this conclusion is difficult to say. Doubtless Taylor tried to be as reassuring as possible, and Stephens in his anxiety either misread him or heard what he wanted to hear. Few southerners shared Stephens' confidence, how-ever. Their prevailing mood was grim, Little Aleck reported, and talk of secession proliferated, even among formerly cool men. [35]

As day after monotonous day passed with no agreement on a way to break the impasse in the Speaker's contest, congressional tempers frayed to the breaking point. On December 13 the House was thrown into bedlam when two representatives had to be physically restrained from coming to blows. A defiant Toombs was the first to speak after order had been restored. The scenes just witnessed, he said grimly, might have been "disgraceful," but he did not regret them. Clearly the South's interests were in danger, and he would not allow a Speaker to be chosen until they were secure. For years he had attempted to stem sectional agitation at the cost of scorn by his enemies and misunder-standing by his friends. Even now all he desired was a guarantee that the organization of the House would not endanger his constituents' rights. If this security were refused, "as far as I am concerned, 'let dis-cord reign forever.'" He loved the Union under the Constitution as much as any free man, roared Toombs, but if the North insisted on legislating the South out of the new territories or abolishing slavery in

34. *Ibid.*, December 3, 4, 1849.
35. *Ibid.*, December 5, 1849.

the District of Columbia, thus fixing "a national degradation" on half the states, then *"I am for disunion."*[36]

Edward D. Baker of Illinois replied just as hotly. "As long as an American heart beats in an American bosom" dissolution of the Union would be "impossible." Stephens rose to his feet, shaking with emotion. His shrill, piping voice cut through the hall like a knife. "The day in which aggression is consummated upon any section of the country, much and deeply as I regret it, this Union is dissolved." Stephens the moderate sounded as radical as any Calhounite. "I tell this House that every word uttered by my colleague meets my hearty response . . . before that God who rules the universe, I would rather that the southern country should perish . . . than submit for one instant to degradation."[37]

The country listened to the words of these well-known Georgia conservatives with amazement. Although northern Whigs dismissed them as loud-mouthed bluffing, the Southern Rights press exulted. Toombs and Stephens now had *"their eyes wide open,"* cheered the *Constitutionalist.* "Keep it up, gentlemen."[38]

Publicly defiant, in private Stephens was desperately casting about for any allies he could find to convince the administration of its danger. He begged Crittenden to come to Washington. The state of affairs was alarming beyond all measure, but most ominous was the North's refusal to take the South seriously. He knew how excited his countrymen were; their agitation was "much greater" than anyone "at the head of affairs here have any idea of." On the House floor, however, Stephens and Toombs did nothing to calm the waters. Up until the final ballot for Speaker, both obstinately refused to support the caucus candidates. Adopting the plurality rule for the sixty-third ballot, the House finally succeeded in electing Howell Cobb to the post.[39]

With the House at last organized, it could receive the president's first annual message. Although pedestrian and ponderous, it was frighteningly clear. Congress should approve California's petition for statehood, said Taylor. On the crucial proviso question he was silent, simply reiterating that his veto should be used only "in extraordinary cases" or "to prevent hasty or unconstitutional legislation." On January 21, 1850, Taylor sent in another message that amplified the first.

36. *Congressional Globe,* 31st Cong., 1st Sess., 28–29.
37. *Ibid.*
38. Augusta *Constitutionalist,* December 18, 1849.
39. AHS to Crittenden, December 17, 1849, in Crittenden Papers, DU.

Congress should admit New Mexico as well as California to state-hood, the president advised. The Texas boundary question could be settled by the courts after that.[40]

Taylor, then, wanted to admit both California and New Mexico as states upon their application to Congress. Had the territorial aspects of the sectional crisis been the only ones in January, 1850, his plan might have been sound. It was, after all, but a variation on the theme Whigs had played the previous winter. But from any other view of the case, the president's policy was hopelessly shortsighted. The sectional crisis involved other pressing problems—the Texas boundary, the fugitive slave law, and slavery in the capital—that Taylor ignored. Moreover, the president had precluded anything but *statehood* for the Southwest—no other plan such as popular sovereignty or an extension of the 36°30′ line would be acceptable. Thus he denied the South even a symbolic, *de jure* participation in the southwestern territories since both new states would obviously draft free-soil constitutions. In short, Taylor's plan deeply insulted southerners because it foreclosed the least that any of them could accept: some plausible face-saving gesture from the national government that allowed them to preserve their honor intact.

Nonetheless, southerners' reactions to Taylor's proposal revealed serious fissures in their ranks. Southern Rights extremists, of course, damned it as a trick to foist the proviso on them. Moderate Democrats, however, strongly opposed resistance on the California issue—it would be, Cobb said, "against the doctrines of all southern statesmen" to thwart the perfectly constitutional statehood process. The great body of southern Whigs reacted peculiarly. For the most part men of innate conservative instincts, they knew slavery would never go west and were willing to admit a free California—on one condition: resolution of all questions touching the South. To admit California without receiving reciprocal concessions from the North they regarded as a gross injustice. Rhetorically, then, many of these Whigs, Stephens and Toombs included, would sound in the coming weeks as uncompromising as any Calhounite. But wild speeches characterized this session, and angry words often cloaked the desperation of men seeking only a formula by which to preserve their pride, their political careers, and what they regarded as their honor.[41]

40. Richardson (ed.), *Messages and Papers of the Presidents*, V, 9–24, 27–30.
41. Cobb to Joseph Henry Lumpkin, January 11, 1850, in Joseph Henry Lumpkin Papers, UG; Cole, *Whig Party in the South*, 163–64.

Deeply troubled throughout January, Stephens began once more to brood on the future. All he could see was the inevitability of civil war. He had no objections to admitting California, he told Linton in a long, thoughtful letter, but this would still leave all the "great questions of the day" up in the air. Even a general settlement, he feared, would not end the troubles because the causes of southern discontent were widespread and growing. The admission of new western states would give the North majorities in Congress that would continually "harrass, annoy and oppress." Such "continual reproach" would become unbearable. He himself would do nothing to hasten disunion, but he considered it "almost inevitable." Ultimately, the South would have to "*submit* or *fight*." If he were in the legislature, he said, he would introduce bills strengthening Georgia's military apparatus. Stephens simply could not understand how important the proviso was to northern consciences. To him it was nothing but "a humbug . . . a dispute about 'goats wool.'" The only real issue was preserving southern honor. Passage of the proviso could only be properly resisted as "an *insult* to the South," and, he ruefully conceded, such a "public censure and national odium" on southern institutions "would be no small outrage."[42]

That Stephens, a man of profound conservatism, could harbor such thoughts indicates just how volatile the sectional strife had become. But he wrote during one of his gloomiest moods, amid a riotous session in Congress, when not a glimmer of hope appeared on the horizon. Civil war seemed inevitable to him now not because slavery's existence was threatened or because its expansion was necessary for southern security—reasons other southerners would advance—but because he foresaw only continued "degradation" for the South. The moral opprobrium being heaped on the South by what he considered self-righteous northern hypocrites personally and deeply insulted him. As a man always acutely sensitive of his dignity and integrity, he could react but one way to threats on his honor—with instant defiance, the same way he had reacted to Judge Cone's insults.

If Stephens really believed sectional war inevitable, his every action from this point until 1861 was inconsistent if not hypocritical. But Stephens' regard for his honor was only one facet of his complex makeup, and his anger when he felt it breached was almost always transitory. Compromise, adjustment, explanation, mutual forbearance—these were always possible. Stephens was no revolutionary. His anger at per-

42. AHS to LS, January 21, 1850, in Stephens Papers, MC.

sonal or collective slight was no more instinctive than his commitment
to preserving what he regarded as the eternal and immutable principles
of law, order, and justice. And in the end, this commitment overrode
everything else. Only when he perceived these principles to be in mortal danger could Stephens ever countenance rebellion against the established order. And once compromise seemed possible, Stephens
never perceived such mortal danger—not now or in 1860, when,
over his impassioned objections, thousands of his fellow southerners
launched a rebellion in the name of justice and honor.

Ironically, it was Henry Clay, whose influence in the capital Stephens
most feared, who laid the groundwork for the Compromise of 1850.
Clay, again in the Senate, introduced his famous resolutions on January 29. They provided for admission of California as a free state, organization of the rest of the Mexican cession into territories without
congressional restriction on slavery, curtailment of Texas' western
boundary in return for assumption of her debt by the national government, abolition of the slave trade in the District of Columbia, a stronger
fugitive slave law, and a congressional statement that it had no power
to interfere with the interstate slave trade.

When Clay defended these resolutions in a two-day speech in early
February, Stephens, seated on his cloak on the floor near Clay's desk,
joined the throng mobbing the Senate chamber to listen. His view of
Clay softened. He pronounced the speech "great" and the Kentuckian
himself "a more remarkable man and much greater orator" than he
had ever supposed. For the moment at least, Clay's plan provided an
alternative to Taylor's and therefore some hope for a comprehensive
settlement of the slavery problem. It was just what the southern Whigs
sought. Like the editor of the Columbus *Enquirer*, they had reservations, but they recognized a life ring when they saw it.[43]

The administration and the president, however, were anything but
pleased, seeing in Clay's action only an attack on Taylor's policy and a
blatant bid for leadership of the party. Consequently, Taylor supporters
in Congress joined others implacably hostile to the compromise proposals—northern abolitionists and the Calhounite southerners. It
would take six long months for Congress to fashion a compromise.
The histrionic Senate debate, which pitted three heroes from the na-

43. *Ibid.*, January 28, February 10, 1850; Columbus *Enquirer*, February 5, 1850.

tion's golden age—Webster, Clay, and Calhoun—in their last titanic struggle, has often overshadowed the violent struggle engaging the House at the same time. And here Alexander Stephens played a key role.[44]

On February 13, Taylor submitted California's free state constitution to Congress. The next Monday, the eighteenth, Representative James Doty of Wisconsin introduced in the House a resolution instructing the Committee on the Territories to frame a bill for California's admission. To get California admitted without addressing the other slavery questions, Doty immediately moved the previous question. Had his resolution come to a vote it would have passed easily, but southern Whigs, led by Stephens and Toombs, thwarted a vote on the motion. Stephens drew up a list and scurried about the hall securing the pledges of more than the requisite one-fifth of the members to demand roll calls. Then, by making endless dilatory motions, all requiring a call of the 230-man roll, Stephens and his cohorts prevented a vote. The session dragged on until after midnight, when Cobb ruled the legislative day over. Doty's resolution would not be regular business on the morrow.[45]

At one point during the day's boisterous proceedings, John A. McClernand of Illinois, a Douglas lieutenant, approached Stephens and Toombs seeking a way out of the deadlock. There certainly was a way, the Georgians replied, and Stephens set it down in writing. No objection would be made to California's admission, he wrote, *after* settlement of other territorial issues. Not only must the proviso be excluded, but the people of the territories "should be distinctly empowered" to make laws allowing slavery and to write a proslavery constitution if they chose. When the time came to admit these new states, Congress must forego its attempts to restrict slavery and admit them. McClernand looked over Stephens' scrawl, nodded, and agreed that this might form the basis of an arrangement.[46]

The preliminary negotiations on the House floor spawned a conference on the following night at Speaker Cobb's house, with five Democratic representatives (two southern, three northern) plus Stephens and

44. Crittenden to Clayton, February 18, 1850, in Clayton Papers, LC.

45. *Congressional Globe*, 31st Cong., 1st Sess., 375–85.

46. Alexander H. Stephens, *A Constitutional View of the Late War Between the States: Its Causes, Character, Conduct and Results. Presented in a Series of Colloquies at Liberty Hall* (2 vols.; Philadelphia, 1868–70), II, 201–202.

Toombs attending. After McClernand pronounced Douglas' blessings on the proceedings, the group agreed to act in concert to admit California and organize New Mexico as the southerners wanted, to oppose any attempt to abolish slavery in the capital, and to reduce Texas' boundary but provide compensation. The plan essentially embodied ideas Douglas had been mulling over. Like Stephens, the Illinois senator realized the importance of a comprehensive settlement of sectional issues.[47]

Most striking about the bargain just made was that Stephens, almost offhandedly, had embraced the Democratic principle of popular sovereignty he had so scorned during the presidential campaign. But the intensity of the crisis had opened Stephens' eyes about popular sovereignty. It offered what the South needed at this juncture: a palatable alternative to the proviso and a "settlement" of the flaming territorial problem that preserved southern honor. Although he would not yet openly espouse the doctrine, Stephens recognized its immediate political benefits. The working alliance the Georgian forged with Stephen A. Douglas and the northwestern Democrats this night would shape Little Aleck's political thought for years.

A few days after their nocturnal meeting, Stephens, Toombs, and Thomas L. Clingman, a North Carolina Whig, called on the president to warn him of the serious dangers attending his policy of admitting California alone. Although the specifics of the conversation are unknown, it is likely that they urged Taylor to veto any enactment of the proviso. But Taylor was adamant; he would sign any constitutional measure presented to him, he said. At this point, the southerners referred, no doubt excitedly, to the danger of disunion Taylor was courting. What was simply a statement of fact to them—none of the three wanted secession, and all were working for a compromise to avert such a disaster—was a threat to Zachary Taylor. He would take command of the army himself to execute the laws, the president shot back angrily, and would hang traitors with less reluctance than he had spies and deserters in Mexico. If these Young Indians of 1848 still needed proof that they had seriously misjudged Old Zack, they had it now.[48]

47. *Ibid.*, 203–204; Robert W. Johannsen, *Stephen A. Douglas* (New York, 1973), 271–73.

48. Thurlow Weed Barnes, *Memoir of Thurlow Weed* (Boston, 1884), 176–81; Charles E. Hamlin, *The Life and Times of Hannibal Hamlin* (Cambridge, Mass., 1899), 201–203.

Although not apparent in March 1850, the mood of the country was gradually becoming more receptive to a peaceful adjustment of the crisis. Daniel Webster's famous and eloquent Senate speech on March 7, which urged settlement along the general lines Clay had outlined, both illustrated and helped shape this state of mind. On May 8, a special Senate committee chaired by Clay reported out two bills. One, the so-called "Omnibus," lumped together the admission of California, settlement of the Texas boundary, and organization of New Mexico and Utah territories; the second outlawed the slave trade in Washington, D.C. Debate on the Omnibus bill began in mid-May and lasted till August.

Meanwhile, the House was locked in rancorous debate of its own on Doty's bill for admitting California. On June 11, the day set for ending debate on the bill, the southern bloc had still found no way to defeat it. Having failed to extend debate, the southerners resorted to a filibuster, offering endless amendments and supporting them with five-minute speeches. On the next day Stephens added his bit to the process of obstruction, smugly reminding his colleagues that he had always opposed acquiring territory from Mexico and had never voted a single dollar to carry out the treaty provisions. But the House had not listened. "If we had come to a distinct understanding at first," he said, "we should have none of these difficulties."[49]

But he willingly compounded difficulties now. Congress, Stephens said the next day, was the only "competent authority" to pass laws protecting slaveholders' rights in the territories. Neither Cass's policy of nonintervention nor an extension of the Missouri Compromise line without "all necessary protection" for slavery south of it would do. Both, he concluded, would be "a perfect mockery of right." Fixed on a "comprehensive" settlement of the slavery issue, Stephens now espoused, at least publicly, a position few southern extremists could fault.[50]

But he spoke in heat, and indeed the interminable oratory had worn everyone's nerves to a frazzle. Even northern representatives now abetted the delay by renewing amendments to Doty's bill so they would have a chance to speak. On June 15, Stephens delivered another angry little speech in reply to one of these northerners. It was Toombs,

49. *Congressional Globe*, 31st Cong., 1st Sess., 1189.
50. *Ibid.*, 1194.

however, who created a sensation. Uncharacteristically quiet during most of the short speeches, he finally exploded. Neither he nor the South opposed California's admission because of her antislavery clause. The issue was the South's right to "equal participation" in the territories, her political equality in the Union. "Deprive us of this right and appropriate this common property to yourselves," he shouted in angry conclusion, "it is then your government, not mine. Then I am its enemy, and I will . . . bring my children and my constituents to the altar of liberty, and like Hamilcar I would swear them to eternal hostility to your foul domination." Refuse the South its just rights, "and for one, I will strike for *Independence*."[51]

According to Stephens, this speech caused "a perfect commotion" in the House. It may also have sobered the congressmen temporarily because for the next six weeks Doty's bill reposed quietly in the Committee of the Whole. The Stephens-Toombs bloc had triumphed. It had staved off a vote on California's admission, thus serving notice to the Senate that the House would await its action on the compromise proposals.[52]

The acerbic congressional debates may not have perceptibly advanced the cause of compromise, but other events outside the capital building did. On March 31, John C. Calhoun died. According to the Washington rumor mill, he had been preparing a strong argument for secession even up to the day of his death. Meanwhile, the Calhoun-inspired Nashville convention fell flat on its face. What had seemed in late 1849 a formidable current for militant southernism had by spring degenerated, in the Milledgeville *Southern Recorder*'s mocking words, to "the creature of a few politicians." Only nine of fifteen slave states were represented, and the delegates took no overt step toward disunion. If the convention signified anything, it showed that the South was far more interested in securing its safety within the Union.[53]

Stephens rarely waxed reflective about slavery, but during the crisis of 1850 he occasionally mused about it to Linton. For a man so naturally compassionate toward the unfortunate, weak, and poor, he betrayed little sensitivity to the fate of the millions of southern blacks. The in-

51. *Ibid.*, 1216, 1219.
52. Stephens, *Constitutional View*, II, 217.
53. Milledgeville *Southern Recorder*, April 30, 1850.

stitution—even in the abstract—had long since ceased to be debatable for him. He accepted all the standard proslavery arguments without question. The economic benefits of the system were so obvious that slavery's spread would be all but inevitable. He would not be surprised if England reinstituted the slave trade, he wrote. Cotton had so "revolutionized" England that a year's embargo on cotton exportation from the South would "ruin" her. This fact would save the Union. Rather than lose southern cotton, Britain would forsake both the North and Canada. She would probably develop her South American colonies as cotton-producing areas and then sell black slaves to tend the crop.

Stephens admitted that slavery, "one of the greatest problems of this interesting age," was at least imperfect. "What is to be the fate of the poor African God only knows. His condition as a slave is certainly not a good one but" far better in the South than "in his own barbarous clime." Simple arithmetic proved this. "If the comforts of a people or race are to be comported according to their natural increase and rapid multiplication the race is certainly vastly better off in this country in their present condition than it ever was in their own with all the liberty of nature." [54]

Moreover, ending the institution in America posed a horrendous practical problem. The cost would be astronomical. He had just read an article by Thomas Carlyle on the slave trade. "In this respect Carlyle is right," he observed. "If it is the duty of [a] Christian nation to put an end to the slave trade they should go directly to those people who are buying the raw Africans and tell them to quit it or be shot." But according to figures he read, it cost England about $1.2 billion to combat the slave trade, "quite enough to give a pretty liberal price for every slave in the United States . . . it would allow $400 a piece." [55]

Stephens considered dishonesty, corruption, and lack of virtue far greater problems than slavery. He felt totally betrayed by the Whigs and the administration culprits. "All parties are corrupt," he wrote angrily, and "kept up by bad men for corrupt purposes." The conduct of men he had helped put in the cabinet particularly incensed him. His old friend Crawford, he said, was "wholly unfit" for his office, took "no interest in public affairs," and "consulted nobody." He loathed

54. The preceding paragraphs are from AHS to LS, March 25, 1850, in Stephens Papers, MC.
55. *Ibid.*, April 20, 1850.

"scheming intriguing" Ballard Preston even more. Preston, in his opinion, had done more to ruin the administration than the rest of the cabinet together because of his dominant influence over the "pure and honest" Taylor. Allied with the malevolent Seward, Preston had set his
head against compromise because of his jealousy and dislike of Clay—
and he had convinced the president to do likewise. For months, said
Stephens, he had warned the Virginian that his advice would ruin Taylor and "leave him with a smaller party than Tyler had." [56]

People like Preston had brought the Whig party to its knees by
utterly changing its character. "You will remember last fall when I first
came here," he continued to Linton, "I told you Taylor in my opinion
would sign the Proviso. You may now understand why I thought so.
That part alone would not have caused me to break with the Whig
party. But I soon saw that Winthrop was to be elected by a coalition of
the Southern Whigs with the *Freesoilers*. And the Whig party was to
be the anti-slavery party. Against *that I kicked*." [57]

In other words, Stephens might have forgiven Old Zack for signing
the proviso, but he could not remain a Whig when the party stood
ready to forsake its nationalism by cooperating with the leprous
northern sectionalists, as it did in the contest for speaker. Even informal association with Free-Soilers would be the political kiss of death at
home. He had thus been forced to bolt the party.

But the party was not the president. "Very few men scan character
more closely than I do," he told Linton. Stephens had long since
judged Taylor pure, and even now, with the president himself spear-
heading opposition to the compromise, Stephens still argued that Taylor was being duped. To do otherwise would be to admit how grossly
he had misjudged the man, and few men would go to the lengths Stephens did to avoid such an admission. What really angered him was
the incongruity of his situation. Fully expecting to wield influence in
the administration, he found himself being driven into direct opposition. Taylor wasn't consulting any of his "*original friends*" except Preston, he complained. And Preston and his cronies "have no objects now
but to elevate themselves upon the sacrifice of those who made Taylor
President." [58]

56. *Ibid.*, April 15, 1850.
57. *Ibid.* Massachusetts Whig Robert C. Winthrop had been the party's candidate
for Speaker.
58. *Ibid.*, May 6, 1850; AHS to Crittenden, May 7, 1850, in Crittenden Papers, DU.

Within a single short year Stephens had found himself first power-less, then partyless. "I am almost an outsider," he told Linton, "and am beginning to feel but little interest in . . . party politicks." But even as a self-styled outsider, Stephens still retained his formidable constituency in Georgia. Party lines in the state throughout 1850 fluctuated wildly with both Whigs and Democrats dividing into pro- and anti-compromise factions. Once Stephens and Toombs bolted the Whigs and Cobb declared for compromise, party labels signified little. About all that was clear was that the mass of Whigs supported Clay's measure and that all the prominent Southern Righters were Democrats.[59]

So Stephens actually had little choice once Clay offered his proposals and the Senate committee made its report. He would support the compromise in almost any form, he decided, as long as the proviso got squelched. In fact, he did not like the territorial part of Clay's plan since it prevented territorial legislatures from passing any laws on slavery. He still believed Mexican law had banned slavery in the cession "and that without some law passed by the governing power it is useless to speak of the constitutional rights of the South." But since "a majority of the South" had failed to concur, he was "willing for the matter to be tested." He supported Clay's plan not "as a *compromise*," he said, "but simply as a measure to quiet the country."[60]

Even as Stephens wrote, events in New Mexico triggered another crisis. On May 15 a convention met in Santa Fe, drew up an anti-slavery constitution, and dispatched it to Washington along with a petition for statehood. As Texas, which claimed the Rio Grande as its boundary and thus about half the New Mexico territory, prepared to use force to assert its rights, southerners in Washington reacted angrily. When word of New Mexico's statehood petition reached the capital, their anger turned to rage. The "usurpation of New Mexico," if admitted with California, wrote one southern radical, would fill "the Cup of humiliation to the brim." At the same time, nothing could have so dismayed the moderates. For if New Mexico's petition were presented, the Omnibus bill, with its heart cut out, would be dead.[61]

The southerners acted quickly. At a caucus on the night of July 1, they appointed a three-man committee—Toombs, Humphrey Mar-

59. AHS to LS, May 14, 1850, in Stephens Papers, MC.
60. *Ibid.*
61. W. F. Gordon to R. M. T. Hunter, July 2, 1850, in Ambler (ed.), *Hunter Correspondence*, 114.

shall, and C. M. Conrad (all "original Taylor men")—to go to Taylor singly and warn him that his policy of immediate statehood for California and New Mexico would cost his last vestige of southern support. Each got the same answer: the president would stick by his policy. Moreover, if he had to sacrifice one wing of his party, Taylor said, he could hardly be expected to abandon eighty-four northerners for twenty-nine southerners.[62]

Stephens' dismay over this news can well be imagined. But Crawford's report that the cabinet had supported using the army if necessary to oppose Texas forces in New Mexico shocked him even more. Crawford had offered to resign rather than countenance this action, but Taylor had refused the offer and signed the order himself. Still smoldering over Crawford's report, Stephens picked up his copy of the *National Intelligencer* on July 3 and read an infuriating editorial. If Texas advanced on Santa Fe, it said, it would be the "duty" of the army to defend it.[63]

Convinced beyond doubt that Taylor would use force to carry out his policy, Stephens sat down at his desk in the House and wrote a blistering reply to the editors. "The first Federal gun that shall be fired against the people of Texas, without the authority of law, will be the signal for the freemen from Delaware to the Rio Grande to rally to the rescue." Whatever doubt there might be about the Texas boundary, "nothing can be clearer than that it is not a question to be decided by the *army*." In case of conflict, the Texas cause would be the cause of the entire South.[64]

While Stephens wrote, Toombs rushed up to the White House for a talk with Taylor. The president had to be convinced that a clash of arms between federal and Texas troops would be catastrophic. Toombs found Taylor "in fine health and spirits" but also "quite determined" to hew to his course. Upon Toombs's return, both he and Stephens left the House and sought out Preston, desperate enough at this point to hope that a man in whom both had lost all faith would help them change Taylor's mind. They encountered the secretary on the steps of the Treasury Building. Preston was hardly cooperative, and at the end of a heated discussion Stephens lost his temper. If troops were sent to

62. AHS to LS, July 10, 1850, in Stephens Papers, MC.
63. Washington *National Intelligencer*, July 3, 1850.
64. AHS to the editors, July 3, 1850, in Washington *National Intelligencer*, July 4, 1850.

New Mexico, he warned, the president would be impeached. "Who will impeach him?" Preston asked frostily. "I will if nobody else does!" Stephens shot back.[65]

Two days after the angry confrontation, Taylor was stricken with acute gastroenteritis. Stephens never saw him again. He, Toombs, and Crawford called at the White House at six o'clock in the evening of Tuesday, July 9, to learn how the president was doing, but they had been turned away. Taylor died four hours later.

Although admitting "respect and sincere regard" for Taylor, Stephens wasn't exactly prostrated by grief for Old Zack. He realized that a mammoth obstacle to sectional compromise was gone and thought it best that "Providence has removed him." Yet even after Taylor's death he refused to admit he had misjudged the man. Taylor had been honest, well-meaning, and patriotic, he wrote. Had he followed his own impulses instead of his cabinet's "foolish counsels," all would have been well.[66]

But Taylor *had* followed his own impulses, and he had clung like a bulldog to the course he charted for the country in his December message. His devotion to the American Union had been no less unflinching than his morbid jealousy of Clay. Whether the Union could have survived his obstinacy is a moot question, but many Americans agreed with Daniel Webster. "If General Taylor had lived," he said, "we would have had civil war."[67]

But Taylor was dead—and the Compromise of 1850 was alive.

65. AHS to LS, July 10, 1850, in Stephens Papers, MC; Avary (ed.), *Stephens Recollections,* 26.
66. AHS to LS, July 10, 1850, in Stephens Papers, MC.
67. Webster quoted in Hilliard, *Politics and Pen Pictures,* 231.

VIII

Stumping for the Union

The Omnibus bill survived Zachary Taylor by a little over two weeks. Fittingly, as indigestion had killed Taylor, Clay's bill expired because too many legislators could not stomach it in one piece. By lumping his proposals together in one bill Clay had made a serious tactical error. Neither he nor any other senator could save the bill when it came up for a vote on July 31. One by one, sections were lopped off until only the Utah territorial provision remained. This part passed the next day, and the day after that, after delivering an angry speech, Clay left Washington for an extended vacation.

"What do you think the 'old fogies' have done?" Stephens wrote Linton disgustedly. "They have made a complete fry of the Compromise." He intended to come home, he said, and "I dont care what they do or fail to do." Clay's last speech blasting southern senators for not voting for his bill had not pleased him. He thought the Senate might pass the compromise piecemeal, but he wasn't sure. "The world is made up of fools," he angrily concluded, "great fools, incorrigible fools, and incomprehensible fools." [1]

Little Aleck did not leave Washington until mid-August, and even then, just as he had suspected, Clay's compromise measures, under

1. AHS to LS, July 31, August 2, 1850, in Stephens Papers, MC.

Douglas' skillful tutelage, were being passed singly in the Senate. President Fillmore's conciliatory message on Texas, upholding national authority around Santa Fe but urging immediate settlement of the boundary question, helped defuse the dangerous situation in the Southwest.

Stephens decidedly favored the new president's approach, although he still remained defiant on the use of national force against the Texans. And he insisted that other sectional problems, especially defining southern rights in the territories, be dealt with. "I am no enemy to the Union," he reminded the House, but "it is time for mutual concessions." The "radical nature" of the differences between the sections, he confessed, had caused him "unpleasant apprehensions" for the future. The House had to deal with the present, however, and both sides had to make concessions now.[2]

Stephens' apprehensions did not prevent his leaving Washington for a month, even as the compromise measures made their way through the Senate. Exactly why he left isn't clear. Maybe he failed to foresee how quickly the compromise would pass. He had already told his brothers that he wanted to come home "to see how our people really talk and feel" and to attend the court sessions. Whatever his reason, Stephens was not in Washington to vote on almost all the compromise laws. (He got back to the capital on September 13, in time to vote for the last of the compromise measures in the House, the bill abolishing the slave trade in Washington, D.C. He voted "nay," but the bill passed, and with its approval the Compromise of 1850 was complete.)[3]

The situation Stephens found in Georgia in mid-August must have shocked him. The sectional crisis had almost completely wiped out Georgia's traditional party lines, and a call by the state's extremists for a mass resistance meeting in Macon in August only hastened the process. After their failure at Nashville, Southern Rights men determined to force matters to a head by agitation in the states. "They expect to manufacture public opinion," scoffed Cobb's uncle, John B. Lamar.

2. *Congressional Globe*, 31st Cong., 1st Sess., Appendix, 1082–84.
3. AHS to LS, July 15, 1850, in Stephens Papers, MC; AHS to JLS, August 6, 1850, in Stephens Papers, EU. Besides abolishing the slave trade in the capital, the Compromise of 1850 admitted California as a free state, established territorial governments in New Mexico and Utah under the popular sovereignty principle, enacted a stringent fugitive slave act, and adjusted Texas' western boundary with $10 million compensation to Texas for giving up her claims to New Mexican territory.

"God damn 'em how I wish old Jackson was alive & President . . . for the next twelve months."[4]

Lamar's anger was understandable. Georgia's Democrats were completely demoralized, while most Whigs clung desperately to hopes for the compromise. "Who will attempt to predict the consequences [if the compromise were lost]?" moaned the *Southern Recorder*. "We shall not—we have no heart for such a subject." Even Whigs inclined to resist the compromise abhorred the blatant opportunism among the Southern Rights men. Using resistance "for sinister and selfish purposes at home" so disgusted Iverson L. Harris that he decided to support the compromise if it passed. It was clear to him that neither Georgia nor the South was united. Instead, both sides were fomenting division with an eye to "ascendancy at home."[5]

The mass meeting in Macon on August 21 climaxed the campaign against the compromise. Spurred by angry speeches from William Yancey and Barnwell Rhett, the extremists completed destruction of Georgia's time-honored Democracy and constructed the new Southern Rights party on its ruins. Although its stand on secession was never clearly defined, a determined minority in the new party consisted of out-and-out disunionists, which prompted many influential Democrats to repudiate the new organization and join forces with Stephens, Toombs, and Cobb. "Party harness sets very loosely on the people of Georgia at this time," commented one Democrat. Whether a man was for or against the Union had become the overriding concern.[6]

Although Stephens had long since embraced the compromise, he soon discovered how his temerarious rhetoric in Congress had confused the home folk. One of Stephens' correspondents even attributed all "the present dissensions in Georgia" to the "fact that our people do not understand the position of their representatives." Once home, Stephens moved quickly to correct any misapprehensions. In speeches at Warrenton and Crawfordville, he defended the compromise bills and counseled moderation. The admission of California was no reason to disrupt the Union, he said.[7]

4. John B. Lamar to Cobb, July 5, 1850, in Cobb-Erwin-Lamar Papers, UG.
5. Milledgeville *Southern Recorder*, July 30, 1850; Harris to Berrien, August 2, 1850, in Berrien Papers, SHC/NC.
6. James Meriwether to Cobb, August 24, 1850, in Phillips (ed.), *TSC Correspondence*, 211.
7. S. T. Chapman to AHS, August 31, 1850, in Stephens Papers, LC; Columbus *Enquirer*, September 10, 1850.

Nor was holding fast to an unpopular position, he might have added. Without any discernible discomfort he repudiated his view that Congress was required to pass laws protecting slavery in the Mexican cession. Congress did have the power to legislate on slavery in the territories, he said, but the right to legislate on it did not imply the power to abolish it. Southerners differed on this point, he conceded; many espoused the principle of nonintervention. If he had been wrong previously, the compromise territorial bills were "as good as they need be for the South." True, they did not open territory to slavery "in express terms," but "in principle" they extended the Missouri Compromise line and were therefore acceptable. He no longer believed it Congress' duty to establish slavery by law, Stephens announced, and he now accepted that conquest had abrogated Mexico's antislavery laws in the territories. So southerners, under the Senate bills, now had "a perfect right" to enter the territories with their slaves "outside of California up to 42nd deg[ree]."[8]

By coloring the compromise territorial bills as a *de facto* extension of the Missouri Compromise line, Stephens avoided accepting the popular sovereignty principle outright. Yet this is what he had done. This was not the same man who had rejected nonintervention out of hand in 1848 or who had recently declared the doctrine "a perfect mockery of right." The vicious struggle for the compromise measures had not changed his mind about southern "rights"—he still believed the South by right entitled to congressional protection of slave property in the territories. But the terrifying vision of disunion had changed it about the wisdom of making this abstract right a point of resistance. "Non-intervention is not the full measure of our rights," he wrote later, but "the only proper point of resistance is some hostile legislation or positive aggression."[9]

This was the position Stephens would hold for the rest of the decade. Profoundly shaken by the violence of southern reaction to the sectional crisis, he came to realize that his original position only abetted his worst foes. Only southern extremists espoused it. He also recognized the nonintervention formula for what it was: a *modus vivendi* that at least preserved the color of southern rights in the territories. It was clear by August, 1850, that a pledge of nonintervention in Utah

8. Milledgeville *Southern Recorder*, September 10, 1850; Augusta *Chronicle and Sentinel*, September 5, 1850.
9. AHS to John Steele, April 9, 1859, in Stephens Papers, DU.

and New Mexico was the most the South could expect from the North, and the least his constituents would accept. A face-saving accommodation for the South in the territories was really the only requirement for Stephens and the other moderates. The nonintervention formula, distasteful as it might be in theory, averted the Wilmot Proviso in practice. On these grounds alone it was more than enough to enlist Stephens' support. But the formula also averted the real possibility of disunion, to Stephens a catastrophic breakdown of the rule of law and order of unimaginable proportions. And what was true for Little Aleck was also true of thousands of middle Georgia Whigs, who accepted a Democratic prescription to avert a much greater disaster.

The long struggle in Congress was over, but in Georgia a fierce one was about to begin. In accord with the legislature's February resolutions requiring a state convention upon California's admission, Governor George Towns ordered a special election of delegates on November 25, 1850. Towns's proclamation sounded the radicals' clarion call: "Your institutions are in jeopardy . . . and the Federal Constitution violated by a series of aggressive measures, all tending to the consummation of one object, the abolition of slavery." The Georgia campaign had national significance. Hers would be the first collective southern voice to speak in response to the compromise and hence would greatly influence other southern states, especially South Carolina and Mississippi, both poised for secession.[10]

Arriving home in October, Stephens, Toombs, and Cobb immediately threw themselves into the campaign for acceptance of the compromise. The Stephens-Toombs-Cobb Triumverate, as the local press dubbed it, wielded formidable influence. Politics in the antebellum South was an intensely personal affair between a leader and his constituents. Had these three counseled resistance, Georgians might well have listened. These giants would then have been leagued with a host of influential leaders: Towns, former governors Wilson Lumpkin, Charles J. McDonald, and George M. Troup, former senators Herschel Johnson (who, in the most quotable and aromatic phrase of the campaign, termed the compromise "a fecund box of nauseous nostrums") and Walter T. Colquitt, not to mention Berrien. Opposed to this array

---

10. Milledgeville *Federal Union*, September 24, 1850.

were state and local leaders such as Charles J. Jenkins, John E. Ward, Eugenius Nisbet, and Dr. Richard Arnold—all men of ability but far below the Southern Rights men in prestige.[11]

"A fiercer political campaign I have never passed through," confessed Dr. Arnold. The radicals, often heartened by Stephens' and Toombs's congressional rhetoric, had been stung to boundless fury when both accepted the compromise. Although Stephens came in for his share of abuse, "Hamilcar" Toombs absorbed the choicest Southern Rights invective. Not that this bothered either one, for they readily challenged extremist leaders to a joint debate on November 2 in Columbus, a Southern Rights stronghold. Upon their arrival the two congressmen found no one to debate, but several effigies of Toombs hanging about clearly indicated the town's mood. Undaunted, Toombs proceeded to insult the hostile crowd: he was wearing the first white shirt ever into a Democratic gathering, he cried. And these scruffy followers of Calhoun now wanted to overthrow the Union! Why, these people didn't have the strength to overturn an eight-by-ten smokehouse. Maybe not, but they did have their pride. At one point during the boisterous proceeding, knives and pistols appeared and fist fights broke out in the crowd. "Toombs and Stephens," said the Columbus *Times* with marvelous understatement, "have operated like sparks on a tinder box in this community. . . . We deem it fortunate there was no serious accident to report."[12]

The fury only intensified because Toombs and the other "Unionists"—a term the procompromise men applied to themselves—systematically misrepresented the Southern Rights position. At the beginning of the campaign the triumvirate purposely limned the issue in glaring contrast: accepting the compromise, they said, would preserve the Union; rejecting it would dissolve the Union. Indeed, early in the struggle the "infuriated madmen" of the opposition press and its "partially demented" public speakers made this easy to do. *"We despise the Union, and the North as we do hell itself,"* raged the Columbus *Sentinel.* "WE ARE FOR SECESSION, FOR RESISTANCE, OPEN, UNQUALIFIED

11. Johnson quoted in Augusta *Constitutionalist,* August 3, 1850.

12. R. D. Arnold to John W. Forney, December 18, 1850, in Richard H. Shryock (ed.), *Letters of Richard D. Arnold, M.D., 1808–1876, Mayor of Savannah, First Secretary of the American Medical Association* (Durham, N.C., 1929), 44; "Autobiography of R. J. Moses," in SHC/NC, 47; Columbus *Times* quoted in Augusta *Chronicle and Sentinel,* November 9, 1850.

RESISTANCE," roared the Macon *Telegraph*. Even the normally circumspect Milledgeville *Federal Union* came close to endorsing disunion.[13]

Unqualified radicalism did not typify all compromise opponents, however. Herschel Johnson, for example, never favored separate state secession. The issue, he insisted, was "resistance or submission," not "union or disunion." The editor of the *Federal Union* echoed this sentiment, arguing that "resistance now" might save the Union. But resistance in what form? That was the unanswered question.[14]

The most vocal Southern Rights men favored outright secession, but the cry for disunion steadily waned. In late October, Stephens reported its disappearance. The opposition leaders, he said, now advocated "Southern Rights" within some constitutional redress. What any anticompromise man meant by "resistance" varied widely. Some, like Berrien, favored commercial nonintercourse with the North; others demanded an extension of the Missouri Compromise line or nothing more than a petition for redress to the national government. But no matter where individual Southern Rights men stood, the triumvirate labeled them all disunionists.[15]

By his own reckoning, Stephens traveled three thousand miles during the campaign, and once again he let his flinty temper get the best of him. The Augusta *Republic*, seeking to embarrass Stephens, printed several of the angriest excerpts from his recent speech on the Texas boundary. Inadvertently, an inexperienced copy boy labeled the excerpts as coming from Stephens' speech against the Clayton bill. The innocent mistake spurred Little Aleck to impute in a public letter that both James M. Smythe, the editor, and his paper were chronic liars.[16]

Smythe quickly explained the error, but Stephens refused to withdraw the insult. An affair of honor was only narrowly averted: it took more than three weeks and at least nine delicately phrased letters before Little Aleck would publicly retract his offensive remarks. Stephens had been childish and petty, as he almost always was when his hypersensitive pride was pricked. But this time, when his opponent was

13. Macon *Journal and Messenger* quoted in Allan Nevins, *The Ordeal of the Union* (2 vols.; New York, 1947), I, 355; Columbus *Sentinel*, September 12, 1850, and Macon *Telegraph*, September 17, 1850, quoted in Augusta *Chronicle and Sentinel*, September 20, 1850, Milledgeville *Federal* Union, October 1, 1850.

14. Johnson quoted in Percy Scott Flippin, *Herschel V. Johnson of Georgia: State Rights Unionist* (Richmond, 1931), 30; Milledgeville *Federal Union*, November 19, 1850.

15. AHS to Crittenden, October 24, 1850, in Crittenden Papers, DU.

16. *Ibid.*, November 11, 1850; Augusta *Chronicle and Sentinel*, November 6, 1850.

clearly in the wrong, he proved just how hateful he could be. For all his pretensions to virtue and superiority, he could rarely forego the malevolent delight in making an opponent squirm.[17]

On November 25, by a smashing vote of 46,616 to 24,499—the greatest majority in state history—Georgia voters endorsed the Compromise of 1850. Only ten of ninety-three counties elected Southern Rights delegations, and of the 264 delegates, only 23 favored "resistance." Less than half of Georgia's Democrats had supported the extremists.

Moderates throughout the country rejoiced. Georgia had "crushed the spirit of discord, disunion and Civil War," said Henry Clay. A Connecticut committee wrote Stephens a letter of effusive praise. Pro-compromise northern papers quickly credited Georgia with averting a national disaster. Southerners reacted quickly too. On the day after the election, South Carolina's governor—who bore the intriguingly aqueous name of Whitemarsh Seabrook—advised his legislature to avoid impetuous action. It did, and thus did South Carolina's many secessionists acquiesce in Georgia's vote for the Union.[18]

No other convention in Georgia's history, the secession gathering of 1861 excepted, would have as profound an effect on the state as the august body gaveled to order in Milledgeville on December 10, 1850. After its five-day session, Georgia had a new political party and the South a new statement of principles, the famous Georgia Platform. Neither Stephens nor Toombs served on the committee that wrote the document—Charles J. Jenkins wrote it—but both saw the draft and suggested changes later incorporated into the final copy. The convention adopted Jenkins' report and accompanying resolutions by an overwhelming 237 to 19 vote. Georgia would abide by California's admission, said the preamble, although not fully satisfied with it. Next came the five resolutions, the Georgia Platform.

The first resolution declared the Union "secondary in importance" only to the rights and principles it was formed to preserve. The next two endorsed the compromise: Georgia would abide by it "as a permanent adjustment" even though she did not "wholly approve" of it. But

17. Augusta *Chronicle and Sentinel*, December 22, 1850. AHS to LS, November 25–December 16, 1850, in Stephens Papers, MC, discuss the Smythe affair.

18. Clay to A. H. Chappell *et al.*, February 13, 1851, in Milledgeville *Southern Recorder*, March 4, 1851; Francis Ives *et al.* to AHS, December 9, 1850, in Stephens Papers, MC.

she would resist "even (as a last resort) to a disruption of [the Union]," said the fourth resolution, any of the following: abolition of slavery in Washington, D.C., or federal areas in the South, suppression of the interstate slave trade, refusal to admit a new slave state, passage of any act prohibiting slavery in Utah or New Mexico, or any repeal or dilution of fugitive slave laws. The preservation of the Union, the final resolution said bluntly, depended on "faithful execution of the Fugitive Slave Bill." [19]

Depending on what one emphasized, the platform served the interests of both Unionists and Southern Rights men. Each group hailed it as a vindication of its own creed. Throughout the nation, papers praised Georgia's patriotic stand. In the outpouring of elation, however, many were apt to overlook the rigorously conditional nature of Georgia's—and by extension, the South's—acceptance of the Compromise of 1850. The Georgia Platform was anything but a "submissionist" document.

The South had not submitted. The defeat of the southern radicals did not mean that the South had accepted "either the finality of the Compromise or accepted the Union if the Compromise was in fact final." Several hundred thousand southerners were willing yet to entrust their rights, safety, and honor to the Union only so long as the bitterly forged "settlement" lasted. But the crisis had also galvanized thousands of others into radicals bent on dissolving the Union. Defeated for the moment, they lay in wait for the proper time. "There is not the smallest respect or affection for the 'Union' even lingering among Representatives or People in this State," wrote one South Carolinian in December, 1850, "and the Question of dissolving it . . . is only one of time, and expediency." [20]

With traditional party lines in Georgia sundered, it was likewise only a matter of time before Unionist Whigs and Democrats coalesced into a common organization. That happened between sessions of the December convention. At the first meeting, December 11, Stephens and Toombs delivered eloquent Union speeches. Fanatics from both sections still endangered the Union, Stephens warned. The only way to arrest this fanaticism was for all friends of the Union to join in one

19. Royce McCrary (ed.), "The Authorship of the Georgia Platform of 1850: A Letter by Charles J. Jenkins," *Georgia Historical Quarterly*, LIV (1970), 585–90.

20. Potter, *Impending Crisis*, 129; J. Townsend to Henry Lumpkin, December 20, 1850, in Henry Lumpkin Papers, UG.

great national organization "upon a principle as broad as the Constitution." This hazy principle proved broad enough for the assembled Georgians, so in meetings on the following two nights they formally organized the new Constitutional Union party and adopted the Georgia Platform as its own.[21]

Stephens and Toombs thus returned to Washington as members of a new political party. But whether this organization was necessary—had not disunion been checked?—or could last for long remained to be seen. After all, both of Georgia's new parties shared the objective of protecting and preserving southern interests. All that separated them was the question of method. The Constitutional Unionists, in the mainstream of the historic pattern of American two-party politics, envisioned a national organization to carry on an adversary relationship with sectional "fanatics." A balance-of-power scheme ensured by party discipline would safeguard southern interests. The Southern Rights men, on the other hand, heirs of Calhoun, distrusted and despised the traditional two-party system. Only through a strictly southern party, a united South, they believed, could southern rights be preserved.

So much for theory. In practice, however, neither party achieved more than local prominence. The Union party existed only in Georgia, Mississippi, and Alabama—places where state governments had endorsed resistance and local disunion sentiment ran strong. The Compromise of 1850 had not disrupted political alignments in the North. Although extreme antislavery elements damned the new fugitive slave law, the overwhelmingly procompromise Democrats did well in the elections. The administration also stood firmly behind the compromise, and by the summer of 1851 Whig and Democratic conventions in most northern states pledged faithful adherence to it as the law of the land.

So the Constitutional Union party stood doomed from the start. Idle Washington gossip in early 1851 speculated on a Clay-Cass ticket in 1852. (Incidentally, Stephens had supped with Cass and now pronounced him "a sociable old fellow.") And on January 22, 1851, a bipartisan congressional group of sorts—five Democrats, thirty-nine Whigs—signed a statement pledging not to support any opponent of the compromise.[22]

21. Milledgeville *Southern Recorder*, December 17, 1850.
22. AHS to LS, February 10, 1851, in Stephens Papers, MC.

But for these two feeble signs, every other showed the traditional two-party system intact. Editors in Washington scorned the third-party movement. The "national" Union convention scheduled for February failed to materialize. And worse, southern Whigs outside of Georgia and Mississippi remained firmly wedded to their old party. "A union of heterogenous bodies!" scoffed one Tennessee Whig. "It is absurd." Even in Georgia, third-party men were having second thoughts. According to the Columbus *Times*, Union Democrats were "wondering how in the damn hell they got into an omnibus with Bob Toombs and Alex Stephens."[23]

If this observation portended the demise of the Union party, an even stranger portent appeared shortly after Congress opened. The Whig congressional caucus, spurred by the cabinet, passed a strong pro-compromise resolution. A nonplused Toombs interpreted it as "a Whig effort at nationalization," a disavowal of "their Freesoil allies." Some northern Whigs stood ready to vote for compromise Democrats, he said, and this strengthened the Union party. Had Toombs analyzed more carefully, he might have seen the caucus vote for what it was: an endorsement of the Fillmore administration—and a clear sign that the Whigs had accepted political reality.[24]

Stephens hardly bothered to mention politics upon his return to Washington, for he had fallen once again into the grip of melancholy, when everything seemed fruitless, especially the machinations of politicians. He would take more pleasure in gardening or farming or even "*ploughing*," he said, "than anything I can think of." He was "heartily worn out" with politics and didn't "care a fig for a single subject."[25]

Little Aleck had good reason to be worn out: his off hours were filled with an almost continuous round of social events. He and Toombs, conspicuous in "saving the Union" in the recent campaign, had become sought-after celebrities on the capital's glittering social circuit. And when not attending receptions and dinners, Stephens found time to take in a circus at the National Theater—and also to move. Forced from their rooms at Willard's Hotel by a case of smallpox, he and

23. Washington *National Intelligencer*, January 23, 1851; Charles Ready to John Bell, January 3, 1851, in John Bell Papers, LC; Columbus *Times* quoted in George V. Irons, "The Secession Movement in Georgia, 1850–1861" (Ph.D. dissertation, Duke University, 1936), 69–70.

24. Toombs to Cobb, January 2, 1851, in Phillips (ed.), *TSC Correspondence*, 219.

25. AHS to LS, January 12, 1851, in Stephens Papers, EU.

Toombs took up new lodgings at the Buckingham house on E Street, four blocks from Capitol Hill.[26]

No doubt Stephens enjoyed his celebrity status, along with the good food, wines, and mirth prevailing at these gatherings. Unfortunately, he also had to endure other guests, one of whom, a young French marquis, he took an "unutterable aversion" to and later deliberately snubbed. He did find words to express his disgust on another occasion, however. "The affair was very pleasant," he reported to Linton, of a tea he attended in Georgetown, "saving and excepting some *flirts* & wriggling of some young ladies in attendance. Some of these were abominable, detestable, just such actions as I would expect to see the vilest prostitutes in a whorehouse perform! These were done in dancing &c, &c." It is doubtless safe to say, given his utterances on this occasion, that had Stephens ever visited a bordello, he would have been struck dumb, if not dead. "I did not dance," he added unnecessarily. "I am particular in telling for fear you might have curiosity to know."[27]

Stephens was always at his most prim and prudish whenever discussing anything remotely sexual, almost as if he were embarrassed for even noticing women—much less himself—as sexual beings. Doubtless his stern religious upbringing had much to do with this reticence, but his extreme discomfort with the subject probably denoted much more than exaggerated moral sensitivities about sex. It is likely that impotence was among his many physical ailments. Trapped in a boy's body, constantly crippled by disease and sickness, he lacked the virility of other men and was denied pleasures they took for granted. He could not accept his own unconscious and completely natural urges. They had to be repressed and condemned because to admit them would be a confession of "weakness," a carnal chink in his self-constructed fortress of rectitude and intellectual superiority.[28]

Stephens was thirty-nine years old in 1851, hardly an age when a man is immune to the beguiling blandishments of young women. And in his own peculiar way, he wasn't *completely* immune. One young lady at the tea, Virginia Semmes, the hostess' daughter, "took my fancy exceedingly," he confessed. "For beauty, intelligence, form, grace and

26. *Ibid.*, January 1, 11, 22, 23, 1851, MC.
27. *Ibid.*, January 23, February 2, 1851.
28. Von Abele, *Stephens*, 136; E. Ramsay Richardson, *Little Aleck: A Life of Alexander H. Stephens, The Fighting Vice President of the Confederacy* (New York, 1932), 57–58.

everything that enters into the composition of a perfect woman she stands number one amongst all the women I ever saw." In one sentence Stephens had summed up his utterly romantic and idealized conception of women. Like Truth itself, the "Perfect Woman" really existed for him. Incorrigible Platonist that he was, how could it have been otherwise? Miss Semmes seems to have come as close to the Ideal as was possible for any corporeal manifestation. But even when discussing near perfection, Stephens found it hard to rhapsodize. He contented himself with this one-sentence description of Virginia's charms. "There is no need for further description," he concluded, "so I will drop the subject." Women and romance made Stephens just as uncomfortable as sex, and the few references he made to women who attracted his admiration were always cryptic. He considered most women frivolous anyway, and all women beneath him in mental and moral attainments. And in this respect only would Stephens have admitted the equality of the sexes: he felt the same way about most men.[29]

His current bout with chills, fever, and toothaches hardly helped Stephens' mood, but he was more than irritable now. He was profoundly sad, a mood unrelated to his health. He could be despondent when he felt fine, or cheerful amid horrible suffering. No, this depression stemmed from loneliness, a realization of how unlike other men he really was. Maybe seeing the young people enjoy dancing at Mrs. Semmes's or the gaiety of the social circuit reminded him of his strangeness, his inability to find joy in situations that brought joy to others. Did he secretly long to be more like other men, to feel a part of humanity? Or was it his physical inferiority and his inability to accept it that so saddened him? It may have been either—or both. It is clear, though, that Stephens was acutely aware of being different, and the thought of it tortured him. So as always, he took refuge behind a mask of superior intellect and moral rectitude. Being better than mankind, or thinking himself so, was the only way that Stephens could live with his own isolation. But consciously setting himself apart only increased his loneliness and sorrow. Stephens lived most of his life in the midst of this fearsome contradiction.

"Man's life," he told Linton, "is but a dreary pilgrimage through an inhospitable clime." And of all men he sometimes thought himself the "most miserable." For along with the normal complement of griefs

29. AHS to LS, February 2, 1851, in Stephens Papers, MC.

and misfortunes he shared with others, he was stalked by another: an "evil genius," an "inseparable companion . . . forever mocking and grinning and making those places which in the lives of others are most happy and agreeable to me most miserable by his fiendish and hideous laughs!" Of bodily agony he had had more than his share. But this was slight compared to the "pangs of an offended or wounded Spirit."

The secret of his life, he wrote, was "*revenge*. Not *revenge* in the usual aceptation of that term. But a determination . . . to meet the world in all its forces to master evil with good." Even as slight a thing as a look or the tone of a remark could arouse his soul from the depths of grief "with the fury of a lion and the ambition of a Caesar." Never did he desire "to *crush* or *trample the vile crew*," he said, "but only to command their respect for my own superiour virtues." His revenge "has nothing in it low or mean." But even "to triumph over the base" while remaining "pure in principle and pure in execution" was, he said, "poor consolation." For the world as often as not remained oblivious to his "superior virtues." This rankled constantly, tempting him to "crush every viper that crosses my path." But he could not bring himself to do this, any more than he could admit his own fallibility. He was not intentionally mean or spiteful; he simply *had* to prove himself before men. Their adulation was life's blood to him.[30]

He certainly had their affection in Georgia. Never had he wielded as much influence at home as he did now, nor had he ever enjoyed so much worshipful attention in the capital. But both situations, as he well knew, could change. Being a big fish in Georgia's small pond pleased him, but he could not abide this position indefinitely. He needed more.

30. The preceding paragraphs are from *ibid.*, February 3, 1851.

IX

New Wine and Old Bottles

In 1851 Georgia for the first time held its congressional and gubernatorial elections in the same year, a conjunction that effectively obliterated the line between state and national politics. Inevitably the voters tended to focus on national issues, which, as sectional troubles mounted, tended to submerge strictly local concerns. This situation played into the hands of the extremists. Meeting in Milledgeville on May 28, 1851, the Southern Rights party again nominated two-time governor and Nashville conventioneer Charles J. McDonald. The party platform denounced the Compromise of 1850 and firmly asserted a state's right to secede from the Union, an issue, it was hoped, that would woo many Union Democrats away from their unholy alliance with the Whigs.

Members of that alliance convened on June 2. Stephens was sick and did not attend, but Toombs, as chairman of the resolutions committee, handled the meeting exactly as his old friend could have wished. The Constitutional Unionists avoided any mention of secession, glorified the Georgia Platform, and warned against the diabolical plots of their opponents to embroil Georgia in a revolution against the government. Then, by acclamation, the convention nominated Howell Cobb for governor. Cobb's nomination had been a foregone conclusion. Running a Whig would have courted trouble, only confirming the insistent Southern Rights charge that Constitutional Unionism was but "a cunning Whig trick to catch gulls."[1]

Back in February Stephens may have found politics uninteresting, but convalescing at the start of the summer campaign, he chaffed under the inactivity. The campaign was strenuous, filled with the usual charges, countercharges, and insults. Southern Righters constantly harped on the secession issue, and although it bore little relation to political realities—its proponents carefully denied any secessionist intentions—it proved effective in both inflaming and indoctrinating the voters.

At first, Cobb tried to ignore the issue, but in June a Southern Rights meeting in Macon posed a series of public questions that he felt compelled to answer. Both Stephens and Toombs quickly offered Cobb advice. In Toombs's opinion, a man's personal thoughts on secession had no practical consequence. A community's political right ultimately rested on "nothing but the blood of the brave," and arguing the issue was "a mere dispute about words." Stephens advised Cobb to play up South Carolina radicalism and treat secession as "an abstract right" of revolution for which no just cause existed. He also urged Cobb to maintain the president's "right and duty . . . to execute the law against all factious opposition."[2]

Despite Stephens' advice to "be pointed not prolix," Cobb's reply to the Macon committee filled three columns of close print in the *Southern Recorder*. Making any sense of this document would confound the most skillful rhetorician, and it is probably safe to assume that the task eluded most Georgians. On one hand, Cobb denied a state's right to secede "at pleasure . . . with or without just cause." But on the other, he admitted a state's right to secede for "just causes, to be determined by herself." Such a right would derive from a state's "reserved sovereignty," not constitutional but "revolutionary" in character. It would not be treasonable action, said Cobb, and military force should not be used to coerce a seceded state except "in defense of the rights and interests of the remaining States." A "kind and indulgent policy" would soon coax a seceding state to return. Cobb concluded that if he

1. Augusta *Constitutionalist*, December 10, 1850.

2. Toombs to Cobb, June 19, 1851, in Cobb Papers, UG; AHS to Cobb, June 23, 1851, in Phillips (ed.), *TSC Correspondence*, 238.

were the governor and asked by the president to furnish militia to co-erce a seceded state, he would call a state convention to decide what to do.[3]

This rank equivocation at least served to hold the disparate wings of the Union party together, despite Southern Rights sneers. Cobb's letter, said the Columbus *Times*, was "a depraved political act" that proved his fear of discussing the issue. Even some of Cobb's friends were dis-appointed. Toombs, for example, approved his positions but not his arguments. But whether or not secession was right, he said, the Union party existed to prevent its necessity.[4]

Once well, Stephens took to the stump. Unlike Cobb and Toombs, who canvassed most of the state, Stephens stayed close to home. But like other Union speakers, he avoided obscurantist dialectics on seces-sion and harped on saving the Union. The compromise had been "*fair, equitable, & just*" and a "Southern triumph," he said. The South had "got '*all* she asked for and more too.'" Anyone denying this was *ipso facto* a disunionist in league with the mad revolutionaries of South Carolina. Electing McDonald would ensure South Carolina's seces-sion, Stephens reminded his rural audiences, and when Georgia fol-lowed her lead, "you wool hat boys would have to do the fighting."[5]

Southern Rights men countered these tactics with withering scorn. "The ceaseless clamor of Union!" raged Herschel Johnson, obscured the real issue: the right of peaceable secession. Southern Rights editors concentrated their fire on the triumverate. Cobb, charged the Colum-bus *Times*, was "a grand criminal before the bar of an insulted South." Toombs's "diabolical somersets" had bewildered the South. "Hamil-car," suggested one editor, should stay at home for the next two years and study the Constitution rather than sell out the South for the sake of office.[6]

Stephens got the same rough handling. The *Constitutionalist* em-ployed a familiar tactic, printing great swaths of Stephens' belligerent

3. Cobb to John Rutherford *et al.*, August 12, 1851, in Phillips (ed.), *TSC Corre-spondence*, 249–59.

4. Columbus *Times*, July 11, 1851, quoted in Augusta *Constitutionalist*, July 15, 1851; Toombs to Cobb, June 9, 1851, in *Georgia Historical Quarterly*, V (1920), 47–48.

5. C. Daugherty to Berrien, August 24, 1851, in Berrien Papers, SHC/NC; Augusta *Constitutionalist*, August 5, 1851.

6. Johnson to Robert A. White *et al.*, August 30, 1851, in Augusta *Constitutionalist*, September 10, 1851; Columbus *Times* quoted in *ibid.*, July 3, 1851.

speeches of the past three years. Little Aleck's former patriotism, scoffed the editor, had disappeared under his "cowardly fears" and "selfish ambition." The *Federal Union* remarked, in pointed if awkward prose, on his vanity: "Those only that have heard his political speeches, can imagine how much egotism, self-conceit, and impudence, can be contained in one small body. Big I, is the Alpha and Omega, the beginning and end of his speeches."[7]

Shall Georgia be governed "by an irresponsible and insolent triumvirate, or act for herself?" shrilled the *Federal Union* as election day approached. Apparently, the Georgians who turned out in record numbers in October didn't fear the triumverate. The Union party won an unprecedented victory. Winning all but ten counties, Cobb triumphed by an unheard-of margin of over 18,000 votes. Union candidates won 39 of 47 seats in the state senate, 105 of 132 in the House. In the Seventh District Stephens crushed Sparta lawyer David W. Lewis by 4,744 votes to 1,955—over 70 percent of the vote, his largest antebellum victory. Toombs also swamped his opponent in the Eighth District.[8]

Unionists in Alabama and Mississippi also won big victories. In a special convention Mississippi affirmed the compromise and flatly denied the right of secession. Even in South Carolina moderates defeated secessionists, and by the time the state's convention met in April, 1852, the secession movement, such as it was, was a dead letter across the South. For reasons of expediency, South Carolina declared, she would forbear exercising her right to leave the Union. The Carolinians had waited too long, a mistake her fire-eaters vowed not to repeat.

"Save us—Merciful God—save us from being represented in the United States Senate for six years by either Toombs or Stephens," the Southern Rights press had fervently prayed. But when the Georgia assembly met in November that prayer went unanswered. No sooner had the election results been published than Toombs declared his candidacy for Berrien's Senate seat, and on November 10, 1851, the legislature bestowed it on him. Although legal, this was sharp politics. Berrien's term did not expire until March, 1853; the next legislature could have filled the seat.[9]

7. Augusta *Constitutionalist*, September 13, 1851; Milledgeville *Federal Union*, September 16, 1851.

8. Milledgeville *Federal Union*, August 26, 1851.

9. Macon *Telegraph* quoted in Rabun, "Stephens," 313.

The Unionists continued to move with unseemly haste. After electing Toombs, the new assembly undid a recent Democratic gerrymander of the congressional districts with one of its own. In the resulting shuffle, Stephens' Seventh District became the Eighth. Only two of its old counties remained, Taliaferro and Oglethorpe. To these were added nine more counties, all but one solidly Whig. The character of Stephens' constituency barely changed. His district shifted to the east by roughly two tiers of counties. Six of the new district's counties bordered the Savannah River, and one of them, Richmond, contained one of Georgia's few sizable cities, Augusta. Little Aleck would be identified with this district for the rest of his life—and he would rule it just as he had the old Seventh.[10]

The Union party's hold over the state was far more tenuous, however. Humiliated for the second time in less than a year, the Southern Rights group ditched the idea of a separate state party and moved to reunite with the national Democrats. At their state convention in late November, 1851, they agreed to send delegates to the next Democratic convention, scheduled for Baltimore in June, 1852. Caught completely by surprise, the Unionists raised an anguished howl. Revive the Democracy in Georgia?—an outrageous proposal! wailed the *Recorder*. The triumphant Unionists hardly expected to be thrown on the defensive so soon after their crushing victory. This new gambit upset all the plans their leaders had carefully staked out for the coming presidential election.[11]

Toombs had outlined the program in his acceptance speech to the legislature in early November: the Constitutional Union party would retain both its name and separate organization, would attend neither major party convention, and would not decide who to support for president until after both parties and candidates had stated their principles. Naturally, endorsement of the Compromise of 1850 would be a prerequisite for the party's support. Only then would the Georgia Unionists consider merging with a national party. He expected more cooperation from the Democrats than from the Seward-led Whigs, Toombs had continued, but if Democrats proved reluctant, he would

10. The nine counties added to Taliaferro and Oglethorpe to form the new Eighth District were Elbert, Lincoln, Wilkes, Warren, Columbia, Richmond, Burke, Jefferson, and Scriven. Only the last was Democratic.

11. Milledgeville *Southern Recorder*, December 2, 1851.

appeal to "sound" men of both organizations to form a national Union coalition.[12]

Governor Cobb also confidently expected that Democrats in Washington would "do what is right" and endorse the "finality" of the compromise. For Cobb, they had to or his political throat would be cut because, paradoxically, even as he occupied the throne in state politics, his influence on the national level steadily fell. While Herschel Johnson's minions busily reorganized the state Democratic party, Cobb's other Georgia enemies were directing a concerted campaign to discredit him with the party in Washington. It was thus vital to Cobb that the Democratic party endorse the compromise to ease the way for the Constitutional Unionists, with the governor at their head, to merge with the national party. "*Dont let these Southern right men get the start on us there*," Cobb warned Stephens immediately after the latter's return to the capital.[13]

If Cobb expected Stephens to be enthusiastic about uniting with the Democrats, he was sadly mistaken. "There is a great deal to be done here," Stephens wrote on his return to Washington. "The *mission* of the Constitutional Union party is not fulfilled yet." Stephens relished the prospect of an angry split in the upcoming Democratic caucus on the finality of the compromise question. But even if the caucus passed procompromise resolutions, Stephens continued, "it will only be done with a mental reservation on the part of some and with the absence of others. . . . There is a great unsoundness with a large portion of the Northern Democrats on slavery."[14]

The six Union congressmen from Georgia attended neither party's caucus. On Saturday, November 29, the Democratic caucus addressed a resolution declaring the compromise the "final" and "permanent" settlement of the slavery question. After angry discussion the resolution was tabled by a coalition of Free-Soil and Southern Rights Democrats. Two days later, however, the Whig caucus unceremoniously passed resolutions affirming the compromise as a "final" settlement.[15]

"*What does all this mean?*" a distraught Cobb asked Stephens.

12. Rabun, "Stephens," 316.
13. Cobb to AHS, November 22, 1851, in Stephens Papers, DU.
14. AHS to Cobb, November 24, 26, 1851, in Phillips (ed.), *TSC Correspondence*, 265–66.
15. Thomas D. Harris to Cobb, November 29, 1851, in *ibid.*, 267–68.

Matters were not going "as smoothly as we had hoped." To say the least. The Democratic caucus had dealt Cobb a nearly fatal blow. Perfectly aware that his Southern Rights enemies had torpedoed the caucus resolutions, he was also receiving assurances that "the mass of [northern] Democrats . . . are sound and more determined than ever." It was now or never for Cobb. Unless he moved swiftly to align the Union party with the Democrats, his political future was finished. Never one to trifle with technicalities when his own political fortunes were involved, Cobb was determined to make a move, caucus resolutions or no. "We are stationary," he told Stephens. "*That wont do*. Before the legislature adjourns, we must take a stance and make a decided movement."[16]

Stephens, of course, disagreed. For the moment he could afford splendid isolation. The Whig party had purged him and Toombs from its ranks. In the Speaker's election (won by Lynn Boyd, a Kentucky Democrat) Stephens and Toombs had thrown away their votes on Junius Hillyer, one of their own. He regretted, Stephens told Cobb, that he could not vote for Boyd, tainted as he was by Free-Soil support. Little Aleck wanted an absolutely pure party. In his opinion, the Democrats had ignored both "principles" and "the past" in their rage to reorganize the party. He couldn't believe that the "foulest of all coalitions"—"Southern Rights men and Abolitionists"—could possibly succeed. All the Union party had to do was wait for the Democrats' inevitable dissolution over rivalries for the presidency. As for the Whigs, they were "dead"; there would not even be a Whig convention. Party structure was breaking down, he had convinced himself, and the process had begun with the Whigs. Many sound northern Whigs were ready for a new organization, and many northern Democrats soon would be. The best course for the Union party, therefore, Stephens advised Cobb, was "masterful inactivity."[17]

Stephens' advice was useless to Cobb and his opinions just as worthless as a gauge of political possibilities. As skilled a politician as he was, Stephens could sometimes be hopelessly naive about the practical operations of the political system. Most Americans, even extremists, recognized the "finality" of the compromise as a political fact of life.

16. Cobb to AHS, December 3, 1851, in Stephens Papers, LC; George W. Jones to Cobb, December 7, 1851, in Phillips (ed.), *TSC Correspondence*, 271.
17. AHS to Cobb, December 5, 1851, in Phillips (ed.), *TSC Correspondence*, 268; AHS to Cobb, December 8, 1851, in Cobb-Erwin-Lamar Papers, UG.

Moreover, it was because of the compromise that both major parties remained intact, and few men were ready to bolt their party over loss of a political battle at home. Basic political loyalties had not been altered.

Stephens, however, believed they had. In his own mind he had elevated the Union and the compromise to almost the status of transcendent truths ("principles," he would say). Therefore, he reasoned, only the regenerate souls who acknowledged these truths should be admitted to the Constitutional Union church. And Stephens, as an elder in the congregation, meant to keep it pure, untainted by heretics and sinners of any stripe. The Constitutional Unionists had to stand firm: "This is no time to conciliate the *free soil* vote by patching up old parties. If we can not purify the old ones we must make a new party. . . . The Scripture teaches us that 'men do not put new wine into old bottles' and I think the same rule will hold as to putting new principles into the old parties." [18]

Like a righteous seventeenth-century Puritan, Stephens judged men with a harsh intolerance and demanded communion only with the saved. But unlike the Puritans, he never acknowledged the regenerate as few in number. He always expected most men to embrace the truth once it was shown them. He, of course, had shown them the truth; they simply had to follow his lead.

In Stephens' estimation, the Democratic spoilsmen in Washington—the "small fry"—had engineered their "foulest of all coalitions" solely to collect spoils. He expected as much of the Southern Rights men but could not believe the country could countenance "such corruption . . . such a foul conspiracy against their rights . . . and honor." Surely the mass of the people would recognize their danger. If the South and Georgia didn't stand firm against this coalition movement, "we are a gone people," he predicted. [19]

He realized, of course, that eliminating Cobb was all part of the Southern Rights plan, but "those mean rascals little know what is in store for them unless I misjudge the people." Georgia had saved the Union the previous fall, and by forcing a "purgation of National parties" she might do so again. As usual, Stephens expected too much of

18. AHS to William Turner, December 19, 1851, in Stephens Papers, DU.
19. AHS to LS, December 10, 1851, in Phillips (ed.), *TSC Correspondence*, 272–73.

people. Preserving unsullied principles at the expense of political power and the spoils that went with it appealed to few—least of all to such men as Howell Cobb.[20]

With the Georgia Southern Rights men (who now styled themselves "Regular" Democrats) busily insinuating themselves into the good grace of the national party and with Union Democrats urging the party to send representatives to the Baltimore convention, Cobb knew he could delay no longer. On January 19, 1852, at a meeting dominated by Cobb's men, the Union party laid plans for an April meeting to select a delegate slate for Baltimore. Stephens was livid, and he let Cobb and all Georgia know it. In a pair of public letters he assailed the January meeting and reiterated his belief that the "*crisis*" that had created the Union party "has not passed by." Only a national organization based on Georgia's principles could arrest the disunion elements still threatening the country.[21]

Even before Stephens' second letter appeared, Cobb found a pretext for a hurried and transparently political trip north. Only a few days after Cobb had left Washington, one of his mouthpieces in Congress declared in a speech that the Georgia Union party would send delegates to the Baltimore convention and abide by its decisions. Cobb himself drove home the point in a speech at Tammany Hall. "Born a democrat, cradled a democrat, and by the blessing of God, I will die one," he declared. Thank God, he continued, that the Democracy was big enough to accommodate patriotic, Union-loving Whigs.[22]

The Union Whigs, who considered unification with the Democrats out of the question, scorned such fluff. Cobb's followers simply shrugged. The Union party had served its purpose: "Why weaken the Democratic party by divisions and strifes and give over the State to the Whigs?" wrote one. "If we are to be Democrats why not be Democrats, and let past quarrels be forgotten?" Unfortunately for the Union Whigs, their erstwhile Democratic compatriots would find reunification with the national party much simpler. In the first place, it was clear by now that the northern Democrats were sounder on the compromise than the Whigs. In early April, House resolutions affirming

20. *Ibid.*

21. AHS to Cobb, January 26, 1852, in Cobb-Erwin-Lamar Papers, UG; AHS to David Reese, February 7, 1852, AHS to Messers. Fisher & De Leon, February 28, 1852, in Milledgeville *Southern Recorder*, February 24, March 9, 1852.

22. *Congressional Globe*, 32nd Cong., 1st Sess., Appendix, 255–58; Milledgeville *Southern Recorder*, March 23, 1852.

the finality of the compromise had passed with two-thirds of the northern Democrats in support and a like percentage of northern Whigs opposed. Moreover, on the eve of its party convention, the Whig caucus had twice refused to repass its December resolutions on the compromise. Upon the second failure, thirteen southerners bolted the caucus, and Georgia Senator William C. Dawson immediately wired the Union convention in Milledgeville to avoid both major party conventions and call a national Union convention in Washington.[23]

Second, Stephens unalterably opposed dismantling the Union party and was working mightily to keep the crumbling edifice intact. Three days after Cobb's New York speech he hurried home, arriving on March 18, ostensibly to attend to some court cases. He remained almost a month, during which time Union party conclaves all over middle Georgia passed resolutions against sending a delegation to Baltimore. On April 22, 1852, when the Constitutional Union convention met in Milledgeville, Stephens' confederates succeeded in carrying his position. Unperturbed, Cobb's men, the Union Democrats, dubbed the "Supplementals" by the state press, simply held their own convention the next day and drew up a slate of delegates for Baltimore. At least one Union paper thought cleansing the "Democratic Augean stables" would prove impossible and confidently expected the errant Unionists to return to the fold shortly and support a "true Constitutional candidate" with ties to neither party.[24]

This editor obviously believed in miracles. Most Georgia Democrats found pragmatic arguments far more compelling than allegiance to a party that had outlived its usefulness. The Regulars, the old Southern Rights party, had already selected a Baltimore slate, and even though they had passed over the compromise in ominous silence, most Union Democrats were ready to cooperate with them. Distasteful as this might be, it was still infinitely preferable to allowing Whigs to regain control of the state. As one of Cobb's men said, the choice was the lesser of two evils: "The democratic party with *much soundness* and *little rottenness* rather than the Whig party which . . . has not good men enough to save it from destruction."[25]

Alexander Stephens could not abide a "little rottenness" anywhere,

23. William Hope Hull to Cobb, February 14, 1852, in Phillips (ed.), *TSC Correspondence*, 281.
24. Milledgeville *Southern Recorder*, April 27, 1852.
25. W. C. Cohen to Cobb, April 29, 1852, in Cobb-Erwin-Lamar Papers, UG.

however, and in a long speech in the House on April 27, he argued earnestly for a party organized on the "right principle and basis." Neither Whigs nor Democrats agreed on the "paramount questions": the permanence of the Union, fidelity to the compromise, and enforcement of the fugitive slave law. "I am here to advocate great principles," he said. The people should support neither candidate nor party that did not unequivocally support the compromise. Southerners going to Baltimore for the conventions should render a "great and essential [national] service" and either purge their respective parties of "Barnburners, Freesoilers, and Abolitionists" or break them up.

Mention of the abolitionists led him easily into discussion of another great principle: "the radical difference by nature between the races." The "sickly sentimentalism" of those opposing the fugitive slave laws sprung "from a spirit at war with the works of the Creator," he said. Different "mentally, morally, and socially" from whites in the scale of creation, the black man occupied "an inferior grade"—"his natural place." This was hardly an unusual position, of course; most northern congressmen agreed with it. But the little sermon on race was unusual for Stephens. Till now his public defense of slavery had been mild. But as the 1850s wore on, he increasingly exhibited characteristics of the siege mentality afflicting the South. Slavery had become tangled up in southern thought on almost every subject. Shortly, no southern speech, no matter what the subject, would be complete without a defense of slavery. The compromise may have applied a temporary palliative to the country's political problems, but it had done nothing to treat a national obsession.[26]

Several old Whig newspapers heartily applauded Stephens' dogmatism. Like him, their editors believed that a Union convention would be called in Washington unless both parties eliminated their anticompromise elements. Obviously, though, if both national parties endorsed the compromise—even without purging their discordant members—Georgia's old Whigs would be placed in a position of intolerable ambivalence.[27]

This is exactly what happened. The national Democrats convened on June 2, 1852, with a plethora of presidential candidates clamoring

26. AHS speech in *Congressional Globe*, 32nd Cong., 1st Sess., Appendix, 459–64.
27. Rome *Weekly Courier*, May 13, 1852; Columbus *Enquirer*, May 18, 1852.

for the prize. The convention found it much easier to decide what to do with the two slates of Georgia delegates (it admitted both) than to settle on a candidate. None of the front-runners (Senators Cass, Douglas, and James Buchanan) succeeded; not until the forty-ninth ballot did the convention choose a dark horse, Franklin Pierce of New Hampshire.

Pierce was an affable, strikingly handsome man of forty-six years of wide political experience. In the Mexican War, he had served as brigadier general of volunteers. Pierce's magnetic charm and conviviality in some ways reflected the inner man, for he was at heart a timid soul, eager, almost desperate to avoid either personal or political disagreement. Until now these qualities had served him well. Unlike the other candidates, he had no powerful political enemies. Moreover, he was a largely unknown quantity, with Delphic qualities almost everyone found reassuring.

After the nomination the convention drew up a platform promising "faithful execution" of the Compromise of 1850 and specifically the fugitive slave law. Democrats throughout the country rejoiced. Successful for the moment in patching up its quarrels, the exultant party confidently departed Baltimore with the smell of victory—and spoils—overpowering the odoriferous aroma of bargain that lingered about the hall.[28]

Both Pierce and his platform were "entirely satisfactory" to Stephens and Toombs, according to reports. Toombs, plagued with rheumatism for months, had returned to Congress early in May and since had repeatedly intimated that both he and Stephens would support a Democratic nominee on a procompromise platform. Indeed, after the convention, Toombs had commended the candidate and platform, although he still envisioned cooperating with Georgia's Union party. Because the Whigs were expected to nominate Winfield Scott without a platform, Toombs suggested that the Unionists wait until after the Whig convention, when all Pierce's friends—Whigs, Democrats, and

28. The preceding paragraphs are based on Nevins, *Ordeal of the Union*, II, 18–22, 41–42. Georgia's delegates had split in the convention, the Regulars favoring Douglas and the Supplementals supporting Cass. Unable to agree, the Georgians cast their votes for Buchanan, and even this was part of a larger southern strategy to ensure nomination of a candidate friendly to the South. See James Jackson to Cobb, June 8, 1852, in Phillips (ed.), *TSC Correspondence*, 300.

fire-eaters—could endorse him at a mass meeting. This course, he thought, would be least likely to alienate Georgia's old-line Whigs.[29]

But most Georgia Whigs already were alienated, and the Whig convention would drive away more. The bolt of the Union Democrats had inspired a similar move by some angry Whigs under Senator Dawson's lead, who met in Savannah on June 7—nine days before the national Whig convention—and selected a slate of delegates pledged to President Fillmore. Naturally, Stephens and Toombs took no part in these proceedings.[30]

The once proud party of Clay and Webster presented a sorry spectacle when it convened in Baltimore on June 16, 1852. The slavery issue had torn it asunder. Southerners in the convention managed to postpone nominations until they got a procompromise plank in the platform, but the ensuing balloting for a candidate was bitter and protracted. After fifty-three ballots the Whigs finally chose General Winfield Scott, Mexican War hero and favorite of the northern Whigs. Most southerners, who despised Scott as nothing but a tool of Seward and the free-soilers, had doggedly held out for Fillmore.[31]

Stephens and Toombs believed the worst about the general. And Scott's letter, in which he merely accepted his nomination "with the resolutions annexed," only confirmed their suspicions. Chastened by experience, they could hardly support a candidate who from all indications was even more untrustworthy than Taylor. Two days after the nomination they advised the Georgia Unionists by telegraph not to support Scott.[32]

To drive home the point, Stephens elaborated in a public letter. Georgians should only support someone "unequivocally in favor of the Compromise," he said. The best way to maintain Union party principles was to support neither national candidate because free-soilers still tainted both parties. Still chasing the will-o-the-wisp of absolute purity, Stephens hoped the election would be thrown into the House, which would be a decisive step toward ending the present party system and founding new parties on "legitimate and correct principles." Run-

29. Toombs to Cobb, May 27, 1852, James Jackson to Cobb, June 8, 1852, both in Phillips (ed.), *TSC Correspondence*, 297, 300; Toombs to Cobb, June 10, 1852, in Cobb-Erwin-Lamar Papers, UG.

30. Horace Montgomery, *Cracker Parties* (Baton Rouge, 1950), 63–64.

31. Cole, *Whig Party in the South*, 245–55.

32. Washington *National Intelligencer*, June 29, 1852; AHS and Toombs to James W. Jones, June 23, 1852, in Augusta *Chronicle and Sentinel*, June 25, 1852.

ning an independent ticket, Stephens concluded, would be the most advisable course.[33]

Although Stephens still placed his hopes in the Union party, it had been ludicrously factionalized. The party's Democratic wing, Cobb's men, was united behind Pierce but fiercely at odds with the Regular Democrats, who refused to withdraw their own slate of electors. The Whig wing of the party floundered in even more deplorable disarray. The largest group refused to cooperate with Democrats and supported Scott for the presidency. Another group, the Stephens-Toombs adherents, favored running an independent ticket. On the day before the Union convention, Stephens' organ, the Augusta *Chronicle*, declared its support for Daniel Webster. A third, and much smaller, Whig faction supported Pierce.[34]

Inevitably, the Constitutional Union party failed to survive the first day's proceedings at its mid-July convention in Milledgeville. Cobb's forces controlled the convention, and when they succeeded in pledging the party to Pierce, Stephens' and Toombs's followers walked out. Meeting the next day, they passed resolutions endorsing Daniel Webster and set August 17, 1852, as the day they would meet in Macon to select an electoral slate. Georgia papers promptly dubbed the Webster men the "Tertiam Quids."[35]

One reason for delaying the convention until August was the necessity of securing Webster's consent to the nomination. Stephens' brother John had received no reply from the "god-like Daniel" when he queried him by letter. A Webster intimate, however, had assured Little Aleck that a "good blow" in Georgia would be followed up elsewhere. This assurance sufficed for the Georgians. Delaying the Macon gathering had other advantages. The Scott Whigs would also be meeting then, and with the split among Democrats as wide as ever—two slates for Pierce were in the field—a strategic merger of Whigs might be possible.[36]

Cobb's Supplementals muddled the complicated jockeying even

33. AHS to editor of the *Chronicle and Sentinel*, June 28, 1852, in Phillips (ed.), *TSC Correspondence*, 304–306.

34. Augusta *Chronicle and Sentinel*, July 14, 1852.

35. Convention reports in Augusta *Constitutionalist*, July 20–23, 1852; Milledgeville *Federal Union*, June 29, 1852.

36. Robert F. Dalzell, Jr., *Daniel Webster and the Trial of American Nationalism, 1843–1852* (New York, 1975), 287–88; George T. Curtis to AHS, August 13, 1852, in Stephens Papers, LC.

more. The Whigs had forced Cobb's hand. On August 10, the executive committee of the Union party officially dissolved the party. Cobb's men then withdrew their slate of Pierce electors and issued a call for a mass meeting of all Union Democrats in mid-September. Unable to count on Whig support, Cobb now had to beg at the Regular Democrats' door and hope for compromise on the electoral slate. For a time it looked hopeful for Cobb: initial reports indicated that harmony was being restored between the Democrats. "There will be a regular love feast in Atlanta," he bubbled happily.[37]

As Cobb confidently contemplated the future, the two Whig groups convened separately in Macon. Despite sincere efforts, they had not been able to reconcile their differences. Stephens remained unalterably opposed to Scott. Let the Whigs lose, he told Linton. It would teach them to rally under wiser heads. So the two Whig factions went their predetermined ways, drawing up slates for Scott and Webster. There were now three electoral tickets in the race. By the time the Democrats finished meeting in Atlanta, there would be five.[38]

Governor Cobb's predictions of an Atlanta love feast proved grossly inaccurate. The Regular Democrats refused to change their electoral ticket. A handful of irreconcilable Southern Rights Democrats, meeting in Columbus on September 2, had chosen yet another slate of electors (pledged to George M. Troup, Georgia's venerable old former governor, and John A. Quitman, a Mississippi radical). This new twist had stiffened the Regulars' backs. Cobb's sins were not to be expiated so easily.

Cobb and many of his followers were willing to swallow this acrid wedge of humble pie. If humiliating submission to former enemies was the price for reentering the Democracy, they were prepared to swallow their pride and pay—many, but not all. When at the September 17 meeting in Atlanta most Cobb men declined to put up another electoral slate, a small band of disgusted Cherokee delegates stalked angrily out the hall. The next day they drew up their own slate of electors for Pierce, the so-called "Tugalo" ticket (after a river in the Cherokee counties).

The bolt of the Tugalo Democrats arrested, at least for the time being, the bewildering perturbations in Georgia politics. Five electoral slates now confronted the state's voters: the Whig slate for Scott, the

---

37. Cobb to his wife, August 27, 1852, in Phillips (ed.), *TSC Correspondence*, 318.
38. AHS to LS, July 16, 1852, in Stephens Papers, MC.

Tertiam Quid for Webster, the Southern Rights for Troup, and two for Pierce, the Regular and Tugalo. Georgia law required the legislature to decide the state's electoral vote if no candidate achieved a majority in the election. If the election were ever thrown into the assembly, which the now defunct Union party coalition still controlled, the possibilities of political wheeling and dealing were endless. Georgia's electoral struggle in 1852 was far less a disagreement in principle—everyone, save the most rabid Southern Righters, accepted the compromise—than a contest for spoils of victory and control of the state.

The Tertiam Quid movement had no chance of winning, but Stephens campaigned for Webster as if he were a front-runner. Everywhere he spoke he eulogized Webster as the "greatest man of his age" and a staunch friend of the compromise, who had braved the savage attacks of free-soilers in his own section. He handled Pierce gingerly, concentrating instead on the "mongrel association" that had nominated him. Against Scott and the northern Whigs he reiterated all his old arguments on their "unsoundness." [39]

Toombs, less enthusiastic than Stephens, delivered only two half-hearted speeches during the campaign. In October he told Crittenden that politics in Georgia was "dull." But Toombs did expect the election to be decided by the assembly. His prediction might have come true had not Webster died on October 24, ten days before the election. A national movement in his favor had never materialized, despite contrary rumors in Georgia. Nothing daunted, the *Chronicle*, the leading Quid paper, immediately placed the names of "Crittenden or Fillmore" on its masthead and urged Webster supporters to "stick by the ticket." [40]

Remarkably, 5,302 voters did just that. But Webster's death undoubtedly kept voters home: one authority estimates that as many as 20,000, fully half the state's Whigs, did not vote. In Brunswick, according to the local paper, the polls did not even open on election day, the voters believing that no candidate deserved their support. Widespread apathy was the rule. Only 61,000 people voted in 1852, 63 percent of the previous year's turnout. But the voters' preference was clear. The Pierce ticket had a majority of more than 33,000 votes. But middle Georgia had as usual followed Toombs and Stephens. Four counties there, including Taliaferro, delivered striking majorities for

39. Augusta *Chronicle and Sentinel*, September 2, 1852; Milledgeville *Federal Union*, September 7, 1852.

40. Toombs to Crittenden, October 9, 1852, in Crittenden Papers, LC; Augusta *Chronicle and Sentinel*, September 22, October 27, 1852.

Webster. Scott carried only one county in the state. Beyond a shadow of a doubt the once mighty Whig party of Georgia was finished.[41]

In fact, the election had been the death knell of the party nationwide. In the South alone a hundred thousand Whigs spurned Scott and stayed home on election day. Pierce romped to a smashing popular victory in the South and a crushing electoral win in the nation. But the raw figures were misleading. Although he lost only four states in the electoral college, Pierce had only a fifty-thousand-vote majority in popular votes and was actually a minority candidate in the North. Hundreds of thousands there remained committed to free soil, and Pierce's victory had not changed their minds.

During the campaign, Stephens had blasted national parties as "dead carcasses." The Whig party fit that description now, and it's doubtful that Stephens shed many tears over its demise. Toombs certainly didn't. If the Whig party could not rise to the same national standards as the "motley crew" of Democrats, he wrote, "it is entitled to no resurrection. It will have none." The prospect of Democratic rule, however, hardly cheered him. Pierce was unqualified, Toombs thought, and "surrounded by as dishonest and dirty a lot of political gamesters as ever Catiline assembled."[42]

Some of the gamesters were already hard at work in Georgia. The election of 1852 had been a singular triumph for the Southern Rights Democrats. Crushed two years in a row, they now found themselves atop the jumbled pile of fragments that was once Georgia's two-party system. Pierce had barely been elected when they began warning the incoming administration: they would not tolerate being ignored in favor of Cobb's people.[43]

Although not perceived then, the most important result of this baffling Georgia election soon became apparent: it had a profound effect on the Democratic party. Georgia was on its way to becoming a one-party state—and the heirs of Calhoun, not Jackson, were in control. State politics would never be the same again.

41. Cole, *Whig Party in the South*, 274; Washington *National Intelligencer*, November 10, 1852. Vote totals were as follows: Pierce Democrats, 33,888; Scott Whigs, 15,798; Tugalo Democrats, 5,800; Tertium Quids, 5,302; Southern Rights Democrats, 1,026 (Augusta *Constitutionalist*, December 2, 1852).

42. Rome *Courier*, September 23, 1852; Toombs to Crittenden, December 15, 1852, Phillips (ed.), *TSC Correspondence*, 322.

43. Johnson to Hunter, November 8, 1852, in Ambler (ed.), *Hunter Correspondence*, 151.

X

The Greatest Glory of My Life

"If it were not for you," Stephens told Linton in May, 1853, the world would be a "perfect waste." Linton was the only "congenial spirit" Stephens had for "full communion of thoughts." Such daily expressions of endearment attained a special poignancy after February, 1852, for Linton had married and moved away from "Bachelor's Hall." Stephens was alone as he had not been since his youth.[1]

Linton's bride was a young widow, Emmeline Thomas Bell, the only child of Stephens' good friend Judge James Thomas. As befitted the daughter of a wealthy planter, "Sister Emm," as Stephens called her, brought a handsome dowry of land, slaves, and securities with her. Linton and Emma made their home in Sparta, in Hancock County, a few hours' buggy ride from Crawfordville. The 1850s were generally kind to planters, and Linton's estate prospered, along with his law practice. In Sparta he took on a partner, Richard Malcolm Johnston, who soon became one of the Stephens brothers' dearest friends.

While Dick Johnston took care of the office, Linton handled courtroom duties. Like his brother, Linton had compelling talents in the courtroom, and he far surpassed him in legal knowledge. But if anything, Linton was even more independent than Aleck and ill-suited to

1. AHS to LS, May 28, 1853, in Stephens Papers, MC.

the chummy camaraderie of politics. Linton had rigid convictions. Compromise was foreign to his nature. "He worked badly in joint harness," commented one observer, and was too outspoken to appeal to the people. He never could command their affection as his brother did. Linton lost the first of his two bids for national office when he ran for Congress in 1855. The advice his brother gave then suggests why people did not warm to him. Keep "perfect command of your temper," Stephens had warned. Always be in good humor on the stump. And don't speak boisterously or too slowly—be "warm, fe[r]vid, and earnest." Linton lost this election, but he did serve in the General Assembly several times and also for a time on the bench of the state supreme court.[2]

Linton always had Aleck's confidence; the other brother, John, never did. Money from his law practice in LaGrange rarely met John's family's needs, so he constantly borrowed money from Aleck. Although generous by nature, Stephens sometimes chafed at having to bail John out of financial difficulties. "You must give me some evidence of a change in your conduct and management of your affairs," Stephens once lectured him, "or I shall *never* let you have another picayune from me."[3]

Of course, the threat was hollow. Stephens could no more abandon his brother than he could stop advising him on how to manage his affairs. John's weakness for alcohol—one shared by Linton incidentally—only exasperated Stephens even more. Worse, John could not claim any demonstrated ability or success in his profession to compensate for this disability. John was the kind of person Stephens had little patience with under any circumstances, blood relative or not. Nonetheless, he still expected his family to follow his lead in politics. In 1853, a still partyless Stephens was "deeply mortified" to discover that John considered voting for a Democrat and threatened never to visit him again. The Whigs had never done anything for him, John had explained. He had little use for anybody with such principles, retorted Stephens, much less a relative.[4]

"Sister Emm," Linton's wife, however, seemed to meet Stephens' exacting standards. The mere fact that Linton had chosen her no doubt

2. *Ibid.*, June 23, 1855; I. W. Avery, *The History of the State of Georgia from 1850 to 1861 . . .* (New York, 1881), 33.
3. AHS to JLS, May 11, 1852, in Stephens Papers, EU.
4. *Ibid.*, September 8, 1852, September 30, 1853, in Stephens Papers, DU.

earned Stephens' esteem, but even apart from this, he thought highly of her. As a wife and mother, Emma had few equals, Stephens thought. "Her intelligence, refinement, good taste and gentleness, amicability and everything that gives and adds charms to womans character endear her to me as a sister not only *in-law* but in feeling, in sympathy and almost in blood." [5]

But Emma's presence in his brother's life took some getting used to. After the marriage, Stephens' relationship with his brother underwent a small but definite change. Now, having to share Linton's affections with another, he seemed at least at first to feel himself displaced. For awhile he wrote less fulsomely and frequently as before. "I am apprehensive," Stephens delicately explained when Linton inquired about the change, "that your time[,] pursuits[,] and occupation will not allow you to take the same interest in my empty scrolls that your former 'solitude' did." [6]

Actually Stephens had no reason to be concerned about losing his place with Linton. The affection between them was mutual. Linton often spoke of Aleck with "great tenderness and reverence." The younger brother realized Stephens' dependence upon him and accepted it. Within a year or so, Stephens had accommodated himself to the new situation, and "Sister Emm" accepted him as part of her family. There never was any question that Aleck approved of Linton's marriage. In fact, Stephens purchased Emma's beautiful nine-diamond wedding ring in Washington. It cost eighty-five dollars and was, he said proudly, "the most splendid thing of the kind in this city." [7]

5. AHS to LS, January 16, 1857, in Stephens Papers, MC.
6. *Ibid.*, May 15, 1852.
7. R. M. Johnston to AHS, July 25, 1861, in Stephens Papers, LC; AHS to LS, January 14, 1852, in Stephens Papers, MC. Von Abele is not convincing when he argues that by Linton's marriage "a triangle had been created. Linton's love was divided, whereas his own could never be. . . . The most catastrophic thing that could happen to him would be the falling of a shadow between him and Linton; and with instinctive strength he fought to retain Linton's perfect confidence" (*Stephens*, 139). Evidence such as Von Abele cites, Stephens' May 28 letter to Linton, cited above, can be found many times before Linton's marriage. See, for example, AHS to LS, April 21, 1850, in Stephens Papers, MC. Richard Johnston, Stephens' contemporary biographer, says simply that Stephens' loneliness was "made deeper" by Linton's marriage, and that "to some extent" Linton was "lost" to him. (Johnston and Browne, *Stephens*, 269). This view is closer to the truth. Stephens did not become the point of a triangle by Linton's marriage, but rather a point outside of a circle containing Linton and his wife. This saddened him rather than aroused him to fight with "instinctive strength" for Linton's confidence. There is no evidence to suggest that Stephens ever lost Linton's perfect confidence or affection.

Politically, 1853 was a quiet year for Stephens. He spoke only once in Congress, in January, when he delivered a short speech against acquiring slaveholding Cuba, a favorite project of the expansionist "Young America" Democrats and ardent proslavery southerners. Stephens denounced filibustering as "lawless aggressions" against a peaceful neighbor. And although he opposed even peaceful acquisition of the island for the moment, he admitted that future policy would depend on contingencies. Further, if Cuba should be acquired "in the national interest," the nonintervention principle established in the Compromise of 1850 would prevent sectional strife. Popular sovereignty had become an article of faith for Stephens, and like many another convert to a new faith, he upheld its dogma tenaciously.[8]

Curious about Pierce, Stephens lingered in Washington after Congress adjourned instead dashing directly home, as was his custom. Although uneasy about reports that the president lacked a "stern nature," Stephens resolved to give him a "fair trial." He soon discovered much to admire in Pierce, whose inaugural address pleased him, as did his conversation and bearing when they met personally. Stephens also admired Pierce's simplicity. He walked the capital streets "just like any other man," Stephens reported. "I am better pleased with him than I expected to be."[9]

Only in selecting his cabinet—"a great blunder" in Stephens' opinion—had Pierce fallen short. Stephens had a point: several of its members were mediocrities with little experience. Even worse, from Stephens' point of view, were the extremists in the cabinet: fire-eating southerners Jefferson Davis and James Dobbins of North Carolina, and Robert McClelland of Michigan, a Wilmot Proviso man and late convert to the compromise. In making his appointments Pierce disregarded men's past principles, requiring only a promise to abide by the compromise.[10]

This policy was charitable, perhaps, but hardly wise. Men who had stood the heat of furious battle in 1850 now witnessed the elevation of their enemies. Pierce's deliberate course of attempting to reconcile all party divisions necessarily required appointing many free-soilers and Southern Rights Democrats to various offices. Instead of healing party

8. *Congressional Globe*, 32nd Cong., 2nd Sess., 192–93.
9. AHS to James Thomas, February 23, 1853, in Stephens Papers, LC.
10. AHS to LS, March 8, 1853, *ibid.*, MC.

wounds, Pierce's policy only made them worse. In Georgia, for example, a great gulf of bitterness separated the two wings of the Democracy. A mortified Cobb had been spurned by the new administration. The governor had no choice but the degrading one of continuing public penance until the Southern Rights men deigned to admit him once more into full communion in the party. Cobb had to fight for his political survival for the rest of the decade, not against Whigs but against extremists in his own party, most of whom would never forget or forgive his renegade course of 1850–1852.[11]

So Cobb decided not to seek reelection and in a public letter in March, 1853, declared a reorganization of the Union party impracticable. Georgia's Democrats, he piously hoped, would soon enjoy a peaceful reconciliation. Although a few of the staunchest Union-loving Democrats, like Tugalo editor Hopkins Holsey, found Cobb's position "totally *repugnant*," Georgia's party structure fell rapidly into its familiar pattern.[12]

Georgia's Union Whigs perforce had no future except in continuing opposition to their traditional foes. Hence they summoned a convention for the last week of June to nominate a candidate for governor. Deciding what to call themselves, however, presented problems: Conservatives, Constitutional Unionists, or Conservative Union Whigs were all suggested. (Eventually the Democrats tired of word games and simply called the opposition "Whigs.") Stephens didn't particularly care what the opposition was called. Parties aren't judged by their names, he told a Crawfordville crowd on June 6. If supporting the Georgia Platform and opposing those against it "will . . . make us *Whigs*, then we . . . have reason to be proud of the distinction." Delighted, his hometown audience promptly appointed him a delegate to the upcoming convention.[13]

Taliaferro County almost lost its delegate, and Stephens his life, the next night. On his way to Columbus to defend an accused murderer, the railroad car in which he was riding derailed, plunged down a fifteen-foot embankment, and smashed to pieces. Stephens suffered a

11. Cobb to AHS, February 23, 1853, *ibid.*, LC; Cobb to John [B. Lamar?], February 23, 1853, in Autograph Letters of the Signers of the Constitution of the Confederate States, DU.

12. Cobb to Thomas Morris, March 21, 1853, in Augusta *Chronicle and Sentinel*, April 11, 1853; Holsey quoted in Montgomery, *Cracker Parties*, 97.

13. Augusta *Chronicle and Sentinel*, June 8, 1853.

broken right arm, head lacerations, and a severely bruised left shoulder. One passenger was killed. For a short while Stephens was unconscious and reportedly delirious. But Macon was only two miles down the line, and he received prompt medical attention there as both his brothers rushed to be with him. Although painful, his injuries were not serious, and within a week he was up and hobbling about. When the Whig convention met in Milledgeville on June 22, 1853, the delegate from Taliaferro was present, his head bandaged and his arm in a sling.[14]

Largely a group of Stephens-Toombs supporters, the "Republican men of Georgia," as they called themselves, invited men of all parties to join them. The resolutions of Toombs's executive committee, however—which condemned the policies of both national parties—were not exactly calculated to win converts. Freed from any taint of national Whiggery in its statement of principles, the convention made certain its position by denying the orthodox Whigs who had supported Winfield Scott any significant statewide nominations and on the first ballot nominated Charles J. Jenkins for governor.[15]

Jenkins' Democratic opponent was Herschel V. Johnson, who proved an amiable foe. It was one of the strangest and quietest campaigns Georgia had ever seen. Part of the time Jenkins and Johnson even ate, traveled, and roomed together. The Whigs' old charges of secessionism against Johnson had worn thin by the summer of 1853. But Jenkins, the soul of urbanity and grace, was still a powerful opponent. As author of the hallowed Georgia Platform and promoter of the recently completed, state-owned Western and Atlantic Railroad, he was popular with north Georgians. An energetic campaigner, he soon began making significant inroads in the traditionally Democratic Cherokee counties.

To counter the threat, the Democrats wheeled out one of their biggest guns, Governor Cobb. Not without some soul-searching did Cobb consent to take the stump for Johnson, for such action could hardly enhance his already besmirched image among the old Union party stalwarts. But Cobb could not deny his party's call. He took the stump in September, canvassing the Fifth and Sixth districts. The Pierce administration, he claimed, now espoused the true Union position. Some voters found Cobb's logic compelling. His intervention

14. *Ibid.*, June 10, 1853; Milledgeville *Southern Recorder*, June 14, 1853.
15. Augusta *Constitutionalist*, June 26, 1853.

probably saved the election for the Democrats in the end. Although dull by previous standards, the election drew out more than 95,000 Georgians to cast ballots—and a paltry 510 votes separated the two candidates for governor. The Democrats also won a substantial majority in the assembly and carried six of the eight congressional districts.[16]

They lost the Eighth District, of course. Stephens easily defeated his opponent, 5,634 votes to 2,444. Still nursing his injuries, he didn't even take to the hustings until September and even then made only about half a dozen speeches. Still intent on remaining aloof from national parties, he harped on Pierce's patronage policies as proof of the administration's untrustworthiness. As a prime example of the administration's folly, Stephens pointed to the appointment of John A. Dix of New York, a Barnburner bolter of 1848, as minister to France.[17]

So disingenuous had Democrats become that they did not even try to deny that Dix was a free-soiler. Instead, they drew a distinction between being a free-soiler and an abolitionist, which no Democrat had ever before admitted—nor ever would again, once free-soilers banded together to form the Republican party. The *Federal Union* calmly acknowledged Dix as opposed to slavery's extension. But did the Whigs fear only Democratic free-soilers? What about Webster and Fillmore, especially Fillmore, an outright abolitionist? Recalling for the umpteenth time Stephens' Texas speech ("I am no defender of slavery in the abstract"), the editor concluded that Stephens was "every whit as bad a free-soiler as Mr. Dix." The campaign may have lacked real issues, but partisan claptrap, as usual, abounded.[18]

Stephens had more important things than ridiculous Democratic charges to worry about. He spent the rest of November at home writing political advice to Linton (who had been elected to the assembly from Hancock) and preparing a new will. This last task raised a host of melancholy reflections, his brother Aaron's death, for example, and what might befall his black family should he die. On this matter Stephens was explicit. He wanted his slaves to pass only into Linton's hands or those of his children. If Linton were to die before him, or if none of his children were of age, Stephens instructed, his slaves were to

16. Augusta *Chronicle and Sentinel*, September 21, 1853; Milledgeville *Southern Recorder*, November 15, 1853.

17. AHS to LS, July 24, September 15, 1853, in Stephens Papers, MC; Milledgeville *Southern Recorder*, November 15, 1853.

18. Milledgeville *Federal Union*, September 27, 1853.

WITH AN AMBITION AS TOWERING AS THOUGHT—STEPHENS IN 1833
COURTESY GEORGIA DEPARTMENT OF ARCHIVES AND HISTORY

A MERE SHADOW OF A MAN—
STEPHENS AS A GEORGIA
LEGISLATOR ABOUT 1840
PRIVATE COLLECTION OF ROBERT G.
STEPHENS, JR.

FRESHMAN WHIG CONGRESS-
MAN—STEPHENS IN 1843
PRIVATE COLLECTION OF ROBERT G.
STEPHENS, JR.

FELLOW WHIG AND LIFELONG
FRIEND—ROBERT TOOMBS AT
THE TIME OF HIS ELECTION TO
THE SENATE
COURTESY SPECIAL COLLECTIONS DIVISION,
UNIVERSITY OF GEORGIA LIBRARIES

FICKLE FRIEND—HOWELL COBB
IN THE MID-1850s
COURTESY SPECIAL COLLECTIONS
DEPARTMENT, ROBERT S. WOODRUFF
LIBRARY, EMORY UNIVERSITY

LINTON STEPHENS IN 1858
COURTESY GEORGIA DEPARTMENT OF
ARCHIVES AND HISTORY

**ON THE EVE OF "RETIREMENT"—
STEPHENS IN 1858**
COURTESY SPECIAL COLLECTIONS DIVISION,
UNIVERSITY OF GEORGIA LIBRARIES

LIBERTY HALL, STEPHENS' BELOVED HOME
COURTESY GEORGIA DEPARTMENT OF ARCHIVES AND HISTORY

**ENEMY TURNED FAST FRIEND—
HERSCHEL V. JOHNSON ABOUT
1860**
COURTESY GEORGIA DEPARTMENT OF
ARCHIVES AND HISTORY

HE ALWAYS LANDED ON HIS
FEET—JOSEPH E. BROWN IN THE
1870s
COURTESY SPECIAL COLLECTIONS DIVISION,
UNIVERSITY OF GEORGIA LIBRARIES

LINTON STEPHENS IN 1871,
THE YEAR BEFORE HE DIED
PRIVATE COLLECTION OF ROBERT G.
STEPHENS, JR.

FORMER VICE-PRESIDENT—STEPHENS IN 1866
PRIVATE COLLECTION OF ROBERT G. STEPHENS, JR.

ONLY HIS BLACK EYES STILL BLAZED—STEPHENS IN OLD AGE
COURTESY GEORGIA DEPARTMENT OF ARCHIVES AND HISTORY

be sent to Liberia. Under no circumstances would they been given to John L. Stephens. Linton was to ensure that John's children got an education; that was all. And Linton was also to look after Rio.[19]

Rio, one of the most beloved members of Stephens' household, was a large, silken-haired, white Spanish poodle, a gift from a Maryland admirer to Stephens in 1850. Little Aleck always had several dogs about the place, but Rio far surpassed the others in his affection, touching wellsprings of love in him that few humans did. At home the dog was his inseparable companion, trotting alongside his master on long walks, lying at his feet in the house, sleeping at the foot of his bed at night. Rio's loyalty was matched by his intelligence. When commanded, he would close doors or fetch hat, cane, or umbrella. Rio always had the place of honor on the buggy seat next to Stephens on travels about the county; the less-favored hounds had to walk.[20]

As Stephens prepared to depart for Washington, the assembly set about electing a U.S. senator. With Stephens and Toombs looking on, a hopeful Howell Cobb soon received another lesson on the present perils of past heterodoxy. After seven ballots the Democratic caucus nominated fire-eating former governor McDonald for the seat. Southern Rights Democrats still hated Cobb, despite his recent services in the election. But neither could the Union Democrats abide McDonald, despite Cobb's personal pleas for party unity. Stephens and Toombs had both returned to Washington before the assembly unsnarled itself. Eventually the Democratic caucus was forced to withdraw McDonald, and in January, 1854, the assembly elected Alfred L. Iverson, a former one-term congressman and Southern Rights man from Columbus.

"Cobb poor fellow! is down, down!" clucked Stephens after Cobb's defeat. Stephens did not so much regret Cobb's defeat as his ignoring warnings about Southern Righters' treachery. Stephens felt sorry for Cobb, despite the "infinite mischief" he had done his allies of 1850–1851. Cobb's error was one of the head rather than the heart, he decided. Naturally, Stephens had no use for Iverson, a "mouse" brought forth by a mountain long in labor.[21]

19. AHS to LS, November 3, 20, 1853, in Stephens Papers, MC.
20. Rabun, "Stephens," 341–42.
21. AHS to LS, December 4, 1853, January 25, 1854, in Stephens Papers, MC.

Given the state of his health, Stephens might well have felt sorry for himself. Since the second week in December he had been ill with a raft of old complaints: high fever, coughing, chest congestion, and vomiting. This latest illness confined him to bed for two months; not until February 10, 1854, was he able to leave his room. Staying in his room did have some compensations. He had many callers and, as he told Linton, "a fine time to read, write and reflect." Besides, things were dull, both in the House and in the city, as dull as a whittling crowd before a village grocery.[22]

Stephens wrote to Linton on January 11, eight days after Stephen A. Douglas introduced into the Senate a bill to organize the territory of Nebraska. This bill was destined to raise a storm the likes of which the country had never seen before. Congress would soon be anything but dull.

Organization of Nebraska, the only territory still without a government, had long been one of Douglas' pet projects. Since before the Mexican War he and others had been trying to get Congress to agree on a territorial arrangement for the area. The surging tide of American expansionism lent urgency to Douglas' task. Already pioneers were trickling out onto the plains; they would soon require government. But the territory's organization was tangled up with an even larger question, that of communications with the Pacific coast, specifically a transcontinental railroad. Prospective terminal cities of the Mississippi Valley had been lobbying for the prize for years, not least among them Douglas' own city of Chicago. But because neither section wanted to grant the Pacific route to the other—and only one route could be financed, or so everyone believed—Congress had been unable to pass a Pacific railroad bill.[23]

It was against this backdrop of previous failures that Douglas, as chairman of the Senate's Committee on the Territories, framed his Nebraska bill. It was not an easy task. To secure a central route across the continent for the railroad, Nebraska would have to be organized. But to do this and counter powerful eastern antirailroad interests, Douglas would have to entice southern support. So he set about trying to win the most influential southern senators. One of these was his

22. *Ibid.*, January 5, 11, 1854.
23. Potter, *Impending Crisis*, 145–46.

friend David Atchison of Missouri, president *pro tem* of the Senate and messmate of several powerful southern colleagues. Atchison, then engaged in a fierce reelection campaign, had his price, a stiff one: removal of the slavery restriction in the new territory.

All of Nebraska lay above the line of 36°30', an area closed to slaveholders by the Missouri Compromise. Although loath to tamper directly with a law on the books since 1820, Douglas resolved to pay Atchison's price, albeit as niggardly as possible. The way Douglas handled the prickly slavery problem was to apply to Nebraska the same language used in the Compromise of 1850: states formed out of the territory would be received "with or without slavery, as their constitution may prescribe at the time of admission." This language conceded little to the South. It allowed settlers to choose slavery upon statehood, but the Missouri Compromise would keep slaveholders out of the area during the territorial stage. This was bogus currency the southerners refused to accept. So they forced the Little Giant to cough up a few more coins.

On January 10, 1854, the Washington *Union* printed a section of the bill, which it claimed had been inadvertently omitted in an earlier edition. The new section said that all questions of slavery in the territory or in the states formed from it would "be left to the people residing therein." In other words, the bill now incorporated the popular sovereignty principle and at least implicitly repealed the Missouri Compromise. But some southerners still were not satisfied. On January 16, Whig Senator Archibald Dixon of Kentucky offered an amendment explicitly repealing the Missouri Compromise. The following day abolitionist Senator Charles Sumner of Massachusetts offered his own amendment affirming the Missouri line. With the question of repeal now out in the open, Douglas was on the spot. Dixon's move had shaken his southern Democratic supporters, who above all could not let the Whigs appear more vigilant for southern interests than themselves.

Events moved swiftly to a climax. Douglas now committed himself to outright repeal of the Missouri Compromise and at a White House meeting on Sunday, January 22, 1854, he secured the president's reluctant written support. New language, which Pierce helped write, was added to the bill. The Missouri Compromise, it said, had been "superseded" by the principles of 1850 and was therefore "inoperative." With the administration's stamp of approval the Nebraska bill had

taken on a new character: it now became a test of Democratic ortho-
doxy and, as such, extremely pleasing to southerners.[24]

On January 23, Douglas introduced his new bill. To make it resemble the older compromise and appear to be an equitable division,
the territory was divided into two: Kansas to the west of Missouri, and
Nebraska, the rest of the area. The Missouri Compromise, said the
bill, was "inoperative" in both territories.

Douglas had expected his bill to "raise a hell of a storm," but even
he was unprepared for the fury of northern reaction. A long diatribe
appearing on January 24 in the capital's abolitionist paper, the *National Era*, opened the outraged chorus. Signed by Salmon Chase,
Sumner, Giddings, Gerrit Smith, and two others, the "Appeal of the
Independent Democrats in Congress to the People of the United States"
arraigned the Kansas-Nebraska bill as a "gross violation of a sacred
pledge," "a criminal betrayal of precious rights," and "an atrocious
plot" to exclude free labor from the two territories. Not content with
denouncing the bill, the Independent Democrats also flayed its author,
accusing him of truckling to the South to further his presidential ambitions. Although voicing ideas antislavery radicals had been dispensing
for years, the "Appeal" made devastating propaganda nonetheless, not
only because it circulated so widely, but also because its charge of an
atrocious slaveholders' plot to encircle the free states seemed so plausible. It struck a raw nerve in the North.[25]

Slavery, long branded by abolitionists as sinful, now appeared as the
tool of odious despots bent on destroying freedom itself. The South
had long feared for its own safety; now the North shared that fear. A
new element had been introduced to the long slavery struggle; henceforth it would be waged in a corrosive atmosphere of suspicion, anger,
and hatred.

Congressman Stephens, sick in his room, carefully followed the
progress of Douglas' bill in the papers, noting with disgust the *Union's*
"*disgraceful*" vacillation on the issue. Three days after the inflammatory "Appeal" appeared, Stephens noted laconically that "the Nebraska
bill is making a stir here now." Stephens supported the bill and was

24. The preceding paragraphs are based on Johanssen, *Douglas*, 405–15; Potter,
Impending Crisis, 158–60; Roy F. Nichols, *Franklin Pierce: Young Hickory of the Granite Hills* (Philadelphia, 1931), 321–23.

25. Douglas quoted in Potter, *Impending Crisis*, 160; *Congressional Globe*, 33rd
Cong., 1st Sess., 281–82.

confident it would pass. To him it simply carried out the principles of the Compromise of 1850 by keeping Congress out of the territorial slavery issue and allowing the people to choose their state's status at the time of admission to the Union. What delighted him most, however, was the prospect of seeing his fire-eating southern enemies "with their noses to the grindstone" vote for bill. Those who had damned the compromise would now see that it "*got back* all that we lost in 1820." "Verily the *truth* is mighty and will prevail," he exulted.[26]

Stephens soon decided that truth might require an assist. Senate debate had not even begun but northern outrage was apparent. The New York and Ohio legislatures passed resolutions against the bill, and the anguished howl from thousands of pulpits, editors' offices, and hamlet conclaves was almost audible in Washington. "You may look out for squalls ahead," Stephens warned Linton. Try to get the Georgia assembly to endorse the bill, he advised his brother, but only if he could be sure it would. He would be very gratified to see supporting resolutions come from "'old Whig line,'" he said. If there were local political capital to be made on this issue, Stephens wanted to be sure it went to the right side.[27]

Stephens had reason to fear Georgia's reaction to the bill. Initial southern reaction had been decidedly cool, particularly among old-line Whigs. "We had enough, and too much excitement during . . . 1850," said the Richmond *Enquirer*. Other papers professed to see no vital southern interests in the measure. Both Democratic and Whig papers agreed that slavery had no chance of actually being established in the new territories, as Douglas also hotly contended. Most were content that the pernicious stigma of inequality imposed by the Missouri Compromise was at last being removed from the South and that the principle of congressional nonintervention was finally being securely established.[28]

There was no such agreement on the popular sovereignty principle, however. The bill's southern proponents, both Whig and Democrat, denied that the bill enacted "squatter sovereignty," the right of a territory to exclude slavery before forming a state constitution. But both friends and foes of the bill clearly recognized that its language also

26. AHS to LS, January 22, 25, 1854, in Stephens Papers, MC.
27. *Ibid.*, January 27, 1854.
28. Richmond *Enquirer* quoted in Avery O. Craven, *The Growth of Southern Nationalism, 1848–1861* (Baton Rouge, 1953), 196.

allowed the contrary northern construction. Southern Whig opponents of the measure quickly complained of the "subtle, circumlocutory, and tautological wording" that allowed a diversity of opinions on what the bill really meant.[29]

No major Georgia paper opposed the bill outright; most of the press endorsed it as consistent with the Georgia Platform. Nor did the congressional debates occasion any great outcry. Most Georgians doubtless agreed with the *Southern Recorder*'s editor. Slavery would never go into the new territory, he said, but it was imperative that "the equitable, and vital, and republican principle contained in the Compromise of 1850, and which removed the odious Missouri restriction, shall be faithfully adhered to."[30]

Important as the "vital" principle may have been, southern assertion of it in January, 1854, was hardly urgent. Some southerners in Washington privately judged the bill as "a most impolitic and mad movement for the South." "No practical good can come of it because there is none in it," wrote one. "It has been concocted by politicians for political and personal purposes," he concluded. "But," he remarked ruefully, "it is upon them."[31]

"It is upon them." These words are the key to understanding the South's support of a measure many had not wanted, most regretted, and almost all believed of no tangible benefit. The virulence of the northern outcry totally transformed southerners' perception of the measure. What had begun as an unremarkable bill to secure a railroad route had in a matter of days become a sectional issue. Regardless, then, of its merits, the Kansas-Nebraska bill had to be upheld on the abstract and highly arguable grounds of equality and justice. And because northern reaction tended to focus on the despicable slaveholders supposedly behind the measure, southerners rallied to the bill in self-defense. In their eyes, northern opposition was simply a plot to rob the South of the principle of equality so arduously won in 1850. Surrendering the principle was unthinkable; it would be the first step on the road to ruin. "The South has no alternative," said the Charleston *Mercury*. "When the North presents a sectional issue, and tenders battle upon it, she must meet it or abide all the consequences of a [northern]

29. Quote in Cole, *Whig Party in the South*, 291.
30. Milledgeville *Southern Recorder*, March 21, 1854.
31. G. W. Jones to Cobb, February 16, 1854, in Cobb-Erwin-Lamar Papers, UG.

victory." Conservative Whig papers voiced similar sentiments. If the bill were defeated, the Savannah *News* predicted, divisions in the South would end and "all hope and faith in compromises will be abandoned."[32]

Georgia quickly made her feelings known. Linton's resolutions supporting the bill promptly passed in the assembly with only five dissenting votes in the senate. In Washington Little Aleck was "delighted," especially in seeing the Southern Rights crowd eat crow. "You have perfectly lassoeed your opponents," he told Linton gleefully. "How often they will be raked for that vote."[33]

In his smugness Stephens overlooked the even more obvious fact that Georgia's old-line Whigs had supported, practically en masse, a measure bearing an unmistakable Democratic impress. The Stephens brothers strained to find party significance in a vote where there was none. The Southern Rights men were not the ones being lassoed; it was the Whigs—with Alexander Stephens in their midst. This truth was not lost on the Democrats. If a "more healthy sign" did not soon appear in the body politic, observed the *Federal Union*, southern Whigs would have to join the Democrats simply to associate with other southerners.[34]

It was true. Democrats could not have asked for more staunch supporters of the Kansas-Nebraska bill than two former bitter enemies, Stephens in the House and Toombs in the Senate. The latter, who had just taken the seat he had been elected to in 1851, presided over the bipartisan caucus that met to map parliamentary strategy on the bill. He wrote letters to Whig editors urging their support of the measure and spoke passionately in its favor many times in the Senate.[35]

The struggle in the Senate to pass the Kansas-Nebraska bill raged for six weeks. Finally, after a numbing seventeen-hour session, the heavily Democratic Senate passed the bill at five o'clock in the morning of March 4, 1854, by a vote of 37 to 14. The Senate vote had been expected, but the fate of Douglas' bill in the House was doubtful from the first. Despite a large Democratic majority there, support for the

32. Charleston *Mercury* quoted in Craven, *Growth of Southern Nationalism*, 204; Savannah *Morning News*, March 22, 1854.

33. LS to AHS, February 24, 1854, AHS to LS, February 28, 1854, in Stephens Papers, MC.

34. Milledgeville *Federal Union*, May 23, 1854.

35. Toombs to W. M. Burwell, February 3, 1854, in William M. Burwell Papers, LC.

bill among the ninety-two northern Democrats, most of whom were put in terrible political jeopardy by the issue, was very shaky.

A House version of the bill had reposed on the Speaker's desk since the last day in January. Although not officially under consideration, the bill sparked debate nonetheless. An uncommonly pale Stephens had no opportunity to speak until February 17, only a week after he had resumed his seat. He had been careful to claim the floor at the close of the previous day's session, and word had circulated that Stephens of Georgia would speak on the morrow. This news always drew a large throng, as Stephens never failed to notice. Doubtless the presence of several senators on the floor pleased him this day. While William H. Seward spoke to a half-empty chamber across the rotunda, Stephens transfixed the House with his shrill voice.

Northerners had argued that the Kansas-Nebraska bill would violate the Missouri Compromise, a solemn compact honorably adhered to for thirty-four years, causing a breach of faith that would destroy the peace of the country. Stephens set out to demolish this contention point by point. The Missouri Compromise had never been a "compact" between the sections, he said. It "was nothing but a law, with no greater sanction than any other statute." The South had voted for the 36°30′ line as a "lesser evil" to the total exclusion of slavery from Missouri and even then had been forced to agreement by the North's superior numbers in Congress.

Stephens scornfully denied that the North had honorably adhered to the supposedly sacred compact. When considering the Oregon and Mexican cession questions, northern representatives had voted time after time against extending the Missouri Compromise line. "Honor, indeed!" he snapped, quoting Shakespeare: "I thank thee, Jew, for teaching me that word." In the heat of eloquence, Stephens had left logic behind. Northern refusal to extend the line hardly violated the compromise.

But Little Aleck pushed heedlessly on, basing his whole argument on the fallacy. Having been repeatedly refused an extension of the Missouri line, he continued, the South in 1850 "was thrown back *upon her original rights under the constitution*" and forced to demand that Congress totally abandon territorial exclusion of slavery. The South's present position—that the people of the territories decide the slavery question themselves—rested on a principle that was the "very foundation of all our republican institutions," the "principle of the Whigs of

1775 and 1776." Stephens carefully waived the constitutional question: whether Congress had the power to impose restrictions on the people of territories. "The question of power is not the question," he said, "the question is, is it right to thus exercise it?" Where, he asked disdainfully, did the "latter-day Whigs" of the North stand upon this "great question of popular rights?"

Everyone knew the answer—but why should the North be so opposed to popular sovereignty? It had a population advantage of two to one over the South, an advantage it would surely maintain in the new territories. "Are your '*free-born* sons,' who never 'breathed the tainted air of slavery,'" Stephens asked with scathing sarcasm, "such *nincompoops* that they cannot be 'trusted without their mother's [*i.e.,* Congress'] leave?'" The only other possible inference was that slavery was not so bad after all and that the only way to keep "wise, intelligent, and Christian men, even from New England itself, from adopting it" was to have Congress prevent it.

As for the contention that passing the bill would convulse the country, Stephens saw no reason for excitement. How would letting the people of Nebraska and Kansas determine their own institutions excite the country? And who was excited anyway? No one but "fragments of the old 'Wilmot proviso,' 'Free-Soil,' and 'Abolition Phalanx'" with their "hypocritical cry about the sacredness of compacts." "Let them rage on," Stephens said.

The political threats against northerners voting for the bill frightened nobody but "old women and timid children." These dire predictions were but "'ravings' and 'howlings' and hissings'" of beaten "factionists and malcontents [afflicted with] negromania." With the principle of 1850 vindicated, agitation would cease. Exhibiting monumental blindness to the emotional power of the issue, Stephens advised his northern colleagues to stand upon great American republican principles. "Meet your constituents, if need be," and tell them face to face that "they are wrong, and you are right." [36]

How utterly simple the whole problem was to Stephens. And how rigid his solution: simply enshrine a constitutional principle and then pay it the homage usually offered Holy Writ. But what if a political problem involved values? Although he would have been the last to ad-

36. Quotations in the preceding paragraphs are from speech in Cleveland, *Stephens*, 394–415.

mit striving for anything but right, Stephens ultimately defined the highest value, and therefore what was right, as what was lawful and constitutional. Slavery was both; so was popular sovereignty. To question either on moral grounds could only be attributed to stupidity, malevolence, or madness. That the right transcends written laws and constitutions, and that many man (even the Whigs of 1776 he so revered) perceived it this way, never for a moment occurred to him.

He was too busy savoring adulation. "I have been wonderfully lionized on account of this speech," Stephens boasted to Linton. Requests for copies poured in from all parts of the United States. Members of Congress alone requested thirty-four thousand copies, and within a few weeks fifty thousand copies were broadcast over the country. To make sure constituents of his new district fully appreciated his efforts, Stephens was careful to request "an extensive list" of Burke County residents so he could send copies of the speech there.[37]

Vindication of Stephens' glorious principles would be no easy task in the House. Douglas, his fighting instincts aroused to fever pitch, was, like Stephens, sure the storm would abate as soon as the northern people understood the bill. But as the storm roared on, Stephens began to doubt seriously that the bill would pass the House. He still didn't trust Democrats—even when they espoused correct principles. The administration wanted the bill defeated, he told Linton, because they "think it will make Douglass president. Jeff Davis also fears it will make Union men from the South two [sic] prominent." Interestingly, after all his talk about northern malcontents, Stephens feared defeat at the hands of his southern antagonists. "The bill is a bitter pill for Southern Fire eaters," he remarked.[38]

Stephens had been around the House too long to believe the bill anywhere near coming to a vote, so near the end of March he returned to Georgia for the spring court sessions. He had probably despaired of any House action on the bill during the present session. He had not yet left for home when William A. Richardson, chairman of the Committee on the Territories, moved on March 21 to take up the Kansas-Nebraska bill. Had the normal course been followed, the bill would have been referred to Richardson's committee, whence it could be re-

37. AHS to LS, February 27, 1854, in Stephens Papers, MC; AHS to Joseph B. Jones, May 9, 1854, in Joseph B. Jones Papers, EU.
38. AHS to LS, April 2, 1854, in Stephens Papers, MC.

ported out at any time and moved by the previous question. Once seconded by a majority, this motion would end debate and bring the bill to a vote at once.

But the Democratic majority remained seriously divided. Hence when Richardson moved that the bill be referred to his committee, he was immediately challenged by a motion that the bill be referred to the Committee of the Whole House. If successful, this maneuver would effectively snatch the bill from Richardson's control by burying it too far down on the House calendar to be reached during the present session. Despite a desperate fight, friends of the bill failed to defeat this motion, losing by a vote of 110 to 95. Only 26 of 92 northern Democrats voted with Richardson in opposing it.

The Kansas-Nebraska bill had received a crippling blow, but not a fatal one. In the following weeks, while Stephens was in Georgia, Pierce, Douglas, and administration forces exercised all their ingenuity to force dissenting Democrats back into line. Stephens returned in the last week of April, shortly before Richardson and Douglas finally succeeded in forging a working majority in the House. On May 2, Richardson announced his intention to try to clear the House calendar on the eighth. The House version of the Kansas-Nebraska bill was nineteenth on the calendar. To succeed, Richardson would have to carry eighteen consecutive motions to lay bills aside. Then he would substitute the Senate version of the bill (the one fiftieth on the calendar) and try to bring the measure to a vote.[39]

Stephens, rested and feeling well, threw himself wholeheartedly into the struggle. Back in February he had spoken of the great national principle which the Kansas-Nebraska bill embodied. Now, as he wrote the editor of the Baltimore *Patriot*, "as a Southern man" he wanted it to succeed. The issue, he said, "has arrayed the *freesoilers* in solid ranks against the South. The moral effect of the victory on our side will have a permanent effect upon the public mind whether any positive advantages accrue by way of the actual expansion of slavery or not. The effect of such a victory at this time is important." Apparently Stephens now thought even "principle" secondary to symbolism. It did not matter whether a single slave ever entered the territory; "moral victory" for the South was all that counted.[40]

<hr/>

39. The preceding paragraphs are based on Roy F. Nichols, *Blueprints for Leviathan: American Style* (New York, 1963), 107–10.
40. AHS to Burwell, May 7, 1854, in Stephens Papers, LC.

On May 8, Richardson, with substantial help from Stephens, succeeded in digging the Kansas-Nebraska bill out from its grave in the calendar. But his problems remained, for by a previous House vote, all pending legislation would be set aside on May 16 to consider a Pacific railroad bill and the usual appropriations bills, matters that would consume the rest of the session. Richardson, therefore, had to secure a vote on the Kansas-Nebraska bill before then or somehow engineer a two-thirds majority vote for suspension of the rules. His motion to end debate on Nebraska on May 12 signaled a frantic display of dilatory tactics by the bill's opponents that tied up proceedings for thirty-six hours. The session dragged on all afternoon on Thursday, the eleventh, through Thursday night, all day Friday, and into Friday night.

It was one of the most riotous sessions in House history. The Senate, unable to keep a quorum, adjourned to watch the engrossing spectacle on the other side of the Capitol. Disregarding proprieties, Senator Douglas stalked the House floor almost constantly. Enduring this grueling session naturally frayed nerves and shortened tempers. More than once physical violence threatened. Several congressmen, insufficiently numbed by the proceedings, further addled their wits and sensibilities with copious draughts of alcohol. A few managed to remove themselves beyond the reach of argument or fatigue by drinking themselves into a stupor. Stephens exchanged hot words with the obstructionists several times during the debate but was no more successful than anyone else in ending it. Finally, at 11:33 P.M. on Friday night, the limits of human endurance were reached and the House adjourned.

Forced to negotiate, Richardson agreed over the weekend to allow another week's debate in exchange for enough votes to postpone the railroad bill. Formal debate was now scheduled to end at noon on the twentieth. But even then the Kansas-Nebraska bill might not come to a vote, for it would be open to an infinite number of amendments, which under House rules could each be supported with a five-minute speech—the same tactics Stephens and his cohorts had used to defeat the California bill in 1850. Sure enough, with the close of formal debate, the bill's opponents began offering amendments. The Kansas-Nebraska bill appeared doomed.

But Stephens, who knew his way through the tangle of rules and procedures better than almost anyone in the House, had devised a way out the impasse. He would use the 119th rule of the House, an obscure and seldom used regulation that allowed a motion to strike the enacting clause of a bill to take precedence over all pending amendments.

The majority would pass this motion, which would take the bill out of the Committee of the Whole and report the bill unfavorably to the House. This report, however, would be of no consequence, for the bill's supporters, reversing field, would then refuse to concur in the committee's report and would pass the bill under the previous question.[41]

The plan was consummate parliamentary tactics, and Stephens, according to one observer, had been "more excited" for a week than ever before, understandably, for despite the soundness of his plan, he had not been able to sell it to Douglas and the other managers. The Little Giant, bitterly assailed for his recent dictatorial tactics in the Senate, wanted to avoid similar charges in the House. Stephens could not contain his disgust. Not only was he "vexed at their vacillating, timid, foolish policy," he told Linton, but he was also "getting chafed in spirit at the thought of following the lead of such men. I am getting insubordinate and losing my self-respect." If he had not come back to the House, he said, they probably wouldn't even have gotten the question up again.[42]

Apparently compelled by concern for his self-respect, Stephens decided the next day, May 22, to take matters into his own hands, managers' approval or not. The minute the House resolved itself into the Committee of the Whole, Stephens claimed the floor and moved to strike out the enacting clause of the bill. He then proceeded to read the 119th rule and explain to his mystified colleagues how damning the bill in committee would ensure its passage in the full House. "It is time this measure was brought to a final vote," he said. It had been discussed enough.

Shocked opponents of the bill realized they had been outmanuevered. Most refused to vote on Stephens' motion, and the bill was reported to the House. The minority's last-ditch attempts to stave off a vote were finally exhausted near midnight, and the Kansas-Nebraska bill passed by a vote of 113 to 100. An even 100 of the majority votes were Democratic, but 58 northern Democrats deserted the party. Thirteen southern Whigs had provided the winning margin.[43]

41. The preceding paragraphs are from Nichols, *Blueprints for Leviathan*, 111–17; *Congressional Globe*, 33rd Cong., 1st Sess., 1162–63, 1183, has samples of Stephens' rhetoric during the debates.

42. D. A. Reese to LS, May 20, 1854, in Stephens Papers, LC; AHS to LS, May 21, 1854, in Stephens Papers, MC.

43. *Congressional Globe*, 33rd Cong., 1st Sess., 1241. The Senate passed the House version of the bill on May 26, 1854. Pierce signed it on May 30.

Stephens was beside himself with glee. "Hurrah for the Compromise of 1850," he wrote exultantly. "Is not this glory enough for one day[?]" He had been absorbed "night and day" for two weeks with the measure, he reported, and without his efforts the bill would have failed. "I took the reins in my own hand and drove with whip & spur until we got the 'wagon' out of the mire." Stephens now decided everything would return to normal, observing a few days later that no one seemed excited but the abolitionists. "Let them howl on," he said smugly. "Tis their vocation." [44]

Convinced that the Kansas-Nebraska Act was one of the greatest laws in the history of the country, Stephens still basked in glory a few weeks later. "I feel as if the *Mission* of my life was perfomed . . . the cup of my ambition was full." He was particularly gratified that time had proven him right and his "bitterest assailants" wrong. Wasn't the South much better off than when he had taken his seat in 1843 and "infinitely better" than had the Clayton compromise passed? [45]

The Kansas-Nebraska Act now joined the Compromise of 1850 and the Georgia Platform to form a trinity Stephens would revere for the rest of his antebellum career. On the stump in 1855 he would call passage of the bill "the greatest glory of my life." Stephens, too, had come a long way since 1843. Then a national Whig, defending Clay, the tariff, and the bank and assailing Tyler, a southern states'-rights president, he now sounded more and more like a sectionalist, for all the world like the Southern Rights men he professed to despise. [46]

One might suppose that after his close cooperation with the Democrats in this session Stephens would have seriously considered formal affiliation with them. But he did not. What he really thought about the party situation and what his own plans were are difficult to ascertain. The Whigs were dead. What little was left of the party had been destroyed by Kansas-Nebraska. Apparently Stephens still hoped that by some mysterious process a new national party purged of free-soilers would emerge. "There are really no parties in this country," he wrote in mid-1854. He had no wish to build up parties himself, but he fervently hoped that no southerners would affiliate with any party containing free-soilers. "This is what I wanted done in 1852. The country is in better condition for this plan or *reorganization* than it

44. AHS to James Thomas, May 23, 1854, in Stephens Papers, LC; AHS to J. W. Duncan, May 26, 1854, in Dreer American Statesman Collection, HSP.
45. "Alexander H. Stephens to Robert Sims Burch, 15 June 1854," in *American Historical Review*, VIII (October, 1902), 91–97.
46. Augusta *Chronicle and Sentinel*, July 29, 1855.

has ever been before." Obviously, though, the Democratic party was not being "reorganized" to his satisfaction. Pierce, although "*individually* sound," had not made the free-soil issue a party test. "He will fall," Stephens predicted.[47]

Actually Stephens had redefined his "national" principles. What was in the South's interest was now, by definition, in the national interest. His views on Cuba, for example, had changed. "I am for Cuba," he announced in mid-1854; he also now favored filibustering, which he had once denounced as lawless aggression. Rescuing the island from "Spanish misrule and English abolition policy" had suddenly become compelling reasons to interfere in the internal affairs of another country.[48]

That Stephens could so easily abandon his isolationism in just eighteen months demonstrates how far he had moved toward becoming a Democrat. But he never would have admitted it. Instead, he seemed to envision the tattered remnant of the southern Whigs as the foundation for a general party restructuring. Southern Whigs had to stand firm outside the party structure, he wrote. "What we want is a sound national organization upon broad National-Republican principles." Nothing would lead more quickly to a "speedy purification" of northern parties than remaining aloof from them until they made the Compromise of 1850 and the Kansas-Nebraska Act tests of membership. So for the moment Stephens did not become a Democrat; he had yet to find the party pure enough for him. He was not alone. Thousands of southern Whigs declined to consider affiliating with their ancient enemies when the slightest hope remained of salvaging their party. The best policy for all southern Whigs, counseled the *Southern Recorder,* was to "watch and wait."[49]

Most of Georgia's Whigs heeded the advice. Breaking a lifelong habit of opposing everything Democratic was not easy. Considering themselves the only true nationalists and defenders of southern rights, they required only some new and plausible standard under which to do battle with the ancient foe. Their rallying point soon appeared. A new national party, with rabid adherents both North and South, rose on the shards of the Whigs: the Know Nothing party. Rooted in bigotry and prejudice, it fed on political and social unrest, and with amazing rapidity it began to sweep the old Whig areas of the South.

47. "AHS to Burch," 91–97.
48. AHS to Burwell, June 26, 1854, in Stephens Papers, LC.
49. *Ibid.*; Milledgeville *Southern Recorder*, June 12, 1854.

XI

With His Principles on His Forehead

Exhausted by the long congressional struggle, Stephens returned to Georgia in the first part of July, a few weeks before Congress adjourned. He always relished being at home, in the midst of his household family, black and white. Stephens took family responsibilities seriously. During this fall he brought his brother's son, John Alexander Stephens, over from LaGrange to live with him and enrolled him in the academy at Woodstock. Young John not only bore the name of his illustrious uncle but also the same nickname. Stephens promptly ended that. He enrolled the boy in school as John A. Stephens. "I have a sort of aversion to any other 'Ellick Stephens' besides myself," he explained.[1]

Stephens cared about his black family too. At the end of November, at the urging of his slave Betsey, he purchased her sister, along with *her* daughter and a male cousin. "They begged me out of it," he told Linton. This act of kindness toward his slaves was characteristic. As a slaveholder, Stephens was the soul of benevolence. Linton was not. With the same flinty impatience with human frailty as his brother but without his ameliorative disposition to charity and instinctive identification with misery and suffering, Linton was often tempted to resort to the usual sanctions of the slave society: the whip and sale of recalcitrant blacks. What restraint he did exercise can probably be attributed to Aleck, who always carefully praised Linton's forbearance

1. AHS to LS, November 21, 1854, in Stephens Papers, MC.

in such matters. Stephens did not believe in physical punishment of slaves. "To err is human," he reminded Linton. If the best could err, "what better could be expected of a poor negroe with a mind very little above those attributes called instincts?" [2]

How Stephens reconciled his racist presumptions with the evidence of his own senses is difficult to say. He certainly treated blacks as if they possessed something more than instincts. In November, for example, he spent the better part of a night and a day in deep, sorrowful reminiscing with "old Ben," a former slave of Aaron's who now belonged to John. They sat side by side in rockers before the fireplace and the next day went down to the graveyard together. Ben desperately wanted to return to Crawfordville, and Stephens assured the old man he would intercede with his brother about it. [3]

Stephens violated the southern canon on proper management of blacks too. He never employed an overseer on his place. When he was in Washington, he simply wrote to Harry, Eliza's husband, and gave instructions through him. Several of Stephens' slaves knew how to read and write, by contemporary southern lights extremely dangerous knowledge for black slaves and against the law in the slave states. The law made no difference to Stephens; he managed his household by his own rules.

Stephens invariably followed a fixed routine at home. Up about sunrise, he would "take a shower bath," and in good weather he would take a buggy ride before breakfast. During the ferocious heat of midday, he would sit on his porch reading or tending to his correspondence. He spent hours with Rio wandering about his property, supervising the farm work, or sitting in quiet reverie on the new stone wall he had had installed around the family graveyard. [4]

Forty-two years old, prosperous, and even moderately famous, Stephens was just as unhappy as ever. "Everything seems stamped with the impress of decay," he dolefully told Linton. "Life is rapidly passing away and soon all of us will be in the grave. There is very little in this world worth the attention of one who must so soon take his departure." [5]

Stephens was nowhere near "departing," but he was ill again—with dysentery this time—which perhaps accounted in part for his glum-

2. *Ibid.*, November 27, July 12, December 11, 1854.
3. *Ibid.*, November 25, 26, 1854.
4. *Ibid.*, July 6, 1854.
5. *Ibid.*, October 13, 1854.

ness. As always, only Linton knew of his despondency. Oddly, Stephens took no solace from organized religion, toward which, by his own account, he had for some years felt "skeptical [and] callous." He had been a member of the Presbyterian church since 1827 but never attended regularly. Nor did he ever talk or write much on the subject. "I have always had an aversion to what I consider the cant of religion," he once explained. Evidently this aversion led some uninformed men to suspect Stephens of being an atheist. Nothing could have been farther from the truth. Stephens had an abiding, conventional faith in divine providence. During the 1850s he began praying daily, and his faith became more pronounced as he grew older. But he spoke of it only rarely. Apparently at some time during his early life Stephens had run afoul of a minister and "came near to being *shipwrecked* in religious feeling" because of it. Thereafter preachers had little effect on him. Most of them, he said, were "poor, erring mortals" to whom he extended charity "as a superior always should to an inferior." "Even the religion of the best," he observed, "is exceedingly earthly."[6]

Despite his insufferably egotistical attitude, Stephens practiced prodigious charity toward "inferiors." Thousands of other Americans during these years did not. The late 1840s and early 1850s brought a veritable flood of immigrants to the country. Most of these newcomers were "inferiors"—poor, illiterate, and worst of all, Catholic—whom men less magnanimous than Stephens despised and feared. Their presence in ever-increasing numbers spawned nativism, a movement dedicated to preserving "pure" Protestant Americanism, which found its political expression in the American, or Know Nothing, party, also commonly referred to at the time as "Sam." By 1854 the party had a platform and was organizing rapidly in almost every state. It found fertile ground in the South. The region had few immigrants or Catholics; but Sam evinced irresistible appeal for many southerners. The party promised reform and an end to selfish, unscrupulous politicians. It espoused Unionism above all and was "sound" on slavery. But most important, it offered former Whigs a national organization in opposition to the Democrats. For this reason alone, thousands of politically homeless southern Whigs flocked to Sam's dens and took its secret oaths.[7]

6. AHS to Johnston, March 29, 1863, in Johnston and Browne, *Stephens*, 439–40; AHS to LS, November 16, December 24, 1854, in Stephens Papers, MC.

7. Cole, *Whig Party in the South*, 316–17.

Know Nothingism appeared in Georgia in the spring of 1854, and it promptly flourished, especially in the old Whig districts across the middle of the state—Stephens' and Toombs's territory. Stephens and many of his constituents watched this growth with interest, and during the winter of 1854–1855 he received many requests from home for advice. Knowing little about the order, he remained noncommittal but was inclined on principle to oppose all secret political societies. "In a republic every man should wear his principles inscribed on his forehead," he said. But if the Know Nothings meant to drive out the "Federal Union fire-eating [Herschel] Johnson Democracy," he and they were pursuing the same end by different roads.[8]

In a prophetic mood as usual on New Year's Eve, Stephens predicted nothing but doom for the Democrats, "the foulest coalition known in our history." Old parties, names, and issues were passing away, he said. A day of new organizations was dawning. About parties he could not have been more correct, but he was dead wrong about the issues. The slavery controversy had again assumed center stage in American politics. The issues had not changed; what had was the way men would deal with them. Until now the slavery question had been debated within a national two-party structure. But the Kansas-Nebraska Act had shattered national Whiggery, and the Know Nothings had rushed into the vacuum. In the North, however, the law had inflamed antislavery feelings that organized nativism could not contain. Thus was born the Republican party. Unlike the Know Nothings, who, as befitted their mysterious and somewhat conspiratorial character, sprung up mushroomlike overnight, the Republicans formed more slowly.[9]

In every northern state antislavery Democrats who had bolted the party over the Kansas-Nebraska bill began to gravitate under a variety of labels toward common organizations in which to oppose the administration. The process took longer in states where the Whigs were strong. Nonetheless, anti-Nebraska coalitions enjoyed amazing success in the summer and fall elections of 1854. "The Democratic party has been literally slaughtered," moaned Cobb.[10]

But neither Stephens nor Toombs appeared too concerned. Despite its formidable appearance, thought Toombs, this new antislavery organization would die out after the fall elections. Stephens agreed. He

8. AHS to LS, December 25, 1854, in Stephens Papers, MC.
9. *Ibid.*, December 31, 1854.
10. Cobb to James Buchanan, December 5, 1854, in Phillips (ed.), *TSC Correspondence*, 348.

blamed the troubles on the Whigs. "Hundreds of thousands" of these Seward-led Whigs, he confidently expected, would cease their agitation if southern Whigs simply held fast to the principles of the Compromise of 1850 and the Kansas-Nebraska Act.[11]

Stephens still discerned no cause for alarm when he returned to Washington in December, 1854. "Everything is flat" and nobody seemed the least interested in public affairs, he reported. As a hardworking congressman, however, it was not his nature to be unconcerned. During this session his position on the Ways and Means Committee kept him particularly busy. Not too busy to be miserable, however. Stephens could always find time for brooding. "I am utterly enveloped in gloom," he wrote on Christmas Eve. He could stand the workaday duties of a congressman, but the "ordinary civilities and courtesies of life" he found most oppressive. Constantly having to hide "the aching void within" was almost unbearable. And the world offered him no sympathy; even its praises were frequently "gall and wormwood" to him.[12]

As usual, Stephens oozed loneliness. He could not share "feelings, tastes and sentiments with the world." Few men were virtuous. "My habitation should be solitude," he concluded. Unfortunately, solitude in Washington was a luxury a popular congressman could not afford. He was still glum several weeks later. "It seems to me if it were not for an effort that no other mortal on earth would make I should sink into profound insensibility—upon all things connected with men & their affairs. But with that effort that I daily exert, to the *senseless herd* about me I have no doubt I appear to be one of the most cheerful and happy men on earth." If this was the impression Stephens conveyed, his daily effort must indeed have been taxing.[13]

Despite his aversion to the senseless herd, Stephens made the usual round of holiday dinners. He and Toombs even gave a small dinner for Senator William Dawson and his new bride, which, according to Stephens "passed off elegantly." But the social whirl pleased him little. "If I had consulted my own inclination," he wrote after one magnificent dinner, "I should have spent the time in some solitary cell."[14]

But he did consult his own inclination in Congress, refusing to allow

11. Toombs to George N. Sanders, June 13, 1854, in Rabun, "Stephens," 383; AHS to Burwell, June 26, 1854, in Stephens Papers, LC.

12. AHS to LS, December 4, 24, 1854, in Stephens Papers, MC.

13. *Ibid.*, January 8, 1855.

14. *Ibid.*, January 4, 8, 1855.

unchallenged attacks on the Kansas-Nebraska Act. On December 13, 1854, when an Indiana representative notified the House of his intention to introduce a bill restoring the Missouri Compromise line, Stephens claimed the right to reply. He did so the next day before a packed gallery that doubtless got what it came for: vintage Stephens histrionics. What history got, though, was a prime example of how disjointed Stephens' speeches could be sometimes. The address wandered from the recent northern elections—not at all affected by the Nebraska bill, Stephens claimed—to defense of southern policy on internal improvements and the popular sovereignty principle to the obligatory defense of slavery.

Blacks occupied their position in society in accord with a "great immutable law of nature," he said. A wise and just Creator had assigned blacks their place; the relation of the races in the South was "best for both of them." Moreover, southern blacks were not only better fed, clothed, and provided for but were also happier and enjoyed a "higher civilization" than blacks anywhere else. Stephens buttressed his case with a cascade of statistics from the latest census, "proving," at least to his own satisfaction, not only how much better off southern slaves were than northern free blacks but also how far superior Georgia's agricultural output was to Ohio's—one of the most prosperous northern states. "Away, then," he concluded triumphantly, "with this prating cry about slavery paralyzing the energy of a people, and opposing the development of the resources of a country." [15]

This rambling and discursive address had been by almost any logical or aesthetic standard one of Stephens' worst. Nevertheless, Stephens reported proudly, he had been "very much complimented" on it. Probably he had—most men in Congress by this time heard only what they wanted to hear. But Lewis Campbell, Cincinnati's congressman, answered Stephens in remarks anything but complimentary. Declining to try to follow the Georgian "through the various mazes in which he has groped his way," Campbell offered a few derisive comments upon earlier points in Stephens' speech and then took up with pleasure the statistical battle between Ohio and Georgia. Two could play this game, and Campbell evinced a fair skill. After Campbell's turn, to no one's surprise, Ohio had bested Georgia not only in value of agricultural products but also in many other categories: livestock production, rail-

15. Speech in Cleveland, *Stephens*, 416–32.

road mileage, value of manufactures, and number of colleges, public schools, churches, and newspapers. The Ohioan conceded the lead to Georgia in only one area: the number of adult white illiterates.[16]

Having satisfactorily disposed of Stephens in the "blackberry and crab-grass arena," as another Georgia congressman jocularly called it, Campbell then attempted to engage him in another, that of constitutional disquisition. On Little Aleck's home turf, however, the Ohioan was much less successful. Campbell attempted to pin Stephens down to a direct answer on the question of congressional power to exclude slavery from the territories. He failed, and for good reason. Stephens had never questioned congressional power to exclude slavery, preferring instead to maintain discreet silence on the subject. But he had persistently opposed the exercise of this power on the grounds of justice. Denying the power would have proved Stephens logically inconsistent because several times he had voted to extend the Missouri Compromise line, a sanction, of course, of congressional power over slavery north of $36°30'$. Specifically affirming the power, however, would have grossly departed from Calhoun's position that Congress had no power over slavery in the territories. And by 1855, this belief had attained the status of divinely inspired doctrine in the South. To deny this argument would have been to declare the Wilmot Proviso, not to mention the Missouri Compromise, constitutional. Even if he did believe this, no southern politician with an ounce of regard for his political neck could say so publicly.[17]

The most Campbell could elicit from Stephens was an indirect answer. On this question of power, Stephens said, he stood "where Chatham stood in the British Parliament upon the subject of taxing the Colonies without representation. . . . Not so much looking to the question of power as to the justice and propriety of its exercise." Without discussing the question of the power, Chatham said that if he were an American he would resist. Stephens gave the same answer. Unsatisfied, the Ohioan pressed for a direct answer. He never got one.[18]

It wasn't in Stephens' nature to allow an opponent the last word, particularly when, as now, it appeared that he had been made to look

16. AHS to LS, December 15, 1854, in Stephens Papers, MC; *Congressional Globe*, 33rd Cong., 2nd Sess., Appendix, 39–42.

17. *Congressional Globe*, 33rd Cong., 2nd Sess., Appendix, 328.

18. *Ibid.*, 42–45. Stephens did, in fact, believe the Wilmot Proviso was constitutional. "You were right," he told Linton, "in your inferences as to my reason for not

foolish. Newspaper reports of the Ohioan's speech had infuriated him. Following time-honored custom, Campbell had embellished his remarks with additional matter inserted into the record. Stephens was outraged with the *Congressional Globe*'s account. "Not one word" of the reported statistics had Campbell uttered, he said.[19]

Stephens, possessed by a consuming drive to vindicate his superior mental agility, prepared his reply for days. He was ready on January 15, 1855, and despite cold and nasty weather a huge throng crowded the galleries to enjoy the show. Campbell had allowed Stephens to interrupt his remarks in December, a courtesy the Georgian did not extend now. He had "a great deal" to say in reply to Campbell's statistics and would not be halted. After a long digression on Cuba, he got to the heart of his address, refuting the invidious comparison of Georgia and Ohio.

Not only did he recapitulate his first list of products, quantities, prices, and valuations, but he also called upon the weighty authority of Adam Smith to defend his "sliding" price scale. It was absurd, he argued, to assign New York prices to Georgia and Ohio products. But "for the sake of argument" he would use a set of prices prevailing in Ohio a little more than two years ago. With a flourish Stephens produced a paper he had dug out of his files—a price list of Ohio's chief agricultural products produced by none other than Campbell himself. Using this list, Stephens accused Campbell of doing some "sliding" of his own.

Naturally, the new computations once more put Georgia in the lead. But this was mere prelude. In a fantastic display of sophistical statistical juggling, Stephens proceeded to bury Campbell, the House, and the crowd under an avalanche of figures. By Stephens' reckoning, Georgia had more hogs, more debt-free railroad track, more colleges and students and churches per white inhabitant, less crime, fewer convicts and paupers than Ohio did. At one point Campbell tried to question the accuracy of Stephens' figures and got his head bit off for it. "No, sir," Stephens snapped. "I am never wrong upon a matter I have given as close attention to as I have given to this."

---

answering Campbell's question as a general proposition[,] to wit[:] Has Congress the power to prohibit slavery over a territory? My opinion is that if they were to do it the Supreme Court would hold it to be constitutional. Hence I always fought the Wilmot provisio because I thought there was something in it" (AHS to LS, January 6, 1855, in Stephens Papers, MC).

19. AHS to LS, January 6, 1855, in Stephens Papers, MC.

Stephens closed this remarkable performance with a deep bow to the throne of King Cotton. Campbell had had the temerity to compare Georgia cotton unfavorably with Ohio hay. Refuting this argument called for yet more figures: on workers and seamen and tons of shipping engaged in cotton transport; on the numbers of mill men involved and the millions of dollars invested in its manufacture; on wages these workers earned; on the hundreds of thousands of southerners engaged in cotton production. Who, he exclaimed, in the face of such facts, could dare compare cotton with a hay crop, "cow food?" [20]

Stephens thought his speech "capital," but the Washington press largely ignored it because in truth it had been tedious and boring. Stephens, however, discerned other reasons for the slight. "The whole [northern] press" was free-soil, he said. Morbidly sensitive on any point touching his mental prowess, he dwelled incessantly on the speech for the next few days. Despite his having "utterly extinguished" Campbell, praise had been less fulsome than usual. Stephens even suspected such Georgia friends as Toombs and David Reese, both of whom had praised the speech, of secret jealousy. As for the southern press, only a (for him) rare scatalogical image could express Stephens' contempt. Southern papers constantly revamped northern news, ideas, and sentiments, he said. "Its daly food is that which the Northern press has not only eaten first but thrown out as excrement . . . thrice digested sh—." [21]

Although even Linton found parts of the speech "somewhat Bentonian" in tone and therefore "somewhat out of taste," he had immediately discerned its purpose. Because it so admirably vindicated the slave system, he told his brother, it was the greatest speech he had ever made. It marked "more distinctly than any other in American history, the commencement of a *new era*." [22]

No new era was commencing, but Stephens was about to embark on a new political course. He left Washington in late January to defend an accused murderer in court at Augusta. Traveling about the circuit that

20. Speech in Cleveland, *Stephens*, 432–58.
21. AHS to LS, January 18, 21, 1855, in Stephens Papers, MC.
22. LS to AHS, January 24, 1855, in Stephens Papers, MC. Despite Stephens' blanket condemnation of the southern press, Georgia's editors praised the speech to the skies. As sectional tensions increased in the late 1850s, and Georgians became increasingly paranoid, the speech reassured them about the merits of their social system. It was reprinted several times in the following years, and according to one editor, it gave Stephens "more character than any he ever delivered in Congress" (Atlanta *Southern Confederacy*, June 7, 1861).

spring, Stephens was stunned to discover that the Know Nothings had made inroads among his constituents. As if to confirm it, on April 9 the Know Nothings swept the local election in Augusta. A week later Stephens decided to retire. He would not be a candidate for reelection, he told the courthouse crowd in Oglethorpe County: "The old Whig party is about to be sold out to the Know Nothings." Far from proscribing foreigners and Catholics, said Stephens, he would hail them as political allies in the fight against the real enemies: free-soilers and abolitionists. "*To crush them* out I would join with any honest man." A few days later he repeated the same words in Augusta.[23]

Privately, too, Stephens condemned the secret order. It was incredible that the South could find any merit in it, he said, especially when it could see what Know Nothing rule meant. The Massachusetts Know Nothings, for instance, had just passed laws proscribing naturalized white foreigners while at the same time permitting blacks the franchise. "They are for elevating the black man and degrading their own kith and kin. This is but a Yankee notion—a new patented idea for making white men *slaves*—menial servants at least—instead of following the order of nature."[24]

Till now only a few knew Stephens' opinions, but rumors abounded in the press. Georgia's Whig papers had generally maintained an attitude of benign neutrality toward the secret order. But as the Americans began demonstrating political potential against the Democrats, many Whig editors felt compelled to join Sam's ranks. One such editor was William S. Jones of the Augusta *Chronicle*, for years a sturdy adherent of the Stephens-Toombs line in Georgia politics. Not yet a Know Nothing but weakening fast, Jones hoped that Stephens and Toombs shared sympathies with the order in its efforts to rid the country of the administration and its "miserable tricksters and time serving demagogues."[25]

Stephens detested the administration, but he shared no other sympathies with Sam, as Jones and the rest of the state would soon discover. In early May Stephens received a letter from Elberton lawyer and his longtime friend Thomas W. Thomas, soliciting his opinions on the new party. Rumors had it, Thomas wrote slyly, that because so many in his district had joined the order Stephens declined to run for fear of

23. AHS to LS, April 20, 1855, in Stephens Papers, MC.
24. AHS to Warren Aiken, April 22, 1855, in Stephens Papers, LC.
25. Augusta *Chronicle and Sentinel*, April 8, 1855.

being defeated. Nothing raised Little Aleck's hackles more than an insinuation of cowardice, and Thomas received his reply immediately in a thundering letter, prominently published in every important state paper.[26]

The retirement rumors were true, Stephens acknowledged curtly. Since so many of his constituents had entered the secret order, he had concluded that "they had no further use for me" in Congress. He would not become "a dumb instrument" for accomplishing secret aims. He would never solicit votes "with my principles in my pocket." The order's secrecy repelled him. "*Truth* never shuns the light nor shrinks from investigation." No one unwilling to openly avow his purposes and principles was fit to represent a free people. "Political ruin" would "inevitably" result from the triumph of a secret party. No less repugnant were the order's "two leading ideas": proscription of Catholics and foreigners. As a basis of party organization these ideas were ruinous, looking "not to *how* the country shall be governed, but *who* shall hold the offices." And as a basis of public policy they were un-American. "I am utterly opposed to mingling religion with politics in any way whatever," Stephens said. "As a citizen and a member of society, a man is to be judged by his *acts*, and not by his creed."

Catholics especially, he continued, were the last people southerners should proscribe. As a church, they had never attacked slavery. "No man can say as much of New England Baptists, Presbyterians, or Methodists." Cooperating with New England puritanism to strike down the South's best friends struck Stephens as little short of insanity. Catholics could not be worse than the "same puritanical accusers, who started this persecution against them, say that *we are.* They say that we are going to perdition for the enormous sin of holding slaves . . . for my part, I would about as soon risk my chance for heaven with [the pope], and his crowd, too, as with those self-righteous hypocrites who deal out fire and brimstone so liberally upon our heads."

Proscription of foreigners, Stephens continued, was not only "at war with all my ideas of American republicanism" but positively perilous in its consequences. Persecuting foreigners would not halt immigration, and if the Know Nothings succeeded in greatly extending the period of naturalization as they proposed, a class of potential revolutionaries would be created.

26. Thomas W. Thomas to AHS, May 5, 1855, in Cleveland, *Stephens*, 459.

As Stephens saw it, the purpose of the movement was nothing less than "an insidious attack upon the general suffrage." Northern capitalists had seized upon the movement to effect "their old, long-cherished desire . . . to have a *votingless* population to do their work." Whole cargoes of foreigners would be "bought up" in Europe and shipped to America, all as part of a diabolical plan: "The whole *sub stratum* of northern society will soon be filled up with a class who can work, and who, though *white* cannot *vote*. This is what the would-be lords of that section have been wanting for a long time. It is a scheme with many of them to get *white slaves* instead of black ones. No American *laborer*, or man seeking employment there, who has a *vote*, need to expect to be retained long when his place can be more cheaply filled by a *foreigner* who has *none*. . . . This is the philosophy of the thing."

In the final part of his letter Stephens turned his attention to more immediate dangers. Organic law in the territories allowed the vote to any person who declared his intention of becoming a citizen. But since Know Nothings would allow only native-born or naturalized citizens to vote, they would ultimately betray the rights of the South, despite their promises. For when Kansas applied for admission as a slave state (which Stephens took for granted because of two territorial elections recently carried by proslavery forces there) southern Know Nothings would unite with their northern brethren to defeat it. "A more insidious attack was never made upon the principles of the Kansas and Nebraska bill." [27]

As could have been expected from a man who revered the Constitution and the charter of liberties it guaranteed, Stephens had argued strenuously against the secret order because it espoused principles both un-American and unconstitutional. But most noteworthy was the main thrust of the argument. It was purely sectional. Not only did he score the order as the cat's-paw of all the old familiar northern demons, but he had already convinced himself that Kansas would "doubtless" become a slave state—a possibility, it will be recalled, the entire South denied only a few months before—and seized upon this issue to criticize his domestic political antagonists.

27. Preceding paragraphs from AHS to Thomas, May 9, 1855, *ibid.*, 459–71. Toombs denounced the Know Nothings in a public letter a month later (Toombs to T. Lomax, June 6, 1855, in Phillips [ed.], *TSC Correspondence*, 350–53).

Stephens' lengthy letter speaks volumes for the intensity of the sectionalization occurring in the mid-1850s. Under the pressure of northern attacks, the ante for staying the game of southern politics had been perilously hiked. Men were now being forced to wager their political careers on but a single blue chip, Kansas as a slave state. And the game was just beginning—it would be two years before those bets were called.

Stephens' blasts against the Know Nothings rolled like a thunderclap across Georgia. Some papers friendly to the Know Nothings rejected Stephens' ideas but hoped that he could still serve his constituents in Congress. Others, like the *Southern Recorder*, less kindly stopped just short of declaring Little Aleck "hopelessly mad." Democratic reactions to the letter occasioned particular disgust. These, shivered the *Recorder*, were "startling monstrosities in the political world."[28]

As the *Recorder*'s reaction suggests, Democratic editors universally approved Stephens' letter. Some, carried away in their enthusiasm, even bestowed on him such unwonted accolades as "an honest man" and "a deep thinker and a profound politician." The Savannah *News*, an independent paper, suggested Stephens' nomination for governor by "THE CONSERVATIVE MEN OF ALL PARTIES." And the *Chronicle*, not yet ready to desert Stephens, decided it the better part of valor not to oppose him. The Know Nothings, it said, had neither the power nor the will to eject "*the ablest man in Congress*" from his post.[29]

Nor did Stephens have the will to remove himself. Two weeks after his letter, he decided to enter the race. Repeated taunts that he was afraid to run had made up his mind. "I may be beaten," he told Linton, "but I may sow seeds of truth in the canvass that may hereafter save the country." Stephens declared his candidacy for Congress in a fiery speech from the City Hall steps in Augusta on May 28, 1855. He was not afraid to run, he shouted. "I am *afraid* of nothing on the earth, or above the earth, or under the earth, except to do wrong . . . I would rather be *defeated* in a good cause than to *triumph* in a bad one." He was presenting his name "by myself," he said, not as the candidate of

28. Milledgeville *Southern Recorder*, May 22, 29, 1855.
29. Macon *Telegraph*, quoted in Savannah *Morning News*, May 17, 1855; Milledgeville *Federal Union*, May 22, 1855; Savannah *Morning News*, May 15, 1855; Augusta *Chronicle and Sentinel*, May 5, 1855.

any party. His sole pledge if elected was to maintain the rights, interests, and honor of the district and state. He then launched into a two-
hour tirade against the Know Nothings.[30]

After a one-year respite Georgia was again embroiled in a political
donnybrook just as furious as the memorable clashes of 1850–1852.
Given the consensus of the parties on the slavery issue—both Democrats and Know Nothings endorsed the Kansas-Nebraska Act and the
Georgia Platform—the campaign inevitably degenerated into vicious
mudslinging. And Stephens played a prominent role in the unedifying
spectacle. At first, the middle Georgia Know Nothings had not opposed his reelection, but his incessant, savage attacks roused them to
rage. Stephens refused to temper his fury. The disease was "not for
plasters," he said, "but for the knife."[31]

Despite the unusually hellish heat and his own poor health, Stephens
embarked on his most vigorous and wide-ranging canvass since 1850.
This campaign was vitally important to him, and he fought it furiously.
It was a crusade for the Constitution and personal vindication of his
own judgment—either of which could rouse him to passionate heights.
Moreover, Linton was running for Congress in the Seventh District
and facing opposition as stiff as his own.

Stephens' voice in the Eighth District had been partially muted. Editor Jones of the *Chronicle* had finally fallen off the fence and into the
Know Nothing camp. But Democrats were beginning to discover virtues in Stephens they had never before suspected. A man who denounced the American party as "revolutionary," "anti-American,"
"anti-republican," and as worse than the seven-headed hydra of the
Apocalypse must, they reasoned, be sound. So for the first time in his
long career, Stephens received a Democratic endorsement. On July 31,
the *Federal Union* ran his name on the masthead as its "Independent"
choice for congressman, Eighth District.[32]

Stephens maintained the fiction that he belonged to no party, but he
had become a Democrat in all but name. Stalwart Democrat James
Gardner, editor of the *Constitutionalist*, claimed after private conversations with the congressman that Stephens "is heart and soul with

30. AHS to LS, May 26, 1855, in Stephens Papers, MC; Cleveland, *Stephens,*
472–89.
31. Johnston and Browne, *Stephens,* 298.
32. Augusta *Constitutionalist,* June 8, 1855; Milledgeville *Federal Union,* July 31,
1855.

us." For "personal reasons" (the long-standing feud), explained Stephens, he could not vote for Herschel Johnson, who was running for reelection as governor, but he would have supported any other man in the party. But he "might" vote for the other candidate, Garnett Andrews, he wrote later, if he would disavow the Know Nothing creed. "Every man in this campaign," Little Aleck concluded, "must 'tote his own skillet.'"[33]

And so he did—with unparalleled pomposity. "Follow the truth, and you will find *me* in the crowd," he declared in Appling. Only "demagogues and small men" were charging him with having switched parties, he averred in Sparta. "By the truth, by the Constitution, and by your rights and my own, I will stand or fall." Late in the canvass, Stephens still avowed his magnificent independence: "As well might the morning owl attempt to locate the eagle, or the wolf attempt to locate the majestic lion, as [anyone] to locate ME."[34]

Such boasting drove some Know Nothings positively wild with fury. One "Ivanhoe," for instance, accused Stephens in the *Chronicle* of being a "polygamist in principle," "a Mormon missionary," "a licentious reprobate," and "a hideous deformity of a man." Even by Georgia's none-too-exacting standards such scurrility was unprecedented. Appeals to Georgia voters' prejudices were hardly new, but in 1855, with unblushing appeal to religious and national bigotry in addition to the old standbys, Georgia politics reached its slimiest nadir.[35]

But in this fierce campaign Stephens made a magnificent display of political skill and personal courage. Undeterred by the possibility of defeat, which he thought likely at first, he fought bare-knuckled, just like his opponents. And he consciously did it alone—without a party, without a newspaper. By the summer of 1855 Stephens realized that the national Democracy offered the only secure bastion for southern rights. He had to make his move. But to do so without first obtaining his faithful constituency's sanction would have been gross political disloyalty. Stephens had an even more important reason for remaining independent in this campaign, however. He could not betray himself—at

33. James Gardner to Cobb, June 12, 1855, in Cobb-Erwin-Lamar Papers, UG; AHS to LS, June 30, 1855, in Stephens Papers, MC.

34. Augusta *Chronicle and Sentinel*, July 4, 1855; Milledgeville *Federal Union*, July 17, 1855; Wilkes *Republican* quoted in Milledgeville *Southern Recorder*, September 25, 1855.

35. Augusta *Chronicle and Sentinel*, September 18, 1855.

least his own conception of himself—as a leader of unshakable integrity and honor.

He fought the Know Nothings with such savagery because the secret order wasn't just a political threat but also a personal affront, a garish trollop seducing hundreds of his faithful disciples from the path of righteousness they had so long followed under his lead. To hide behind the Democracy in the face of such an affront was to Stephens unthinkable. He had to wage this last campaign on his own. To have done less would have been an open admission that his political course for the last five years had been wrong. Frank admission of error never was one of his virtues. Even worse, it would have been an act of cowardice— and a coward he was not.

About halfway through the campaign, Stephens knew he would win by at least a small majority. Linton, however, was fighting an uphill battle in the Seventh District, where the Americans were particularly potent. He had entered the race in June, also as an Independent, much to his brother's delight. "In you and about you," Stephens had told him, "are centered all my hopes and aspirations." Linton's success was more important than his own.[36]

Stephens hoped in vain. Linton lost by about two hundred votes despite his brother's and Toombs's best efforts in his behalf. Little Aleck won a smashing victory in his own district, defeating Lafayette Lamar, a Lincolnton lawyer, 5,808 votes to 3,079. Out of eleven counties he lost only one—Augusta's Richmond County. Know Nothings had done well only in the cities; otherwise Democrats ran rampant over the state. Johnson won reelection by more than 10,000 votes. Counting the Eighth District ("ONE THOUSAND CHEERS FOR THE UNTERRIFIED AND INDEPENDENT WHIGS—ONE THOUSAND AND ONE FOR A. H. STEPHENS!!" hosannaed the *Federal Union*), Democrats had carried six of eight districts and also won large majorities in the General Assembly.[37]

Once vindicated by his constituents, his honor secured, Stephens had no reason to delay longer his entrance into the Democratic party. Rather than announce his conversion straightaway, he did so by indirection, in a speech at Milledgeville on November 16, the night before Johnson's inauguration. The address castigated Know Nothings and

36. AHS to LS, June 23, 1855, in Stephens Papers, MC.
37. Milledgeville *Southern Recorder*, October 16, 1855; Milledgeville *Federal Union*, October 9, 1855.

profusely praised victorious Democrats all over the country, especially those in Georgia. Toombs, too, announced his conversion in characteristic fashion. The South's fate, he roared, was inextricably bound with that of the national Democratic party. Never again, he vowed, would he fight Democrats.[38]

Toombs and Stephens' new associates were ecstatic. Capturing these two luminaries along with most of their followers had been a cherished goal for national-minded Democrats since the early 1850s. Not least gratified was Governor Johnson, who had himself migrated from fire-eater to national Democrat. At Johnson's urging, Cobb had encouraged the new converts' presence in Milledgeville. The governor especially wanted Stephens there; he intended to patch up their nine-year estrangement. But Stephens acted first, calling on Johnson with Toombs to congratulate him on his reelection. The handshake the two men exchanged that day sealed a friendship between them that would end only with Johnson's death in 1879. "*The fires are out*," wrote Stephens, "and let them stay so." Only Toombs shared as close a friendship with Stephens than Johnson through the years ahead.[39]

The elated Democrats waived baptismal rites for Stephens and Toombs and bestowed immediate confirmation. At their caucus on November 8, both men—and Linton Stephens—were placed on the resolutions committee to draw up platform planks for the upcoming state convention. A fearful new menace loomed up in the North—the Republican party, and against this danger the Georgia Democracy primed its guns. Congressman Alexander Stephens, Democrat, was about to enter the most tumultuous years of his career.

38. Milledgeville *Federal Union*, November 13, 1855.
39. Johnson to AHS, November 17, 1855, AHS to Johnson, April 19, 1856, both in Stephens Papers, LC.

XII

The Devil to Pay in Kansas

No sooner was Stephens back in Washington in late November, 1855, than he began complaining that public life was not "worth the candle." Not only was the cost of living too high, but he missed home, where both his farm and his expanding law practice demanded more of his time. But most galling about being in the capital was having to witness the perfidy of his fellow southerners, who in the midst of a bitter contest for the speakership were voting with the enemy.[1]

So many jumbled elements composed the House in December, 1855—Know Nothings, temperance men, avowed Republicans, anti-Nebraska and administration Democrats—that for the first time the *Congressional Globe* abandoned denoting members by political party. The administration, with only seventy-five to eighty supporters, lacked the requisite majority to organize the House. The opposition, however, could not agree on a candidate, so the contest for Speaker dragged on for two months and through 133 ballots before being resolved in favor of Nathaniel P. Banks, a Massachusetts Republican.

For Stephens, never a patient man, the contest was one long irritation. For some unknown reason, he did not attend the first Democratic

1. AHS to LS, November 30, 1855, in Stephens Papers, MC.

caucus on December 1, but he drew up the resolutions for the group and had them sent in. The caucus passed his resolutions unanimously—affirming the Kansas-Nebraska Act and deprecating Know Nothing secrecy and bigotry—and then it nominated William A. Richardson, the Illinois Democrat, as its candidate for Speaker.[2]

After 122 ballots, Richardson withdrew, and the Democrats shifted their support to James L. Orr of South Carolina. Throughout the balloting Banks consistently fell short of a majority by a dozen or so votes. The balance of power lay with thirty southern Know Nothings, doggedly voting for Henry M. Fuller, an anti-Nebraska former Whig from Pennsylvania. Although these southerners were as loath as their Democratic colleagues to help elect an antislavery Speaker, the Democrats had imperiously refused to strike any reasonable accommodation with them. Ill disposed to sacrifice themselves as a party, even for the sake of preventing Banks's election, the Americans reiterated their lone condition: the nomination of a "national" Democrat, that is, one not put up by the Democratic caucus, behind whom they could unite.

If Stephens' attitude is any indication of Democratic thinking, it is not difficult to understand the enmity between the two groups. To him, Banks was "the best specimen of Black Republican Fusionist" in the House, but he would as soon vote for him, he said, as for Fuller. But the Georgian recognized the political imperatives in the situation, and he was one man resourceful enough to break the impasse.[3]

As the weeks of fruitless balloting and furious bombast dragged on, it became obvious that the House would have to resort to the plurality rule, as it had in 1850, if it were ever to organize. Stephens had foreseen this possibility late in December, but not until a month later was he able to propose a plan Democrats would support. Customarily, when the House set aside majority rule, it would pass a resolution requiring three more ballots. If these failed to produce a winner, the candidate receiving the most votes on the next ballot would be declared Speaker. Stephens' plan was to nominate Democrat Warren Aiken of South Carolina at the last moment on the last ballot. Orr would then withdraw his own name, and the contest would be between Aiken and Banks. Quietly Stephens conferred with Democrats and southern Know Nothings. His scheme "took well," he reported.[4]

2. *Ibid.*, December 2, 1855.
3. *Ibid.*, December 11, 1855.
4. *Ibid.*, December 29, 1855, February 1, 1856.

But it went for naught: before the House adopted the plurality rule Alabama representative Williamson Cobb offered a straight resolution to make Aiken Speaker. It failed by a vote of 110 to 103. Stephens was livid at the "*blather skited* fool" who had foiled the plan. As it was, Banks was elected the next day by 103 votes to Aiken's 100. Southern Know Nothings had voted for Aiken at the crunch, but Fuller got half a dozen northern votes, enough to prevent Aiken's election. The vote had been "*purely sectional*," wrote Stephens angrily. Banks had not received a single southern vote. "The election of Banks," Toombs observed, "has given great hopes to our enemies, and their policy is dangerous in the extreme to us."[5]

It certainly was, from the southern point of view. Committed to preventing the extension of slavery into any part of the national domain, the Republicans had determined to prevail in the only part of that domain where the issue was still in doubt. The congressional struggle between the pro- and antislavery forces during the winter of 1855–1856 mirrored the more elemental struggle that had been raging in faraway Kansas almost since the passage of the Kansas-Nebraska Act.

Even before then, free-soil forces had been mobilizing to ensure their triumph in Kansas. In late April, 1854, Eli Thayer, a Massachusetts politician and entrepreneur, organized the Massachusetts Emigrant Aid Society to subsidize New England settlers traveling to Kansas. Although by the end of 1855 the society had transported only 1,240 settlers, it quickly became a *cause célèbre* among antislavery partisans and, in turn, an object of utmost suspicion and hatred among southerners.

Not least among these southerners stood the rough, hard-drinking, and violently proslavery population of northwestern Missouri. Not only did they consider eastern Kansas theirs by right of eminent domain (indeed, many had land claims there), they also judged it vital to the continuance of slavery in their own state. To safeguard the area, angry groups of border Missourians had convened during the summer of 1854 to form protective associations and vigilance committees.[6]

A chief organizer for one of these associations was none other than Senator David Atchison, who, it will be recalled, had staked his po-

5. *Ibid.*, February 4, 1856; *Congressional Globe*, 34th Cong., 1st Sess., Pt. 1, 334–35, 337; Toombs to Thomas, February 9, 1856, in Phillips (ed.), *TSC Correspondence*, 361.
6. The preceding paragraphs are from Nevins, *Ordeal of the Union*, II, 306–11.

litical future on the triumph of slavery in Kansas. He was blithely matter-of-fact about his intentions. Northern abolitionist hirelings would not be tolerated in Kansas: "We will before six months rolls round, have the Devil to play in Kansas and this State, we are organizing, to meet their organization we will be compelled, to shoot, burn & hang, but the thing will soon be over. we intend to 'Mormanise' the abolitionists."[7]

Most Kansas settlers hardly shared Atchison's passion on the slavery issue. They were probably far more intent on securing title to their land, much of which was encumbered by treaties with various Indian tribes. Undeterred, settlers had simply moved in and staked out claims, but disputes inevitably arose between rival claimants, and the slavery issue exacerbated the problem. Individual settlers thus became symbols of opposing socioeconomic systems, pawns in a gigantic sectional struggle for stakes far beyond the simple possession of their own little plots of farmland. "We are playing for a mighty stake," growled Atchison, "if we win we carry slavery to the Pacific Ocean if we fail we lose Missouri Arkansas and Texas and all the territories."[8]

With both sections of the Union viewing the Kansas struggle as apocalyptic, any governor would have been hard-pressed to maintain order and rule judiciously. Unfortunately, neither of Pierce's first two appointees proved equal to the task. The first, Andrew H. Reeder, who arrived in Kansas in October, 1854, promptly alienated the proslavery element by delaying elections for a territorial legislature until spring to allow a census of the territory to be taken, a necessary step in establishing the number of qualified voters.

Five thousand heavily armed Missourians made a mockery of the February census, however, by crossing into Kansas the following month and casting ballots. Some sixteen hundred of these so-called "border ruffians" had entered Kansas the previous November and cast ballots for the territorial delegate to Congress. Thus by March, 1855, the Kansas territory had "elected" a proslavery legislature and congressional delegate.

Reeder, fearing for his life, allowed two-thirds of the fraudulent March ballots to stand and then left for the East to seek the president's

7. D. R. Atchison to Jefferson Davis, September 24, 1854, in Jefferson Davis Papers, DU.

8. Atchison to Hunter, March 4, 1855, in Ambler (ed.), *Hunter Correspondence*, 161.

support. With the press of both sections in an uproar, Pierce temporized. When he failed to convince Reeder to resign, he allowed him to return to Kansas. Upon the governor's return, the new legislature, over his repeated vetoes, proceeded to shackle slavery onto the territory, adopting Missouri's slave code and passing draconian laws to punish anyone speaking against slavery, harboring fugitives, or aiding slaves to escape. The assembly then expelled its few free-soil members and petitioned the president for Reeder's removal. With some of the governor's shaky land speculations as pretext, Pierce complied. The free-soilers were furious. The removal, raged Thomas Hart Benton, was "the lawless destruction of every principle in the Nebraska act." [9]

Reeder's successor was Wilson Shannon, former governor of Ohio, minister to Mexico, and congressman, and an even worse appointment than Reeder. He immediately sided with the proslavery forces, prompting the free-soil settlers to set up a territorial government of their own. After establishing the Free State party and repudiating the "bogus" legislature, the free-soilers convened in Topeka and drew up an antislavery constitution. By January, 1856, in elections in which only free-soil voters participated, the constitution had been "ratified" and a "legislature" and "governor" chosen, and by March this legislature had taken steps preparatory to statehood. [10]

It was against this backdrop of fraud and lawlessness in Kansas that Congress met in December, 1855. Fully aroused to their peril, southerners were putting intense pressure on their legislators to maintain the proslavery cause. Georgians, for example, were being urged to form emigration societies of their own, and southern representatives were being pointedly reminded of "what may be lost by their unworthiness." [11]

Georgia Know Nothings gleefully seized on the Kansas issue at their December convention, branding the Kansas-Nebraska Act as dangerous to southern institutions and excoriating the Democrats for devising it. Clearly southern Democrats were vulnerable to the charge: if Kansas came into the Union as a free state, any connection with the

9. Kansas narrative from James E. Rawley, *Race and Politics: "Bleeding Kansas" and the Coming of the Civil War* (Philadelphia, 1969), 86–92; Thomas H. Benton to Clayton, August 2, 1855, in Clayton Papers, LC.

10. Rawley, *Race and Politics*, 92–95.

11. Columbus *Times* and Charleston *Courier* quoted in Savannah *Daily News*, October 9, 29, 1855.

Douglas and administration forces might well prove a fatal political liability. Stephens, of course, recognized this danger. He, like other Democrats, had dangled the prospect of a new slave state before the voters during the last campaign. The confused and menacing Kansas situation cried for a clear, unequivocal interpretation of popular sovereignty. What good was the doctrine if in practice it led to the election of two territorial delegates to Congress—John W. Whitfield, elected with the aid of sixteen hundred illegal Missouri voters in December, 1854, and Andrew H. Reeder, chosen by the free-soilers in an illegal election the following fall?[12]

Both men were now in Washington demanding admission to the House as Kansas' only legal representative. Southern Democrats had only one choice: to uphold Whitfield's election, however spurious, at all costs. If they didn't do so, political disaster loomed at home. If Kansas came in as a free state, Thomas W. Thomas warned Stephens, "the true southern rights party, of which I consider you and Toombs the head and front—will go down." Only success would satisfy the masses on this question. The Know Nothings at home had branded the Kansas-Nebraska Act a free-soil measure. Proving that the status of Kansas was truly antislavery and "that the repeal [of the Missouri Compromise] gave us at least a chance" would be fruitless, Thomas continued. The Know Nothings "will bring up their prophecies and the result and all the reasoning and truth in the world cannot withstand the effect that will be made upon the popular mind. . . . The effect will be the utter prostration of every man at the South who has stood up for us and the complete triumph of a set of traitors and fools."[13]

Stephens didn't need the warning. He had already taken steps to protect both himself and his party during a debate on January 17, 1856, with Felix Zollicoffer, a Tennessee Know Nothing. Southern Know Nothings had charged that the Kansas-Nebraska Act enacted squatter sovereignty, a charge Stephens hotly denied. At issue was the hoary question of congressional power over territorial slavery, always important but now under a different guise. Direct congressional power

12. Luke Fain Crutcher, III, "Disunity and Dissolution: The Georgia Parties and the Crisis of the Union, 1859–1861" (Ph.D. dissertation, University of California, Los Angeles, 1974), 28–29.

13. Thomas to AHS, February 25, 1856, in Phillips (ed.), *TSC Correspondence*, 362.

had supposedly been settled by the Kansas-Nebraska Act. But enacting popular sovereignty had raised a host of other troublesome questions: when would the people be permitted to exercise the power of excluding slavery? And from whence did they derive the power? From the Constitution? From Congress? From their own inherent sovereignty?

Stephens had no trouble providing answers. Contention in such abstract realms never failed to stir his greatest powers of legalistic and rhetorical inventiveness. Zollicoffer had contended that Congress had no constitutional power over slavery in the territories; therefore, southerners who had voted to extend the Missouri Compromise had sanctioned a violation of the Constitution. He had never maintained that Congress had the "general original power" over territorial slavery, Stephens retorted. On the contrary, he had pledged to resist any attempt by Congress to exercise such power. But he had supported extending the Missouri line as "an alternative," a compromise based on an equitable division of common territory. Congress could, under these circumstances only, exercise a constitutional power to exclude slavery from territories. But just because it could in this case did not mean it had the unlimited power to exclude slavery totally: "I deny, *in toto*, the existence of such unlimited or unqualified power in Congress."[14]

For the first time Stephens allowed himself to be drawn into public debate on the question of congressional power over slavery, a subject he had studiously avoided till now. What he said was consistent with ideas he had held since at least 1846. He had already told Linton privately that he had always opposed the Wilmot Proviso because he believed "there was something in it," that the Supreme Court would declare the proviso constitutional if the question were ever tested. Then he had been on firmer logical grounds. His death-grip embrace of popular sovereignty—not to mention the many times he had voted for extension of the Missouri Compromise—had foreclosed consistency, however. So he was forced into an argument so attenuated and sophistic that people not inclined to dance with angels on the head of a pin found impossible to accept. Either Congress possessed the power, or it did not—Calhoun's position exactly.[15]

Zollicoffer, who pressed Stephens into some snappish replies to repeated questions, could not understand the Georgian's position. For

14. Cleveland, *Stephens*, 489–94.
15. AHS to LS, January 6, 1855, in Stephens Papers, MC.

what he argued essentially was that Congress could constitutionally exercise a power it did not constitutionally possess, and even then it could exercise it only over half a territory and under particular circumstances.

These dialectical gymnastics were but prelude. The formation of the free-soil government in Topeka had wrenched the question of squatter sovereignty out of the theoretical realms and down to earth. For if the people of the territory were to be left entirely free under the Kansas-Nebraska Act to determine their own domestic institutions (as Stephens had so strenuously argued in the past), could it not be contended (as indeed thousands of northerners did) that the Topeka constitution and the government elected under it were true expressions of the people's will? Not by Stephens' lights. To him squatter sovereignty meant the "*inherent and sovereign right*" of settlers on common domain to establish governments for themselves, "without looking to Congress, and independently of Congress." This idea was nonsense, Stephens said. The Kansas-Nebraska Act had "not a particle" of squatter sovereignty in it. "Their whole organic law emanates from Congress. . . . Every department and the whole machinery of their government proceeded from Congress." As for the people's power over slavery in Kansas, the bill gave them only "the power that Congress had over it, and no more." The people had no power at all, then, it would seem.

But he added a startling qualification. Whatever the people of a territory did about slavery—whether they protected or excluded it or simply left it without protection—"I should for myself abide by their acts." Several congressmen had become confused by now. Where did the people get the power to exclude slavery, asked one, if Congress did not have it and the people possessed only those powers that Congress had given them? They possessed it, Stephens replied, "only in a State capacity, or when they form their State constitution." In the territorial condition the people were "but new States in *embryo*" with only a "latent power of full sovereignty," which did not develop until "the proper time," like the butterfly from the chrysalis. The image was a pretty one, but Stephens had dodged the question by the old rhetorical trick of arguing by analogy.

All this was beside the point, Stephens went on to say. For the sake of the public peace he was willing to be magnanimous. If the people's power to exclude slavery was not theirs "by absolute right," he would grant it to them "as a matter of favor." The House ought to drop the question because the people could dispose of it so much better. All he demanded was "a fair expression of the popular will" unaffected by "emigrant aid societies, or other improper interference."[16]

Just how magnanimous Stephens intended to be soon became apparent. Widespread violence in Kansas had been threatening for months, and with the new year came news that the free-soilers in Kansas had proceeded with their elections. Kansas now had two governors, two legislatures, and two territorial delegates. Civil war now seemed as inevitable as the spring thaw. On January 24, 1856, a distressed president sent an angry special message to Congress. Pierce laid most of the blame for the unrest on his own, now defrocked, appointee Governor Reeder and on the abolitionists with their "propagandist colonization." Although frauds in the election of the legislature were likely, he admitted, the governor's decisions on the returns were not only final but a matter of local jurisdiction as well. Pierce saved his strongest language for the Topeka movement, branding it "revolutionary" and, if it attempted to oppose the national authority, "a treasonable insurrection." Although suppressing insurrection would require force, he continued, it was not his duty to use force "to preserve the purity of elections" or to question the wisdom or justice of territorial laws. Despite his purposeful tone, however, the only solution Pierce could recommend was for Congress to pass an enabling act for the formation of a state constitution in Kansas.[17]

The president was just as inept a few days after his message when the free-soil government in Topeka pleaded with him for protection from the Missourians. The president responded by issuing a proclamation ordering all irregular combinations in Kansas to disperse. All good citizens should help suppress violence, Pierce urged, and he put the troops at Forts Leavenworth and Riley at Governor Shannon's disposal.[18]

The House, too, was up to its neck in Kansas problems. No sooner had it organized than Andrew Reeder presented his credentials as the legal representative of the territory. Whitfield's election was void, he claimed. It had been accomplished by hundreds of illegal votes and under the laws of a legislature that was itself a creature of fraud and

16. The preceding paragraphs are from Cleveland, *Stephens*, 510–12.
17. *Congressional Globe*, 34th Cong., 1st Sess., Pt. 1, 296–98.
18. Nichols, *Pierce*, 443–44.

violence. The House, after two months of wrangling over the speakership, now launched into six months of disputation over the untying of this latest Gordian knot. Like his Macedonian namesake, Alexander Stephens preferred to solve the puzzle with a single bold stroke—that is, to deny any dispute, any puzzle at all. Unfortunately for the Georgian, however, his sword lacked the requisite keenness: although the ranking Democrat on the House Committee on Elections, Stephens was in the minority.[19]

Nevertheless, he threw himself energetically into opposing Reeder's claim. On February 19, 1856, when the committee majority requested authorization of the House to call for persons and papers in its investigation (that is, to go behind the returns), Stephens opposed the resolution in a biting little speech. How absurd, he said, that Reeder should claim Whitfield's election invalid when he himself, as governor, had certified the election of the legislature whose law he now pronounced invalid. Stephens saw no need to investigate anything; the validity of the law in question was plain. The House disagreed and refused to recommit the resolution to committee, but the session ended before any further action could be taken.[20]

At stake was far more than the legal claims of Reeder and Whitfield. Recognition of either man legitimized the government he represented. Clear-thinking southerners, away from the capital's charged atmospher, could see that resistance to the investigation was bad policy. The South should show impartiality and "faith in its own cause," wrote one, by allowing the House to investigate. Resistance did not promise to halt an investigation anyway.[21]

Impartiality was the last thing Stephens and the southern Democrats in Congress wanted, however. Haunted by the threat of Know Nothing ascendancy at home if popular sovereignty failed to deliver the slave state they had so rashly promised, they craved only victory. And to achieve it they were prepared, even as Atchison's ruffians, to use whatever means were necessary. On March 5, the House Committee on Elections renewed its request for authorization to investigate the election and present its report. Stephens, who had been up till two in the morning writing the minority's report—"blindly," he angrily told Lin-

19. *Congressional Globe*, 34th Cong., 1st Sess., Pt. 1, 427.
20. *Ibid.*, 455–58.
21. George D. Prentiss to Clayton, February 28, 1856, in Clayton Papers, LC.

ton, because the "knaves" of the majority had refused to let him see their report—read his own first. Reeder's case was insufficient, it said. By settled House precedent, mere evidence of illegal votes was not enough to unseat a member. A contestant must prove that he himself had received more *legal* votes. Reeder did not even pretend to have accomplished this, basing his claim instead on denying the legal authority under which Whitfield had been elected. But the House lacked jurisdiction in this matter. By similarly long-established principle, legislative bodies themselves were the only proper authorities to settle questions about their own membership. The House could consider the validity of Kansas laws, Stephens acknowledged, but not by probing the membership and elections of the legislature that passed those laws.[22]

Stephens' excellent legal argument was, of course, entirely secondary to which side wielded the power at the moment, a proposition as true in Congress as in Kansas. And in the House the antislavery coalition commanded the votes. Realizing this, Stephens was in a foul mood when he rose on March 11 to deliver yet another speech against investigating in Kansas. Neither the compliments he received after the speech nor the presence of one of the largest crowds in House history pleased him. "I spoke with perfect indifference and contempt of the whole concern," he said.[23]

But he did not sound indifferent, for the speech was long, learned, and, at the end, bitter. The real culprits behind the Kansas agitation, he charged, were "the original enemies of the Kansas bill," still determined to cause strife and discord. Having lost at the polls, they now resorted to physical force and collecting arms, money, and volunteers in open "hostility to the existing legally-constituted authorities. . . . "What is this but treason?" he exclaimed.[24]

What one Georgia editor considered Stephens' "unanswerable argument" didn't deter the House majority. On March 19 it appointed a three-man committee (two Republicans, one Democrat) to go to Kansas, collect evidence, and make inquiries—not only on the disputed election but on the whole Kansas problem. Disgusted and beaten, Stephens left for home to attend the spring court sessions.[25]

22. AHS to LS, March 4, 11, 1856, in Stephens Papers, MC; *House Reports*, 34th Cong., 1st Sess., No. 3 (Serial 868).
23. AHS to LS, March 11, 1856, in Stephens Papers, MC.
24. Cleveland, *Stephens*, 515–31.
25. Milledgeville *Federal Union*, April 8, 1856.

While the House debated, administration forces in the Senate had been preparing a statehood bill for Kansas. In due time Douglas' Committee on the Territories reported a routine bill, which was introduced on March 17, 1856. Free-soilers spurned the bill, however, because it left the Kansas government in the hands of Shannon and the proslavery legislature for an indefinite period. Their spokesman William H. Seward proposed an equally unacceptable solution: the admission of Kansas under the free-soil constitution drawn up by the illegal government at Topeka. Congress was at an impasse.[26]

Springtime returned to the plains of Kansas, and with it the final shattering of the fragile peace between two heavily armed groups of settlers. The proslavery men struck first. On May 21, 1856, a sheriff's posse of hundreds of whiskey-fueled Missourians, armed with indictments, arrest warrants for three free-soil leaders, and no fewer than five cannon, rode into the free-soil stronghold of Lawrence. Thwarted in its attempt to make the arrests, the posse contented itself instead with destroying the presses and type of the town's newspapers and burning and looting the town. Amazingly, only one person was killed—a proslavery man, accidentally crushed by a falling wall. Three days after this outrage, a fifty-six-year-old abolitionist fanatic named John Brown took revenge for the free-soilers. On the night of May 24, 1856, he led a self-proclaimed "Northern army" of eight men through the darkness to the banks of an insignificant stream called Pottawatomie Creek. Within an hour or so five proslavery men had been marched unarmed from their homes and hacked to death with swords.[27]

The massacre ignited the Kansas tinderbox. Within days violence convulsed the territory. Shootings became common. Armed bands of men rode freely over the countryside burning, pillaging, and killing. A desperate Governor Shannon issued a proclamation against the violence, which both sides ignored as they poured reinforcements and munitions into the territory. As the nation prepared to choose its fifteenth president, "Bleeding Kansas" dominated the news.

Bloodshed was not restricted to the territory. The war in Kansas had its analogue on the floor of the United States Senate. During the week of the Pottawatomie murders and the sack of Lawrence, Senator Charles Sumner, a Massachusetts Republican, was beaten senseless at

26. Johannsen, *Douglas*, 495.
27. Nevins, *Ordeal of the Union*, II, 434–36; 474–75.

his desk by a South Carolina congressman. The Republican party could scarcely have hoped for a more spectacular incident with which to indict the barbarous slaveocracy.

What occasioned the attack was Sumner's two-day speech, begun on May 19 and entitled "The Crime against Kansas." Throughout it had crackled with Sumner's indignation at the depredations of the slave power in Kansas and the "infamous" and "absurd" apologies being offered for them. But Sumner had far transcended the boundaries of propriety and tradition by grossly insulting, sometimes in lurid sexual imagery, three of his colleagues: Andrew P. Butler of South Carolina, Douglas, and James M. Mason of Virginia—not to mention the entire state of South Carolina, which was accused of "shameful imbecility" for its devotion to slavery.[28]

Even less rigorous codes than that of southern chivalry demanded a reply to this phillipic. Douglas, Mason, and Cass all rose to excoriate Sumner for his disgraceful performance. But Butler was absent, so after two days of brooding, his kinsman, Representative Preston Brooks, raised not his voice but his gutta percha cane in Butler's defense. Walking up to Sumner's desk in the Senate, Brooks announced his intentions and then rained almost thirty blows upon Sumner's head, shattering the cane, knocking his helpless victim unconscious, and creating a martyr—all in about thirty seconds.[29]

The repercussions of the attack were ominous. Shock and outrage swept the North. Hundreds of protest meetings and rallies denounced "Bully Brooks" and his outrage on free speech. Reaction in the Republican press was frenzied. Like almost all the Republican editors, Horace Greeley portrayed the assault as the first step of a foully conceived plan of attack by the entire slaveholding South on the democratic, freedom-loving North.[30]

But the southern press hardly stood as a model of detached, objective journalism. In South Carolina, Brooks, inundated with canes from thoughtful admirers, was lionized, feted, and praised; the state press almost universally proclaimed him a hero. Only a few southern papers questioned Brooks's "honorable" intentions, although some editors expressed reservations about the time, place, and manner of the as-

28. *Congressional Globe*, 34th Cong., 1st Sess., Appendix, 529–47, 1119.
29. David Donald, *Charles Sumner and the Coming of the Civil War* (New York, 1960), 289–311.
30. Avery Craven, *The Coming of the Civil War* (rev. ed., Chicago, 1957), 369.

sault. The Milledgeville *Federal Union,* for example, regretted the place of the attack but also maintained that for some kinds of slander "no office or station should protect a man from deserved punishment." The Columbus *Enquirer,* on the other hand, thought the attack "disgraceful" and sure to inflame the South's enemies.[31]

A few southerners had an even more rarefied conception of honor. Gazaway Lamar, a prosperous Savannah banker, told Cobb that Brooks had "so outraged decency, propriety and manliness" that he should be expelled from the House. He too foresaw disaster if the South attempted to sustain the act. Lamar's voice, however, was a single puppy's yap in a pack of baying hounds. And in the middle of the pack were two of Georgia's most influential legislators. "Brooks whipped Sumner the other day," Stephens reported casually. "It is all right *me judice.* The abolitionist[s] howl over it—and cry out for liberty of speech. I have no objection to the liberty of speech when the liberty of the cudgel is left free to combat it." Toombs was even more callous. "The yankees seem greatly excited about the Sumner flogging," he said. "They are afraid the practice may become general & many of [their] heads already feel sore. Sumner takes a beating badly. He is said to be ill, tho' I don't believe it." Later, during a Senate investigation of the incident, Toombs said flatly that he "approved" of Brooks's action.[32]

A third influential Georgian, Cobb, served on the House's investigating committee. Although the committee majority voted to expel Brooks, Cobb chose not to follow Lamar's advice. He wrote the committee's minority report denying that the House had jurisdiction over the conduct of its members outside the hall. After heated debate, the House eventually voted, 121 to 95, to expel Brooks. But the vote fell short of the required two-thirds majority. Stephens and every other southerner but one voted against the expulsion. Brooks resigned his seat after the House vote but returned to it, triumphantly reelected, seven weeks later.[33]

While the country attempted to digest the overabundance of depressing and infuriating news, Congress was trying to get Kansas admitted

31. Milledgeville *Federal Union,* June 3, 1856; Columbus *Enquirer,* June 3, 1856.
32. Gazaway B. Lamar to Cobb, May 31, 1856, in Phillips (ed.), *TSC Correspondence,* 366; AHS to Thomas, May 25, 1856, in Stephens Papers, EU; Toombs to Crawford, May 30, 1856, in Toombs Papers, LC.
33. *Congressional Globe,* 34th Cong., 1st Sess., 1305, 1628.

as a state. To counter Douglas' bill in the Senate, free-soilers in both houses had introduced bills to admit Kansas under the Topeka constitution. It was altogether more likely at the moment that Henry Clay would rise from his grave to propose another Union-saving compromise than that either of these proposed solutions to the Kansas problem would pass both houses of Congress.

On June 24, however, the most constructive piece of legislation yet proposed came from an altogether unlikely source. As early as April, Toombs had despaired of passing the Douglas bill, but by June he had devised, with the Little Giant's approval, what appeared to be an ideal way out of the impasse. His bill provided for direct federal supervision (by a five-man presidentially appointed commission) of the preliminary stages of state making: the census and registration of voters. Delegates to a constitutional convention, elected by these voters, would meet in November and draw up the governing document. Congress would then admit the state immediately under whatever constitution, free or slave, had been submitted. To safeguard against unlawful incursions by the Missourians, election day for the convention would be set to coincide with the presidential election day. A week after Toombs introduced his bill, Stephens introduced an identical one in the House as a substitute for the free state measure there.[34]

Not only might the Toombs measure have worked, it offered southerners the undeniable advantage of blunting the Republicans' most potent issue in the upcoming presidential campaign. Both Stephens and Toombs were privately convinced that the South had a majority of the legal voters and actual residents in Kansas. Firsthand reports from their Kansas informant had not only stressed this point but had even contended that the House investigation committee's report would uphold the southern settlers. Proslavery Kansans were confident about their prospects, Stephens told Linton.[35]

Southern prospects in Congress, however, weren't nearly so rosy. After a bitter all-night struggle, the Toombs bill passed the Senate by a vote of 33 to 12, but the House barely considered it. The day after the Toombs bill passed the Senate, the House, by a close vote, passed a bill to admit Kansas under the Topeka constitution.

Several days before, on June 28, Stephens had delivered a long,

34. Toombs to Crawford, April 26, 1856, in Toombs Papers, DU.
35. AHS to LS, June 26, 1856, in Stephens Papers, MC.

closely attended speech in the House in support of his own bill. All he wanted, he said, was "a fair expression of the will of the *bona fide* residents of Kansas," which would naturally be ensured by the Toombs measure. Who could object, he asked, to dealing with the problem "upon principles of fairness, of justice, of law, of order, and the constitution?" Many were objecting, as Stephens well knew. The Republican party had recently met in its first national convention. All its clamor about "bleeding Kansas," he charged, was transparently political and sectional. Republicans meant to alienate one portion of the Union from the other. "Are you going to allow this subject to be used for such purposes?" he asked.[36]

The Republicans certainly did intend to use the Kansas question, even though some of them admitted the fairness of Toombs's bill. Had their suspicions of Pierce and Douglas been the only forces operating against the bill, it still might have passed. But their party platform had flatly declared against any further extension of slavery. Any bill allowing a territory to choose slavery, no matter how slight the possibility that it would, violated the party's cardinal tenet. Seward spoke for all Republicans when he said he would never allow Kansans the "ruinous privilege of choosing an evil and a curse." He neglected to say that for Republicans the Kansas question offered too many political benefits to allow its settlement on the eve of a presidential election. "They do not mean that there shall be peace," said Douglas bitterly. "An angel from heaven could not write a bill to restore peace in Kansas that would be acceptable to the Abolition Republican party previous to the presidential election."[37]

Douglas was right. The Kansas issue had been sucked into presidential politics. By July, when the Toombs bill failed in the House, three parties were in the field. The Know Nothing party had been the first to enter the contest. Having already fallen into disarray over the slavery question, the party split completely when its national convention gathered in February of 1856. Southerners and a few northerners

36. Speech in Cleveland, *Stephens*, 531–60.

37. Van Deusen, *Seward*, 172–73; Johannsen, *Douglas*, 527. Toombs's bill even appealed to some Know Nothings. Preeminent racists in a racist society, northern Know Nothings deplored Republican intransigence. "The people are heartily sick of the 'nigger worshipping' party," wrote one. "All conservative men thus may favor the settlement of the Kansas question in some such way as is proposed by the bill of Tombs" (James McCallum to J. Scott Harrison, July 15, 1856, in J. Scott Harrison Papers, LC).

defeated a resolution favoring restoration of the Missouri Compromise. This vote precipitated a walkout by eight northern delegations, who met separately and issued a call for another convention. The rump of the original body nominated Millard Fillmore for president, causing more northerners to withdraw. The American party had failed to survive even its first national convention.

Conversely, the Republicans gathered for their first convention in mid-July in an atmosphere of revivalistic fervor. The party platform, thunderously endorsed, declared the right of Congress to bar from the territories "those twin relics of barbarism—slavery and polygamy," demanded admission of Kansas as a free state, and called for construction of a government-subsidized railroad to the Pacific. As its candidate, the party selected forty-three-year-old John C. Frémont. Frémont was little known in politics but had achieved a modicum of fame as an explorer and soldier in the Mexican War and for his romantic marriage to Jessie Benton, the beautiful and gifted daughter of Missouri's former senator.[38]

The Democrats had held their own nominating convention six weeks earlier in Cincinnati. For months Stephens had been engaged in a favorite election-year sport—attempting to guess the party's nominee. During the winter Stephens had thought it "bad policy" to supplant Pierce, but he really didn't "give a fig" who was nominated. It was the principles involved—sustaining the proslavery government in Kansas—that he considered most important. Thomas R. R. Cobb, in the capital in early March to lobby for a southern candidate (his brother, perhaps?), reported both Stephens and Toombs "very warm for Pierce," with Douglas as their second choice. But by the eve of the convention, Stephens had changed his preference to Douglas, "an original friend of the Kansas bill." But Pierce was all right too. So was James Buchanan of Pennsylvania, "one of the soundest states in the Union" because of its support of the Kansas-Nebraska bill.[39]

Stephens, supposedly so concerned with principles, was thinking exactly like a back room manager. Although not at the convention, he doubtless would have fit in perfectly. The conclave was a manager's affair from beginning to end, with Buchanan's lieutenants eventually suc-

38. Platform quoted in Nevins, *Ordeal of the Union*, II, 462.
39. AHS to Thomas, February 29, 1856, in Stephens Papers, DU; Thomas R. R. Cobb to Cobb, May 25, 1856, March 4, 1856, in Cobb-Erwin-Lamar Papers, UG; AHS to Thomas, May 25, 1856, in Stephens Papers, LC.

ceeding in the back room bargaining. Playing up Buchanan's lack of identification with the Kansas problem—a claim Pierce and Douglas could not make—and his long experience in government, Buchanan's forces put him over on the seventeenth ballot. Douglas had withdrawn to avoid prolonged and heated deadlock; and to mollify both him and his southern supporters, the convention had nominated for vice-president a handsome, elegantly mustachioed, bourbon-loving Kentuckian, John C. Breckinridge. The platform, too, was all Douglas—or Stephens—could have wished. It affirmed the Compromise of 1850 and praised the Kansas-Nebraska Act as the only sound and safe solution to the slavery question.[40]

Stephens, unlike his friend Thomas W. Thomas, was perfectly satisfied with the candidate. Thomas considered Buchanan nothing but a low political charlatan willing to sell out southern rights in Kansas to conciliate northern free-soilers, and he hated the nominee with ferocious passion. Supporting such a man, he warned Stephens, would be courting political ruin.[41]

Little Aleck did his best to allay his friend's fears. In glaring contrast to his demands for party purity in the early 1850s, Stephens now professed himself willing to affiliate with anyone committed to the Kansas-Nebraska Act as the basis for present and future territorial policy. And why not? His demands for party purity in 1850 and afterward had been visionary but of no personal or political consequence to him. He belonged to no national party but stood safely atop a powerful state organization. The issue had been cleaner then: union or disunion, for the compromise—the one guarantee against the unspeakable catastrophe of disunion—or against it. Now, however, the situation was different. Political disaster at home loomed as a real possibility. And popular sovereignty in Kansas was a real issue, not a theoretical abstraction being applied to the deserts of New Mexico and Utah. The Kansas-Nebraska Act, in his eyes, belonged to him—personally—quite as much as it did to his party. If it failed, he would be proven wrong, a public humiliation he could never allow.

So it was enough that Buchanan and every man of the party supported the bill. "To get the whole country" similarly committed, he said, "is the height of my ambition." The coming election would be an

40. Roy Franklin Nichols, *The Disruption of American Democracy* (1948; rpr. New York, 1967), 17–31.
41. Thomas to AHS, June 11, 1856, in Stephens Papers, EU.

"almost death struggle" between "the friends of the Union under the constitution" and the "open and avowed enemies of both." Duty, therefore, demanded that he support Buchanan, and he could not care less, he said, if it brought about his own political downfall.[42]

There was little danger that supporting the nominee would have so dire a result, even in Georgia, where Douglas sentiment was strong and the Know Nothings were preparing an energetic campaign. Every day more and more southerners were realizing that the Democracy offered their last safe haven and that the coming campaign would be almost a death struggle. Evidence of this perilous situation screamed out of the daily papers, whose pages bristled with reports of the civil war in Kansas and of the interminable Kansas fracas in Congress.

At the moment, the congressional fracas occupied almost all Stephens' time. The House investigating committee had returned to Washington. The report of the two Republican members, made public on July 1, 1856, upheld their party's position in every particular. The bitter dissent of the committee's lone Democrat was just as partisan, but through it the nation learned the gruesome details of the Pottawatomie killings. This information had not the slightest effect on the majority of the Committee on Elections, which, it will be recalled, had been grappling with the Whitfield-Reeder dispute since February. On July 24, it, too, brought in its expected report declaring Whitfield not entitled to his seat because his election had been "without authority of law." Reeder's election had been too, the report continued, but he *was* entitled to the seat because he was "the choice of a much larger number of [Kansas] residents." On the twenty-seventh, therefore, the committee offered resolutions to seat the free-soil representative.[43]

Stephens, the minority's spokesman, savagely attacked the majority opinion both in his own report and in a speech he delivered against the resolutions on July 31. He had spent a week digesting the mass of testimony gathered in Kansas, and it had "not changed the merits of the case one iota." With the majority report before him, he proceeded to dissect the testimony—"sift it a little"—with characteristic thoroughness and legal analysis. Naturally, after the sifting not a single committee conclusion stood. Stephens argued as he had before: bare proof of illegal voting was insufficient to set aside an election. To do

42. AHS to Thomas, June 16, 1856, in Phillips (ed.), *TSC Correspondence*, 367–72.
43. *House Reports*, 34th Cong., 1st Sess., No. 200 (Serial 869).

this, he said, it must be proved that illegal votes had been cast and had actually changed the result. The committee had done neither. His own painstaking analysis of Kansas census reports had indicated that in February, 1855, southern settlers had outnumbered northern ones. These data proved, at least to his own satisfaction, that the result "upon all reasonable and rational grounds" would not have changed. After some obligatory swipes at the Republicans as the true cause of Kansas' troubles, he pleaded once again for passage of the tabled Toombs bill and for faithful application of the principles of the Kansas-Nebraska Act.[44]

The speech "took well," Stephens told Linton. It obviously had among Democrats: House members quickly ordered fifty thousand copies for campaign use, and there was talk of having one hundred thousand more printed. Stephens' logic did not convince the Republicans, however. The day after his speech, the House voted to unseat Whitfield. But then, spurning the election committee's logic too, the majority refused to seat Reeder. After eight months of discussion, investigation, and debate, the Kansas delegate's seat still stood empty. The Kansas problem was no nearer solution than it had been in December.[45]

Meanwhile, Kansas Governor Shannon had celebrated the Fourth of July by using federal forces from Leavenworth to disperse the Topeka legislature. The purge proved to be his undoing. An embarrassed administration disavowed his action, and in late July Pierce replaced him with John W. Geary of Pennsylvania. Geary did not depart immediately for the frontier. Furious at Shannon's action, House Republicans had tacked an amendment onto a routine army appropriations bill forbidding the president use of federal troops to enforce the territorial laws of Kansas. The new appointee understandably declined to descend into a pit of vipers without protection. The Senate had stricken the rider, but the House had reinstated it, and three separate conference committees had failed to resolve the matter. With it still unresolved on August 18, the day set for adjournment, Speaker Banks allowed things to stand as they were and adjourned the House *sine die*. Pierce, not about to let Kansas completely shackle the army in the territory, promptly called a special session to deal with the appropria-

---

44. *Ibid.*, No. 275 (Serial 870); *Congressional Globe*, 34th Cong., 1st Sess., Appendix, 1070–76. Illegal votes had not been proven, Stephens contended, because the committee had simply asserted them, not giving numbers or where they had been cast.

45. AHS to LS, August 2, 1856, in Stephens Papers, MC.

tions bill. This unusual presidential resolve angered even most Democrats. They, like their opponents, preferred to leave the issue just where it was and use it during the campaign.[46]

Not the least upset was Congressman Stephens, already on his way to the Potomac docks for a steamship south when he got news of the president's call. Court cases at home required his attention, but "*I must stay*," he wrote. No loyalty to Pierce prompted him; he had lost all faith in the president. "The miserable little creature in the White House is lapsing back into his original [Kansas] policy," he told Linton. To prevent such a "relapse," Stephens, unlike Toombs, endured the steamy confines of Washington for yet another twelve days.[47]

The apparent indifference of his southern colleagues got Stephens more than a little overheated himself during the ensuing session. Absent congressmen were bad enough; southern congressmen so drunk they missed votes were intolerable. Because of them the bill, or votes to reconsider it, was several times lost. "I sometimes fear the glory of the South has departed," Stephens fumed. "A miserable set of drunken *debauchees* fill the places once filled by statesmen."[48]

While Stephens raged, the House refused to retreat from its rider. Another conference committee, on which Stephens served, got nowhere. Finally, on August 30, shortly before the scheduled adjournment, two Know Nothings changed their votes and enough Democrats were scraped up to pass the army bill without amendment. So Pierce had his way, the country had its unfettered army, and Congress at last had respite from the heat and frustration of one of its most fruitless sessions on record. There would be no respite from politics, however. The presidential campaign was in full swing. Stephens, like most of his colleagues, fully appreciated its importance. But as he hurried back to Georgia in early September he had even more important personal matters on his mind—duties that even the fate of the republic must await.

For two and a half months these matters had been weighing heavily on him. On June 16, his brother John had died of apoplexy in LaGrange. He left a wife, six children, two slaves, more than $43,500 in debts—and one grief-stricken older brother. Indeed, only shortly before John's death, Aleck had severely scolded him for his conduct of a

46. Nichols, *Pierce*, 478–79.
47. AHS to LS, August 19, 1856, in Stephens Papers, MC.
48. *Ibid.*, August 24, 1856.

lawsuit. To this characteristically testy blast John had replied with re-
pentant submission, promising to try "to conform to your view of
things" in the future. These were the last words Stephens ever heard
from John.[49]

John Stephens was now well beyond the reach of Aleck's anger—and
his remorse. He was "overwhelmed with grief," he told Linton, and
suffering all the more because he had often lost his temper with John:
"If I could recall any unkind word, look or reproof ever given it would
afford me relief as well as consolation." Denied this opportunity, he
resolved to help John's family as much as he could. Immediately upon
learning of his death, he decided to adopt John's entire family.[50]

Stephens had determined to take this step before learning that his
brother's will had entrusted that very task to him. He was named not
only executor but sole heir and manager of his brother's meager estate
and virtual guardian of his children. Despite the severe pressures of
campaigning, by November Stephens had untangled John's debts (clearing over two thousand dollars worth with his own money), moved the
family from LaGrange, and installed them in a house he bought for
them in Crawfordville. He remembered only too well the suffering the
breakup of his own family had caused. He refused to let it happen to
John's family.[51]

In his initial shock over his brother's death, Stephens had canceled a
speech in New York and had intimated that he might not speak at all
during the summer. But he couldn't stay off the stump for even a
month. On July 16, he made a speech in Alexandria, Virginia, and
early in August he spoke again at Chambersburg, Pennsylvania. He
was evidently in fine form. Even though one observer was astounded
by his appearance—"a well-preserved mummy"—he thought Stephens "an unusually earnest, incisive and impressive speaker." The
Democrats needed such talent this summer, especially in the North.[52]

The party's prospects in the North were tenuous enough, but
Georgia's Democrats worried about home too. The Know Nothings
had refused to roll over and die, despite their recent rout. Some be-

49. AHS to JLS, June 24, 1856, in Stephens Papers, DU; AHS to LS, July 20, 1856,
in Stephens Papers, MC.
50. AHS to LS, July 20, 1856, in Stephens Papers, MC.
51. *Ibid.*, November 14, 15, 1856; John L. Stephens' estate papers in Norwood, *Liberty Hall*, 210–12.
52. Alexander K. McClure, *Colonel Alexander K. McClure's Recollections of Half a
Century* (Salem, Mass., 1902), 357.

lieved Fillmore "the first choice of the masses," but other Fillmore men in the South attacked their enemies' suicidal course in repealing the Missouri Compromise. It was a potent argument, which the southern Americans soon recognized as their strongest weapon.[53]

Consistency had never been the rule among Georgia's politicians. Convincing the voters that southern rights were safer in one's own hands than in one's opponents' had been the time-honored political stratagem since 1844. If such a course required inconsistency, so be it. Except for a few hard-core southern radicals, none of Georgia's politicians ever hesitated to swerve into the most expeditious political channel if circumstances seemed to warrant it. This was the course Cracker Know Nothings took in 1856. They repudiated the Kansas-Nebraska Act, which as a bill most of them had hailed two years before.

Fillmore had already given them the nudge by implying that he favored restoring the Missouri Compromise, and the northern Know Nothings maintained the same attitude. Undismayed, Georgia's American party, all the while claiming to be the only national party in the race, met in Columbus in July and coolly condemned a restoration of the Missouri line, damned the administration's twin heresies of squatter sovereignty and alien suffrage, and announced its adherence to "the principles of the Utah and New Mexico territorial bills" as the government's true territorial policy. Whatever this last platform plank meant— it seemed to envision some vague notion of popular sovereignty—the hazy formulation served Know Nothing needs admirably, for it allowed them to attack the Kansas-Nebraska Act and Pierce's policy as dangerous to southern rights. Not only had it unleashed squatter sovereignty, but it had also granted the franchise to odious, ignorant foreigners.[54]

Stephens, who regarded the election as a life-or-death matter for the South, at first granted the Know Nothings a condescending but irritated pity: "When I see Southern men[,] Georgians, large slaveholders doing all in their power to strike down the only men at the North who stand between them and those who would cut their throats and put their negroes over them I do not know that it ought to be a matter of such personal interest to me what fate befalls them. . . . Some of them

53. Milledgeville *Federal Union*, January 15, 1856; McCallum to Bell, January 15, 1856, in Bell Papers, LC.

54. Columbus resolutions in Haywood J. Pearce, *Benjamin H. Hill: Secession and Reconstruction* (Chicago, 1928), 13.

I believe know better. Those I abhor, but as a class I pity them. I know they are deceived and act from passions and prejudices that they are not conscious of. They are nothing but . . . erring mortals who may see their error when it is too late to remedy it." [55]

But as these poor mortals persisted in error, Stephens' compassion changed to revulsion. His longtime supporter Jones of the *Chronicle* now proclaimed the principles of the Kansas-Nebraska Act more odious than those of the Wilmot Proviso. He was probably a free-soiler at heart, Stephens said. What these traitors really wanted was to restore the Missouri restriction, a course Georgians had pledged to resist under the Georgia Platform. "If they are for putting [the restriction] back let them openly say so—and let them no longer pretend to be G. Platform men but let them go over to the *freesoilers* where they belong." [56]

His mood was even more foul at the end of August as he prepared to return home for the campaign. Political intelligence from the North indicated a most alarming state of affairs, "and yet thousands of Georgians would sing hosannas at the triumph of our enemies. Oh human nature how frail, how weak & how ignorant thou art." Once home, Stephens threw himself into the fight. Toombs had already been bloodied. "The order is vigilant and untiring and fight for their necks," he warned his friend, and moreover "were making some impression on the 8th Dist." "The great fight is in the 8th," echoed Thomas. "*This district is not safe unless you put in strong.*" [57]

After visiting John's grave in LaGrange and seeing to his family's needs, Stephens began his campaign on the eleventh in Chattanooga, where with Cobb he spoke to a large crowd of Tennesseans and north Georgians. Despite what he considered a "great speech," Stephens confessed that he felt "self abused" and "mortified" because so many of his old Whig friends "were not giving me their wonted smiles." [58]

Few of his old Whig friends close to home were smiling either. The Kansas-Nebraska Act, charged the Rome *Courier*, was a "double headed monster" sired by Douglas and Stephens. "If Mr. Stephens and

55. AHS to LS, August 2, 1856, in Stephens Papers, MC.
56. *Ibid.*, August 10, 1856.
57. *Ibid.*, August 31, 1856; Toombs to AHS, September 3, 1856, Thomas to AHS, September 5, 1856, both in Phillips (ed.), *TSC Correspondence*, 380, 381.
58. Milledgeville *Federal Union*, October 21, 1856; AHS to LS, September 15, 1856, in Stephens Papers, MC.

his coadjutors had let the Compromise alone, this Union would not be in imminent peril of disruption." Stephens deceived the people by denying that the bill had not enacted squatter sovereignty, said the *Chronicle*. How could he now defend the same principles he had denounced in 1848 as "*treachery to the South?*" Taking its cue from the Democratic editors of bygone days, the *Chronicle* now chastised Stephens by reprinting his Texas speech several times. And at least one American editor branded Little Aleck with the all-purpose expletive: abolitionist.[59]

The victim of all this vituperation countered with his accustomed energy. Over and over he denied that the Kansas-Nebraska Act had a particle of squatter sovereignty in it. Wasn't it plain that the enemies of the bill and the enemies of the South were one and the same? Only once did he let his guard down. On October 22, a few days before the election, he shared the platform at Lexington with Benjamin H. Hill, the Know Nothings' brightest young luminary.

Since Berrien's death in January of 1856, Hill stood alone as the American party's most magnetic leader. He had served one term in the Georgia General Assembly (1851–1852) and was narrowly defeated for a second in 1855. Thirty-three years old in 1856, the tall, fair-haired, blue-eyed lawyer-planter from LaGrange epitomized noble southern manhood. Bright, rich, and fearless, he had already campaigned for Fillmore all over the state, had met Linton in debate three times, and was not ruffled by the prospect of debating Linton's famous older brother.

Stephens erred seriously by underestimating his young opponent, who was more than a match for his rhetorical wiles. Instead of concentrating on issues, Stephens tastelessly abused both Fillmore and his party. Although Little Aleck maintained himself in what argument there was, he was decisively bested in the insult-trading. Hill delighted especially in turning Stephens' villification of his former Whig friends back upon him. It ill became him now, Hill charged, to abuse his conscientious former friends. Why, Stephens himself was a turncoat. He had deserted the men who had supported him for thirteen years, the men who had made him what he was. "Men did not make me," Stephens shot back hotly. "God Almighty alone made me." "If God alone

59. Rome *Courier* quoted in Augusta *Chronicle and Sentinel*, September 6, 1856; Augusta *Chronicle and Sentinel*, October 8, 15, 21, 1856; Wilkes *Republican* quoted in Augusta *Constitutionalist*, August 8, 1856.

made you," Hill retorted, "He did not pronounce you good." The crowd loved it.[60]

Hill's next encounter—with the indomitable Toombs at Washington the following day—showed what poor tactics Stephens had chosen to deal with his opponent. Constantly kept on the defensive, Hill achieved no better than an honorable draw at best. But the state's American press agreed that Stephens had been badly beaten. Hill "met him on his own dunghill," crowed the Athens *Southern Watchman*, and "humiliated him and whipped him badly in the presence of his warmest admirers." Stephens, gloated the *Chronicle*, had been completely "used up and demolished." Democrats lent credence to the boasts. Hill's conduct toward the sainted Little Aleck, reported one correspondent, was "disgustingly rude." Outraged citizens of Atlanta promptly burned Hill in effigy.[61]

If these reports pricked Stephens' thin skin, he gave no immediate indication of it. Election day, November 4, was fast approaching. For the moment at least, dealing with the young LaGrange upstart would have to await the singularly more pressing task of carrying Georgia, and especially the Eighth District, for Buchanan.

Had any of the Know Nothings at the huge rally in Atlanta on October 2 been disposed to see omens, the fall of a delegate to his death from atop an eighty-foot flagpole might have given them pause. His swift descent from the heights and his unfortunate end mirrored exactly the fate of the national American party. The Know Nothings failed to survive their first presidential election. They had lost all pretensions to national stature, and as the campaign progressed the party was steadily weakened by desertions. Many southern Know Nothings, such as reluctant former Whigs Charles Jenkins and Eugenius Nisbet, gradually came to believe that defeating Frémont might well be critical to preserving the Union, a point Democrats unceasingly emphasized. Similar fears had a like effect among northern Know Nothings. Men who feared for the safety of the Union above all gravitated to Buchanan, and in the end they provided him with his margin of victory. He won the election with 174 electoral votes.

60. Augusta *Chronicle and Sentinel*, October 29, 1856.
61. *Ibid.*; Athens *Southern Watchman* and F. Z. Landrum quoted in E. Merton Coulter, "Alexander H. Stephens Challenges Benjamin H. Hill to a Duel," *Georgia Historical Quarterly*, LVI (Summer, 1972), 179, 180.

Buchanan's victory in the South had never been seriously in doubt, despite the heated campaign. With the lone exception of Maryland, Buchanan carried every slave state. Fillmore had run much better in the South than in the North, but Buchanan had won only five northern states: Pennsylvania, New Jersey, Illinois, Indiana, and California. Frémont took the rest, a total of 114 electoral votes. Little Aleck had reason to be pleased with the results in Georgia. "Old Buck" had carried both his district and the state. But the national totals could not have failed to shock him. In its first presidential contest the Republicans had demonstrated astonishing strength—more than 1.3 million voters had cast their ballots for an avowedly sectional party that in southern eyes personified all the hateful forces of northern fanaticism. And as the election demonstrated, Democrats had precious little room for error in dealing with this threat.

For the moment, however, Stephens had to deal with a threat closer to home, a threat to his reputation as a man of honor, and worse, a blow to his monumental ego. While in court at Augusta in mid-November Stephens heard reports that Hill had publicly boasted of charging him and Toombs with betraying the Whig party and acting toward it worse than Judas Iscariot. Hill, so ran the reports, "had thundered this in [their] ears and [they] cowered under it."[62]

Although busy settling John's family into its new home and preparing to depart for Washington, Stephens could not ignore this intelligence. On the seventeenth he wrote Hill a cold note. Were the reports true? His reply came on the twenty-second, a turgid missive in which Hill denied abusing anybody or making personal issues in public speeches. But, he continued, "I generally reply to anything which I consider merits a reply." This should have satisfied Stephens but it didn't. He pressed Hill in another letter for a specific denial of imputing treachery to him. Hill's long reply awaited him on his arrival at Washington. One glance at this insolent response prompted Stephens' usual course in such cases. Through Thomas he dispatched a challenge to a duel to the "grand liar" and "arch knave" in LaGrange. Not only was Hill's latest letter unsatisfactory, but it also levied more none-too-subtle insults. Stephens was furious. If Hill's previous letters had angered Stephens, his response to the challenge must have set Little Aleck's frail frame aquiver with rage. Hill refused to fight. To take Stephens' life, he said, "would be a great annoyance to me afterwards." "I

62. AHS to LS, November 26, 1856, in Stephens Papers, MC.

never engage in farces," he continued, and besides, dueling was against the law—both God's and Georgia's.[63]

The controversy was anything but farcical to Stephens, who considered himself "deeply and grossly wronged." Matters would be righted even at the cost of his life, he vowed. More than in any of his previous near-duels, Stephens was motivated in this one by a consuming hatred. He longed to shoot Hill, and Linton, Thomas, and Toombs egged him on. Stephens had already decided to release the correspondence to the newspapers in hopes of drawing Hill out, but Hill's refusal of the conventional challenge had convinced him that a more effective prod was required.[64]

He applied the prod in a card to the *Constitutionalist*. Before the entire state he branded Hill a coward, "an impudent braggert and unscrupulous liar," and "a despicable poltroon besides." Up to this point, Stephens had carefully observed all the intricate amenities of the code duello. Now he wondered if he had overstepped the bounds of propriety in his rage. He had not known what course to take, he told Thomas. Had his language been too coarse?[65]

Stephens received his answers soon enough, from both Hill and Thomas. Hill replied in a public letter to the *Chronicle*. It was long (two full columns of close type), wonderfully sarcastic, and more insulting than ever. Adroitly Hill turned all Stephens' accusations back upon him. A braggart? Why, Stephens had compared himself to Moses in one speech, to an eagle soaring above owls in another. And who had not heard him boast continually about his role in passing the Compromise of 1850? A liar? Hill ticked off five instances in which Stephens— "a perfect 'Colt's *repeater*' in the matter of telling falsehoods"—had taken liberty with the truth. A poltroon? "He *forged* his grievance, *manufactured* his excuse, acted only a *pretender* in his challenge, and is therefore a poltroon!" As for dueling, said Hill, he considered it "no evidence of courage, no vindication of truth, and no test of the character of a true gentleman."[66]

63. The entire Stephens-Hill correspondence is in Benjamin H. Hill, Jr., *Senator Benjamin H. Hill of Georgia: His Life, Speeches and Writings* (Atlanta, 1893), 20–31.

64. AHS to LS, December 9, 13, 1856, in Stephens Papers, MC; LS to AHS, December 5, 1856, Toombs to AHS, both in Stephens Papers, EU.

65. Augusta *Constitutionalist*, December 17, 1856; AHS to Thomas, December 12, 1856, in Phillips (ed.), *TSC Correspondence*, 384.

66. Hill to the editor, December 18, 1856, in Augusta *Chronicle and Sentinel*, December 23, 1856.

With this masterly shot, the duel in the mails ended. Hill gave the entire correspondence to the newspapers, and soon all Georgia and most of the surrounding region were chuckling with delight. Stephens' challenge was taken as a joke, and Hill's classic comment—"I have a family to support and a soul to save, while Stephens has neither"—set Crackers to guffawing from Atlanta to Savannah.[67]

Democratic papers found the whole affair embarrassing, running the correspondence with little or no comment. The American press naturally had a field day. The *Southern Recorder* extolled Hill (a bit extravagantly) as "an exemplary man of the church," respectful of the laws of God and men. William G. "Parson" Brownlow, the acerbic editor of the Knoxville *Whig*, suggested that Hill accept the challenge and fight Stephens with "dung-forks" in a hog pen after a hard rain. "In this event, Hill will *toss out* the *feverish ambitious shadow of a man*, and leave the so-called field of honor, without the shedding of blood!"[68]

Despite the general opinion of his card—it had been judged "too severe," said Thomas—and Hill's devastating rejoinder, Stephens still refused to let the ridiculous affair end. Stephens was unconcerned about the public's reaction. Perhaps, he suggested to his erstwhile second, he should publish his version of the Lexington speech so the public could have all the facts. Even Thomas, not among the coolest-tempered men himself, had by now seen the futility of protracting the controversy further. He advised Stephens to drop it.[69]

He did, but the whole affair continued to rankle him. Weeks after Hill had allowed the argument to sink into a well-deserved oblivion, Stephens still seethed. He could not let the issue rest until he had gathered the testimony of enough admirers and sycophants in Washington and at home to convince himself that "men of honor" regarded Hill "as a cowardly blackguard and nothing else." By way of contrast, he told Linton, "I stand higher I think in the opinion of all men here at this time than I ever did before."[70]

It was fortunate for Stephens that he had such associates. Gigantic

67. Hill quoted in Rabun, "Stephens," 456.

68. Milledgeville *Southern Recorder*, February 10, 1857; Knoxville *Whig*, December 27, 1856, clipping in Stephens Papers, LC.

69. Thomas to AHS, December 29, 1856, AHS to Thomas, December 29, 1856, both in Stephens Papers, LC.

70. AHS to Thomas, January 16, 1857, in Stephens Papers, DU; AHS to LS, January 15, 1857, in Stephens Papers, MC.

though it might be, his ego was still fragile, protected only by his own self-constructed defenses—his habitual guises of intellectual superiority and moral rectitude. Hill had battered both and, worst of all, made Stephens look like a fool in the process. Of all his political opponents, the many past and future, Stephens despised Ben Hill above all. He would not forgive him until twenty-five years later, when Hill was on his deathbed. By that time, this infuriating encounter, so important to him now, had long since disappeared behind the mists of time and great clouds of acrid gunsmoke.

XIII

Little Balm and Much Outrage: Dred Scott, *Buchanan, and Walker*

Instead of repose, what the country got when Congress met in December was more recrimination. President Pierce had touched off an explosion among the Republicans by blistering them severely in his last annual message to Congress. For the next month yet another angry debate on slavery and Kansas convulsed Congress. House Republicans would not allow the message to be printed until they had their say. At least one southern paper found the spectacle "disgusting" because southern representatives so lacked self-respect and regard for the public interest to be seduced "into this disreputable squabble."[1]

Congressman Stephens' own considerable self-respect did not deter him from adding his voice to the dissonant chorus. "The conflict is now over," Stephens announced grandly to the House on January 6, 1857. The popular verdict in the election had sustained his most cherished principles. "Sectionalism has been signally rebuked and constitutionalism gloriously triumphant." Luxuriating in constitutionalism triumphant, Stephens made a disarming admission. Defense of principle had been the "main point" of the Kansas-Nebraska Act, he said. He had not supported the bill because he expected Kansas to become a

---

1. Richardson (ed.), *Messages and Papers of the Presidents,* V, 397–404; Savannah *Republican*, December 22, 1856, quoted in Rabun, "Stephens," 462.

slave state. In fact, he did not expect any slave states to be formed out of the western territories. The laws of "climate, soil, and productions," as well as population, would prevent it. He would prefer that Kansas come in as a slave state, but he had supported the Kansas-Nebraska bill only to maintain a principle essential to national peace and the security of the South.[2]

With a Democrat safely in the White House, Stephens obviously believed the time right for announcing what he really thought about slavery's chances in Kansas. He had been told by proslavery people there how optimistic they were, but he had also seen the reams of evidence the House investigating committee produced. He could read the census reports as well as anyone; he knew how few slaveholders had chosen to immigrate to the plains. Like most of them, he believed that slavery depended on demographic and climatic conditions. Moreover, he knew that the sole reason slavery had attained even a foothold in Kansas was through the Missourians' machinations in defiance of all laws: climatal, geographic, and statutory. Until now at least, Stephens had been able to maintain the southern cause in Kansas only by the narrowest reading of the statute law and by the manifestly illegal operations of the free-soil forces. But resolving the issue could not long be postponed. If the question were dealt with fairly—say, in accord with the Toombs bill—it was almost certain that Kansas would be free. The southern people ought to be prepared for that result.

In his sudden zeal for forthright recognition of the facts, Stephens momentarily forgot how irrelevant the truth was to current political reality in the South. Southern Democrats, including Stephens, had long since painted themselves into a corner by dangling the prospect of Kansas as a slave state before the voters. Simply by following the logical imperatives of slave state politics they had placed themselves in a logically untenable position. People who, like Stephens, took even tentative steps toward trying to dispel the sectional self-delusion they had fostered quickly discovered that facts now had little bearing on the situation.

Southern Know Nothings instantly pounced on Stephens' speech as evidence of what they had long contended: the Democrats meant to surrender Kansas to the free-soilers. "The poor South has again been deluded—humbugged—swindled," wailed the *Recorder*. "Why did

2. Cleveland, *Stephens*, 561–80.

we make an effort to dedicate Kansas to slavery," raged a Memphis editor, "when Democratic leaders knew that [it] was in rebellion against the immutable law of Heaven?" Stephens knew this. Why didn't he tell the truth? "Can the people of the South ever trust the Democracy after this?"[3]

The ever-alert Thomas quickly, almost frantically, reminded Stephens of the political quicksands. *"Kansas must come in as a slave state or the cause of Southern rights is dead."* The Know Nothings had foretold free-soil triumph in Kansas. "If their prediction is fulfilled . . . we go down and such knaves as Ben Hill & Co will rule. . . . We can't afford to lose the point. We must have it our way or we are ruined." Know Nothing papers had also been charging that Buchanan secretly favored the Kansas free-soilers. If this were true, thought Thomas, he "richly deserves death, and I hope some patriotic hand will inflict it." Thomas hated Buchanan with inexplicable passion, but thousands of his fellow Democrats shared his paranoia.[4]

Stephens, however, remained calm, confident that Buchanan's Kansas policy would follow the southern reading of popular sovereignty. With "fair play" the South would get Kansas. But amazingly, the southern people didn't seem to realize the magnitude of the question. They were not emigrating to Kansas with their slaves. If the South lost Kansas, it would be her "own fault or inability as the case may be." The South could demand only that the federal government allow "the right of expansion equal to our capacity." This was a law "we cannot change or modify."[5]

This was certainly a different Stephens than the one who had intimated publicly a few weeks earlier that inexorable laws of nature would declare Kansas free. In private he seemed to recognize only one immutable law—simple numbers. He realized that slavery's hold on the territory was only technical, and its grip was being steadily weakened as free-soil settlers continued to arrive. Iron laws of nature or no, it remained to be seen how he would react if, by some feat of legerdemain, the proslavery settlers in Kansas managed to annul nature's laws.

Stephens' apprehensions about Kansas suddenly came to a halt. Letters from Linton since early in the month had grown increasingly

3. Milledgeville *Southern Recorder*, January 20, 1857; Memphis *Eagle & Enquirer*, January 21, 1857, quoted in Milledgeville *Southern Recorder*, February 3, 1857.
4. Thomas to AHS, January 12, 1857, in Phillips (ed.), *TSC Correspondence*, 392.
5. AHS to Thomas, January 16, 1857, in Stephens Papers, DU.

hysterical. His wife, Emma, had contracted puerperal sepsis, a virulent childbed fever, after giving birth to their fourth child. After two weeks of suffering, she died, and Linton nearly went mad with grief. Stephens, who understood his brother's high-strung temperament and his dependence on Emma, prepared immediately to leave for home. Everything else, even Kansas, would have to wait. Linton needed him. But for an anxious week the weather and his own precarious health stymied his plans. The Potomac was choked with ice, and for the first time in his sickly life Stephens was coughing up blood. Fortunately, the affliction lasted only two days, and as soon as the weather broke, February 4, 1857, he hastened home. In the meantime, he offered Linton what comfort he could. Do not despair, he urged. God's ways were inscrutable, but suffering His dispositions with meekness and faith led to purity and growth. Do not surrender to passion, he pleaded.[6]

Stephens' advice went unheeded, and for a while James Thomas, attempting in Aleck's absence to console his son-in-law, feared for Linton's sanity. Once in Georgia, Stephens went immediately to Sparta and stayed with his brother for three weeks before going home. His presence did little to ease Linton's pain. In his grief Linton turned to drinking, and liquor only depressed him more. "I do daily and fervently pray for death," he wrote upon Aleck's return to Crawfordville. Nor did prayer and faith in God's providence provide any comfort. They were "*humbugs*," he declared. "God has blasted me and I verily believe He intends to damn me eternally."[7]

Doggedly, the elder Stephens kept up a steady barrage of multipaged letters. It was wrong to despair, he warned. God chastised those He loved: "Remember Job in his afflictions." God allowed afflictions for man's ultimate good: "They subdue our passions, restrain our appetites, smother our temper, increase our confidence in an all ruling power and render us more obedient to his will." Just as earnestly he begged Linton to stay away from alcohol. "You may not think you drink too much, I tell you you ought not drink any." Keep busy, Stephens exhorted. Remember your children, who now need you so much. And over and over again: do not despair; everything is for the best.[8]

6. LS to AHS, January 15, 19, 1857, AHS to LS, January 28–31, 1857, all in Stephens Papers, MC.

7. James Thomas to AHS, February 7, 1857, in Stephens Papers, LC; LS to AHS, February 27, 29, 1857, in Stephens Papers, MC.

8. AHS to LS, February 27, March 2, 1857, in Stephens Papers, MC.

While Stephens was at home—he had no intention of leaving with Linton in such distress—James Buchanan took the oath of office as the United States' fifteenth president. Ordinarily the accession of a new president and the general air of expectation would have dominated the newspapers and gossip in Washington for days. But not this time, for two days after the inauguration the Supreme Court announced one of its most momentous decisions of the nineteenth century.

Buchanan might have had trouble attracting attention even without judicial competition, although he was a man of fair ability and a forty-year veteran of public service. Tall, white-haired, and inclined to corpulence, Buchanan was the first bachelor to occupy the White House. He, like Pierce, subscribed to the time-honored and increasingly shopworn Jacksonian creed: laissez-faire economics, frugality in government, and extreme hostility to antislavery fanaticism. But in many ways Buchanan contrasted sharply with earlier Democratic presidents. He had little of Pierce's affability, even less of Polk's determination, and none of Jackson's unyielding defiance of southern extremism.

This is not to say he was weak. Once decided upon a course of action, he held to it with bulldog tenacity. He could be a mean and petulant opponent, a man little inclined to trust people, especially those who disagreed with him. His tragic flaw was not weakness of character, although to be sure, he lacked the steel so conspicuous in Jackson or Lincoln or even old Zack Taylor. Like Taylor, Buchanan lacked vision, that elusive quality possessed by all great leaders that allows them to see their own role in shaping the future.

Like Stephens and thousands of others, James Buchanan was imprisoned in an outdated conception of the Union. The real problem he confronted was not, in the final analysis, a specific one like the Kansas question or rising antislavery sentiment but a crisis in the American Union. It was Buchanan's sorry fate was to preside over a rapidly changing nation when all the old ideas in which he believed—of a confederated republic, of a central government of severely limited powers, and of the rights of individual states to define for themselves their own spheres of sovereignty—were becoming increasingly anachronistic. The president naturally gravitated toward men who believed as he did: southerners, products of an agrarian society that resisted change and whose economy rested on an institution that was itself an anachronism.

"Old Buck's" prosouthern proclivities had long been known. He had never voted against the South on a sectional issue; his best friends, personal and political, were southerners. Naturally, his cabinet—three northerners and four southerners—reflected his beliefs. None of the men, save Howell Cobb, who got the premier post at the Treasury Department, stood much above commonplace. Cobb, a close friend of Buchanan's, accepted his post eagerly. Not only would he control vast patronage, but he would also be close to Buchanan's ear, where he could continue to nurture his own presidential ambitions.[9]

The president's inaugural address was as ordinary as his cabinet. Only one striking passage illuminated the dull, familiar litany of Democratic encomiums, and it dealt with the Supreme Court. Opinions differed, Buchanan said, about when a territory might decide the slavery question. It was a judicial question anyway, now before the Supreme Court. He would abide by the Court's decision, although he personally believed that a territory could not decide the question until writing its state constitution. The president's remarks, as it turned out, were a trifle disingenuous, for through correspondence with Robert C. Grier, one of the justices, he knew the general contours of the decision even as he spoke.[10]

Two days after the inauguration, on March 6, 1857, the Supreme Court rendered its decision in the case of *Dred Scott* v. *Sanford*. Scott was a black slave of Missouri owners whose suit for freedom had reached the Supreme Court after a tortuous route through lower courts. For several years in the 1830s Scott had been held by his army surgeon master in Illinois, a free state, and Wisconsin, a free territory. Because of his residence in these places, Scott contended he should be free. In 1852 the Missouri Supreme Court disagreed with him; the federal Supreme Court got the case on appeal in 1856.

The case presented three questions to the justices: first, was a black slave a citizen of the United States and therefore entitled to sue in federal courts? Second, did Scott's residence in Illinois and Wisconsin entitle him to freedom? And third, was the Missouri Compromise restriction, which governed the Wisconsin territory, constitutional? In other words, did Congress have the power to exclude slavery from the territories? Ever since the Clayton bill in 1848, Congress had been attempting to get a judicial answer to this question. Now it was given.

9. The preceding paragraphs are based on Allan Nevins, *The Emergence of Lincoln* (2 vols.; New York, 1950), I, 61–79, and Elbert B. Smith, *The Presidency of James Buchanan* (Lawrence, Kan., 1975), 11–22.

10. Richardson (ed.), *Messages and Papers of the Presidents*, V, 430–36.

With varying degrees of agreement, the justices answered "no" to all three questions. Chief Justice Roger B. Taney delivered the majority opinion; two northern justices vigorously dissented, but the other northerner, Grier, joined Taney and four southern justices in declaring that the Missouri Compromise had always been unconstitutional.[11]

Had Stephens been in Washington there is little doubt he would have tried to squeeze into the packed Court chamber. He was more than casually interested in the case, having followed it closely since the previous winter, when it was argued for the second time before the Court. He had done more than just listen, for what Stephens, Buchanan, and the entire South wanted was a clear-cut ruling on the constitutional power of Congress over territorial slavery. It first appeared that they would be disappointed. In June, 1856, the Court had ignored the constitutional question and divided evenly on the issue of its jurisdiction in the case. It had agreed to a request for reargument, and on the opening day of that argument, December 15, 1856, Stephens wrote Linton:

> I have been urging all the influences I could bring to bear upon the Supreme Court to get them no longer [to] postpone the case on the Mo. restriction before them, but to decide it. . . . If they decide as I have reason to believe they will that the restriction was unconstitutional, that Congress had no power to pass it then the question, the judicial question as I think will be ended as to the power of the people in their Territorial Legislature. It will in effect be "res adjudicata[.]" The only grounds upon which that claim of power then can rest will be Genl. Cass['] "squatter sovereignty" doctrine, that is they possess the power not by delegation but by sovereign right—and you know my opinion of that.[12]

Two weeks later Stephens joined the throng jamming the small courtroom in the Capitol basement to hear reargument of the case. George Ticknor Curtis, one of Scott's lawyers, argued a legal justification for congressional power over territorial slavery that even Stephens admitted to be "chaste, elegant, and forensic." But however elegant, the argument did not convince him. Like many other Democrats, Stephens expected a broad ruling in the case, one that would address the Missouri Compromise question and decide it in the South's favor. And having been privy to some of the Court's thinking, he had good

    11. See Don E. Fehrenbacher, *The Dred Scott Case: Its Significance in American Law and Politics* (New York, 1978), 239–388.
    12. AHS to LS, December 15, 1856, in Stephens Papers, MC.

reason for his expectation. "From what I hear *sub rosa*," he told Linton, the decision "will be according to my own opinions upon every point as abstract original questions. The restriction of 1820 will be held to be unconstitutional. The judges are all writing out their opinions I believe *seriatim*. The Chief Justice will give an elaborate one." [13]

Stephens' source (accurate, as it turned out) and what "influences" he brought to bear on the Court are impossible to determine. Grier was a distant relative of Stephens' mother, but Little Aleck was not particularly friendly with him. His closest acquaintance on the Court was James M. Wayne of Savannah. Perhaps Wayne was both informant and "influence." Back in the 1840s, Stephens had shared a mess with several justices, but of these only Taney and McLean remained on the bench. McLean, a Republican, was impervious to Stephens' opinions, and no evidence suggests that Stephens approached Taney on the case.

It is probably safe to assume that Stephens pressed his opinions upon anybody important who would listen. The Georgian had argued cases before the Court several times and was at least casually acquainted with all the justices and most of the Court's functionaries. But Stephens could not have had much effect on the ruling; his contacts with the Court were not that solid. Without question, he made no secret of his desires and opinions, and it would have been typical of him to characterize whatever conversations he may have had with the justices or men even remotely connected with the Court as "influences." Such statements ought to be regarded with skepticism: Stephens never regarded his own opinion as anything but weighty and influential.

For only the second time in its history the Supreme Court of the United States invalidated an act of Congress, and for the first time a substantial segment of the country refused to accept the decision. Never before had the Court received such a torrent of abuse as descended upon it from the North. Just as much moral weight should be given the decision, thundered Greeley's *Tribune*, as the majority judgment of a Washington barroom. The decision had transformed the Constitution into "nothing better than a bulwark of inhumanity and oppression." Frenzied abolitionists condemned the decision as yet another link in the chain forged by the slave power conspiracy to shackle the odious

13. *Ibid.*, January 1, 1857.

institution upon free men. "If the people obey this decision," Henry Ward Beecher pronounced, "they disobey God." Fellow abolitionist Gerrit Smith recommended hanging Taney. Northern legislatures also pilloried the decision. New Hampshire passed a law granting citizenship to all Negroes and freedom to all slaves. New York's legislature condemned the decision, and Pennsylvania's declared it nonbinding. A large portion of the northern press believed that the Court had declared slavery a national institution: now the very existence of American liberty, so long tested by the slave power, had been jeopardized.[14]

Relative calm pervaded the South. The volume of the northern uproar hardly seemed to affect the Savannah *News*. Natural laws of climate and population would decide the territorial question, it observed with typical southern pietism, "for Congress henceforth can have nothing to do with the subject." The *Constitutionalist* had a firmer grip on reality. Far from quieting the antislavery fanatics or curing their madness, it said, the decision would only make them "more lawless and insane." Supreme Court rulings did not faze such men; they would simply plead "higher law." Almost overlooked in the excitement was the decision's effect on Douglas' popular sovereignty doctrine, which the ruling had not clarified at all. Both northern and southern Democrats could thus applaud the decision and still maintain their inimical positions on the powers of territorial legislatures over slavery.[15]

Court decision or no, the true meaning of popular sovereignty was the most pressing question confronting the new administration. After six frustrating months Governor Geary had resigned his post in Kansas. Over Geary's veto the territory's proslavery legislature had rigged a bill for a June election for delegates to a constitutional convention. The law barred from the polls anyone arriving in Kansas after March 15, 1857, and worst of all, it made no provision for submitting the constitution to the voters for ratification.

This was the grim situation confronting Buchanan's appointee as Kansas governor, Robert J. Walker, who arrived in Kansas in late May. Walker, an experienced politician of national stature, was a small, somewhat sickly man. But he made up for it in energy and ambition.

14. New York *Tribune*, March 7, 1857, quoted in Craven, *Coming of Civil War*, 385; New York *Tribune*, March 7, 1857, and Beecher quoted in Rabun, "Stephens," 470.

15. Savannah *Morning News*, May 6, 1857; Augusta *Constitutionalist*, March 18, 1857.

He had not wanted the post, and before accepting it he demanded a clear statement of administration policy and had it printed in a public letter. He, the president, and the cabinet had agreed, Walker wrote, that "the actual bona fide residents of Kansas, by a fair and regular vote, unaffected by fraud or violence must be permitted, in adopting their State Constitution, to decide for themselves what shall be their domestic institutions." Buchanan and Douglas also approved at least parts of Walker's proposed inaugural address, which reiterated this idea and promised that Congress would not admit Kansas unless this condition were met.[16]

Walker went to Kansas as an agent of Democratic policy: to secure Democratic ascendancy in the territory and have it admitted as a state as soon as possible. Neither he, Buchanan, nor Douglas believed Kansas would ever be anything but a free state, but preserving the basic forms of popular sovereignty was essential. Walker's job was to ensure the participation of the free-soil Democrats in the process, thus locking up Kansas for the party.

Unfortunately, none of Walker's blandishments could persuade the free-soilers to participate in the election. Even his inaugural address in Lecompton failed to woo them. Slavery in Kansas was doomed, Walker had said. An "isothermal line" (climatic law) had rendered the territory unfit for slave labor. But even if this were not so, the governor pledged that Congress would refuse to admit Kansas unless a majority of the people decided the slavery question for themselves by a direct vote on the proposed constitution. He himself would ensure that the elections were fairly conducted, a course that both the president and his cabinet had approved.[17]

Neither Walker nor Buchanan could have anticipated the ear-splitting squall these remarks engendered in the South. Walker had "delivered Kansas into the hands of the abolitionists," roared the Richmond *South*, a sentiment echoed in a thousand variations across Dixie.[18]

Besides playing into the hands of Georgia's Americans, the new Kansas clamor caused consternation among the state's Democrats. Anti-Cobb, southern rights men, and inveterate Buchanan-haters all leaped

16. Robert J. Walker to Buchanan, March 26, 1857, quoted in Potter, *Impending Crisis*, 298.

17. *Ibid.*, 301.

18. Richmond *South* quoted in George Fort Milton, *The Eve of Conflict: Stephen A. Douglas and the Needless War* (Boston, 1934), 266.

to the attack. Administration supporters such as Toombs and Stephens found themselves caught in the middle. Just when everything was quiet, Walker's folly had raised the devil all over the South, fumed Toombs. Even worse, the administration seemed disposed to sustain him. Toombs was enraged by Walker's presumption in advising the Kansans and threatening that "unless they carried out his will in the business Congress *ought not* & *would not* admit the state." This was intolerable "direct government interference," said Toombs, and Walker should be recalled immediately.[19]

Once more Georgia Democrats had to come up to the mark and defend southern rights against outrage. None of them, including Stephens, approved Walker's address, but they differed widely on how best to handle the problem. Stephens, silent on Walker till now, received opinions from all sides. Martin Crawford, a delegate to the upcoming Democratic convention, favored a resolution denouncing Walker and reminding the administration "what *neutrality* is." Party survival depended on it; Walker's address had hurt them badly. Thomas W. Thomas, detecting the administration's malevolent hand in the business, was in a lather. "*We are betrayed*," he stormed. Surely, he told Stephens, the administration could not be sustained in this policy. Secretary Cobb also worried about Stephens' intentions. A united state party was vital to his own political future, and Little Aleck's influence was indispensable. So in the weeks before the convention he too plied Stephens with letters defending the administration and casting Walker's intentions in the most favorable light.[20]

But Cobb's hopes were dashed when Georgia's angry Democrats convened on June 24, 1857. Only the first of their five platform resolutions praised Buchanan; the rest excoriated Walker and demanded his recall. Stephens stayed home during the convention, but he was present in spirit, because Linton was there, and he drafted the critical anti-Walker resolution. Not only did the Stephens brothers ignore Cobb's plea, they also refused to support his candidate for governor, John H. Lumpkin, Stephens' old congressional crony. But neither their favorite—James Gardner, editor of the *Constitutionalist*—nor any of the other four candidates could secure a majority, and after twenty bal-

19. Toombs to Burwell, July 11, 1857, in Toombs Papers, LC.
20. Martin J. Crawford to AHS, June 19, 1857, in Stephens Papers, LC; Thomas to AHS, June 15, 1857, Cobb to AHS, June 17, 18, 1857, all in Phillips (ed.), *TSC Correspondence*, 400–403.

lots the convention appointed a committee to select a compromise candidate.

As a member of this committee, Linton Stephens performed probably the most momentous act of his political career. He moved the nomination of Joseph E. Brown by acclamation. Both the committee and the fragmented convention liked the idea. Brown was nominated unanimously and thus launched on a career that would put him at the center of Georgia politics for the next thirty-five years. Characteristically, even at the onset of his career, he benefited from an important political connection. Having the support of the Stephens brothers—one of whom, Aleck, he had never met—was no mean achievement. Most of Georgia reacted as Toombs did. "Who the devil is Joe Brown?" he exclaimed.[21]

Toombs and Stephens, along with the rest of Georgia, soon found out. At the time of his nomination, the thirty-seven-year-old Brown was serving as judge of the superior court of the Blue Ridge circuit. Born in South Carolina, eldest of eleven children, Brown had worked on the family's north Georgia farm until he was nineteen. After three years in South Carolina academies, Brown, like Stephens, taught for a while, read law, and then, in 1845, attended Yale Law School for a year on a patron's money. Upon his return to Canton, Georgia, he began a remunerative practice. He won a seat in the state senate (where he met Linton Stephens) on his first venture into politics in 1849 as a Southern Rights man. Brown next served as a presidential elector for Pierce in 1852 and was elected to the superior court bench in 1855.

Joseph E. Brown was a man of determined eccentricity, utterly devoid of humor. He took three things seriously: his Baptist religion, his business affairs, and his own political survival. He neither drank, smoked, chewed, nor swore; and he just as religiously excluded any principle that threatened either his political or monetary fortune. Like a cat, Joe Brown always landed on his feet. Opinions on the man varied greatly, and Stephens received them from both ends of the spectrum. From Linton came glowing reports of Brown's speaking abilities and fine personal character. Bob Burch, Stephens' old law partner, knew Brown better. He could not vote for him, he told Stephens. Not only did Brown lack "open candor and untarnished character for fairness

21. LS to AHS, June 29, 1857, in Stephens Papers, MC; Stovall, *Toombs*, 154.

in the transactions of this life (including *politics*)," but he was also "a complete demagogue."[22]

What Cobb thought of Brown is unknown, but he made no secret of his opinion of the convention that nominated him. The party's course, he confessed, had been "inexplicable. They have lost all their good sense & seem bent on self destruction." The distress in administration circles did not bother Stephens. He was delighted with Walker's censure and especially with Linton's nomination for the Seventh District congressional seat. He would help in Linton's campaign any way he could, he promised his brother.[23]

That campaign promised to be volatile. Most Georgians were not aware of the president's reservations about Walker's inaugural, and the American party, which nominated Benjamin Hill for governor in July, made Walker's and Buchanan's perfidy the keynote of its campaign. Many Georgia Democrats, especially the southern rights men, agreed with the Americans about Walker. So to preserve party unity Democrats praised the president while damning his appointee.

But Cobb's supporters remained bitter. The convention had rebuked them roundly. Hostility from the Southern Rights crowd could have been expected; Cobb had never made peace with the ultras. But for the first time since 1850, Cobb found himself seriously on the outs with Stephens. His associate Lumpkin angrily blamed Little Aleck both for the anti-Walker resolutions and for denying him the nomination.[24]

Lumpkin's suspicions were well-founded. Defending slavery had already corroded Stephens' once pristine principles of party purity. He could now approve an avowed southern rights man over one who had stood firmly for the Union in 1850. Linton had lamely explained to Lumpkin that "justice" demanded a division of state offices between unionists and southern rights men. It would have been more candid had he pointed out that, unlike Cobb, neither he nor his brother was married to the administration. In fact, Linton blamed the president for Walker's indiscretions. For his part, Aleck, always less combustible than Linton and far the better politician, still expressed undiminished friendship for Cobb, and the secretary did his utmost to assure Ste-

22. LS to AHS, June 29, 1857, in Stephens Papers, MC; Burch to AHS, June 30, 1857, in Stephens Papers, LC.

23. Cobb to his wife, June 27, 1857, in Cobb Papers, UG; AHS to LS, June 26, 1857, in Stephens Papers, MC.

24. Lumpkin to Cobb, July 14, 1857, in Cobb Papers, UG.

phens of Buchanan's fidelity to popular sovereignty. Cobb had good reason to be concerned: some of his sources reported Stephens on the verge of deserting the administration.[25]

Stephens *was* behaving peculiarly. It was mid-July, and he had not yet declared his candidacy for Congress. During the spring the press had been rife with rumors that he meant to retire. Since then local Democratic meetings all over his district had passed laudatory resolutions urging him to run again. Cobb added his voice, warning Stephens that disaster would befall the ticket if he retired. "Your place cannot be filled in the House," he wrote.[26]

Still Stephens said nothing. Maybe he did consider retiring. He had good reasons to do so. During the twenty years he had been in public life his estate had grown. With more time to devote to it, it might prosper even more. Then, too, the Americans in his district hated him more than ever. The prospect of another grueling campaign against them could not have been inviting. Until his last term, Stephens had ruled his district like a fiefdom, but the task was daily becoming more difficult.

Moreover, yet another of his bouts of gloom had settled upon him. First had come Emma's death; and now, for the second year in a row, a drought threatened to ruin his crops. And then came another family death: his last surviving sister, Catherine, died during the summer. A buggy accident on the way home from the funeral had only worsened his mood. Aleck had luckily escaped unhurt, but Linton wrenched his knee so badly that it hampered him throughout the campaign. None of these dreary events could have helped his mood, but Stephens never required any particular reason to feel melancholy. On July 18, he told Linton that he felt more low spirited than he had for years. He felt no better at the end of the month. "Never was one more *corroded* with those things that make life a living anguish," he wrote. The world knew nothing of his "mental agonies and sufferings." "I have been a poor miserable being all my life. Miserable all the time."[27]

Miserable or not, Stephens could not ignore the vicious assault on his principles, so on August 18, he announced for Congress in a public

25. LS to AHS, July 16, 1857, in Stephens Papers, MC; Cobb to AHS, June 10, 1857, T. R. R. Cobb to Cobb, July 15, 1857, both in Phillips (ed.), *TSC Correspondence*, 400, 404.

26. Augusta *Constitutionalist*, June 2, 1857; Cobb to AHS, June 10, 1857, in Phillips (ed.), *TSC Correspondence*, 400.

27. AHS to LS, July 18, 31, 1857, in Stephens Papers, MC.

letter to his constituents. Despite the storms of the previous session and the triumph of the nonintervention principle in the election of 1856, the enemies of the Kansas-Nebraska Act continued their agitation. Stephens could hardly quit the fight now. Whatever his private wishes, he said, he would not retire as long as a fight over that act lasted. He would make no new pledges; he would simply see to the Kansas-Nebraska Act's faithful execution in all the territories.

The most interesting feature of the long letter was Stephens' interpretation of the Walker affair. In his view the Kansas governor had violated the Kansas-Nebraska Act, plainly trying to sway public opinion by arguing against the possibility that slavery might thrive in Kansas. And he had committed an even "grosser violation of principle" by prescribing how the state constitution should be formed and by declaring that Congress would not admit the state unless its constitution were submitted to the voters. The people decided such questions. Congress' duty was simply to ensure that the constitution came from legally constituted authorities and was republican in form.[28]

The question of Congress' proper duty struck at the foundation of government and involved "everything recognized as State Rights and State Sovereignty," Stephens continued. And since this question would likely come before the next Congress, this was why he was running again. It would have been impolitic had Stephens mentioned that the great question also involved more immediate matters—such as the fate of Georgia's Democratic party. Despite his bluster against Walker, Stephens carefully excused the administration. If the administration sided with Walker, it would share Walker's fate. But not for a moment did he believe this would happen. He would not condemn the president without a hearing, he said; for the present, men of principle ought to stick by the party.[29]

If Stephens was to steer a middle course, as he was trying to do, he had to condemn Walker. But even as he professed his undying devotion to "principle" he had to forget remarks similar to Walker's that he himself had made on the House floor not eight months before. Paradoxically, a consistent defense of southern rights, particularly for a moderate, demanded a certain malleability in one's principles, which Stephens, even as he exemplified it, would have categorically denied.

28. AHS to the voters of the Eighth Congressional District, August 14, 1857, in Phillips (ed.), *TSC Correspondence*, 409–20.
29. *Ibid.*

He chose not to notice that the middle ground was tilting, and at a pretty severe angle. Solid ground lay in only one direction—toward Calhounism and its adherents, men whose principles were as fixed as granite.

In short, Stephens' position was vulnerable. On one hand, nothing he said could please the Americans and the fire-eating Democrats who demanded both Walker's and Buchanan's heads. On the other, Cobb's friends remained suspicious. Both Stephens and Toombs, some thought, might desert the administration. Stephens' arguments, said one, were nothing but "veriest affectation." [30]

From Washington, Secretary Cobb ruefully contemplated the state of his party. All the news he got was bad. Extremism seemed rampant again, and his best friends bore the brunt of the attack. Georgia's Democratic candidate for governor, along with Stephens, his brother, and Toombs, condemned Walker as vigorously as the Americans. Patiently Cobb tried to explain to Stephens that Walker, according to firsthand reports, "is fully sustained by our friends in Kansas," and that neither Buchanan nor the cabinet had approved the inaugural. All this may have been true—but Cobb wasn't running for office in Georgia that summer. [31]

Actually, the Democrats were in no danger. With some early help from Toombs, Brown proved to be an adroit campaigner, at the least a match for Hill. Stephens campaigned only in his own district, with a few forays into the Seventh to help Linton. Linton needed help, but Aleck, facing his roughest campaign ever, also had to canvass vigorously. His opponent, Thomas J. Miller, former mayor of Augusta, was an able, energetic enemy. The *Chronicle*, once Stephens' staunch defender, now almost daily delivered withering attacks upon him. Any man with a record as long as Stephens' was bound to be vulnerable, and the American press concentrated its fire on every weak spot it could find, especially his insufferable vanity. "Apart from Mr. Stephens own bragging, what has he ever done for the country," the editor sneered. [32]

The campaign thoroughly wore Stephens out, but when the ballots were counted he defeated Miller by 1,261 votes, 54.6 percent of the

30. William H. Stiles to Cobb, August 26, 1857, in Cobb-Erwin-Lamar Papers, UG.

31. Jackson to Cobb, August 27, 1857, in Cobb-Erwin-Lamar Papers, UG; Cobb to AHS, September 12, 1857, in Phillips (ed.), *TSC Correspondence*, 422.

32. Augusta *Chronicle and Sentinel*, September 30, 1857.

tally. Although a personal low, Stephens' margin of victory had surpassed Brown's in the district. Hill had been beaten by almost 10,000 votes, but as a candidate for a near-defunct party he had done well. This was cold comfort for the Americans, however. Democrats won six of eight congressional seats and large majorities in the assembly. One Democrat they had defeated, though: Linton Stephens, beaten by fewer than 300 votes. Evidently one Stephens in Congress was all the Americans could tolerate.[33]

The Democracy lost no time in consolidating its hold. A few weeks after Brown's victory the legislature reelected Toombs to the Senate on the first ballot. Several days later the party assembled in Milledgeville for its usual postelection convention. Both Stephens and Toombs gave speeches. Little in the former's remarks distinguished it from his campaign orations: silent on Buchanan, loud in denunciation of Walker, and profuse in praise of the party. He did, however, moderate his scorn for the Americans, urging them to "bury the hatchet" and join the Democrats in presenting "an unbroken front to the enemies of the Union and constitutional rights of the South." Everyone applauded; no one seemed to notice the irony, except perhaps the shade of Calhoun. Only seven short years before, Stephens had denounced men who advocated this course as "enemies of the Union."[34]

Stephens did more than deliver speeches at the convention. As chairman of the committee on resolutions, he framed the state party's position on national issues. Cobb had warned him frantically several days before against "the fatal blunder of committing the democracy of Ga. against the submission of the constitution of Kansas to the people." This time Stephens heeded the advice. But his resolutions (which the convention adopted unanimously) left little room for maneuver. First, the convention demanded Walker's recall. It then went on to declare that Congress had no power either to question a territory's proposed state constitution or its mode of adoption. Congress could only ensure that the document was republican in form, that it legally expressed the majority's will, and that it had met the requirements of territorial law in its adoption. Only rigid adherence to these principles, the party concluded, could preserve the Union's peace and safety and the rights of the South.[35]

33. Milledgeville *Federal Union*, October 20, 1857.
34. Stephens' speech in Augusta *Chronicle and Sentinel*, November 14, 1857.
35. Cobb to AHS, November 2, 1857, in Stephens Papers, DU; Milledgeville *Southern Recorder*, November 17, 1857.

What had been going on in Kansas was no secret to anyone. The free-soilers had boycotted the June election for the constitutional convention, thus handing control of that body to the proslavery faction. But in a pivotal point in the territory's history the free-soilers voted in October elections for legislative seats, county offices, and territorial delegates to Congress. Not only did they elect the territorial delegate by a two-to-one margin, but they also succeeded in electing Kansas' first free-soil legislature after Governor Walker threw out thousands of spurious returns.

The constitutional convention assembled at Lecompton on October 19 and proceeded to draw up a document guaranteeing property rights for slaveholders. Although furious at Walker and initially disposed to submit the constitution directly to Congress, a majority of the delegates realized that some sort of popular ratification would be essential for at least a patina of legitimacy on their handiwork. But rather than submit the entire constitution to the voters, who would surely reject it, the convention left to Kansans a choice between "the constitution with slavery" or "the constitution without slavery"—in effect, a referendum on slavery's future. Voting for either proposition approved the *entire* constitution. Moreover, control over the "ratification" balloting (set for December 21, 1857) had been placed not with Walker but with designees of the convention. An astounded Walker pronounced the plan "vile fraud, a base counterfeit, and [a] wretched device to keep the people from voting." He left almost immediately for Washington to consult with Buchanan.[36]

Obviously the president faced a fearsome choice. To accept the Lecompton constitution was to bestow his blessing on a rancid piece of political trickery. In a territory with more than twenty-four thousand people eligible for the franchise, representatives of a mere 8 percent of the voters had drawn up a document offering the overwhelmingly free-soil majority a choice between strychnine and cyanide. Lecompton was the grossest perversion of popular sovereignty Kansas slaveholders had yet devised. And hundreds of thousands of northerners—Republicans to a man and a substantial portion of an outraged Democracy—were having none of it.

But rejecting the document would not only spurn the work of a perfectly legal convention, whose legality the president had repeatedly defended, but would also court political ruin for the Democratic party.

36. Potter, *Impending Crisis*, 307; Walker quoted in Rabun, "Stephens," 487.

For the southern wing, two-thirds of the party, stood solidly behind Lecompton and demanded that he accept it. Other points also argued in Lecompton's favor. Technically it fulfilled the president's pledges to Walker and the party's platform by offering voters a choice on slavery. The document itself was legal. And finally, swift admission of Kansas would probably end the interminable territorial hassle. Once a state, Kansas could do as it pleased about slavery and no one, North or South, could do anything about it.

Buchanan wasted little time making up his mind. He moved firmly to support the Lecompton formula. And in the process he destroyed his party beyond all hope of redemption. What was farce in Kansas would be tragedy in Washington.

XIV

The Fraud Was Glaring: Lecompton and Its Aftermath

Arriving back in Washington on November 29, 1857, Stephens promptly conferred with Cobb, who had disquieting news. Several days earlier Buchanan had broken with Walker; worse yet were persistent rumors that Douglas, en route to the capital, opposed Lecompton. Stephens didn't believe it, but he had noticed unusual silence among Illinois Democrats. Anticipating trouble, Stephens told James Thomas that "if we can get [the Lecompton constitution] through Congress it will be a great triumph of a great principle." It's hard to imagine what "principle" Stephens meant. The triumph was what mattered. Indeed, in his mind the two had become identical.[1]

Douglas had principles, too—and a political career to protect. But his principles came into direct conflict with official administration policy. Even before reading the Lecompton constitution Douglas told friends he suspected that "trickery & juggling have been substituted for fair dealing." If this were true, he said, the only course would be to vindicate both the Kansas-Nebraska Act and the party platform by referring the whole matter back to the people. Once he had read the docments and conferred with Walker, the Little Giant did not hesitate. He could not sanction Lecompton, he later said, without "repudiating all

1. AHS to James Thomas, December 1, 1857, fragment in Stephens Papers, LC.

the acts of my life, and doing a political act that I did not believe was moral and just." And he told the president the same when they met after his arrival. Already suspicious because of several snubs and irritated that Buchanan had released the Kansas portion of his forthcoming message without consulting him, Douglas believed that the president meant to destroy him. The meeting only confirmed his views and resulted in a complete break between them.[2]

No one was as anxious to find out where Douglas stood than Stephens, and within a day of the White House confrontation, he had met twice with the Illinois senator. Dejectedly but without rancor, Stephens reported to Linton, "He is against us, decidedly, but not extravagantly." There was no foreseeing the result now.[3]

On the brink of his most taxing congressional session ever, Stephens might have spared himself a multitude of headaches had he accepted the party's nomination for Speaker. For several months there had been a strong movement for him in the South, and friends like Toombs urged him to accept the post. But Stephens resisted. With a protracted House battle looming up, he valued his freedom to speak as he pleased more than being honorably gagged as Speaker. So the Democratic caucus nominated James Orr of South Carolina, and, once elected, Orr appointed Stephens chairman of the most important committee, Territories.[4]

The caucus vote that nominated Orr was the last vestige of unanimity the Democratic party would exhibit for years. Numerically the party held healthy majorities in both houses of Congress, but two-thirds of the Senate's 37 Democrats and 75 of the House's 128 were southerners, all infected with the incurable Lecompton virus. On December 8, 1857, Congress received Buchanan's first annual message, the expected strong endorsement of the Lecompton constitution. When Kansas was admitted, all the excitement would pass away, the president said. But, he warned, Kansans should not spurn this opportunity to settle the slavery issue fairly; otherwise they themselves would be responsible for the consequences.[5]

2. Stephen A. Douglas to John McClernand, November 23, 1857, in Robert W. Johannsen (ed.), *The Letters of Stephen A. Douglas* (Urbana, Ill., 1961), 403–404; Johannsen, *Douglas*, 582.

3. AHS to LS, December 4, 1857, in Stephens Papers, MC.

4. Toombs to Burwell, in William M. Burwell Papers, LC; Toombs to AHS, November 18, 1857, in Avary (ed.), *Stephens Recollections*, 50.

5. Richardson (ed.), *Messages and Papers of the Presidents*, V, 449–54.

Kansans took their own counsel, however. That same day their legislature voted to submit the entire Lecompton constitution to the voters along with the two alternatives offered by the convention. This election was set for January 4, 1858. Events now moved rapidly. On December 9, to the horror of southern Democrats and the amazement of Republicans, Douglas blasted Buchanan's message in a fiery speech in the Senate. He did not care whether slavery was "voted up" or "voted down," he thundered, but the method of submitting the question was a "mockery and an insult." Governor Walker resigned on the fifteenth. Six days later, in an election boycotted by the free-soilers and replete with the usual frauds, more than 6,000 Kansas voters approved the constitution "with slavery" while 529 voted for it "without slavery." Then on January 4, 1858, Kansans voted again in the election called by the legislature and boycotted by proslavery men. This time 10,226 voters rejected the Lecompton document outright, and only a handful chose one of the convention's options. Popular sovereignty, it was clear, had declared Kansas free—popular sovereignty, that is, as Douglas understood it.[6]

The Little Giant's actions may have stunned Georgians, but judging by Stephens' mail, Buchanan had few friends there either. Most of Little Aleck's closest associates either despised or distrusted the president and held him responsible for the renewed strife. Even levelheaded Herschel Johnson found little to praise in the annual message. He agreed only with admitting Kansas under the Lecompton constitution and only if the voters ratified the slavery clause. If they did not, Johnson continued, "I believe we have a perfect right to take advantage of the situation and send it back as a rebuke to the administration."[7]

By comparison with the president, even Douglas looked good to Thomas. The South only appeared to agree with Buchanan, he wrote. In principle it did not: "Indeed the position of Douglas is more reasonable and consistent. Buchanan has bullied and bribed the jury—if we get the verdict notwithstanding, we have a right to hold the benefits— if it is against us we have the right to repudiate it." Convinced that southern Democrats had been far too easy on the president, Thomas tried to get the Georgia senate to censure him, but the resolutions were promptly tabled. Most Georgians (including Stephens) realized that

6. *Congressional Globe*, 35th Cong., 1st Sess., 17–18.
7. Johnson to AHS, December 24, 1857, in Herschel Johnson Papers, DU.

to get Kansas they had to have Buchanan as an ally. Not Thomas. He did not blame Douglas for "looking to his interest at home," he said, "when southern men persisted in shouting hosannas" to the man who had betrayed them.[8]

Stephens bore Douglas no grudges either, but the Little Giant's defection presented him with serious problems. As chairman of the Committee on Territories, Stephens would be responsible for forging an administration majority in the House over Douglas' opposition. It would be a fearsome task and Stephens knew it. Buchanan knew it too, and Stephens noticed the strain on the president even before the battle started, when he went to the White House to confer with him on his Lecompton message. Buchanan's careworn expression softened Stephens. "He really means to do right," he told Linton. "What he needs most is wise and prudent consellors."[9]

It was a cogent observation. Unfortunately, Buchanan ignored prudent advice he was getting. Fully half of the northern House Democrats opposed Lecompton and had formed their own caucus under the lead of Thomas L. Harris, a close Douglas ally. They had warned the president that Lecompton could not pass, that he should heed the true voice of the Kansas people. To no avail. Buchanan's message recommending the admission of Kansas under Lecompton arrived on February 2, 1858, and it immediately became apparent how closely the House was divided. Normally the message would have been routinely referred to Stephens' committee. But Harris moved to have it sent to a special investigating committee instead. This would not only bottle up any bill indefinitely but would also provide reams of evidence for the opponents to take before the people. Sensing danger, Stephens moved to refer the bill to his committee and then to adjourn, but both motions lost, 109 to 105. Harris' motion was held over.[10]

For the moment Stephens chose not to read the dark omens. He did not yield authority gracefully. A nervous, touchy individual, contemptuous of mankind most of the time, Stephens spent a good deal of this session bemoaning the weaknesses of his southern colleagues. Three had been absent from their seats during these important votes,

8. Thomas to AHS, December 25, 1857, January 12, 21, 1858, all in Stephens Papers, EU.

9. AHS to LS, February 3, 1858, in Stephens Papers, MC.

10. Richardson, *Messages and Papers of the Presidents*, V, 415; Nichols, *Disruption of Democracy*, 162–63.

and he deplored such "inattention and culpable negligence." Stephens might not have been so harsh had he realized how some of his colleagues judged him. "Members are afraid of him," said one. It was useless to argue with him when he opposed one of their measures. If he took charge of a bill, though, "you have to let him take his own course—he will not take any suggestions." Stephens had few peers in plotting parliamentary strategy. Throughout this session he would recognize none.[11]

Even so, he had no easy task. Attempting to cram Lecompton through the House in early 1858 would have tried the patience of men far closer to sainthood than he was. The situation was highly flammable, and when the president's message came up again on February 5, the House exploded. For almost twelve hours, from 3 : 30 in the afternoon till past 2 : 00 the next morning, Stephens tried to get a vote for adjournment. Harris' motion to establish a special investigating committee had been called, and there were not enough administration votes on the floor to defeat it. Even at that late hour men were ready to fight, and a pair of traded insults between Republican Galusha Grow and Carolinian Laurence Keitt finally sparked one. One retort led to another. Keitt lunged for Grow's throat, and that started a general melee.

At least fifty of the people's servants joined in, oblivious to Orr's cries for order, to James B. Clay's drunken shouts of "Gentlemen, remember where you are!" and to the sergeant-at-arms' flailing mace. Viewing the ruckus from his front row seat, Stephens witnessed one of the strangest sights of the night. Out of the mass of grunting, punching humanity there suddenly emerged, airborne, a dark, furry object—Mississippi congressman William Barksdale's toupee—with its embarrassed and enraged owner in hot pursuit. In his haste to replace his errant scalp, in the meantime being trampled under foot, Barksdale put the wig on wrong side out. This absurd sight was enough to break up the fight and the legislators.[12]

"Such a row you never saw," Stephens reported. Although no one was injured, animosity lingered. If weapons had been present, there probably would have been bloodshed, he thought. Stephens began to

11. AHS to LS, February 3, 1858, in Stephens Papers, MC; L. F. Grover to Asahel Bush, March 5, 1859, quoted in Von Abele, *Stephens*, 168.

12. The preceding paragraphs are from Nichols, *Disruption of Democracy*, 163–64.

get an inkling of what it all meant: "All things here are tending to bring my mind to the conclusion that this Govmt. can not or will not last long." [13]

It took two more days of bitter bickering before Harris' motion to establish a special committee finally carried the House by a close vote. But the Lecompton opponents' victory was short-lived. Speaker Orr packed the fifteen-man committee with eight Lecompton men and put Harris and Stephens in the number one and two spots. Without much ado, the committee voted, eight to seven, against conducting a protracted investigation. At least for now the administration had matters precariously in hand. [14]

It was a good thing it did. The mood in Georgia was ugly. Thomas still raged about Buchanan. "Nothing short of seeing the Holy Ghost descending on Old Buck in the form of a dove patent to my eyesight could ever make me trust him again," he vowed. Governor Brown began hinting ominously that if Kansas were rejected he would call a state convention to determine Georgia's status in the Union. And Linton had worked himself into a frenzy. If Kansas were refused admission, "I am for dissolution," he announced. He would not submit to "a brand of sin and infamy and degradation" at the hands of the government. [15]

Brother Aleck studiously refused to notice this outburst until several weeks later, and only then at Linton's prodding. In the grips of one of his black moods, he advised Linton not to get so upset: "It is not worth the troubles. Fame is a poor thing, a miserable po[or] thing, patriotism is a poor thing. All the things of this world are poor beggarly elements—ashes and emptiness." [16]

Sick in body and spirit, Stephens gave himself over to his gloom, a mood broken only by intermittent spells of "patriotism" for the next two months. In mid-February, after about a week laid up in his room with "something like rheumatism," Stephens considered resigning his seat: "The strife, vexation, wear and tear of public life here is nothing but a useless sacrifice of ones self for nought and nought only." His

13. AHS to LS, February 5, 1858, in Stephens Papers, MC.

14. *Congressional Globe*, 35th Cong., 1st Sess., 621–23.

15. Thomas to AHS, February 7, 1858, in Stephens Papers, EU; Joseph E. Brown to AHS, February 9, 1858, in Phillips (ed.), *TSC Correspondence*, 431; LS to AHS, February 9, 1858, in Stephens Papers, MC.

16. AHS to LS, March 29, 1858, in Stephens Papers, MC.

arms and elbows hurt, he complained. "Overwhelmed" with hard work, he had no time for recreation. Even politics gave him no pleasure. He wished he had never run for Congress. Nothing in Washington interested him, and he was disgusted with selfish men to whom patriotism meant nothing. Once Kansas came in, he vowed, he was through with it. All he wanted was "quiet retirement and uninterrupted solitude."[17]

If Kansas came in, Stephens should have said, for clearly by this time he strongly suspected that Lecompton would fail. "We have so many fools," he sighed resignedly, "and from the South too, that there is no counting upon what will be done." With the right men there would be no difficulty. But patriotism, statesmanship, and public virtue were all either gone or "fast dying out."[18]

The biggest "fools," of course, were the Know Nothings, although Stephens hardly excused drunken Democrats either. Stephens found it disgraceful having constantly to cope with southern allies in the clutches of demon rum. But far more vexing was dealing with the southern Americans, who, though small in numbers, held the balance of power in the House. They had not yet rallied behind Lecompton, and the question of how they would vote plagued Stephens continually.

Part of what had been keeping Stephens so busy was writing his report endorsing the Lecompton constitution for the special Kansas committee. On March 3, the committee accepted it by an eight-to-seven vote, but House rules prevented its immediate publication. Faced with months of delay, Stephens had the report printed himself, and it appeared in the Washington *Union* on March 11, 1858. Under the Kansas-Nebraska Act, Stephens argued, the people could form their constitution "*in their own way.*" Who participated in the convention's election and whether the convention submitted the constitution to voters were immaterial questions. Congress could examine only the *form* of the proposed constitution. Of course, the Kansas free-soilers' vote in January had nothing to do with the inquiry. Ignoring sensitive southern opinion, however, courted real danger: "Will not [Kansas'] rejection tend to weaken the bonds which hold the States together?"[19]

17. *Ibid.*, February 14, 19, 28, 1858.
18. AHS to LS, February 28, 1858, in Stephens Papers, MC.
19. *House Reports*, 35th Cong, 1st Sess, Rept. No. 377. Under House rules reports of standing committees took precedence over those of special committees, unless the House gave unanimous consent to suspend the rule. Republicans naturally objected to receiving Stephens' report.

Stephens had reason to fear for the Union. Governor Brown again threatened to call a convention if the Lecompton constitution was rejected. Many southerners were angry, but, as Stephens well knew, many more were simply confused. If our leaders differ, wrote one perplexed Georgian, how could the home front be united? Good question, Stephens might have mused; he himself did not know what to do if Lecompton failed.[20]

The rich irony of the situation escaped Stephens. Unity before the northern enemy was what he wanted now, the very thing he had denied Calhoun in the crisis of 1849–1850. Now, as then, political differences among southerners prevented that unity. The only change since Calhoun's death was the number of southerners who perceived a dire threat from the North and decided that unity offered the only hope for survival. The southern Know Nothings, however, stood outside this growing consensus and its vehicle, the southern Democratic party. The central paradox of southern politics had not changed: each party championed southern rights and urged solidarity in the face of the enemy, but each insisted that the battle be fought only on its terms, thus ensuring continued divisions. Indeed, the only force unifying southerners in 1858 was paranoia, and even that was a matter of degree.

Stephens' pleas for the safety of the Union had no effect on the northern congressmen. The same day that his report appeared in the *Union*, Harris charged that the special committee had not investigated Lecompton properly. Stephens protested instantly, and two days of heated debate followed. On a procedural vote some southern Americans, to Stephens' disgust, voted with the Republicans. Even worse, twenty-two Lecompton Democrats, over half southerners and some completely immobilized by whiskey, had been absent. Such laxity sent Stephens into a fit of helpless hand-wringing. "Alas for my country," he wrote Linton, "—for the South. . . . How shamefully she is represented." He still agonized the next day. Lecompton forces lost another close vote, again with southern Know Nothings against them and some southern Democrats so drunk they had to be held off the floor until time to slobber their "yea" or "nay." "Oh my country my country my own native Georgia. . . . What is to become of you?"[21]

Lecompton supporters could do nothing now but await Senate ac-

20. Brown to AHS, February 18, 1858, H. Fielder to AHS, February 24, 1858, both in Stephens Papers, EU; AHS to LS, April 3, 1858, in Stephens Papers, MC.

21. *Congressional Globe*, 35th Cong., 1st Sess., 1075; AHS to LS, March 11, 12, 1858, in Stephens Papers, MC.

tion on the bill. And it was clear that southern Americans would follow their most revered leader, Senator Crittenden of Kentucky, who denounced the Lecompton constitution and suggested that it be resubmitted to the voters. Lecompton would be lost, Stephens told Linton and Brown: Know Nothings would vote with the enemy. Brown replied swiftly. It made no difference how the Kansas constitution was rejected; he would have to call a state convention. Many Georgians agreed with him. "I trust that our Southern representatives will leave in a body when Kansas is rejected," wrote one. With such advice arriving daily, Stephens lost all hope. He was, he confessed, "on the verge of that deep dark and gloomy abiss" of despair.[22]

The administration had its votes in the Senate, however, and it approved the bill admitting Kansas under Lecompton on March 23. The House dawdled a week before addressing the bill. Twice Stephens tried to set a date for voting on the measure, finally announcing that he would move on April 1 to take the bill up for a vote. In the meantime, he was doing his best to keep Democrats in their seats and to win back deserters. He succeeded at least partially because only one southern congressman missed the crucial vote on the first. The vote itself, however, went against the administration. By a 112 to 120 tally, the House accepted an amendment that sent the constitution back to the Kansas voters. Twenty-two Democrats and six southern Americans voted with the majority.[23]

Stephens almost despaired. Even the firmest northerners, he told a friend, resented having to fight both Republicans and southern Americans. But he refused to give up and continued working feverishly. There was yet a glimmer of hope: Congress had reached an impasse. The Senate rejected the House substitute and sent it back. The House refused to recede, and the Senate again rejected the amendment, this time asking for a conference. By the narrowest of margins on April 14, Orr's vote breaking a tie, the House agreed to confer. To save itself from utter humiliation, the administration had used every means of suasion it could to shake loose enough Democratic anti-Lecompton men for even this paltry victory.[24]

22. AHS to LS, March 17, 19, 1858, in Stephens Papers, MC; Brown to AHS, March 26, 1858, in Phillips (ed.), *TSC Correspondence*, 432–33; M. C. Fulton to AHS, March 30, 1858, in Stephens Papers, LC.

23. *Congressional Globe*, 35th Cong., 1st Sess., 1437, Appendix, 194–201; AHS to LS, April 2, 1858, in Stephens Papers, LC.

24. AHS to G. F. Burton, April 5, 1858, in Stephens Papers, DU; AHS to LS, April 3, 1858, in Stephens Papers, MC.

Stephens now had his chance to salvage as much as he could out of the mess. Orr appointed him to the conference committee, along with Republican William A. Howard of Michigan and Douglas supporter William H. English of Indiana. Passing Lecompton was out of the question, but trying to save a shred of face for the administration would not be easy either. Fortunately for Buchanan, he had one of the cagiest men in Congress working on the problem.

Even before the deadlock, Stephens had foreseen it and sized up the opposition. English, an ambitious man, had proven amenable to both flattery and persuasion. Stephens therefore kept him in tow until the saving formula passed. But strain was beginning to tell. Stephens fell ill, and twice the conferees postponed meeting because of it. In the meantime, however, he devised the plan that would bear English's name.

The so-called English bill in effect resubmitted the Lecompton constitution to the Kansas voters, but instead of coupling admission with slavery it focused on the size of the land grant the new state would receive. If the voters accepted the normal land grant (about 4 million acres instead of the extravagant 23.5 million Lecompton's authors had requested), she would be admitted; if they refused, the territory would have to wait until her population reached about ninety thousand, enough to entitle her to one congressional representative. Rejecting Lecompton would thus delay Kansas' admission for two years or more. The bill was ingenious: with the resubmission question buried under the acreage, proslavery diehards could be mollified—the choice would not be a referendum on slavery but on acceptance of Congress' stipulation on the size of the federal land grant. Moreover, if Kansas voters rejected Lecompton, admission of another free state would at least be postponed for several years. But the anti-Lecompton Democrats could also support the bill because it did submit the entire constitution to the voters under a federally sanctioned procedure.[25]

The conference committee submitted its report on Friday, April 23, 1858, but it took several more days to get the bill passed. Before signing the report, Stephens had carefully cleared it with every important southern senator, including bedridden Jefferson Davis. In the House, however, the bill ran into trouble, and it took another weekend of frantic cajolery to right matters. Although "exceedingly harrassed," Ste-

25. The preceding paragraphs are based on Johannsen, *Douglas*, 610–11.

phens told Linton, he was "as patient as Job." He knew the bill still might fail, that all his work would have been for nought. He was obviously tired of the whole wretched business. He spoke once, briefly, in favor of the bill.[26]

On the last day of April the administration finally succeeded in passing the compromise. The vote in the House was 112 to 103; in the Senate, 31 to 22. After wavering, Douglas voted against it. Buchanan signed it on May 2. In the House, 9 of the 22 anti-Lecompton Democrats voted with the administration. It was no secret how the votes were obtained. "The progress of this business has been damnable corrupt," said Thomas Harris. "The Adm. has bought men like hogs in the market." For Stephens the victory was barren. He hoped that the new vote would split the Kansas free-soilers, he said, but even if not, slavery in Kansas would at least be assured for a few more years under the *Dred Scott* decision.[27]

So it had finally come to this. For the sake of slavery's existence for only a few more years, and in a territory he believed unsuited for it, Stephens had stretched his vaunted principles to the vanishing point. He who had once proclaimed himself no defender of slavery in the abstract had become so blind to reality as to suppose that the few slaves in Kansas really made a difference. The truly sad part about Stephens' support of the Lecompton constitution was that even later, when the issue had long since been forgotten, he could admit his shame but not that he had been wrong. "[Douglas] knew, as we all did, that the Lecompton constitution was procured by fraud," Stephens told his friend Dick Johnston. "I supported it, not because it was fairly obtained, but because it was right when obtained. The fraud was glaring. I feel when looking back at it, like the sons of Noah when they saw their father naked—I wished it might be covered up from the world. Douglas would not support it. I thought it ought to be, and think so yet, because it gave us only what we were entitled to under the Kansas act."[28]

His construction of the law was bizarre, to say the least. The South was entitled to *nothing* under the Kansas-Nebraska Act. That legislation addressed the people of the territory, and it granted them a choice.

26. AHS to LS, April 26, 1858, in Stephens Papers, MC.
27. Harris quoted in Johannsen, *Douglas*, 613; AHS to LS, May 1, 1858, in Stephens Papers, MC.
28. Johnston, *Autobiography*, 151.

But Stephens, like so many southerners, construed it as practically a promissory note from the government for another slave state in the Union. Then with recklessness beyond all reason, to combat ruthless and unscrupulous opponents at home, he enticed the voters into believing this fiction too. Once having done this, he had no choice but to play the game out to the end, regardless of how slimy the game was. At least there was an aura of remorse about what he did. Stephens' conscience could not let him forget that he had supported a dishonest, morally repulsive political instrument. Only because the ratification of Lecompton could be construed as strictly legal, and only because his perception of right and wrong had been so skewed by his emotions— "The election was legal, and the result gave to the South only what was just and right," he contended—did his conscience allow him any rest at all.[29]

And this was why he could not bring himself to blame Douglas for opposing him. Stephens may have relaxed his own moral standards during the Lecompton struggle, but he didn't lose his respect for Democrats who refused to. Throughout the bitter fight he uttered not a single word of recrimination against Douglas. Unlike the crisis of 1850, which he had regarded a truly life-or-death matter, Stephens approached Lecompton as simply a political struggle, to be lost or won with political weapons, however sharp.

Stephens understood Douglas. Once the issue was joined, he had anticipated the Illinois senator's tenacity—and incidentally had won a bet with Cobb on it. Douglas made an issue out of the election that had ratified Lecompton; the administration did not, as Stephens (and Douglas) came to believe, because it meant to ruin the Little Giant in the North. Stephens knew well what political struggles against heavy odds were, and he recognized Douglas' as a life-or-death fight. Tenacious as he was, Stephens had never been an uncompromising sectionalist. He had always tempered his sectionalism with a certain moderating wisdom. He deprecated the war Cobb and Buchanan waged on Douglas and advised against it. The administration, after all, had been responsible for promising the voters of Kansas that their constitution would be submitted to them for ratification, assurances Stephens believed it "had no right to give." Stephens dutifully fought the administration's battle, but deep down he always held Buchanan responsible for the whole debacle.[30]

29. Johnston and Browne, *Stephens*, 428.
30. *Ibid.*

Stephens' views on Douglas were, to say the least, unusual among southern Democrats. Most loathed the Little Giant as the rankest traitor. "We propose to take his political life," vowed the Columbus *Times* with consummate savagery, "dissecting the body, and dividing the good from the evil." The good would be buried with honor, but the evil "we will hang on the gibbet, where the vultures of the air, and the wild beasts of the forest, may devour it." Douglas had paid a stiff price for his integrity—but the Democratic party had paid an even higher one.[31]

The English bill finally removed the Kansas issue from Congress (in August the Kansans overwhelmingly rejected the constitution), but Lecompton had crippled the Democrats. Not only had the issue created thousands of Republican converts, but it had also hopelessly split the last reamining national party. For the moment, however, orthodox Democrats basked in their victory. At the White House signing ceremony, Toombs spoke glowingly of the "peace and harmony and prosperity" the party had won. Stephens also collected his share of praise. The Washington *Union* expounded on his "higher qualities of statesmanship" and "faithful devotion" to "great principle." One Georgia editor called the English bill "the most brilliant idea I ever heard of in politics." Thomas called it "*inspired*," and of course Linton approved. Governor Brown sighed with relief. After congratulating Stephens, he went on to say how "truly glad we are rid of this vexed question." Brown had reason to rejoice. "Had not the bill passed," he observed in classic understatement, "there would have been great confusion in Georgia."[32]

There was confusion enough in Georgia as it was. The American press, which had spent months raking the southern Democrats and sometimes even finding flattering things to say about Douglas, universally condemned the bill. The South, it claimed, had once again been betrayed "by her own recreant sons," foremost of whom was Alexander H. Stephens.[33]

Worn out, Stephens wanted to go home, but several matters delayed by the Kansas imbroglio now required that he stay in Washington. The

31. Columbus *Times*, March 13, 1858, quoted in Irons, "Secession Movement in Georgia," 217.

32. Milledgeville *Southern Recorder*, November 2, 1858; Washington *Union*, May 4, 1858, quoted in Rabun, "Stephens," 508; Hull to Cobb, May 30, 1858, in Cobb-Erwin-Lamar Papers, UG; LS to AHS, May 9, 1858, in Stephens Papers, MC; Brown to AHS, May 7, 1858, in Phillips (ed.), *TSC Correspondence*, 434.

33. Augusta *Chronicle and Sentinel*, May 5, 1858.

delay didn't help his mood, which had been foul for several months. In addition to his usual raft of physical ailments, his eyes had been troubling him, so before he left Washington he laid out ten dollars for a pair of gold-rimmed spectacles, his first pair. These may have improved his vision, but they hardly helped cheer him up. "Thus life passes away," he told Linton. "Wrinkles in the face, gray hairs on the head, and dimmed vision in the eyes. In a few more years, loss of teeth, bending shoulders, and trembling limbs will close the scene." [34]

For almost six months Stephens had been particularly miserable. He had ushered in 1858 "looking back on the misfortunes and miseries of the past" and reflecting on the future. What he had seen since then could hardly have encouraged a brighter outlook. He was ill, tired, disgusted with politics, and ready to quit. More than once during this session he had said so. [35]

Perhaps, then, it was general discontent that prompted him to travel during the break between sessions. He hoped, too, that a trip would improve his health. With Kansas out of the way and his mind almost made up not to seek reelection, the time seemed propitious for touring a section of the country he had never seen, the Northwest. Besides, he had business there. Back in the early spring, while having his portrait painted by the famous artist George P. A. Healy, he made arrangements to have Linton's and his late wife's done, too. Healy, however, was a busy man and could not fit Linton into his schedule until the summer—in Chicago. [36]

The two brothers left Georgia on July 20, 1858, and made their leisurely way up to Cincinnati, taking in the sights along the way. It was impossible for a man of Stephens' repute to pass unnoted through any part of the country, much less Illinois, where a senatorial campaign of national interest was in progress. About the time the brothers began their trip, Republican Abraham Lincoln and Douglas began a series of debates. The campaign generated extraordinary interest, for Douglas, in addition to fending off the surging Republicans, had to cope with the administration, which was ruthlessly wielding all the patronage and pressure it could to purge him from the party. Naturally the reporters wanted to know Stephens' opinion of all this. In Cincinnati, he

34. AHS to LS, June 11, 1858, in Stephens Papers, MC.
35. *Ibid.*, December 31, 1857.
36. Rabun, "Stephens," 514.

gave it. Not only did he favor Douglas, it was duly reported, but he regarded the administration's war on him as "wickedly foolish."[37]

As he made his way north, the purpose of Stephens' trip engendered feverish speculation in the nation's press. Some thought he went as an agent of the administration to patch up its quarrel with Douglas; others suggested he was a stalking-horse for Cobb's presidential ambitions. Some said that Stephens himself sought the 1860 nomination and wanted Douglas as a running mate. Other rumors claimed that he had allied with Douglas against the administration or that he simply wanted to help the Little Giant defeat Lincoln. Stephens' remarks in Cincinnati put an end to several of the more fantastic speculations.[38]

Little Aleck's statement that he favored Douglas stunned the South. At first neither Democratic nor American editors could believe it. Soon, however, most of the Democratic papers in Georgia, the *Constitutionalist* excepted, raked Stephens as if he had been in league with Moloch himself. With one voice, orthodox southern Democrats prayed for Douglas' defeat. The idea that the South should turn its back on the administration "merely to save an ambitious and reckless politician" was "monstrous," said the *Federal Union*. "It would be just as reasonable," echoed the Mobile *Register*, "to lay down our arms and surrender to the Black Republicans as to abstain from making war upon Mr. Douglas," who was every bit as hostile to the South as the Republicans.[39]

Stephens was hardly the only Georgia Democrat who saw little sense in attacking Douglas, however. These men recognized that Douglas had done only what was politically necessary, and they tended to be philosophical about recent events. "We have made all out of niggers thats to be made," said Martin Crawford, "there's nothing left." Kansas, he continued, had been "*a great investment*" that had paid handsome dividends until the expiration of the charter. All debts due were now canceled. The Lecompton fraud still bothered some consciences. Had there been no fraud in Kansas, wrote Augustus Wright, who could doubt that Douglas would have voted for her admission? All Douglas' friends in Georgia believed he was "*sound on niggers*," and

---

37. Savannah *Morning News*, August 13, 1858.
38. J. Henley Smith to AHS, August 3, 1858, in Stephens Papers, LC.
39. Milledgeville *Federal Union*, September 7, 1858; Mobile *Register* quoted in Savannah *Morning News*, July 22, 1858.

few were blind to Cobb's presidential aspirations—or that Cobb's papers were the ones most critical of Stephens.[40]

Much to Stephens' distress, several newspapers concluded that he too was angling for the 1860 nomination. After a pleasant trip home by way of Mammoth Cave and Memphis, he arrived to find his "nonpolitical" trip the prime topic in the press. He didn't "care a button" for the "ill-grounded surmises and unjust suspicions," he told Dick Johnston. Politics had nothing to do with his trip: "I was, in reality, running away from politics." Moreover, he had been misquoted. He had characterized the war on Douglas as "unwise and impolitic," not "wickedly foolish." "This is my deliberate judgment," he concluded, "and it is perfectly immaterial with me who approves and who disapproves it."[41]

The trip had not been entirely free of politics, despite Stephens' denial. In Chicago, for example, the Georgian had found time to confer with James Sheahan, the editor of Douglas' chief organ, the Chicago Times. And he had written Cobb remonstrating against the administration's war on Douglas. Cobb was not listening. "Don't allow your kind feelings and past confidence in him to deceive you," he replied. "The Democratic party and the South have nothing to hope for in his success."[42]

Stephens and Cobb had finally reached an inevitable parting of the ways. Little Aleck's estrangement from the state party was already apparent. He found it necessary to disavow presidential ambitions publicly. Seeing his name bruited about in such a way, said Stephens, mortified and annoyed him almost as much as seeing it printed "in a list of suspected horse thieves" would have. Cobb's partisans didn't believe him. Disclaimers aside, the fact remained that Stephens continued to defend Douglas, an unforgivable apostasy. Several Cobb papers began muttering ominously about former Whigs in the party showing "leniency" toward Douglas. Their "fidelity" was not in question, the Federal Union silkily explained; it simply wanted to warn them against "error." The Cassville Standard did not mince words. The party had

40. Crawford to AHS, September 8, 1858, Smith to AHS, August 3, 1858, both in Stephens Papers, LC; Augustus R. Wright to C. P. Culver, August 23, 1858, in Milledgeville Southern Recorder, September 7, 1858.

41. Rabun, "Stephens," 518; New York Times, August 24, 1858; AHS to Johnston, September 3, 1858, in Johnston and Browne, Stephens, 338.

42. Cobb to AHS, September 8, 1858, in Phillips (ed.), TSC Correspondence, 442.

too many former Whig leaders, it said: "They are giving the Democracy trouble, and the sooner their places are filled by 'Simon Pure' Democrats, the better it will be for us."[43]

Democratic dissension naturally delighted Georgia's Opposition (as the Know Nothing/American remnant now came to be known). One Opposition editor, in mock bewilderment, listed seven discernible factions in the state party and asked for enlightenment. Most honest Democrats would have had to admit that their party was in shambles. About all that was certain was that the vast majority of the party despised Douglas.[44]

Grievously troubled, Stephens made his way back to Washington in November, 1858. Linton and Rio and a crowd of well-wishers had seen him off at the station, and as he gazed at them Stephens was struck with the thought that he might never see any of them again. By the time he reached Augusta, the presentiment of death became overpowering. He wrote Linton a long letter enclosing a list of notes owed him and instructing him to do his best for "Harry and his family" if he were to die. Harry, Stephens' most trusted slave, whom he loved greatly, looked after all the workaday tasks at the plantation in his master's absence. Stephens relied on him implicitly and, indeed, thought more of him "than the great majority of white men" he had to deal with.[45]

The president doubtless belonged to this majority. Stephens noticed how quiet he was during his courtesy call and suspected that his support of Douglas had annoyed Old Buck. Maybe Buchanan viewed him as an "insidious rival." Had he been aware "of how I *pitied him*" despite his powers, Stephens mused, he surely would have thought differently. But all Buchanan knew was what he heard, and the capital buzzed with rumors about Stephens' presidential aspirations. Genuinely vexed, Little Aleck denied it to everyone who would listen, but it did no good. "I do wish an end put to all such use of my name," he wrote irritably.[46]

43. Augusta *Constitutionalist*, August 26, 1858; Milledgeville *Federal Union*, October 5, 19, 1858; Cassville *Standard* quoted in Milledgeville *Southern Recorder*, October 12, 1858.
44. Milledgeville *Southern Recorder*, October 26, 1858; R. P. Thweatt to AHS, December 15, 1858, in Stephens Papers, LC.
45. AHS to LS, November 30, 1858, in Stephens Papers, LC.
46. *Ibid.*, December 8, 1858.

Cobb had found Stephens in better humor the night before, but the secretary burned with bitterness against Douglas. If the Georgia Democrats ever forgave him, Cobb promised, it would be over his dead political body. This remark struck Stephens as funny. If Cobb persisted, both his feelings and his policy would be run into the ground, he joked. Cobb did not know it, but Stephens had a reason to be jovial: he had decided to retire, and the prospect seemed to lighten his mood—at least temporarily.[47]

The House, however, had its own annoyances. After months of delay, it had finally taken up the Oregon statehood bill, only to be bogged down by Republican objections. (Oregon was a Democratic state that barred free blacks and was to be admitted with sixty thousand population, thirty thousand less than had been required of Kansas.) Five times during January and February Stephens had tried to bring up the bill and each time was stymied. The bill finally got to the floor on February 10, 1859.

By this time it was common knowledge that Stephens meant to retire, so the high point of the short debate came on February 12, when Little Aleck spoke. Onlookers jammed the galleries and even the floor itself, but everyone fell silent when Stephens' shrill voice pierced the hall. After disposing of Republican and Know Nothing objections to the bill, he reached the most interesting part of the speech. Several southerners opposed Oregon's admission simply because it was a free state and would further tip the balance of power against the South. "That balance is already gone," Stephens told them, "lost by causes beyond your or my control." No statesman should ever consult his fears. Great changes were crowding in; the West would continue to grow. "Nothing in the physical world is still. . . . Progress is the universal law governing all things." Since he had been in Congress, the country had witnessed amazing changes: six new states, 1.2 million miles of new territory, astonishing increases in manufactures, exports, cotton, railroads, telegraph, colleges, the arts. The South had no reason to fear such progress. The Constitution guaranteed her security. The fabric of the nation rested on the dissimilarity of its members. The South's safety lay in strict conformity to the country's laws of existence, and "growth is one of these." New states would come in under constitutions people made for themselves. The South had always de-

47. *Ibid.*, December 7, 1858.

fended this principle; it should not abandon it now. At one point Stephens waxed so eloquent on the glories of the Union and the near divinity of the American political system that the crowd burst into tumultuous cheering and applause. Even veteran legislators stood up and joined in. It was a singular tribute. For all his faults, Stephens had the respect, if not the affection, of his colleagues.[48]

The Washington *Union* gave his speech a rave review—"one of the most eloquent and effective ever delivered in Congress"—and credited Stephens with passing the bill. Even Linton, always Stephens' most exacting critic, thought the speech "the most powerful I ever read from you." After spending a few weeks with Aleck in Washington in January, Linton had come home almost awed, "more impressed with your *intellect*" than ever before. "You seem to me to be a benign and superior intelligence moving among the rest."[49]

Extravagant praise was probably just what Stephens needed to hear; he was in the midst of a profound depression. As was true so many other times, the exact cause of his sorrow on this occasion is impossible to pinpoint. Linton, who normally saved his brother's letters like a pack rat, actually destroyed one Stephens wrote near the end of January, so much did it trouble him. At first Linton felt sure he knew the cause of the sorrow. His analysis hinted at a profound sense of insecurity in Stephens, a feeling Aleck would have repressed at all costs:

> In my judgment it is the foundation of your highest virtues and the source of your greatest faults. If I know you, one of your leading virtues is a resolute, determined, almost dogged kindness and devotion of service to mankind who have in your judgment no *claims* to your affection and whom your *impulses* lead you to despise and hate. This is the great battle which often rages, the conflict between your resolution to be kind, and your impulse to be almost vengeful. . . . One of your greatest faults which has been more and more corrected from year to year . . . is a *residium* of "what's *not* resisted"—an imperiousness which loves to show the vile herd how immeasurably they are your inferiors in certain points. . . . Your philosophy has failed to cure the unhappiness of your constitution. . . . The opinions of people have too much power to affect your happiness. . . . Besides, you impute to them sometimes opinions which they do not have.[50]

48. Speech in Cleveland, *Stephens*, 621–37.
49. Washington *Union*, quoted in Rabun, "Stephens," 523; LS to AHS, February 19, 26, 1859, in Stephens Papers, MC.
50. LS to AHS, January 29, 1859, in Stephens Papers, MC.

The next day, upon rereading his brother's letter, Linton was no longer so sure. Never, he marveled, had he seen anything like it "in its energy, its despair and yet its unearthly resolution to bear on, and despair on. . . . You must allude to something I don't understand." He had always thought it in the nature of human beings to share misery. His brother, however, was different. In him he discerned a conscious desire to hoard unhappiness: "A desire from your earliest remembrance to keep it to yourself, is what you say." For his own peace of mind, Linton burned the letter. Stephens' dark secret was lost.[51]

Linton was correct, of course. Stephens cared desperately about others' opinions, far more than his frequent scorn for them indicated. And his innate disposition to kindness clashed constantly with his self-protective hauteur. But Linton hardly suspected the real pangs his brother suffered. For Aleck was immersed in an affair of the heart, and he knew he had to give it up.

Stephens never was comfortable discussing such matters. They were too private to share with anyone else: Toombs, Dick Johnston, even Linton. Just why can never be known for sure. As a very young man Stephens had resolved to remain a bachelor, and the only time he deigned to discuss the reason why, he blamed his health. He would not burden any woman with lifelong care of an invalid, he told Johnston. Even when pressed, Stephens refused to elaborate. He answered with but a single word—"*pride.*"[52]

What mysterious facet of Stephens did this laconic reply conceal? Maybe it was an agonizing consciousness of his own inadequacy as a man, a sexual inadequacy perhaps, or an inability to deal with women emotionally. Or was it really pride—a massive, monumental pride that forever prevented him from becoming dependent on anyone? Did this single word contain the clue to the source of Stephens' profound loneliness and despair? Only Stephens knew. But this much is sure: several women found him more than ordinarily attractive—and in 1859, even as he wrote from the depths of despair, he had the same feelings about Elizabeth Church Craig, a comely Athens widow.

This was not the first Georgia lass whose heart Stephens had captured. Another, known to us only as Constance, had once enjoyed a relationship with him that clearly went beyond simple friendship. But

51. *Ibid.*, January 30, 1859.
52. Johnston and Browne, *Stephens*, 499–500.

Stephens had ended that one too—abruptly. "Constance has just left me," he wrote to Linton in 1849. "She wept sorely and bitterly. The conflict of feeling between a desire to stay and a duty to go seemed to be exceedingly strong, or rather perhaps I should say that the consciousness that we *had* to part caused her great pain and mortification of spirit. I bid her good bye with a heavy heart and suffered upon the last wound that must be—'farewell.' . . . But she is gone." [53]

His relationship with Elizabeth Craig ended similarly but not before it had reached the stage of strong mutual affection. Thirty-seven years old in 1859, Elizabeth was the youngest and prettiest of the three daughters of Alonzo Church, the president of Franklin College. Stephens had first met her when she was a child and he a sixteen-year-old freshman boarding with Church. Stephens had been kind to her then, as she gratefully remembered. The years intervened. Stephens went on to fame, and Elizabeth grew into a beautiful woman. In 1843 she married a young army officer, Lewis Craig, who was killed by Indians in New Mexico ten years later. Shortly thereafter, his widow renewed her friendship with Stephens, writing him a sympathetic note after his train accident in 1853. The correspondence continued, and the affection between the two deepened. By 1857 Stephens was seasoning his letters to Elizabeth with the "spice of flattery" and "kindly sentiments," which, she confessed, "affected her heart." [54]

About the time of his despairing letter to Linton in January, 1859,

53. AHS to LS, November 28, 1849, in Stephens Papers, LC. One of Stephens' early biographers sheds a possible ray of light on the mysterious Constance, although he does not mention her name. At the time he wrote, in 1883, there lived in Atlanta an unmarried woman who had once been linked romantically to Stephens. The pair had first met around 1840, when the girl was only sixteen or seventeen years old. Ten years later they met again and became more serious, their relationship "amounting to an engagement." "Occurrences of a private nature, delays and disappointments intervened and prevented their marriage," he says, but in the best romantic tradition both remained single for each other's sake (Frank H. Norton, *The Life of Alexander H. Stephens* [New York, 1883], 86). The last statement is, of course, fanciful, but it is possible that the woman referred to is Constance because the date of the supposed romance coincides with the hard evidence. There is abundant evidence that Stephens had great charm with women, and several would have welcomed a serious relationship with him. He had a number of secret admirers too, some of them more bold than others. "My dearest friend," wrote one of these in the 1840s. "Will we never meet? Will our happiness never be complete?" ("Carrie" to AHS, n.d. [1840s], in Stephens Papers, LC).

54. Rabun, "Stephens," 546–49, contains the account of Stephens' relationship with Elizabeth Craig; E. C. Craig to AHS, June 21, 1853, 28 January 1857, in Stephens Papers, LC.

Stephens was working to push a bill through the House to pay her more than $800 in back pay due her late husband. More than simple gratitude prompted her to call Stephens "the greatest man now living" when the bill passed. Mrs. Craig must have been much on Stephens' mind during these months—way too much on his mind. Their relationship was growing dangerously warm on both sides. It had to end.[55]

He had tried to bow out gracefully, sending her some jewels with the hope that they would establish "a place" for him in her "memory." Elizabeth was delighted but assured him that the gift could not "compare with that jewel which beyond all other I prize and which I hope I shall never lose—your friendship." Because it was more than friendship, Stephens found it impossible to extricate himself immediately. Twice during the summer of 1859 he stayed as a guest with the Church family. Elizabeth was captivated, thrilled with Stephens' visits. After his last stay she visited Dick Johnston, "looking uncommonly beautiful," he told Stephens, "and saying many beautiful things of you." That Stephens found it desirable to stay with Elizabeth and her family twice in three months suggests that his resolve may have weakened. It is clear that he did not end the relationship then; indeed, it seems to have grown stronger. Was he unable to confront Elizabeth face-to-face with his crushing news? Or was he having second thoughts about marriage? Johnston, for one, was "suspicious."[56]

Stephens could not bring himself to end the relationship in person; he did it by mail. Elizabeth left Athens in October, 1859, to visit a friend in Pennsylvania; she never saw him again. Her last letter to him is both pathetic and poignant. It came with a gift, a copy of Giovanni Ruffini's sentimental novel *Dr. Antonio*. In his "noble charities, devoted friendship and other good qualities," Elizabeth told him, he came nearer Dr. Antonio's goodness than anyone she knew. This, she said, was "the sincere and just tribute of my heart to one who has always been this, and more, in my estimation."[57]

As she suspected, however, the book was a parting gift. She had already received intimations from him that even simple friendship with her could not continue. His last letter had saddened her greatly. In it he had alluded to his sufferings, which she had been unaware of. Besides,

55. Johnston to AHS, April 27, 1859, in Stephens Papers, LC.
56. Craig to AHS, January 28, 1857, in Stephens Papers, EU; Craig to AHS, July 20, 1859, Johnston to AHS, August 12, 1859, both in Stephens Papers, LC.
57. Craig to AHS, October 2, 1859, in Stephens Papers, LC.

"it seemed a farewell letter." It was. She had wanted to see him before leaving, but he avoided her. In the only way he could, Stephens had said good-bye. Within six months Elizabeth had remarried. He never forgot her. Years later, when a prisoner in a northern cell, just the sight of a handwriting similar to hers brought Elizabeth immediately to mind. Her absence and all that might have been were pangs he carried in secret the rest of his life.[58]

He made no secret of his desire to be free of politics, however. By February, 1859, his habitual foreboding for the future at least had foundation. Sectional tensions increased daily, while the administration continued its unremitting war on Douglas, much to Stephens' distress. The last time Stephens saw the president he had warned that his policy would lead to a disruption of the government. He did not think the current session would end without a "general smash up." But, for once, he was unconcerned. He meant to go home for good and devote himself "to pursuits more congenial to my tastes and nature."[59]

"The state cannot fill your place in Congress," wrote Governor Brown, a sentiment Democratic papers throughout the country echoed. Stephens' own colleagues extended the most impressive tribute. On March 1, 1859, sixty members of Congress, "personal friends" they ascribed themselves, invited him to a testimonial dinner to be held the following Friday, March 4. Among the signers were almost half the Senate, the vice-president, and many friends from the House. But Stephens declined the invitation, pleading the press of personal business at home. He wanted no public tribute this time; he just wanted to leave quickly. So on March 5, without ceremony, he departed the capital for home.[60]

Why had he left Congress at the peak of his power and influence? Quite simply, he was tired, harassed, and terribly unhappy. He had given up on his own power to affect the future and wanted to be home for good. He was fed up with Congress, tired of being pestered by favor seekers, and, by his own reckoning, overworked and unappreciated by a "restless, captious, and fault-finding people." He longed for

---

58. Ibid.; Avary (ed.), Stephens Recollections, 398–99.
59. Avary (ed.), Stephens Recollections, 29; AHS to LS, February 3, 1859, in Stephens Papers, MC; AHS to Johnston, February 28, 1859, in Johnston and Browne, Stephens, 342.
60. Brown to AHS, February 14, 1859, in Stephens Papers, DU; Augusta Constitutionalist, February 5, 1859.

Crawfordville and the idyllic life of reflection and repose it offered. He was much too lonely and provincial a man ever to have found much contentment away from home. Simply enjoying Rio gave him more pleasure than "all of the honors this world has ever seen fit to bestow upon me," he said shortly after his arrival home. "I am content."[61]

Stephens had flirted with the idea of retiring ever since 1855. All that had ever brought him back since then was what he saw as an unavoidable battle for the principles of the Kansas-Nebraska Act, a bill he considered himself responsible for. That bill, like the Kansas question itself, was a dead letter now, and with it went his main reason to stay. "I am out of politics and intend to stay out," he wrote in April, a statement the nation's gossip mongers would have scoffed at. His retirement, they were saying, was just a prelude—either for a try at the presidency or for the Georgia senate seat coming up for election in the fall.[62]

Unfortunately, Stephens' return coincided with the start of Georgia's biennial gubernatorial campaign. Stephens had about as much chance of giving up politics as of renouncing breathing. He was a pivotal figure in the state party whether he liked it or not. He and Toombs (who also deplored the war on Douglas) led one of the party's recognizable factions, a group lukewarm toward the administration and at best ambivalent to Cobb's presidential hopes. Arrayed against this faction was Cobb's large proadministration group and a small southern rights splinter. The governor had his own cadre. For the past two years Brown had deftly built his own formidable patronage machine based largely on the state-owned Western and Atlantic Railroad. Concerned chiefly with consolidating state power, Brown kept a wetted finger to the breeze on national issues and sailed with the prevailing gusts.

The governor carefully kept his lines open to both major factions of the party. He courted Stephens almost obsequiously, constantly soliciting advice and counsel. Brown had gushed when Linton presented him with a portrait of his brother. One copy of the distinguished countenance was insufficient; he wanted another to hang in the executive office in Milledgeville. By this time Brown had already sealed his friendship with Stephens, for in May, 1859, he had appointed Linton

---

61. AHS to Johnston, January 28, March 15, 1859, in Johnston and Browne, *Stephens*, 341–42, 344–45; AHS to LS, March 16, 1859, in Stephens Papers, MC.
62. AHS to John Steele, April 9, 1859, in Stephens Papers, DU.

Stephens to the state supreme court bench. Stephens was ecstatic. "I am truly gratified," he burbled to Linton. "My very heart overflowed." More objective observers saw through this transaction immediately. "Gov. Brown is proving himself to be a pretty good diplomatist," the Rome *Courier* observed. "We suppose there are a hundred men in Georgia better qualified for a seat on the supreme bench than Linton Stephens, but none of them have got 'little Alec' for a brother."[63]

Brown had also secured his other flank by coming to terms with Cobb. In return for unofficial assurance of a friendly delegation to the national convention, Cobb persuaded Lumpkin to cease his grumbling about patronage and forego his usual quest for the gubernatorial nomination. The governor had struck the far better deal.

Secretary Cobb, his eye constantly on 1860, had his own flanks to guard. Needing Stephens' support, he had his followers lobby him before the state's June convention. Stephens hedged, refusing to endorse proadministration resolutions or commit himself to further definition of southern rights in the territories. The 1856 national platform was sufficient, he said. Far more intent on preserving party unity than on promoting Cobb for president, Stephens favored a middle course that neither blasted Douglas nor praised Buchanan too extravagantly. Cobb's people could not accept this ambivalence. Indeed, for the next year and a half they suspected everything Stephens did or said. Little Aleck, they concluded, was Cobb's worst enemy.[64]

Meanwhile, despite his assurance to Cobb, Governor Brown also wanted Stephens' advice on how the party should treat the administration. Stephens gladly obliged him—with a twenty-five-page letter. Generally, he told Brown, the party's many differences with Buchanan ought to be soft-pedaled and the administration sustained as far as possible "without injury to the cause or sacrifice of principle." Resolutions praising Buchanan's "patriotism and integrity," would be enough, he thought. At all costs, though, the Democratic party should be sustained, for only in it, and not without, were "corrective elements" to be found.[65]

63. LS to AHS, June 21, 1859, in Stephens Papers, MC; AHS to LS, May 13, 1859, in Stephens Papers, MC; Rome *Courier*, May 25, 1859, quoted in Joseph H. Parks, *Joseph E. Brown of Georgia* (Baton Rouge, 1977), 80.

64. Jackson to Cobb, May 30, 1859, in Cobb-Erwin-Lamar Papers, UG.

65. AHS to LS, June 2, 1859, in Stephens Papers, MC. The letter to Brown has been lost, but according to Stephens, he had told Cobb's man James Jackson the same thing.

Although hardly staying out of politics entirely, Stephens did take steps to crush a move by some of his more exuberant supporters to have the convention endorse him for the presidency. Through Brown, Stephens informed them he would not accept nomination at Charleston even if it were tendered. Remarking upon their disappointment at this news, Brown insinuated that he, too, thought Stephens' determination a trifle hasty. Characteristically, he saw Stephens' "position as no aspirant" as a pose. It was "correct," he said, but duty might require his accepting.[66]

The Democrats met in Milledgeville on June 15. Brown's address to the gathering followed Stephens' advice, and the convention followed his lead. The party unanimously affirmed its faith in the Cincinnati platform and called for Brown's renomination by acclamation. Except for the convention's extremely tepid endorsement of Buchanan, Cobb was pleased. Stephens, of course, got all he wished.[67]

Shortly after his nomination, Brown announced that he would not canvass the state. At that point it would have been silly, for not until August did the Opposition find a candidate willing to run. Georgia's American party had officially disbanded in early June but then scheduled an "Opposition party" convention for the next month. After several false starts, the Opposition finally convened in August and named Warren Akin, an obscure Cass County lawyer, for governor. The Opposition platform was a ringing southern rights declaration demanding positive congressional protection for slavery in the territories.

As usual, the Opposition had seized the main chance. Georgia's anti-Democratic vote had stabilized at around 40 percent of the electorate. Only by luring enough disgruntled Democrats could the Opposition hope to survive. The Democrats' intramural spat played right into their hands. Strategy demanded that they antagonize the pro-Douglas and administration wings of the Democracy as much as possible. Neither would protect southern rights, they charged; both had cheated the South in Kansas. Adherence to the Democracy and its imbecile leaders endangered the Union. This was a line astutely calculated to keep the Democrats from ever uniting.

And it worked. While the Opposition, again with Ben Hill in the forefront, harped on national issues, the splintered Democrats had to

66. Brown to AHS, June 21, 1859, in Phillips (ed.), *TSC Correspondence*, 445.
67. Milledgeville *Southern Recorder*, June 29, 1859.
68. The preceding paragraphs are based on Montgomery, *Cracker Parties*, 227–35, and Crutcher, "Disunity and Dissolution," 36–54.

fall back on Brown's state record. Fortunately, he had a good one, and he proved invincible, running up a startling victory of more than twenty thousand votes. But the Opposition had not failed completely. Its campaign tactics had almost forced the Democrats to take an aggressive southern rights position. The Democratic party was beginning to move perilously in the direction Calhoun had charted ten years before. Two nagging questions haunted the party. Could it survive a Douglas candidacy in 1860? Could it afford *not* to demand congressional protection for territorial slavery in its next platform? [68]

Neither question particularly concerned Stephens at the moment. He was thinking about a speech he had to give. For the first time in twenty-three years he wasn't running for office. So the speech would not even bear on the campaign. It would be just a simple little farewell to his constituents.

XV

A Damned Strange Disease

A few days before the speech Stephens fretted about what to say, but in Augusta on July 2, 1859, he managed to hold forth for three hours to a large, respectful assembly at his testimonial dinner. The occasion naturally lent itself to a review of the past—Georgia's, the country's, and his own—and to some glimpses of the future. After conventional expressions of gratitude, Stephens launched into a paean to progress in both the state and nation. He took particular pride in the advance of education in Georgia, especially the Georgia Female College at Macon, established with his "warm support." The progress of the nation had also been phenomenal, without parallel in history. Not surprisingly, during the exhaustive review of his own career, he found nothing to regret. Every great and vexing sectional question had been "amicably and satisfactorily adjusted"; there wasn't "a ripple upon the surface."

If this remark indicated Stephens' self-delusion, what followed amplified the proof. This happy state of affairs, he soon made clear, had come about in no small measure through his own diligence and foresight. Resolutions embodying his and Milton Brown's ideas had brought Texas into the Union, he recalled, with the guarantee that four additional slave states could be carved out of her territory. (Though this was true, in 1845 Stephens had emphasized closing the slavery question, not the possibility of slavery's expansion.) In 1850, the principle of nonintervention had been established, not "the full measure of our rights" he thought then, but he had yielded to prevailing opinion in the South.

Since establishment of that hallowed principle, he had done nothing but defend it. All the ensuing struggles had been "for abstract principle on both sides." Principle was paramount, Stephens emphasized, even if it led to no practical results. So the bloodshed in Kansas, the Lecompton fraud, all the hours he had spent trying to circumvent the true expression of the popular will in that unhappy territory had been for nothing but abstract principle. Stephens conveniently forgot how vital the "practical result"—another slave state—had been. It was what he had promised these voters four years ago, what he had labored mightily for since then, what he had sacrificed his honesty and integrity for. He now said that Kansas never had been important. It's a wonder he could say these words with a straight face. Even all the fearful agitation this struggle for abstract principle engendered had not harmed the South, he said. The South had "repelled assault, calumny, and aspersion, by argument, by reason, and truth." In fact, slavery had grown stronger. The odious Missouri restriction had been removed, and the Court had prevented both Congress and territorial legislatures from excluding slavery from the territories.

Stephens had no fear for the future. So long as the constitutional equality of the states was maintained and "virtue, integrity, and patriotism" ruled in public office, the Union would stand. "I see no cause of danger, either to Union, or to southern security in it." And a secure South seemed destined to achieve an even more glorious future. The northern provinces of Mexico beckoned, and even more important, so did Cuba. American neutrality toward Cuba no longer concerned him. Spain's possession of the island presented only a minor inconvenience, for she held it by "force and conquest." The remedy, said Stephens, was to repeal antifilibustering laws and allow Americans to "go and help" the Cubans achieve independence if Spain refused to sell the island. In the past few years, Cuba, a land that permitted slavery, had become an increasingly attractive prospect to ardent southern expansionists. Stephens had never agreed with these radicals, who argued that southern security depended upon the spread of slavery. His concern had always been with southern equality in the territories. Yet he could see no harm in spreading slavery "to the extent of population and capacity."

He might have left the subject with this innocuous observation, but instead he plunged heedlessly into a subject long taboo among all but the most radical proslavery zealots—reopening the African slave trade:

> You may not expect to see many of the territories come into the Union as slave States, unless we have an increase of African stock. . . . It takes people to make States; and it requires people of the African race to make slave States. . . . I very much question whether . . . we can furnish the requisite number to secure more than the four states to come out of Texas in the present territories. . . . To look for, or expect many more, is to look in vain, without a foreign supply. This question the people of the South should examine in its length and breadth. It is one deserving of consideration of the gravest character. It deeply concerns our internal interests and domestic policy, as well as the growth and extension of our institutions. It should not be acted on or decided hastily, but calmly and deliberately.

This iron law of population was so obvious, he continued, that it was utterly useless to wage war on northerners who denied slaveholders' rights in the territories or for southerners to quarrel among themselves "unless we get more Africans to send there to be protected." If the prohibition against the slave trade continued, the South would have to abandon its race with the North for colonizing new states.

Stephens continued at length, justifying the institution of slavery and finally taking lofty leave of his constituents. Not a single one of his past actions would he change, he said. All important questions had been settled, so he was retiring. He would not, of course, declare that under no circumstances would he abandon politics, but he wanted no "office under Heaven." Apologizing to anyone he may have offended in the heat of party battles, he took his leave.[1]

Perhaps only an announcement from Stephens that he had become a Republican would have created a greater sensation than his remarks on the slave trade did. He had scrupulously avoided advocating reopening the trade, but almost everyone, North and South, read his remarks that way. One eyewitness said that part of the speech "brought down the house."[2]

1. The preceding paragraphs are from speech in Cleveland, *Stephens*, 637–51.
2. Augusta *Chronicle and Sentinel*, July 3, 1859.

Although pleased with his speech, Stephens bristled at the careless way it was reported. So despite severe rheumatic pains in his fingers, he began writing it out for the press. The job was "a great bore," but he wanted the record kept straight. He had not endorsed reopening the slave trade, he told Linton angrily. "I offered no opinion. . . . But if they decided against bringing in more Africans they must cease mouthing against the loss of new states." The *Chronicle*'s acid comments on his arrogance and excessive "self-laudation" particularly galled him. He expected such critism from the Augusta sheet but was "*really astonished*" to see similar editorials in other papers. "There is a good deal of self will about me," he confessed to Linton, "and an earnest spirit to have my way, but I do know that I am not *vain* however I may appear to others."[3]

Linton, hardly a discerning critic on this occasion, reassured his brother. He had found nothing "arrogant" in the speech. He thought it contained "important truths and sound philosophical views." Few shared this opinion. In fact, Stephens had confused everyone but the most militant southern rights men—and they were delighted. Edmund Ruffin, the Virginia radical, wrote for a copy of the speech, and others who shared Ruffin's views also expressed their approval.[4]

These opinions represented only a tiny minority in the South. One Georgia editor averred that he had yet to meet anyone opposed to the laws prohibiting the slave trade. Martin J. Crawford, who knew Stephens well, offered to bet eighty-five slaves that he had not endorsed reopening the trade. Others, however, had read his remarks much differently. Peterson Thweatt, one of Brown's placemen, warned Stephens that the country strongly opposed the slave trade, much less agitation for repeal of laws against it. Discussing the matter divided the South, he said. Stephens' enemies could scarcely contain their delight. Nine-tenths of the people, reported Howell Cobb's younger brother Tom, opposed the trade, and many of Stephens' friends were condemning him outright.[5]

With southern opinions at variance, it can well be imagined how the

3. AHS to LS, July 5, 9, 1859, in Stephens Papers, MC.
4. LS to AHS, July 3, 17, 1859, *ibid.*; Edmund Ruffin to AHS, August 3, 1859, *ibid.*, LC.
5. Milledgeville *Southern Recorder*, July 11, 1859; Crawford to AHS, July 7, 1859, Thweatt to AHS, July 8, 1859, both in Stephens Papers, LC; T. R. R. Cobb to Cobb, August 24, 1859, in Cobb-Erwin-Lamar Papers, UG.

North received Stephens' speech. It created "quite a sensation," said one Republican paper, especially among moderates, who had been deluded into believing that respectable southerners opposed the slave trade. Northern Democrats were plainly distraught; several warned Stephens that raising the issue would bring disaster on the party.[6]

Naturally, Stephens refused to acknowledge how foolhardy he had been. As controversy over his speech heightened, he got angrier. "I certainly meant to say nothing except what is clearly expressed," he fumed, "—that was that unless we get immigration from abroad we shall have but few more slave states. This great truth seems to take people by surprise."[7]

Was Stephens so naive as to believe that belaboring the obvious would pass for a simple declaration of fact and nothing more? Hardly. He rarely spoke publicly without purpose, and he had mulled over this speech for several days. Not a shred of evidence suggests that he had changed his mind on the slave trade question since December, 1856, when he voted for a resolution condemning the reopening of the trade. Nor could he possibly have hoped to win friends in the North with these remarks. If he *were* interested in the Democratic nomination for 1860, he had chosen a most bizarre way of demonstrating his national appeal.

What, then, was his point? It appears that in his own convoluted way Stephens hoped to promote southern unity, especially among Democrats. Belaboring the obvious in this case was a backhanded way of undermining his enemies' position. Both the Opposition and the Democratic hotheads still used the loss of Kansas not only to embitter southerners against each other but also to crucify Stephen A. Douglas. Stephens had foreseen the loss of Kansas months before it happened and for the very reason he emphasized in this speech: lack of population. There was nothing inherently wrong with popular sovereignty, in other words, and by extension, nothing to condemn its northern champion Douglas for. It made no sense, he argued, for southerners to rail about each others' "unsoundness" if they refused to admit basic demographic facts. Surely the southerners could see that the region lacked enough blacks to expand without a substantial increase from

6. New York *Commercial Bulletin* quoted in Savannah *Morning News*, July 15, 1859; James J. Steele to AHS, August 29, 1859, in Stephens Papers, LC.
7. AHS to Smith, July 29, 1859, in Phillips (ed.), *TSC Correspondence*, 446–47.

abroad. But were they willing to consider what means would actually be necessary to allow southern expansion?

As reaction to the speech showed, everyone missed Stephens' point. It had been a terrible mistake for him to raise this explosive issue, much less in a way that only a metaphysician could sort out what he was really trying to say. In his compulsion to expound great truths to the ignorant masses, he took leave of his good sense. If everything were as rosy as he said, the worst possible issue to raise was the slave trade, one of the few questions the sections agreed on. If he meant the speech to have a calming effect, he had virtually guaranteed that no one would remember its soothing parts. He had even guaranteed that most people would miss the real point of the speech, his copious self-congratulation for the triumph of his principles. Ultimately, his foolish remarks served no one's cause but the radicals'.

But then Stephens had retired. Others might have to suffer for his bad judgment, but for the moment he delighted in being home. "Liberty Hall," as Stephens began to refer to his house around the end of 1859—"Because here I do as I please and all my guests are at liberty to do the same"—was an unpretentious yet comfortable dwelling, atop a low ridge north of Crawfordville, in the shade of numerous oak, locust, and hickory trees, grown (like their owner) venerable with age. Since 1845 Stephens had made no major structural alterations, but his retirement required some. So in the summer of 1859 he added two rooms in the back, with a small breezeway separating them from the rest of the house. One new room housed his large library—eventually more than sixty-five hundred volumes, mostly law and history. The other room was a combination bedroom-office for himself. Except for carpeting, the new addition was completed by September, and Stephens had moved himself and all his impedimenta—masses of papers, several old trunks into which he tossed his huge daily receipt of letters, his desk and writing paraphernalia, his numberless odd-shaped medicine bottles—into his "new apartments."[8]

From his window Stephens could enjoy a magnificent view of his garden and the trees of his orchard. Like his father, he took special pride in his fruit trees: peaches, apples, pears, figs, and pomegranates. His garden, tended by the household slaves whose cabins bordered it, produced a sizable crop of vegetables: corn, potatoes, beans, tomatoes,

8. AHS to LS, September 2, 1859, in Stephens Papers, MC.

and (his favorites) peas and okra. Stephens believed in agricultural experimentation. He constantly tried different fertilizers and grasses to enrich the soil, for example. His most successful experiment adorned the same slope as the fruit trees—a beautiful stand of Catawba grapes. He had planted the vines in 1848 at the suggestion of immigrants who had settled in Crawfordville. Twelve years later the vineyard yielded over five hundred gallons of wine.

Like the grounds, the home reflected a quiet prosperity, from the parlor, with its Healy oils of family members in massive gilt frames, its Italian marble bust of Stephens on a marble pillar, and its mementoes of the years of public service scattered here and there, to the four simply furnished guest rooms upstairs. Stephens' house bespoke an owner of conventional tastes and comfortable circumstances. By the county's standards, Stephens was well-to-do. Taliaferro's largest planter in 1860 owned fifty-five slaves and an estate valued at $81,000. Stephens' wealth ranked him thirteenth that year. His estate was valued at $53,000, with a little over a third of its worth in his thirty-four slaves. Six parcels of land he owned in and about Crawfordville were worth another $3,800; $7,702.55 in notes outstanding and other property accounted for the rest.

Stephens was not meticulous about keeping records (the dusty office trunks were his only filing system), so it's impossible to tell how profitable his farm was. Although the 1856–1857 drought had hurt, by 1860 the farm produced its best cotton crop ever—twenty bales, about $1,000 worth—plus large quantities of hay, peas, potatoes, wheat, and corn. Although he enjoyed farming and knew a great deal about it, the law was his real profession. In 1859–1860 Stephens earned $22,000 from his practice. His prowess at the bar by this time enabled him to charge a standard fee of $1,000. Stephens' practice, however, earned him nothing while he was in Washington. Upon entering Congress in 1843 he had made it a scrupulously observed rule never to make any money as a congressman beyond his salary. He refused pay from constituents for any work he did for them with various departments of the government. Nor did he take any of his cases to the state courts while in Congress, although if his public duties allowed it he would appear as an advocate in trials of causes. His earnings, sometimes as much as $2,000 at a time, he gave away to needy people, some penurious student, or another charitable cause. Money never meant much to Stephens, even now, when he made a lot of it. "I like law better than politics," he wrote near the end of 1859, "but I like being home better than either . . . very soon I shall quit the courts, and devote all my time to myself. Not this year; but very soon—if I live."[9]

The pessimism was chronic, but in fact his health was "very good." He had put on six pounds and was working twelve to fourteen hours a day. Nor was he showing much inclination to forget about politics, except that he had reason to fear the worst. Southern support for the administration's incessant war on Douglas embittered many northern Democrats. Those who had been Douglas' chief champions in Cincinnati four years before now demanded his head, one indignant Democrat told Stephens. They themselves would guarantee a Republican president, and then "these same gentlemen will be for dissolving the union . . . whenever they do, they will find the North will scorn them as traitors."[10]

Characteristically, Douglas defended himself vigorously. In response to repeated southern demands that he make his position clear, in September he sallied forth with a long article in *Harper's Weekly*. The article, which upheld the northern construction of popular sovereignty in every particular, created an immediate sensation. The South was outraged. The essay, said one Alabama congressman, gave Douglas "a death blow in the South." A Richmond editor called it "an incendiary document." Many of Douglas' southern editorial friends abandoned him, and the cadre of Douglasites, small in any case, shrank even further. Few southerners agreed with Stephens' assessment of the matter. After carefully reading all the papers, he concluded that Douglas had displayed admirable consistency, standing "just where he has always stood."[11]

If southerners had been enraged by the Douglas manifesto, another event occurring close on its heels horrified them. On the night of October 17, 1859, fanatical old John Brown led a small group of armed raiders into the village of Harpers Ferry, Virginia, and seized the U.S. arsenal there. His avowed purpose was to foment a slave insurrection that he hoped would spark a general revolt in the South. Despite

9. The preceding paragraphs are based on Cleveland, *Stephens*, 21–24; Rabun, "Stephens," 541; "List of Taxable Property for 1859," MS in Stephens' hand, in Stephens Papers, DU; quotation in Johnston and Browne, *Stephens*, 349–50.

10. AHS to Smith, November 10, 1859, in Phillips (ed.), *TSC Correspondence*, 448; J. H. Grundel[?] to AHS, October 7, 1859, in Stephens Papers, LC.

11. Johannsen, *Douglas*, 710; AHS to Smith, November 10, 1859, in Phillips (ed.), *TSC Correspondence*, 448.

Brown's expectations, no slaves revolted, and within thirty hours after it began the raid ended in a flurry of gunfire. More than a dozen men—raiders, innocent bystanders, and marines—lost their lives. Several weeks later the state of Virginia hanged Brown for treason.

It is impossible to overestimate the effect of Brown's raid on the southern psyche. Brown's purpose was heinous enough—visions of a slave revolt were unspeakably horrible to southerners. But the episode was made even more despicable in the South's eyes by northern reaction to it. Instead of condemning him, many northerners praised Brown's courage and sanctity. The day he was executed thousands of northerners in hundreds of cities and towns gathered to mourn. Abolitionists extolled Brown as a martyr; some even approved slave insurrection. As it turned out, abolitionist fanatics had been more than casually involved with Brown. More than four hundred of Brown's letters discovered shortly after his arrest revealed that he had received moral and financial support from several prominent New England abolitionists.

The South found only one conclusion possible: Brown was the inevitable product of Republicanism. It mattered little that responsible northern men condemned the raid and tried to reassure the South nor that leading Republicans such as Lincoln and Seward repudiated Brown. The South could never have hoped to forge for itself the unity that John Brown had given her, literally overnight.

Across Dixie people talked about disunion, about the impossibility of peaceful coexistence with fanatics bent on destroying the South. Several southern legislatures passed resolutions declaring the election of a Republican president sufficient grounds to dissolve the Union. South Carolina called for a convention of southern states and dispatched a commissioner to Virginia to press for joint measures of defense. Mississippi sent her own commissioner to Virginia and readily accepted the plan for a southern convention. Legislators in Alabama, Mississippi, and South Carolina voted military appropriations.[12]

Georgia also got caught up in the hysteria. The *Federal Union* blamed key Republican leaders for at least "indirect encouragement" of Brown. Life for nonsoutherners in Georgia became very uncomfortable. Anyone "who does not boldly declare that he believes African slavery to be a social, moral, and political blessing" would be regarded

12. The preceding paragraphs are based on Craven, *Growth of Southern Nationalism*, 305–11.

as an enemy, growled the Atlanta *Confederacy*. The Savannah *News* reported that suspected abolition sympathizers were being run out of town, sometimes ridden out on a rail. "The torrents of insult and abuse heaped upon the South by the public speakers, preachers, and presses of the North," continued the *News*, "are exasperating to our people beyond forbearance."[13]

Stephens' immediate reaction to the Brown raid is not known. No doubt he agreed with Toombs, who denounced the Republicans on the Senate floor as "in moral complicity with the criminal himself." Thirteen months later Stephens rebuked the Republicans for sympathizing with "such exhibitions of madness." And after the war he concluded that by their sympathy for Brown the Republicans had proved their revolutionary intentions.[14]

Georgia's newly elected legislature responded swiftly to an angry message from the governor. After passing resolutions declaring Georgia's willingness to join with the other southern states in concerted action to secure their rights in the Union, or if that were impossible, "their independence and security out of it," the lawmakers sharply reversed previous policy and appropriated seventy-five thousand dollars to improve the militia and make other military preparations.[15]

Amid all this excitement Cobb's supporters decided the time was right to move decisively in his behalf. Exactly what Cobb was thinking is difficult to say. While still trying to convince Stephens that Douglas was finished and that "policy requires the nomination of a Southern man," he was telling closer associates that "the days of the Union are numbered." The truth was that Cobb lusted for the nomination himself, and he was willing to play sharp politics to get it. The Union, with Howell Cobb as president, would be safe enough.[16]

Accordingly, his legislative supporters, perhaps two-thirds of the assembly, gathered after their session on the night of November 21, 1859, and passed resolutions for a Democratic convention in Milledgeville on December 8 to nominate delegates for the national convention. The

13. Milledgeville *Federal Union*, November 1, 1859; Atlanta *Confederacy* quoted in Nevins, *Emergence of Lincoln*, II, 108n.; Savannah *Morning News*, November 26, 1859.

14. Toombs quoted in Rabun, "Stephens," 550; AHS to Abraham Lincoln, December 20, 1860, in Stephens, *Constitutional View*, II, 259, 269.

15. Kenneth Coleman (ed.), *A History of Georgia* (Athens, Ga., 1977), 146.

16. Cobb to AHS, November 14, 1859, in Stephens Papers, EU; Cobb to Lamar, November 19, 1859, in Cobb Papers, UG.

next day, Governor Brown, who knew about sharp politics himself and who no longer needed Cobb for reelection, directed the state executive committee to call for another convention, this one to be held on March 12, 1860, six weeks before the Charleston convention opened. Brown's move was unprecedented. Since 1842 the legislature had summoned conventions, and as a rule they had been composed largely of assembly members.

Cobb's people had tradition on their side, but their unseemly haste proved their undoing. The December convention duly met, and after passing resolutions to support the party's nominee if the platform upheld southern rights in the territories and the *Dred Scott* decision, it voted (not without acrimony) to support Cobb as the party's nominee at Charleston. It then drew up a slate of delegates and adjourned. This attempt to ramrod Georgia's endorsement of Cobb for the presidency shattered the party's fragile unity. Full scale war erupted in the Democratic ranks. Fifty-two members of the legislature signed and published a solemn protest. Four appointed delegates refused to serve, and in the ensuing weeks several counties repudiated their nominees. Newspapers sprang to the attack, accusing the convention of being "arrogant, presumptuous, and insulting" to the Democratic masses.[17]

Cobb papers tried to defuse the issue. The *Federal Union* piously expressed its belief that the delegation already appointed would carry out its duty faithfully, but it also agreed not to oppose the March convention. Georgia's vote at Charleston should be cast for a Georgian, it declared, and it did not care who: Cobb, Stephens, or Toombs. Now was no time to quarrel about men; it was time to work for party unity.[18]

While Cobb's editor penned this drivel, the governor was writing confidential letters to Stephens. The short-notice December convention had thwarted the freely expressed will of the people, he said. What should be done? Since he had already taken steps to cripple Cobb, the question was more than a trifle gratuitous, but Brown never missed a chance to play up to Stephens' vanity. It was probably inconceivable to Brown, a habitual grasper after power, that anyone so often spoken of as an ideal candidate for the president as Stephens could be indifferent to the prospect. The executive committee had effectively blunted Cobb's gambit, thus leaving the door open for an un-

17. Americus *South-Western News* quoted in Augusta *Constitutionalist*, December 15, 1859.
18. Milledgeville *Federal Union*, December 27, 1859.

committed delegation to Charleston that might swing to Stephens if circumstances warranted. But Stephens was having none of it. Party unity was essential, he told Brown. The March convention should ratify the December delegate slate and reappoint all its members. Brown hastened to agree that "it would be a great misfortune" for the party to divide on the delegate question, and he professed himself willing to do anything to promote harmony—well, almost anything. If the March convention failed to unite, he said, "I should doubt the propriety of re-appointing all of them."[19]

Stephens celebrated Christmas in his usual fashion—by enveloping himself in gloom. "The greatest happiness I see," he said, "is in work." Neither the state nor the country's affairs presented a happy picture. The House was embroiled in another of its vicious fights for the speakership, and according to one of Stephens' capital informants, even once cool border state men talked openly of secession. The situation in Georgia was almost as bad. Cobb's enemies and Little Aleck's own friends persisted in pushing his name for the presidency, despite his repeated denials of any such aspirations. Not unnaturally, Cobb's partisans blamed Stephens for their woes. From Washington, J. Henley Smith wrote that Cobb's friends "look upon you as moving heaven and earth to defeat him." None of them believed Stephens' denials of presidential aspirations. Stephens certainly looked like an enemy to Cobb, especially when several Georgia papers suggested that the March convention draft the former congressman. Allowing his enemies to triumph in March, Cobb insisted, would be as fatal to him as outright defeat. This had to be prevented at all costs.[20]

Cobb could not have known about Stephens' tough letter to Brown. Nor was he aware of the steady pressure Stephens' closest friends exerted on him. Smith and Toombs, both in Washington, apprised him often of preconvention intelligence. From what he saw, Smith said, nothing could avert Stephens' nomination in Charleston. "You are to be our next president in spite of yourself." Toombs was more explicit:

19. Brown to AHS, December 29, 1859, January 5, 1860, both in Phillips (ed.), *TSC Correspondence*, 453–54.
20. AHS to LS, December 29, 1859, in Stephens Papers, MC; Crawford to AHS, December 13, 1859, Smith to AHS, December 10, 1859, both in in Stephens Papers, LC; Cobb to James M. Spullock, January 14, 1860, in James Madison Spullock Collection, GDAH.

Douglas would be strong at Charleston, not enough to win but enough to nominate whom he chose. "His friends are very strongly for you and I regret very much if we are to continue the govmt. that you have taken the position not to accept. I think [it] very unwise of you and hurtfull to the country." Receiving the nomination would be no problem, he said; two weeks later he repeated the message. Linton also plied his brother with rosy reports. One Kentuckian, for example, had said that it would be shameful for Georgia not to nominate Stephens "when so many other States are only waiting for your own State to take the lead."[21]

Stephens discounted the Washington rumors. He was unaware of any ground swell for him, he told Smith, and felt confident that there would be none once his views were "really understood." He could understand others' suspicions and distrust, he said, but these too were groundless. "But how I pity and commiserate all such. Their eyes will be opened in due time."[22]

"In due time." The words help explain why so many people suspected Stephens, for he had not unequivocally renounced aspirations for the presidency in writing. True, he had written the "horse thieves" letter back in August, 1858, and since then he had privately made his position clear to anyone who would listen. None of Stephens' friends doubted his sincerity; even Linton was positive his mind was made up. Still, there had been no public letter.

The reason for this is not hard to see. If Stephens had irrevocably removed himself from the preconvention speculations in Georgia he would have assured triumph for Cobb and the administration and at the same time killed any chance Douglas' southern supporters had of contesting the prevailing southern rights sentiment. Even with Stephens silent, these chances were slim, but they were better than none. Political strategy, then, dictated silence. For all his ill-considered posturing for southern solidarity, Stephens remained just as opposed to an all-southern party as he had been ten years before. Southern rights were as dear to him as to any other Georgian, but only within the Union, he believed, could they be secured. And to control the govern-

21. Smith to AHS, December 10, 1860, in Stephens Papers, LC;, Toombs to AHS, December 26, 1859, January 11, 1860, in Phillips (ed.), *TSC Correspondence*, 452, 455; LS to AHS, February 7, 1860, in Stephens Papers, MC.

22. AHS to Smith, December 17, 1859, in Phillips (ed.), *TSC Correspondence*, 451.

ment, the South needed the northern Democrats, the last barrier between her and the hated Republicans.

Even so, Stephens could not allow the March convention to nominate him. Permitting it to do so would sunder the state party and cripple Douglas almost as terribly as allowing Cobb's nomination. Several counties were preparing to send Stephens delegations to the state convention in Milledgeville. They had to be muzzled. Stephens took care, therefore, to write letters to two prominent convention delegates, Jack Lane of Hancock and Dr. H. R. Casey of Columbia County. He did not want his name "connected with the proceedings of the convention in any way," he told Casey. "I wish it distinctly known that I have no aspirations for that high office, none whatever. . . . I assure you I would not assume its great trusts if my own volition were all that were to secure it." Casey should read this letter to the convention, instructed Stephens, if it were necessary to get the point across.[23]

When the three hundred plus delegates, representing 90 of Georgia's 132 counties, convened in Milledgeville on March 14, 1860, they immediately began a two-day wrangle that would have done a pack of dogs proud. Cobb's supporters succeeded in electing the presiding officer, but this was their last victory. Fully 47 counties repudiated the December convention, and at one point the anti-Cobb delegates withdrew and nominated their own slate for Charleston. Cooler heads, horrified by the prospect of a party split on the eve of the national convention, ultimately prevailed. A reassembled convention voted to combine the new slate with the December one and then imposed the unit rule on the enlarged delegation. During bitter debate over the resolutions, Cobb's forces did their utmost to secure an endorsement for him. They failed because Cobb had too many enemies, Stephens too many friends, and the southern rights men too little faith in either. Cobb had been killed off, but the state party, on the eve of one its most fateful contests, was in pitiful shape.[24]

Stephens approved the convention's results. But the papers had mentioned neither of his letters. "I wrote one to Dr. Casey which I *expected* him to read. This I suppose he did not do." Casey had not. The anti-Cobb forces had found it expedient to withhold Stephens' letter and use his name freely. If unable to get the nomination, Douglas

---

23. AHS to H. K. Casey, March 9, 1860, in Stephens Papers, LC.
24. Avery, *History of Georgia*, 109–10.

would support Stephens, it was alleged. Keeping such rumors afloat held the anti-Cobb men together. With opposing forces almost evenly matched, there was no sense in confusing anybody with an excess of candor.[25]

Unlike his fanatical supporters, Stephens was hardly weighing his own chances at Charleston. The way had now been cleared for Douglas' nomination, he told Samuel J. Anderson, one of several odd characters with whom he habitually corresponded. His only fear was that "the Caliban of the White House" would persuade Cobb to bolt the party. Nevertheless, Stephens continued his outspoken support for Douglas, convinced that the Little Giant was the only man who could be elected.[26]

Stephens could savor Douglas' "victory" only briefly, for Cobb's friends raised a an immediate ruckus and charged that the devious little sage of Crawfordville had engineered their defeat. Stephens not an aspirant? sputtered the Cassville *Standard*. Such "chaff" could "deceive no sane man for a moment." Cobb's closest associates considered Stephens the main enemy, but even they admitted the opposition to their man had been widespread. "Every combination was formed and brought to bear that could possibly be," fumed John B. Lamar, including every paper south of Athens but the *Federal Union*.[27]

The Opposition knew exactly what had happened at Milledgeville: "The Stephens alias Douglas Democracy won the day." Georgia had surrendered to a contemptible squatter sovereignty candidate. As if it might have found any hope in the Democrats otherwise, the Rome *Courier* announced that there was none in the Democratic party. "It is demoralized—Douglasised." Opposition editors did not excuse Stephens. He wanted the nomination for himself, they said, and if not for 1860, then for 1864, the *Chronicle* ingeniously argued. But a Stephens candidacy would be as bad as a Douglas one. (Maybe it would be even more dangerous because of Stephens' former popularity among many

25. AHS to LS, March 16, 1860, in Stephens Papers, MC.

26. S. J. Anderson to Douglas, March 20, 1860, quoted in Milton, *Eve of Conflict*, 413. Anderson, who reached the pinnacle of his career when he served for a day as secretary of war *ad interim* in Fillmore's cabinet, was a Georgian now living in New York City. He was a genuine eccentric: chronically jobless, an atheist, a dabbler in politics and literature. In 1874, after three previous failures, he would finally succeed in killing himself.

27. Cassville *Standard* quoted in Rabun, "Stephens," 555; Lamar to Cobb, March 17, 1860, in Cobb-Erwin-Lamar Papers, UG.

in the Opposition. Some bitter former Know Nothings were prepared to vote for Stephens now, one of them claiming that he would willingly forego ever voting for president again if he could cast one hundred or one thousand votes for him in 1860.) The time had come to overthrow the party tricksters. What was needed was a "Constitutional Union party," based on the principles of the *Dred Scott* case.[28]

All the abuse upset Little Aleck. He had not headed opposition to Cobb, he said. His accusers were ignorant of all he had done "to harmonize that opposition." Had his own name been substituted for Cobb's, he thought with his usual modesty, "a large majority" would have supported him, but he did not wish it. Several of his own friends had voted for Cobb for just this reason. Cobb simply was hardly the choice of Georgia's Democrats, Stephens said, "not as between me and him but as between me and any other prominent man in the party."[29]

Stephens was hardly being entirely candid, for Cobb's defeat could hardly have "surprised" him, as he claimed. But he was "mortified" by having to shoulder sole blame for it. Most galling of all were charges that he and Douglas had some secret understanding. To set the record straight, he wrote a long letter to James Sledge, the editor of the Athens *Banner*, Cobb's hometown sheet. He had no deal with Douglas and he did not want to be president, Stephens told Sledge. He had been "exceedingly annoyed" by the free use of his name in the convention. People ought to be concerned with party unity, not with pushing individual favorites.[30]

Sledge should not make this letter public, Stephens instructed. He did not want to open himself up to ridicule. Announcing that he would spurn a nomination he could not possibly get could only "be looked upon as the grossest exhibition of personal vanity and presumption upon the record." Even after Sledge entreated him to allow the letter's publication to clear the air with Cobb's people, Stephens refused. But he did allow it to be circulated privately in Washington—evidently to good effect. Smith reported that Cobb's men and even the secretary himself were finally doing Stephens "justice."[31]

28. Rome *Courier*, March 20, 1860; Augusta *Chronicle and Sentinel*, March 27, 1860; S. McJunkin to Smith, March 10, 1860, in J. Henley Smith Papers, GDAH; Columbus *Enquirer*, March 27, 1860.

29. AHS to Smith, March 18, 1860, in Phillips (ed.), *TSC Correspondence*, 466–67.

30. AHS to James Sledge, March 25, 1860, in Stephens Papers, LC.

31. *Ibid.*; Smith to AHS, April 3, 1860, in *ibid.*

While Georgia's Democracy cracked at the seams, the country did likewise. Months ago Stephens had observed how little the people seemed to care what was happening in Washington. Congress and the government gave the people little reason to be interested. Sectional hostility had practically paralyzed the government. It took the House nine acrimonious weeks to elect its Speaker; fisticuffs among the legislators occurred frequently; members of Congress commonly went armed to their work. The strain was beginning to tell, especially on Democrats. The Republicans, on the other hand, reported Toombs, were "stern, confident and defiant." Crawford pronounced the House "*a magnificent failure*." Democratic members had become unmanageable.[32]

Toombs had already broadcast his feelings, treating the Senate on January 24, 1860, to his most radical utterances since 1850. The Republican party, he charged, had been guilty of "open, shameless, and profligate perfidy" in its war on the South. It was "unfit to rule over a free people," and if it ever gained control of the government, "the people whose safety is thereby put in jeopardy" would be justified in going to war. Never let the Black Republicans gain control, he warned his fellow Georgians. "Defend yourselves, the enemy is at your door . . . meet him at the doorsill, and drive him from the temple of Liberty, or pull down its pillars and involve him in common ruin."[33]

Practically buried in the bluster was Toombs's pledge to labor for southern security within the Union till all hope was gone. Stephens spied it though and thought the speech "exactly on the right line." Choosing to focus on the speech's "true national patriotism" rather than his friend's fiery warnings, Stephens overlooked the obvious point: Toombs meant to disrupt the Union if a Republican were ever elected president.[34]

For the present, however, Toombs labored as diligently as Stephens to keep the Democratic party together. It was a hopeless task. Within a few days of Toombs' speech, Jefferson Davis introduced into the Senate a set of administration-approved resolutions designed to crush the political life out of Douglas forever. At their heart was the assertion that

32. AHS to Smith, January 5, 1860, in J. Henley Smith Papers, GDAH; Toombs to AHS, December 26, 1859, in Phillips (ed.), *TSC Correspondence*, 452; Crawford to AHS, March 14, 1860, in Stephens Papers, LC.

33. *Congressional Globe*, 36th Cong. 1st Sess., Appendix, 88–93.

34. AHS to Smith, February 4, 1860, in Phillips (ed.), *TSC Correspondence*, 459.

neither Congress nor a territorial legislature had the power to exclude slavery from the territories. Moreover, Congress had the duty to provide "needful protection" for slave property there if the Court could not enforce its ruling. The resolutions were transparently political, aimed at binding the Democratic party to the extreme southern position. So Toombs and other southerners who valued the goodwill of the northern Democrats fought them vigorously in caucus. It was folly, Toombs argued, to bring up such issues now. True, the Court had ruled for the South, but the issue was moot; it might never come up. The Douglas-haters had inspired this foolishness, and although he wanted to see the Little Giant defeated at Charleston, Toombs certainly did not want him and his friends humiliated. Despite Toombs's plea, the congressional Democrats approved the resolutions. A crucial showdown loomed at Charleston.[35]

Toombs's favorite candidate was Robert M. T. Hunter, a bland but solid Virginian, whose nomination would have pleased Stephens too. But Little Aleck also said he would "cordially" support Douglas should he get the nomination. For his part, Douglas had made no secret of his preference of Stephens as his running mate. Many northwestern papers had, in fact, tacked Stephens' name on their mastheads below the Little Giant's. The vice-presidential rumors did not disturb him, but Stephens continued to figure prominently in public speculations about the ticket's top spot. And this did not please him at all.[36]

To silence his still vociferous Georgia enemies, Stephens reluctantly decided to allow publication of his letter to Casey, the one he wanted read at the March convention. At the same time, he reiterated his demand to his own supporters. "I do not wish my name put in nomination at Charleston," he told one of the delegates. "I not only do not wish it done but I protest against its being done. The presidency is an office I do not want." He may not have wanted it, but when Dr. Casey, also a delegate to Charleston, pressed him for an answer about what he would do if the nomination were tendered him, he refused "to give a *determined* and *irrevocable* negative" before the convention: "I can conceive of circumstances in which that nomination might be . . .

35. Toombs to AHS, February 10, 1860, in *ibid.*, 461.
36. AHS to Smith, February 24, 1860, in *ibid.*, 463; Crawford to AHS, March 14, 1860, in Stephens Papers, LC.

tendered to me wherein I would consider myself derelict of all duty and obligation which as a citizen I owe to my country were I to withhold my assent." This sphinxlike statement was all the encouragement Stephens ever offered his supporters.[37]

Had the Democrats deliberately set out to pick the worst place in the country for their 1860 convention, they would have chosen Charleston. The city's Old World charm, beautiful homes, and shaded walks hardly compensated for its glaring deficiencies: the most radical citizenry in the South, abysmal accommodations for large numbers of people, and a convention hall barely suitable for half the number of people crammed into it each day. Even the city's weather—alternately hot, rainy, and unseasonably cool—seemed to conspire during this last week of April to make the delegates as uncomfortable and belligerent as possible.

Few delegates could have expected a tranquil convention. Unlike the southern-controlled congressional caucus, the convention's majority belonged to Douglas, and his people meant to secure him the nomination. On the other side, the Gulf states were just as adamant: they would not abide a Douglas candidacy, and to preclude it they meant to build a platform embodying the antithesis of Douglas' popular sovereignty doctrine.

The southern radicals had never been in such a position of tactical superiority. Back in February, Alabama extremists under the lead of William L. Yancey had managed to pass resolutions in their state party conclave demanding that the national party affirm the radical southern position in its platform. The party must not only deny the power of Congress or territorial legislatures over slavery, but it must also declare it Congress' duty to pass laws protecting the rights of slaveholders in the territories. If the party refused to do this, the Alabama delegation was instructed to bolt the convention. On the eve of the convention, six other states (Louisiana, Texas, Mississippi, Florida, Georgia, and Arkansas) agreed to stand with her.

The ensuing tragedy was played out in three acts in nine days, from April 23 to May 2. The slave states, plus Oregon and California, both secured by copious administration patronage, controlled the resolu-

37. AHS to Henry Cleveland, April 8, 1860, in Stephens Papers, DU; AHS to H. R. Casey, April 4, 1860, in Stephens Papers, LC.

tions committee. (The convention had already broken with tradition by agreeing to formulate its platform before selecting its candidate.) The divided committee submitted three separate reports on April 27. The majority report embodied the Alabama platform; the minority report affirmed the Cincinnati platform but also declared that questions of territorial power over slavery were judicial and that the party would abide by decisions of the Supreme Court. Benjamin F. Butler of Massachusetts, his whole life a majority of one, submitted a third report simply reaffirming the Cincinnati platform.

The second act began with floor debates on the resolutions, highlighted by Yancey's eloquent and uncompromising speech. The South, he declared, would at last demand her full constitutional rights. Yancey was answered by George E. Pugh of Ohio, who perfectly epitomized the Douglas men, pushed to the limits of their patience and now to the abyss of political suicide by southern demands. The South now insisted that they take the leap. "Gentlemen of the South!" Pugh protested. "You mistake us—you mistake us. We will not do it." And they didn't. When the crucial vote on the reports took place on Monday, April 30, by a seventeen-vote margin, 165 to 148, Douglas' men substituted the minority's report for the majority's—and six southern delegations, led by Alabama, took their promised walk. The next day they were joined by twenty-six of Georgia's thirty-six delegates plus a scattering of others from the border states.[38]

The closing act was anticlimax. Democrats now met in two separate conventions. The rump of the original convention proceeded to the balloting, but after fifty-seven ballots Douglas still fell short of the requisite two-thirds majority. The convention therefore adjourned, agreeing to reconvene in Baltimore on June 18. There was nothing for the bolters to do but follow suit. After adopting the Alabama platform, the southerners also adjourned and agreed to meet in Richmond on June 11.

The Charleston fiasco threw the southern Democracy into absolute turmoil. Georgians, as was their custom, immediately solicited the views of all the state's leading men. What was to be done? Should the

38. Narrative of the convention based on Nichols, *Disruption of Democracy*, 296–308; Pugh quoted in Nevins, *Emergence of Lincoln*, II, 217. Of the ten Georgia delegates who remained in the main convention, four (Henry Cleveland, H. R. Casey, Hiram Warner, and James Thomas) were staunch friends of Stephens. The rump of the Georgia delegation voted steadfastly for Douglas on all of the ensuing fifty-seven ballots.

state send a delegation to Baltimore? If so, who should represent her? For the next few weeks the papers ran the replies. Stephens, Toombs, Cobb, Brown, and a host of others all agreed that Georgia should be represented at Baltimore. Beyond this, however, the opinions spanned the spectrum, from the cool violet moderation of Stephens and Johnson to the flaming red defiance of Toombs and Iverson.[39]

Stephens was appalled. Perfectly satisfied with the Cincinnati platform, he would have demanded no more. Since 1850 he had supported nonintervention. "I shall never change my views," he told J. Henley Smith, "so long as ink will not blush at human inconsistency." After fighting the extremists for so long, Stephens loathed seeing them triumph. The trouble, he said, was having in power men with "no loyalty to principle, no attachment to truth for truth's sake," reckless graspers after office, position, and power.[40]

Stephens' public letter was less explicit on this point, but withal a sober appraisal of the situation. The question in dispute was essentially juridical, he wrote. The South had supported nonintervention for years. How could she discard it now? Under nonintervention slavery would go where the people wanted it and where natural laws of soil, climate, and population allowed it to go. No congressional act could contravene those laws "any more than it could make the rivers run into the mountains instead of the sea."

The betrayal of the South's northern allies offended his sense of justice; he appealed to his countrymen's sense of honor. Why should the South want anything more than the Cincinnati platform? "For my life I cannot see it, unless we are determined to have a quarrel with the North anyhow on general account. If so, in behalf of common sense, let us put it on more tenable grounds! These are abundant. For our own character's sake, let us make it upon the aggressive acts of our enemies, rather than upon any supposed shortcomings of our friends, who have stood by us so steadfastly."

Stephens, unlike others, had no fears for the future of slavery. The "great truths" upon which slavery rested could withstand all assaults from without. It was danger from within that really threatened the nation. "We have grown luxuriant in the exuberance of our well-being

39. Montgomery, *Cracker Parties*, 238.
40. AHS to Smith, May 8, 1860, in Phillips (ed.), *TSC Correspondence*, 470.

and unparalleled prosperity," he warned. "There is a tendency every-where, not only at the North, but at the South, to strife, dissension, disorder, and anarchy." All sober minded men had to resist it to the utmost.[41]

Unwittingly, Stephens had bared his deepest fears: the thought of disorder and anarchy chilled him to the marrow of his conservative bones. To Stephens, even a threat to slavery, a threat that terrified and angered so many of his fellow southerners and which they discerned so clearly, paled by comparison. The Cassandra of Crawfordville had glimpsed the future, and the vision repelled him. For the threat he saw was the destruction of order and law, an unbridling of men's dark and murderous passions. Before this cataclysm everything, slavery included, would be swept away.

Anarchy held no terrors for Toombs. For the first time in their long association he and Stephens stood diametrically opposed. Toombs had executed a 180-degree turn since his February pledge to do everything possible to promote party unity. From now to the end of his life Toombs personified southern intransigence. His public letter was inflammatory. "Our greatest danger today," he warned, "is that the Union may sur-vive the Constitution. . . . Look to the preservation of your rights." On the Senate floor he professed to see a "terrible practicality" in con-gressional protection for territorial slavery. Refuse the South this pro-tection, then let the Union be dissolved, "and the sooner the better."[42]

Toombs's sudden reversal, seemingly mysterious at first blush, was actually characteristic. Without Stephens' personal influence to mod-erate him Toombs had done well to maintain his balance until now. He had come to believe that only a southern man on a "good" platform would be acceptable. He had advised the bolt at Charleston by tele-graph from Washington and resolved now to "stand by the bolters and let things rock on." Unable to abide Douglas' strength in the party, Toombs made intransigence his own point of honor. Douglas seemed to believe that "our fear of Black Republican rule will make us submit to anything," he told Stephens. "As to me he is mistaken." Rather than support the nebulous nonintervention formula and admit "weakness,"

41. The preceding paragraphs are from AHS to Thirteen Gentlemen of Macon, May 9, 1860, in Johnston and Browne, *Stephens*, 357–64.

42. Toombs to Robert Collins *et al.*, May 10, 1860, in Phillips (ed.), *TSC Corre-spondence*, 475–77; *Congressional Globe*, 36th Cong., 1st Sess., Appendix, 339–45.

Toombs demanded that Douglas accept the radicals' reading of the *Dred Scott* case. And even at the cost of "disaster & defeat" he meant to have his way.[43]

For the first time in months the Georgia Opposition had something to cheer about. The Democratic chaos delighted them. National suicide, so long as it included Democrats, was perfectly acceptable. "Dissolution of the Union," said the *Chronicle*, could be no worse than the continued rule of "that corrupt, demoralized, imbecile, extravagant and plundering organization." Until now even the Opposition would have hesitated to make such a statement. By June of 1860, however, talk of disunion had become as common as cotton market quotations in Georgia's newspapers.[44]

Georgia's crumbling Democracy, however, was perfectly capable of working its own dissolution, without prodding. There was little doubt that the party would send a delegation to Baltimore. The character of that delegation was what embroiled the delegates at the rancorous Democratic convention on June 4. Unfortunately, Georgia's foremost "national" Democrat, Stephens of Taliaferro, was ill, unable to attend. His absence, wrote a distressed Herschel Johnson, left the moderates "almost without an advocate, certainly without a Champion."[45]

Stephens' influence would not have mattered had he been there. He wanted an entirely new delegation composed only of men who repudiated the Charleston bolt and its bastard offspring, the Richmond convention. Instead, by a substantial vote, the Georgians reappointed the original Charleston slate and instructed it to bolt again if the party refused to accept the Alabama platform. At this point Herschel Johnson led a walkout of angry conservatives. This group drew up its own slate of delegates for Baltimore pledged to uphold the original Charleston platform.[46]

Stephens could not believe the South really intended to abandon nonintervention, and he attributed the growing madness to ignorance. Thousands, he thought, misunderstood Douglas' position: "He holds that all property, negroes and all, should stand upon the same footing

43. Toombs to AHS, May 5, 12, 16, 1860, in Phillips (ed.), *TSC Correspondence*, 468, 477–78.
44. Augusta *Chronicle and Sentinel*, May 11, 1860.
45. Johnson to AHS, June 9, 1860, in Johnson Papers, DU.
46. AHS to J. P. Hambleton, May 18, 1860, in Hambleton Papers, EU.

in the territories." The only real question was how far a territorial leg-islature could go in discouraging one particular species of property. The Supreme Court had not decided this question; it might never have to. By the time of the Baltimore convention he had lost all hope. It would "blow up in a row," he predicted. For once, Stephens proved a perfectly accurate seer.[47]

All the southern radicals at Baltimore needed was a pretext to repeat their walkout, and they got it on the fifth day, June 21, when the con-vention voted to seat newly elected Douglas delegations from Alabama and Louisiana. By the time this bolt ended, all or part of fourteen state delegations had left. Meeting in a separate hall, the seceders nomi-nated Kentuckian John C. Breckinridge for president and Senator Joseph Lane of Oregon for vice-president on a platform demanding congressional protection of slavery in the territories. The Richmond meeting a few days later merely ratified these proceedings. What re-mained of the original Baltimore body swiftly completed its work, nominating Douglas for president and Senator Benjamin Fitzpatrick of Alabama for vice president. Within a week, Fitzpatrick succumbed to fierce pressure and declined his nomination. In his place the Demo-cratic executive committee named Herschel Johnson.[48]

The name of Alexander Stephens had played a prominent role dur-ing the Baltimore proceedings. Douglas partisans made plain their es-teem for the Georgian, and at one point Douglas even offered to with-draw in Stephens' favor. But the senator's managers refused to consider the idea. To forsake their man now was unthinkable; besides, some of the Georgians only stiffened their resolve. None other than Toombs and Cobb led denunciations of Stephens among the delegates. (Cobb, of course, approved the Charleston bolt and had found it just as painlessly expedient to repudiate nonintervention, a doctrine he had supported since 1848, and embrace the positive protection formula. Up until the last minute, Cobb believed that in its extremity the party would turn to him as its savior.) Stephens was as offensive as Douglas, they asserted. While Cobb dredged up Stephens' opposition to the Mexican war, a record that would cost southern votes, he claimed, Toombs harped on his erstwhile friend's poor health. Stephens suffered

47. AHS to Smith, June 17, 1860, in Phillips (ed.), *TSC Correspondence*, 481–82; AHS to Johnston, June 19, 1860, in Johnston and Browne, *Stephens*, 365.
48. Nichols, *Disruption of Democracy*, 312–18.

from a "want of blood in the head," said Toombs; he would never survive the campaign.[49]

This ailment, commented one of Stephens' bitter friends, struck him
as "a damned strange disease." But the southern Democracy suffered a
malady far stranger. For the sake of an absolutely pointless abstraction, the "full measure of Southern rights," protection of virtually non-
existent property in territories most believed utterly inhospitable to
slavery, the southern Democrats had put their party, the vehicle of their
power and bulwark of their rights, to the sword. For the sake of be-
heading Douglas, they had eviscerated themselves.[50]

Irony capped irony. Utterly lost in all the furor of the anti-Douglas
vendetta at Richmond was the fact that his popular sovereignty doctrine had been all but abandoned. The Baltimore platform declared
that the Supreme Court would be the final arbiter of a territorial legislature's power over slavery: exactly the position maintained by James
Buchanan.

It was quiet around Liberty Hall, still and hot. The rhythms of life continued their ageless pace: regular, slow, predictable, secure. It was
comfortable in the shade of the oaks; peaches ripened and dogs lazed
in the sun. The master of the house was home, as he had been for several weeks, suffering from dizzy spells that prevented his traveling. But
Alexander Stephens was not too ill to recognize the sickness in the
South, and it was from an almost bottomless pit of gloom that he now
surveyed the political scene.

The southern people, those patriotic lovers of justice and the Constitution he had so often extolled, had deserted their principles, had lost
their sense of justice, their devotion to truth. They had deserted him
and every principle he stood for. Instead of heeding his advice, they
doted now on "prating demagogues." Stephens felt personally betrayed. Just such an ignorant mob had crucified Christ, he wrote
furiously. The mob had passed beyond the reach of reason. Well, the
people could do as they pleased. He would have nothing to do with
their "worrying, profitless, factious demagoguical strifes." With the
battle raging around him, the sage of Crawfordville chose to sulk in his
tent.[51]

49. Douglas to William A. Richardson, June 20, 1860, in Stephen A. Douglas
Papers, DU; Johnson to AHS, June 19, 1860, in Johnson Papers, DU; LS to AHS, June
28, 1860, in Stephens Papers, LC.
50. LS to AHS, June 28, 1860, in Stephens Papers, MC.
51. AHS to Hambleton, July 2, 1860, in Stephens Papers, LC.

XVI

We Are Going to Destruction as Fast as We Can

Before the final Democratic split at Baltimore in mid-June, two other parties held their own conventions. The first of these was a short-lived aggregation called the Constitutional Union party. Less a party than an ad hoc assembly of former Whigs and Know Nothings who could abide neither of the other parties, Constitutional Unionists from twenty-three states convened in Baltimore in early May. Decidedly southern in complexion, with its chief strength in the border states, the party selected Senator John Bell of Tennessee as its candidate. Following the old Whig custom of presenting men rather than programs for the country's consideration, the party adopted an enigmatic platform endorsing the Constitution, the Union, and enforcement of the laws.

One week later the jubilant Republicans convened in Chicago. The delegates passed over William H. Seward and Salmon P. Chase of Ohio, the preconvention favorites for the nomination, whom some considered too radical and controversial. On the third ballot, amid thunderous approval from the partisan galleries, they nominated instead Abraham Lincoln of Illinois, a moderate, and just about everyone's second choice. The party pledged to oppose the extension of slavery and reopening of the slave trade. It also denounced John Brown's raid and promised no interference with slavery in the states. Other platform planks endorsed a homestead law, a transcontinental railroad, and a modest tariff. One month later the Democracy split itself in twain. The stage was set for the most crucial presidential election in American history.

The stunning events in June left Stephens numb. The Democratic party was in shambles. For the life of him Stephens could not understand why, with defeat almost certain, Douglas even consented to run. He might take enough votes from Lincoln, Stephens thought, to throw the election into the House, where Breckinridge would win. "What honor this will be to Mr. Douglas would be difficult" to imagine, he commented wryly. Stephens resolved to take no part in this campaign. In the first place, his health was very poor. And in the second, he had lost all faith in his fellow southerners. Their present fever simply had to run its course. Trying to talk reason with them was pointless. At best all he could hope for was a "profitless victory." He had foreseen these troubles in 1859, Stephens sadly told Dick Johnston, and they were the reason he left Congress. He had searched in vain for evidence of patriotism anywhere. "Exclusive selfishness and personal ambition had taken possession of all." The situation was much worse now than he had ever expected it to be. Disunion was certain. And a deluded people, once horrified at the mere idea of revolution, "will as circumstances change be ready and willing for it."[1]

And why? Why? He kept returning to the question. All because of a trumped-up war on Stephen A. Douglas, who, Stephens marveled, was safer on slavery than any man who had ever been president, who held blacks inferior to whites, who denied that the Negro was included in the Declaration of Independence, and who, at great personal political peril, had expounded this "great truth" in the North; a man, further, who believed slavery to be the Negro's normal condition in a white society.[2]

But Douglas also held that slavery ought not to be forced upon people against their will. Suppose the idea were wrong in theory, Stephens posited. What great principle of states' rights did he violate in holding it? Stephens, a zealous guardian of such principles, could find none. Natural laws were far surer than any man-made legislation. This being the case, was it "not wiser & better more conversant with our republican institutions to let the people exercise [the power of excluding slavery] even though they have it not under the Constitution than

1. AHS to Smith, July 2, 1860, in Phillips (ed.), *TSC Correspondence*, 485; AHS to Hambleton, July 2, 1860, AHS to Johnston, July 5, 1860, both in Stephens Papers, LC.
2. AHS to Johnston, July 5, 1860, in Stephens Papers, LC.

to withhold it from them?" Would it not be better to let them have the power as a matter of "favour" rather than one of justice or right? What harm to the South could possibly result? "None whatever, for if the people want slavery under his ideas they can & will have it and if they do not no power on Earth will be likely to make them have it." [3]

Stephens had undergone a remarkable change since the year before, when he had tried to cram Lecompton down Kansans' throats against the very natural laws he knew as well then as now. With the hounds of revolution baying all over the countryside, it was only too apparent what the vile fruits of the South's perversion of popular sovereignty in Kansas had produced. The furies of passion had been released upon the land, and they, Stephens knew, followed a natural law of their own. Never had he seemed so paralyzed by gloom. His friend Herschel Johnson, the vice-presidential candidate, had no illusions either. Douglas' cause was "hopeless," but to preserve at least a fragment of the party in favor of nonintervention, he said, would be worth his own political suicide. So Stephens' sulking, and particularly his refusal to endorse Douglas, saddened him greatly. He had hoped Aleck would consent to be an elector at large and at least make a few speeches. [4]

Mortified that a friend could doubt his allegiance, Stephens quickly set matters straight by announcing his support for Douglas publicly. It had been rumored that Stephens meant to support Breckinridge. "Never," he scoffed, "could I do such a thing until I became as inconsistent" as the radicals. Others might eat their words, he told Dick Johnston, "but I do not feed upon such a diet." But he still refused to campaign among a people running mad. "The surest sign that a dog is going mad is to see him eat his own ordure," he explained, "and this eating of words and old party principles is . . . a like sign of approaching *rabies* among the people." He was adamant. "I am out of politics, and mean to stay out." [5]

3. *Ibid.* When Stephens referred to republican institutions he meant the whole complex of representative forms of government, from the municipal body to the Congress. These institutions, as he stated in 1854, rested on the vital principle "that the citizens of every distinct and separate community or State should have the right to govern themselves in their domestic matters as they please, and that they should be free from intermeddling restrictions and arbitrary dictation on such matters from any other power or government in which they have no voice" (Johnston and Browne, *Stephens*, 552). In granting the people of a territory the right to bar slavery, Stephens was simply allowing them a right—not a "favour"—he had conceded them already.

4. Johnson to AHS, July 4, 1860, in Johnson Papers, DU.

5. AHS to Smith, July 15, 1860, in Phillips (ed.), *TSC Correspondence*, 488; AHS to Johnston, July 12, 1860, in Johnston and Browne, *Stephens*, 365–66.

He had been repeating the same words for months. A grinding campaign was the last thing he wanted. On the face of it this campaign seemed like all the rest. Partisan editors still inked their pens in acid; orators sweated and shouted from stumps at almost every crossroads. But this campaign was different. This time the Union was at stake. And despite Stephens' scorn, the arguments of the Breckinridge supporters were not without merit. They appealed to a basic characteristic of southerners, their highly developed, exquisitely sensitive sense of honor. The South demanded equality, said the Breckinridge men. To accept Douglas' position that the people of a territory could bar the southerner and his slaves from the nation's common property before that people convened a constitutional convention would be to admit inferiority. It was degrading, odious, and unthinkable because it was cowardly and dishonorable.

Popular sovereignty was as bad as the Republican heresy that the national government could do what the people of a territory could not. Republicans were not even worth arguing with. They were a group of fanatics who had pledged themselves as a party to the destruction of southern society—in complete disregard of the Constitution, the laws of humanity and God, and the principles of human decency. Could the South in honor—not to mention sanity—allow this party to dominate the national government? To God-fearing Tom Cobb the matter was simple. "They are *different* people from us, whether better or worse and *there is no love* between us. Why then continue together? No outside pressure demands it, no internal policy or public interest requires it." Thus ran the Breckinridge argument in logic. On the emotional level its appeal was even more basic, for there it prompted fear, hatred, and anger. Thousands in the South found Breckinridge irresistible.[6]

But thousands more found appeals to simple love of the Union or to ancient political loyalties even more compelling, as was the case with Douglasites who, like Stephens and Johnson, rejected the logic of the Breckinridge position and loathed its appeal to the baser instincts. And so, too, did the Bell men. With customary dexterity the Georgia Opposition had flip-flopped into its usual adversary relationship with the Democrats. The Opposition men began a silent retreat from their position in favor of congressional protection of slavery after Bell's nomination, and most made the transition from rabid southern righters to

6. T. R. R. Cobb to his wife, October 11, 1860, in T. R. R. Cobb Letters, UG.

almost unconditional unionists easily. But from the first, the Bell campaign in the South was schizophrenic. Constitutional Unionists detested Lincoln as much as Democrats did, but they also claimed to be the true guardians of southern rights. As such, they had to castigate Democrats, both as enemies of the Union and as fools for their position on territorial slavery. Not unnaturally, they began to discover previously unsuspected virtues in the Douglas Democrats.

Breckinridge Democrats indignantly rejected the disunionist charges. A vote for their man was a vote to *preserve* the Union, they claimed; indeed, the only way to preserve it was by electing the man who demanded full protection for southern rights. The Union's real enemies were those who divided the South. A vote for Bell or Douglas, ran the argument, was essentially a vote for Lincoln. Nonetheless, relentless pressure eventually forced Breckinridge to deny publicly that he or any of his followers espoused disunion.[7]

Most of his adherents belied the claim, however. As their hopes for victory faded, pro-Breckinridge papers returned zestfully to a familiar theme: the abolitionists' hellish machinations to incite a slave revolt in the South. Great furor erupted all over the South in the wake of a reported slave insurrection in Texas. If only the prospect of an "Abolition ruler" caused such horrors, wailed the Athens *Southern Banner*, "what will be our condition when he is actually in power?" Another Georgia paper trembled at the prospect of "vast hordes" of abolitionist agitators pouring into the South if the Republicans got control of the government. The South would never submit to such an insult.[8]

Breckinridge's Georgia leaders sounded the same theme. At a Milledgeville gathering in early August, Toombs declared for "open unqualified disunion" if the South were denied protection in the territories, a theme he repeated on the stump for the next three months. Toombs considered disunion a foregone conclusion. The people stoically anticipated the "probable downfall" of the government, he told J. Henley Smith. "I hope they will continue in that temper until the time for action comes." Toombs, however, had about as much chance of encouraging stoicism as he did of taking the temperance pledge. Cobb was

7. The preceding paragraphs are based on Crutcher, "Georgia Parties," 90–97, and Craven, *Growth of Southern Nationalism*, 341–42.

8. Athens *Southern Banner*, September 6, 1860, Carrollton *Advocate*, September 7, 1860, both quoted in Ollinger Crenshaw, *The Slave States in the Presidential Election of 1860* (Baltimore, 1945), 103, 104n.

more calculating and less excitable, but he did nothing to promote calm either. He returned home in August to campaign and publicly advocated secession if Lincoln were elected.[9]

Against the formidable array of Breckinridge talent in Georgia— the entire congressional delegation, former governors Lumpkin and McDonald, Cobb's extended family, and Governor Brown (who admitted the impracticality of protection but recognized the side with the strongest battalions), plus a host of other influential politicos and editors—the Douglas men could claim Herschel Johnson, James Gardner, Augustus R. Wright, Eugenius Nisbet, and Hiram Warner, plus only three major papers: the *Constitutionalist*, the Rome *Courier*, and James A. Hambleton's *Southern Confederacy*. By any standard the sides were sorely mismatched, particularly with Stephens on the sidelines.

And it seemed likely he would remain there. None of his friends' entreaties had budged him, and in late July he suffered a painful accident that promised to hobble him even if he did decide to campaign. Tripping over the rug at the doorway of Liberty Hall, Stephens had pitched headfirst down an eight-foot flight of steps, landing on his face in the gravel. The fall left ugly bruises and scabs on his face and pain in both his wrists and hands. Fortunately, his wounds were not serious, but they did provide another excuse to avoid the canvass.[10]

Privately, however, he followed the campaign avidly. The terrible slanders of Lincoln, his old congressional crony, he knew to be false. He didn't fear Lincoln; indeed, he thought the Republican would administer the government "just as safely for the South and honestly and faithfully *in every particular*" as Buchanan had. "I know the man well. He is not a bad man." Nor did he fear for slavery's safety; it was clear to him that slavery would be much more secure in the Union than out of it. If people were not wise enough to see this, then what hope was there for more security out of the Union under the South's present reckless leaders?[11]

Stephens had returned to his old persistent theme. For months he had argued that sectional strife arose not from some defect in the government or "irrepressible conflict" but from the character of the country's leaders and their effect on public opinion. The South's present

9. Toombs to Smith, August 5, 1860, in Smith Papers, GDAH.
10. AHS to Smith, August 8, 1860, in Phillips (ed.), *TSC Correspondence*, 491.
11. *Ibid.*, July 10, 1860, 487.

leaders would prove no more virtuous guiding a southern confederacy than they had in the national government. Even worse, these same leaders would unleash the passions of the mob, when "without control legal or moral, there is no telling to what extent of fury they may lead their victims." Stephens had long shuddered at such a prospect. By July, 1860, when the revolution he had so long feared seemed infinitely closer, he had crystallized his objections to the South's course in a few telling phrases: "We have nothing to fear from anything so much as unnecessary changes and revolutions in government. The institution is *based* on *conservatism*. Everything that weakens this has a tendency to weaken the institution." Nowhere else did Stephens ever state his political philosophy so pithily.[12]

The nature of his fears made it altogether unlikely that Stephens would remain passive in Crawfordville indefinitely. Two midsummer events shook him out of his lethargy. The first was Linton's retirement from the supreme court bench. Muttering about the "divided sceptre" among the judges and complaining about fatigue, Linton resigned his seat in late July. About a week later, he undertook an extensive speaking schedule for Douglas. With Linton on the stump, could Aleck be far behind? Then, in August, largely at Johnson's instigation, a group of Douglas Democrats meeting in Milledgeville unanimously named Stephens an elector on the Little Giant's slate. Stephens wasn't exactly pleased by the honor, calling it "a great embarrassment." And he was miffed that his friends had ignored his express wishes. But having to choose now between his "individual feelings" and the "principles which lie so near to my heart" left him no choice. He accepted an invitation to speak in Augusta.[13]

The news that Stephens had been named a Douglas elector immediately heartened the senator's supporters everywhere. Simply a letter from his pen, one ecstatic Georgian told Stephens, "will do an inconceivable amount of good." And from all over the state and country, letters poured in requesting him to speak. He declined all the invitations from outside Georgia; the crisis at home required his undivided attention. Fortunately, his health had improved remarkably, and only a small scar on his cheek recalled his recent accident. Healthy and fit, Stephens hoped "to go the rounds." The rounds began, aptly enough,

12. *Ibid.*, January 22, July 10, 1860, 457–58, 487.
13. LS to AHS, July 23, 1860, in Stephens Papers, MC; *ibid.*, August 25, 1860, 492.

in Crawfordville, where he filled in for his brother on August 27. His first real speech of the campaign came at Augusta, five days later.[14]

The hometown effort had been a short, pithy defense of Douglas; the Augusta one was a patented Stephens extravaganza, three hours long. The crush of humanity around the speaker's rostrum in City Hall Park made a stifling evening even more unbearable. At one point an exhausted Stephens had to sit down and rest for half an hour before going on. The crowd waited patiently, pleased by what it had been hearing: a forthright defense of Douglas and a heartfelt plea for wisdom and reason.

One by one Stephens ticked off the objections to Douglas and turned them aside. He defended the regularity of his nomination and his platform. The South did not need additional safeguards, he said. The Cincinnati platform of 1856 more than sufficed. Speaking of the candidate himself, Stephens readily admitted that he differed with Douglas on the power of territorial legislatures over slavery, but "practically, [this power] amounts to nothing." It involved neither the South's equality in the Union, its honor as a people, nor any principle vital to its future security and safety. No law of Congress or of territorial legislatures would keep slavery from expanding to its natural limits. Therefore, he would willingly grant a territory's people the "favor" of prohibiting slavery if they chose. This was simply self-government as practiced since the dawn of the republic. "If these opinions make a man a 'squatter sovereign,'" he concluded defiantly, "then I am one." But how could he support Douglas after differing so widely with him on Lecompton? In short, because Douglas acted from unsullied motives. For the first time publicly, Stephens admitted how greatly he had differed with Buchanan, "much more radical on principle," than with Douglas. It had been "a great and radical error" for the president to require submitting the Kansas constitution to the voters. Douglas had opposed Lecompton because of its mode of submission, not because of its slavery clause. Stephens had not questioned his patriotism then, nor would he now.

Having dealt with the objections to Douglas, Stephens addressed his many virtues. He was a strict constructionist, a states'-rights man. He was sound on slavery, and particularly on race, believing that blacks

14. Culver to AHS, August 18, 1860, and profusion of letters requesting Stephens to speak, in Stephens Papers, LC; AHS to Hidell, August 24, 1860, in Stephens Papers, HSP.

were inferior, not citizens, and not included in the Declaration of Independence. And this man was being castigated all over the South! "Was there ever blacker ingratitude, since Adam's first great fall?"

Finally Stephens came to the heart of his argument. He was weak now, scarcely audible; men had to strain to catch his words. But they rasped with urgent warning. He would not question the patriotism of Breckinridge's followers, Stephens said. But "those who begin revolutions seldom end them." The Breckinridge movement tended to disunion and civil strife. Only "the virtue, intelligence, and patriotism of the people" could prevent such a disaster.[15]

Perhaps the prolonged ovation in Augusta momentarily clouded Stephens' view of reality, or maybe it was that old familiar rush of adrenalin. Whatever the reason, for the next few days Stephens sounded optimistic. After four speeches in north Georgia, he thought Douglas was "gaining very fast" there. And a few days later, he discerned growing "*tendencies*" for him across the state. A week later Stephens returned to normal, seeing only "gloom and darkness." "I have almost despaired of the Republic," he told Smith. "Passion and prejudice rule the hour; reason has lost its sway." Once again his health had failed him, but even "weak and debilitated" he continued his exhausting speaking schedule. Often he had to stop speaking, sit down, and rest before continuing. The pathetic spectacle did not lack heroic aspects. Daily, as returns from state elections in the North arrived, it became apparent that Lincoln would sweep the North. By the end of September Stephens admitted as much to a correspondent of the New York *Herald*. And after that? "I hold revolution and civil war to be inevitable," he said. "The demagogues have raised a whirlwind they cannot control."[16]

News of Republican triumphs shattered Georgians' last illusions. With sudden toleration spawned by desperation, Constitutional Union papers began to suggest a fusion of all Georgia parties in the hope of defeating Lincoln. For about two weeks the press furiously discussed the plan. Both Ben Hill and Herschel Johnson gave it their blessing, and the Stephens brothers favored it too, although Aleck was skeptical

15. Speech in Cleveland, *Stephens*, 674–94.
16. AHS to Hidell, September 7, 1860, in Stephens Papers, HSP; AHS to Smith, September 12, 15, 1860, in Phillips (ed.), *TSC Correspondence*, 495–96; AHS to Lanman, September 17, 1860, in Lanman Papers, LC; New York *Herald*, September 27, 1860, quoted in Rabun, "Stephens," 579–80.

of its success. The Breckinridge camp, however, refused the overtures, and the scheme ingloriously collapsed.[17]

The certainty of Lincoln's election seemed to fire Stephens with new determination. The issue was no longer who would be president but whether the Union would survive. Stephens found hope where he could. Democrats, he noted, had retained enough seats in the House to keep it out of Republican control, which was all the more reason, he thought, that secession if Lincoln were elected would be groundless: the new president would be powerless to do harm.[18]

Southern disunionists were the real danger, and no one realized it better than Douglas. In Iowa, when he heard the bad news about Republican sweeps in Pennsylvania and Indiana, he resolved immediately to take his campaign south. "We must try to save the Union," he told his secretary. Douglas had no illusions; he was beaten and he knew it. But he still had faith in the basic good sense of the southern people, and to them he would appeal over the heads of their leaders. On his only other southern swing during the campaign the Illinois senator had branded secession as treason, so the Breckinridge camp was naturally enraged by the prospect of another visit from Douglas. Toombs predicted violence if Douglas dared repeat such statements in Georgia, and the Memphis *Avalanche* warned ominously of the "incendiary" soon to turn "his bloated visage" toward the South.[19]

Stephens had already urged Douglas to come to Georgia, believing it would change the minds of "thousands" who had been "kept in dark" about his views. Even at this late hour, Georgia's Douglas men hoped that the Little Giant's personal appearance might make a difference. To ensure that the senator came—some feared he might change his mind— Linton Stephens was dispatched to Memphis to escort him back.[20]

His older brother met Douglas in Atlanta on October 29 and the next day introduced him to a crowd of ten thousand. The Little Giant returned Stephens' compliments with interest. Back in June, he said, he had been willing to withdraw from the nomination race at Baltimore and had advised his supporters to rally around Stephens. The crowd roared its approval. Despite the apprehensions of some and the

17. Johnson to AHS, October 1, 1860, in Flippin, *Johnson*, 144; AHS to LS, October 14, 15, 1860, in Stephens Papers, MC.
18. AHS to LS, October 15, 1860, in Stephens Papers, MC.
19. Johannsen, *Douglas*, 798.
20. AHS to Douglas, September 26, 1860, quoted in *ibid.*

tight-lipped fury of others, Douglas completed his tour of Georgia without incident. Stephens accompanied him to his other two stops, Macon and Columbus, and delivered a speech in the latter city after his guest had crossed over into Alabama. Characteristically, both men blasted the secessionists in their speeches. They had fought fiercely, but now it was over. The country went to the polls on November 6, 1860.[21]

Two days later, it was clear to Stephens that Lincoln had won, just as he had feared from the beginning. And although returns were not yet in, he was just as sure that Georgia had gone for Breckinridge. For the moment he had energy only for bitterness. "Sometimes I think I will let them do as they please," he told Linton. "I fear we are going to destruction anyhow, and that nothing can arrest our course."[22]

Stephens was right about the vote tally in Georgia. Breckinridge had carried the state, but only by a plurality. (The legislature later awarded the state's ten electoral votes to him.) The Kentuckian had received 51,889 votes (48.5 percent), Bell 42,886 (39.9 percent), and Douglas 11,590 (11.6 percent). Thus slightly over half of Georgia's voters endorsed conservatism, or, alternatively, refused to endorse secessionism, protectionism, or extremism. Most striking about the returns was the persistence of long-standing voting patterns in the state: 116 of the state's 132 counties voted for the same party they had in 1856.[23]

Traditionally strong Democratic areas in the north Georgia mountains, the southeastern pine barrens, and the coastal counties near Savannah returned heavy majorities for Breckinridge. Bell ran poorly in the mountains, but he won about 45 percent of the vote in the middle Georgia Piedmont, where the Whigs had always been strong. Characteristically, too, the Eighth District, Stephens country, followed its leader. Douglas carried six of it twelve counties outright while winning a plurality in the district as a whole. Breckinridge took only 22 percent of the district's vote.[24]

But these returns did nothing to alter the results of the election. Lincoln carried every free state but New Jersey (which Douglas won)—more than enough to win in the electoral college—although his popular vote (1,864,735) was only a little over 39 percent of the total for the country. In the South Breckinridge won eleven states; three border

21. Rabun, "Stephens," 584.
22. AHS to LS, November 8, 1860, in Stephens Papers, MC.
23. Milledgeville, *Federal Union*, November 27, 1860.
24. Crutcher, "Georgia Parties," 108–109; Rabun, "Stephens," 585.

states went to Bell; Douglas took Missouri. But again the popular vote totals told a slightly different story. Bell and Douglas polled 55 percent of the popular vote in the slave states. If the election of 1860 is regarded as a test on sentiment for secession, the majority of the southern people rejected the extreme remedy.[25]

Moderation, however, was not in season. South Carolina could almost count its unionists on one hand. Thwarted several times by the refusal of its sister slave states to stand with them, the state's secessionists would brook no delay this time. "We must rely on ourselves in moving off," wrote Laurence Keitt. Keitt had stated the key tactical motif: speed. Carolinian radicals intended to move quickly. Delay meant discussions, resolutions, and proposals. Delay would allow consolidation of conservative strength. The radicals did not intend to let this happen again.[26]

Under other circumstances, the haste with which the South reacted to Lincoln's election might have appeared unseemly. But in November, 1860, the southern extremists had momentum. Six cotton states promptly called conventions to which voters would elect delegates. How these conventions would be constituted and who would control them still remained crucial questions the voters would answer in a series of December and early January elections.

Lincoln's election "with its hideous deformities . . . stares us in the face," said the Rome *Courier*. "*What shall be done?*" Countless Georgians in early November puzzled over the question. One did not: Governor Brown. The legislative session that opened on November 7, 1860, received a special message from Brown on the eighth. In typically verbose fashion, for he never said in one word what he could say in ten, the governor recited a long litany of northern crimes against the South. Then he offered his recommendations: the state should immediately secede; the legislature should appropriate $1 million for defense; and it should call a state convention to deal with the crisis. The assembly quickly appropriated the funds, but Georgians never acted hastily in such a crisis. The lawmakers therefore formally requested twenty-two of the state's most prominent citizens to address them and offer advice for the emergency. Naturally, Stephens was invited to speak.[27]

25. Potter, *Impending Crisis*, 442–43.
26. Keitt quoted in Craven, *Growth of Southern Nationalism*, 348.
27. Rome *Courier*, November 10, 1860; Brown's message in Allen D. Candler (ed.), *The Confederate Records of the State of Georgia* (5 vols.; Atlanta, 1909–11), I, 19–57.

Stephens had spent the past few days brooding on the futility of further resistance. First had come the news of Lincoln's election, then Brown's message, and now word that Savannah had overwhelmingly passed resolutions favoring immediate secession. And from everywhere came signs that a strange frenzy had taken hold of the people: minutemen companies being organized, suspected abolitionists being tormented, opponents of immediate secession being intimidated. Worst in Stephens' view were indications that people had succumbed to the secessionist argument. The news from Savannah fell particularly hard. Judge William Law, he had learned, formerly a "breastwork of conservatism" in the city, had shared both the sentiments and the podium with Frank Bartow, a flaming secessionist. With the ramparts being overrun, disaster seemed inevitable. "So we go," Stephens sighed wearily. "I really apprehend that no power can prevent it. Our destiny seems to be fixed." [28]

Whatever his private feelings, Stephens appeared anything but dispirited when he addressed the legislature on the night of November 14. He could not have been unaware of the importance of this speech. The fate of the republic, and certainly of Georgia, might well depend on his talents as an advocate this night.

Counsel for the opposition had already spoken. Judge Henry L. Benning had opened on the sixth, followed by Governor Brown on the seventh. Then on two succeeding nights, November 12 and 13, the secessionists' heavy artillery boomed. Tom Cobb spoke on the first night. A gifted jurist and erudite writer on the law of slavery, Cobb was also an eloquent, impassioned speaker. The South had been "robbed," "threatened," "abused," and "vilified," he said. She had been denied all voice in electing the president; she was being bound "in vassalage more base and hopeless than that of the Siberian serf." Lincoln could not be trusted, even on his oath. Again and again he returned to his theme: no delay—strike now—don't wait—secede now. Toombs had added his majesterial appearance and baronial voice to Cobb's on the thirteenth. Delay invited ruin, he contended: "Strike, strike, while it is yet time." And if resisted, "make another war of independence." [29]

It was thus to a legislature already aroused to rafter-ringing huzzas

---

28. AHS to LS, November 9, 1860, in Stephens Papers, MC.
29. Candler (ed.), *Georgia Confederate Records*, I, 157–82; Phillips, *Toombs*, 201.

by these vintage southern histrionics that Alexander Stephens addressed his appeal. The smoky chamber, eerily yellow in the sputtering gas light, was jammed to capacity, buzzing with anticipation. As the last words of introduction died, a crescendo of applause greeted the familiar figure striding deliberately to the podium. On the dais behind the speaker a stern-faced Toombs folded his arms and waited. "My fellow citizens, . . ." The buzz became a hush, and the shrill voice enveloped the chamber.

He had come, Stephens said, not to appeal to passions, but "to your good sense, to your good judgment. . . . Let us, therefore, reason together." The argument Stephens led his audience through was familiar to most of them, only now it had ceased to be an academic exercise. The peril so long potential was actual; form had taken substance. As was his wont, Stephens constructed a compelling argument and delivered it forcefully. He appealed first to their hearts, to tradition. "We are all launched in the same bark," he said. It had been a trustworthy craft, which still floated, even after all the tempests of the past seventy-five years. "Don't abandon her yet," he pleaded. "Let us see what can be done to prevent a wreck." "The ship has holes in her," came a voice from the crowd. Stephens quickly agreed—"But let us stop them if we can; many a stout old ship has been saved with richest cargo after many leaks; and it may be so now."

The South had hardly been blameless for the fearful result of the election, Stephens reminded them. Had she stood firm on the old platform at Charleston, Lincoln, obviously elected by a minority, would have been defeated. Hastiness and rashness ill became men who had brought an evil on themselves. Stephens had reached the core of his argument. Lincoln's election simply was not sufficient grounds to break up the Union. His election had been constitutional. How could the South, which had always boasted of her devotion to the fundamental law, leave the Union when the Constitution had not been violated? "If all our hopes are to be blasted, if the Republic is to go down, let us to be found to the last moment standing on the deck with the Constitution of the United States waving over our heads. Let the fanatics of the North break down the Constitution." Do not, he begged, let history record that the South had committed the aggression.

If a constitutional election was insufficient to provoke secession, then fear of anticipated evils was even less so. It would be time enough to strike when the Constitution had been violated. To do so sooner would be "injudicious and unwise." Besides, even the anticipated evils were chimerical. Lincoln, bound by constitutional checks, would be "powerless to do any great mischief." For example, the Republicans would not control either house of Congress. Moreover, the Senate had to approve cabinet officers. Theoretically the Democrats there could compel Lincoln's choices by refusing to confirm his nominees. Under these circumstances it was even conceivable that a southerner could hold office under him. "Should any man, then, refuse to hold office that was given him by a Democratic Senate?"

"If the Senate was Democratic," snapped Toombs, "it was for Breckinridge." Stephens riposted cleverly: "Well, then I apprehend that no man could be justly considered untrue to the interest of Georgia, or incur any disgrace to hold an office which Breckinridge had given him, even though Mr. Lincoln should be president." The hall exploded into prolonged applause. Georgians of all political persuasions loved this verbal cut and thrust. Stephens impatiently silenced the hubbub. He was addressing their good sense, he said. Let those who disagreed with him speak later.

Toombs minded the stricture for about five minutes. Then he interrupted again as Little Aleck harped on one of his persistent themes, the glory of the Union. Where on earth, Stephens asked, was a better government to be found than the present one? "England," Toombs interjected. "Next best, I grant," Stephens replied, but the United States was better. Compare the blessing of liberty enjoyed here, he suggested, with Turkey, Spain, France, Mexico, South America, Ireland, Prussia, and China. Americans, enjoying a "surfeit of liberty," failed to appreciate what they had. None of the evils his friend Toombs mentioned yesterday—navigation laws, tariffs, fishing bounties to New England—could possibly outweigh the benefits Georgia or the South had derived from the Union. The government had defects, he conceded, but even so, Georgia had prospered mightily. Was the South willing to risk this prosperity? He shuddered to think that passion would endanger "this Eden of the world," that instead of becoming more prosperous and happy, "instead of becoming gods, we shall become demons, and at no distant day commence cutting one another's throats."

He had finally arrived at the point to advise the legislature. Obviously he could do nothing in the atmosphere of hysteria but counsel delay. Secession was a last resort; it ought to be resisted while hope remained. Admittedly, great dangers might arise from Lincoln's election, but "wait for the act of aggression." Georgia's platform of 1850 was perfectly explicit and perfectly applicable. If the Republicans should exclude slavery from the territories by congressional action or weaken the fugitive slave law, these would be acts of aggression justifying action by Georgia. By all means, let a convention of the people be called, Stephens urged. The legislature was not the proper body to decide the state's course. Sovereignty belonged to the people; they should decide. "Our constitution came from the people. They made it, and they alone can rightfully unmake it."

From behind the podium Toombs interrupted again. "I am afraid of conventions," he boomed. (What he really feared was that secession might not carry if people were given time for reflection and for their conservative instincts to assert themselves.) "I am not," Stephens retorted. Such fundamental questions could be answered only by representatives of the people. But the question should not be presented as Toombs had suggested—"'Will you submit to abolition rule or resist?'"

Toombs broke in again: "I do not wish the people to be cheated." This time his rudeness gained him a barb of Stephens' quick wit: "Now, my friends, how are we going to cheat the people by calling on them to elect delegates to a convention to decide all these questions?" The question his honorable friend proposed smacked of unfairness, if not cheating. Was putting the question this way a fair means of getting an expression of the popular will? "I think not. Now, who in Georgia is going to submit to abolition rule?"

The question was so patently ridiculous it evoked a guffaw from the assembly. Toombs tried to recover. "The convention will." Stephens turned serious again. "No, my friend, Georgia will not do it. The convention will not recede from the Georgia platform. Under that there can be no abolition rule in the General Government." Only his friend's "excessive ardor" accounted for his readiness for violence. "When the people in their majesty speak, I have no doubt he will bow to their will, whatever it may be, upon the 'sober second thought.'" He himself would do the same, he reminded them. If Georgia decided to leave the Union, "I shall bow to the will of the people. Their cause is my cause, and their destiny is my destiny."

But "I am for exhausting all that patriotism demands before taking the last step," Stephens said in summary. A convention of the people should be called, South Carolina and the other southern states invited to a conference, and one additional plank (demanding repeal of the personal liberty laws) added to the Georgia Platform. If all these measures failed, then so be it. "We shall at least have the satisfaction of knowing that we have done our duty and all that patriotism could require."

Toombs led the legislature in three cheers for Stephens when he resumed his seat. "We have just listened to one of the brightest intellects and purest patriots that now lives," he shouted.[30]

In Herschel Johnson's opinion, the legislature might have seriously considered stampeding Georgia out of the Union had Stephens not spoken. Johnson was as overwrought as Stephens. (Perhaps even more so: being Douglas' running mate had not been pleasant or easy. He had been vilified, insulted, and hanged in effigy all over the state.) Both he and Ben Hill also argued for delay, Hill in a stirring speech to the legislature the night after Stephens' and Johnson in a public letter. Three days after Stephens' address the legislature passed a bill calling for a state convention to meet on January 16, 1861. Election for delegates would take place on January 2.[31]

Back home in Crawfordville Stephens sifted through the mountain of mail that arrived in the wake of his speech. It had produced an extraordinary effect upon conservatives' hopes. Virtually every important big city northern daily printed it in full. Even the London *Times* ran most of it. The letters poured in for weeks from all parts of the country and from citizens of every class, every party. In Washington Douglas praised the speech to the skies. If the country would but heed Stephens' advice, he said, all might yet be well.[32]

Several letters came from Republicans and northern Bell voters. Most pointed out what Stephens knew well already: that equating Republicanism with abolitionism was wrong. Ohioans had voted for Lincoln, wrote one Buckeye, because they opposed Buchanan, not because they wanted to interfere with southern slavery. And no less than the president-elect himself said the same thing. Lincoln's request for a copy of the speech initiated a brief exchange of letters between the two old friends. Stephens had warned him in a short note about the great peril the country faced and his own heavy responsibilities.

Lincoln acknowledged the dangers but was genuinely puzzled by all the excitement in the South. Did the southern people really fear that a

30. Speech in Cleveland, *Stephens*, 694–713.

31. Percy S. Flippin (ed.), "From the Autobiography of Herschel Johnson," *American Historical Review*, XXX (1925), 323–24.

32. Smith to AHS, December 2, 1860, in Stephens Papers, LC; letters, November–December, 1860, on the speech are in *ibid*.

Republican administration would "*directly* or *indirectly* interfere with the slaves, or with them about their slaves? If they do, I wish to assure you, as once friend, and still, I hope, not an enemy, that there is no cause for such fears." There was only one major difference between them, Lincoln continued. "You think slavery is *right*, and ought to be extended; while we think it is *wrong* and ought to be restricted."

Lincoln had not bargained for the long, sharp reply his letter elicited. Stephens was not discourteous, but he was pointed. He was far from holding Lincoln an enemy personally, he replied, however wide apart their political opinions. "We both have an earnest desire to preserve and maintain the Union" if it could be done upon the principles on which it was founded. And this was the rub as Stephens saw it. The South did not fear interference with its slaves, nor did it fear Lincoln because of his personal antislavery views. People feared Lincoln's party, whose "leading object" was "to put the institutions of nearly half the States under the ban of public opinion and national condemnation." On general principles this aim justified "general indignation," if not "revolt" in the South. Differences over slavery had existed when the Constitution was written, Stephens continued, and parties had not been formed over them. Why should they now? For only one reason—"fanaticism." It was "neither unnatural nor unreasonable" that the South should be apprehensive, "especially when we see the extent to which this reckless spirit has already gone"—laws against the return of fugitive slaves, for example, or open sympathy for John Brown.

Stephens concluded sharply: Lincoln should not underestimate the danger. "The Union under the Constitution" could not be maintained by force. "Independent, sovereign states" had formed the Union, and they could resume their sovereignty whenever "their safety, tranquility, and security" demanded it. The federal government had no power to coerce a state. Force might perpetuate the Union, but it would not be the Union of the Constitution. "It would be nothing short of a consolidated despotism."[33]

As Stephens had made plain, he may have questioned the policy of secession but never its constitutionality. And even as he penned his reply to Lincoln the question of coercion had assumed a "terrible practicality." South Carolina had already left the Union, and Mississippi

33. The Lincoln-Stephens correspondence is in Stephens, *Constitutional View*, II, 266–70.

was sure to follow. The Carolinians had provided for their convention immediately upon Lincoln's election, and on December 20, 1860, in Columbia, amid much ballyhoo, they unanimously passed an ordinance of secession. Stephens, who had loathed South Carolina radicalism for years, scorned her action now. But the shock wave sent its tremors across the country—and the vibrations in Georgia, just across the Savannah, were particularly strong.

Georgia's unionists had expected and feared South Carolina's action, but once it happened it caused scarcely a perceptible change in the conservative leaders. The three major unionists—Stephens, Hill, and Johnson—had all sunk into a profound and inexplicable lethargy. The legislature had allotted six weeks for the convention campaign, during which time the three leading unionists of the South's richest, most populous state delivered one speech apiece, each in his hometown, where their views could hardly have been influential in the state at large.

Johnson later wrote that a "fair and energetic canvass" would have produced a large majority against secession. Possibly it would have; it is difficult to say what might have happened had he, the Stephens brothers, and Hill labored as strenuously as the famous triumverate had in 1850. But they did not, and their failure to act largely explains Georgia's eventual secession. The secessionists' margin of victory in the convention was thin enough to suppose that a determined canvass at the county level, out among the simple farming folk at the villages and crossroads, might have altered the complexion of the convention. Of course, the conservatives' lassitude was only part of a larger complex of circumstances contributing to the secessionist victory, but no political campaign was ever won by apathy. And the top conservative leaders made no attempt to win this one.[34]

Stephens still hated Hill and refused to speak to him. He did correspond with Johnson, but they confined themselves to swapping gloomy reflections. Vague rumors had circulated around Milledgeville about the formation of a Union party; nothing came of the idea. Aside from the one- and two-man editorial operations in a few papers, the conservatives remained unorganized and voiceless, like cowed rabbits in the gaze of a snake.[35]

34. Flippin (ed.), "Johnson Autobiography," 324.
35. AHS to LS, January 1, 1861, in Stephens Papers, MC; Rabun, "Stephens," 596.

Stephens presented a pathetic spectacle. Aside from writing letters to his usual correspondents, he did nothing, wrote nothing, said nothing. Shortly after the Milledgeville speech Stephens apparently decided his cause was lost and gave up completely. Sorrowfully he watched the last major conservative Democratic paper, the *Constitutionalist*, desert to the other side. "We have fallen on sad times," he sighed. "And I doubt if there is enough patriotism in the country to save us from anarchy either in the Union or out of it." He was having nothing to do with it. "Let those who sowed the wind reap the whirlwind, or control it if they can," he wrote bitterly. "It does seem we are going to destruction as fast as we can." [36]

While sparing no words of execration for the secessionists, he had few words at all for his fellow townsmen. His one address was a spiritless effort, hardly more than a "talk," delivered impromptu to a county meeting in Crawfordville on November 24. Stephens had a bad cold, spoke briefly, and left disgruntled. His neighbors had selected him as a delegate to the forthcoming convention. He wasn't even sure he wanted to go. [37]

Aleck's attitude appalled Linton, who was convinced that Georgians largely opposed immediate secession. Go the convention, he urged. Do your best and leave the result to God. A few days later Linton allowed himself a rare burst of impatience with his brother. Stephens' steadfast refusal to canvass had so exasperated him that for once he let it show. "I think you are too much disposed to despair," he wrote. "Your despair will be the *cause* of defeat." The demagogues had not yet taken full control of the people. Indeed, never had the people's confidence in Stephens been higher. "Don't disappoint them," Linton begged. "You can save the country, I do firmly believe." [38]

Stephens ignored the pleas. The vaunted people, preferring to follow canting demagogues, had spurned his leadership and his warnings. Let them all go to perdition. He left Crawfordville during the crucial six weeks only once—to attend a supreme court session in Athens during the first week in December. The rest of the time he stayed home, living his life as if everything were normal: supervising the slaughter of his hogs, playing euchre with callers, reading Dickens and Macaulay, and

36. AHS to LS, November 21, 1860, in Stephens Papers, MC; AHS to Smith, November 23, 1860, in Phillips (ed.), *TSC Correspondence*, 504.

37. AHS to LS, November 24, 1860, in Stephens Papers, MC.

38. LS to AHS, November 26, December 2, 1860, *ibid.*

taking his beloved Rio, now blind and decrepit, on long walks through the woods and fields to the ruins.[39]

While Stephens sought refuge from the terrible present in memories and familiar routine, Georgia's disunionists campaigned as if they expected their opponents to appear on the hustings at any moment. The secessionists were "active and noisy" all over the state, reported Johnson, and more than "zealous," they were "frenzied." Tom Cobb adhered to a daily schedule of three, sometimes four, speeches. His brother joined him in late December. Secretary Cobb finally tendered his resignation to Buchanan on December 8, but not before penning a public letter for the Georgia press. Although he privately believed the Republicans presented no real threat to southern interests, Cobb told the Georgians that "degradation" and "certain and speedy ruin" were assured if Georgia remained in the Union. On his way home, Cobb, at Brown's request, stopped off in South Carolina to impress upon the Carolinians the importance of immediate action—an unnecessary meeting, if there ever was one. Secession would carry in Georgia's elections, Brown wrote, if given this push; otherwise "we are beat and all lost."[40]

Reams of argument, bombast, and cajolery in the Democratic press, which with but few exceptions was tirelessly disunionist, reinforced indefatigable secessionist speakers. The Opposition press, however, including the powerful *Chronicle*, remained staunchly opposed to secession. The real battle for Georgia was being waged at the county level, where in all but nineteen counties two slates of delegates were offered the voters, one pledged to immediate secession, the other opposed to it. The secessionists' position contrasted sharply with their opponents'. It presented a clear-cut line of policy and an argument of compelling simplicity: the Republicans meant to abolish slavery. The safety and security of the South required that she secede immediately. Their opponents, the cooperationists, however, labored under the weight of one insurmountable difficulty: they could not agree on what should be done, much less how to do it. They did agree to cooperate with other slave states in presenting an ultimatum to the North—hence their name—and their goal was clear: they wanted delay. But they had no

39. Rabun, "Stephens," 597.
40. Johnson to AHS, November 30, 1860, in Johnson Papers, DU; Cobb to the people of Georgia, December 6, 1860, in Augusta *Constitutionalist*, December 16, 1860; Brown to Cobb, December 15, 1860, in Cobb Papers, UG.

unified policy. Instead of providing answers, their position raised a host of questions. How should the South reach agreement? How many slave states should agree? Was an all-southern convention necessary? When and where should it meet? Who would choose the delegates and how? What would constitute a believable demonstration of northern support for the southern cooperationists? How long should the South wait for such a demonstration?[41]

Hurt badly by South Carolina's secession, the cooperationist cause was further crippled by the failure of compromise efforts in Washington. Upon convening in early December, both houses of Congress named special committees to try to devise a workable compromise. Neither of these committees, thirty-three men in the House, thirteen in the Senate, demonstrated anything but the utter impotence of the national government to arrest the slide into chaos. Georgia's congressional delegation was adamant. Rather than allow the executive department to be ruled by a Black Republican, stormed Crawford, "we ought to make a grand charnel house in Geo[rgia] from the Savannah to the Chattahoochie." Efforts at compromise in his opinion were pointless.[42]

It took the Senate almost two weeks of arguing even to agree on forming a committee; it took the committee six days to reject every proposal considered. On the other side of the Capitol the Committee of Thirty-three deliberated until almost the end of February. Even had all its final proposals been accepted, the gesture would have been as barren as Abraham's wife. Indeed, just such a divine intervention as had changed her condition would have been necessary to reconstruct the Union at that point: seven states had already formed a new Confederacy.

By mid-December southern hotspurs in Congress had had enough. In a telegram sent to every major southern newspaper, thirty-three cotton state senators and representatives advised their constituents that "the argument is exhausted." Southern safety and honor could be found only in a southern confederacy, "a result to be obtained only by separate state secession." Six Georgians signed this telegram, but not Toombs, who had not yet arrived in Washington. Whether he would have signed is a matter of conjecture. For before leaving home he had written a public letter that, for all his previous blustering, seemed to

41. Michael P. Johnson, *Toward a Patriarchal Republic: The Secession of Georgia* (Baton Rouge, 1977), 10–58; Crutcher, "Georgia Parties," 113–223.
42. Crawford to AHS, December 8, 1860, in Stephens Papers, LC.

indicate his receptiveness to certain adjustments. Remedy of the South's grievances, Toombs argued, might still be possible within the Union. It would be "reasonable and fair" to delay secession if a majority of the Republicans in Congress endorsed constitutional amendments guaranteeing southern rights and security.[43]

The letter flabbergasted almost everybody in Georgia. Secessionists understandably approached apoplexy in their outrage. With a few strokes of his pen Toombs had immeasurably damaged their cause. Toombs "deserves the exoration [*sic*] of every man in Geo who has a regard for truth virtue morality & integrity," wrote one angry citizen of Columbus. In Augusta, enraged secessionists voted Toombs a tin sword. "Traitor" was about the mildest epithet radicals could find to describe him.[44]

Stephens professed not to be fooled. Toombs's letter, "a masterstroke to effect his object," would lull conservatives to his support and then propel them into favoring secession when the Republicans, as they must, rejected his constitutional amendments. The Constitution needed no amending, Stephens said. "The Constitution as it is with a discharge of all its present obligations is what I want." As it turned out, Stephens was correct. Toombs, at his own request, was placed on the Senate Committee of Thirteen. He proposed six amendments, all embodying the extreme southern position, which the committee's five Republicans found obnoxious and summarily rejected.[45]

Even before this, though, Toombs had reverted to form. On December 23, the Senate voted down a set of milder resolutions proposed by Crittenden. The Republican party would obviously offer no guarantee, much less one Toombs would consider minimally acceptable. That night the senator wired his advice to the state, and on Christmas morning his message blared out from the pages of the newspapers. Any more looking to the North for security ought to be "instantly abandoned," said Toombs. Secession "should be thundered from the ballot box by the unanimous vote of Georgia on the second day of January next. Such a voice will be your best guarantee for liberty, security, tranquillity, and

43. Telegram quoted in Nevins, *Emergence of Lincoln*, II, 387; Toombs to E. B. Pullen *et al.*, December 13, 1860, in Milledgeville *Southern Recorder*, December 25, 1860.

44. W. N. Hutchins to "Dear Fitz," December 19, 1860, in Nathan L. Hutchins Papers, DU.

45. AHS to Johnston, December 22, 1860, AHS to LS, December 29, 1860, in Johnston and Browne, *Stephens*, 370.

glory." "THE LAST REFUGE OF CONSERVATISM IS DESTROYED! GEORGIA MUST SECEDE," shrilled the *Constitutionalist*. Seasons greetings. . . .[46]

Against such stirring appeals Stephens could offer only wishes that the people would exercise "a patriotic forbearance for a while relying upon the good sense and patriotism of the conservative masses of the North." If the people "united in a common effort for a redress of grievances," Stephens told a northern friend, "with an intent to be satisfied with it when it was obtained," he would feel confident that Georgia would prove equal to the crisis. Even though the actions of other states dimmed these expectations, he still had hope—or so he said. "All I can do to that end will be done."[47]

But when? If Stephens thought sitting home in funereal contemplation was all that he could do, then his idea of effective political action had undergone radical revision. The truth was he had simply given up. The only redress he thought necessary was revocation of northern personal liberty laws. But the extremists, he was convinced, didn't want redress. They meant to destroy the government, and the movement they had spawned now ran out of their control. In Washington a distraught Buchanan, his cabinet and his country crumbling around him, could think of nothing better to recommend then prayer for divine aid. Even this resort Stephens considered hopeless. "It is past praying I fear. Mr. Buchanan has ruined the country. His appeal to heaven was made too late."[48]

Two days after Stephens wrote these New Year's Eve reflections Georgians went to the polls. Perhaps "sloshed" would be a more accurate description, for the day of the most important election in the state's history was the worst in anyone's memory. Torrential rains and windy, bone-chilling weather prevailed over the entire state. "The elements of nature seemed to be in accordance with the distemper of the times," Stephens remarked the next day.[49]

He had buggied into town in a downpour to cast his ballot the previous afternoon. At the courthouse he found a drenched and woebegone-looking crowd of about a hundred huddled around the stoves. Moved

46. Toombs to the people of Georgia, December 23, 1860, in Phillips (ed.), *TSC Correspondence*, 525; Augusta *Constitutionalist*, December 25, 1860.
47. AHS to Bradford Wood, December 24, 1860, in Simon Gratz Collection, HSP.
48. AHS to Smith, December 31, 1860, in Phillips (ed.), *TSC Correspondence*, 527.
49. AHS to LS, January 3, 1860, in Stephens Papers, MC.

by their forlorn expressions, Stephens made a little speech. Keep calm, he urged. Fear and panic were the worst enemies. He didn't know what the convention would do, but he himself had only two objects: first, to maintain the "right, honor, safety, and security of Georgia," and second, to preserve the Union. If this proved impossible, he favored cooperation with the other states to form a new union based on the federal Constitution. "Three cheers for South Carolina!" yelled a local zealot. And in return—silence, broken only by the steady drip, drip, drip of water from the hats and cloaks of the grim-faced crowd.[50]

Stephens was always convinced that the weather had cost the conservatives the election. In 1867, he estimated that so many country voters had been forced to stay home that "we lost at least twenty Union members [in the convention]." A recent quantitative study of the results supports Stephens' judgment. Secessionist candidates, historian Michael Johnson concludes, polled at the most 44,152 votes to 41,632 for the cooperationists. A "more realistic" estimate, he says, is 42,744 for the secessionists to 41,717 for their opponents. "Georgians were so equally divided by the question," he writes, "that the voters' judgment can just be termed a paralyzing indecision."[51]

The "official" returns reported by Governor Brown—four months after the election and then only at the specific request of some citizens—claimed 50,243 votes for secession to 37,123 for cooperation. Had the actual results of the election been published immediately as was customary, the secessionists even then might have been given pause. Obviously, sentiment for immediate secession in Georgia, despite the conservatives' apathetic campaign, was anything but the "unanimous" thunder Toombs desired. So Stephens' lament about the weather has real substance. As it was, even in the downpour over 87,000 Georgians struggled to the polls—more than 80 percent of the turnout in November's presidential election. The voters at large were anything but apathetic.

Although individual exceptions existed, counties that went for Breckinridge in 1860 generally tended to vote secessionist, those for Bell the opposite. Generally, too, the more slaves in a county, the more likely it was to support disunion. Two conspicuous exceptions were the strongly Democratic counties of north Georgia, which voted over-

50. *Ibid.*
51. New York *Times*, July 16, 1867; Johnson, *Patriarchal Republic*, 63.

whelmingly cooperationist, and the southeastern wire grass counties, also strongly Breckinridge in 1860, which split evenly on the secession question. The Georgia Piedmont provided the third exception. Here, in the black belt, where slaveholding counties predominated, so did cooperationism. Voter turnout in the state, higher than in any other, indicates that the secession question was hardly an open-and-shut case. In the final analysis, the results in Georgia hinged on a host of intangible, unmeasurable, unquantifiable factors.[52]

And it is likely that the voter who stayed at home that day would have voted against secession. Why? Because that voter's leaders had not convinced him that his vote was crucial, that hope for the Union was not dead. Had Georgia's leading cooperationists demonstrated just half the tenacity of their followers and their opponents during the campaign, the results of the crucial election might have been reversed. The approach of the convention, however, still found these leaders gripped by paralyzing indecision and pessimism. After the rain, Stephens concluded that the conservatives' bad luck had been engineered by God. The series of misfortunes since last April, he wrote, had led him to believe "that a severe chastisement for sins of ingratitude and other crimes is about to be inflicted upon us." His despair had reached its nadir. With God against him, what could he possibly do?[53]

Governor Brown was anything but indecisive, however. The day after the election he ordered the occupation of Fort Pulaski at the mouth of the Savannah. The bewildered cooperationists could only look on in horror. Brown was being pressured into such rash actions, said Stephens, by Toombs and other ultras who meant to make secession inevitable. Johnson agreed. Brown was obviously attempting to influence the convention, but wasn't this act "technically & practically treason?" A perplexed Johnson shook his head in disbelief. "For my life I cannot understand how they expect secession to be peaceable, when they make war against the Govt of the·U States, in advance of the act of secession."[54]

"Technically & practically" Johnson may have been right, but such bothersome details hardly deterred secessionist leaders any longer.

52. The preceding paragraphs are based on Johnson, *Patriarchal Republic*, 64–65, 189–233.

53. AHS to LS, January 3, 1861, in Stephens Papers, MC.

54. *Ibid.*, January 7, 1861; Johnson to AHS, January 9, 1860, in Johnson Papers, DU.

Three more states left the Union during the first two weeks in January: Mississippi on the ninth, Florida the next day, and Alabama two days later. Louisiana and Texas voted for their conventions. On the tenth, Louisiana state troops seized the federal arsenal at Baton Rouge; the Pensacola naval yard fell to Florida troops on the thirteenth.

Less than a week before Georgia's convention Stephens concluded "that the State will secede." However wrong, the policy was impossible to resist. All he intended to do now was "maintain my principles to the last." He didn't want to be part of the proceedings and regretted he had ever consented to be a delegate. "I am getting to be a thorough home man," he told Linton. He used to like trips, but "such trollopings" greatly annoyed him now. But complain as he might, he could hardly consider betraying a public trust. And had he not gone, he would have been about the only political luminary in Georgia not there. Besides, Linton was also a delegate, and where Linton went, Stephens went. What he must bear, so must Aleck.[55]

Just as in 1850, Georgia now occupied a pivotal position in the South's destinies. Had she rejected secession, even at this juncture, the effect on the movement would have been incalculable. For without Georgia there could be no southern confederacy worthy of the name. That only one state, and particularly the Empire State of the South, could cripple the movement by voting secession down was always the weakest point in the separate state secession movement. The secessionists' success depended entirely on unity and swift execution. Any faltering by any state during the process might well have proved fatal.

On the other hand, by mid-January, 1861, the Georgia conservatives occupied an extremely anomalous position. They too had argued for unity, but four of the Gulf states were already arrayed against them. The pressure for Georgia to join them was overwhelming. Moreover, the conservatives were despondent, demoralized, unorganized, and confused. They had let eight weeks go by without the first move toward concentration on a common strategy, much less a concerted attack on their enemies. Momentum was the paramount advantage the radicals took into this convention. And in the end, although the contest was far closer than most of them desired, it sufficed for victory.

Every one of Georgia's major politicians was on hand as the Milledgeville convention came to order on January 16, 1861. Three of them,

55. AHS to LS, January 10, 1861, in Stephens Papers, MC.

Brown, Howell Cobb, and superior court judge Charles J. Jenkins, although not delegates, had been voted seats on the floor. In all, eight former congressmen, two former senators, two former governors, one former cabinet member (Cobb), and the state's entire present congressional delegation were there, plus a gaggle of state politicians and judges. The cream of Georgia's aristocracy would render her decision, for it was a rich, illustrious assembly, its median wealth $24,000. Only two delegates in ten owned no slaves; over half owned more than twenty. Similar aristocratic commissioners from already-seceded states also attended—James Orr of South Carolina and John G. Shorter of Alabama, both of whom would address the convention on its first day, and Rhett and Yancey, too—buttonholing delegates on the floor, exhorting, pressuring, arguing in low, intense tones. These men knew well what was at stake.[56]

So, supposedly, did the conservatives, but not one had come to the convention prepared. Immediately upon Stephens' arrival, Johnson had conferred with him and had been, so he says, "surprised" to discover that his friend had not written a word—not a speech, not a plan, not the first line of a resolution. Johnson need not have been so surprised. He had been corresponding with Stephens for weeks; neither had so much as mentioned convention strategy. Stephens' adamant refusal to take the lead at the convention itself, however, is more puzzling. Johnson urged him to, told him the Union delegates looked to him for leadership—to no avail. By all means write up the resolutions yourself, Stephens told him, and he would support them. So at the penultimate moment Stephens abdicated, absolved himself of all responsibility for what he regarded as inevitable tragedy. Not only did he concede the defeat of his cause, in a special way he surrendered to an enemy he had fought all his life. Despair had finally conquered him.[57]

The convention offered him its presidency, an honor he politely refused. But he did suggest that his old friend former governor Crawford be named. For probably the last time in his life, one of his suggestions was unanimously adopted. Stephens helped escort Crawford to the chair.[58]

56. Ralph A. Wooster, *The Secession Conventions of the South* (Princeton, 1962), 28–29, 84–86.
57. Flippin, *Johnson*, 177.
58. Augusta *Chronicle and Sentinel*, January 18, 1861.

Events now moved swiftly. On its third day, the eighteenth, the convention received two sets of resolutions, the first by Eugenius Nisbet of Macon, a former Whig, American, and Douglas man, declared it Georgia's duty to secede from the Union and join a southern confederacy. Johnson immediately countered by offering his own resolutions as a substitute. They sought delay, calling for a convention in Atlanta of all the unseceded states and "independent Republics" to consider relations with the federal government and promising prompt action if redress were not forthcoming.[59]

If delegates expected a long, passionate address from Stephens when he rose to speak for these resolutions, they were soon disabused. He spoke barely fifteen minutes. One delegate who heard it didn't think Stephens meant it to influence anyone; he simply expressed his opinion. Johnson judged more harshly. Stephens' support had been "half-hearted and ineffective," he said, and his speech a "surrender of the contest." Both critics were correct.[60]

Stephens began by saying that since his views against secession were well known, no good could come of repeating any of the arguments. All delegates' minds were made up anyway, and the arguments had all been heard in the canvass. In the first sixty seconds, he admitted defeat. As Stephens had precluded trying to sway anyone's opinion, he went on quietly to recite the reasons he opposed immediate secession. The gist of it was that the "point of resistance should be the point of aggression." He remained confident that a united South could obtain redress of grievances in the Union, and if the convention passed these resolutions he would do all he could to perfect a plan for cooperative action. In closing, Stephens made it clear that he would not vote for secession. No existing cause warranted it, he repeated, but if the "Sovereignty of Georgia," the majority of the convention, went against him, then he would "bow in submission to that decision." Despite the convention's ban on such demonstrations, Stephens' submissive patriotism received a burst of applause.[61]

Others—Nisbet, Tom Cobb, Johnson, Hill—spoke, but it is doubtful that anyone's mind was changed. The vote, when it came, was 166

59. Convention proceedings in Candler (ed.), *Georgia Confederate Records*, I, 229ff.

60. F. C. Shopshire to Mary Wright Shopshire, January 18, 1861, in Wright-Shopshire Family Papers, LC; Flippin, *Johnson*, 177.

61. Johnson and Browne, *Stephens*, 380–82.

for Nisbet's resolution, 130 against. The convention promptly appointed a committee of seventeen, including Stephens, to draft an ordinance of secession. The conservative cause twitched twice more before expiring. On January 18, a cooperationist motion that Governor Brown publish the county vote totals was defeated, 168 to 127. The next day Ben Hill tried again to substitute Johnson's resolutions for Nisbet's. This time the vote was 133 yeas, 164 nays. A switch of 16 votes—a very narrow margin—would have kept Georgia in the Union.

The struggle was over. The ordinance of secession now passed by a vote of 209 to 89. Alexander H. Stephens, delegate from Taliaferro, voted "nay."

XVII

Heroic Patience

Signing the ordinance of secession on January 21, 1861, had been mere formality for Stephens. The sovereignty of Georgia, the only unquestioned, indivisible sovereignty had spoken. Scrawling his name across that parchment, however distasteful to him, was a duty he could not avoid. Three days later the assembled Georgians selected ten delegates to a convention of the seceded states scheduled to begin in Montgomery, Alabama, in early February. To Stephens' chagrin, he was chosen, along with most of Georgia's other prominent leaders: the Cobb brothers, Toombs, Nisbet, and Hill. Only the "earnest solicitations" of the many in the convention convinced him to go, Stephens claimed. Even so, it took him several days to make up his mind, and when he finally did, he insisted on a condition. Everyone knew the convention would form a new government for the seceded states. Stephens wanted to ensure that it would resemble the old republic as much as possible. Not until the convention had passed a pair of resolutions he offered, stating that any government formed be based upon the United States Constitution, did he consent to go.[1]

But even as he prepared to leave, Stephens was filled with forebod-

---

1. Candler (ed.), *Georgia Confederate Records*, I, 331; AHS to Johnston, February 2, 1861, in Johnston and Browne, *Stephens*, 383–84.

ing. He would go to Montgomery, he told Dick Johnston, and do his duty. But the future appeared grim: the movement's leaders lacked "integrity, loyalty to principle, and pure, disinterested patriotism." At Montgomery he would do all he could to "prevent mischief, if possible." If he failed, he was mentally prepared for the worst. And from what he knew of the likely leaders in this new venture—men "selfish, ambitious, and unscrupulous"—he wasn't sanguine about the future.[2]

Amid the wild euphoria greeting secession, few southerners shared Stephens' fears. Most had become captives of their own dreams. Free at last from the domination of northern society to build a nation in their own image, the leaders of the South chose to ignore the hatreds, bitterness, and distrust rife in their own. The secessionists' triumph, celebrated with fireworks and champagne toasts all over the Gulf South, for the moment obscured the narrowness of that triumph. Dreams had become reality. It was a new epoch, a *tabula rasa*, a revolution. Southern unity, indeed a new southern nation, would exist not by everyone's choice, but by necessity—and necessity sometimes dictates strange choices.

For the hotspurs would not lead this revolution. In fact, almost half the fifty delegates at Montgomery were cooperationists or Unionists. On the whole a moderate body of men, the delegates had far less revolutionary zeal than a sense of urgency to present a united front to the North and the world and to put a stamp of legitimacy on their movement as soon as possible. Had they been anything else, Stephens would hardly have pronounced them the "ablest, most intelligent, and conservative body I was ever in." True to its intentions, the convention accomplished the formidable tasks of writing a provisional and permanent constitution, selecting a president and vice-president, and setting a government in motion all in about six weeks' time. And true to his own resolve to do good and prevent mischief, Stephens played a prominent role in the proceedings.[3]

The trip to Montgomery had not been auspicious. Three miles outside town the train carrying the Georgia and South Carolina delegations had three of its cars derailed. For Stephens, who would have preferred to stay home anyway, the vexing delay presaged greater discomforts in the future. First was the Exchange Hotel and his quar-

2. AHS to Johnston, February 2, 1861, in Johnston and Browne, *Stephens*, 384.
3. AHS to LS, March 3, 1861, in Stephens Papers, MC.

ters therein. Stephens liked neither—too crowded, too cramped, too noisy—so he took a room at a boardinghouse about half a mile from the state capitol building where the convention met. Within a few days Stephens was complaining about the annoyance of curious crowds, the burden of work he had, and his health. He had caught a bad cold.[4]

He might have been even more annoyed had he realized the bitterness his enemies still harbored toward him, Cobb's men in particular. The ink from his pen on the secession ordinance had barely dried before John B. Lamar reported Stephens and other cooperationists forming a "reconstruction party" dedicated to rebuilding the Union by having the seceded states rejoin if they could get the right terms. Other friends of Cobb worried that Stephens and his friends would garner positions for themselves in the new government at the expense of dedicated secessionists.[5]

Holding an office was about the furthest thing from Stephens' mind. Since his arrival he had done little but work. After electing Howell Cobb its president, the convention, on Stephens' motion—"because the crowd generally seemed green and not to know how to proceed," he explained—appointed him and four others to a committee on rules. That night the committee met in Stephens' room and accepted a set of rules he had drawn up; he then brought them to a printer and paid for enough copies for the next morning's session.[6]

The next day, February 5, Stephens was appointed to the committee charged with drafting the constitution for the new republic. Within four days—the document was approved near midnight on the eighth— Stephens and his associates produced a provisional framework of government based on the Constitution of the United States. Aside from affording slavery national recognition and protection, and a few other changes aimed at improving the prototype, the Confederate Constitution was a virtual replica of the document southerners had so long revered.

Stephens played a key role in the process of constitution making. He was directly responsible for a provision allowing cabinet members seats in Congress to answer legislative inquiries and another forbidding Congress to appropriate funds unless at the express request of the

4. *Ibid.*, February 4, 6, 8, 1861.
5. Lamar to Cobb, January 21, 1861, in Cobb Papers, UG; Charles C. Jones, Jr., to his father, January 28, 1861, in C. C. Jones Collection, UG.
6. AHS to Johnston, February 5, 1861, in Johnston and Browne, *Stephens*, 385.

president or the heads of executive departments. Later, when the convention had resolved itself into the Provisional Congress, he led the successful fight to include provisions in the permanent Constitution to allow the admission of free states into the Confederacy.[7]

Despite his energetic participation in the convention's business, Stephens' private views had not changed. He regarded war as "almost certain," and he still entertained great apprehensions about the selfishness and ambition of the South's leaders. Even Linton, no stranger to Aleck's moroseness, was concerned about his "hopeless" tone and tried to be encouraging.[8]

Fearful as he was, Stephens had nevertheless reconciled himself to the present state of affairs. The country was "in the midst of a revolution," he told one correspondent, and a wise man ought to accept it "and do the best he can under the circumstances." It was "bootless" to argue about secession now; separation was a "fixed fact." Even Cobb, lately a bitter foe, noted with pleasure that Stephens and other cooperationists in the Georgia delegation stood "as strong against reconstruction as any of us." The whole group, he continued, "are acting with perfect unanimity on all questions."[9]

Except on the question of who was to be president, that is. On that there was hardly unanimity, only the pressing necessity for maintaining a facade of unity. For this reason there had been no public discussion of the question, just closed-door conferences and semiprivate speculations among the delegates. From the first, it appears, there was a strong current in favor of Jefferson Davis, although his election was not assured until two hours before it took place, around noon on February 9. The South had several other eminent candidates, and each had some support in the convention. Yancey of Alabama and Robert Barnwell Rhett of South Carolina, paramount in the secession movement, were now considered by most to be too ultra to lead a conservative revolution or win the sympathies of the uncommitted slave states. Cobb and Toombs both had support too. Cobb, however, let it be known that he didn't want the office. (He shrank from its responsibilities, his brother explained.)[10]

7. *Ibid.*, February 9, 1861.

8. AHS to D. Cotting, February 6, 1861, in Joseph F. Burke Papers, EU; LS to AHS, February 9, 1861, in Stephens Papers, UG.

9. AHS to Samuel R. Glenn, February 8, 1861, in Stephens Papers, LC; Cobb to his wife, February 6, 1861, in Phillips (ed.), *TSC Correspondence*, 537.

10. T. R. R. Cobb to his wife, February 3, 6, 1861, in T. R. R. Cobb Letters, UG; Cobb to his wife, February 6, 1861, in Phillips (ed.), *TSC Correspondence*, 537.

Finally there was Stephens, who had not even considered the idea until James Chesnut, a South Carolina delegate, mentioned it on the train over from Crawfordville. His state was looking to Georgia for the president, Chesnut said. Stephens nodded and mentioned several names, Toombs and Cobb among them, and was astonished to hear that Chesnut had meant Toombs or Stephens himself. Stephens hastily declined; he had not been part of the "movement," he said.[11]

Stephens soon discovered that other delegates agreed with Chesnut. Barely an hour after his arrival in Montgomery, two Mississippi delegates—Josiah A. P. Campbell and Wiley P. Harris—approached him and after two hours of arguing got him to say he would consider the presidency. The next day Alabamans Colin McRae and William P. Chilton urged him to consider the office, and another Carolinian, Laurence Keitt, reiterated what Chesnut had said on the train. This time Stephens wavered: only if his election were unanimous and if he could form his own cabinet would he possibly accept, he told Keitt.[12]

Although most of these men had supported secession in their states, all wanted to weld the Unionists and cooperationists to the new government. What better way to do it than by naming the South's foremost unionist president of the Confederacy? The idea was not uncommon. The Augusta *Chronicle*, critical of Stephens since the mid-1850s, endorsed it. Its editor told Stephens that "many people" favored him for president and urged him to accept the office. Louis T. Wigfall, the leading Texas fire-eater, whose delegation would not reach Montgomery until after the election, wired ahead urging Stephens for president as a way to placate the conservatives. Judging by the reaction of some secessionists, Stephens' name must have been mentioned often enough to cause them considerable concern. William Henry Trescot said that the Stephens rumors had created a "general and very unpleasant surprise" in South Carolina. And Tom Cobb, who loathed Stephens heartily, reported on the day before the election that Little Aleck was "*looming up*" for the office since his brother had withdrawn.[13]

The actual discussions among the delegates in the last few hours before the election will probably never be known. There seems to have

11. Johnston and Browne, *Stephens*, 389–90.

12. David Hamilton Twiggs, "Presidency of the Confederacy Offered Stephens and Refused," *Southern Historical Society Papers*, XXXVI (1908), 141–44.

13. Augusta *Chronicle and Sentinel*, February 6, 1861; William H. Trescot to William Porcher Miles, February 6, 1861, in Miles Papers, SHC/NC; T. R. R. Cobb to his wife, February 8, 1861, in T. R. R. Cobb Letters, UG.

been agreement only that the election must be unanimous. Evidently Stephens wasn't eliminated entirely from consideration until late at night on February 8. Meeting in the hotel with a group of delegates from all six states, Stephens refused to commit himself to striking the first blow against the Union. Since border state radicals, many of whom were in Montgomery, considered this commitment essential to prod their lagging states out of the Union, the remaining support for Stephens—and it had been scattered at best—withered away.[14]

The way was now clear for Davis. At ten the next morning, when Georgia's delegation caucused, an incredulous Toombs learned that the other delegations had lined up behind the Mississippian. A quick check confirmed it. Ironically, Georgia's abundance of political talent had preempted her most available candidate: the state's own delegation had never united behind one of its own. While awaiting confirmation of the report on Davis, the delegation agreed to put Stephens forward for the vice-presidency instead of Toombs for the top spot. Obviously Georgia could not be slighted. And so it was that Alexander Stephens became the Confederacy's second highest official. He and Davis were unanimously elected that afternoon. By prearrangement, Stephens did not attend the session.[15]

On February 11, 1861, a Monday, Stephens took the oath of office as vice-president. It was his forty-ninth birthday, and the fact struck him as curious. The night before, serenaded by a crowd outside the Exchange Hotel, he had spoken briefly. That crowd heard more of a speech than this one did. Stephens spoke perfunctorily. Davis would address public affairs when he arrived, he said, and he would support whatever policy the new president's "superior wisdom and statesmanship" might indicate. It was hardly an auspicious beginning, and Stephens sensed the crowd's disappointment with his brevity. But a long speech, he thought, would have been injudicious. Besides, he seemed a little bewildered by all that had happened. He had not even wanted to come to Montgomery, much less be elected to office. After the war he would come to see himself as a creature of destiny—like "Lafayette at Olmute"—a victim of the policies of others.[16]

It was true. Even Stephens' bitterest enemies, like Tom Cobb, were

14. Twiggs, "Presidency Offered Stephens," 144.
15. Johnston and Browne, *Stephens*, 390.
16. AHS to Johnston, February 11, 1861, in *ibid.*, 385–86; *The American Annual Cyclopedia and Register of Important Events of the Year 1861* . . . (New York, 1864), 156; Avary (ed.), *Stephens Recollections*, 138.

unable to stem the "maudlin disposition to conciliate the union men" that had swept Stephens, the most available conservative, into office. Similarly disgusted, Howell Cobb consoled himself with the thought that the vice-presidency was an "empty compliment" and Stephens would have nothing to do.[17]

For the moment, however, Stephens wasn't thinking about destiny. Nor did he give any indication that he considered his election meaningless. He almost shrank from the magnitude of his responsibilities, he told Governor Brown. And he told Dick Johnston he would much rather be at home. Only his concern for the public weal had ever induced him to accept the office. And this too was true, but had he ever claimed to hold any office except in the public interest?[18]

No, Stephens' motives in accepting this office were a bit more complicated. For months he had railed against the lack of virtue and true patriotism among the South's leaders. Virtue, as Stephens conceived it, meant honesty and dedication to public service for its own sake, not for personal gain or power. Like the abolitionists, Stephens scorned the extremist leaders in the South as dishonest men, hypocrites more interested in seizing power than in wielding it responsibly. And true to his predictions, these deficient leaders had brought on revolution. Now, however, cooler heads prevailed. Virtue and patriotism just might triumph after all. Stephens must have savored the delicious irony as he thought about his new office. He was now the second highest elected leader in a nation that embodied the fondest dreams of the Calhounites from Texas to Carolina. Surely he knew the political imperatives that had prompted his election; nevertheless, could the South have erred in choosing him? He of all men knew what disinterested public service was. Obviously, the country realized it too. In every election he ever won Stephens had viewed victory as a personal vindication. This one was no different.

Jefferson Davis arrived in Montgomery on February 15 and was inaugurated three days later. His inaugural address, delivered to a large, appreciative crowd in front of the Alabama statehouse, sounded just the right notes of assertive nationalism. The seceded states, he declared, had merely upheld the rights of all sovereign states under the Declaration of Independence to resume the authority they had once

17. T. R. R. Cobb to his wife, February 9, 1861, in T. R. R. Cobb Letters, UG; Cobb to John A. Cobb, February 10, 1861, in Cobb Papers, UG.
18. AHS to Brown, February 13, 1861, in Stephens Papers, EU; AHS to Johnston, February 21, 1861, in Johnston and Browne, *Stephens*, 387.

delegated. Reunion was neither "practical nor desirable." The guiding policies of the Confederacy would be peace and free trade, but it would fight for its existence if necessary. To underscore the point, he urged speedy establishment of a large, well-trained army. He also paid due reverence to the Constitution, changed in its "constituent parts," he admitted, but still the "Constitution framed by our fathers." [19]

Not only did he sound like a president, he looked like one. Tall and slender, with slate-gray hair and beard and finely chiseled features, Davis looked every inch the plantation aristocrat and former soldier he was. In fact, the fifty-three-year-old Mississippian would have much preferred a military position in the Confederacy. A West Point graduate (1828), he had served seven years in the frontier army before retiring to his Mississippi Delta plantation. Elected to the House in 1845, Davis had left to lead a volunteer regiment in the war with Mexico. There he had fought well, especially at Buena Vista, where he was painfully wounded. In 1847 Davis entered the U.S. Senate but left to run for governor of Mississippi in 1851. Narrowly defeated, he was out of public life until President Pierce appointed him secretary of war in 1853, a post he filled with distinction. In 1857 Davis returned to the Senate. By 1860 he was acknowledged by all as one of the South's foremost leaders. After his resignation from the Senate during the general exodus of southern lawmakers in early 1861, he had accepted command of Mississippi's state forces.

Now he found himself the leader of a self-declared nation with no army, no executive departments, no laws. There was much to be done, so Davis naturally turned to Stephens for help and counsel. In the early weeks the two men met daily, much to the disgust of Tom Cobb, who complained that everybody else from Georgia was being ignored. Anyone consorting with Stephens aroused Cobb's ire, so it was equally disconcerting for him to see that Little Aleck and Ben Hill had apparently settled their differences and were "now as thick as brothers." [20]

Stephens—aside from "company and calls," which "bored me to death," he said—thoroughly relished his privileged status. Only Christopher Memminger of South Carolina, soon to be appointed secretary of the treasury, seemed to enjoy as much of the president's confidence. At the center of power, and entirely cordial with Toombs again after a

19. James D. Richardson (ed.), *The Messages and Papers of Jefferson Davis and the Confederacy Including Diplomatic Correspondence, 1861–1865* (2 vols.; New York, 1966), I, 32–36.

20. T. R. R. Cobb to his wife, February 20, 1861, in T. R. R. Cobb Letters, UG.

few months' lapse, Stephens seemed momentarily oblivious to the incongruity of his equally cordial relationship with such a man as Davis.[21]

The president was a lifelong Democrat, and of the Southern Rights variety at that. True, he had not been an ultrasecessionist in 1860, having migrated a bit from the fiery anticompromise stance he had taken ten years before. But he detested Douglas and all his works. As a senator he had been largely responsible for ousting the Little Giant from his chairmanship of the Committee on Territories and for demanding positive protection of slavery in the territories. So, except for their joint support of the Lecompton constitution in 1858, Davis and Stephens had been at odds on every important political measure since 1845. Robert E. Lee, who in the next few years would come to know Davis well, admired his character but still judged him as "of course, one of the extremist politicians."[22]

Indeed, there was much to admire in Davis' character: a high sense of loyalty, rock-ribbed honesty, courage, an exquisite sense of personal honor. Intelligent and energetic, Davis had a vision for the Confederacy and a willingness to sacrifice himself totally in its cause. But most of these manifest excellencies were counterbalanced by other, less laudable facets of his character. Few people knew Davis well because his icy aloofness froze out all but members of his immediate family. He was notoriously hard to get along with. Humorless and self-conscious, he appeared stiff and imperious to most people, a common trait among people who take themselves too seriously. Davis' self-righteousness easily equaled Stephens', and, if anything, the president was even more irritable and quick-tempered than his vice-president. The rigidity Davis sometimes displayed defied common sense, and, as might have been expected, he was absolutely graceless about accepting criticism.[23]

These were hardly the traits of a skilled politician, much less a man needed to lead 5 million stiff-necked southerners. In a position demanding political skills and instincts of the highest order, the South had installed a colorless stolidity. Only those who knew him well realized his shortcomings. "He did not know the arts of the politician," said his wife, "and would not practise them if understood."[24]

This failing would become painfully clear later. For the moment,

21. AHS to LS, February 21, 1861, in Stephens Papers, MC.
22. Lee quoted in Charles Bracelen Flood, *Lee: The Last Years* (Boston, 1981), 220.
23. On Davis, see Paul D. Escott, *After Secession: Jefferson Davis and the Failure of Confederate Nationalism* (Baton Rouge, 1978), *passim*.
24. Davis, *Jefferson Davis*, II, 12.

most of the South was too enthralled with independence to question the suitability of its choices for executive office. Linton Stephens was not. Immediately after the election, he told Aleck that judging by "his *looks* and some of his conduct," Davis was "a *mean* fellow." What Linton failed to notice was how alike Davis and his brother were, which boded ill for the prospects of long-term cooperation between them.[25]

The vice-president had no time to think about such petty matters. The sleepy little river town of Montgomery, home for eight thousand people at the beginning of February, had doubled in population in the past month. Office-seekers, potential officers and enlistees for the army, and a ragtag aggregation of opportunists crowded the streets and buildings. When Stephens wasn't busy fending these people off or answering his voluminous correspondence, he had to attend to business in Congress, which had appointed him chairman of the Committee on Executive Departments. Congress continued to debate the permanent Constitution, a duty Stephens considered more important than a place on the three-man commission the Confederacy was sending to Washington to obtain recognition and settle other points of dispute. So when the president offered him a place on the commission, he declined. He did not think the mission would do any good, he told Linton. Nonetheless, he was disappointed when Davis ignored his suggestions in naming the commissioners.[26]

So for the time being Stephens stayed in the capital, where debate on the permanent Constitution lasted until March 9. Although the final document did not meet all of his expectations, Stephens was generally satisfied. He would have preferred that the wording of the "necessary and proper" clause remain as he had written it in the draft: that Congress had the power to make all laws necessary and proper to carry out the specified powers and all other powers "expressly delegated" by the Constitution. "Expressly delegated" had been dropped and the founders' "vested by" substituted.[27]

This was a minor defeat. Stephens and his allies had won the biggest fight over the new Constitution: the one over the admission of free states to the Confederacy. Most of the ultras, fearing reconstruction of the old Union either through subterfuge or dilution of the pure experiment,

25. LS to AHS, February 12, 1861, in Stephens Papers, MC.
26. AHS to LS, March 10, 1861, in Stephens Papers, MC.
27. Von Abele, *Stephens*, 196.

had argued for restricting future state admissions to slave states alone. But the confluence of interests of the old Northwest and the South, not to mention their common trade and transportation ties, might attract future states to the Confederacy. Moderates did not want to preclude this possibility arbitrarily, and they had eventually prevailed.[28]

With the Constitution finished, Stephens seized his first opportunity to leave crowded Montgomery and go home. It had been a momentous five weeks. Leaving Crawfordville a reluctant revolutionary, he returned the second executive officer in a government embodying that revolution. He might have had time to remark the irony of his situation had he not been so worried about the fate of his new country. He realized how out of place his fears appeared to some. Most, he admitted, did not share his view. "Still," he wrote, "I cannot divest myself of deep anxiety, and a consideration that we have more troubles ahead than many of our more sanguine friends see or realize."[29]

At first Congress had presented a ray of hope. It had not seemed "a set of revolutionists" at first blush. But after the acrimonious debate on the admission of new states, Stephens wasn't so sure. "Some very bad passions and purposes [are] beginning to develop themselves here," he told Linton. On top of his fears for war, then—a certainty, in his opinion—Stephens had seen a frightening reality behind the flimsy facade of southern unity. Few in Montgomery had worried about the latent hostilities between moderates and radicals as much as Stephens. All would go to ruin "should dissensions, strifes, and factions spring up among us," he wrote the day after his return home. The tumultuous welcome he had received in Atlanta the day before ("acres of enthusiastic admirers") and his optimistic remarks on the occasion seemed slightly unreal to him now.[30]

But he had his duty. The die had been cast, and Stephens was not looking back. No one in Montgomery, including himself, he told a correspondent, favored compromise or return to the Union "on any terms." "Virtue, patience, and patriotism" among the people, he knew, would ensure the success of even this risky enterprise. And if he could

28. Charles Robert Lee, Jr., *The Confederate Constitutions* (Chapel Hill, 1963), 116.
29. AHS to Johnston, February 21, 1861, in Johnston and Browne, *Stephens*, 387.
30. AHS to LS, March 3, 10, 1861, in Stephens Papers, MC; AHS to Johnston, March 13, 1861, in Johnston and Browne, *Stephens*, 393; Atlanta *Southern Confederacy*, March 13, 1861.

promote those virtues, he would. So he did not hesitate to accept an invitation by the Georgia convention to give a speech in Savannah on the night of March 21, 1861.[31]

This address probably gained Stephens more notoriety than any he ever gave. The Athenaeum was jammed beyond capacity, and outside an even bigger crowd pressed around, straining to hear. As Stephens began to speak, police on the streets had to hush the throng. After that they were his. To this partisan crowd Stephens' words were gospel. They interrupted him several times with outbursts of whistling, foot-stomping applause.

This was Stephens' first chance to expound at length on fresh themes: the excellence of the Confederacy's Constitution; the patriotism and conservatism of its Congress; its breadth, wealth, and power. Older themes beckoned too: the perfidy of the Republicans and the great dangers of factionalism and party spirit in the South. If divisions and schisms were allowed to spring up, Stephens warned, "I have no good prophecy for you." No representative government could stand without "intelligence, virtue, integrity, and patriotism" among its people.

This was standard fare, but Stephens soon got caught up in his own eloquence. Unlike the abolitionist northern government, which be-lieved in the equality of the races, "our new government is founded upon exactly the opposite idea; its foundations are laid, its corner-stone rests upon the great truth, that the negro is not equal to the white man; that slavery—subordination to the superior race—is his natural and normal condition." Not content with uttering this seem-ingly self-evident truth, Stephens dilated on the theme at some length.[32]

Stephens had always found great truths irrepressible. Once they popped into his brain—and they did so much more frequently than among ordinary mortals—he had to utter them. Davis was dismayed. His vice-president's emphasis on slavery had shifted attention from the primary issue he and other southern spokesmen had been harping on for weeks: state versus national sovereignty. Stephens had seriously compromised the Confederacy's public political stance. The northern press roundly condemned the speech, and it received wide coverage in Europe. Outraged abolitionists seized on it to demand Draconian measures from Lincoln. How much the speech had helped the North

31. AHS to A. R. Wright, February 18, 1861, in Stephens Papers, LC.
32. Speech in Cleveland, *Stephens*, 717–29.

could not even be estimated, one Yankee paper later said: "It was of incalculable value to us."[33]

Many years later Stephens was still defending his by then infamous "Cornerstone Speech." The metaphor, he explained, had been borrowed from a decision of the U.S. circuit court in 1840s, the case of *John* v. *Thompson*, in which Supreme Court Justice Henry Baldwin had declared that the foundations of the government rested in rights of property in slaves. By then Stephens was an old man, still as loath to admit error as ever. But he wasn't courting embarrassment either. His official biography omitted the offensive sentence, providing only a pallid paraphrase. It claimed the speech had been "grossly misinterpreted" and "imperfectly reported." It had been neither, of course; Stephens had meant exactly what he said.[34]

Barely three weeks after the speech, Davis had much bigger problems on his hands. Stephens had spent most of his time at home, enjoying Linton's company, except for a brief foray on court business into Atlanta, where he again extolled the Constitution and the country's prospects before a "dense" crowd. The guns at Sumter blasted away the lingering hopes of moderates on both sides. As Stephens had long feared, the price of independence was to be measured in blood. Lincoln promptly called for seventy-five thousand volunteers to put down the insurrection. In a fever of war lust, patriots North and South rushed to enlist lest the war end before they got a chance to fight.[35]

Even before he had gone to Montgomery, back when the foreign affairs committee of the sovereign republic of Georgia was considering the Sumter question, Stephens stood unequivocally for peace. Had he been in the capital with the rest of the cabinet, he would surely have sided with Toombs, the secretary of state, and Leroy P. Walker of Alabama, the secretary of war, in opposing the president and others, who saw no choice but to attack Sumter. It seems odd that Stephens never questioned this momentous decision. But after all, he had long believed war to be inevitable. If it didn't come one way, it would come

33. Hudson Strode, *Jefferson Davis* (3 vols.; New York, 1955–64), II, 24–25; New York *Daily Tribune*, December 3, 1873.

34. Alexander H. Stephens, "Reminiscences of Alexander H. Stephens vs Those of General Richard Taylor," *International Review*, V (March, 1878), 152–53; Johnston and Browne, *Stephens*, 394. See also Avary (ed.), *Stephens Recollections*, 172–75.

35. Atlanta *Southern Confederacy*, April 9, 1861.

another. And Sumter had irrevocably shut the door on questions of peace. War would raise more than enough questions of its own.[36]

An urgent telegram from Davis summoned Stephens to Montgomery two days after Sumter's fall. Among the thousand other pressing details of putting the Confederacy on a war footing, Davis had one particular problem he needed Stephens' help with. He had received an important wire from John Letcher, governor of the just-seceded state of Virginia. The Old Dominion would soon join the Confederacy, but meanwhile Letcher wished to form a military alliance with the southern nation as soon as possible. Davis wanted Stephens to head a commission to Richmond immediately. As he had before, Stephens argued against accepting the job. For a change, his health had been good, and he did not want to risk it on a long miserable train ride. This time, however, he had to give in to the persistent promptings of Davis and the whole cabinet.[37]

Nervous and tired, Stephens arrived in Richmond early in the morning of April 22. All along the way at whistle stops in Georgia and the Carolinas he had been forced out onto dusty platforms to speak to knots of frenzied patriots. That night at the Ballard House another excited crowd refused to go home until he made them a rousing little speech. The next morning he addressed the Virginia convention—at much greater length.[38]

The Virginians had stayed in session just to hear this address. What Stephens gave them might have caused some to wonder why they bothered. It was a strange mixture: fulsome praise for Virginians, past and present, and their renowned reverence for the Constitution; more exposition of southern race theory; redundant rehashings of reasons why he had followed Georgia out of the Union; prompting to sign the military alliance they had already decided to sign; and some thoughts on the war prospects. He hoped it would be short, Stephens said, but he feared otherwise.[39]

Stephens had been so busy in Richmond that even the train he boarded on the twenty-sixth to go back to Montgomery must have seemed a relief. The four days in Richmond had been nonstop work. The mass of mail he was getting was ridiculous. Everybody, it seemed,

36. "Memoirs of Augustus H. Hansell," in SHC/NC.
37. AHS to LS, April 17, 19, 1861, in Stephens Papers, MC.
38. *Ibid.*, April 22, 25, 1861.
39. Speech in Cleveland, *Stephens*, 729–45.

had a plan to win the war or wanted a position in the army or government. And then there were the callers. Some, like old Edmund Ruffin, already a secessionist while Stephens was still a pup, just wanted to meet the vice-president. Others, like Major General Robert E. Lee, came at Stephens' request. The problem Lee and Stephens had to discuss was minor—would Lee accept the authority of a Confederate commander whom he outranked? (The highest-ranking general in the Confederate army at the time was a brigadier.) Lee graciously said he would, winning permanent respect and admiration from Stephens.[40]

It is difficult to say what Stephens thought of a strange visitor from Washington who also called on him—although who could have been stranger than that grizzled old radical Ruffin with his shoulder-length white hair and blazing black eyes? The visitor was Rudolph Schleiden, minister of the German Republic of Bremen to the United States. Perhaps he wasn't as strange as his mission. With both Lincoln and Secretary of State Seward's blessing, Schleiden came as a self-appointed envoy to arrange a temporary armistice between the sections. Stephens spent three hours with him, politely listening. The North was the aggressor, the vice-president said; the Confederacy intended to maintain "absolute jurisdiction" over its soil.[41]

Virginia ratified the military convention with the Confederacy on April 25, and Stephens returned to Montgomery, stopping over for a day at home on the way. All of his public speeches had been buoyantly optimistic. It would take seventy-five times the seventh-five thousand volunteers Lincoln had requested to subdue the South, he declared in North Carolina. Hyperbole was for the public, however. Privately Stephens expected a long, murderous conflict. At a gala reception in the capital shortly after his return he sounded so pessimistic that Mary Boykin Chesnut, the wife of prominent South Carolinian James Chesnut, Jr., accused him of being "half-hearted." Twice before this she and Stephens had discussed the Confederacy's prospects. His views were "deeply interesting," Mrs. Chesnut admitted, but far too gloomy for her tastes.[42]

40. Stephens, *Constitutional View*, II, 382–85.

41. AHS to R. Schleiden, April 26, 1861, in Phillips (ed.), *TSC Correspondence*, 563–64; Ephraim Douglass Adams, *Great Britain and the American Civil War* (2 vols. in one; New York, 1958[?]), I, 122.

42. Rembert W. Patrick, *Jefferson Davis and His Cabinet* (Baton Rouge, 1944), 112; C. Vann Woodward (ed.), *Mary Chesnut's Civil War* (New Haven, 1981), 56.

Stephens remained in Montgomery for the next three weeks while Congress, in special session, passed the necessary spate of laws to prosecute the conflict, measures to raise both troops and money foremost among them. From all indications Stephens was satisfied with the session's work. Though not feeling well, he dutifully presided over the debates, and when he could, made the rounds of the executive departments trying to secure commissions and appointments for his friends and constituents. By the end of May, although still certain the South faced a severe test, he pronounced himself cured of depression. "All that is past," he told Dick Johnston. "I am now nerved for the conflict."[43]

Congress adjourned on May 21, deciding on that date to transfer the Confederate capital to Richmond and reconvene there in July. Thoroughly exhausted, Stephens stayed an extra day in Montgomery to finish business and then went home, only to be stricken with dysentery. Once able to be up and about, however, he took off again on a whirlwind tour of nearby communities in support of the so-called "produce loan." This law, passed in mid-May, was the Confederacy's second major financial bill. The first, on February 28, had been an issue of $15 million worth of twenty-year 8 percent bonds. The new law authorized an additional issue of $50 million worth. Because of the dearth of hard money in the South, the new law authorized payment for the bonds in military supplies or in the "proceeds of sales of raw produce, or manufactured articles," as well as specie. In effect, farmers and planters pledged to lend the Confederacy part of their anticipated proceeds from sale of their current crop. The law also authorized the secretary of the treasury to issue, in lieu of bonds, $20 million worth of non-interest-bearing treasury notes, paper currency, that would be redeemable in specie in two years.[44]

Stephens' foray out into his old district was part of a plan whereby each congressman functioned as an agent to promote the loan. No one could have accused Little Aleck of being halfhearted during June and July. He made at least a dozen speeches to large crowds in Augusta, Atlanta, and other places. In Washington, Toombs's hometown, he se-

---

43. AHS to Johnston, May 25, 1861, in Johnston and Browne, *Stephens*, 405.
44. AHS to LS, May 22, 1861, in Stephens Papers, MC; James M. Matthews (ed.), *The Statutes at Large of the Provisional Government of the Confederate States of America from the Institution of the Government, February 8, 1861 to Its Termination, February 18, 1862, Inclusive* (Richmond, 1864), 117–18. On August 19, 1861, Congress extended the produce loan by authorizing issue of an additional $50 million in bonds.

cured pledges for two thousand bales of cotton, including a hundred bales from the secretary of state himself.

Since his election Stephens had given over forty speeches. It had become increasingly clear to him what this conflict really meant. It was a struggle for constitutional liberty, the right of a state to determine its own destiny, the right of individuals to be secure against encroachments by their government. This subject called forth all his eloquence. That the North would eventually succumb to anarchy he did not doubt. All Lincoln's actions, from the unconstitutional blockade of southern ports to the suspension of civil liberties to the monstrous attempt to subjugate the South, proved that the Confederacy stood as the last bastion of constitutional liberty and democratic government on the continent. Upon its fate rested the fate of individual liberty. Support the government, he urged. Buy bonds, if for no other reason than to avoid the heavy taxation that would surely come if the loan failed. Like thousands of wartime orators before him and since, he assured his listeners: "God is on our side. . . . None but his omnipotent hand can defeat us in this struggle."[45]

Southern farmers and planters responded well to the produce loan drive. Intended to help both the farmers and the government, the loan did neither. It did not provide what the government most needed: food products for the army. In this situation the temptation to fill the gap with paper money was almost irresistible because farmers accepted treasury notes that could be circulated as cash much more readily than bonds. So increasingly the Confederacy relied on issuing paper money to pay its bills and on intensely unpopular measures like impressment to secure supplies. The $20 million issue of notes this May barely cracked the lid of a Pandora's box, which by the end of the war would spew forth over a billion dollars worth of paper money. By then it literally wasn't worth the paper it was printed on.

But the produce loan had not solved the cotton planters' main problem either. With the blockade already threatening their former markets, cotton planters needed another outlet for their crop, so as early as the summer of 1861 they began urging the government to buy their cotton for cash. From the treasury's point of view, the scheme was impossible. Such a purchase would require an issue of up to $175 million in notes, irreparably shattering the country's credit and the value of its

45. *American Annual Cyclopedia for 1861*, 139.

currency at the onset of what might be a protracted war. Moreover, the plan contravened fundamental law. In October, Memminger declared the proposal unconstitutional.[46]

Although hardly a financial expert, Stephens took considerable interest in the economic affairs of the Confederacy. The planters considered him a friend because from the beginning he favored government purchases of cotton—but not for cash. The government, Stephens said, should pay for the cotton with 8 percent bonds. Using the cotton as credit, the Confederacy could then buy warships in Europe to break the blockade. Stephens first proposed his plan in the Provisional Congress, and as late as November 1862 he was still urging its feasibility. He said later that he would not have supported the produce loan so strongly had he known the Confederacy would stick by its original policy.[47]

At least Stephens realized that the South's most valuable agricultural asset had to be used. And if his plan to use the cotton was visionary, it was no more so than official government policy, which aimed at forcing European intervention by creating an artificial cotton shortage. Foreign powers would never break the blockade, Stephens believed. He was right about this and another thing too. From the first, his shrill voice was one of the few raised in favor of stiff taxation to hold down inflation. As the months dragged on, Stephens grew progressively more disenchanted with Congress' refusal to pass a tax bill. "Independence and liberty will require money as well as blood," he said. "The people must meet both [needs] with promptness and firmness."[48]

No one could complain about Linton's promptness in responding to the crisis. In early May, he volunteered for service in the army, and, as befitted a gentleman of refinement and property, was elected captain of his company. Soon thereafter he was elevated to the rank of lieutenant colonel. Linton's company formed part of the 15th Georgia Regiment, commanded by Stephens' old friend Judge (now Colonel) Thomas W. Thomas. Mustered into service in late July, the regiment eventually be-

---

46. The preceding paragraphs are based on John Christopher Schwab, *The Confederate States of America, 1861–1865: A Financial and Industrial History of the South During the Civil War* (New York, 1901), 10–16.

47. Committee of Sandersville Planters to AHS, October 3, 1861, in Stephens Papers, LC; R. Barnwell Rhett, "The Confederate Government at Montgomery," in Robert U. Johnson and Clarence C. Buell (eds.), *Battles and Leaders of the Civil War* (1887–88; rpr. New York, 1956), I, 110; Avary (ed.), *Stephens Recollections*, 352.

48. AHS to Johnston, May 14, 1861, in Johnston and Browne, *Stephens*, 403.

came part of Toombs's Brigade after the secretary of state decided his talents could be better employed on the battlefield. The whole time Linton was in the army—about eight months—Aleck naturally fretted himself half to death about his safety. His only reaction to the news that Linton had enlisted was the laconic statement that he was "glad." But then, even when Linton wasn't in danger, Aleck worried about him. "I think of you day and night," he wrote in February. "May our Heavenly Father watch over and protect you and inclose you to him."[49]

Had Stephens had to worry about affairs at home as much as he did about Linton, he might not have been able to function at all. As it was, plantation business rested in Harry's capable hands, and George Bristow, a young lawyer whom Stephens had educated and who lived at Liberty Hall, took care of matters Harry was unable to handle. Bristow's reports about all the slaves and their families, the crops—the melons did fine that summer—the weather, and the town gossip arrived regularly among Stephens' huge complement of mail.[50]

So did intelligence from Milledgeville, for although the vice-president busied himself with national affairs, he kept a close watch on Georgia's capital. One of his most frequent correspondents was Peterson Thweatt, the comptroller general of the state. Thweatt, an inquisitive, fat little man, kept Stephens posted on political gossip and financial affairs. In addition to being good friends with Governor Brown, Thweatt idolized Stephens; he had recently named his infant son after him.[51]

Along with Thweatt's long, chatty letters, Stephens often received some from Brown himself. The governor, however, usually came right to the point, most often with a complaint about something the Confederate government was doing. It had not taken Brown long to realize that a central government in Montgomery or Richmond could be as threatening to Georgia's sovereignty as one in Washington. And as representative of that sovereignty, Brown guarded his executive prerogatives with grim intensity. Like a scorpion, he applied his stinger to the administration every time he felt his nest threatened.[52]

The War Department was hardly a month old before Brown assailed its policy on raising troops. In the following months he clashed with

49. AHS to LS, February 15, May 13, 1861, in Stephens Papers, MC.
50. G. F. Bristow to AHS, April 27, July 22, August 5, 1861, in Stephens Papers, LC.
51. Thweatt to AHS, March 16, 1861, in Stephens Papers, LC.
52. Brown to AHS, March 28, 1861, *ibid.*

the secretary of war on several other questions. And almost always, by dint of perverse intransigence, the governor's view prevailed. Even before the first clash of arms, then, the course of intrastate politics in Georgia was set. People either supported Brown, which as the war dragged on meant opposing the Confederate government, or they supported the government and its increased wartime powers. Perforce, these people despised Brown, all his works, and all his friends. Howell Cobb, for example, thought Brown a "miserable demagogue who . . . disgraces the executive chair of Ga." Even some of Stephens' friends hardly entertained more lofty opinions of the man. J. Henley Smith, editor and part owner of the Atlanta *Southern Confederacy*, called him a "dirty low-down man . . . a mighty mean man and low slung with it."[53]

Stephens followed his own counsel. Ever since Brown had first been elected governor in 1857, he and Stephens had been, if not good friends, at least congenial associates. Brown, an oleaginous politician, who when cornered could have taught a chameleon some tricks, recognized Stephens' popularity with the people. So he had assiduously courted his opinions and played shamelessly to his vanity. Little Aleck always found such blandishments difficult to resist. Moreover, the vice-president shared Brown's low opinion of the War Department. Secretary of War Walker, he thought, was "rash," "lamentably irresolute," and "inefficient." (Stephens didn't hold a high opinion of the rest of the cabinet either. Toombs was "the brains of the whole concern," he said.)[54]

But Stephens thought Brown was doing a good job. At Little Aleck's request, Smith of the *Southern Confederacy* agreed to temper his criticism of the governor. And he sympathized with Brown, who had to endure such criticism. He had been "much pained," he told him, "at seeing the expression of discontent and dissatisfaction at some quarters." There was no question in Stephens' mind that Brown should continue in office, and for months he had been urging him to do just that. But the governor had been coy. No other Georgia governor had ever run for a third term. Tradition was strongly against it, and Brown didn't know how powerfully he would be opposed, both on this count and because of his altercations with the government.[55]

53. Cobb to his wife, May 18, 1861, in Phillips (ed.), *TSC Correspondence*, 568; Smith to AHS, October 16, 1861, in Stephens Papers, LC.

54. Johnston and Browne, *Stephens*, 467.

55. Smith to AHS, June 3, 1861, AHS to Brown, September 2, 1861, both in Stephens Papers, LC.

He found out in mid-September, when his enemies managed to get up a nominating convention of sorts in Milledgeville and chose Eugenius Nisbet, a strong supporter of the administration, to run for governor. This helped Brown make up his mind fast; he repudiated the convention's choice and then went on to win the election handily despite savage opposition from most of the state press. To the governor's friends his reelection had been a "triumph of the people over the newspapers." Others, like Cobb, viewed the prospect of two more years of Brown with loathing. "I feel humiliated in the dust," he wrote his wife. "Our state is disgraced and if you will consent I will arrange to bring my family out of the state and if the war should last for two years I will not return whilst the miserable wretch disgraces the executive chair." [56]

On one point, however, both sides seemed to agree: the war would not end with a short, easy victory. Some were already beginning to worry. "I am afraid the people will *flinch* when we begin to feel the war severely, two or three years from now," Henley Smith told Stephens. As long as Lincoln could raise money and men, the war would never end. And the Richmond administration, he thought, was doing its best to alienate the old Douglas and Bell men in the South. The exhilarating feeling of unity, so evident just months before, had vanished. War began forging its own hostile alliances in the South. [57]

From his vantage point in Richmond, Stephens listened to his friends and remained silent, for the moment keeping his own reservations about the course of events to himself. His duties kept him occupied. When the Provisional Congress convened for its third session on July 20, 1861, the vice-president sat in the presiding chair. Only duty could have kept him there. Accustomed to the idyllic peace of Crawfordville, Stephens must have been appalled by the capital. A bustling commercial center of forty thousand, Richmond would see its population double before the end of the year. Already the city teemed with an influx of refugees, government workers, visitors, office-seekers, and other hangers-on and parasites—gamblers, thugs, and whores. Hotel lodgings were impossible to find; debris from recently departed troops choked the streets along with huge clouds of dust. Stifling heat, deadly as a curse, lay over everything. And as the war went on, life in Richmond grew progressively more grim. Prices and crime soared. Depri-

56. Thomas to AHS, October 10, 1861, in Phillips (ed.), *TSC Correspondence*, 580; Cobb to his wife, quoted in Parks, *Brown*, 163.

57. Smith to AHS, October 16, 1861, in Stephens Papers, LC.

vation and scarcity stalked the streets and alleyways. To its normal commerce of foodstuffs and tobacco Richmond soon added the vast and ghastly traffic of war: the wounded and maimed, the dead and dying from hundreds of outlying battlefields. Shortly after Manassas, when the city received its first consignment of wounded, the vice-president began his daily practice of visiting the hospitals.[58]

This ritual he found far more fulfilling than his official duties. When his own health allowed, he made his daily rounds, little packages of candied fruits and other delicacies under his arm. "There goes Mr Stephens to a hospital," passers-by would remark as the frail little figure trudged down the street. As president of the Board of Managers for the Georgia hospitals, Stephens concentrated on his home state's wounded and sick, but upon request (and there were many) he would seek out other wounded to offer what succor and comfort he could. Stephens, of all men, understood physical anguish. All his life the sufferings of others affected him deeply. What he saw in these overcrowded and woefully supplied hospitals seared his soul.[59]

Room and board in Richmond seared his pocketbook. In June rent ran $100 a month; by October it had risen to $135. While in the capital during 1861 and 1862 Stephens lived at the Bruce house at the corner of Clay and 12th streets. None other than the "rash" and "irresolute" Secretary Walker split the rent with him—almost literal confirmation of the old saw about politics and bedfellows. Louisianian Thomas J. Semmes, with whom Stephens developed a close friendship, also lived there. Diagonally across the intersection stood the president's house; three blocks to the south and toward the James River lay Capitol Square.[60]

Stephens' messmates saw little of him during the summer. Linton's regiment came to Virginia just days after the war's first big battle at Manassas and encamped near the battlefield. No sooner had Linton arrived than he contracted measles. Aleck rushed out from the capital to be with him. Fortunately, Linton recovered enough within a few days to be up and around—only to get sickened in another way by re-

58. Johnston and Browne, *Stephens*, 407.
59. Edward Morrisson Alfriend, "Social Life in Richmond During the War," *Southern Historical Society Papers*, XIX (1891), 384; AHS to Johnston, January 12, 1862, in Johnston and Browne, *Stephens*, 410.
60. David K. Whitaker to AHS, June 20, 1861, L. P. Walker to AHS, October 30, 1861, both in Stephens Papers, LC; Emory Thomas, *The Confederate State of Richmond: A Biography of the Capital* (Austin, 1971), 22.

minders of the recent carnage. The oppressive stench of partially buried men and animals permeated everything. And a mere glimpse of a field hospital with its mounds of severed limbs, Linton said, made him sick to his stomach.[61]

Aleck, for his part, had never been happy with his brother's decision to join the army. He confessed to lying awake nights worrying about it. "I have felt intensely for you in your position," he wrote, hinting broadly that had it been his decision, Linton would never have become a soldier. "I felt too much to talk to you freely about it, for fear I might influence you improperly."[62]

Having found that he despised everything about military service, Linton hardly needed such prodding. In late June, from his vast perspective of less than two months in uniform, he pronounced all military science "humbug." Further experience hardly tempered his view. The physical discomforts were bad enough. His piles hurt. Then there was the rain, the leaky tents, the mud, the smoke from the green wood fires, which almost put out his eyes and deprived him of his senses, he sputtered on one occasion. But the incompetence and inefficiency of the army leadership finally drove him to distraction. Like many another hot-blooded southern patriot, Linton wanted action. Instead, all he got was boring camp routine and false starts. In early November, he finally exploded. "The administration of the business part of this army is miserable beyond belief," he told Aleck. The daily bulletins of the generals "have fallen into perfect contempt and have about as much impression on the soldiers as the generals could provide by turning up their backsides and *farting* at this great army." Within just a few more weeks Linton had had enough; he resigned his commission and got home in time for Christmas.[63]

Other voices joined the dissident chorus. Not any happier as a brigadier general than as a cabinet officer, Robert Toombs, like Linton, chaffed at inaction. The army was dying of lethargy, he thought, and he adjudged its commander, General Joseph E. Johnston, was "as incompetent [an] executive officer" as he ever knew. The president, pronounced Toombs, should concentrate the army on the Potomac instead of frittering away its strength on "panic expeditions." Colonel

61. AHS to Hidell, July 22, August 23, 1861, in Stephens Papers, HSP; LS to AHS, July 27, 1861, in Stephens Papers, MC.
62. AHS to LS, June 29, November 7, 1861, in Stephens Papers, MC.
63. LS to AHS, June 2, November 5, 7, 1861, *ibid.*

Thomas blamed all the army's troubles on President Davis, "the prince of humbugs." How in the world could the nomination of such a man for the country's first permanent president meet with such universal acceptance?[64]

Thomas erred about the president's universal popularity, but in fact the nomination of Davis and Stephens as the Confederacy's first permanent executive officers had occasioned little excitement. Since the provisional government would function for only one year, Congress had mandated an election for the permanent officers on the first Wednesday in November, 1861. Both Stephens and Davis had critics. The Richmond *Examiner*, an implacable foe of Stephens throughout the war, opened its attack in mid-September. Stephens was basically a reconstructionist, said the *Examiner*, and a vain and egotistical one besides. The Augusta *Chronicle* leveled similar charges against Davis, but the worst salvos issued from the Rhett-controlled Charleston *Mercury*. Davis, proclaimed the *Mercury*, was grossly incompetent in military affairs; the South ought to be pursuing a more aggressive military policy. And even at this stage, it began ominous rumblings about executive usurpations.[65]

Most southerners ignored such criticisms on election day; indeed, many ignored the election altogether. The listless affair produced a predictable unanimous vote for Davis and Stephens. "Political matters are quiet here," a Georgian told the vice-president, "the most remarkable unanimity prevailing throughout the state in support of our new government." The unanimity would not last for long.[66]

"It does my soul good to see how you are appreciated in Richmond," the ever obsequious Thweatt told Stephens on the eve of the election. "You are making *so many* feel good by your kindness to their suits &c." After months of being ignored by the president, Stephens must have smiled wanly. Truly, he had been attentive to requests from constituents throughout the South, but aside from a few Georgia patron-

---

64. Toombs to AHS, September 30[?], 1861, Thomas to AHS, October 10, 1861, both in Phillips (ed.), *TSC Correspondence*, 577–78, 580.

65. Harrison A. Trexler, "The Davis Administration and the Richmond Press, 1861–1865," *Journal of Southern History*, XVI (May, 1950), 184; Dunbar Rowland (ed.), *Jefferson Davis: Constitutionalist, His Letters, Papers, and Speeches* (10 vols.; Jackson, Miss., 1923), V, 51–53.

66. W. T. Thompson to AHS, November 2, 1861, in Stephens Papers, LC.

age questions and even fewer consultations on military affairs, Davis and the cabinet had ceased to rely on his advice.[67]

Even worse, no one in the executive department bothered to keep Stephens informed. The president usually kept military matters to himself—"perhaps wisely," Stephens remarked—but he did solicit the vice-president's advice in November, 1861, on the choice of an officer to organize defenses on the Georgia and South Carolina coasts. Stephens suggested P. G. T. Beauregard or Joseph E. Johnston and was surprised to learn that both were estranged from Davis. This embarrassing incident simply underscored Stephens' isolation. Ultimately he had to poke around the newspaper and telegraph offices like any ordinary citizen to find out what was going on. This conference between Davis and Stephens would be their last for over a year.[68]

The vice-president was still intensely interested in public affairs, and despite the growing coolness between him and Davis, he tried to temper his friends' harsh criticism of the president. What was needed, he told Thomas, was "heroic patience." But a man of his pride, not to mention conspicuous lack of patience, could take only so much. He too began to have serious misgivings about the direction of events. By late November, Linton was burning his brother's letters to keep prying eyes from discovering how disillusioned Aleck had become.[69]

Jefferson Davis was never noted for either political astuteness or personal warmth. A little more of either might have spared him the doleful results of this growing estrangement from the intense, pale little Georgian who so needed to be appreciated. But Stephens had become just one of several important men the president had alienated in one way or another. Beauregard, Joe Johnston, Senator Wigfall of Texas, Yancey, Toombs, Rhett—the list went on and on—and the administration had been in office barely a year. The carefully contrived unanimity of Montgomery wasn't just fraying around the edges, it was fast unraveling.

The military situation, however, appeared brighter. After the first nine months of war, Confederate territory remained basically intact. Aside from the loss of portions of western Virginia and Missouri, and

---

67. Thweatt to AHS, November 1, 1861, in Stephens Papers, LC.
68. AHS to Johnson, August 15, 1861, in Johnson Papers, DU; J. Cutler Andrews, *The South Reports the Civil War* (Princeton, 1970), 512.
69. Thomas to AHS, October 17, 1861, in Phillips (ed.), *TSC Correspondence*, 582; LS to AHS, November 27, 1861, in Stephens Papers, MC.

a few small enemy encroachments on the Atlantic coast, the new nation appeared robust and healthy.

Unfortunately, the same could not be said of its vice-president. Near the end of December, Stephens suffered a severe attack of facial neuralgia: his face, teeth, and neck "an agony of pain." It got so bad in mid-January that he had to remain in bed for two weeks. None of the practical remedies he tried—steam baths, quinine, extraction of a wisdom tooth—offered relief. Linton suggested a poultice of red pepper and sweet potatoes applied on the chest, which produced no better result. Near the end of January, Stephens struggled manfully to spend a few hours at his office but had to return quickly to bed. "I fear I shall always be sick," he told Linton sadly. The climate in Richmond was bad for him, he thought. As soon as he could, he would go home.[70]

As it turned out, Stephens stayed longer than planned, all the way till early April. By the first week in February his health had improved enough for him to resume smoking his customary cigars and attend the glittering dinner parties at the Toombses, where, as always, he charmed all the young belles in attendance.[71]

Why Stephens stayed in Richmond is unclear. The new Congress, elected the previous November, convened on February 18, 1862. Six days later, Davis and Stephens were inaugurated for their six-year terms of office. Neither event interested Stephens much. After nearly a year's association with the Provisional Congress, he had come to regard it as distinctly mediocre. Even administration supporters such as Nisbet and Tom Cobb agreed, although the latter characteristically attributed antiadministration sentiment in Congress to Stephens' malevolent influence. Actually Stephens had reasons of his own to deprecate the factionalism developing around him. He greatly feared a "break-down of the war spirit on our part. . . . We have a fiery ordeal to go through yet. It is that patience under wrong and suffering to which our people are so little accustomed." The test, he knew, still had to be endured, and it would be "the severest to which human nature can be subjected."[72]

70. AHS to LS, December 27, 1861, January 19, 23, 28, 29, 1862, in Stephens Papers, MC.

71. Sally [Gratten] to Alexander Brown, February 11, 1862, in Alexander Brown Papers, DU.

72. T. R. R. Cobb to his wife, January 12, 24, 1862, in T. R. R. Cobb Letters, UG; Nisbet to AHS, February 6, 1862, in Stephens Papers, LC; AHS to LS, January 12, 1862, in Stephens Papers, MC.

He had never been shy about expressing his opinion, however, and he was constantly being asked to do so. It embarrassed him, he said, to differ with the administration; he preferred not to be put in such a position. But when he was, he always tried to answer frankly, without the least appearance of "asperity." Apparently Stephens never considered remaining silent, but then no one in the administration valued his opinion anyway.[73]

The new Congress pleased Stephens even less than the old one. Neither House nor Senate had many good men in it, he thought. Increasingly restive in the capital, he began to feel an acute sense of isolation. "I meet with but few persons that I feel the liberty to communicate freely & cordially with," he told Linton. And yet, for the present, he was stuck in Richmond. Virginian Robert M. T. Hunter, the president *pro tem* of the Senate, had gone home, and Stephens had to preside in his absence.[74]

Just in time for the inauguration, the Confederacy was staggered by a series of crippling blows. In the west, Forts Henry and Donelson, key points on invasion routes into Tennessee, fell to Union forces, as did Roanoke Island off the North Carolina coast. Within a week, Columbus, Kentucky, had to be evacuated, and federal troops occupied Nashville.

The weather in Richmond on inauguration day, February 22, 1862, appeared as bleak and gray as the nation's prospects. A chilly, day-long downpour failed to dampen the spirits of huge crowds that turned out for the ceremony, however, nor the military band that blared out martial airs along with "Dixie" and the Marseilles hymn. Capitol Square was jammed, the throngs spilling out into the streets beyond its ornate iron gates. Mounted marshals had to clear a way for Stephens and the other dignitaries to get to the covered platform beside the equestrian Washington monument. Few people heard the invocation, the oaths, or the president's address—not memorable by most accounts—for the racket of the rain beating down on countless umbrellas and carriage tops. Stephens, garbed for the occasion in a suit of homespun denim woven by two Taliaferro County women, did not speak. He simply bowed deeply to the crowd and returned to his place. After the cere-

73. Johnston and Browne, *Stephens*, 414–15.
74. AHS to LS, February 25, 1862, in Stephens Papers, MC.

mony he pushed his way through the crush of people and walked home alone in the rain.[75]

What could he have said to them, his state of mind being what it was? The fall of Forts Henry and Donelson had plunged him into one of his most despairing moods. "The Confederacy is lost," he had told Martin Crawford one night as they were leaving Congress. "We may not meet again, and you are leaving." Yet duty required him to stay. He tried to go on but could not. At this, Crawford said, "he laid his head upon my shoulder and wept, and said that he did not care to survive the liberties of his country." Stephens' mood had not noticeably shifted when he wrote Linton a few days after the inauguration. "I am very sad," he confided. As bad as things were, he expected them to get worse. He had said so from the beginning.[76]

Davis' first message to Congress on February 25 hardly helped lighten the burden. The president, brief and businesslike, offered an alarmed and apprehensive public no explanations for the recent disasters. The reports of the executive departments had all the specifics, he told the new legislators. Manpower requirements for the army were being sufficiently met by the system of furloughs and reenlistments. That was it. Not a line a patriot could hang a hope on. Little wonder the message disappointed Stephens, but he was philosophic. "We have to bear what we cannot mend," he told Linton. If the country could survive the next two or three months, it might weather the storm, but even then survival would "depend on the wisdom and statesmanship of our public men." [77]

Two days later statesmanship dictated that Congress suspend the writ of habeas corpus. As a wartime measure against spies, traitors, and saboteurs, this act afforded a modicum of protection for the smooth operation of the government in certain areas. This law, the first of three passed during the war, allowed the president to suspend the writ and declare martial law in cities and military districts he judged in danger of attack. The act was faulty in that it implied that suspension of the writ and martial law were the same thing (a flaw Congress later corrected), but it applied for only a limited time. And Davis, unlike his counterpart in Washington, used the power sparingly and with

75. Andrews, *South Reports the War*, 166–67.
76. Avery, *In Memory*, 11; AHS to LS, February 25, 1862, in Stephens Papers, MC.
77. Richardson (ed.), *Messages and Papers of the Confederacy*, I, 189–92, 215–16; AHS to LS, February 26, 1862, in Stephens Papers, MC.

great caution. Unfortunately, several of his generals, especially in the West, overstepped their authority. Citizens of Richmond, in fact, suffered under one of the most oppressive of these generals, John H. Winder, the city's provost marshal.[78]

Later in the war, the suspension of the writ would raise Stephens to the heights of outrage. And yet, on February 27, 1862, it passed the Senate over which he presided without his raising a discernible protest. In light of his later actions, this inaction seems curious. Evidently he must have thought the law had some temporary utility and in his great concern for the fate of the country chose to overlook what he would later recognize as a grievous threat to personal liberty. Of course, he could not have foreseen that suspension of the writ would soon be used to ensure effective enforcement of an even more radical piece of legislation: the conscription bill.

On April 16, 1862, the Confederate Congress passed the first national conscription bill in American history. Under its provisions every able-bodied white male in the Confederacy between the ages of eighteen and thirty-five became liable for service in the army. Several days later Congress provided for a series of exemptions to the law. At the time, the bill was clearly imperative: a gigantic federal host was assembling at the foot of Virginia's peninsula southeast of the capital. And the volunteer system, which had filled the ranks with thousands of eager recruits the year before, was sputtering. Generous inducements passed by Congress the previous December to stimulate reenlistments had failed miserably. Not only were volunteers barely trickling in, but most of the twelve-month veterans planned to go home at the end of their enlistments.[79]

The argument that the act was vital could not be countered. With General George B. McClellan's army of more than a hundred thousand beginning its ponderous advance on Richmond, a host of administration critics joined to support the bill. Both the Charleston *Mercury* and the Richmond *Examiner*, virulent anti-Davis sheets, supported the measure. So did various Davis enemies in Congress, including Wigfall and Yancey. Both of Georgia's senators, Ben Hill and Herschel Johnson, also voted for the bill, although Johnson did so with reservations.[80]

78. Emory Thomas, *The Confederate Nation, 1861–1865* (New York, 1979), 150–52.
79. *Ibid.,* 152–53.
80. Albert Burton Moore, *Conscription and Conflict in the Confederacy* (New York, 1924), 25–26.

Exactly two weeks before the conscription bill passed, Alexander Stephens left for home. For months he had been listening to a steady barrage of criticism about Davis and his military policy. All that time he had been little more than a cipher in a government he had helped build. Even as he departed, attacks on Davis continued. Congress had exploded in mid-March when Davis, standing on his constitutional prerogatives, vetoed a bill creating the office of commanding general of the armies. The House secretly debated the propriety of deposing the president. Rumor had it that only widespread mistrust of Stephens prevented the lawmakers from acting. The vice-president's advice, though seldom solicited by either the president or his cabinet, had always been given earnestly. He would have burned with indignation had he known that some members of the cabinet considered his views "puerile."[81]

And so he left, knowing that he would not be missed. Hunter could take care of his duties in the Senate; they bored him stiff anyway. He needed to escape from this dusty, noisy place. Back home he went to tranquil Crawfordville, where he was loved and respected, where he could at least feel he exerted some control over events. As he had foreseen, things were getting worse. The war had taken on a life of its own, and it was beginning to raise fundamental questions about the nature of freedom, republican government, and constitutional liberty. As yet, with the chattering clamor of discontent swirling in the background, he had done no more than mull these matters. But the time was coming when his heretofore "heroic patience" would have to give way to action.

81. Thomas Bragg Diary, March 7, 1862, in SHC/NC.

XVIII

My Dear Sir, It Is the Principle Involved

Davis proposed the conscription bill in a message to Congress on March 28, 1862, and its shocking ramifications struck many Georgia editors. Conscription would "override all the barriers of the Constitution and every vestige of State Rights," remarked one, and would undoubtedly lead to military despotism. But once the bill passed, the same editor decided that "it becomes our duty to receive it without discussing the whys and wherefores . . . those who should be good judges think it absolutely necessary to our safety." If the policy worked, he continued, there would be time enough to discuss the act's constitutionality after the war was won.[1]

Unfortunately for the Confederacy, the "whys" and "wherefores," not to mention the "howevers" and "therebys," were crucially significant to some people. And the subject demanded immediate discussion. Governor Joe Brown dallied less than a week before penning a long letter of protest to Davis. Little did the president suspect when he replied promptly and courteously that he had just begun a lengthy correspondence with Brown on the subject. From April 22 to the end of July, when an exhausted Davis ended the exchange, the two men

---

1. Milledgeville *Southern Federal Union*, April 8, 22, 1862.

argued over the constitutionality of the measure, over the meaning of the word "militia," over who should be exempted, and over the law's necessity.

Brown contended that the plea of necessity did not apply to Georgia. The state had fielded sixty thousand men and would supply more if called upon. Moreover, the act was exceedingly dangerous because it put into the president's hands the power to destroy the state government by enrolling its employees as well as troops raised by the state above her quota. It also stripped Georgia of her constitutional prerogative to appoint militia officers. Therefore, said the governor, he would refuse to enforce conscription in Georgia, nor would he allow his state officials to enroll. Eventually Brown relented and allowed the conscription officers to work in Georgia, but he steadfastly prevented enrollment of his civil and militia officers. And to obstruct the smooth operation of the law, he began padding the rolls of state employees, who were exempt from the draft, a practice he continued—with increasing vehemence—throughout the war.[2]

After Brown's first interminable blast at the conscription act, most Georgia editors declined to print more of the same. To fill up his pages with controversy over "mere *abstract principle*," remarked one, would risk taxing readers "beyond all reasonable endurance." The vice president, however, infinitely patient when discussing abstract principle, had followed the Brown-Davis controversy avidly in the *Chronicle*, one paper that ran the entire correspondence. And from the first he agreed with Brown. Conscription was bad policy, Stephens thought, because it depressed the natural patriotism of the people. Despite ample evidence to the contrary, he insisted that a call for volunteers for the duration of the war would have supplied all the men the army needed.[3]

He also agreed with Brown about the law's constitutionality and his construction of the term "militia." According to English and American colonial history, Stephens argued, the militia was the only force that could be raised by compulsion. If the central government had the power to force every fighting man in the states into service, then "there could be no such thing as militia—and with such a construction of the Constitution it is a mockery to talk of State Rights and will soon be not much short of mockery to talk of Constitutional liberty." Clearly

2. Brown-Davis correspondence on conscription in Candler (ed.), *Georgia Confederate Records*, III, 193–302.
3. Milledgeville *Southern Recorder*, July 1, 1862.

Stephens was about to draw his line in the sand. Indeed, Linton probably heard the sword being unsheathed when his brother expressed his "surprise" at some of Davis' arguments "coming from a strict constructionist." Stephens had already noted with satisfaction how Brown had "demolished" Davis in his first reply to the president. And he had staunchly defended the governor against critics who for some unfathomable reason found him "cranky" and "unsafe" and governed as much by "vindictiveness . . . and other bad impulses as by patriotism or correct views."[4]

But Brown was just warming to the task. Encouraged by a letter from Stephens, the governor wasted no time soliciting his suggestions for protracting the controversy with Richmond. Brown was irked because Davis had released only part of the correspondence to the papers. Davis would never get the last word in this discussion, he vowed.[5]

Although he had been pressed to speak out, Stephens said nothing publicly, a reticence his friends interpreted as a clear sign that he had nothing encouraging to say. They were right. Stephens was very gloomy. Conscription was bad enough, but the fall of New Orleans and other Confederate setbacks in the West made matters worse. "The day for a vigorous policy is past," he told Dick Johnston. "It is too late for anything. . . . I think we are ruined irretrievably." It appeared to him that Davis had lost confidence in winning independence. Even if the government were to devolve upon himself, it would be too late. He should never have stood for office last November: "I don't know how I came to make the mistake, but I hoped it would do good in the way of preserving harmony."[6]

Stephens spent four and a half months at home, a decidedly pleasant interlude. Aside from the absence of hundreds of young men, the middle Georgia countryside showed not a trace of war. Stephens' plantation pulsed peacefully with the slow, ancient southern rhythms: the crops, the weather, and the family, both black and white. The legendary hospitality of Liberty Hall beckoned many—relatives, friends, strangers—to drop by, chat, and stay. And when he wasn't entertaining callers, Stephens had plenty to keep him busy. The farm needed tend-

4. AHS to F. W. Thomas, June 23, 1862, in Stephens Papers, LC; AHS to LS, June 25, 28, 1862, in Stephens Papers, MC.
5. Brown to AHS, July 2, 1862, in Stephens Papers, EU.
6. Smith to AHS, June 21, 1862, Thweatt to AHS, May 11, 1862, both in Stephens Papers, LC; Johnston, *Autobiography*, 159–61.

ing, as did his legal business. There were always letters to write, books to read.[7]

But the war would not go away. It intruded with every piece of mail arriving up his tree-shaded drive: acrid outbursts from Toombs about the lamentable incapacity of Davis, the baseness of Congress, the idiocy of regular army officers; passionate observations from Herschel Johnson about the unwisdom of conscription; pleas from ordinary citizens, high and low, displaced, disconnected, wounded, or suffering from the war. And Linton would come over with the children and stay for days. Far into the night the brothers would discuss the baleful trend of events. Linton had flirted briefly with returning to the army but had decided he could better serve the glorious cause at home. In the fall he would once again be elected to the state assembly, the staunchest ally Brown could want.[8]

The Stephens who returned to Richmond in mid-August was not the same man who had left in April. The months of cumulative disappointment and frustration had taken their toll, but the recent time at home had hardened him. Nothing he had heard cheered him, and everything he saw happening seemed to confirm his worst suspicions about the capacity of his fellow southerners to recognize real danger when they saw it. If the government's cotton policy was unwise, its resort to conscription was positively perilous.

He had long been convinced that the most promising element for the Confederacy's eventual success was that it fought for personal liberty, not just independence. Not only did conscription disregard this element, but it brought the full power of government to bear against it. Moreover, the states, individually, had formed the nation. Conscription threatened the rights of these states, individually, by wresting their very life's blood from them. Stephens could not let such a policy go unchallenged. He had left the Union with Georgia, the ultimate government authority in his life then—and now. A threat to Georgia's sovereignty was a threat to his own personal liberty. Ultimately Stephens could not separate the two. Important as Confederate independence might be, it was far less basic than this.

7. AHS to Thomas, April 18, 1862, AHS to Linton A. Stephens, June 19, 1862, both in Stephens Papers, DU; AHS to Hidell, April 26, 1862, in Stephens Papers, HSP.
8. Toombs to AHS, May 17, July 14, 1862, in Phillips (ed.), *TSC Correspondence*, 595, 601; Johnson to AHS, May 4, 1862, in Johnson Papers, DU; J. J. Harris to AHS, n.d. [1862], in Stephens Papers, LC.

Even so, he did not consider speaking out publicly against conscription, at least not yet. Instead he tried to exert what influence he had with the government to aid individuals affected by the law. All summer long he tried to help anybody who asked him in dealing with the War Department. From his vantage point in Crawfordville, many army regulations appeared petty and arbitrary, and he gladly jousted with the military bureaucracy about its silly rules. It wasn't until he returned to Richmond that he learned more news that really made him angry.[9]

Congress had authorized the suspension of the writ of habeas corpus to last until October 13, 1862. Unfortunately, because the legislation was confusing, many field officers confused martial law with suspension of the writ and were only too willing to clap on both in areas under their control. Martial law was an extreme measure, whereas suspension of the writ simply prevented the civil courts from freeing a person held by the military authorities. General Braxton Bragg, for example, had declared martial law in Atlanta, and Major General Earl Van Dorn had issued a similar edict for parts of Mississippi.

The vice-president, who had arrived in Richmond on August 16 and promptly come down with a bad cold, was hardly in a mood to tolerate these abuses. He had been snubbed again, for Davis and the cabinet were too busy to see him during his first few days back in the capital. Now came this news about overzealous generals. Over the past few weeks he and Linton had decided the country was drifting "towards the merging of all power and authority in the hands of the military." The drift, it appeared, had become a precipitous rush.[10]

Stephens wasted no time throwing himself in its path. "I have not been idle in attempting to arouse our members of Congress," he told Linton. "A reaction is in active progress here." This may have been a typical exaggeration of his own influence, but Stephens could point to some small successes. First, he convinced Secretary of War George W. Randolph to admonish a general who had been impressing commissary stores by force. He then persuaded Senator Semmes, chairman of the judiciary committee, to introduce a resolution calling for Senate investigation of the question of martial law. According to Stephens, martial law was an impossibility. "No power in this country can estab-

9. AHS to George B. Randolph, May 1, 6, June 3, 30, 1862, in Letters Received by the Confederate Secretary of War, 1861–65, Record Group 109, Microcopy 437, Roll 71, NA.
10. AHS to LS, August 17, 1862, in Stephens Papers, MC.

lish martial law; neither the President, nor Congress, much less a general in the field." Suspension of the writ was as far as Congress could go, but even this power was hedged with conditions. Arrests had to be made upon probable cause supported by oath. Moreover, the accused had a right to speedy trial with a full redress under the law for false detention. An "excess of patriotism" had blinded the people to "great vital principles," Stephens thought. To save their constitutional liberties, Congress had to be awakened from its slumber.[11]

Ironically, while Stephens feared for liberty's survival, the Confederacy's armies were winning a series of stunning victories. Shortly after Thomas J. "Stonewall" Jackson befuddled and defeated several Union generals in the Shenandoah Valley, Lee checked McClellan's advance on Richmond in a week of vicious fighting around the capital. Then Lee turned on another Union army under John Pope at Manassas and routed it. By September Confederate armies were invading Union territory in both the East and West—Lee into Maryland and Bragg into Kentucky. If ever a time beckoned southerners to hope, it was now.

But the vice-president could find little room for optimism. Like most of his countrymen, he waited expectantly for the European powers to recognize Confederate independence after Lee's victories. He had even believed the North might realize the futility of trying to defeat the South. But after two weeks in the capital he reverted to his earlier opinion: the war would drag on interminably and England and France would never intervene. Domestic affairs, if anything, were even worse. Constitutional liberty had already been destroyed in the North, and the same thing was happening in the South. If the people continued to submit to such "palpable and dangerous usurpations" as impressment orders, establishment of martial law, and appointments of provost marshals and military governors in some locales, he said, then as sure as the sun rose and set, military despotism would result. "Better, in my judgment, that Richmond fall, and that the enemies['] armies should sweep the whole country from the Potomac to the Gulf, than that our people should submissively yield obedience to one of these edicts of our own generals."[12]

He did not doubt the patriotism of the generals, he told Dick Johnston, "but, my dear sir, it is the principle involved. We live under a

11. *Ibid.*, August 27, 1862.
12. AHS to Johnston, September 1, 1862, in Johnston and Browne, *Stephens*, 419–20.

constitutional government, with clearly defined powers." The lawmaking power under the Constitution belonged to Congress, and even its power was limited. "Martial law sets at defiance the Constitution itself. It is over and above it. It is directly against its most important prohibitions, put there for the protection of the rights of the people." But the people seemed perfectly willing to submit to these usurpations. "They do not consider what they are doing. . . . They forget that the first encroachments of power are often under the most specious guises." The people of the North, having gone to war to make free men of slaves, had succeeded only in making slaves of themselves: "We should take care and be ever watchful lest we present to the world the spectacle of a like free people having set out with the object of asserting by arms the correctness of an abstract constitutional principle, and losing in the end every principle of constitutional liberty, and every practical security of personal rights." His "whole soul," Stephens concluded, was engaged in arousing the people to the danger. He was working on it "day and night, in season and out."[13]

Johnston agreed with his friend, but he had more immediate worries. Rumor had it that a new conscription law would raise the draft age to forty-five. An anxious Johnston, a family man and teacher with twenty pupils, pleaded his case with Stephens, who conferred with the secretary of war and learned that Randolph opposed raising the age limit. (Which didn't matter, of course, future conscription acts—one in September, 1862, and another in February, 1864—raised the age limit to forty-five, then fifty.) Johnston feared losing the exemption allowed him under the present law. At any rate, Stephens gladly exerted what influence he had to keep his friend out of the army, a service he performed for several others.[14]

During the war Stephens spent countless hours handling similar problems for friends. But at no task did he labor more assiduously than the one of sounding the alarm about the disregard of "great vital principles," the dangers to liberty his unwitting countrymen courted under the specious guise of necessity. The South had taken up arms to defend "an abstract constitutional principle"—state sovereignty. The

13. *Ibid.*, 420.
14. Johnston to AHS, August 25, 1862, February 4, 1863, both in Stephens Papers, LC. Stephens also interceded for his secretary Hidell and a shoemaker in Crawfordville. See AHS to Hidell, October 15, 18, 21, 1862, in Stephens Papers, HSP, and AHS to Randolph, May 1, 1862, in Letters Received by the Confederate Secretary of War, Record Group 109, Microcopy 437, Roll 71, NA.

same Constitution also enshrined the precious guarantees of individual liberty. To Stephens these were the reasons the South fought. He was as dedicated as any other southerner to achieving independence, but not at the cost of trampling underfoot the Constitution he had revered all his life.

It never occurred to him either now or later that war operates under a certain mad logic of its own. There is nothing more malleable in war than principles, which may launch wars but rarely end them. To thousands of southerners war's own logic was compelling: anything necessary for the war effort was by definition correct, honorable, patriotic, constitutional. To men who, like Stephens, unswervingly subscribed to the philosophy that the end never justifies the means, the argument from "necessity," the pragmatist's position, would always be specious— and dangerous.

For a deductive thinker as Stephens was, such arguments were incomprehensible and could be explained only by ignorance. "It is strange what ignorance prevails on this subject," he lamented to Linton, "and how little the representatives of the people know of the nature of the Government under which they live." Congress, it now appeared, was the real problem. Struggling vainly to get some of its "lamentably ignorant" members to recognize dangers he saw so clearly frustated him constantly. Even after being convinced by irrefutable argument, a representative could have an idea knocked out of his "weak head" by some uninformed military man. Then "the whole ground has to be gone over [again] with these children in politics and statesmanship." [15]

Although Stephens might have logically expected Georgia's governor to join him in protest, Brown had been uncharacteristically silent. As he explained to the vice-president, he feared being judged "too refractory for the times." So he had decided to await the meeting of the legislature and let it decide how far he should go in defense of Georgia's rights. Unless he had the legislature's approval, Brown feared he would expose himself to censure "without the moral power to do service to the great principles involved." In other words, the great principle of his own political welfare dominated for the time being. There was no advantage to be gained in complaining while Confederate armies won victories and public opinion bubbled with hope. [16]

15. AHS to LS, August 31, September 7, 1862, both in Stephens Papers, MC.
16. Brown to AHS, September 1, 1862, in Stephens Papers, EU.

The vice-president had no such compunctions. With Congress lagging, he put his case before the public. On September 7, 1862, he wrote a lengthy letter to the *Constitutionalist* detailing his reasons for opposing conscription. Although he signed this letter "Georgia," Linton and Dick Johnston (and presumably others politically knowledgeable) immediately recognized his handiwork. Ten days later he wrote again, this time over his own signature, approving Brown's refractory course on the conscription question and repudiating the government's policy. "The citizen of the state owes no allegiance to the Confederate States Government . . . and can owe no 'military service' to it except as required by his own state. His allegiance is due his State." [17]

Forceful as this statement was, it paled before the blistering response Stephens gave James M. Calhoun, whom Bragg had appointed "civil governor" of Atlanta under martial law. Calhoun had queried Senator Ben Hill about the extent of his duties under martial law, and Hill passed the letter on to Stephens for reply. "Your office is unknown to the law," Stephens told Calhoun. It was a "nullity." "General Bragg had no more authority for appointing you civil governor of Atlanta than I had; and I . . . have . . . no more authority than any street walker in your city." The Constitution governed the country, during either war or peace, and until it were set aside, there was no such thing as martial law. It could not be established by anyone, anywhere. [18]

Stephens returned to Crawfordville in early October with little to show for his efforts. True, generals in the West had, on Davis' orders, revoked their martial law orders. But Congress had refused to act on the question. Then, on October 13, 1862, it passed a new law authorizing suspension of the writ of habeas corpus. Like the first law, this one would be in effect until thirty days after the next meeting of Congress. This law omitted all reference to martial law. In subsequent guidance the war office stressed the importance of respecting the civil liberties of the populace. [19]

This bow to the South's civil libertarians afforded them little comfort; less than a month after the new suspension Congress passed a second conscription act. Although the new draft law raised the age

17. Augusta *Constitutionalist*, September 7, 17, 1862.

18. AHS to James M. Calhoun, September 8, 1862, in Cleveland, *Stephens*, 747–49.

19. John A. Campbell to Maj Gen Samuel Jones, October 27, 1862, in U.S. War Department, *The War of the Rebellion: A Compilation of the Official Records of the Union and Confederate Armies* (Washington, D.C., 1881–1901), Ser. I, Vol. XVI, Pt. 2, 980. Hereinafter cited as *Official Records*.

limit for potential draftees, it also allowed the president to suspend its operation and receive troops under the old voluntary system in areas where the draft proved impossible. This concession hardly appeased Brown, who decidedly ended his silence. Until the legislature met and passed on the constitutionality of conscription, he told Davis, he would not allow the law to operate in Georgia. No law ever passed by the United States had endangered constitutional liberty more than the conscription acts, he continued. Georgia would not yield her sovereignty to usurpations. She would instead force the central government to operate "within the sphere assigned it by the Constitution." Sounding much like the vice-president, Brown confided to a fellow governor that the South had more to fear from "consolidation tendencies" in the government than she did from the Yankees.[20]

Brown repeated these words to the legislature when it convened in early November. According to the *Recorder*, his message set off a "long and profitless discussion" in the House that neither changed anyone's mind nor shed any light "over that impenetrable domain, State Sovereignty." Linton Stephens did his passionate best to aid the governor on the House floor. If the central government could take all of Georgia's fighting men without her consent and against her will, state sovereignty had become a mockery, he said. Georgia had an absolute right to retain troops for her own protection. As a "monument to Georgia's sovereignty" he would march forty thousand militiamen to Savannah and stand them on the seacoast.[21]

Most legislators understandably preferred to follow Ben Hill's counsel; he addressed them on December 11 and calmly shredded the governor's arguments. Brown, he noted archly, had been the first Confederate governor to resort to state conscription—without even bothering to consult the assembly. (Early in 1862 Brown had imposed a draft on any county not meeting its quota of volunteers.) A few days before the legislature met, Georgia's supreme court had made Hill's case all the more persuasive by declaring conscription constitutional. In response to Brown, about all the assembly did was pass a resolution authorizing the state to raise two regiments for local defense and a law appropriating $1 million for defense.[22]

20. Brown to Davis, October 18, 1862, in Candler (ed.), *Georgia Confederate Records*, III, 294–302; Brown to Zebulon Vance, September 26, 1862, in Joseph E. Brown Collection, LC.

21. Milledgeville *Southern Recorder*, December 9, 1862; Atlanta *Southern Confederacy*, November 16, 1862.

22. Parks, *Brown*, 222–23.

Brown, however, chose to read these moves as an endorsement of his conscription policy. Actually, all the resolution did was authorize replacement of state troops the new national law had just declared eligible for the draft. The assembly had said nothing about the constitutionality of conscription, much less forbade the law's operation in the state. Nonetheless, Brown continued to thwart the law by granting as many exemptions to the draft as he could. Before the war ended he had exempted more than fifteen thousand men one way or another.[23]

Stephens remained silent during the assembly's session. Linton, however, was anything but quiet. He saw nefarious plots everywhere. In his opinion, the supreme court's decision had been fixed, "a *sham*" got up solely to influence the legislature. Conscription, he had decided, formed part of a gigantic conspiracy against liberty. The law had been expressly designed "to decitizenize the whole army . . . degrade them into mere machines . . . for the unquestioning execution of the designs and commands of their masters." According to Linton, the "monstrous impolicy" of the law far overshadowed even its unconstitutionality.[24]

Aleck would have demurred at this, although he would not have denied that conscription was bad policy. Governor Brown had simply been trying to "save the Constitution," he told Dick Johnston. The governor might be old-fashioned, but he knew what he was doing. In fact, he "had more sense than the whole legislature." With Brown doing perfectly well on his own, Stephens declined an invitation to address the legislature. Everyone knew his views anyway, he said. Some weren't even interested in hearing them. (One legislator had scribbled, "provided he does not speak on the Conscript Acts," after his name on Stephens' invitation.)[25]

Or perhaps Stephens had tired of speaking. Upon returning from Richmond he had embarked on a tour around central Georgia. Few hearing him could have believed he had serious doubts about the country's policies. Extolling the southern cause, he reminded people that the American Revolution had been won even though several states had been overrun by the enemy. Everywhere he urged the "importance of providing clothes, shoes & blankets for the men from each county." In Hancock County "about two thousand dollars were raised on the

23. *Ibid.*, 226–27.

24. LS to AHS, November 12, 1862, in Stephens Papers, MC; LS to J. A. Stewart, December 28, 1862, in Waddell (ed.), *Linton Stephens*, 246–47.

25. Johnston, *Autobiography*, 168; 148 Members of the Georgia Assembly to AHS, December 5, 1862, in Stephens Papers, DU.

spot," he proudly reported. Yet he couldn't resist reminding the crowds that had his cotton policy been followed a year before, there would be no need now for destroying cotton in the face of the enemy. He still thought his cotton plan had merit and said so.[26]

Unfortunately, some Georgia editors failed to appreciate the subtleties of Stephens' argument. To them it seemed that he was urging people to plant cotton against the administration's policy of encouraging the raising of corn and grain. "What will corn be worth next year if a large cotton crop is planted?" groused the Columbus *Times*. "God only knows what will become of us if Mr. Stephens' policy finds favor with the planters."[27]

The criticism stung Stephens and his friends. Several papers had misrepresented his remarks. He had not meant to discourage raising food. On his own farm he was planting as much wheat, corn, and peas as possible and was encouraging everyone else to do likewise as their highest patriotic duty. But this policy met only immediate needs. He did not agree with those urging destruction of cotton as an instrument of foreign policy to force recognition from the European powers. After raising an abundance of provisions for home consumption and the army, the more cotton the South could raise the better, he believed. For cotton meant foreign credit; its destruction would only force England to find other sources.[28]

For Stephens, the plight of destitute Confederate soldiers, many of them shoeless and in tatters, overshadowed even mistaken administration policies. Indeed, his primary object on the speaking tour had been to try to rectify this deplorable situation. In Crawfordville he put up two hundred dollars of his own money to buy shoes and clothes for Taliaferro County soldiers. And if it took more, he told the aid committee, he would put up to a thousand dollars. The bill would be paid regardless of what it took. He didn't know who was to blame for the miserable supply situation, but surely, he thought, they lacked qualifications for the job.[29]

Not everyone misunderstood what Stephens had said about cotton.

26. Cleveland, *Stephens*, 749–60; AHS to Hidell, October 26, 1862, in Stephens Papers, HSP.

27. Columbus *Times*, October 17, 1862, quoted in Milledgeville *Confederate Union*, October 26, 1862.

28. AHS to Hidell, October 26, 1862, in Stephens Papers, HSP.

29. *Ibid.*, November 18, 19, 1862.

An assistant secretary of the treasury had written to compliment him, and it pleased him that someone in the executive branch was listening to him. Davis had consulted him only once since the capital had been moved to Richmond, Stephens reflected ruefully. Nonetheless, he had to admit that personal relations between them seemed as cordial as ever. Still, he wasn't interested in going back to Virginia any time soon. He had spent three delightful weeks in December visiting relatives, and aside from some touches of rheumatism in his knees, his health was good. Going to Richmond in the middle of winter might aggravate this, a personal discomfort he would tolerate, he told his secretary, "if there was any necessity . . . any call of duty." He discerned none, so he decided to stay home and let Hunter attend to his duties in the Senate. Having to sit and listen to debates without being able to express his opinion by even so much as a vote, he said, was "the most tantalizing and worrying position in life." So Stephens stayed in Georgia as Congress went into session on January 12, 1863. If necessity required it, he reminded correspondents, he would come straight to Richmond.[30]

Stephens began the new year contented, even optimistic, from all indications. Success continued to bless Confederate arms: Bragg had held his own in a bloody engagement at Murfreesboro in Tennessee; Lee had shattered the latest attempt to dislodge his army in Virginia; and the Union campaign against Vicksburg on the Mississippi was stymied. Moreover, Republican setbacks in northern elections had raised doubts about Lincoln's reelection. The North would not hold out another year, Stephens predicted in a speech at Culberton.[31]

But Stephens also recognized the dangers confronting his own country. Within a year, he told Linton, there would be a "smashup," and not necessarily peace. If the South could hold out until May, the North would lose three hundred thousand nine-month volunteers. But perseverance would not be easy: the country's enormous expenditures were being met solely by new issues of treasury notes that inflated prices to frightful levels. According to the latest reports he had seen, $400 million more was needed, far too much to raise by direct taxation. It would be better, Stephens thought, to tax in kind, simply taking produce and supplies, rather than issuing more paper money.[32]

30. Johnston and Browne, *Stephens*, 426; AHS to Hidell, December 22, 1862, in Stephens Papers, HSP; AHS to Thomas Semmes, March 29, 1863, in Semmes Papers, DU.
31. R. M. Johnston to AHS, January 24, 1863, in Stephens Papers, LC.
32. AHS to LS, January 18, 1862, in Stephens Papers, MC.

Money was on everybody's mind. The Confederacy's financial condition was in a shambles. By the end of 1862 the government had issued over half a billion dollars in treasury notes. Funded and unfunded debt exceeded $567 million; inflation ran rampant, and the produce loan and funding act of October, 1862, had barely dented the problem. For some time a plan to enable the Confederacy to fund its debt, reduce the amount of paper money in circulation, and sustain the credit of its securities had been bandied about Congress and the press. The proposal would combine a heavy war tax and a new bond issue, with the debt from the new issue being guaranteed by the states on a *pro rata* basis. Davis liked the idea and recommended it to Congress in his message at the opening of its session.[33]

The vice president, on the other hand, opposed the idea. Only stiff taxation could answer the crisis, he believed, and there was only one way to reduce the amount of currency in circulation: take it up and either fund it or put it into another form of debt. The Davis plan would do nothing toward reducing the volume of currency, and he did not think state legislatures had the nerve to vote the taxes necessary to back up their promises. Furthermore, he thought the responsibility for creating and paying debt ought to rest on the same shoulders. With Congress free to appropriate at will while the states endorsed the debt, "our situation would be like that of a rich father giving an unlimited line of credit to a profligate son . . . general bankruptcy would ensue if the war should last long."[34]

Stephens had even less faith in the upper-class bondholders. State guarantee of national debt could threaten the independence of the Confederacy. Holders of Confederate bonds that depended on state credit for redemption might easily get nostalgic for the benefits of the old Union. "Capital by itself has little patriotism above the brute instincts of self preservation," he told Senator Semmes. "I would not have it led into the great temptation of leaning towards any terms of Peace short of independence. I have heard much of *reconstruction* since the war began but . . . this scheme if adopted would be the most dangerous step in that direction," especially since its proponents lacked "the slightest conception of its natural tendency."[35]

33. Richardson (ed.), *Messages and Papers of the Confederacy*, I, 294.

34. AHS to LS, April 3, 1862, in Stephens Papers, MC; AHS to Semmes, January 4, 1863, in Semmes Papers, DU.

35. AHS to Semmes, January 4, 1863, in Semmes Papers, DU.

Stephens was still remonstrating with Semmes a couple of weeks later. State endorsement of the debt would stimulate only short-term investment, he predicted. A much better prod to investment would be to "declare at once that all outstanding treasury notes not funded by a particular day shall after that be funded in bonds" at a low interest rate. Only substantial taxation, he reiterated, could save the country's finances. But how could the taxable property of the states be reached? That was the problem. Under the Constitution, Congress could not levy *ad valorem* taxes. And direct taxes had to be apportioned among the states by representative population, an inequitable course to take, Stephens thought, because "the property will not bear the burthen as it ought." The wealthiest would for the most part escape their responsibility. Stephens had a solution: by using its power to support armies, Congress could reach taxable property "with as little violation of either the spirit or letter of the clause as . . . is now used in the conscription of men." If the clause allowed taking men, then it also permitted taking money or goods. Stephens was not prepared to say how far Congress should go in providing for compulsory seizure of needed goods, but it was clearly necessary to reduce the horrendous inflation. Of course, better security for confiscated goods ought to be given than the depreciated paper money then being used. Cotton would do just fine, he thought.[36]

Whether Stephens' plan would have worked—and there were many who agreed with him—is not the point. (In fact, the Confederacy did attempt to regularize its *ad hoc* system of impressments with legislation later in 1863.) What is striking about the vice-president's position was his fierce devotion to the independence of his country, not to mention his extraordinary willingness to sanction a broad reading of the Constitution if it would help stabilize the currency and produce goods or wealth for the government's use.

It's much more facile than illuminating to tar Stephens with an always-a-unionist-at-heart brush or to brand him a "fanatic," an "obstructionist," an "emotionalist," a "supreme egoist," and an "agitator" than to deal critically with the abundant evidence that, in opposing certain policies of the government, he did not harbor a traitor's heart. By the same token, to insinuate that Stephens' unremitting hatred of Davis ultimately accounted for his opposition to the policies of the

36. *Ibid.*, January 17, 1863.

government does little justice to his obvious sincerity and devotion to civil liberties.[37]

Stephens always denied personal antipathy to Davis. Indeed, the files of his correspondence contain little evidence of a personal hatred of the president. Compared to men Stephens *really* despised—James K. Polk and Ben Hill come immediately to mind—Davis comes away favorably. Relations between the two men certainly were (or later became) very frosty, but this was as much the president's choice as it was Stephens'. At this point, early 1863, Stephens described his relations with Davis as "cordial," although they admittedly saw little of each other.[38]

The president's latest message to Congress pleased Stephens greatly. Except for the part that urged state guarantee of Confederate debt, Stephens judged it the best message Davis had ever presented: "strong, clear, and pointed and in admirable taste tone and temper." It had "fewer faults and more excellencies" than any previous Davis pronouncement and would do much good both at home and abroad. Among other subjects, Davis discussed at length Lincoln's Emancipation Proclamation, which had been issued on New Year's Day. Lincoln's action, said the president, had rendered reconstruction of the Union forever impossible. Discussing the Emancipation Proclamation with Linton a few days later, Stephens did not quibble with Davis' assessment.[39]

Linton had become obsessed with the conscription question, which he argued with anyone having the stamina to stand it. Twenty-five pages of constitutional discourse from his pen was not unusual. Aleck, of course, happily explored the question with his brother, but he refused to countenance some of Linton's hasty schemes to oppose the policy. Near the end of January, for example, he suggested modifications to a series of resolutions Linton intended to introduce in the assembly. His brother should forego any allusion to repeal of the conscription acts, Stephens advised, and resolve instead "under existing circumstances

37. E. Merton Coulter, *The Confederate States of America, 1861–1865* (Baton Rouge, 1950), 25, 137; Burton J. Hendrick, *Statesmen of the Lost Cause: Jefferson Davis and His Cabinet* (New York, 1939), 420–21; Frank Lawrence Owsley, *State Rights in the Confederacy* (Chicago, 1925), 184; James Z. Rabun, "Alexander Stephens and Jefferson Davis," *American Historical Review*, LVIII (January, 1953), 290–321.

38. AHS to Johnson, April 15, 1864, in Johnson Papers, DU; Johnston and Browne, *Stephens*, 426; AHS to Hidell, January 19, 1863, in Stephens Papers, HSP.

39. Richardson (ed.), *Messages and Papers of the Confederacy*, I, 291–93; AHS to LS, January 18, 22, 1863, in Stephens Papers, MC.

[to] waive all opposition to their present execution," reserving remedies for the future. As egregious as the law was, Stephens refused to
sanction radical measures to oppose it.[40]

But editorial attacks on Linton irked Stephens, and he himself took
pains to explain their position on the question. Sometimes, though, he
wearied of the whole tiresome business. He had hoped the war would
soon end, he told his secretary William Hidell, and with it "all of these
questions" about conscription. But most of all he hoped that disagreements about policy might be expressed with "candor and without passion and that we shall be saved from the evils of parties & factions
upon them." "I am no grumbler, no croaker as the cant phrase is," he
assured Herschel Johnson. "I am a patient silent cool man." He would
aid the administration in anything "that meets the approval of my
judgment," but unless his views were requested, he would keep silent.
The cabinet knew his views and had since November of 1861.[41]

Patient and cool, perhaps; no grumbler, surely; but he was not completely silent. The *Constitutionalist* had used some of his ideas (exactly
as he had written them, Stephens noted) in opposing state endorsement
of the Confederate debt. And in private letters to many in Richmond
he had been frank in his opinion of certain government policies: state
endorsement, suspension of the writ, conscription, impressment.[42]

Like many other Georgians, Stephens abhorred the way the impressment system worked. The system operated arbitrarily and set prices
the government paid for seized goods far below market value. Although
he admitted the constitutionality and necessity of impressment, Stephens believed the system needed major overhauling to distribute its
burdens equally. Unfortunately, a complicated law passed by Congress
in March, 1863, failed to stem the system's inherent abuses. Impressment remained a colossal burden and major irritant to the populace
throughout the war. One particularly egregious case Stephens knew
about—government agents paid a Georgia woman fifteen cents a pound
for beef worth three times that price—was "but a straw," one of ten
thousand such straws that sapped popular morale and support for the
government.[43]

40. LS to Landrum, February 9, 1863, in Stephens Papers, LC; AHS to LS, January
15, 29, 1863, in Stephens Papers, MC.
41. AHS to Hidell, February 22, 1863, in Stephens Papers, HSP; AHS to Johnson,
February 29, 1863, in Johnson Papers, DU.
42. AHS to LS, January 15, 1863, in Stephens Papers, MC.
43. AHS to Johnson, February 29, 1863, in Johnson Papers, DU.

Occasionally Stephens spoke out publicly; not often, but then anything from his pen received wide notice. He wrote one such letter in March, 1863, to a woman in Raymond, Mississippi. Only those intimately acquainted with Stephens could have discerned more than slight annoyance with the government in what he said. Stephens meant to be encouraging, and so the South perceived him. (Northern papers interpreted the letter as a sign of Stephens' confidence in victory.) The Confederacy had the means to resist just as long as the federals continued the war, he wrote: "No equal number of people on earth ever had more of the essential elements of war at their command than we have. . . . All that is wanting with us . . . is the brains to manage and mould our resources." Only if the South failed to devote enough care to producing food and other supplies could she fail. Meanwhile, everyone had to bear the privations and sacrifices with "patience, patriotism, and fortitude." These were "the price of independence." John B. Jones in the War Department assured Stephens that "thousands . . . had taken new courage" from his words. Stephens should speak out again, he urged, against widespread illicit trade with the enemy.[44]

While Confederate congressmen wrestled with near intractable problems of finance in Richmond, down in Milledgeville Joe Brown tussled less mightily with a personal decision: whether to run again for governor. (Perhaps the warm letter from Davis congratulating him for an assembly resolution partially prohibiting the cultivation of cotton momentarily convinced him that he was losing his grip.) Brown, who learned all he ever knew about candor from a sphinx, never did reveal why he decided to forego a fourth term in late January, 1863—more than six months before the election—or exactly why he changed his mind a few months later. At any rate, on January 30, 1863, the governor informed Stephens that he would not run again. To maintain state sovereignty unsullied Brown suggested Linton as his successor. What did Stephens think? Apparently Aleck or Linton (likely both) opposed the idea, for within a couple of weeks Brown was suggesting Toombs as his second choice.[45]

Brown could not have wished for anyone more suited to carry on in his own inimitable tradition than Bob Toombs. Since his resignation

44. AHS to "A Lady of Raymond, Mississippi," March 14, 1863, in Augusta *Chronicle and Sentinel*, April 12, 1863; New York *Times*, April 26, 1863; John B. Jones to AHS, May 20, 1863, in Stephens Papers, LC.

45. Davis to Brown, January 22, 1863, in Jefferson Davis Papers, LC; Brown to AHS, January 30, 1863, in Stephens Papers, EU.

from the cabinet and entry into the army, Toombs had established himself as probably the most outspoken malcontent in the Confederacy. His military career had proceeded ingloriously from its beginning: its high points—aside from innumerable instances of intoxication in camp—consisted of a challenge to Major General D. H. Hill, his division commander, to a duel; being placed under arrest by General James Longstreet for disobeying orders; an inept performance during the Seven Days campaign; and a creditable one at Sharpsburg. Wounded shortly thereafter, he convalesced slowly, waiting for a promotion that never came. Burning with hatred for Davis ("a false and hypocritical . . . wretch"), Toombs resigned his commission in early March, 1863.[46]

He had made no secret of his contempt for the president and his West Point generals. He also made a *cause célèbre* out of planting as much cotton as he pleased on his Georgia properties in the face of local protests and government policy. If for no other reason than this, wrote Thweatt, the voters would reject Toombs, and the "timid" were "horrified" at the prospect of him as governor. They preferred Brown as one less likely to run the state against the administration.[47]

Toombs had no interest in running for governor. He preferred to stand for Congress, the best place to oppose Davis' "illegal & unconstitutional course." With Brown silent, several trial balloons for other possible candidates floated aloft, a few feeble ones for Stephens himself. Thweatt promptly scotched the "absurd" idea among legislators and urged Stephens to "insist" that Brown run again. Evidently Stephens took the hint, for a few days later the governor told him that his recent letter and verbal message "had much to do with shaping my course." Friends had assured him that no other states'-rights man could win. Before having Georgia back down from her position, he would "submit to any personal sacrifice." Having manfully shouldered the burden in one sentence, he requested Stephens in the next to help him carry it by writing his friends in the army on his behalf. Almost as an afterthought Brown wrote that he had "negatived the idea of an antiadministration party" in his letter accepting the nomination for governor.[48]

46. Thompson, *Toombs*, 175–204; Toombs to AHS, March 2, 1863, in Phillips (ed.), *TSC Correspondence*, 611.

47. Thweatt to AHS, March 21, 1863, in Stephens Papers, LC.

48. Toombs to Burwell, June 10, 1863, in Burwell Papers, LC; Thweatt to AHS, May 14, 1863, in Stephens Papers, LC; Brown to AHS, May 21, 1863, in Stephens Papers, EU.

Stephens replied promptly to commend Brown both for his decision and his acceptance letter. His had been one of the most influential voices counseling Brown, for by now he and the governor had developed a bit more than a marriage of convenience and a bit less than a warm friendship. For some unaccountable reason, Stephens, a man of unblemished integrity, felt drawn to Brown, whose principles were as malleable as putty. For the present the two men found each other mutually useful, and the vice-president loved the tunes Brown crooned in his ear. "I agree with you fully," the governor told him, "that independence without constitutional liberty is not worth the sacrifices we are making." Maintaining constitutional liberty meant maintaining Georgia's sovereignty.[49]

It seemed to occur to neither man that an antiadministration "party," or something similar, would naturally form around leaders who opposed almost everything the government did. It certainly appeared so to Herschel Johnson, who shared Stephens' constitutional scruples but considered it his patriotic duty to support Davis, the commander in chief, whether men liked him or not. Johnson supported the war effort and confined his protests to the Senate chamber.[50]

But he never ceased to remonstrate, cajole, flatter, and argue with Aleck and Linton. Johnson knew his friends well; he knew what tone he could take and what persuasions were most likely to be effective. For his part, Stephens respected Johnson's opinions and occasionally listened. Much more often, though, he spent pages explaining himself, as if by sheer weight of superior arguments he might get Johnson to understand that some principles were even more dear than victory.

For some weeks Johnson had been trying to get Stephens to come to Richmond. Near the end of March, with the funding act already passed and Congress debating a comprehensive tax bill, Johnson wrote again. He regretted that Stephens had not come at the first of the month: "I know it was unnecessary, but there are hundreds all over the Confederacy, who criticize you unjustly." The tax bill was "*the* great measure of the session;" his counsel was sorely needed. All his frinds agreed. Senator Robert Johnson of Arkansas pleaded with Stephens in a similar vein. The country had a right to the advice of its vice-president, he said.[51]

---

49. Brown to AHS, May 29, 1863, in Phillips (ed.), *TSC Correspondence*, 618–19.
50. Johnson to A. E. Cochran, March 4, 1863, in Flippin, *Johnson*, 231.
51. Johnson to AHS, March 25, 1863, in *ibid.*, 234; R. W. Johnson to AHS, April 8, 1863, in Stephens Papers, LC.

No doubt these entreaties helped convince Stephens to undertake the trip, however painful the prospect. He had not been disposed to go before for a variety of reasons, and at this point, with his neuralgia bothering him, he decided to wait for warmer spring weather. Even aside from his aches and pains and his vexation with Confederate policy, it had not been a good month for Stephens. He had lost one of his truest friends. Old, deaf, blind, and infirm Rio, who had been devoted to his master with all the passion of his canine heart, breathed his last just as Stephens was boarding a train to visit a very sick Bob Toombs.

For over ten years Stephens had loved the animal with a fervor he vouchsafed to few humans. He had already wept much at the piteous spectacle of Rio's painful old age, and even as he left for Toombs' place, he sensed that the dog might die. So in accordance with the master's instructions, George, a household servant, laid the body in the library overnight, placed it in a box the next morning, and buried it behind the house, just a few yards from Stephens' office.[52]

For Stephens Rio's death meant losing a part of himself. Whenever he was home, the dog followed him everywhere: to town and on the long walks to the old homestead and the graveyard. Rio had slept at the foot of his master's bed, had curled up at his feet when he read or played whist or scribbled one of his many letters. Even old age and blindness had not altered this routine. The dog's sufferings only further endeared him to Stephens. And so Stephens cried, more than once, out in back by the grave. "You, nor I, nor anyone will ever see his like again," he told Dick Johnston. "Who that knew him as I did could refrain from shedding a tear for Rio?"[53]

Linton and Johnston did what they could to comfort Stephens, both writing long letters of sympathy. These didn't help much; Stephens fell into one of his moods of black melancholy. But a mood that in former days might have lingered weeks or even months this time passed quickly. In about a week Stephens had shed it, by simply willing it away, he said. Indulging feelings of melancholy or misanthropy, which, he confessed, had been the "Scylla and Charybdis in my life," only made matters worse. He had finally escaped both, he told Linton, with God's help.[54]

52. AHS to LS, March 19, 1863, in Stephens Papers, MC.
53. AHS to Johnston, March 20, 1863, in Johnston and Browne, *Stephens*, 438.
54. LS to AHS, March 19, 1863, Johnston to AHS, March 20, 1863, both in Stephens Papers, LC; AHS to LS, March 29, 1863, in Stephens Papers, MC.

Once launched into reflection, Stephens found it difficult to still his pen. Like the subject of women, the subject of religion made him uncomfortable. Indeed, so reticent had he been about it, and so obviously unchurched, that some men had suspected him an atheist. Stephens admitted that after his youthful piety he had become "skeptical [and] callous." But his continual misery had prompted extensive self-examination, which in turn had led him to conclude that "the error might be in myself." A human frailty he could seldom admit to men he found comforting to confess to God. He had given up "finding fault with, or thinking about" what he could not understand. And he had begun to pray daily, a practice that "soon appeared to bring a certain inexplicable satisfaction to the spirit. . . . It seemed to elevate the soul and put it in union with its Maker." The practice of daily prayer and communion with the inward spiritual power had made him much more contented and happy. "Such is the character of religion," he said, and few people knew of it. This was exactly the way he wanted it, for he had always hated the "cant of religion" and had consciously suppressed what he really thought and felt about such things.[55]

Aleck's new-found religion did not prompt charity in Linton's heart toward at least one frail human, the "sly, secretive, malignant hypocrite" in the executive chair in Richmond. It was "a delusion," Linton fumed, to let preconceptions about Davis' character blind them to the evil. Davis' policy looked to absolutism; he raced Lincoln "in usurpation and madness." The recent bill to have the states endorse the Confederate debt was but another link in a chain of "rapidly accumulating and gigantic usurpations." The "personal pussillanimity" of the citizens, the Congress, and Georgia's assembly filled him with dread. "I believe we are lost!" Stephens received these uplifting thoughts on the eve of his departure for the capital. He left on the night of April 20, 1863, informing Davis and sending ahead a letter about a court martial case he wished to discuss. In Augusta, where he stopped for some private business, he met Yancey and learned that Congress was about to adjourn. After some hesitation Stephens decided to go on. He did want to see Congress, and he had business in the war office.[56]

Stephens arrived in Richmond on the twenty-fifth, the day after

55. AHS to LS, March 29, 1863, in Stephens Papers, MC.
56. LS to AHS, April 6, 1863, in Waddell (ed.), *Linton Stephens*, 257–59; AHS to Davis, April 20, 1863, in Jefferson Davis Papers, DU; AHS to LS, April 23, 1863, in Stephens Papers, MC.

Congress passed the tax bill. His business took only a few days. On the twenty-ninth he spent an amiable two hours with the president at his home discussing matters of state. Davis, Stephens reported, had talked more freely with him than he had for some time. Then Stephens was off to take care of business in the War Department. He felt good—at least so he told clerk Jones. Jones, however, confided to his diary that Stephens appeared "afflicted with all manner of diseases." Only his blazing eyes betrayed a mind "in the meridian of intellectual vigor."[57]

By May 9, 1863, Stephens was back home in Crawfordville. Presumably by this time he had heard of Lee's great victory at Chancellorsville, for he had been concerned and had asked Hidell to wire him a report the minute he had news. He worried too about his secretary trying to pay the atrocious rents in Richmond on his limited salary. Stay in Richmond a month or so and take care of the mail, Stephens told him, especially the mail about the wounded. Then come on down to Crawfordville to live with him if he couldn't find affordable boarding. It was a typical gesture of Stephens' kindness, one that Hidell gratefully accepted for a few months.[58]

If this trip to Richmond accomplished little, Stephens' next visit to the capital proved even more fruitless. But it was destined to have a great effect on Stephens' later thinking, especially his regard for the president. Having just returned from a place he despised, Stephens might have surprised even himself when, scarcely a month after getting home, he proposed to Davis that he return and undertake a diplomatic mission for the Confederacy.

In a letter to Davis on June 12, he stated two reasons for wanting this mission. The papers had printed correspondence between Davis and federal Major General David Hunter on the sore subject of prisoner exchange. Not until mid-1862 had Washington and Richmond even agreed on any prisoner exchange at all. The United States had refused even this tacit recognition of its enemy until public opinion and sheer numbers of captives on both sides compelled it. But the prisoner exchange cartel had never worked smoothly, and after the Emancipation Proclamation, it had broken down completely amid blood-curdling threats of mutual retaliation.[59]

57. AHS to LS, April 29, 1863, in Stephens Papers, MC; J. B. Jones, A Rebel War Clerk's Diary at the Confederate States Capital (2 vols.; Philadelphia, 1866), I, 306.

58. AHS to Hidell, May 4, 9, 1863, in Stephens Papers, HSP.

59. William B. Hesseltine, Civil War Prisons: A Study in War Psychology (Columbus, 1930), 7–33, 69–96.

The possibility of barbaric treatment of innocent prisoners horrified Stephens, so he volunteered his services to Davis to see if he could re-establish the cartel. But as his letter continued, it became obvious that Stephens had larger purposes in mind. He phrased it delicately: "I think *possibly* I might do some good—not only on the *immediate* sub-ject in hand; but were I in conference with the authorities at Washing-ton on *any point* in relation to the *conduct* of the war, I am not with-out hopes, that *indirectly*, I could now turn attention to a general adjustment, upon such a basis as might ultimately be acceptable to both parties." The only such basis, he continued, was "recognition of the Sovereignty of the States." He might fail, but he wasn't without "*some* hopes of success." Of course he didn't believe the federals "ripe" for such an acknowledgment, but that "the *time has come* for a proper presentation to the authorities at Washington, I do believe." This "presentation" could only be made diplomatically. In other words, Stephens thought the time propitious to extend a peace feeler to the North—and himself the proper instrument to do it. The arrangement of the cartel would provide the proper diplomatic cover.[60]

Back in January Stephens had not been hopeful about peace. Peace on the basis of "our separate independence" wasn't in sight, he said. Evidently the Stephens brothers began discussing peace feelers shortly afterward, for in February Linton sounded out Herschel Johnson about suggesting negotiations to the North. The South meant to se-cure peace on the basis of its independence with no conditions, Linton said. But the time had to be right to offer negotiations; the South should not ever be suspected of acting out of fear. The offer to negoti-ate, if it were made "on the right basis and under fitting circum-stances," would be to the South's advantage whether accepted or re-fused. The time was not yet right, Linton and Johnson agreed.[61]

It was now June, and "fitting circumstances" had appeared: the South had just won another striking victory in the East; active opera-tions by Confederate armies were for the moment suspended; and there was discontent in the North over the defeat at Chancellorsville and the Union's first conscription act, which had passed in March.

Stephens was not the only Confederate thinking about peace. Gen-

60. AHS to Davis, June 12, 1863, in Stephens, *Constitutional View*, II, 558–60.
61. AHS to Johnston, January 29, 1863, in Johnston and Browne, *Stephens*, 435; Johnson to AHS, February 15, 1863, LS to Johnson, February 22, 1863, both in Johnson Papers, DU.

eral Robert E. Lee had also recently written to the president. Lee did not usually discuss politics, but for some time he had been bothered by "the manner in which the demonstration of a desire for peace at the North has been received in our country." Some southern responses had weaked the northern peace advocates in his opinion, and that was not good. Northern advantages in manpower and material would continue to bear down on the South while southern resources diminished. Under the circumstances, the South should use all honorable means of dividing the enemy. Encouraging the peace party in the North was "the most effectual mode of accomplishing this object."[62]

Making "nice distinctions" between northern unconditional peace men and those who wanted peace as a means of reunion was foolish, Lee said. Political necessity determined the latter's course: "Should the belief that peace will bring back the Union become general, the war would no longer be supported, and that after all is what we are interested in bringing about." It was imprudent for the South to spurn peace offers from any quarter. As was his wont when dealing with Davis, Lee closed deferentially: "If the views I have indicated meet the approval of Your Excellency you will best know how to give effect to them. Should you deem them inexpedient or impracticable, I think you will nevertheless agree with me that we should at least carefully abstain from measures or expressions that tend to discourage any party whose purpose is peace."[63]

The conjunction of these two letters from important leaders could not have failed to affect Davis, who knew, as Stephens did not, that Lee was preparing to invade the North again. Suddenly the idea of peace feelers had merit. Stephens could accompany Lee's army, which once victorious on northern soil could conceivably threaten Washington. Obviously, Davis' view of "fitting circumstances" differed considerably from his vice president's. Stephens preferred the open-handed approach: suasion during a time of relative quiescence on the battlefields. Davis believed in the fisted-glove method: a blow with the fist, then a soft stroke with the glove. Upon receiving Stephens' letter, therefore, Davis wired him to come at his earliest convenience.[64]

62. Robert E. Lee to Davis, June 8, 1863, in Clifford Dowdey (ed.), *The Wartime Papers of R. E. Lee* (New York, 1961), 507–508.

63. *Ibid.*, 508–509.

64. John Raymond Brumgardt, "Alexander H. Stephens and the Peace Issue in the Confederacy, 1863–1865" (Ph.D. dissertation, University of California, Riverside, 1974), 76–77.

Stephens got the telegram on the evening of June 18, a Saturday, and responded immediately that he would leave on Monday. In a hurried letter he warned Linton "not to speak of my being called to Richmond as a matter of very serious importance." The real purpose of the trip Linton was to keep to himself.[65]

Upon arriving in the capital on June 26, 1863, Stephens discovered to his shock and dismay that Lee's army had crossed the Potomac onto northern soil and that the capitulation of Vicksburg could come at any time. The next day he met with Davis, who received him cordially but curiously said nothing about the feasibility of Stephens' proposed mission. The vice-president brought up the subject immediately. The new military situation since he had written had changed his mind about the mission. He was even more incredulous when he learned that Davis planned to send him to Lee's headquarters whence he would pass through the lines under a flag of truce. Stephens thought this a preposterous idea. Why, by the time he reached Lee his army might be threatening Washington! He would hardly have a chance of being received under such circumstances, much less succeed in extending a discreet peace feeler. Davis agreed that Stephens' chances of being received were slim, but, he argued, accompanying a victorious army enhanced rather than diminished prospects of Stephens' success. Stephens continued to disagree, so Davis decided to call a cabinet meeting before making a decision.[66]

Stephens spent the next three days in the "laborious and exhausting" work of poring over documents relating to the prisoner exchange cartel. He had begun to fret; it appeared that he would be unable to leave for two or three days. Frankly, he was ready to go back home. He thought of home more than anything else except this miserable business at hand. He would do anything he could to avert the "barbarous system of retaliation" that threatened, he told Linton, but he wasn't hopeful. He seemed to have put his "ulterior views" out of mind entirely.[67]

---

65. AHS to Davis, June 20, 1863, in Keith Reid Collection, UG; AHS to LS, June 22, 1863, in Stephens Papers, MC.

66. James Z. Rabun (ed.), "A Letter for Posterity: Alex Stephens to His Brother Linton, June 3, 1864," *Emory University Publications, Sources and Reprints*, Ser. VIII, No. 3 (1954).

67. AHS to Hidell, June 29, 1863, in Stephens Papers, HSP; AHS to LS, June 28, 1863, in Johnston and Browne, *Stephens*, 443.

On the morning of July 1, 1863, Stephens met again with Davis. The president, although ill with dysentery, conversed "very freely, unreservedly, and most confidingly," Stephens reported. The cabinet agreed: the mission ought to be attempted. Secretary of War James A. Seddon was particularly anxious that something be done about the prisoner cartel before the fall of Vicksburg and its thirty thousand-man garrison. Pressed by the entire cabinet, Stephens reluctantly agreed to go, but he told them flatly that under present circumstances "I could effect nothing."[68]

Little Aleck received his instructions the next day. He was to try to establish a cartel for the exchange of prisoners and attempt to deal with other matters of illegal warfare. Since the weather had turned rainy, mucking up the roads, instead of going to Lee's headquarters, Stephens would travel to Washington on a small packet steamer, the *Torpedo*. The letter from Davis to Lincoln that Stephens carried with him described his mission as "humanitarian" with "no political aspect." The *Torpedo* steamed out of Richmond at noon on July 3. Miles to the north, Confederate gunners prepared for a gigantic cannonade on Union positions south of a little Pennsylvania town called Gettysburg. In the woods, behind the artillery, General George E. Pickett's infantrymen waited, their charge into history less than three hours away.

Not until noon the next day did the little steamer under its white flag make contact with a ship of Admiral S. Phillips Lee's North Atlantic Blockading Squadron at Newport News. Both Lee and the commander of Fortress Monroe had received identical notes from Stephens describing his mission and requesting permission to proceed to Washington. Admiral Lee responded promptly: he would telegraph Stephens' arrival and purposes on to the capital and reply as soon as he got an answer. The *Torpedo* dropped anchor in calm seas to wait. The admiral's dispatch created a somewhat bigger splash in the northern government. Secretaries William H. Seward and Edwin M. Stanton—who "swore and growled indignantly"—heatedly opposed having anything to do with Stephens. President Lincoln, elated with the news from Gettysburg and Vicksburg, did not seem to think the matter very important and proposed to take it up with the cabinet the next day.

Sunday, July 5, 1863, dawned clear in Washington. While Stephens bobbed on the waves and endured the steamy heat of his cramped ves-

---

68. AHS to LS, July 1, 1863, in Johnston and Browne, *Stephens*, 444.

sel, Lincoln sat down with his cabinet to decide what to do about the distinguished envoy. Having slept on the matter, he now thought it would be a good idea to send someone, or even go himself, to Fortress Monroe. No one but Navy Secretary Gideon Welles agreed. Stephens, said Seward, was "a dangerous man, who would make mischief anywhere." After some more haggling about how to respond, the cabinet agreed to postpone the question another day.

By now Stephens was growing impatient. A little before noon on July 6, he sent another message to Admiral Lee: how long before he could expect an answer to his note of two days before? Not long, it turned out. At two-thirty that afternoon he received his answer. His request, said the curt little notes transmitted through both army and navy channels, was "inadmissible. The customary agents and channels are adequate for all needful military communications and conferences between the United States and the insurgents."[69]

And so his mission had ended—in failure, as he predicted it would. He could not have known the reasons behind the Lincoln government's rude rebuff to his ever so slight hopes. All he knew at that moment was that once again his advice had been disregarded, his objections overruled. Sad news awaited him in Richmond. Lee had been decisively beaten at Gettysburg; Vicksburg had fallen. The fortunes of his country had taken a drastic downturn.

69. The preceding paragraphs are based on material in *Official Records*, Ser. II, Vol. VI, 74–76, 79–80, 94–95, which contain the official correspondence on the mission, Stephens' instructions and report, Davis' letter to Lincoln; reactions of Lincoln cabinet in Howard K. Beale (ed.), *The Diary of Gideon Welles: Secretary of the Navy Under Lincoln and Johnson* (2 vols.; New York, 1960), I, 358–60.

XIX

A Towering Passion

Stephens stayed in Richmond only briefly. He wrote his report on the failed mission and left town within a few days. He never would have approached Davis in the first place, he disgustedly told Linton, had he known Lee's army would go north. At this point nobody in the South even knew if Lee's army had escaped, and Stephens was as anxious as anybody for some news.[1]

On his way home, at Charlotte and Augusta, and then again at Sparta shortly after his return, Stephens did his best to rally dispirited fellow citizens. The fall of Vicksburg and Port Hudson (both within days of the disaster at Gettysburg) was not insurmountable. People determined to be free would be, as the American revolutionaries had proven. Support the government, he urged, and don't listen to the grumblers and croakers who advocate reunion. "The idea of reconstruction is obsolete," he told the Sparta crowd, and people who talked about it were dreamers. Foreign intervention was also a chimera. The South would have to weather the crisis on its own.[2]

Stephens' public fervor for the cause had long been missed, judging

1. AHS to LS, July 10, 1863, in Johnston and Browne, *Stephens*, 444.
2. *American Annual Cyclopedia and Register of Important Events of the Year 1863* . . . (New York, 1866), 218.

by the amount of reaction it stirred. The acerbic Colonel Thomas, recuperating after an epileptic seizure, rejoiced at the "'entiente [*sic*] cordial'" between Stephens and Davis. As long as it lasted, Davis would be unable to harm the country, he said, and the government would have the benefit of Stephens' experience and knowledge. Several people, including Governor Brown, wrote urging Stephens to speak, and various editors, sensing that he might be ready to help them rally the people, asked Stephens to write articles for their papers. He ignored all such requests.[3]

His private opinion of Davis' course had not changed. Stung by his rebuff at Hampton Roads and shocked by the staggering defeats at Vicksburg and Gettysburg, he reacted instinctively to encourage steadfastness. He spoke his heart, not his head, his faith, not his doubts. At home he reverted to silence. The Confederacy's situation seemed to be deteriorating. In early July, Bragg's army, flanked out of its position in middle Tennessee, fell back into north Georgia. The new threat prompted the administration to call for eight thousand six-month volunteers from Georgia. The effort flopped miserably. Hancock County, for example, with a quota of only sixty men, came nowhere close to meeting that goal after two public meetings. Only Toombs's personal efforts enabled Wilkes County to meet its quota. "Our volunteering has turned out wretchedly," Toombs told Stephens. "They shall have to call out the 'melish.'" Some anti-Davis extremists claimed the call had simply been a trick to get men into the army permanently, a charge even Toombs branded as ridiculous.[4]

Stephens too defended the president—after a fashion. The difficulties attending the military arrangements were not Davis' fault, he told Dick Johnston, but his subordinates', especially Adjutant General Samuel Cooper. But he suspected the call for volunteers had been a ploy to "make conscription appear to be indispensable." The effort was intended to fail, Stephens contended, coming as it did on the heels of a similar call for volunteers from Brown.[5]

Brown, who had just organized his draft-exempt militia, resisted the new encroachment fiercely. And as usual he succeeded. Unwilling to engage in a prolonged tussle with Brown, the administration allowed

3. Thomas to AHS, July 31, 1863, Benjamin H. Dill to AHS, September 19, 1863, both in Stephens Papers, LC; Brown to AHS, August 12, 1863, in Stephens Papers, EU.
4. Toombs to AHS, July 14, 1863, in Phillips (ed.), *TSC Correspondence*, 621.
5. Johnston and Browne, *Stephens*, 445.

the troops to be organized as the Georgia State Guard and permitted Brown to name most of the officers. The Guard was one of the Confederacy's most curious army units. Its troops were divided into three categories, depending on how much of the state they chose to defend—all, certain districts, or only the local community. But it was a national unit, and the administration evened scores with Brown by placing his bitter enemy Howell Cobb in command.

Oddly enough, Davis had appointed Cobb at Stephens' suggestion, a measure of how well the two men were getting along lately. For the past few weeks their relationship had been about as cordial as it would ever be. Stephens had readily agreed when Davis asked him to confer with Brown about dispatching the local defense forces to cooperate with Bragg's army. Once these forces entered Confederate service, Davis got to name their commander.[6]

Obviously Stephens had not held Cobb's political opinions against him when he proposed him for the job. The two men had recently exchanged letters on political topics. Although agreeing with Cobb on some points in foreign policy, Stephens disagreed on every other: conscription, financial policy, appointment of officers, impressment, provost marshals, and passports. All these were wrong "in principle and in policy."[7]

He could barely find words to rebuff another of Cobb's suggestions. "After the most mature reflection," Cobb had become convinced of the "vast importance" of appointing a dictator to rule the country. Stephens almost had apoplexy. "No language at my command could give utterance to my inexpressible repugnance at the very suggestion of such a lamentable catastrophe!" he wrote. The only way to secure constitutional liberty was to uphold constitutional limits on authority. Maintaining that document in all its purity was the war's chief object. Even the country's independence was secondary. The only reason the South had struck for independence in the first place was to secure its rights under the Constitution, and now Cobb made this insane suggestion. "Nothing could be more unwise than for a free people, at any time, under any circumstances, to give up their rights under the vain hope and miserable delusion that they might thereby be enabled to defend them."[8]

6. Davis to AHS, August 31, September 18, 1863, in Rowland (ed.), Davis, VI, 20.
7. AHS to Cobb, August 29, 1863, in Stephens Papers, EU.
8. Cobb to AHS, September 1, 1863, in Stephens Papers, LC; AHS to Cobb, August 29, 1863, in Stephens Papers, EU.

Ordinary citizens lacked Stephens' facility with language, but thousands shared his sentiments. "If we are not to have moore liberties than we are now allowed we had better have remained in the Union," one Georgia farmer told Governor Brown, "for we ware allowed much more liberty while we ware under Yankee rule than we are now[.] if we are still to bee brought down from this time on as we have been since the establishment of the Confederate govrment to this time I for one hail the day of its overthrow."[9]

After more than two years of war, countless individual sacrifices, and thousands of deaths, many in the Confederacy saw no point in continuing. Until now most had borne the burden of increasingly harsh government policies, if not without a whimper, at least with resignation. It appeared, however, judging from the present military position, that the government could not fulfill its most fundamental duty: protection of its citizenry. And yet it continued to press for more sacrifices, for continued resistance, which only alienated people further. With the war at their doorstep, Georgians were especially likely to doubt the wisdom of unquestioning fealty to their government.

Disaffection and outright disloyalty flourished in many parts of Georgia, as in other sections of the Confederacy. J. Henley Smith had seen too much evidence of a large reconstruction element in the country to be deceived. "Thousands of men in Georgia, Alabama and Miss look upon slavery as doomed" no matter how the war ended, he wrote Stephens. "These men are willing to give up their slaves tomorrow and go back into the Union with slavery abolished if it will bring peace and security to them in their other property." One North Carolinian told Stephens that people in his area did nothing to organize to meet the enemy. Union flags had been raised within six miles of Asheville, he said. People in eastern Alabama and western Georgia, although not openly hostile to the government, could easily get that way, warned J. W. Warren, the editor of the Columbus *Times*, especially if the army met another defeat.[10]

Compared to other parts of the Confederacy, the sentiment around Columbus was almost benign. In the mountain areas of east Tennessee, northern Georgia and Alabama, and western North Carolina, dis-

9. "N.D." to Brown, August 26, 1863, in Brumgardt, "Stephens and the Peace Issue," 100.

10. Smith to AHS, August 20, 1863, A. W. King to AHS, September 9, 1863, J. W. Warren to AHS, September 5, 1863, all in Stephens Papers, LC.

loyalty flourished. Not only did citizens resist conscription and im-pressment, they openly advocated reunion. Peace societies had sprung up in various locales throughout the South. By December of 1863, W. W. Holden, editor of the Raleigh *Standard*, had become an unoffi-cial spokesman for the movement, proposing through his paper that North Carolina begin peace negotiations with the North through a separate state convention.[11]

In the wake of Bragg's retreat into Georgia and the impending invasion of the state, Linton Stephens returned to the colors. During the sum-mer he raised a company of cavalry for the Georgia State Guard, was elected major, and put in command. In mid-September he and his unit reported to Atlanta. Linton's faith in the government had long since died, and the view from camp further enraged him. The South was "cursed with incompetency," he told his father-in-law, and success would be impossible "without a radical and early change in the mode of conducting our affairs."[12]

Linton's hatred of Davis had passed beyond the realm of reason. The president's continued confidence in Bragg, who had just allowed a Union army he had defeated at Chickamauga to escape back into Chattanooga, sparked a classic outburst. "We are a doomed people," he told Aleck. Davis was "*mad, infatuated*," "a bloated piece of incom-petence," "a fool," almost a traitor in his misguided policies. Linton had almost run mad himself thinking about the "tyrant" dedicated to the ruin of popular liberty. "I am *greatly troubled*," he continued. "I don't know what to do. I don't know what my *duty* is. . . . I see no hope in *anything* but God. It seems to me the case calls loudly for a Brutus." His brother's apparently good relations with the president only made him angrier. Aleck had been far too patient with Davis: "You have allowed his hypocrisy to impose on your charity." Near the end of this tirade, Linton caught himself, admitting that only "*per-haps*" would the knife of Brutus solve the problem, in fact, it "may render the confusion more confounded."[13]

Stephens heartily agreed with this final statement. Linton had un-wittingly raised a subject he had been thinking a lot about lately. What

---

11. Wilfred Buck Yearns, *The Confederate Congress* (Athens, Ga., 1960), 171–75.

12. LS to James Thomas, October 10, 1863, in James Thomas Papers, EU.

13. LS to AHS, October 14, 1863, in Stephens Papers, UG.

if Davis were to die, Dick Johnston had asked him. What would he do if the responsibility fell to him? Davis' death would be "the greatest possible calamity," Stephens replied. He wouldn't know what to do. Obviously he would look to men agreeing with his line of policy and would try "to secure the confidence of the people; to make the Administration acceptable to all classes; to make every man who fights or suffers by privation . . . in any way, feel that it is all for his rights and liberties, and not for mere dynasty." These, he confessed, were his instincts, not the result of long thought on the subject.[14]

As for things he might do, Stephens reeled off several: clearing the hospitals of the sick and wounded to free needed supplies, abolishing the passport system, and dismissing all the provost marshals. Impressment would be instantly stopped, "except in case of actual necessity for the army." Even then, supplies would be bought at fair market prices. Stephens honestly believed these measures would reinvigorate the country. But the truth was, he did not want to have the opportunity to try. He knew only too well how many distrusted him and the fierce opposition he would meet as president. To what extent that opposition would go he could not guess, but he was sure it would be "quite far enough to weaken and cripple my efforts."[15]

And for once he was totally honest with himself. Those who doubted his ability to govern might be right. "On that point I assure you I have the strongest distrust of myself." He knew he would manage affairs differently, "but would they be managed for the better or the worse? I know not." One thing was certain: if he ever had to take the job, "it would be with fear and trembling." Just thinking about the prospect of himself as president put Stephens on edge. "I never wish to avert to the subject again," he told Johnston.[16]

Aside from his few speeches, the vice-president said nothing and wrote nothing public for rest of 1863. If he could not be positive, he would say nothing. Nor did he participate in the November gubernatorial campaign, which like the 1861 contest was carried on mainly in the newspapers. Oddly enough, Joe Brown represented the centrist choice in this election, his two opponents occupying opposite poles on the political spectrum. One was Timothy Furlow, a wealthy planter,

14. AHS to Johnston, October 23, 1863, in Johnston and Browne, *Stephens*, 447–48.
15. *Ibid.*, November 3, 1863, 448.
16. *Ibid.*, 449.

ardent secessionist, and outspoken supporter of the administration. Joshua Hill stood on the other extreme: an out-and-out unionist, he had refused to withdraw with the congressional delegation when the state seceded. Never in any real danger of losing—he had worked industriously and shown constant solicitude to Georgia's soldiers, their families, and the poor—Brown won the election easily. The results revealed some striking facts. The administration candidate, Furlow, ran a miserable third in the balloting, while unionist Hill took over 20 percent. Clearly the administration had few friends in Georgia.[17]

Shortly after the election the Georgia assembly rejected Bob Toombs's bid for a Senate seat. Even disaffected Georgians weren't quite ready to be represented by a Davis-hater like Toombs. "The only question for a patriot," the fiery Georgian had written, was whether opposing the administration or acquiescing in its follies did the most harm to the public good. Since the summer he had damned the administration and Davis at every opportunity. In deciding to run for the Senate, he told Stephens he wanted to offer "whatever resistance I can to the ruin of the revolution and the destruction of public liberty." Stephens lent whatever covert aid he could to Toombs' campaign. But neither this, nor Brown's backing, nor a fiery Toombs oration before the assembly proved sufficient. On the third ballot the legislature elected Herschel Johnson by large margin.[18]

Except for a trip to Sparta to see Linton, Stephens had stayed close to home. In late October, however, he went to Atlanta to meet with Jefferson Davis. So serious had dissension among Bragg's top commanders become that the president came down from Virginia to deal with it personally. He had taken care of this business in mid-October (removing most of Bragg's detractors and leaving the unpopular general in command) and then proceeded west. Stephens caught him as he

---

17. Election results were as follows:

	Brown	Hill	Furlow
County vote	36,558	18,222	10,024
Army vote	10,012	3,324	1,887
Total	36,570	21,546	11,911

(Louise Biles Hill, *Joseph E. Brown and the Confederacy* [Chapel Hill, 1939], 137).

18. Toombs to Burwell, August 29, 1863, Toombs to AHS, November 2, 1863, both in Phillips (ed.), *TSC Correspondence*, 628–29, 630. The Constitution provided for staggered elections of senators to ensure that one-third of the Senate stood for reelection every two years. Johnson currently occupied the short-term seat, the one Toombs had been elected to in 1861 and declined.

passed through Atlanta on his way back. Davis "was in excellent health and spirits," Stephens reported, but he still had confidence in Bragg and the army's positions around Chattanooga, news that Little Aleck found "painful."[19]

Stephens believed the country's prospects were bad and getting worse. Having to endure Davis' baseless optimism pained him almost as much as the thought of having to return to Richmond for the fourth session of Congress. Going there in the midst of winter just to preside over the Senate, he told Herschel Johnson, would be a waste of time. He would "immediately go on any sacrifice of comfort," however, if his advice were needed or he could be useful. Evidently he at least entertained the possibility of being useful, for he had already made arrangements to live with Senator Semmes in Richmond—at a cost of six hundred dollars a month, to begin November 15, whether he was there or not. It was worth the price to Stephens to stay home "unless some call of duty" required him in the capital. Presiding over the Senate no longer fit this category.[20]

Stephens' attitude troubled his friend Johnson. He understood Aleck's position but told him frankly that the country never would. The people respected his wisdom and thought Congress ought to benefit from it by having him in Richmond. The good of the country had to come before personal desires. Johnson had another good reason to want Stephens out of Georgia: to keep him out of harm's way. The senator had heard disturbing news when in Milledgeville for the election. Clearly "a purpose existed to inaugurate open hostility to the President." This would be disastrous, he thought, discouraging the army and dividing the people at home: "One revolution at a time is enough."[21]

It didn't require a weatherman to see which way the wind was blowing in late 1863. The hapless Bragg had just sustained a crushing defeat at Chattanooga and reeled back into Georgia in disorder. So on top of the odious administration policies, Georgia faced invasion by the enemy. Legislators were understandably agitated, and with people such as Linton Stephens, who had been reelected to the assembly, and those of his ilk around, freely venting their fury anywhere they could find an audience, Johnson had heard much wild talk. Brown and Toombs had been particularly vociferous.

19. AHS to Johnson, November 14, 1863, in Johnson Papers, DU.
20. *Ibid.*
21. Johnson to AHS, November 29, 1863, in Flippin, *Johnson*, 249–50.

By contrast, only the yapping of a hound or the shrill whistle of the Georgia Central at its daily stop in town disturbed the peace and quiet of Liberty Hall. Stephens loved this place and its quiet, but Johnson's chiding had evidently spurred second thoughts about his avoiding the session in Richmond. Perhaps he should go, he decided. But he dallied about leaving. In late November he dropped over to Linton's house. His brother was not home, but Stephens stayed anyway, enjoying his nieces' company and entertaining a visitor or two. Back at home, he awaited word from Semmes that his living quarters were ready in Richmond. On December 9, he noted happily in his daily letter to Linton that Bragg had finally been replaced as commander of the Army of Tennessee. Stephens admired the new commander, General Joseph E. Johnston, a cautious man, "who will not fight unless he feels assured of victory." With the South's dwindling resources "our ultimate success now depends as much on not fighting as fighting," Stephens thought.[22]

The same day Stephens wrote this letter, a perplexed Semmes wrote from Richmond wondering where Stephens was. His secretary Hidell had arrived, "& I was surprised to learn that you expect to hear from me before coming on." Semmes had written to Stephens while en route to Richmond that he was going to prepare the house. This should have been "sufficient intimation," he thought, that their quarters would be ready when Congress opened on December 7. "Do come soon," he urged.[23]

Stephens no doubt would have gone but for an urgent note he got from Brown. Linton had fallen ill, perhaps seriously. The governor was caring for him in his own house until Stephens arrived. "He asks that you lose no time." Distraught, Stephens rushed to Milledgeville and to his immense relief found his brother in much better health. But his departure for the capital would be delayed. After a few days in Milledgeville, Stephens accompanied Linton back to Sparta; he did not return to Crawfordville until December 22, and by then he was not in the best of health himself.[24]

Christmas on the plantation, by his own admission, was dull, despite the gaiety of the slaves, who enjoyed their traditional feast and eggnog along with visits from their friends. Stephens had too much on his mind to enjoy the spirit of the season. First there was Linton. Ever

22. AHS to LS, December 9, 1863, in Johnston and Browne, *Stephens*, 450.
23. Semmes to AHS, December 9, 1863, in Stephens Papers, LC.
24. Brown to AHS, December 8, 1863, in Stephens Papers, EU; AHS to Hidell, December 13, 22, 24, 1863, in Stephens Papers, HSP.

since his wife's death seven years ago, his brother had never seemed quite balanced. Merely looking at her picture or simply reflecting in those quiet moments when a father gazes on his children could trigger either morbid or violent spells of grief. Linton had never been able to shed the notion that somehow he had been responsible for her death.[25]

So he punished himself for it. Like the Aleck of former days, Linton would be seized by moods of blackest depression and despair. They came on unexplained, sometimes lingering for days. More than any other person alive Stephens understood these things, and so he too suffered, as much from the knowledge of what Linton endured as from the absolute certainty that nothing he could say would alleviate his brother's pain. Nonetheless, he tried. The secret, he told Linton, was realizing that a man's happiness or misery depended more on "himself than everything else combined." His passions and emotions, "according to their cultivation," could make life either a heaven or a hell. It followed, then, that avoiding everything tending to stir up unhappy feelings was the cardinal rule. The mind had to be turned from disagreeable thoughts. Even when things were worst, "there are some prospects more agreeable than others: let the mind be directed to them." With one's passions "in perfect subjugation," "constant culture of the moral faculties," and a firm reliance on God, anyone could be happy.[26]

Self-control, virtue, and faith, according to Stephens, guaranteed happiness. For all its naivete—because Stephens believed all these qualities could simply be willed into being—this counsel offered a pretty fair prescription, if not for happiness, at least for relative peace in a world of inexplicable suffering. But had Stephens taught this lesson to himself, as he so typically claimed, or had life taught it to him? He had conquered his own depression, and his faith in God deepened with each passing year. But many virtues still eluded him. And so, too, on occasion, did self-control.

Stephens' long delay in getting off to Richmond, a healthy dose of antiadministration bile from Brown in Milledgeville, and now Linton's illness and his own precarious health combined to make him question the wisdom of his ever abandoning his self-imposed retreat. He began slipping his departure date. On Christmas Eve he informed Hidell that

25. AHS to Hidell, December 27, 1863, in Stephens Papers, HSP; Von Abele, *Stephens*, 221–22.
26. AHS to LS, December 31, 1863, in Johnston and Browne, *Stephens*, 450–51.

he would probably leave for Richmond during the next week; three days later he said he would leave the first week in January.[27]

Stephens had decided he could do nothing to arrest the government's precipitous course. Under the circumstances, patriotism seemed to dictate that he stay put and say nothing. Johnson couldn't understand this rationale. He had been prodding Stephens to come for weeks. It was no secret that this session of Congress, held amid the worst crisis of confidence in the country's short history, would address critical issues: finances, impressment, conscription, a possible new suspension of the writ of habeas corpus. Indeed, anticipation of the manifold evils the administration might yet do was what had so agitated Brown and his allies in Milledgeville. And this too gave Stephens pause. He wanted no part of it.

Johnson saw only defeatism in his friend. Stephens' last letter had saddened him "because it shows you have given up the contest in your *judgment*, whilst your patriotic *heart* bleeds over our fate." Purposely holding himself aloof from public affairs was unjust to "yourself . . . to our bleeding cause, and to the country that reposes in your confidence." Just because he saw no possibility of doing good was no reason to give up. The "rash counsels of extreme and ambitious men" imperiled the country. "Why not throw your whole soul and all your gifted powers into the struggle . . . to save her from ruin?" Johnson pleaded. He too saw great errors in policy but for the moment would stay at his post and vote his convictions.[28]

Cobb was more blunt. There was "a lamentable lack of brains and good common sense" in Richmond, he wrote. "You can do good here," he assured Stephens and urged him to go if his health permitted it. "Why isn't Stephens here?" was a question being asked all over Richmond, another correspondent told him. *"You are needed here, much needed."*[29]

From all indications these pleas from friends had persuaded Stephens to make the trip despite his reservations. His health was poor— recent pains in his side had given way to a persistent bladder infection—and the weather was even worse—wet, cold, and nasty. But as soon as it moderated, Stephens told Hidell, he would leave.[30]

27. AHS to Hidell, December 24, 27, 1863, in Stephens Papers, HSP.
28. Johnson to AHS, December 29, 1863, in Flippin, *Johnson*, 250.
29. Cobb to AHS, January 2, 1864, in Cobb-Erwin-Lamar Collection, UG; Jeremiah Morton to AHS, January 5, 1864, in Stephens Papers, LC.
30. AHS to Hidell, January 1, 1864, in Stephens Papers, HSP.

A brief warm spell in middle Georgia right at this moment might have made a great difference for Stephens' future course. And who knows what effect his presence in Richmond might have had on Congress during this fateful winter? It is probably safe to say that had Stephens left Georgia, he would have never embarked on the course he was about to take. As it was, the weather remained miserable, and then on January 7, 1864, Linton got sick again and summoned his brother to his side. He recovered quickly, but Stephens' departure had been postponed again—just long enough for him to be prostrated by what he said was the worst pain he had ever experienced: kidney stones. He had been delirious with it, he told Hidell on the eighteenth, the day after the attack, and had no memory of anything from early afternoon until around midnight, when he passed several granular stones. For a while he seemed so ill that even Davis sent a telegram inquiring about his health.[31]

Obviously Stephens would be confined to his home for an unspecified period of time. And when he finally recovered, the Confederate Congress had already passed a series of measures that settled his mind once and for all about his potential to influence events at the national level. Stephens did his best to make Herschel Johnson understand his position. The contrast between their temperaments was striking. Little distinguished their positions on the major issues. Johnson opposed conscription, suspension of the writ, impressment, and martial law, and he favored a strong national tax on incomes. Like Stephens, he would later support any reasonable proposal for peace. Johnson construed his patriotic duty differently from Stephens, however. Both men fought to promote the national interest, but Johnson believed the honest errors of the government had to be tolerated for the sake of harmony and victory, so he supported it even as he disagreed with almost everything it did.

Stephens, on the other hand, believed that the only way to secure harmony was to remove sources of discontent. Defense of the Confederate cause to him did not mean blind loyalty to its government, but rather unyielding fealty to the principles on which he believed the government rested: state sovereignty, personal liberty, and the Constitution as he understood it. Not for a moment would he tolerate the no-

31. *Ibid.*, January 7, 11, 18, 1864; AHS to Davis, January 22, 1864, in Davis Papers, DU.

tion that independence ought to be purchased at the price of these principles, for without them independence meant nothing.

Herschel Johnson enjoyed cordial personal relations with the president, and unlike Stephens, he revered the man as a "pure patriot." "You have my entire confidence," Johnson had told him in mid-1863, "& my poor prayers to God that he will sustain you." Whether men liked Davis or not, Johnson believed, he was the leader and under him the war would be lost or won. "It is a patriotic duty to sustain him," the senator told a Macon judge, "for in this crisis he is in truth, the government."[32]

Stephens would have choked had he heard such a thing. In effect, this attitude granted dictatorial powers to Davis without even going through the formality of naming him dictator, as Cobb had suggested. Stephens had never trusted centralized executive power, and at this point his distrust of it bordered on obsession. Congress, and only Congress, he believed, constituted "the Governing Power, the law-making Power, the power to regulate the whole policy of Govmt."[33]

The vice-president had not given up—not by a long shot. But try as he might he could not convince Johnson. "We could whip the fight without even fighting it," he told the senator. What ailed the Confederacy was its "present line of 'proceeding' (I will not call it policy for it does not deserve the name.)" With its resources controlled properly, the nation could fight on for "many years." The next day Stephens elaborated on one example, impressment. The government certainly had the right to seize private property for public use, but it should pay just compensation, the same as other buyers would pay "on the spot." Moreover, a property owner should have recourse to the courts if he objected to the government's price. War did not abrogate this peacetime right.[34]

What Stephens said just made Johnson sadder. "I see no prospect of a change in policy," he said. Stephens' ideas, he agreed, should have been adopted in the beginning. Now it was too late. "The crisis is so near that there is not time enough to change the policy or plan."[35]

Stephens simply didn't believe this, nor did Joe Brown. It would

32. Johnson to Davis, August 6, 1863, in Davis Papers, DU; Johnson to Cochram, March 4, 1863, in Flippin, *Johnson*, 233–34.
33. AHS to Semmes, January 27, 1864, in Semmes Papers, DU.
34. AHS to Johnson, January 3, 4, 1864, in Johnson Papers, DU.
35. Johnson to AHS, January 12, 1864, in *ibid.*

never be too late as long as some means of impressing the administration with the urgency of the issue existed. Evidently when Stephens was in Milledgeville in December, Brown had suggested calling the legislature into special session to state Georgia's objections to government policies in the most forceful and visible way possible. Stephens balked at the idea. The time was not right. Congress had just convened and would be addressing almost all the vexatious issues. Better to wait and see what it did. After that the vice-president would be glad to share his views with Brown.[36]

A couple of weeks later, on January 2, 1864, although not "unmindful" of this promise to Brown, Stephens urged him to be circumspect. The idea of a formal protest had "pressed heavily" on his mind. Such a move by Georgia could easily be misconstrued; it was potentially divisive and ought to be approached carefully. Stephens gave no indication whatever that he intended to take an active part, but he didn't openly oppose the idea either. "Every one should do his duty in his own sphere as he from the best light before him understands it." Still, he wanted Brown to be aware of the risks. "Injudicious conflicts . . . in public counsels" that might prompt similar strifes and factions among the people had to be avoided at all costs: "Such a result can be but disastrous."[37]

Sometime within the next two weeks Stephens, as he had promised, wrote to Brown "on the subjects on which we conversed [in December]." Unfortunately that letter has been lost, but judging from Brown's reaction the vice-president had again expressed reservations about the propriety of a legislative protest against administration policies. Brown therefore had decided to follow Stephens' advice and wait before planning any formal protest. But he would not wait long. If the government did not take action to correct its abuses soon, he said, he would call a special session of the legislature and take action himself. Naturally he didn't want his intentions spread about the capital. For the moment, only Stephens and Linton knew what he was planning.[38]

Meanwhile, news from Richmond underscored Stephens' concerns. Aside from a drastic extension of conscription, along with a paring of exemptions to the bone—terrible enough to contemplate—a new suspension of the writ of habeas corpus seemed likely. Stephens' horror at

36. Brumgardt, "Stephens and the Peace Issue," 116–17.
37. AHS to Brown, January 2, 1864, in Stephens Papers, EU.
38. Brown to AHS, January 15, 1864, in Stephens Papers, MC.

this prospect knew no bounds. If the president signed such a bill and the people submitted to it, he told Linton, "constitutional liberty will go down, never to rise again on this continent, I fear. This is the worst that can befall us." [39]

The president's recent telegram gave Stephens an opportunity to lay his concerns before Davis and plead for a change in policy before Congress acted. So three days after Davis' wire, Stephens, feeling "comparatively comfortable," sat up in bed and wrote a long "private" letter to the president. His chief apprehension was that Congress would approve another suspension of the writ. Such an act, he said, would be unwise, impolitic, and unconstitutional, and he hoped Davis would never sanction it. Passage of the act would sap popular morale and undermine confidence in the government. Oddly enough, the "people's" views comported with his own. "They have looked upon [the war] from the beginning as a struggle for constitutional liberty," and just as long as this object was kept in view, they would endure countless trials and deprivations. Their "willing hearts" were the government's greatest hope. It must do nothing to jeopardize their goodwill.

Less straightforwardly, Stephens suggested that extending conscription would also be wrong; it was unnecessary. The country's strength did not lie in numbers. Trying to match forces with the North might even weaken the South: "No people can keep all of its arms bearing population in the field for a long time." The South should not try to increase its present force; the army was already as large as the country could maintain "in view of the probable continuance of the war." Stephens saw no early end to the war—or to the South's continued resistance. In the coming campaigns the North could overrun more territory than ever before—this still would not end the war "if the hearts of the people are kept right." Long wars could be won without much fighting, Stephens contended. But to win the war "we must not collapse for want of subsistence."

Stephens then launched into a long discourse on the inherent ability of the southern economy to support the armies and the abuses and evils of the impressment machinery, complete with extrapolations on how many tithe bushels of corn and wheat the government controlled. None of this produce need be lost for lack of transportation, Stephens said, because it could be fed to government stock in remote places and

39. AHS to LS, January 21, 1864, in Johnston and Browne, *Stephens*, 453.

then the stock could be driven to the armies for slaughter. In his opinion, the government had almost enough food in tithes to support the armies for a year "with proper system & management."

And yet government impressment agents were going through the country buying and impressing. It was "*essential* that the producing capacity & energy of the country not be weakened this year," he said. And two measures would ensure that it would not be: leaving overseers and managers on the plantations (that is, retaining their exemption to the draft) and paying fair market price for everything the government had to buy.[40]

This long epistle must have astonished the president. Apparently his vice-president had completely lost touch with reality. Stephens seemed to have no conception of what waging war on a near continental scale involved. Davis ignored the letter, and rightly so, for most of Stephens' ideas were fanciful. He had little idea of the nature of the conflict the South was engaged in: a multifront war that committed it to defending fixed points and huge swaths of territory. To an extent unknown in previous American history this war had required the mobilization of an entire society: its manpower, its productive capacity, its heart and soul. Davis understood the nature of the war far better than Stephens did, but he erred in believing that the hearts of his countrymen could be further welded to the cause by increasingly burdensome laws ever more capriciously executed. And all in the name of an independence that seemed more distant with each passing day. Having already borne undreamed-of horrors in the name of liberty, thousands of poor and middling yeomen in the South had long since ceased to see a logical connection between the original goal of secession and the privations their own government had forced them to endure. So far that government had done nothing to alleviate those sufferings—except to promise victory and demand further sacrifice. The vast majority had reached the limits of their endurance.[41]

Stephens could see this in every day's mail. However unrealistic his specific ideas for prosecuting the war, he had an instinctive grasp of the common people's concerns. Far better than Davis he knew the hearts of these people. Maintaining morale was more than a high-

40. The preceding paragraphs are from AHS to Davis, January 22, 1864, in Davis Papers, DU.
41. Escott, *After Secession*, x–xi and *passim*.

sounding slogan. For Stephens it was the *sine qua non* for winning the war.

So Davis might ignore some of Stephens' ideas, but he blundered seriously in casting aside the man himself. The vice-president was a political force to be reckoned with. Had Davis been half the politician his masterful counterpart in Washington was—Lincoln had forged an effective administration out of such disparate elements as Chase, Seward, Welles, and Stanton—he might have recognized the foolishness of treating Stephens like a cipher. But then, this had been his practice since the government left Montgomery. He had long believed the worst of what Stephens' enemies said: that the vice-president was a reconstructionist. He could never resign his post, Davis said, unless the vice-president did too, for Stephens, if given the chance, would immediately hand the government over to the enemy.[42]

Stephens had made his case to the president, and within a couple of weeks he received his answer. On February 3, 1864, Davis sent a message to Congress requesting a new suspension of the writ of habeas corpus. Discontent and disloyalty were being exhibited at home, secret leagues were being formed, deserters and conscripts were being freed under the writ, said the president. If the power to suspend the writ did not exist under the present state of invasion, "when can it ever be expected to arise? . . . It may occasion some clamor," he continued, "but this will proceed chiefly from the men who have already been too long the active agents of evil. Loyal citizens will not feel the danger, and the disloyal must be made to fear it." Congress approved the new suspension on February 15, 1864. Like the previous two suspensions, it was limited to six months, but the new law stipulated specific causes to invoke suspension of the writ.[43]

Joe Brown had not waited for this latest outrage to decide to bring his own case before the state assembly. No doubt the certainty of a new conscription bill spurred him on. Besides eliminating most exemptions and ending substitutions, the law that passed on February 17 raised the upper age limit of eligibility for the draft to forty-five and organized all able-bodied men between the ages of seventeen and eighteen and forty-five and fifty into a reserve corps. The new statute threatened Brown's state forces because he had just ordered enrollment of all

42. Strode, *Jefferson Davis*, II, 509.
43. Richardson (ed.), *Messages and Papers of the Confederacy*, I, 395–400.

Georgia's able-bodied men between the ages of sixteen and sixty into the militia.[44]

Conscription was only the worst of Brown's irritants at the moment. There were others: the pending suspension of the writ, Confederate seizures of engines and rolling stock from the Western and Atlantic, and administration indifference to the governor's newest project, a negotiated peace. He had hoped Congress or the president might make a move in this direction, Brown told Stephens, and "obviate the necessity" of his having to do so in a special message to the legislature. "I hope . . . to be able to do some good by proper state action. I thank you for all your suggestions."[45]

The possibility of a negotiated peace clearly had become important in Brown and the Stephens brothers' thinking. Apparently the three men had discussed the subject in December and decided that Richmond's failure to take the initiative to begin peace negotiations constituted another of its many shortcomings. Until now only a few scattered peace proposals had been introduced in Congress, but as war weariness increased, various plans for proposing negotiations with the North began to appear more frequently. The most visible agitation for peace centered in western North Carolina, where proposals for separate state action were being bruited about in the papers. Governor Zebulon B. Vance condemned the idea, but the peace genie was out of the bottle.

Vance, like Brown a jealous guardian of his state's prerogatives against Richmond, inquired about the situation in Georgia. There was considerable discontent with the Confederate authorities, Brown replied, and a sincere desire for peace, but not much disloyalty and "no disposition" to take separate state action to correct the government's abuses. Brown favored sending Confederate peace commissioners at the proper time but deprecated the idea of a convention looking to sep-

---

44. James Horace Bass, "The Attack upon the Confederate Administration in Georgia in the Spring of 1864," *Georgia Historical Quarterly*, XVIII (September, 1934), 234–35. The new conscription act drastically cut legal exemptions from the draft and allowed the administration to allocate manpower by a system of military details. After drafting a man, the government could detail him as a soldier on special assignment to a civilian occupation it considered essential to the war effort. Theoretically at least, the law gave the government practically total control over the manpower pool in the Confederacy (Thomas, *Confederate Nation*, 260).

45. Brown to AHS, January 28, 1864, in Stephens Papers, EU.

arate state action "at the present" as "very unfortunate" and likely to spur internal divisions. He planned to convene the legislature in the spring, when he would review the peace question and "offer some suggestions" that he hoped would win Vance's approval.[46]

While Brown shared his views with Vance, Stephens shared his with many in his vast array of correspondents, friends and foes of the administration alike. He was particularly anxious that people influential with Davis understand the urgency of the situation. Still weakened by his recent illness, he pleaded with Cobb to stop by Crawfordville on his way from Augusta. He had many things he wanted to talk about, Stephens said. Administration supporters didn't seem to realize the dangers they courted by curtailing personal liberties. "We need not think we can trust our own people! We can trust nobody with the wheel if our Liberties are given up." By nature the southern people were "no better than other people." Once they surrendered their liberties, they would be no more reliable than any others.[47]

Agitated as he was, Aleck was the picture of serenity compared to Linton. Where the elder Stephens saw mismanagement, bad policy, and a misguided president, the younger saw a heinous plot contrived by an unscrupulous tyrant to enslave the free men of the South. "If we escape from Lincoln *what* will save us from Davis?" he demanded. The president did not want peace, despite the wishes of the people and the rank-and-file soldiers on both sides. The West Pointers directing the war would lose their importance if peace came. "Is it human nature that [such] men should desire peace," he asked Mrs. Toombs, "or make an effort to obtain it? . . . Have both governments formed designs which can not be accomplished in peace, and which seek opportunity and shelter in the confusion and panic of war? The force of [this question is] not diminished at all by the recent infamous legislation which was passed by our Congress and asked for by our President; nor by the recent appointment of Gen Bragg, the most monstrous military tyrant of the Confederacy, as supervisor of all our military operations. . . . None but very simple or very bad people will be deaf to the voice which [these actions] speak." Obviously, Linton's own ears were ring-

46. Brown to Vance, January 16, 1864, quoted in Brumgardt, "Stephens and the Peace Issue," 122.

47. AHS to Cobb, February 5, 1864, in Cobb Papers, UG.

ing: he fully expected the next usurpation would be the conscription of white women to do whatever the president assigned. "I would strike a thousand blows to pull down this infamous government than one to sustain it," he told his brother. Davis should be impeached; otherwise, a "counter revolution" or "early ruin" was inevitable.[48]

Linton's hysterical tone alarmed Aleck. He too worried about the government's policies, but "for your own peace of mind" he implored his brother to be less emotional. In the long run, if the people wanted to accept Davis' policies, nothing could be done. It was "worse than useless for one to spend sympathy" on those who didn't want it. He had written and spoken and labored in 1860, and "it did no good." The people had to "see & feel the wrong" before remedies could succeed. Keeping cool until then was the only course to follow.[49]

Linton found it impossible to keep cool, but he, Aleck, and Brown were ready to educate the people and try to provide a remedy for the country's fast-deteriorating condition. Brown, having roughed out his message to the legislature, wanted to confer personally with Stephens about the draft. "I wish to act with caution and prudence," he assured the vice-president.[50]

Stephens did too. He realized the possible political repercussions of the impending protest. He had already warned Brown about the dangers of intemperate dissent and believed he would act responsibly. Still, he had no desire to go beyond giving advice and did not want to be personally identified with the protest. So with Linton temporarily away from his home on military duty, he strictly enjoined Cosby Connel, a longtime resident at Linton's house, not to say anything to anybody but Linton about the proposed meeting.[51]

For the convenience of the still weak Stephens and the busy governor, Brown had asked that the meeting be held at Linton's house in Sparta, midway between Crawfordville and the capital. Stephens agreed, setting the date for Thursday, February 25, 1864. In the midst of these preparations Congress passed the suspension of the writ,

48. LS to James Thomas, January 31, 1864, in James Thomas Papers, EU; LS to Julia Toombs, March 3, 1864, in Toombs Papers, UG; LS to AHS, February 9, 1864, in Stephens Papers, MC.
49. AHS to LS, February 10, 1864, in Stephens Papers, MC.
50. Brown to AHS, February 13, 1864, in Phillips (ed.), *TSC Correspondence*, 633.
51. AHS to Cosby Connel, AHS to LS, February 19, 1864, both in Stephens Papers, MC.

which only lent further urgency to the ensuing conference. Brown contemplated the act with "horror," he said. "Every state in the Confederacy should denounce and condemn the wicked act." One state, at least, was about to do just that.[52]

The Stephens brothers and Brown got together as planned in Sparta from February 25 to 27, 1864. On the twenty-seventh Brown issued a proclamation calling the legislature into session on March 10. Despite Stephens' wish to keep the meeting quiet, Davis-backer James Nisbet sounded a warning to the administration through Cobb. The legislature would be called into special session, he said, and Brown, egged on by "Toombs, Stephens & Co.," would put up "some fractious issue with the Confederate government," especially on suspension of the writ. Stephens, Nisbet reported, had treated the Sparta citizens to an "insidious speech, full . . . of poison and bile." Only a "forestalling expression of public opinion" could halt these men from putting Georgia publicly against the government.[53]

Nisbet hardly needed the gift of prophecy to discern the drift of public sentiment. "In Augusta the men of means are all '*hog faced*,'" said one observer. "Long! Long! They look like shipwrecked men just washed upon the strand." The recent laws were the main reason, he contined. "If these acts of Congress do not draw all the blood out of us . . . we need not fear the Yankees or the Devil."[54]

Davis had anticipated hostile reaction to a new suspension of the writ. Even Herschel Johnson, who tried to minimize the extent of the dissatisfaction, reported that the matter had inflamed the people. Brown would succeed in getting the legislature to endorse his position, Johnson feared. The people got more excited about this issue than even conscription: "It is new; it touches the right of personal liberty; the popular mind is sensitive & there will not be wanting those who will use diligently all the elements of strife, in order to organize a party."[55]

Ironically, it was the absence of an organized party system in the Confederacy that had impelled disaffected leaders like Brown and Ste-

---

52. Brown to AHS, February 20, 1864, in Phillips (ed.), *TSC Correspondence*, 633.
53. Nisbet to Cobb, February 28, 1864, in Cobb-Erwin-Lamar Collection, UG.
54. James H. Hammond to William Gilmore Simms, February 21, 1864, quoted in Brumgardt, "Stephens and the Peace Issue," 155.
55. Johnson to Davis, [*ca.* February 27–March 10, 1863], in Davis Papers, DU.

phens to take their present course. Opposition to Confederate policy was not simply manufactured out of whole cloth in Georgia's capital in 1864. It was widespread, of long standing, and growing throughout the South. But lack of legitimate machinery to focus and channel this opposition—thereby exerting pressure on the government to arrive at workable compromise solutions—had diffused its force. Until now the opposition had lacked political cohesion.[56]

Brown and Stephens intended to give it cohesion by a method hallowed and time-honored in American history: state memorialization of the national government. Perhaps by raising the issues in this way, at this high political level, the government could be brought to understand the magnitude of public disaffection. Stephens remembered a similar role Georgia had taken in 1850, when the famous platform drawn up by the legislature had rallied the entire South.

Having advised both Linton and Brown, Stephens returned home. On the heels of Brown's strong message Linton would introduce two sets of resolutions before the assembly. The first would condemn the suspension of the writ, and the second would propose that the South proffer negotiations for peace to the North after its every victory in the field. "I hope you will go to work and fix up your resolutions with great care," Stephens told Linton the day after his return. "The great mission is on you." The main attack, he reiterated, should be made on suspension of the writ. "If the State can be got to stand right upon that all other things will go right." Linton didn't need his brother's encouragement. He would try "to profit by your injunctions," he told Aleck, but even without them the importance of the crisis had compelled him to follow his brother's advice. He was not hopeful of success, however.[57]

While Linton did his part, Stephens would try to get all the help he could "legitimately" get from Georgia's senators. He wrote to Ben Hill and tried to set up a meeting with Johnson in Augusta. Hill answered Stephens quickly. Writing from LaGrange on March 2, he promised to try to visit Crawfordville on the following Saturday. Like Johnson, Hill had voted against suspending the writ and had tried to modify it. But he believed Davis would use his power under the act "very sparingly

56. David M. Potter, "Jefferson Davis and the Political Factors in Confederate Defeat," in David Donald (ed.), *Why the North Won the Civil War* (Baton Rouge, 1960), *passim.*

57. AHS to LS, LS to AHS, February 29, 1864, both in Stephens Papers, LC.

and with great caution." Until that power was abused, he hoped no issue would be made on the question.[58]

Johnson also tried to put the best face he could on the distasteful law. Although he had opposed the bill for no fewer than three reasons, he said, "I hardly believe much harm will grow out of it." The suspension aimed at only two targets: the "spies and traitors in Richmond (it is full of them)" and the "disloyal movement of Holden in N. Carolina." The first was a worthy target, he thought, and the second questionable "because it involves liberty of speech & the press."[59]

But Stephens had no patience left. He was furious. If the government would not voluntarily recede, it should be forced to, he said. Shocked by his friend's anger, Johnson responded quickly. There was only one constitutional way to do this, he said: by impeaching the president. Davis had done nothing to deserve that. Stephens had let his anger get the best of him, Johnson suggested gently: "You are evidently in a towering passion. I say this in no offensive sense . . . & therefore you are liable to be mistaken in some of your views." What good could come from wholesale abuse of Congress and Davis? "It will but weaken us greatly" and would delight the enemy. True, Davis had made errors, but was Stephens prepared to depose him? "I know you are not. And yet, that is the tendency of the counter-revolution likely to be inaugurated" by Brown. And if the governor's purpose was not counter-revolution, what was it? Was destroying confidence in those the people had chosen to lead the best way to resist the enemy?[60]

Stephens had no intention of starting a move to depose Davis or to form an opposition party. Nor would he even urge defiance of the law. He wanted to mobilize public opinion to right what he saw as a monstrous wrong. All along he had advised people to appeal to the courts and obey the laws, no matter how unjust, if the courts sustained them. But under this new suspension the courts could be closed. What remedy would the people have then? "I say appeal to the courts. Speak out. Discus[s]—don't be mum while your chains are being forged. Let the Legislature do its duty. Let county meetings be called & denounce the infamous act. Let all well wishers of the country demand the repeal

58. AHS to Johnson, February 29, 1864, in Johnson Papers, DU; Hill to AHS, March 2, 1864, in Stephens Papers, EU.

59. Johnson to AHS, March 4, 1864, in Flippin, *Johnson*, 247.

60. AHS to Johnson, March 13, 1864, in Johnson Papers, DU; Johnson to AHS, March 9, 10, 1864, in Flippin, *Johnson*, 251–52.

of it and let a common united voice of the great mass go up to the President that in the meantime he do not exercise the power attempted to be conferred on him. Let this be done and all may be well." If the people quietly submitted to this law, he continued, "I see but little difference in any result. . . . I have no choice between tyrannies or master—and shall never have one North or South." The only path to harmony was to condemn this "attempt to overthrow public liberty." The farthest thing from patriotism was to advise his people to submit to "unprovoked wrong and wanton oppression"—especially when they were denied the right to a hearing. As for Holden, Stephens had not read his articles and had no opinion. But discussing public policy was not treason, and if there were a question in Holden's case, he ought to be publicly tried.[61]

Stephens stoutly denied favoring armed resistance to the government or counterrevolution. His language may have been inflammatory in a previous letter, he admitted. "I was certainly not in a very quiet frame of mind—and did not study my phraseology." But he wasn't in a passion now. "I am calm and cool." Stephens went on for pages: he disagreed entirely with Johnson about the purposes of the act, and in this "I cannot be mistaken." The law persecuted loyal and honest men, denying them a court hearing to decide whether they were liable to serve in the army. What greater tyranny could Congress create than closing the courts, denying these men their constitutional rights? The current laws were perfectly adequate for every supposed target the act listed: spies, traitors, and the like. This extensive list was simply subterfuge "to mislead the people" about the act's real intentions: to muzzle dissenters and the press and to force men into the army whom the courts might otherwise have freed.[62]

Stephens wrote these lines as the Georgia assembly entered the fourth day of its special session. Sensing the danger in Georgia, the administration had made certain its own advocates would be on hand. Cobb, Augustus Kenan, Hill, and L. Q. C. Lamar, senator from Mississippi, all attended, and all but Hill addressed the legislators. The War Department had even furloughed a few friendly military officers

61. AHS to Johnson, March 12, 1864, in Autograph Letters of the Signers of the Confederate Constitution, DU.
62. AHS to Johnson, March 13, 1864, in Johnson Papers, DU. The previous letter Stephens referred to was one written to Johnson on March 7, 1864, which has since been lost.

to lobby in its behalf, a privilege it did not extend to eleven members of the assembly in the army when Brown requested it. From the first, Brown realized that he would have a fight on his hands. Even the friendly *Chronicle* had declared Cobb's speech "in excellent tone and temper." None of the legislators wanted a long session; daily board in Milledgeville cost more than twice what they collected in per diem. Moreover, although most of the legislators deplored the recent acts of Congress, few wanted to express their opposition as a body for fear of harming the war effort.[63]

So Brown offered inducements. Besides politicking on the floor himself, he sold cotton cards to the lawmakers for ten dollars a pair. (They were a rare commodity at the going price of forty to sixty dollars.) And he authorized each member of the assembly to exchange up to two hundred dollars in Confederate notes for state notes, which were worth about twice as much. Even with these blandishments, however, Brown knew he needed Stephens' help to succeed. He had already urged Little Aleck visit the capital before the session, to no avail. Once Linton tested the political winds in Milledgeville, he too had tried to get his brother to Milledgeville before the session, with no more success than Brown.[64]

The last few weeks had strained Linton's normally volatile temperament to the breaking point. And once exposed to the "timidity" of his fellow lawmakers, he gave himself over to despair and made himself sick in the process. Writing from Brown's house on the night of the tenth, the day Brown's message had been read and his resolutions introduced, Linton urged Aleck to come over and make a speech. The formality of an invitation from the legislature could be gotten up, "but I don't want you to wait for its arrival. Come right on here at once, if you are well enough, for there is no time to be lost." The session would be short, and the legislators were anxious to get back to their farms. Brown, of course, agreed that Aleck should come immediately.[65]

From all available evidence Stephens had not intended to go to Milledgeville—until now. He wanted to avoid any appearance of impropriety, however, so he disregarded Linton's plea and waited until he

63. Augusta *Chronicle and Sentinel*, March 16, 1864.

64. Brown to AHS, March 4, 1864, in Phillips (ed.), *TSC Correspondence*, 634; LS to AHS, March 10, 1864, in Stephens Papers, DU.

65. LS to James Thomas, March 11, 1864, in James Thomas Papers, EU; LS to AHS, March 10, 1864, in Stephens Papers, DU.

received a formal invitation from the legislature to speak. This arrived at Liberty Hall on the thirteenth. It had become obvious that he would have to lend his voice to the Milledgeville proceedings. Up until the night he spoke—and for some time afterward—the crucial issue hung in the balance. "Outside pressure," Brown commented, had been heavy, and at this point the assembly had heard only from friends of the administration. His message had been attentively received, but the legislature had shown no disposition to act.[66]

Brown's message had artfully blended fervor for the Confederate cause with strong criticism of government policies. He assailed conscription with familiar arguments. In attacking suspension of the writ, Brown echoed all Stephens' arguments. The rest of the message reviewed the causes of the war and the prospects of peace. Since the South had shown itself impregnable on the battlefield, he continued, the only way to peace was through negotiations, which the Confederate government should offer to the North after every important victory. The basis for these proffered negotiations should be the principles of the Declaration of Independence—the right of self-government and state sovereignty.[67]

Forceful as it was, Brown's message had recommended nothing revolutionary or subversive, nothing beyond established practice. Nor did Linton's resolutions and their accompanying preambles. The seven peace resolutions reiterated Brown's position: justifying secession, blaming Lincoln's government for the war, and endorsing the plan of offering negotiations after southern victories and at other times, "when none can impute [our] action to alarm, instead of a sincere desire for peace." The five habeas corpus resolutions denounced the suspension of the writ as unconstitutional. They did not recommend disobeying the law but urged Georgians in Congress to push for repeal. The South, said the fifth resolution, was fighting solely for constitutional liberty. If the Richmond government acted quickly, it would not only inspire the southern people but also convince the northern people to end the war "against our liberty, and as truly, but more covertly, against their own."[68]

---

66. Brown to Ira Foster, March 16, 1864, in Brown Letters, UG.
67. Candler (ed.), *Georgia Confederate Records*, III, 587–655.
68. Johnston and Browne, *Stephens*, 455–59.

A huge press of people filled every nook and cranny of the state assembly hall on the evening of the sixteenth. It had been months since Georgians had heard a speech from Stephens. A spontaneous and warm burst of applause greeted the familiar little figure as he entered the hall and made his way up the crowded aisles to the podium. Then the crowd quieted, settling back. Stephen's high-pitched voice began softly.

The country was in danger, Stephens said, but it was not beaten and never would be if the people displayed the same courage as their revolutionary ancestors. Their country had been invaded and ravaged by superior armies and they had not been conquered; neither would the South, for it was fighting for the same sacred goals: "State rights, State sovereignty . . . the right of every state to govern itself as it pleases." "Discussions of public affairs," he said, in taking up the recent congressional acts, "should be given as friends to friends, brothers to brothers, in a common cause." Disagreements ought never arise except over differences in judgment about the safest course to pursue. It would be in this spirit that he spoke further.

Although he agreed with Brown that the tax and funding acts were not "proper, wise, or just," he was reconciled to them. Conscription, though, presented a much graver issue. This law was both unconstitutional and unwise. The system of details begun by the latest law dangerously extended central government power. Even without the detail system, the law would still be pernicious. Putting one-third of the arms-bearing population of a nation under arms courted disaster because it took these men away from necessary production tasks at home. The war could be won without the draft: the American colonies had done it; so had the Greeks against the Persians, the Netherlands against Philip of Spain, and Frederick of Prussia against most of Europe.

After sitting through this history lesson, the assembly had to endure a long constitutional discourse on the habeas corpus act. The suspension of the writ, an act "unwise, impolitic, unconstitutional" and "exceedingly dangerous to public liberty," proclaimed Stephens, was the most important matter before the legislature. He insisted that the clause granting Congress power to suspend the writ was an implied power, one that was circumscribed by the due process clause and the section prohibiting illegal searches and seizures. Moreover, Congress could not give its own powers to the president.

Georgia had voted against this clause in the constitutional convention, but he admitted that, with restrictions, the right to suspend the writ might be a "wise power." In time of invasion or rebellion, "the public safety may require it." He was not even prepared to say that public safety did not require suspension now. But apparently the presence of several northern armies on Confederate soil did not classify as "invasions" for Stephens. For he went on to say that he didn't know why the president asked for it, nor did he know or had he heard of any reason for it. No, the long list of offenses set forth in the law was but "rubbish verbiage" intended to cloak what was really "the whole gist of the act"—a bludgeon to force men into the army.

Stephens coldly dismissed the argument that Davis would use this extraordinary power with care. "Tell me not to put confidence in the President." The abuses might not come from him because military subordinates all over the country would be executing the law. The president would have to be omniscient as well as omnipresent to prevent all the abuses that would arise. What should the legislature do? It should call for immediate repeal of the act and in the meantime ask the government and the people to let the question of constitutionality be decided by the courts.

At this point Stephens took pains to make his position clear: "I am for no counter-revolution." What he wanted was to keep the present revolution on the right track: "The surest way to prevent a counter-revolution is for the State to speak out." Don't be deterred by the charge of counterrevolution or those who urged support of the government, he warned. The truest supporters of the government defended the Constitution. Protecting the fundamental law would be the best way of helping the gallant soldiers in the field.

Stephens had reached the climax of his speech. His voice cut through the still hall like razor. The legislators must guard always against the argument "independence first & liberty afterward." Like a man's soul, liberty, once lost, could never be regained. "Never for a moment" should they look upon their birthright of constitutional liberty as subordinate to independence. The two were "co-ordinate, co-existent, co-equal, co-eval, and forever inseparable." Independence without liberty he scorned. "Give me liberty as secured in the constitution, amongst which is sovereignty of Georgia, or give me death. This is my motto while living, and I want no better epitaph when I am dead."[69]

69. For the preceding paragraphs, see Stephens' speech in Cleveland, *Stephens*, 761–86.

In his whole life Stephens had never delivered a more impassioned address—or a more fateful one. Less visionary men would have stifled the impulse that drove Stephens to the podium that night. They would have stopped to count the consequences, would have seen how they might be misunderstood, would have realized what a weapon they were placing in the hands of their political enemies. They would have balked at the impropriety, the rashness, of it all. They would have weighed their reputation, both present and future. And ultimately they would have said nothing.

But for Stephens silence in the present crisis would have betrayed his deepest political ideals. Over the years he had largely tempered his impetuosity. His speech had been no rash, spur-of-the-moment impulse. He knew exactly what he was doing, and he realized the grave political risks he ran. Open cooperation with Brown courted political suicide: if it failed he might be forced out of political life forever. For a man to whom politics was almost life's blood, the prospect of death itself might almost seem preferable.[70]

The vice-president returned to Crawfordville anxiously to await public reaction. Back in Milledgeville the Georgia assembly was in an uproar.

70. Johnson to AHS, March 23, 1864, in Stephens Papers, LC.

XX

Malus, Pejor, Pessimus

Pushing Linton's resolutions through the assembly proved every bit as difficult as Brown had feared. On the eighteenth the House passed the peace resolutions 88 to 49, but friends of the administration managed to have an additional resolution tacked on declaring Georgia's dedication to achieving independence. The habeas corpus resolutions also passed the House, but narrowly. On the morning of March 19, 1864, the last day of the session, it began to look as though Brown and Stephens' effort would fail. In the House the pro-administration forces carried a vote for reconsideration of the habeas corpus resolutions. Meanwhile, the senate had taken no action, except to pass a resolution that the governor impose no obstacle to operation of the conscription laws. Linton's resolutions still hung fire, and adjournment loomed. No action at all would have been as bad as defeat for the governor's plan.

Brown refused to be outmaneuvered. If the assembly had not taken action on these issues by the end of the session, he warned, he would call another special session to convene the following Monday. This threat produced results. The House acted first, repassing the habeas corpus resolutions, 71 to 68. Forty-three staunch Davis men signed a special protest to be forwarded to Richmond; then, lest the resolutions be misread as hostility to the president, the House passed a further resolution declaring undiminished confidence in Davis. At its evening session the senate followed suit, passing this resolution and both sets of Linton's (by a 20 to 12 vote on the writ resolves—to which 11 senators appended a special protest—and 19 to 12 on the peace resolutions).[1]

If nothing else, the Brown-Stephens movement succeeded in raising the biggest ruckus in Georgia's press since the memorable election donnybrooks of prewar days. Most of the Atlanta papers approved the move, but Macon and Savannah papers uniformly condemned it. Brown's message, stormed the *Morning News*, was "the most dangerous fire-brand yet thrown in the Confederate camp." The Augusta papers were split, as were those in Athens, Columbus, and Milledgeville. The *Southern Recorder* deplored Stephens' part in the protest. If the vice-president of the United States had made such a speech before the legislature of Maine, it asked, wouldn't the South be justified in thinking he opposed further prosecution of the war? The southern press at large mirrored the diversity of opinion in Georgia.[2]

Northern editors, who generally found the Holden story in North Carolina more interesting, interpreted Georgia's protest variously. Some saw it as an indication of war weariness or as factionalism among the enemy or as a disposition in Georgia to seek a separate peace. Stephens' actual words received little attention, but the northern press delightedly reprinted columns of hostile reaction from the southern papers. This evidence of division among the enemy, they argued, was the best advertisement possible for continuing the war effort.[3]

If the drumfire of criticism Stephens read in the hostile newspapers discouraged him, reading his mail did not. Even before the avalanche of favorable mail began pouring in, Stephens received encouraging words from no less discriminating a critic than Ben Hill. Hill had approved parts of the governor's message, and "I know I must thank you for it." Brown's only trouble was that Stephens' "footprints [were] *too plain not to* be recognized." Hill also recognized Stephens' tracks in the section dealing with the writ. For a strong administration supporter Hill seemed surprisingly receptive to Stephens' ideas. "You in-

1. The preceding paragraphs are based on Brumgardt, "Stephens and the Peace Issue," 206–13.

2. Savannah *Morning News* quoted in Louis Turner Griffith and John Erwin Tallmadge, *Georgia Journalism, 1763–1950* (Athens, Ga., 1951), 79; Milledgeville *Southern Recorder*, April 19, 1864.

3. Brumgardt, "Stephens and the Peace Issue," 238–40.

voke Georgia to move in this [peace] matter *now* and I agree with all my heart." Their differences, he continued, were "not great." Like many other administration supporters, Hill quibbled with Stephens' legal reasoning and contended that Davis would not abuse the suspension power.[4]

Some of Stephens' other critics were less gentle. "We must *win* our independence," wrote one, "before there can be much danger from usurpation of power, or despotism. . . . It is a case of self defense, of life and death, and technicalities must not form barriers." The country expected the vice-president to repair to the capital and counsel those running the government. "Truth must and will prevail. So will *sense*."[5]

Once Stephens' speech hit the southern presses, criticism of the vice-president increased. Why Stephens had embarked on Brown's "wild schemes . . . to accomplish ulterior aims" was a mystery, said the *Recorder*. Advancing his popularity or reputation could not explain it, for he had sullied both by voluntarily joining a "fractious conspiracy" to cripple his own government. Kenan told Davis that the scheme to turn the people against the administration would fail because the legislature had affirmed its trust in the president. And, of course, everyone was "mortified" by Stephens' "unpatriotic & unwise" besmirching of his official position.[6]

No one was more mortified than Herschel Johnson. Although he didn't see a copy of Stephens' speech until early April, he deplored it on principle. How could Stephens feel it his duty to avow open hostility to the government and help array the states against it? It filled him with "gloom and sadness." "You are wrong—*wrong* in policy," he told his friend. He might have expected such rashness from Brown and Toombs, but "I did not expect it of you." Even if he did think as Stephens did, Johnson said, "propriety would have kept me aloof from strife."[7]

Once he had read the speech, Johnson found it "unexceptional in temper and spirit" but clearly hostile to Davis as anyone who knew Stephens' real feelings about the man could see. Stephens' explana-

---

4. Hill to AHS, March 14, 1864, in Phillips (ed.), *TSC Correspondence*, 634–37. Numerous letters, April to May, 1864, praising Stephens' speech are in Stephens Papers, LC.

5. L. R. Cockrill to AHS, March 18, 1864, in Stephens Papers, LC.

6. Milledgeville *Southern Recorder*, May 17, 1864; Kenan to Davis, March 24, 1864, in Keith Reid Collection, UG.

7. Johnson to AHS, March 19, 1864, in Flippin, *Johnson*, 253.

tions had not swayed him. "You asked me if I still think you are wrong? My dear sir, I *know* you are wrong. You have allowed your antipathy to Davis to mislead your judgment." But even if this were not so, Stephens had erred because of his position in the government, because the "whole movement originated in a mad purpose to make war on Davis & Congress," and because it had brought joy to the enemy.[8]

It is a mark of Stephens' maturity (which brought forbearance) that he tolerated such criticism so genially. Naturally he denied being part of a war on Davis. He "knew as much as anybody else" about the purposes of the resolutions. And if anyone were responsible for the protest movement, "no one is more so than myself." He exaggerated his role in the movement's genesis, but his point was clear: he had no intention of forming an opposition party. And though he denied hating Davis—his feelings were "much more akin to suspicion and jealousy," he said— his words betrayed more enmity than he owned up to. He had never regarded the president as a great man or a statesman, Stephens said, but as "a man of good intentions, weak and vacillating, timid, petulant, peevish, obstinate, but not firm."[9]

Johnson, knowing Stephens' extreme sensitivity, hastily apologized for anything he might have said to upset his friend. But he stuck to his guns. Whether Stephens intended it or not, he would be identified with an anti-Davis party. He had a right to speak out if he wished. "I have no quarrel with you for it. But I deplore it." Stephens may have mellowed with age—Johnson had not hurt his feelings, he said—but in one regard he had not changed at all. He had to get the last word. As if sheer volume of argument could establish his point, he subjected Johnson to another twenty-four pages of justification for opposing the habeas corpus act. He was particularly concerned that Johnson understand how he felt about Davis. He denied contempt for him—a feeling Johnson said he had detected in Stephens for the past two years. But the line between contempt and condescension was easily blurred. "I respect Mr. Davis as a man," Stephens said. He had an above average intelligence, but he wasn't fit for the presidency. Stephens had thought so from the beginning, although he couldn't say who would have been a better choice. Even so, he wasn't about to say amen to Davis' errors.[10]

8. Johnson to AHS, April 6, 7, 1864, in Johnson Papers, DU.

9. AHS to Johnson, April 8, 1864, in *Official Records*, Ser. IV, Vol. III, 278–81.

10. Johnson to AHS, April 11, 1864, in Flippin, *Johnson*, 254; AHS to Johnson, April 15, 1864, in Johnson Papers, DU.

Nor would he let critics in the newspapers go unchallenged. In an open letter to the *Southern Confederacy* in early April he assumed a statesmanlike pose. The beauty of the country's system of government, he wrote, was that "all in authority are responsible to the people." Although it was more agreeable to approve of what leaders did, "highest duty" sometimes required voicing disapproval. No harm would come of honest disagreements "when truth alone is the object of both sides. . . . We are all launched upon the same boat, and must ride the storm or go down together."[11]

Not for a second did Stephens grasp what Herschel Johnson had been saying: that no matter how correct his position on the issues, "highest duty" for the vice-president of the country was to support the government, at least tacitly. In publicly assailing administration policy the vice-president had been as mistaken as Johnson had said he was. As he had done so many times before, Stephens had allowed his own understanding of "truth" to blind him to an even more fundamental reality: truth is myriad, "a great ocean," as Newton put it.

Although Davis and his supporters would never have put it so baldly, three years of war had revealed to them the cruel, cold truth of the warrior, a truth Stephens could never accept. Desperate, total wars and individual rights are fundamentally incompatible. The imperatives of the former must always overrule the blessings of the latter. For leaders of a nation at war survival of the state, the body politic, is the highest truth.

But what of its soul? Stephens would protest. What of its animating principles of liberty and freedom, the rule of law and the demands of justice? Were these all to be sacrificed on the altar of Mars? Survival of the body at the expense of the spirit? Unthinkable! Better, as he had said several times, that the spirit live and the body die. Mere survival was no truth at all.

Somehow in his excursions through the ethereal realms of truth Stephens had failed to understand what a shambles war always makes of morality, what an unreasoning activity it is, and what a pitiful weapon philosophy is to oppose the minions of Mars. His intellectual position was pure, even if his motives were clouded by a corrosive suspicion of Davis. And it was eminently defensible, even if only in the realm of abstract thought, which was where he spent most of his waking hours anyway. What could not be defended was his wanton disregard of his

11. Atlanta *Southern Confederacy*, April 3, 1864.

official position. As admirable as his devotion to personal liberty may have been, by publicly excoriating his own government's policy Stephens committed the most reckless act of his life. No evidence suggests that Stephens ever considered resigning his office. But believing as he did, it would have been the most honorable course for him to take.

Indeed, resignation would probably have been far more effective in dramatizing his principles and effecting a political remedy. Dramatic as his action had been in Milledgeville, the political situation as he saw it demanded an even more radical gesture. Instead of sullying his integrity and credibility as his speech had done, resignation from his office would have underscored his devotion to principle. Not incidentally, it likely would have also presented the administration with a much greater spur to address the evils Stephens so deplored.

Why he couldn't see this must forever remain a mystery. Could he have done his country's cause any more harm by resigning? As a private citizen, a former vice-president, would he have sacrificed one whit of the pitifully small influence he had on national policy? These questions never seemed to occur to him. Unalterably convinced of his own pure motives and the perfidy and blindness of his opponents, he didn't stop to heed honor, or the humility that, according the Scriptures he knew so well, has to precede it.

He was too busy noticing how much controversy Georgia's acion had stirred up. Within months of the special session, three more Confederate state legislatures (Alabama, North Carolina, and Mississippi) passed resolutions condemning the suspension act. Stephens took particular satisfaction in Mississippi's action. "Is Mr. Davis['] own State in unanimous opposition to his administration! Are they all factionists and malcontents?"[12]

They were not, of course, but Brown took whatever help he could get from anywhere. Having successfully carried out his plans in Georgia, Brown made sure that the protest got the widest possible circulation. Within weeks of the assembly's action he had copies of his message and Stephens' speech printed and dispatched to newspapers in the North, South, and Europe. Every county clerk in the Confederacy received a copy. So did every captain and lieutenant of every company of Georgia troops. So did Governor Vance in North Carolina.[13]

None of the protest leaders in Georgia were prepared for the violence

12. AHS to LS, April 17, 1864, in Stephens Papers, MC.
13. Brown to AHS, April 5, 12, 1864, in Phillips (ed.), *TSC Correspondence*, 639; Brown to Vance, March 23, 1864, in Joseph E. Brown Collection, LC.

of their opponents' counterattack. Howell Cobb's review of Brown's message had been especially severe. "Thousands of brave men . . . must pay with their blood the price of this infamous man's treason," he told his wife. Some army units in Virginia passed counterresolutions of their own condemning Brown and the legislature. Meanwhile, Ben Hill (who had evidently concluded that the differences between him and Little Aleck were greater than he had first supposed), Lamar, and several other administration supporters branded Stephens a traitor at numerous public forums in the state. The commander of the Conscript Bureau in Georgia told Davis that Stephens was being "very generally condemned" in various conversations he had heard.[14]

Painfully sensitive to criticism, especially when it misconstrued his motives, Stephens wrote several letters to Richmond trying to explain. He was horrified to learn that editors were using his letters to members of the administration as evidence of his "'bitterness, hostility, and malignancy'" against the government. Stephens desperately wanted to convince these people that only his sense of public duty had impelled him to act. He had not been influenced "in the slightest degree," he told the secretary of war, "by feelings of hostility or bitterness, to say nothing of malignancy, toward a single mortal who disagreed with me."[15]

Apparently his concern about his reputation in the capital persuaded him to attend the opening of the first session of the new Congress, which had been elected in 1863. There he could explain his position to Davis and the cabinet and also be on hand when Congress considered repealing suspension of the writ. Accordingly, he made plans to leave Georgia in time to reach Richmond for the opening of Congress on May 2.

A highly curious bit of state business detained him, however. Back in February he had received a letter from one David F. Cable, a Union soldier en route to Andersonville prison. Cable, an Ohio lawyer and supporter of Clement Vallandigham, earnestly desired a personal interview with Stephens. He had been traveling throughout the western states, he said, talking with the leading northern Democrats. He had visited Ohioan Vallandigham, whose outspoken criticism of the north-

---

14. Brown to AHS, April 19, May 5, 1864, in Phillips (ed.), *TSC Correspondence*, 641–42; Cobb to his wife, April 4, 1864, in Cobb Papers, UG; W. M. Browne to Davis, June 7, 1864, in Davis Papers, DU.

15. AHS to James Seddon, April 29, 1864, in Cleveland, *Stephens*, 786–90.

ern government and efforts to promote a peace movement had earned him temporary banishment in Canada. The last hope for constitutional liberty, Cable declared, was Democratic victory in the coming presidential election in the North. But to beat Lincoln the southern people would have to help.[16]

Stephens, who received letters from crackpots daily, ignored this one. Cable wrote again on March 20 explaining the details of his mission. He had been sent south as an agent of the leading northern peace men to implement a plan of action that would lead to an honorable peace. The plan embraced two elements: first, a union of all the northern conservatives against Lincoln to defeat him in the election, and second, "to obtain from the Confederate States authoritatively, or if unauthoritatively from persons of eminent character therein the declaration of the desire for an armistice on the part of the South and her willingness to submit the adjustment of our difficulties to commissioners, to be chosen or appointed from the contending sections," thus confronting the northern people with "the direct issue of *peace* upon rational terms, or *war* upon the principle of Abolitionism." [17]

Stephens had decided long ago that the Confederate government had to seize every opportunity to influence the northern elections as the best way of obtaining peace on the basis of independence. Such a strategy was obvious. Clearly nothing but unrelenting war could be expected from the Republicans. The idea had been abroad in the South for some time, and both friends and foes of the administration had endorsed it. "Lincoln and his fanatical party do not constitute all the North," Ben Hill had written. The South should make it clear to the many sensible northerners that it was ready to meet them in convention to adjust the difficulties "by the rules of reason and right." The *Chronicle*, along with several other papers, heartily endorsed Hill's sword-and-olive-branch plan when he introduced it publicly in LaGrange.[18]

So when Cable's second letter, delayed for a time by the prison bureaucracy, came on April 9, Stephens sensed its potential usefulness to the Confederate cause. He immediately forwarded it to Davis with a cover letter, saying that he deemed Cable's letter sufficiently important

16. David F. Cable to AHS, February 28, 1864, in Stephens Papers, LC.
17. Cable to AHS, March 20, 1864, in Stephens Papers, EU.
18. Hill to his wife, February 7, 1864, in Hill, *Hill*, 89; Augusta *Chronicle and Sentinel*, March 6, 1864.

to call it to the president's "*special* attention." If Cable's story were true, it seemed logical to grant him the interview. It would also be "proper" to tell Cable that the Confederate government earnestly wished a settlement of the conflict on the basis of "State sovereignty" and would negotiate on that principle. If Cable were paroled to carry these ideas North, it might help elect a Democrat in November. At any rate, Stephens couldn't see how talking with Cable could possibly hurt the South.[19]

Alexander Stephens wasn't naive. He wanted peace and independence for the Confederacy, but he also knew most northerners wanted reunion. What most northerners desired didn't matter. Lincoln had to be defeated, and the peace party appeared to be the only way to do it. Promising cooperation with a Democratic president to achieve peace not only would be smart politics but also would capitalize on northern war weariness. When the peace party won the election, an immediate armistice would go into effect and negotiations would begin. Once this happened, reunion would be found "to be out of the question and would ultimately be abandoned," even by the most ardent northern unionists. Maybe the South or the northern peace party or both could do nothing to defeat the Republicans, Stephens continued, but "every effort . . . ought to be made to do it." Cable presented a fine opportunity, and if the president approved, Stephens would invite him to Crawfordville, see what he had to say, and report on it. It was vital that the Republicans be beaten, he repeated.[20]

This was the first time since his speech that Stephens had written the president, and Davis could hardly have been thrilled. He had largely kept his feelings about the vice-president and his speech to himself. Unlike many others, he didn't question Stephens' patriotism, but he was chagrined by the speech and wished the vice-president would abandon his fault-finding in favor of harmony. By midsummer, however, Davis didn't even want to think about his Georgia critics. He forbade all discussion of the matter.[21]

But it would have behooved him to treat Stephens' letter with respect. He replied affirmatively only to the request that Cable be investigated and ignored everything else the vice-president had said. The

---

19. AHS to Davis, April 9, 1864, in C. C. Jones Papers (Georgia Portfolio II), DU.
20. *Ibid.*
21. Burton N. Harrison to William P. Johnston, July 21, 1864, in William Johnston Papers, TU.

truth was that Jefferson Davis did not believe his government had any business getting involved in a "foreign" election, at least not overtly. (He did sanction covert operations to strengthen anti-Lincoln elements in the North.) For Davis there could be only one basis for negotiation: independence. And the best way to force negotiations was to prove the futility of trying to subjugate the South by force of arms.[22]

Davis did not share these views with Stephens, but this didn't seem to bother the vice-president. Upon receiving Davis' letter on April 26, he canceled his plans to leave for Richmond and awaited news from Andersonville. After hearing nothing for several days, Stephens wrote the prison. On May 6 he got his answer from Colonel S. W. Persons. "From what he writes," Stephens told Davis in a letter the next day, "I take it for granted that the examination of Cable did not satisfy the Staff officer" and that no parole would be granted. He would start for Richmond the day after tomorrow.[23]

But he was suspicious. The officer's letter from Andersonville, dated April 30, had taken about a week to reach him. Clearly, he told Linton, "the authorities do not wish the interview to take place." Linton suspected something even more sinister. He wished Aleck had been in Richmond at the opening of Congress because he feared it would not repeal the suspension act. Congress could easily be "affected by a *new panic* . . . got up for their benefit. . . . Has it not occurred to you that you have possibly been *tricked* out of your presence there at the critical moment?" Keeping Stephens in Georgia would be just the sort of ruse Davis' "sly and low cunning" would devise.[24]

Impatient now to get to Richmond, Stephens promptly boarded a northbound train. He almost got no farther than Charlotte, North Carolina. In the middle of the night and in a pouring rain, part of the train in which he rode separated from the rest and plummeted backward down a steep grade. After rolling to a stop, it barely missed being rammed by a following freight. It took ten days for the train to reach Danville, Virginia, over war-ravaged tracks. Halted again by another railroad accident—a collision between two trains that damaged a

22. Johnson to AHS, May 30, 1864, in Stephens Papers, LC; Davis to AHS, April 19, 1864, in Rowland (ed.), *Davis*, VI, 231; Larry E. Nelson, *Bullets, Ballots, and Rhetoric: Confederate Policy for the United States Presidential Contest of 1864* (University, Ala., 1980), 28–29.

23. AHS to Davis, May 7, 1864, in Stephens Papers, DU.

24. AHS to LS, May 7, 1864, LS to AHS, May 6, 1864, both in Stephens Papers, MC.

bridge and killed several soldiers—Stephens learned that his chief reason for going to Richmond had disappeared. Responding to a message from Davis on May 20, the House abandoned efforts to repeal the habeas corpus suspension act. Disgusted and sick, Stephens decided he "wasn't well enough to go on to Richmond with all the discomforts for only a few days of excitement without the prospect of doing any good." So he turned around and went back to Georgia. Along the way he was appalled by the condition of the railroad and even more by the plight of the Confederate wounded making their way south.[25]

No sooner had he reached home than something he noticed in the papers fanned his suspicions of Davis into bitter resentment. Zeb Vance, engaged in a bruising battle with W. W. Holden for the governorship in North Carolina, had released a letter he had written to the president on December 30, 1863, along with Davis' reply of January 8, 1864. Holden had challenged Vance on the issue of whether the state should offer peace terms to the North through a separate state convention. To prove that he too favored negotiations, Vance had published his letter. It suggested that the only way to still discontent in North Carolina would be to make "some efforts at negotiation with the enemy." Davis' reply refuted this idea. He pointed out that in July, 1863, Stephens had offered his "services, in the hope of [promoting] the cause of humanity, and although little belief was entertained of his success, I cheerfully yielded to his suggestion that the experiment be tried." Davis went on to use Stephens' failure as proof that Confederate offers to negotiate invited "insult" and "contumely . . . without the slightest chance of being listened to." As far as he was concerned, he said, the South would never offer negotiations again.[26]

Besides twisting the truth, Davis had used false information to bolster his own point of view. Stephens was furious. Rather than write the president or run a refutation in the papers—"this is no time to bring such matters before the public mind," he reasoned—Stephens poured his anger into a long letter to Linton, which he never mailed. The falsehoods in Davis' letter enraged him. He, not Davis, had opposed the mission; he, not Davis, had had little hope of its success. Davis' whole letter "is in bad tone and temper and shows his utter want of

25. AHS to LS, May 23, 1864, in Stephens Papers, MC; AHS to LS, May 12, 1864, in Johnston and Browne, *Stephens*, 462–63; Richardson (ed.), *Messages and Papers of the Confederacy*, I, 452–53.
26. The Vance-Davis letters are in *Official Records*, Ser. I, Vol. LI, Pt. II, 807–10.

statesmanship." It was exactly on a par with his invasion of Pennsylvania and John Hunt Morgan's 1863 raid into Ohio. Commissioners with full powers to make peace should have been sent north with Lee, Stephens now thought. Even if they had not been received, the South could have published the terms and helped the peace party in the North.

But he had never really seen *any* prospect for peace, said Stephens, because Davis "has but one idea and that is to fight it out." Morgan's raid and Lee's invasion had destroyed the northern peace party, and this was so plain to Stephens "that sometimes I am strongly inclined [to think] it was done partly if not mainly for that purpose." Nor was this the only fantastic suspicion he harbored. He had not seen Davis' letter to Lee during the abortive mission of July, 1863. It had gone by a courier whom the Yankees had captured. That letter, Stephens surmised, must have contained the real intent of his mission, and Davis meant it to be captured to thwart the chance for peace. "A great many other facts" had led him lately to strongly suspect that Davis "is a very unprincipled, untruthful, unreliable bad man! . . . I am now fast approaching the conviction that he is quite as much a knave as fool." Stephens went into paroxysms of adjectival overkill in describing the president: "Since his inauguration his every act is consistent with the course of a weak timid sly unprincipled arch aspirant after absolute power by usurpation." [27]

Less than two weeks after this tirade Stephens discovered more shocking evidence of Davis' duplicity. Another letter from Cable arrived. This one was plaintive. Having heard nothing in reply to his earlier letter, Cable said, he was appealing to Stephens. He had come South as an "earnest champion of peace," an operative for the northern peace party. Expecting to find "open-hearted friends and all due encouragement," he had instead been treated as a prisoner of war and was now "so much reduced" he didn't expect to survive long. Even if his mission in the South were rejected, he had much to do in the Northwest during the election. "At all events," he pleaded, "do not allow me to perish here for my family's sake." [28]

Outraged, Stephens decided to contact Cable directly. It appeared that Davis had promised an investigation merely to humor him, for the

27. AHS to LS, June 3, 1864, in Rabun (ed.), "Letter for Posterity."
28. Cable to AHS, June 21, 1864, in Davis Papers, DU.

commander of prisons, General J. H. Winder, told Stephens that no investigation had ever taken place. Thoroughly angry now, Stephens sent a terse letter to Davis mentioning the Cable and Winder notes and reminding the president of his promise. "It does seem to me that Mr. Cable[']s case is one that deserved prompt attention." [29]

Unfortunately attention didn't come promptly enough. On July 16, Cable died. The president had not ignored Stephens. He told the secretary of war to carry out Stephens' wishes if Cable was telling the truth. But the orders had miscarried somewhere in the mail. At this point, however, Stephens could believe nothing good about Davis. His conduct in the Cable matter "has really outraged my feelings," he told Dick Johnston. "He does not want the war to end until he is absolute military ruler." [30]

Once having launched his state into public controversy with Richmond, Joe Brown pitched into the contest with all his considerable guile and political skill. Shortly after the March session he tried to appoint Linton Stephens to a circuit judgeship so he could render favorable decisions on the conscript act. Although Aleck favored his taking the position, Linton decided to decline it. He could do more against conscription as a lawyer before the supreme court than as a subordinate judge, he thought. [31]

The governor also refused to forward to Richmond the resolution passed by the assembly expressing "undiminished confidence" in the president. Stephens lamely defended this piece of political pettiness by pointing out that this resolution had not been connected with the other two sets on "public affairs." Narrow people had mistakenly assigned to Brown the same "mean & vile passions" they falsely ascribed to him. Having to disapprove of Davis' actions, said Stephens, was as great a "source of deep pain & mortification" to Brown as it had been to himself. [32]

More likely the pain and mortification came from having to deal with the administration's defenders, a greater task than either Brown

29. J. H. Winder to AHS, July 2, 1864, in Stephens Papers, LC; AHS to Davis, July 5, 1864, with note by John B. Sale, July 20, 1864, thereon, in Confederate Autograph Letters, DU.

30. AHS to Johnston, August 26, 1864, in Stephens Papers, LC.

31. AHS to LS, May 5, 1864, in Johnston and Browne, *Stephens*, 462; LS to AHS, May 6, 1864, in Stephens Papers, MC.

32. AHS to Johnson, June 22, 1864, in Johnson Papers, DU.

or Stephens had anticipated. The March session had sparked a fierce war in the state's newspapers, and the governor soon found himself outgunned. To rectify the imbalance, and especially to find a suitable forum to counter administration instransigence on the peace issue, Brown stepped up his efforts to buy controlling interest in an influential Georgia newspaper. Stephens, boiling mad over the Vance correspondence and the Cable affair, gladly lent his aid.

Brown had determined that Georgia's printing patronage go only to friendly papers, but this policy guaranteed neither suitable editorials nor extensive circulation. So in June he began angling for a controlling share of Georgia's most widely read newspaper, the Augusta *Constitutionalist*. Brown believed the necessary money could be raised "on short notice" with only "a little effort on the part of our friends." The Stephens brothers both pledged funds for the project.[33]

Stephens had already been feeling out prospective editors for the newspaper. As fate would have it, a man more than suitable for the job had already offered his services: Henry Cleveland, then working as the editor of the *Constitutionalist* under the watchful eye of James Gardner, the paper's owner and a staunch Davis supporter. A longtime Stephens friend, Cleveland had studied law in Toombs' office and had refused to bolt the party in 1860. Captured and paroled at Vicksburg as a member of the ordnance corps, he had returned to journalism. A savage critic of Davis, Cleveland also harbored extreme (if not treasonable) opinions about Georgia's proper course in the war. He had opposed Linton's peace resolutions because he believed they would not influence either Davis or the North. His solution was for Georgia to secede from the Confederacy immediately: "To win this fight under this Administration would be a result without reason, an effect without a cause." Unfortunately for Brown, Cleveland's days with the *Constitutionalist* were numbered. At the end of June he resigned under pressure from the stockholders. Brown had raised enough money to buy the paper, but Gardner refused to sell. Meanwhile, Cleveland sent friends to Charleston and Savannah to ask about papers there, but what he really wanted, he told Stephens, was to start a "Democratic battery" in New York against Lincoln (and not incidentally, to save his own neck and fortune from the Yankees).[34]

33. Brown to AHS, June 17, 1864, in Phillips (ed.), *TSC Correspondence*, 644; LS to AHS, June 26, 1864, in Stephens Papers, MC.

34. Thweatt to AHS, June 14, 1864, Cleveland to AHS, June 8, 28, 1864, all in Stephens Papers, LC.

Having failed to acquire one Augusta paper, Brown now turned his attention to the other. In mid-July he bought control of the *Chronicle and Sentinel* through Nathan B. Morse, to whom he advanced eighty thousand dollars credit. The governor also arranged to have Morse offer Cleveland a job. Cleveland turned it down and continued to cast about fruitlessly for a paper of his own that Brown would buy.[35]

The exact extent of Stephens' involvement in all this is uncertain. He definitely supported Brown's plans, and he continued to countenance Cleveland's inflammatory utterances without rebuking him. Just as he had seen no inconsistency in his public attack on the administration while serving as its second executive officer, he saw none in helping to set up a newspaper whose sole purpose would be to oppose that government. He had reached the unshakable conviction that Davis' policies were ruinous. And unless a power greater than the government, the power of the people, could change those policies, then the revolution would fail. Stephens had not given up—far from it. The Confederacy was not "whipped," nor could it ever be, he told Hidell, "if our affairs are properly managed." But without "radical changes" in policies, "nothing but Divine Providence can save us."[36]

Many Georgians probably pondered God's inscrutable designs during the summer of 1864. Since spring General William T. Sherman's powerful army had been advancing inexorably toward Atlanta, Joseph E. Johnston's Confederates falling back before him. On the day Stephens wrote Hidell, July 3, Johnston retreated south from Kenesaw Mountain to a new position. Within two weeks Johnston would be relieved of his command and replaced by General John B. Hood; within three Sherman would invest the city of Atlanta. In Virginia, after more than six weeks of frightful carnage, General Ulysses S. Grant had succeeded in pinning down and besieging Lee's army in Petersburg, thirty miles south of Richmond.

For most of the early summer Stephens was severely ill and bedridden—"in very much the same condition, constitutionally, with our

35. Cleveland to AHS, July 15, 16, 1864, in Stephens Papers, LC; Brown to Cleveland, July 13, 1864, in Stephens Papers, LC. Morse was a transplanted Yankee who had come South after his own paper, the Bridgeport (Connecticut) *News*, had been wrecked by an abolitionist mob and a warrant issued for his arrest by the federal government. He became one-third owner and editor of the *Chronicle* in November, 1862. After July, 1864, the paper became virulently anti-Davis and increasingly outspoken on the possibility of a negotiated peace.

36. AHS to Hidell, July 3, 1864, in Stephens Papers, HSP.

country," he told Dick Johnston. "On the decline. *Malus, pejor, pessimus,* applies to the state of public affairs as well as to myself." But if the South could hold her own for six more months, he would be more hopeful. "Temporary invasion is not conquest." The people could bear sufferings and privations "not only for six months, but for years" if only administration policy did not break their spirit. Even in late August, with the fall of Atlanta only days away, Stephens remained guardedly optimistic: if the civil and military leaders made no blunders for the next two months, Lincoln might be beaten by a peace candidate, thus ensuring an end to hostilities "sooner or later." Georgia's resolutions, he was certain, had created these possibilities.[37]

By August 29, 1864, the day the Democrats convened in Chicago, Stephens had worked himself up into a state of considerable agitation. "Very great events" would depend on what the convention did, he said. News from the North took several days to reach war-torn Georgia, and when it arrived it proved disappointing. The Democrats had tried to appease both wings of the party, conciliating the war wing with the nomination of George B. McClellan for president and allowing the peace wing to write the platform. The so-called peace plank demanded cessation of hostilities so that "at the earliest possible moment peace may be restored on the basis of the Federal Union of the States." McClellan, however, promptly emphasized the Union in his acceptance letter and went before the people as a war candidate.[38]

Linton read the results of the convention more clearly than his brother. It guaranteed Lincoln's election and four more years of war, he said. And with hopes for a strong peace party gone, a quick collapse among the southern people was likely. Aleck was much more hopeful. The convention would have done better had the Davis administration backed the leading peace men from the beginning. An out-and-out peace man and platform would have been much better. Still, he thought the result probably the best possible under the circumstances. Barring blunders by the Confederate authorities before the election, he believed that "as matters now stand at the North, McClellan will be elected." The convention had at least presented "a ray of light."[39]

37. AHS to Johnston, June 23, 1864, in Johnston and Browne, *Stephens,* 467–68; AHS to Linton, August 27, 1864, in Stephens Papers, MC.

38. AHS to LS, August 29, 1864, in Stephens Papers, MC; platform quoted in James G. Randall and David Herbert Donald, *The Civil War and Reconstruction* (2nd ed., Lexington, Mass., 1969), 474.

39. LS to AHS, September 4, 1864, in Stephens Papers, MC; AHS to Johnson, September 5, 1864, in Johnson Papers, DU.

Stephens refused to see that it would take more than a change in Davis' stance on the northern elections at this point to save the Confederacy. In his opinion, the administration's firm resolve to stay out of the election was madness. To spurn offers of negotiations because they were not premised on independence was blind obstinacy and bumbling diplomacy. Stephens saw no inconsistency at all in an "*unalterably fixed*" desire for independence and a willingness to entertain negotiations on the basis of reunion. Negotiating on this basis and settling on it, he said, "are very different things."[40]

Stephens believed peace on the basis of separation would be the inevitable result of negotiations commenced on any basis. The key question was how to bring about these negotiations. One way was by a convention of states, a plan the Chicago convention had endorsed. People on both sides had discussed the idea since the war began, but with increasing frequency in 1864. During the summer, Congressman William W. Boyce of South Carolina had asked Stephens to take the lead in proposing an armistice and convention of the states. Unreceptive then, Stephens was willing to explore the idea now.[41]

He got his chance when three citizens of Macon sent identical letters to him and Herschel Johnson. The war could be settled only by negotiation, said these gentlemen, and they asked that the two leaders inaugurate a southern peace movement. Johnson wrote his friend immediately for advice. He would not answer, he said, till Stephens wrote back. Away at Sparta, Stephens didn't get the Macon letter until September 22. He answered immediately and at length. The Georgia resolutions had stated the sole principle on which peace could be based: state sovereignty. The idea that the old Union could be maintained by force was "preposterous." He refused to lead a peace movement himself. Cooperation with the northern peace men was desirable, however, and he did not object to a convention of the states. But making peace could be handled only by the governments. The "properly constituted authorities at Washington and Richmond" might assent to the idea. The convention should not be given any decision-making power. It might, he suggested, formulate a plan for ratification by the states.[42]

---

40. AHS to Johnson, September 11, 1864, in Johnson Papers, DU.
41. William M. Boyce to AHS, August 24, 1864, in Stephens Papers, EU.
42. James Scott *et al.* to AHS, September 14, 1864, in Stephens Papers, LC; Johnson to AHS, September 17, 1864, in Stephens Papers, EU; AHS to Scott *et al.*, September 22, 1864, in Milledgeville *Confederate Union*, October 11, 1864.

Stephens sent a copy of his letter along with a note to Johnson. He didn't know whether the Macon gentlemen would publish the letter, he said, and preferred that they would not. But a week or so later he had second thoughts and sent a copy to the *Chronicle* for publication. He was prompted, he said, by the "almost daily" letters he got on the subject of peace. Maybe so, but this was hardly the whole reason, for he had come to believe that "almost [the] entire press of the country is now completely *subsidized* by the administration" and under its control. The president, he also believed, was at best indifferent to the northern election. Clearly, then, if the public was to be informed, and the administration prodded, Stephens had to publish the letter. It might also offer some encouragement to the Democrats in the North.[43]

Stephens' letter to the Macon gentlemen would cause him no end of trouble in the following weeks, but on the day he wrote it, trouble in another form appeared at his doorstep. While he had been in Sparta, an emissary from General Sherman had come calling with an offer of safe passage for Stephens to Atlanta for a conference. Brown received a similar message. Like everyone else who read the papers, Sherman knew of the breach between the Georgia leaders and Davis. The state had been stunned by the loss of Atlanta; Brown had just furloughed his militia for the fall harvest; despondency lay heavily on the land. What better time to detach Georgia from the Confederacy? He had reason to believe that Stephens and Brown would talk with him, Sherman informed Washington. He had therefore sent them a "hearty invitation." President Lincoln himself heartily approved and awaited the results of Sherman's experiment in diplomacy with interest.[44]

Intrigued, Stephens told Linton he would have liked to have spoken to Sherman's messenger directly. Naturally he would not respond to a mere verbal message. Brown, on the other hand, answered immediately in a public letter. Georgia had the right to make a separate peace, he asserted, but could not honorably do so without the consent of her sister states. "Come weal or woe" Georgia would never withdraw from the Confederacy and leave her sister states in the lurch. The only basis for permanent peace, Brown said, was for the North to acknowledge the sovereignty of the states and let them decide on that basis. If not, the war could rage for generations until mutual exhaus-

---

43. AHS to Johnson, September 22, 25, October 2, 1864, in Johnson Papers, DU.
44. William T. Sherman to Henry W. Halleck, September 15, 1864, Lincoln to Sherman, September 17, 1864, in *Official Records*, Ser. I, Vol. XXXIX, Pt. 2, 381, 395.

tion and ruin justified *all* the states taking "the matter into their own hands and [settling] it as sovereigns in their own way."[45]

Stephens did not reply to Sherman until October 1, when another messenger from the general arrived. In the meantime, Toombs had warned him to avoid the Yankee trap: "If Sherman means to do anything he means to detach Georgia from the Confederacy. Better any fate than that." The fundamental law committed peacemaking powers to Davis, "and nothing could be of more evil tendency" than for anybody else to meet with anyone, especially a general, to discuss peace.[46]

Thus warned, Stephens refused to go to Atlanta. Neither he nor the general had the power to enter negotiations, he wrote. If, however, Sherman thought it possible that they might agree on "terms of adjustment to be submitted to our respective Governments" (even if he had no power to act), then Stephens, "with the consent of our authorities," would be glad to meet with him. So Sherman's little experiment in diplomacy failed. Disenchanted as they might be, Georgia's prominent malcontents would not consider any action on peace apart from the Confederate government.[47]

Although events in Georgia confused many northern observers, the keenest of them soon realized that rumors about peace overtures from there were "bogus and bosh." Apparently Richmond shared in the initial confusion, for in late September Davis decided to make one his periodic forays into the country to shore up public confidence. At the headquarters of General John B. Hood's defeated army, he tried to rally the soldiers with promises that they would soon be in Tennessee. Everywhere else he spoke—Montgomery, Macon, Augusta, and Columbia—he sounded the same note. Do not despond. Support the government.[48]

Only victory could secure peace, he insisted. He was willing to negotiate, but only on the basis of Confederate independence. Naturally he rejected any scheme for separate state action. All such schemes were traitorous and unconstitutional, and even if not, the North would still

45. AHS to LS, September 22, 1864, in Stephens Papers, LC; Brown to Aaron Wilbur, September 22, 1864, in Wilbur Papers, EU; Brown to William King, September 29, 1864, quoted in Brumgardt, "Stephens and the Peace Issue," 304.

46. Toombs to AHS, September 23, 1864, in Phillips (ed.), *TSC Correspondence*, 652.

47. AHS to King, October 1, 1864, in Johnston and Browne, *Stephens*, 472.

48. Allan Nevins and Milton Halsey Thomas (eds.), *The Diary of George Templeton Strong* (3 vols.; New York, 1952), III, 495; Strode, *Davis*, III, 91–96.

demand reunion and emancipation. The enemy's intentions were clear: to subjugate the South. Mentioning Stephens' unsuccessful "peace" mission in 1863, Davis insisted in Columbia that he had attempted every honorable means of settlement. All had been rejected. The president barely alluded to the northern elections.[49]

Stephens found Davis' stance incomprehensible. Prudence and good politics demanded that the South respond favorably to the Chicago platform. Had Davis made such a response, he believed, McClellan's election would have been secured. But, as he wrote to Herschel Johnson, Davis had had no sympathy with the northern peace people from the beginning. "His whole policy has been to weaken, cripple and annihilate them." And he didn't care whether this statement might be "unkind and unjust." He didn't even want to argue about it.[50]

Arguing with Linton presented a different case. If anyone in Georgia favored separate state action, it was Linton Stephens. In early October the vice-president had received a copy of a public letter Congressman William Boyce had sent to Davis. Boyce had urged the president to respond positively to the northern Democrats' state convention plan. The South's only hope lay in a Democratic victory. The weaker party had to make up in sagacity what it lacked in strength, he said.[51]

In discussing this letter with Linton, Stephens found out just how radically they differed on the subject of peace. Stephens naturally agreed with the main thrust of Boyce's letter. The only reason Davis insisted on continued war, he said, was because he feared that if the peace party were elected, it would woo the South back into the Union. But he objected to Boyce's contention that a constitutional amendment would be necessary before a convention of states could be called. This was "all wrong," Stephens told Linton. The two central governments could agree to any form of adjustment they chose, to commissioners appointed by the states or some other way. In any convention the sovereignty of each state should be recognized as the basis for peace. There was no constitutional barrier to this plan.[52]

In Linton's definition of what was constitutional, the states could do

49. Rowland (ed.), *Davis*, VI, 349–56.
50. AHS to George Brook, November 3, 1864, in Stephens Papers, EU; AHS to Johnson, October 9, 1864, in Johnson Papers, EU.
51. Nelson, *Bullets, Ballots, and Rhetoric*, 137.
52. AHS to Boyce, October 13, 1864, in Stephens Papers, EU; AHS to LS, October 9, 1864, in Stephens Papers, MC.

anything they chose. It would not even be unconstitutional for the states to propose a peace plan involving termination of the Confederate government. States had the right to abrogate the Constitution within their borders. Why should the consent of the two governments be necessary? He scoffed at the idea that the Confederate states had pledged their good faith to stand by the central government during the war. "Where is the pledge that would be broken by secession?" he demanded. The supposed pledge "is a cant invented to serve the purpose of usurpation and consolidation."[53]

This wild talk didn't seem to bother Stephens much; by this time he was used to Linton's rantings. Gently but firmly he stuck to his position. He agreed that a state could secede and also that "bad faith" to the central government would be a poor reason for not doing so when the state's interest required it. But secession at this time would be "highly injurious" to any state's welfare. He disagreed that states of the Confederacy could act as free diplomatic agents. The Constitution gave the treaty-making power to the executive. If a convention of states took place, "to have all things done regularly and properly," both governments should accede. This did not preclude a state taking matters into its own hands, but to do so, a state would first have to secede.[54]

Although he often couched his position in careful verbiage, Stephens firmly opposed any separate state action for peace. He realized, much better than most, that if the Confederacy were to succeed it would have to be by default, by somehow getting the two sides together, establishing an armistice, and then letting events take their natural course, which to him meant eventual recognition of southern independence once the parties had agreed to recognition on the basis of state sovereignty. He knew the South could not force peace militarily, though it just might finesse one by diplomacy—but only if the Democrats could carry the northern elections. It all seemed so clear to him that the obtuseness of others astonished him.

Many still misconstrued his words. A longtime friend wrote from North Carolina that people there believed Stephens not only favored reconstruction but wanted Georgia to secede from the Confederacy. Others thought he wanted the states to make peace on their own, without reference to either national government. Unfriendly editors at-

53. LS to AHS, October 13, 1864, in Waddell (ed.), *Linton Stephens*, 284–85.
54. AHS to LS, October 15, 1864, in Stephens Papers, MC.

tacked Stephens in much the same vein. "No such idea entered my head," Stephens protested to Linton. He remained silent until late October, however, when he saw notices of a speech his friend Senator Semmes had made in Mobile. Stephens' convention idea, said Semmes, was dangerous and unconstitutional, an "apple of discord" thrown into the Confederacy by the enemy.[55]

Stephens read the speech on November 3 in the *Constitutionalist* and immediately resolved to set himself right before the public. He sent the newspaper a copy of his long reply to Semmes, and it was printed on November 16. It repeated everything he had been saying privately for six weeks. He had not invited a convention; he had merely responded favorably to the Chicago platform. If the convention reaffirmed the sovereignty of the states, the war would end and Confederate independence would be assured. If Lincoln won, however, there would be no such opportunity. The South, therefore, should do everything possible to aid the Democrats. Unfortunately, many in the South, perhaps even Davis himself, preferred Lincoln to McClellan: "Judging from his acts, I should think that he did." People who favored Lincoln, Stephens continued, feared terms from McClellan that would entice the South back into the Union: "The Ghost of the Union haunts them. The spectre of Reconstruction rears its head at every corner to their imaginations." He did not believe in "ghosts of any kind," Stephens said. "The old Union & the old Constitution are both dead—dead forever." No power short of "that which brought Lazarus from the tomb" could resurrect them.[56]

Three days after Stephens wrote to Semmes, Abraham Lincoln swept to victory in the northern elections. The fate of the Confederacy had been sealed. But it hardly seemed to make any difference to Brown and the Stephens brothers. Evidence suggests that they barely noticed Lincoln's victory. Brown was preoccupied with raking the Davis administration. The regular session of the Georgia assembly had begun on November 3. And before the lawmakers had to scamper out of the way of Sherman's marauding army on its way to Savannah, they got a chance to listen to another of Brown's fulminating attacks on Richmond and an endorsement of the idea of a convention of the states in

55. Andrew H. H. Dawson to AHS, October 6, 1864, in Stephens Papers, LC; Semmes quoted in Augusta *Constitutionalist*, November 3, 1864; AHS to LS, October 15, 1864, in Stephens Papers, MC.
56. AHS to Semmes, November 5, 1864, in Semmes Papers, DU.

accordance with the Democratic platform. During the next several days the legislature heatedly debated several sets of resolutions (including one offered by Linton Stephens) calling on the Confederate government to offer a convocation of the states. The assembly defeated them all.[57]

No doubt Lincoln's reelection and the merciless advance of Sherman's troops through Georgia's vitals helped the lawmakers decide. But Davis had lent his help too, wiring six Georgia senators his own opinion of Linton's resolutions: two "innocuous," the third "possibly injurious," and the rest "objectionable if not dangerous." The president followed his telegram with a more detailed letter, but by the time it arrived in Milledgeville, Sherman had passed through and the session had come to an inglorious and hasty end.[58]

The day before Sherman's army of sixty thousand set out for the sea, the Second Confederate Congress convened in Richmond for what was to be its last meeting. Davis' message to the lawmakers began on an optimistic note. He played down the fall of Atlanta and even found no great reason to be discouraged about the country's finances. But then he went on to urge the strongest war legislation yet proposed: a general militia law and a virtual end to draft exemptions. He also proposed that the government buy slaves for work in the army (thus ending their impressment) and offer them freedom. He even left the door open for eventually employing slaves as soldiers. On peace, however, he refused to budge. The enemy's sole terms had been "unconditional surrender and degradation." The South had no choice but to fight on. Two days later the president requested reinstatement of his authority to suspend the writ of habeas corpus.[59]

From all indications, Congress meant to accede to this request. Contemplating this dire possibility with loathing, Stephens decided to go to Richmond, not only to try to stop a new suspension of the writ but also to foster some sort of peace initiative. The past two weeks had not been pleasant for him. To counter continuing public criticism, he had defended his consistency in the papers with a reprint of the first political speech he had ever made. The 1834 address would prove he was no

57. Brumgardt, "Stephens and the Peace Issue," 314–15, 341–44.
58. Davis to A. R. Wright *et al.*, November 17, 1864, in Rowland (ed.), *Davis*, VI, 403.
59. Richardson (ed.), *Messages and Papers of the Confederacy*, 482–88, 498.

latter-day adherent to states' rights or state sovereignty. Stephens might as well have issued a testimonial by God himself for all the good it would have done. But surreal gestures seemed to be the order of the day. He clipped a copy of his letter to Semmes from the *Constitutionalist* and sent it to the president. What he hoped to accomplish is difficult to say. But justifying himself had become an obsession, and even at this point he expected to convince Davis.[60]

Stephens arrived in Richmond on December 5, suffering from a bad cold and a flareup of his chronic bladder trouble—and no doubt equally from the insufferably long and uncomfortable railroad journey. The capital, like the Confederacy itself, presented a sorry spectacle, its physical shabbiness in harmony with the loud and scruffy denizens of its crowded streets and gaming halls. Everything but liquor was scarce and monstrously expensive. It cost Stephens nine hundred dollars a month for room and board with Semmes, another nine hundred dollars for fuel and extras. "It will not take long to consume my salary," he remarked ruefully. If the task at hand didn't destroy him first, he may as well have observed, for Stephens was destined to be very busy in the next few weeks.[61]

Congress was in a sullen and rebellious mood. Since the beginning of the session, anti-Davis cadres in both houses had been trying to force the president's hand on peace negotiations. Several resolutions to that effect—either instructing the president to act or authorizing Congress to—had been introduced in the House; all were referred to the foreign affairs committee. Stephens immediately got caught up in these machinations. Approached by two Tennessee congressmen, John Atkins and Arthur Colyar, with yet another set of resolutions, the vice-president readily agreed to revise them for presentation to the House.[62]

Only a major interruption could have distracted Stephens from his work, and it came only a few days later: a letter from Davis that Linton had forwarded from Georgia. Stephens had been in Richmond for about a week and as yet had not seen the president. He had attempted a courtesy call, but, as he later told Linton, after pulling at the doorbell three times and receiving no answer he had to hurry on about his business. He intended to call back but got the letter before he could.[63]

60. AHS to the public, November 10, 1864, in Phillips (ed.), *TSC Correspondence*, 654–55; 1834 speech in Augusta *Chronicle and Sentinel*, January 7, 1865.

61. AHS to LS, December 5, 1864, in Johnston and Browne, *Stephens*, 475.

62. Von Abele, *Stephens*, 233.

63. AHS to LS, January 7, 1865, in Stephens Papers, MC.

If Stephens had deliberately intended to pique the president with the clipping of his Semmes letter, he had succeeded. Davis' frosty letter came right to the point. He wanted an explanation of Stephens' imputation that certain acts of his had led the vice president to think he favored the election of Lincoln over McClellan. Stephens claimed he had no idea what Davis meant by this, "but I shall give him a full plain candid & pointed answer." He would "take some pains with it," he told Linton, and wanted it to be as "short as possible."[64]

Full the reply certainly turned out to be, and candid maybe. But the shortest the agitated Georgian could make it was twenty-six pages in his almost indecipherable scrawl. (And for reasons of "tact" he declined to discuss military policy.) Critically, self-defensively, Stephens laid out his grievances. Davis had made no efforts to help the peace party in 1864, as witnessed by his lack of cooperation in the Cable matter and his belligerent remarks at Columbia. His unreasonable policy had aided Lincoln and alienated the northern peace faction. Of course, Stephens said, Davis did not intend to help Lincoln, but that was the effect nonetheless. He was sorry the Semmes letter had offended the president, but he had written it only to defend himself against scurrilous charges.[65]

Having finished the letter, Stephens summoned seven of his congressional allies to his room and read it to them. He wanted to sound them out and let them know his views, he told Linton. Doubtless few of these gentlemen—among them Semmes, Rufus Garland of Arkansas, and William A. Graham of North Carolina—needed to be told, and none demurred at the sniping tone of what they heard.[66]

The correspondence between Davis and Stephens dragged on into the new year. The president, as stiff-necked as Stephens, responded with a twelve-page justification of his own. He denied failing to cooperate in the Cable business and defended his Columbia speech. The inferences Stephens had drawn from it were "strained and unnatural." He closed coldly: the only reason he had departed from his customary rule of bearing criticism in silence, he said, was because Stephens' letter "quite plainly" meant to disparage him, inspire distrust in the people, and do public injury. He sincerely regretted having to bring the

64. Davis to AHS, November 21, 1864, in Johnston Papers, TU; AHS to LS, December 10, 1864, in Stephens Papers, MC.
65. AHS to Davis, December 13, 1864, in Davis Papers, DU.
66. AHS to LS, December 16, 1864, in Stephens Papers, MC.

subject up. It would give him the greatest pleasure, Davis concluded, "to see you devoting your great and admitted ability exclusively to upholding the confidence and animating the spirit of the people." If Davis thought this would end the matter, he simply didn't know Little Aleck. Stephens issued another ten-thousand-word blast in response. This letter never got mailed. It was just as well. Davis had more pressing matters on his mind than this fruitless debate with a man whose mind was as closed as his own.[67]

After his first letter to Davis, Stephens turned his attention to forwarding any reasonable peace plan in Congress. Far from seeking an end to the war on the enemy's terms, Stephens still believed the South might achieve its ends by negotiation. He opposed reconstructing the old Union just as vehemently as ever, remarking to Senator Graham that reconstruction was an "obsolete idea." But before any of the many peace proposals could come to fruition, Stephens got an unexpected chance to strike a triumphant blow for sound policy on another matter.[68]

Responding to the president's urgent promptings, the House on December 7 had passed a bill authorizing a new suspension of the writ of habeas corpus. On the twentieth, with Stephens in the presiding chair, the measure came up for a vote in the Senate and deadlocked in a 10 to 10 tie. With grim satisfaction Stephens prepared to cast the tie-breaking vote to defeat the bill, but first he requested permission to explain his position. Everyone in the Senate already knew his reasons, and several declined to hear them again. One senator objected to Stephens' request, and then another changed his vote, thus defeating the measure and muzzling the presiding officer. Stephens contended that the rules forbade a member from changing his vote without unanimous consent of the Senate. This ruling from the chair sparked "considerable debate." Finally the Senate voted, 16 to 3, to allow the vote change. Stephens, stinging from the public insult, told Hunter that he intended to resign his office at once. His usefulness was ended if the Senate refused to hear his views on important matters.[69]

67. Davis to AHS, January 6, 1865, in Stephens Papers, EU; James Z. Rabun, "Alexander Stephens and Jefferson Davis," *American Historical Review*, LVIII (January, 1953), 318–19.

68. William A. Graham to David L. Swain, January 28, 1865, in Graham Papers, SHC/NC.

69. *Journal of the Congress of the Confederate States of America, 1861–1865* (Washington, D.C., 1904), IV, 385–87; Johnston and Browne, *Stephens*, 478.

Hunter succeeded in soothing the vice-president's wounded feelings for the moment, but Stephens was still writhing in embarrassment several days later. "I am satisfied I can do no good here," he wrote Linton. He still wanted to resign. Worse, he suspected that congressional sentiment for suspension of the writ might eventually prevail. To head off such sentiment he went to the office of the Richmond *Whig* on Christmas Eve and offered the editor two hundred dollars to print a copy of Justice Taney's 1861 decision in the Merryman habeas corpus case. To his chagrin, he could not get a definite answer.[70]

This rebuff and the close vote in the Senate, not to mention the blow to his monumental ego, brought Stephens to the brink of hopelessness. If the suspension act should pass and be upheld by Georgia's supreme court, "I shall feel very little further interest in the result of the conflict," he told Linton. "I have fallen on evil times," he remarked sadly to Hidell. "My opinions & judgments have no influence." Nothing could have been worse for him. He wanted to go home and would "as soon as the road is open." Little did he suspect that his one great act in the entire drama was yet to be played.[71]

As the Confederacy entered its final months of existence in January, 1865, a perceptive observer might have wondered which would evaporate first—Lee's army of gaunt and shivering veterans in the trenches at Petersburg or Jefferson Davis' government. Hood's proud Army of Tennessee, crushed by successive disasters at Franklin and Nashville, had for all practical purposes disappeared. Sherman's army occupied Savannah after a devastating march through the heart of Georgia without benefit of a supply line.

And in Richmond the opposition to Davis grew daily bolder and more strident. Speaker of the House Thomas Bocock informed the president that the state of Virginia wanted a change in the entire cabinet, and if this were not done the House would seriously consider passing a resolution of no confidence in the government. James Seddon, the Virginia-born secretary of war, resigned in dudgeon. Some editors clamored for Davis' removal from office, and almost everyone talked about peace proposals. Down in war-weary Georgia, agitation for

70. AHS to LS, December 23, 24, 1864, in Stephens Papers, MC. On the Merryman case, see Randall and Donald, *Civil War and Reconstruction*, 301–302.

71. AHS to LS, December 24, 1864, in Stephens Papers, MC; AHS to Hidell, December 27, 1864, in Stephens Papers, HSP.

separate state action for peace grew incessant. Congress, always critical of Davis' military policies, had finally coerced him into appointing
a general in chief of all the armies—Lee, who ignored Congress and
thanked the president for the honor.[72]

Stephens found the atmosphere most uncongenial. He still intended
to leave. Longtime Davis critic Louis Wigfall of Texas had arrived,
however, breathing fire against the president, so Stephens decided to
stay "until I see what turn the present agitation may take." If it took
the right direction, and he saw "any prospect of doing any good," he
would stay. Though doubtful of accomplishing anything, Stephens
eagerly embraced any opportunity to try. He got a fine opportunity on
January 6, 1865, when the Senate, much to his surprise, unanimously
passed a resolution that he address it in secret session after adjournment. The invitation did wonders for Stephens' wounded dignity; he
readily accepted. With Hunter in the chair, the vice-president spoke
and held the floor for two hours.[73]

What was needed, Stephens told the Senate, was a complete change
in policy to reanimate the people: an immediate end to conscription
and impressments, a forthright policy of friendship toward the northern Democrats (in other words, negotiations on the basis of the resolutions he had drawn up for Atkins and Colyar), a proclamation inviting
deserters back to the ranks, and a promise to potential draftees that
they could serve under their own elected officers. This course, he said,
would produce more steadfast soldiers in thirty days than compulsion
had from the beginning. A revamped military policy, one in which the
army abandoned its attempt to defend fixed points and offered battle
only when reasonably sure of success, would enable the country to survive for at least a year or two longer. Northern advantages in numbers
could not be matched. "The leading object should be to keep an army
in the field." Eventually war weariness and an inevitable financial collapse in the North would bring the enemy to reason.[74]

Albeit characteristically unrealistic, it had not been a gloomy speech.
That night, writing to Linton, Stephens betrayed his excitement about
again being in the limelight. "The feeling here is better than it was," he
declared. It appeared that the habeas corpus suspension as well as several other "follies" and "mischievous measures" would be dropped.

72. Strode, *Davis*, III, 130–32.
73. AHS to Hidell, January 4, 1865, in Stephens Papers, HSP.
74. Stephens, *Constitutional View*, II, 587–88.

This new turn of events had dispelled his recent hopelessness. Naturally he had never been anything but resolute about the correctness of
his own views, but now that it seemed they might actually be influencing someone, his spirits soared. "I am not sanguine, but not by any
means depressed," he said. "I am prepared for anything."[75]

Stephens gave up the idea of going home, and as January wore on he
found more reason for optimism. On January 12, Congressman J. A.
Orr of Mississippi introduced a set of resolutions Stephens had helped
write. These declared Confederate independence to be "rightful fact"
and urged that a convention of all the states be called "as an advisory
body" with the approval of both governments to agree on a peace
plan. The House refused to consider these resolutions, but on the
twenty-third Congressman James Leach of North Carolina submitted
another set of motions calling for peace and pledging undying resistance if the North spurned the offer. Stephens was ebullient. Rumors in
Richmond suggested that Congress would adopt all his suggestions
on the writ, finance, conscription, and impressment. "A wonderful
change promises soon to come over the spirit" of the government, he
proudly reported.[76]

As Stephens fantasized about the first indications in almost four
years that someone might be taking his suggestions seriously, he was
jolted back to reality by distressing news from Georgia. Widespread
peace sentiment at home had spawned a virulent contagion infecting
thousands: a movement for separate state action promiscuously spread
by Nathan B. Morse of the *Chronicle* and others of his ilk. Stephens
vigorously opposed this movement. For most of January he had been
discussing the matter with Linton. The only convention he wanted
anything to do with was a general convention of the states. Moreover,
he greatly feared creating any more factions in the South. It was clear
to him that only by harmonious action, which would necessarily involve the Confederate government, could the South hope for peace.[77]

People like Morse, however, didn't concern themselves with such
subtleties and freely claimed that Stephens and Brown shared their
opinions. J. Henley Smith, who knew where Stephens and Brown

75. AHS to LS, January 6, 1865, in Johnston and Browne, *Stephens*, 483–84.
76. Orr's resolutions in Johnston and Browne, *Stephens*, 480–82; "Peter Finkle"
[AHS] to LS, January 27, 1865, in Stephens Papers, MC.
77. Augusta *Chronicle and Sentinel*, January 7, 17, 1865; AHS to LS, January 7, 18,
1865, in Stephens Papers, MC.

really stood, was outraged. "You are doing untold harm to these two men," Smith warned Morse, "and I want you to stop it." Morse refused to heed the warning—for all the difference it made. Georgia was in chaos. Governor Brown had called another special session for mid-February, and neither of the Stephens brothers knew what he intended to do.[78]

Stephens had been far too busy in Richmond to pay much attention to what was happening in Georgia. In addition to his full schedule in the Senate and his regular visits to the hospitals, Stephens conferred endlessly with everyone from an incarcerated Georgian accused of murder to gaggles of lawmakers to crackbrained mavericks like Henry S. Foote—who tried to convince him to undertake a one-man peace mission to Washington, failed, and then set out on the venture himself only to be arrested by Confederate agents at Fredericksburg.[79]

A Yankee emissary with similar aims fared much better. On January 12, 1865, crusty old Jacksonian Francis P. Blair arrived in Richmond with a proposal of his own to lay before Davis. Unlike Foote's unilateral venture, the northerner's mission had his president's blessing. Blair proposed that the North and South join forces to maintain the Monroe Doctrine against Napoleon III's puppet government in Mexico. Slavery as an issue was dead, he argued, and with it any reason for Confederate independence.[80]

Davis had no intention of entertaining any such idea, but he immediately recognized a golden political opportunity. He had known about Blair's intended visit since late December but had kept the matter secret. He knew Lincoln's terms, but he made a show of interest nonetheless. Blair went back to Washington with a letter from Davis to Lincoln stating his willingness to enter a conference to secure peace between "the two countries." Lincoln had no interest in the Mexican angle (that had been Blair's idea), but he was willing to talk. He was prepared to receive "informally" any agents to secure peace "to the people of our common country."[81]

Fairly sure envoys would be received, Davis seized the chance to ease

78. Smith to Nathan B. Morse, February 8, 1865, in Stephens Papers, LC; LS to Hidell, January 22, 1865, in Stephens Papers, HSP.

79. Henry S. Foote, *A Casket of Reminiscences* (Washington, D.C., 1874), 305–306.

80. Coulter, *Confederate States*, 551–52.

81. Correspondence of Blair, Davis, and Lincoln is in Richardson (ed.), *Messages and Papers of the Confederacy*, I, 521–30.

his domestic difficulties. From Georgia Cobb had warned that anti-administration sentiment was "so general" that "you know not whom to look upon as a friend." The idea of a separate state convention had many adherents, Cobb continued, but for the present Brown opposed it. For how long no one knew. Faced with incipient unilateralism in Georgia, the growing sentiment for peace in the press and public, and the increasing strength of his congressional opposition—Stephens' resolutions were on the verge of passing in the Senate—Davis saw a chance to solve all problems with a single stroke. And since few besides himself knew the terms of Blair's proposal, he controlled the situation. By responding to Blair's mission the president could satisfy the public, silence and discredit his critics, and thus rally the people once again to support of the government.[82]

Like everybody else in Richmond, Stephens speculated about the meaning of Blair's visits. "Blair is back again," he told Hidell on January 23. "What he is doing I do not know but presume the President is endeavoring to *negotiate* with him for *negotiation*—that same thing which on 17. Nov. seemed to him to be so absurd." Stephens hardly bothered to conceal his contempt for the administration's policies. Even the distinguished Yankee visitor heard of it when Stephens crossed his path one morning at breakfast at Mrs. Stannard's house, about the closest war-wracked Richmond had to a fashionable salon.[83]

Stephens didn't have to wait long to find out about Blair. The day the old man left Richmond, January 27, Davis summoned the vice-president to discuss "special and important" business. The message probably came as a surprise. Not a word save the acerbic exchange of letters had passed between Stephens and Davis since the former's arrival in town. Stephens was convinced that Davis disliked him and had deliberately ignored him the day he had called at the president's house. The president might never have contacted Stephens except for Hunter's urging. Hunter knew about the letters, and he knew that Stephens had written a reply to Davis' last but had not mailed it yet. So to avoid a possibly scandalous break, he engineered this temporary restoration of official relations between the two men.[84]

Stephens met privately with Davis in the afternoon, before the

82. Cobb to Davis, January 20, 1865, in *Official Records*, Ser. I, Vol. LIII, 393–94.
83. AHS to Hidell, January 23, 1865, in Stephens Papers, HSP; James Lyons to W. T. Walthall, July 31, 1878, in Rowland (ed.), *Davis*, VIII, 212.
84. "Peter Finkle" [AHS] to LS, January 27, 1865, in Stephens Papers, MC.

scheduled 4 P.M. cabinet meeting. Only Hunter knew about the meeting. Davis described Blair's plan, showed Stephens the correspondence, and asked his opinion. Given Washington's demand for reunion, would it be proper to enter talks? If so, who should go? Having assured himself that Washington knew Blair's plan and would be open to talks, Stephens advised Davis to do it. It would at least get a conference and might result in an armistice without committing the South to an active role in maintaining the Monroe Doctrine.

Davis himself should confer with Lincoln, Stephens suggested, a proposition the president decidedly opposed. Three commissioners should go, he thought. Stephens suggested three names: Henry Benning, an old Douglas man, former justice of the Georgia Supreme Court, now a brigadier general in Lee's army; John A. Campbell, the assistant secretary of war and a distinguished jurist; and Thomas S. Flournoy, an old-line Whig from Virginia who knew Lincoln. Davis nodded his approval and the meeting ended.[85]

The next morning Stephens met again with Davis, this time with the cabinet present. To his disgust he learned that his suggestions of yesterday had been spurned. Only Campbell remained of the delegation he had proposed; Hunter and Stephens himself had been named instead of the other two. Davis knew perfectly well that Stephens didn't want this job, and originally he had not intended to offer it. The cabinet and Ben Hill changed his mind. At the very least, they argued, sending Stephens would forestall his resolutions in the Senate. Hill offered other good reasons: Stephens was more acceptable to the North, and if the commission failed, the administration's enemies could not say it was because of Stephens' absence. What Hill did not tell Davis was that he and Little Aleck had struck a deal. Georgia's congressional delegation had promised to support Stephens' peace resolutions in exchange for the vice-president's influence in restraining Brown from initiating separate state action. Hill had made a sharp bargain. He fully expected this proposed conference to fail, and once that happened Stephens' resolutions would be a dead letter.[86]

Taken aback, Stephens lamely attempted to avoid the mission. The absence of both the vice-president and the president *pro tem* of the Senate would attract too much attention, he said—as if the Blair visits

85. Account of Stephens-Davis meetings in Stephens, *Constitutional View*, 589–95.
86. Davis to E. L. Drake, 1877, in Rowland (ed.), *Davis*, VIII, 28; Davis to James M. Mason, June 11, 1870, in Davis Papers, DU; Pearce, *Hill*, 103–104.

had not sufficiently stirred the rumor mill already. It seems clear that Stephens feared he would be hamstrung by his instructions. He had already seen the Blair correspondence, knew Davis had no faith in finessing a cease-fire, and had been stung once before on a "peace mission." Stephens was wily enough to recognize a political trap when he saw one—only this one had been sprung before he could avoid it.[87]

He tried to make the best of a bad situation. He wanted to assure that no hopes would be raised too high by this meeting. He had implored Davis "to see that no improper impressions be produced on the public mind North or South by the manner of announcement of what has been determined on in the papers or by telegram." He suggested a simple message for the papers to the effect that three men would go to Washington "to see what can be done in the way of negotiation." He insisted that the word "commissioners" not be used.[88]

Stephens later told Linton that he thought the mission a "humbug" from the beginning. Sure enough, once he had seen his commission, which was not until the three men had set out on the morning of January 29, 1865, he "felt confident" the mission would fail and told his colleagues so. But he thought differently now, and the day before he left he actually sounded hopeful. Lincoln's desire for reconstruction "seems to be in abeyance," he told Linton. Immediately before leaving the next day, Stephens told Hidell there was "some prospect of doing something if we be received." If Stephens had seen the Blair correspondence, how could he have believed this mission would do any good? And how could he have so misjudged Lincoln?[89]

The truth was that Stephens didn't want to understand Lincoln. He had been talking about the advantages of negotiation for so long that he could hardly admit their futility, especially if he were one of the negotiators. But at the same time he was cautious and realistic. He realized the informal nature of the mission, as he stressed to Linton, and strongly urged that its importance be downplayed in the press. Unduly arousing people's hopes at this juncture would do no good. This game had to be played carefully, for it held out the promise of the only thing

87. Von Abele, *Stephens*, 237.

88. AHS to Davis, January 28, 1865, in C. C. Jones Papers, (Georgia Portfolio II) DU.

89. AHS to LS, February 18, 1865, "Peter Finkle" [AHS] to LS, January 28, 1865, both in Stephens Papers, MC; AHS to Hidell, January 29, 1865, in Stephens Papers, HSP.

Stephens believed could save the South: an armistice—on whatever pretext the South needed to get it.

Davis, however, was not thinking along these lines. It was to his advantage to have the mission understood as a full-blown peace initiative. For months there had been clamor for such a move. But the president could envision peace only on his terms, and he drew up the commission's instructions accordingly. The object of the mission was explicitly spelled out: an "informal conference . . . for the purpose of securing peace to the two countries." Secretary of State Judah Benjamin had advised less constricting terminology—an informal conference on the "subject" of Lincoln's letter—but the president had been adamant.[90]

Whether Stephens wanted it or not, the commission immediately became the talk of the South, and most people, if not all, hoped it would herald peace. John B. Jones, the War Department clerk, was hopeful; so were the editors of both Augusta papers, although Morse at the *Chronicle* expected "total failure" if the commissioners carried any ultimatum. A North Carolina diarist reported many people there "greatly cheered" at the prospect of an early peace. The soldiers in the trenches most longed for peace. When the Confederates crossed the shell-pocked no-man's-land between the lines, men on both sides stood up, waved their hats, and yelled "Peace! Peace!" at the top of their lungs.[91]

The ensuing meeting would be one of the greatest anticlimaxes of the war. And had it not been for Ulysses S. Grant, it would never have happened. The Confederates traveled by rail to Petersburg (the original plan to go by steamer from Richmond to Washington had been thwarted by Potomac ice), arriving on the afternoon of January 29. Because Grant didn't receive their request to cross the lines until the next day, the three men did not reach Grant's headquarters at City Point until the evening of the thirty-first.

Stephens had never seen Grant and was struck by his simple appearance and unaffected manner. He was "one of the most remarkable men" he had ever met, Stephens later acknowledged. The general's actions over the next two days only reinforced his favorable impression.

90. Rowland (ed.), *Davis*, VIII, 540–41, 570–71, 585.
91. Augusta *Chronicle and Sentinel*, January 31, 1865; Earl Schenck Diary, quoted in Brumgardt, "Stephens and the Peace Issue," 360; Shelby Foote, *The Civil War, A Narrative* (3 vols.; New York, 1958–74), III, 773.

For his part, Grant, like so many others laying eyes on Stephens for the first time, couldn't help being dumbfounded by the man's appearance. He wore a thick gray overcoat, thicker than anything Grant had ever seen—"even in Canada"—that reached almost to his ankles. And then when he saw what a ghastly, emaciated figure emerged from the endless wraps, the general had to stifle a secret amusement. (Later one of the Union soldiers around the headquarters, less reticent than the commander, exclaimed upon seeing Stephens, "My God! He's dead now, but he don't know it.")

Grant apologized for the delay; he had been in Washington and had not returned until that morning. Grant's manner was so easy that the four men soon found themselves in amiable discussion about the politics of peace, a subject supposedly *verboten* for generals. They were soon joined by General George G. Meade, commander of the Army of the Potomac; he too showed no compunction about discussing peace. Grant found himself quite taken with the frail little Georgian. It had not taken them long to discover that they liked each other and shared an equal enthusiasm for the conference. Grant wanted it to happen as badly as Stephens did.

Grant's instructions were to hold the delegation until a special message arrived from the capital. Since no other suitable accommodations were available, Grant had arranged comfortable quarters for his guests aboard his dispatch steamer, *Mary Martin*. The accommodations were almost as elegant as the dinner the three commissioners enjoyed with Grant, his wife, and about fifty other Union officers: "fish, meats and vegetables of every variety . . . an abundance of champagne, hock, sherry, madeira . . . other varieties of wine and the best French brandy." Grant sat at the head of the table, Stephens at his left. During coffee and cigars, the general took his leave. He had not drunk anything during the meal, Stephens noted. Others had, though, and Stephens had trouble getting to sleep that night in his stateroom, which adjoined the dining room. The hilarity there, heartily joined in by Hunter and Campbell, did not subside until after 1 A.M.

The next morning, February 1, Grant introduced his family and took the rebels to see his horses. They all politely declined his invitation to take a drive with him, preferring to stay around and aboard the steamer. The thorough civility of the occasion got rudely interrupted when Lincoln's emissary, Major Thomas T. Eckert, arrived from Washington that night. He had been instructed to allow passage of the Confederates only on the basis of Lincoln's January 18 letter to Blair ("our common country"). The letter the Confederates carried with them did not comply with these instructions, Eckert said.

Grant was greatly disappointed, Stephens noticed, and at the general's urging he attempted twice to frame letters of intention that would satisfy Eckert. Neither did. At this point the general in chief of the Union armies took matters into his own hands. Secretary of State Seward already awaited them at Fortress Monroe, he told the Confederates. He would telegraph Lincoln and allow them to pass on his own authority. Actually, Grant had already sent the wire, to Stanton not Lincoln, claiming the commissioners' intentions were "good and their desire sincere to restore peace and union." The president, he hinted broadly, should talk to the southerners if he could.

As it turned out, Lincoln granted the necessary permission himself once he saw Grant's wire. On the morning of the second, with the *Mary Martin* drifting into the James's current under a full head of steam, an elated Grant hurried to the dockside waving a piece of paper. "Gentlemen, it's all right," he hollered across the water. "I've got the authority." "Say to the gentlemen," he read, "I will meet them personally at Fort Monroe as soon as I can get there. (signed) A. Lincoln." And so with the sight of the most powerful man in the Union army waving them good-bye, the three commissioners steamed off to Hampton Roads. Travis, Stephens' body servant, whom Grant had allowed to accompany the Georgian, must have wondered what sort of enemies these were.

The long-awaited meeting took place aboard Lincoln's steamer on February 3, 1865. Only the president, Seward, the three Confederates, and an unobtrusive black steward were present. Lincoln, his eyes glinting with merriment, remarked when Stephens removed his coat what a small nubbin had emerged from such an immense husk. The two old Whig compatriots had not seen each other for years. They spent a few minutes talking over old times. How were Toombs, Flournoy, and Preston, Lincoln asked. And Truman Smith, Stephens countered.

Once the meeting settled down to business, it became apparent that Lincoln would not be budged. Restoration of the Union and an end to the rebellion was the only basis on which he would entertain discussion. Stephens tried several times to explore the question of an armistice to allow a cooling-off period and possible joint action against the French in Mexico. Blair had no authority, Lincoln said. He had not endorsed his ideas; he had only issued him a passport. Stephens pressed. With hostilities suspended to contend with France, the idea of reunion would have time to work on people's minds. Seward pointed out practical difficulties: who would control the Mississippi meanwhile? How would the law be administered in the states if there were two national authorities? By military convention, Stephens answered. Lincoln repeated his terms—nothing without reunion. Campbell inquired how this would be done. Lincoln's answer was simple. The armies would disband and national authority would resume.

The talk now turned to the slavery question. Stephens reminded his old friend that he had just reiterated to the U.S. Congress that emancipation would not be modified. Indeed, Campbell cut in, what about all the slave property that had already been confiscated? That would be for the courts to decide, replied Seward, and he had reason to believe that Congress would be liberal in making restitution for confiscated property. Stephens asked about the slaves not yet freed. This too would be a matter for the courts, Lincoln said, and since emancipation had been a war measure it would probably be declared inoperative for the future. The president sat silently while Seward outlined a startling possibility. The Thirteenth Amendment, barring slavery forever, had just passed the U.S. Congress and was on its way to the states for ratification. With the southern states back in the Union, ratification could be blocked.

Lincoln had another suggestion to make. If he were Stephens, he said, addressing his old friend, he would go down to Georgia, persuade the governor to call a state reconstruction convention, elect senators and representatives to the U.S. Congress, recall Georgia troops from the war, and ratify the Thirteenth Amendment "prospectively," say, to take effect in five years. Slavery was doomed, he said. The main objective now was to avoid the evils of immediate emancipation. This would be nothing less than unconditional surrender, snorted Hunter. Seward immediately protested that no degradation of the South was contemplated, and Lincoln quickly agreed. Northerners were as guilty as southerners for tolerating slavery and should be willing to bear the costs of freedom. He himself would be willing to be taxed for the remuneration of southern slaveowners. He knew many in the North who felt the same way, and he had heard sums as large as $400 million mentioned. But again he could not offer assurances to those in rebellion against the government.

The conference had reached its inevitable dead end. After a cordial four hours, there was nothing left to say. Stephens, trying to salvage something from the conference, asked Lincoln about a prisoner exchange; the president referred him to Grant. As they all rose to leave, Lincoln asked Stephens if there was anything else he could do. Little Aleck thought a moment or two. Yes, his young nephew John A. Stephens had been a prisoner on Johnson Island since the fall of Port Hudson. Perhaps. . . ? Lincoln wrote the name in his notebook and promised to check on the matter. As the president shook hands with Stephens, the little bundled-up Georgian made a last earnest effort to press the armistice idea. Lincoln promised he would reconsider, but he didn't think he would change his mind.[92]

The conference was over. All that had been decided was that the killing would continue. A disgusted Stephens could take joy only in the release of his nephew. True to his word, Lincoln had secured Lieutenant Stephens' release almost immediately upon his return to Washington. The president gave the young man a five-day pass to visit friends in the capital before sending him on his way with a note to his uncle requesting that a Union prisoner of equal rank "whose physical condition most requires his release" be sent to Washington. Old Abe also presented John with an unusual souvenir—an autographed portrait of himself. "Don't have these where you're from," read the wry inscription.[93]

Jefferson Davis' purposes had been admirably served. When the commissioners returned he insisted that they submit a written report. Stephens objected strongly to any report, much less one that went beyond a bare recital of the facts. And a terse report was all Davis got, which was more than enough for the moment. Not since 1861 had the administration enjoyed such an upsurge of support. A Georgian observed that since the conference "our people have become united and are determined to die together rather than submit to Yankee rule." "Will any Georgian accept these terms?" raged a Milledgeville editor.

92. The preceding account of the Hampton Roads conference is based on AHS to editor of the Philadelphia *Times*, undated MS, in Stephens Papers, LC; Stephens, *Constitutional View*, II, 597–624; U. S. Grant, *The Personal Memoirs of U. S. Grant* (2 vols.; New York, 1886), II, 422; William S. McFeely, *Grant: A Biography* (New York, 1981), 199–208. Official correspondence is in *Official Records*, Ser. I, Vol. XLVI, Pt. 2, 290–92, 301–302, 311–14, 341–43, 505–13.
93. Lincoln to AHS, February 10, 1865, in Stephens Papers, PHS; Lincoln's inscription in Edward L. Cashin, "Alexander H. Stephens' Concept of the Confederacy" (M.A. thesis, Fordham University, 1957), 74n.

"Forbid it, Almighty God! Now, let us cease all bickerings, and strike for life and liberty." Stephens' enemies particularly relished his embarrassment. From Macon, Hill wrote enthusiastically of the revival of the war spirit in Georgia. Brown, it was said, had given up all idea of a state convention. Everybody was delighted, Hill said, with the "master-stroke" that had put Stephens on the commission.[94]

Capitalizing on this final surge of desperate resistance, Davis scheduled a massive public rally at Richmond's African Church on the night of February 9. Torchlights, parades, a great noisy crowd—an incongruous prelude to disintegration. How Davis ever convinced Stephens to appear on the podium with him is a wonder. But Stephens refused to say a word to the throng. How could he encourage hopes he lacked himself? Davis had no such problem. Even Stephens admitted that his defiant speech had been "brilliant . . . but little short of dementation."[95]

Stephens may have been right, but he was hardly thinking rationally anymore. He had not approved of the rally with its spread-eagle oratory. The "only politic" way to respond to Lincoln's intransigence, he told Linton, was to try to "make allies of all friends of Constitutional Liberty on the continent and have all questions touching the future relations of the States to be settled . . . between the States hereafter." The Republicans, the "consolidationists," and not the whole North were the real enemies. He tried to get Wigfall and Hunter to introduce another set of state convention resolutions. To no avail. The Senate had no hope left in resolutions.[96]

No question about it, Stephens was going home now. His last interview with Davis, proper and formal, marked the end of his participation in the Confederate government. What would he do, the president asked. He would go home and stay there, Stephens said. He would make no speeches, write no letters. Fortune would decide the issue now, and he intended simply to await her decree.[97]

Joe Brown still spewed vitriol. As Stephens traveled back to Georgia, the governor harangued the assembly with another of his foaming attacks on the administration. Castigating Davis for all his familiar sins,

94. Charles A. L. Lamar to his wife, February 14, 1865, in Charles A. Lamar Papers, GDAH; Milledgeville *Confederate Union*, February 14, 1865; Hill to Davis, February 17, 1865, in Keith Reid Collection, UG.

95. Avary (ed.), *Stephens Recollections*, 241.

96. AHS to LS, February 18, 1865, in Stephens Papers, MC.

97. Stephens, *Constitutional View*, II, 625.

he urged the legislators to call a convention of the states to amend the Constitution to correct manifold abuses. And while they were at it, they should depose Jefferson Davis as commander in chief of the armed forces. Significantly, Linton Stephens did not support this idea. He wanted a convention but thought it ought to be called only by the people of the state. The Georgia assembly didn't like either idea and defeated them both by large margins. The final chimerical panacea had vanished.[98]

Stephens no longer cared. He disapproved of Brown's idea to amend the Constitution, convinced that the other states would not go along. As always, he opposed separate state action. He had not cooperated with either Brown or his brother this time. Rumor had it that Stephens had reacted to the Hampton Roads failure the same way many other southerners had and would be returning to Georgia to fire zeal for patriotic resistance. Nothing could have been further from the truth. Stephens was through talking. Pleas for speeches came in daily; he ignored them all. Words were pointless. Stephens had accepted the inevitable.[99]

But his enemies sniped at him still. "If Mr Stephens cant write anything hopeful or say anything encouraging he might at least say something *manly*," wrote E. P. Alexander, Lee's chief artillery officer. Hill was vicious. While assuring the president that Georgians still solidly supported the war, he accused Stephens of supporting Brown's latest attempt at "revolution." "Under every obligation of honor and patriotism" Stephens should have spoken up for renewed resistance after Hampton Roads, he told Davis; his silence had earned Hill's "utter abhorrence." On the other hand, "his failure has at least *silenced his* pernicious tongue about 'brains.'"[100]

As the Confederacy tottered to its death, others wondered why Stephens said nothing. There was nothing to say. By mid-March the Confederate Congress had ceased to function. On April 1, 1865, Lee's ragged army evacuated Petersburg and fled westward to its appointed destiny at Appomattox. Richmond, burned and looted by its own citizenry, fell to the Yankees the next day.

98. Candler (ed.), *Georgia Confederate Records*, III, 818–55.

99. AHS to LS, February 18, 23, 1865, both in Stephens Papers, MC.

100. E. P. Alexander to his wife, March 20, 1865, in E. P. Alexander Papers, SHC/NC; Hill to Davis, March 25, 1865, in [Mrs. John Osborne Summer], "Georgia and the Confederacy—1865," *American Historical Review*, I (October, 1895), 100–101.

"I wish you would come over here," Stephens wrote Linton on hearing of Lee's surrender, "and let us stand or fall together. Organized war is, or soon will be, over with us." If he knew where to write Governor Brown, he said sadly, he would advise him to call the legislature together and issue a call for another state convention to provide for the future. He loathed the idea of any further bloodshed. "Almost anything is better than guerilla warfare."[101]

Incredibly, almost pitifully, Stephens clung to his faith in states' rights. Call the state legislature to provide for the future! It never occurred to him that Georgia's future was no longer in her own hands. In many ways the last four long, bloody years had taught him nothing.

It was as natural as breathing for Stephens to think only of his family in times of greatest crisis. On May 1, 1865, almost the entire Stephens clan in Georgia—Linton and three children, John's widow, Elizabeth, and her three boys, Confederate veterans all—gathered at Liberty Hall (providentially, Stephens thought). Something in their blood seemed to draw then together in this hour of crushing defeat. Perhaps it was the same force that drew them all—all but William Grier Stephens, still hobbled by a leg wound—to the old cemetery, there to stand in solemn stillness by the gravesides.[102]

101. AHS to LS, April 20, 1865, in Johnston and Browne, *Stephens*, 487.
102. Avary (ed.), *Stephens' Recollections*, 141–42.

XXI

The Man No Longer

They put him in a cell, like a common criminal, a damp, chilly cell slightly below the waterline at Fort Warren in Boston harbor. And they clamped on many restrictions. He stayed in his cell except for a one-hour daily walk; he was forbidden communication with anyone, verbal or written. On his walks no one could approach him, least of all the other rebel prisoner at the fort, former postmaster general John Reagan.

He had arrived on May 25, 1865, two weeks to the day after a detachment of the 4th Iowa Cavalry had arrested him at his house in Crawfordville. They took him to General Emory Upton's headquarters in Atlanta. On the fourteenth, on the way to Savannah and the packet steamer that would carry him North, Stephens stopped again at Crawfordville to fill a trunk with everything he thought he might need. Saying good-bye nearly broke his heart; all his slaves wept, and so did many in the huge crowd at the train platform, "old friends," he described them, who had come from miles around to grasp his hand and wish him well. Two young black servants, Anthony and Henry, whom he intended to release at Washington, were allowed to go with him.

In Augusta, Stephens joined a group of other Confederate prisoners: Davis, Senator Clement C. Clay, Reagan, General Joseph Wheeler and several of his officers, plus assorted wives, children, and servants. On the tug from Augusta to Savannah Stephens finally had to confront Davis, a meeting he had been avoiding ever since he had learned of his capture. Their conversation, though not unfriendly, was "far from cordial," Stephens said.

The trip from Savannah to Fortress Monroe on the steamer *Clyde* passed pleasantly enough. Most of the passengers got seasick, including young Anthony, whom Stephens tended in his own cabin for most of the trip. What some passengers interpreted as standoffishness—he took fewer turns on the deck than others—was in fact Stephens' habitual concern for one of his "people." Even so, Stephens ate his meals with the rest of the captives up on deck and from all indications got along well with everyone. Davis even came down to Stephens' cabin for a "long and friendly talk" the second day out from Savannah.

The captives were separated at Hampton Roads. Stephens and Reagan were taken aboard the steam-propelled war sloop *Tuscarora* for the voyage to Boston. Stephens' final meeting with Davis stuck in his mind. Davis "gave my hand a cordial squeeze," Stephens wrote shortly afterward, and spoke but a single word—"goodbye." They might have been enemies before, but now for all they knew, the same fate awaited them both. Defeat had been a great leveler.[1]

As it turned out, Davis suffered a far worse ordeal than Stephens—a two-year incarceration at Fortress Monroe, at times manacled in leg irons, constantly guarded, his cell illuminated twenty-four hours a day. By contrast, Stephens spent only four months and nineteen days in prison. He was confined to his cell until July 29, 1865. From then until mid-August he was given free run of the fort and allowed visitors and "indulgence in fruits, food, and beverages" he found agreeable. Rarely after this did a day pass without the arrival of a fruit basket or box of other treats from kindly Bostonians. On August 20, by special order of President Andrew Johnson, he was removed to a more comfortable room, where he stayed until his release on October 13.[2]

The first few weeks were the worst: coarse food, close confinement,

---

1. Official correspondence on Stephens' trip to Fort Warren and the terms of imprisonment are in *Official Records*, Ser. II, Vol. VIII, 558, 559, 562, 568, 572, 574–75; Avary (ed.), *Stephens Recollections*, 99–126, contains the account of his arrest and trip to Fort Warren; see also Leeland Hathaway Recollections, Vol. 8, in SHC/NC.

2. E. D. Townsend to Joseph Hooker, July 27, 1865, in *Official Records*, Ser. II, Vol. VIII, 712.

no letters, and loneliness. He wept frequently, pining for Linton, for the sight of his family, his servants, his home. Naturally his health suffered. "The Prisoner," as he called himself, blamed his physical problems on the lack of conversation with friends. This "natural nourishment of the mind," he said, would have strengthened the body.

But he quickly adjusted to the routine. Never in his entire life did he admit to boredom. Even in prison he kept himself occupied. His captors permitted him newspapers and books from the fort's library from the first. During his confinement he read an astonishing number of books. Characteristically, none was light, fluffy stuff: Cicero, Aristotle, Bacon, Matthew Arnold's *Essays in Criticism*, Horace Greeley's *American Conflict*, William H. Prescott's histories of Spain and Mexico, Swedenborg, not to mention biographies and poetry. He read the Bible daily, mostly the New Testament, and Psalms and Job from the Old Testament. He also wrote letters—although he was not allowed to receive any until June—and kept a detailed diary.

He noticed how white his hair had turned and how badly he needed his glasses. He paced his room for exercise. And he thought. His mind flitted from here to there—his boyhood; his father and mother, so long dead; secession and how foolish it had been; Davis and how miserably he had handled things; the little mouse in his cell that try as he might he couldn't tame; the bouquet of flowers from the prison commandant's pretty little girl; friends; God; home; and Linton, always Linton.

The minute they let him, Linton came to Boston to be with his brother. He arrived on September 1 and stayed until Aleck's release. During the last few weeks Stephens had all the "natural nourishment of the mind" he could have wished. Several other Georgians also visited. Citizens of Boston and other northerners called. When he took his leave of them, Stephens left a host of friends behind—his guards, orderly, and the fort's commandant and physician not the least among them.[3]

Under the provisions of President Johnson's amnesty and pardon proclamation of May 29, 1865, prominent Confederates had to apply to the president directly for pardons. Not sure how Johnson might receive such an application from him, Stephens considered the matter for a few days before writing the president on June 8. It took Stephens

3. The preceding paragraphs are based on Avary (ed.), *Stephens Recollections*, *passim*.

twenty-three respectful pages to present his case. No man had been "less responsible" for the "late troubles" than himself, he argued, reviewing his political career, his devotion to states' rights and the Constitution, his abhorrence for slavery "in the abstract," and his opposition to secession.[4]

The prisoner in solitary confinement waited three long weeks for the busy president to respond, and when he heard nothing, Stephens wrote again, far less deferentially this time. Johnson's silence had proven to Stephens that "my case does not come within the proffered tender of . . . clemency . . . . I did not, and do not, wish to be considered a bare suppliant for mercy." He did not feel he had done anything "criminal before God or man" during the war, Stephens continued, and he would be a hypocrite to pretend otherwise. Having been held without charges for seven weeks, Stephens now demanded his rights under the Constitution to be tried for his crime.[5]

This letter got Johnson's attention. (Indeed, the next time Stephens wrote he thanked the president profusely for easing the terms of his confinement.) The barrage of letters in the Georgian's behalf that the president received from so many people no doubt helped also. The frail little prisoner had a host of friends working to obtain his release. There were Georgians in profusion, of course: Linton, Herschel Johnson, Joe Brown, J. A. Stewart, and provisional governor James Johnson (both prominent unionists during the war). A surprising number of former enemies, including abolitionist politicians Charles Sumner and Henry Wilson, and several Union generals: Grant, George H. Thomas, Nathanial J. Jackson, and James Steedman, the present commander in Georgia, also lent their influence. Secretary of State Seward spoke for Stephens in the cabinet. Even Stanton, hardly a man inclined toward mercy for rebels, had to admit that Stephens had complained bitterly to the Confederate authorities about the treatment of Union prisoners at Andersonville.[6]

By October, when Johnson authorized Stephens' release on parole, the president considered his own plan for reconstructing the southern

4. AHS to Andrew Johnson, June 8, 1865, in Johnson Papers, LC.
5. *Ibid.*, June 27, 1865.
6. *Ibid.*, July 29, 1865; J. A. Stewart to Johnson, July 9, 1865, Thomas Ewing to Johnson, June 29, 1865, in Amnesty Papers, Georgia, Stephens, Alexander H., Record Group 94, Folder 4190, B. F. Nourse to Charles Sumner, June 15, 1865, in Union Provost Marshal's File of One-Name Papers Re Citizens, Record Group 109, all in NA; Stewart to Johnson, Stewart to AHS, August 12, 1865, Francis T. Willis to AHS, August

states well under way. (Johnson would announce the Union restored in his first annual message to Congress on December 6, 1865.) He had already recognized the "loyal" governments Lincoln had set up in four southern states; in the other seven he had appointed provisional governors empowered to call conventions made up of "loyal" citizens. These conventions had to repeal the secession ordinances, abolish slavery, repudiate the Confederate war debt, and set up dates for the election of new state officials and legislatures, which would in turn ratify the Thirteenth Amendment.[7]

Stephens' influence, commented the New York *Tribune*, "was too valuable to be longer compressed within four stone walls." He ought to be freed to "aid in correcting Southern opinion." The president no doubt agreed. Moderates like Stephens, who would support his policy, belonged at home. Indeed, the Georgian had pledged his unreserved support to Johnson during an interview at the White House on his way back to Georgia. Stephens did most of the talking during the ninety-minute conversation, and aside from urging Johnson to release Davis on parole, he stuck to public affairs. As for the slaves, Stephens was "perfectly willing" that they be free. Moreover, he didn't think blacks ought to be excluded from the polls—although he admitted this would be a matter for the states to decide. The franchise should be limited to those who "could come up to some proper standard of mental and moral culture with . . . a specified amount of property." Not only would this help break the strength of the radical Republicans in Congress, who favored a more thoroughgoing political and racial reconstruction policy, but it would offer worthy inducements for the blacks themselves, Stephens thought.[8]

While in prison Stephens had given the new position of southern blacks considerable thought. He of course believed in their inherent

5, 1865, all in Stephens Papers, LC; AHS to Ulysses S. Grant, September 16, 1865, in Avary (ed.), *Stephens Recollections*, 506–507; AHS to Henry Wilson, September 13, 1865, in Henry Wilson Papers, LC; LS to AHS, August 27, 1865, in Stephens Papers, LC; Thomas T. Eckert to Edwin Stanton, September 12, 1865, in *Official Records*, Ser. II, Vol. VIII, 746.

7. Executive order for Stephens' release in *Official Records*, Ser. II, Vol. VIII, 763–64.

8. New York *Tribune*, quoted in Jonathan Truman Dorris, *Pardon and Amnesty Under Lincoln and Johnson: The Restoration of the Confederates to Their Rights and Privileges, 1861–1898* (Chapel Hill, 1953), 250; AHS to John A. Stephens, March 16, 1878, in Stephens Papers, EU; Avary (ed.), *Stephens Recollections*, 136, 536–37.

inferiority to whites. But unlike many of his fellow white southerners, he candidly admitted that to deprive this large population of any "direct or indirect" voice in the government "would not only be an anomaly in Representative Government but would be manifestly wrong upon the principles of wisdom and justice." Without some representation, "their condition," he thought, "will be worse than that of the Astects in Mexico and not much better than that of the Gipsies in all countries of Europe. Ultimate extinction would probably be their doom."[9]

Stephens envisioned a rather curious basis for black participation in the government. Writing to Linton in June, while Georgia considered its new state constitution, Stephens proposed a novel system of representation. The population would be "divided into classes according to professions, pursuits, interests, and conditions." Blacks would be one of these classes but could choose their representatives from any other class. It might be necessary at first to restrict their franchise or limit their choice to white men only or delay putting the plan into effect for a few years, but Stephens believed political rights ought to be given the freedmen for the South's own future good. Under such a system, he thought, the blacks "for years to come" would probably choose white men to watch over their interests.[10]

It never occurred to Stephens that the "inferior race" might have difficulty seeing the justice of this plan. Maybe it should have. He had always believed the black race as a whole should be kept in proper subordination but never could reconcile this dogma with his own experience. He loved and trusted Harry and his wife Eliza implicitly, as he did almost every other black on his place. Once his people had been freed, the vast majority of them stayed and worked individual plots Stephens rented to them for one-quarter of the crop. (Stephens divided his thousand acres into five individual farms, each rented to the head of a family.) He still treated them like family, and they still doted on him. The war and freedom had not changed that.[11]

But both these forces had wrought a social and economic revolution in the South. Moderate southerners may not have realized the extent of the change, but they did know that racial harmony, not to mention future southern prosperity, required substantial concessions from

9. AHS to LS, July 4, 1865, in Stephens Papers, MC.
10. AHS to LS, June 27, 1865, in Avary (ed.), *Stephens Recollections*, 273–74.
11. Johnston and Browne, *Stephens*, 488–89.

whites. Stephens was prepared to make quite a few, beginning with un-trammeled property rights for blacks. Beyond this he even envisioned qualified blacks being allowed to hold office after a relatively short time. Education, too, ought to be extended to as many blacks as wanted it, to whatever level they could achieve. As the superior race, he thought, whites had a moral obligation to protect and care for the former slaves. If white southerners lived up to their obligation, not only would racial harmony be assured, but so would the immemorial *status quo* between the races.

And this, after all, was what Stephens wanted. The evil ("in the abstract") institution of slavery had arisen inevitably, unfortunately, out of peculiar historical circumstances in the South as an absolutely necessary method of racial control. With slavery gone the South would have to devise another method, a humane and generous one, of course, but one that preserved the basic antebellum racial arrangement nonetheless. The war and the demise of slavery had not changed that aim—not in Stephens' mind.

Nor had many other southerners' minds changed either. Bill Arp, the pseudonymous mock hard-scrabble scribbler, voiced the feelings of thousands: "I'm doin my durndest to harmonize, [but] when I see a black guard goin around the streets with a gun on his shoulder, why right then, for a few minutes, I hate the whole Yanky nation. . . . Why the whole of Afriky has come to town, women and children and babies and baboons and all. . . . They won't work for us, and they won't work for themselves. . . . The truth is, my friend, sumbody's badly fooled about this bizness. . . . These niggers will have to go back to the plantations and work. I ain't agoin to support nary one of 'em." [12]

Stephens never would have been so crude or vulgar; he deplored the thinly disguised undercurrent of violence in such views. The South, he believed, had much more effective ways to ensure her protection. She could stand as she had always stood: on her rights under the Constitution.

After four years of bloodshed and destruction, hundreds of thousands of deaths, millions of dollars in property damage, 4 million slaves freed, the South ravaged from one end to the other, Alexander Stephens still refused to see the truth: it simply did not matter how he interpreted the Constitution. It had not mattered before, and it would

12. Bill Arp to Artemus Ward, in Rome *Courier*, September 21, 1865.

matter least of all now. The world he had once helped rule was gone. He had become a relic.

And yet for the rest of his life he would pretend it wasn't so. For him it could not be so. Now more than ever he felt compelled to prove himself before the people. Only once before in his long public life had he ever spurned public office, at his retirement from Congress in 1859. He never would again. Only office, the repeated endorsement of the people, their stamp of approval on his worth, met Stephens' deepest needs. He had to have it, had to stay in the public eye—and its heart. He had to keep his bony hands on what levers of power he could still reach. Either that or confront the awful truth: that the South no longer needed him—or his ideas.

Stephens arrived back in Crawfordville on October 26, 1865, appalled by the devastation he had seen on his journey. "Change, change, indelibly stamped upon everything I meet, even upon the faces of the people!" he remarked sadly. Even Liberty Hall and the surrounding grounds, though familiar, seemed bleakly different. But it was home, and for the moment he needed nothing else.[13]

While Stephens bustled about catching up on his many neglected affairs, a state constitutional convention got down to business in Milledgeville, revising Georgia's fundamental law to meet President Johnson's minimal demands for restoration to the Union. A conservative body, elected only by voters who met Johnson's general amnesty provisions, it wasted no time in repealing Georgia's secession ordinance, abolishing slavery, and repudiating over $18 million in Confederate debt. Other articles in the new constitution directed the legislature to pass laws protecting the personal, property, and legal rights of the freedmen, as well as forbidding interracial marriage. Six days after the convention adjourned on November 9, Georgians went to the polls to elect a governor and legislature. Charles L. Jenkins, an old Whig and antisecessionist, ran unopposed for governor. Since the election was held under the new constitution (under which all normally eligible Georgians could vote) the legislature elected with him contained a goodly number of former Confederates.[14]

The composition of the assembly did not bode well for the future of

13. Avary (ed.), *Stephens Recollections*, 538–39.
14. Alan Conway, *The Reconstruction of Georgia*, (Minneapolis, 1966), 42–58.

sweet reason in Georgia's dealings with the national government. War-time unionists had fared badly even in the poll for the convention. Stephens was already receiving ominous warnings about the probable fate of "the true Union men, if [the secessionists] get the reins once more." His friend Henley Smith declared himself "disgusted at finding the people everywhere so disgracefully whipped and so much like vile spaniels." Henry Cleveland evidently ran with a different pack. "Our people are yet crazy," he told Stephens. People who had favored peace were being denounced as "d——d reconstructionists." A "large class" believed slavery would be restored. "Linton is cursed here on the report he favors Negro suffrage, Negro evidence, and Negro equality all through." [15]

"Why don't they rekonstrukt the niggers if they are ever goin to?" sneered Bill Arp. "If the abolishunists had let us alone we would have fixed it up right a long time ago, and we can fix it up now." Arp despised the president and all his plans. "Who's sorry? Who's repentin? Who ain't proud of our people? Who loves our enemies? Nobody but a durned sneak. I say let 'em be hanged and be hanged to 'em, before I'd beg 'em for grace." [16]

For people who, like Stephens, favored Johnson's reconstruction policy, such attitudes courted real danger. At all costs Georgia's chief executive had to steer the state toward compliance with this policy. Stephens had even been ready to assume the disagreeable burden himself, despite the obligatory denial of his interest in the office issued to the press. An old friend, Judge O. A. Lochrane of Macon, however, knew Stephens would accept and was supposed to convey this to the convention. He didn't speak soon enough, according to one witness. When word got out that Little Aleck would not run against Jenkins, the latter got the nomination instead. Besides Stephens and Jenkins, only one other person had support in the convention—the old chameleon himself, Joe Brown, who by this time had already received his pardon from Johnson and was testing the political waters again. [17]

Brown claimed, as "emphatically" as Stephens had, that he didn't want the office. But the truth was that Jenkins had been put up to head

15. Stewart to AHS, October 14, 1865, Smith to AHS, October 20, 1865, Cleveland to AHS, October 28, 1865, all in Stephens Papers, LC.

16. Rome *Courier*, October 26, 1865.

17. *Ibid.*, November 2, 1865; Milledgeville *Federal Union*, November 7, 1865; J. B. Dumble to AHS, November 17, 1865, in Stephens Papers, EU.

off Brown. Both would have withdrawn promptly had they known Stephens would accept. Brown said he would have nóminated Stephens himself had he known where to reach him after his release. A few days later, Brown explained that he had let his own name be used only to control matters enough "to give you or some other friend the place without a contest."[18]

This disingenuousness failed to satisfy Stephens, who for once was suspicious of Brown. It took a letter from Linton, to whom Brown gave a "very full and very satisfactory" explanation of his convention machinations, to mollify him. Jenkins also described the quandary the convention had faced. According to him, Stephens' envoy (presumably Lochrane) was "not in good odor" or credible with Georgians.[19]

Stephens lost little time mourning his lost opportunity. Another even more glittering office beckoned. Many Georgians wanted to elect him to the United States Senate. Even before the new legislature convened on December 4, 1865, Stephens had received many letters on the subject. He wasn't sure what to do. Linton decidedly opposed the idea. To him the "whole *new* regime [was] a usurpation and an iniquity." Toombs, in self-imposed exile in Paris, offered even stronger advice. "I deeply regret your purpose to go back to Federal councels," he said. He saw no difference between Johnson and Sumner's radical followers. Both favored black suffrage, and for Toombs that made them guilty of the most heinous sin imaginable.[20]

In his correspondence Stephens seemed uncertain about running, but he clearly wanted the office. His most troublesome problem was his inability to take the test or so-called ironclad oath required of all federal officials, swearing that he had not willingly aided the Confederacy in any way. Another obstacle was the as yet unresolved charge of treason against him. If the right people in Washington could be reached, however, even these problems could be solved. And he was working on it. Along with the excellent political contacts his rejuvenated legal business afforded, Stephens cultivated the friendship of important army officers in Georgia. General Steedman, the army commander,

18. Brown to AHS, November 9, 1865, in Phillips, (ed.), *TSC Correspondence*, 670–71; Brown to AHS, November 14, 1865, in Stephens Papers, EU.

19. LS to AHS, November 20, 1865, in Stephens Papers, MC; Jenkins to AHS, November 17, 1865, in Stephens Papers, EU.

20. AHS to LS, November 12, 1865, LS to AHS, November 22, 1865, both in Stephens Papers, MC; Toombs to AHS, December 15, 1865, in Phillips (ed.), *TSC Correspondence*, 673–75.

was one, Davis Tillson, the head of the Freedmen's Bureau, another. Steedman, just as interested in Little Aleck's prospects as many Georgians, asked the president directly whether running for the Senate would violate Stephens' parole.[21]

The president replied by wire promptly and pointedly. It would be "exceedingly impolitic" for Stephens' name to be put forward. He would not be allowed to take his seat; he could not take the test oath. Stephens could do far more good as an influential private citizen. Steedman should feel free to confer with Stephens, Johnson continued, but "not as coming from me." Johnson hardly needed to have Georgia elect the former vice-president of the Confederacy to the Senate. Other southern states had already begun making a mockery of his policy by electing similarly prominent rebels. "It seemed something like defiance," Johnson remarked, "which is all out of place at this time."[22]

Out of place or not, Stephens persisted. He had seen the president's telegram, but it had been equivocal enough for him to probe further. Herschel Johnson had just returned from Washington. Had he heard how the "Administration" might view his election to the Senate? Indeed, Johnson told him, he had mentioned to the president that Stephens would probably be elected senator but received no reply. Others in the capital had been enthusiastic.[23]

Despite this encouraging news, Stephens tacked his course again in early January. Martin J. Crawford, who had also gone to Washington to secure a pardon, warned Stephens that the Republicans would not seat any southern congressmen. Nor would Stephens' election help him get a pardon because the president would fear northern reaction. On the eighth Stephens told a friend he had determined to take no public position; he would do all he could privately "for the earliest possible restoration of civil law."[24]

Several days later he reiterated this decision in a public letter to several members of the assembly. Declining a request that he speak, he issued an "explicit and emphatic" prohibition against his being nominated for the Senate. Much as he desired a speedy restoration of peace

21. Rebecca Latimer Felton, *My Memories of Georgia Politics* (Atlanta, 1911), 38; Davis Tillson to AHS, December 26, 1865, in Stephens Papers, LC.

22. Johnson to Steedman, November 24, 1865, in *Official Records*, Ser. II, Vol. VIII, 818.

23. AHS to Herschel Johnson, December 23, 1865, in Johnson Papers, DU; Johnson to AHS, January 8, 1866, in Flippin, *Johnson*, 272.

24. Crawford to AHS, January 10, 1866, AHS to S. J. Henderson, January 8, 1866, both in Stephens Papers, LC.

and harmony, he saw no hope that his services would be available. He didn't even want a complimentary vote. The legislature refused to listen, however, and claimed the right to bestow the public trust on whomever it chose. It asked whether Stephens serve if elected even against his wishes. Under these circumstances, he could hardly refuse. If the people of Georgia assigned him to the position, he told the assembly, he could not imagine "any probable case in which I would *refuse* to serve."[25]

And so he was elected. Stephens crushed his opponent, wartime unionist Joshua Hill, 152 to 38 on the first ballot. Herschel Johnson was elected with him for the short term. Hill had argued strenuously in a speech to the legislature that it would be a "profound mistake" to elect men who couldn't take the test oath. The assembly thought otherwise. Inability to take the oath did not signify disloyalty to the present government. In fact, Stephens and Johnson were the best possible choices, prominent antisecessionists who had not deserted the state when it left the Union. Whether the North would accept them, the Atlanta *Intelligencer* blandly remarked, it had no way of knowing. But they were offered as representatives of a people "loyal at heart," who would now bear faithful allegiance to the government. Indeed, as sixty members of the assembly said in a public letter, secessionists and original Union men had been united in choosing Stephens, "the Prophet who had warned us against the fatal error, which we all now lament and are anxious to correct. Instead of being an act of disloyalty, [electing them] was just the reverse."[26]

Joshua Hill interpreted his defeat much differently. He told General Sherman that most Georgians, including Stephens and Johnson, refused to trust the wartime unionists. Furthermore, both senators-elect, whom the once-bitter secessionists now honored and forgave, would rather Georgia be unrepresented in the Senate unless the test oath were repealed. "The government will lose nothing by refusing to relax fur-

25. AHS to Messrs J. F. Johnson, Charles H. Smith *et al.*, January 22, 1866, in Augusta *Chronicle and Sentinel*, January 27, 1866; AHS to H. R. Casey, Wm Gipson *et al.*, January 29, 1866, in Johnston and Browne, *Stephens*, 490.

26. Hill's speech in Augusta *Chronicle and Sentinel*, February 6, 1866; Atlanta *Intelligencer*, February 2, 1866, quoted in Michael Perman, *Reunion Without Compromise: The South and Reconstruction, 1865–1868* (Cambridge, Eng., 1973), 159; "Friends of Hon. A. H. Stephens in the Georgia Legislature" to editors of the Macon *Telegraph*, February 2, 1866, in Augusta *Chronicle and Sentinel*, March 9, 1866.

ther in the South at present," Hill warned. "Jeff Davis is today stronger in Georgia than Stephens."[27]

Hill was right on all counts. Shortly after the election, Herschel Johnson urged Stephens to "stand firm" and "keep me company in the agreeable task of staying home until we can be allowed to take our seats." Stephens wanted the seat, but he did not want to stay home. He wanted to go to Washington immediately and confer with the president. The secessionists, he assured Andrew Johnson, "are much more willing to listen to me now." Almost apologetically—but not quite— he explained that he had no desire for office. "Still I could not refuse the call of the people to serve them if I be permitted to do so."[28]

He could have refused of course, but that would have deprived him of this wonderful vindication of his course during the war, and it might spell the end of his political power forever. Besides, Stephens understood the violent intransigence of some of his fellow Georgians and with typical modesty believed himself the best man to counter it.

Practical considerations—Stephens' and the legislature's—meant nothing to the North. To it the election had symbolized everything still wrong with the South, which was supposed to be a thoroughly humbled enemy. Moderate Senator Lyman Trumbull of Illinois was appalled that Georgia would elect men so conspicuously instrumental in the deaths of thousands of northern patriots. Moderate Republican journals such as the New York *Times* thought it "unfortunate" that stauncher unionists had been bypassed and wondered at the "strange system of reasoning" that interpreted Stephens' refusal to be considered for office as the "strongest argument" for electing him anyway. Southern Republican sheets were embarrassed. Georgia's and the other southern states' course could only put weapons in the hands of the radicals.[29]

Stephens didn't trouble himself about such things; he had agreed to deliver a speech to the assembly. He spoke on the night of February 22, 1866, exhibiting both common sense and a clear indication that his understanding of the nature of Union—states " 'separate as the billows but one as the sea' "—had not been changed in the least by the failed

27. Joshua Hill to W. T. Sherman, February 5, 1866, in William T. Sherman Papers, LC.

28. Herschel Johnson to AHS, February 1, 1866, in Flippin, *Johnson*, 273; AHS to Andrew Johnson, February 5, 1866, in Avary (ed.), *Stephens Recollections*, 543–44.

29. Lyman Trumbull to "Mrs. Gary," June 27, 1866, in Lyman Trumbull Papers, LC; New York *Times*, February 7, 11, 1866; Memphis *Morning Post*, February 8, 1866.

"experiment" of the last four years. He urged Georgians to exercise a "spirit of forbearance" among themselves and put their hopes in the president's policy. He pleaded for both North and South to abandon their prejudices. Slavery was dead and gone, and irrevocable change had to be accepted. Moreover, "wise and humane" provisions ought to be made for the freedmen. All rights of person, liberty, and property ought to be secured for them by law. The white race had to accept an increased moral responsibility for the blacks. Hence, not only should their rights be secured, but education should be opened to them as well.[30]

Whatever good Stephens hoped his words would have, his speech garnered almost universal acclaim. He had spoken from both his heart and his head, pleading not only for justice but for mutual charity and generosity. Letters of praise poured into Crawfordville from across the country; the New York *Times* commended the speech; the Georgia assembly passed resolutions endorsing it. Delighted with its reception, Stephens had several hundred copies of the speech printed and sent across the country. Linton observed the "remarkable spectacle" presented by the "extreme men . . . of both sections" uniting in "loud praise for the same *speech*."[31]

Within a month the assembly followed Stephens' lead and passed laws protecting the freedmen's personal, property, and legal rights. Georgia, unlike other southern states, did not pass an outrageously discriminatory black code. The state's new criminal statutes were color blind, as were its vagrancy, apprentice, and enticement laws. Having done this much, Georgia waited expectantly to be readmitted as a full-fledged member of the Union. In proudly reporting to the president, Stephens remarked, "this it does seem to me should be sufficient." The state had done nothing about black suffrage of course. That subject, Stephens remarked blandly, ought to be left where the Constitution left it—with the states.[32]

The United States Congress, however, hardly intended to leave the suffrage question with the states or the reconstruction of the Union in

30. Speech in Cleveland, *Stephens*, 804–18.

31. J. Dent to AHS, March 7, 1866, in Stephens Papers, LC; AHS to LS, February 29, March 4, 1866, LS to AHS, March 6, 1866, both in Stephens Papers, MC; New York *Times*, February 24, 25, 1866.

32. Conway, *Reconstruction of Georgia*, 54–56; AHS to Andrew Johnson, March 23, 1866, in Johnson Papers, LC.

Andrew Johnson's hands. Since convening in December, 1865, it had been searching for a reconstruction policy. A joint fifteen-member Committee on Reconstruction took testimony and was drafting a plan for restoring the southern states. Eventually the plan would be embodied in the Fourteenth Amendment, which was reported to Congress on April 30, 1866.[33]

Congress had entertained several other proposals before framing the amendment. A most promising one had been suggested by Senator W. M. Stewart of Nevada. Its key features called for the southern states to grant universal manhood suffrage with no disfranchisement of anyone eligible to vote in 1860. When a majority of a state's voters ratified this and a couple of other provisions—equal civil rights and repudiation of the Confederate debt—a general amnesty would be proclaimed. On March 17, Stewart sent Stephens a copy of his proposals for his opinion. Stephens pronounced the plan "the best possible settlement." The suffrage provision was undoubtedly a bitter pill, but Stephens surely envisioned a large degree of white control over the freedmen's vote to offset its most objectionable features.[34]

Unfortunately Stewart's proposal failed, a victim of the president's intransigence. On March 27, Johnson vetoed a widely supported civil rights bill that was clearly needed to protect the freedmen. A month earlier Johnson had vetoed another bill—one to extend the life of the Freedmen's Bureau, the only government agency extending direct relief to thousands of freed slaves—on similarly narrow constitutional grounds. Relations between the president and the Republican majority had been deteriorating for months. Now almost the entire party broke with him.

Stephens soon got a firsthand look at the radical Republicans, for he had been called to Washington to testify before the reconstruction committee. Because he was the most prominent southerner appearing before the committee, his testimony, given on April 1, 1866, attracted a large crowd and extensive press coverage. He repeated much of what he had recently said to the Georgia assembly. He accepted the results of the war as final, but refused to concede that secession had been uncon-

33. Eric L. McKitrick, *Andrew Johnson and Reconstruction* (Chicago, 1960), 336–50.
34. W. M. Stewart to AHS, March 17, 1866, in Stephens Papers, LC; McKitrick, *Johnson*, 342.

stitutional. Relations between the races in Georgia, he said, were "quite as good" as those anywhere else in the world between employers and employees. He praised the work of General Tillson's Freedmen's Bureau in the state and presented copies of Georgia's recently passed laws as evidence of her good intentions toward the blacks.

On the suffrage question, though, Georgia would be immovable, he said. She would not ratify a constitutional amendment making congressional representation dependent on voting population. The state had done all it would do for restoration. He personally did not object to a restricted black suffrage, but of course, this matter "belongs of constitutional right to the States to regulate exclusively." The states should be immediately restored to the Union, he said; nowhere did the constitutional power exist to require conditions for their reentry to the Union.[35]

Stephens had taken the position he would maintain for the rest of Reconstruction. Typically rendering the Constitution to suit his own thoroughly entrenched preconceptions, he failed to see how tangled his logic was. He believed the war had been fought solely over a constitutional principle. Now, even as he proclaimed that the South had accepted the results of the war—and thus the defeat of its own construction of the fundamental law—he insisted that the problems raised in the wake of the conflict be solved by the South's understanding of the Constitution. Technically he was correct: the Constitution did leave suffrage requirements to the states. But under the present circumstances this was a malleable point. Unfortunately, he could not rise above niggling over such points. He did not see the law as a living organism, growing and changing in response to history. For him, law, and especially the Constitution, was forever fixed because it rested on immutable, eternal principles that neither history nor men could change.

Congress, however, was dealing with much more than suffrage requirements. It was trying to define the nature of citizenship in the United States. What responsibility did the national government have when a state or group of states denied fundamental rights to a large number of residents? To this Stephens would unhesitatingly reply: "Only such responsibility as the states would allow the federal government to have."

35. Testimony in Cleveland, *Stephens*, 819–33.

The answer had been grossly inadequate in 1861; it was no better in 1866. Unreconstructed rebels came in many guises. Some, like Toombs, kicked and cussed till they died. Others simply could not or would not understand that the war had changed the nation, its Constitution, and the South irrevocably. Stephens was one of these. In his own way he remained as unreconstructed as anyone.

Stephens' intransigence had enraged the radicals. "Your answers," reported a friend, "they say were not only 'defiant,' but 'impudent' & 'insolent.'" This attitude was difficult to discern, however, because at a large reception at the White House on the night of April 8 the radicals treated Little Aleck like an honored guest. People from every point on the political spectrum seemed genuinely glad to see him, Stephens reported. He tried to stay in the background, but men sought him out. Even the "most rabid" radicals conversed "freely and fully" with him and "curiously" said they preferred him in the Senate to any other man in the South.[36]

The only other person at the gathering who attracted as much attention as Stephens was the hero of the hour, Ulysses S. Grant. Stephens had already made it a point to call on the general. "Unsophisticated, honest, and unambitious" though Grant was, Stephens found himself "still well pleased with his whole manner." Grant's assessment of the radicals' policy for southern reconstruction had been even more heartening. It made enemies out of friends instead of the other way around, he said.[37]

While in Washington Stephens learned the substance of the radicals' policy. The South would have to ratify the Fourteenth Amendment. Under its provisions blacks were defined as citizens and congressional representation was circumscribed for states refusing them suffrage. Confederates who had previously held state or federal office would be barred from these offices, but this disability could be removed by a two-thirds vote of Congress. Finally, the Confederate debt had to be repudiated.

Stephens had nothing but contempt for the plan. It arose, he said, not from any "real philanthropic sentiment for the Negroes," but from "nothing but a desire for power." But he realized that the plan would

36. James Hambleton to AHS, May 11, 1866, in Stephens Papers, EU; AHS to LS, April 8, 1866, in Stephens Papers, MC.
37. Johnston and Browne, *Stephens*, 492.

appeal to northern voters in the fall, a situation the South could have avoided by allowing a "wisely restricted" suffrage for blacks in its new state constitutions. He considered the civil rights bill Congress had passed over Johnson's veto less important because it would not affect Georgia directly. But "a great error in principle" had been made when Congress assumed jurisdiction over these matters. The South should "accept and obey the law in good faith," he told a reporter. Obviously it represented the congressional "temper and determination" on civil rights for the freedmen.[38]

"I am the man here no longer," Stephens wrote President Johnson on his departure from Washington. Little did he realize at the time that he was describing the rest of his political career. With the indomitable tenacity of utter certitude, Alexander Stephens would spend the balance of his life defending principles that, like himself, had become casualties of history. Fortunately, he, unlike most his fellow southerners, would abide by a maxim he often quoted to others: "A wise man must take things as he finds them and do the best he can with them as they are."[39]

Heeding his own advice enabled him to survive. Incredibly, Stephens remained basically optimistic through the next seventeen years, through some of the worst physical pain he ever experienced, through Radical Reconstruction—a ravishment of his cherished principles he could not have imagined in his worst nightmares—through the death of Linton, who meant more to him than life itself. Somehow in the midst of all these trials, Stephens managed to find the key to contentment. For old age had graced him with its greatest gift: wisdom. He stopped fighting life and simply lived it, accepting himself and his place in God's mysterious, unfathomable plan. As he grew older, Stephens found solace and strength in the sturdy Protestant faith he had abandoned in his youth. Belief in God's inscrutable providence allowed Stephens finally to believe in himself. It brought him peace.

And, withal, life was not unduly unkind to him. During his final years Stephens enjoyed the love of a host of friends and relatives and the respect and devotion of most of the people in Georgia. His nephews, John and Linton A. Stephens (his brother John's sons), both lived in

38. AHS to LS, April 8, 1866, in Stephens Papers, MC; New York *Times*, April 13, 1866.
39. AHS to Johnson, April 17, May 10, 1866, in Johnson Papers, LC; AHS to LS, January 3, 1866, in Stephens Papers, MC.

Crawfordville, the first serving as his uncle's secretary. Liberty Hall was his, and so was the farm. His legal business prospered, as did a few of his investments. And against all odds, for his writing was undistinguished and his ideas out of season, he made handsome sums as an author. And there was politics, of course, as always almost the breath of life to him.

But for the next few years he almost suffocated. During the summer of 1866, after much vacillation and at the strong urging of some prominent northern Democrats, Stephens accepted his appointment as a delegate to the so-called National Union Convention in Philadelphia. The convention, billed as a bipartisan gathering of all President Johnson's supporters, ended up being dominated by Democrats and southerners. Conservative Republicans, fast becoming an extinct breed, hardly appeared among the rank-and-file delegates. In the end the convention turned out about as consequential as Stephens' attendance. Suffering from "his old disorder of the bowels," Stephens was delayed on the trip, and upon his arrival, he had to stay in his hotel room.[40]

By this time Johnson had burned all his bridges with Congress, publicly proclaiming it and its creation, the Fourteenth Amendment, as revolutionary. His speaking tour across the North to stump for conservative candidates in the off-year congressional elections turned into an unmitigated disaster. Almost everywhere hecklers hounded him and the press raked him. Moreover, his intemperate retorts made him look foolish and debased his office. Northern voters responded to the embarrassing spectacle by electing scores of anti-Johnson men to Congress in the fall.

Initially hopeful after the Philadelphia convention, Stephens soon realized the true direction of events. As the extent of the radical gains became clear, he told Herschel Johnson that prospects looked gloomier than at any time in the past six years. Toombs, still in Paris, said it appeared to him that a large majority in the North intended to keep the South out of the government "for a generation." Radicals wanted to turn the government over to "traitors and negroes"—which was not much different from Johnson, who would give the government to traitors and let them handle the black suffrage question "as they pleased."[41]

40. AHS to Montgomery Blair, July 13, 1866, in Blair Family Papers, LC; AHS to James L. Orr, August 10, 1866, in Patterson-Orr Papers, SHC/NC; AHS to Connel, August 19, 1866, in Stephens Papers, MC.

41. AHS to Johnson, August 31, September 27, 1866, in Johnson Papers, DU; Toombs to AHS, September 28, 1866, in Stephens Papers, LC.

It pleased Georgia's assembly to endorse Toombs's views of black suffrage overwhelmingly. On November 9, 1866, it rejected the Fourteenth Amendment. Only two brave legislators in the House cast votes
in its favor. Stephens no doubt approved the assembly's course, but
some Georgians doubted it. For the past two weeks Little Aleck had
been trying to squelch press rumors that both he and Linton favored
ratification of the amendment as Georgia's most expedient course. Perhaps its plausibility gave the tale currency. After all, both of them had
endorsed limited black suffrage.[42]

But the report was false, and Stephens placed his categorical denial
in several papers. The public had to be content with this because he
refused to be drawn into publicly discussing the question on the eve of
several state elections. But in private correspondence, he spoke more
candidly. The suffrage question didn't rankle him nearly as much as the
injustice, the gross irregularity of what was being done: "The whole
program of this constitutional amendment I consider an absurd mockery of the Southern States. To say nothing of its injustice. If the States
are sufficiently *in the Union* to vote on a constitutional amendment
they are sufficiently *in* to have a voice in proposing it." The South, he
continued, should maintain a dignified silence like a prisoner of war.
Retorts, "even discussion," would do no good. He "utterly opposed"
the "States doing anything as a condition precedent to the restoration
of all their rights."[43]

Practicing what he preached, Stephens now withdrew into a proper
"dignified silence." Rather than fight current battles, he had decided to
relive old ones. Several publishers had approached him while he had
been in prison about writing a book. After several weeks of agonizing
over it—and the obligatory consultation with Linton—Aleck decided
in mid-September to make a "new departure in life" and signed a con-
tract with the National Publishing Company of Philadelphia for a six-
to eight-hundred-page volume on the war. The publishers advanced
Stephens four thousand dollars on his promise to produce the work in
twelve months, and indeed they would have sent "any amount desired." Books on the war were in great demand. A book by a high-

42. Conway, *Reconstruction of Georgia*, 138; AHS to LS, November 2, 1866, in Stephens Papers, MC; New York *Times*, November 8, 1866.
43. Stephens' denial in Macon *Journal* [n.d.], quoted in New York *Times*, November
11, 1866; AHS to Randall, November 2, 1866, in Stephens Papers, LC.

ranking rebel like Stephens, an insider's view on the operations of the Confederate government would make them a fortune.[44]

What the expectant Yankee booksellers got from Stephens, however, was *A Constitutional View of the Late War Between the States*, a ponderous two-volume treatise on the compact theory of government and the legality of secession. Aside from a few pages on the Hampton Roads conference and several more justifying his opposition to Davis, Stephens hardly mentioned the war. Throughout the work the writing sparkled with all the brilliance of a polished mudball, and it went on forever. It wasn't history at all but a lawyer's brief for the antebellum southern interpretation of the Union.

Although most of his argument was "totally defective," according to a modern student of the work, withal the book was the "ablest defense of the Southern position ever made." The work's chief flaw—aside from its numbing length and tediousness—was its "skillful, albeit selective use of evidence." Sovereignty, Stephens argued, was indivisible; the nation had no general powers. The Constitution had not changed the nature of the Union; it had simply improved the Articles of Confederation by conferring incidental powers on the federal government. Going beyond the Kentucky and Virginia resolutions, which had proclaimed *all* states judges of the Constitution, Stephens rested his case on the primal sovereignty of each individual state. What Edmund Wilson wrote of the book was just as true of its argument: it was a "great, cold, old monument."[45]

Stephens finished the first volume on time; the second was not completed until the spring of 1870. "I doubt the spirit of the times will have much relish for the doctrines it will advocate or which it teaches," Stephens had told Mrs. Toombs upon the first volume's appearance. He was right, but it didn't appear so at first. The first volume sold an astonishing 32,289 copies in the first three months after its issue on May 1, 1868. It eventually sold over 64,000 copies, half of these before the

44. AHS to LS, September 16, 1866, in Stephens Papers, MC; AHS to Jones Brothers, September 17, 1866, Jones Brothers to AHS, October 16, December 15, 1866, all in Stephens Papers, LC.

45. Jasper Braley Reid, Jr., "The Mephistopheles of Southern Politics: A Critical Analysis of Some of the Political Thought of Alexander Hamilton Stephens, Vice President of the Confederacy" (Ph.D. dissertation, University of Michigan, 1966), 1–3 and *passim*; Edmund Wilson, *Patriotic Gore: Studies in the Literature of the American Civil War* (New York, 1962), 399.

newspaper notices came out and the public discovered the nature of the tome. Forewarned by bitter experience, not to mention hostile reviews, over half the original subscribers refused copies of the second volume. (In Newark, New Jersey, the publisher's agent actually had to sue "about 30 men of means" to force them to take it.) Even so, the second volume sold more than 20,000 copies, but only in Georgia did it achieve sales anywhere near those of the first volume.[46]

Almost any writer would have been thrilled to earn almost twenty-three thousand dollars on his first book, especially one on such a dreary topic. Not Stephens. Convinced he had penned a "great" and "unanswerable" book, he was enraged by public criticism of it and responded to his critics in maddening detail. (A collection of these long, incredibly somnolent essays was later gathered into a volume called *The Reviewers Reviewed*, which by contrast to the *Constitutional View* sold very poorly.) Even though he admitted his book contained "obsolete ideas," which he, as the "sentinel on the watchtower," felt impelled to promulgate, Stephens could not face the truth about the public's reaction to his work. People who bought the book felt cheated, and worse, bored. The author, however, blamed his publisher for the second volume's poor sales and harangued the poor man for weeks with complaints and advice on how to run his business.[47]

But at least Stephens' literary efforts kept him busy. The fearsome shadow of congressional reconstruction fell over Georgia in 1867, to remain for almost four years. Throughout the ordeal Stephens watched glumly from his house in Crawfordville, too old and often too desperately sick to do more than bemoan what he saw as the dying gasps of constitutional liberty on the continent.

With only a woebegone corporal's guard of Democrats to oppose them, the Republicans proceeded to enact their own reconstruction program for the South. Embodied in a series of bills passed from March, 1867, to February, 1868, congressional Reconstruction mandated a series of requirements before a state could be readmitted to the Union. The "unreconstructed" South—all the states but Tennessee—was divided into five military districts, each commanded by a general

46. AHS to Julia Toombs, December 31, 1867, in Toombs Papers, UG; William H. Lucas to Jones, July 25, 1870, and note of Jones to AHS thereon, July 27, 1870, Jones to AHS, August 16, 1870, both in Stephens Papers, LC.

47. AHS to Hidell, June 9, 1868, in Stephens Papers, HSP; Hidell to AHS, July 19, 1870, J. R. Jones to AHS, July 23, August 15, 1870, all in Stephens Papers, LC.

supported with troops. The Johnson state governments were abolished, and under the supervision of the district commanders the states were required to register all adult black males and all eligible whites not falling under the office-exclusion ban of the proposed Fourteenth Amendment. These voters would elect a constitutional convention, which in turn had to write a new state constitution with provision for black suffrage. After the state's voters had approved this constitution, another election would be held to choose a state government. The legislature thus elected then had to ratify the Fourteenth Amendment. Only then could a state apply for readmission to the Union.

This program was repulsive enough to most white Georgians, but even more vile was the spectacle of their former governor embracing it. In the latter part of February, 1867, just before passage of the first Reconstruction Act, the so-called Sherman bill, Joe Brown published the most sensational letter of his career. Georgia, said Brown, should submit to the law and black suffrage. In bowing to "inevitable necessity" Georgians should remember that the blacks "were raised among us and naturally sympathize with us." If treated fairly, they would "consult our interests at the ballot box." [48]

With his bloodhound's nose for the main chance, Brown certainly consulted his own interest in making this astonishing announcement. Overnight he became anathema; soon he sank even lower: he joined the Republicans, the untouchables themselves. Bob Toombs, back in Georgia from exile, quivered with fury. "He has betrayed his natural and foster mother," he raged in a speech at Cedartown. "What more can I say to commend this wretch to your detestation?" [49]

It hardly mattered to Brown what Toombs or thousands of other outraged Georgians said. He was prospering. In 1868 he was appointed chief justice of Georgia's supreme court. In addition to reaping political benefits, Brown also amassed a considerable financial fortune during Reconstruction. His instinct for the profitable, if not always completely foursquare, business venture seldom failed him. [50]

Brown's timing, more than anything he had said, disturbed Stephens. It would have been better had he waited until "the necessity was

48. Columbus *Daily Sun*, February 27, 1867, quoted in Conway, *Reconstruction of Georgia*, 140.

49. Felton, *Georgia Politics*, 65.

50. Derrell C. Roberts, *Joseph E. Brown and the Politics of Reconstruction* (University, Ala., 1973), *passim*.

more apparent," he thought, for now northern opposition to the radicals might be weakened. Still, Stephens continued in a letter to Linton, although "too hasty" and "indiscrete," Brown had his sympathy. His motives were pure. Stephens told Brown the same thing, but disagreed with his advice. "Our political doom is inevitable . . . we might just as well stand still and take what comes" instead of taking action "that may ultimately make our ruin more complete in the estimation of the world from our having done so of choice." Stephens meant to obey the law and say nothing. But he would not impede anybody feeling "more confident of success in effort of any kind than I do." As he told Brown a few months later, "If I do not do any good I shall certainly do no harm."[51]

Doing no harm meant doing nothing—and admonishing all his correspondents to keep his views to themselves. His views were hardly incendiary. Georgians got enough fire-brand rhetoric from their editors and from the volatile speeches of such people as Toombs and Ben Hill. In the summer of 1867, Hill took the lead in opposing congressional Reconstruction with a widely published group of essays called "Notes on the Situation." The twenty-two long articles raged against the unconstitutionality of the Reconstruction acts and urged Georgians to resist them with every means at their disposal.[52]

Hill and anyone else could do as they pleased as far as Stephens was concerned. He had lost all hope. Constitutional liberty quivered in its death throes. The South's inevitable ruin must eventually spread north. Neither accepting nor rejecting the congressional plan would make the slightest difference. The difference between the two, he said, was akin "to the difference between martyrdom and suicide." Like Caesar, he said, he would wrap himself in his mantle and take the fatal blows without protest.[53]

The South's hallowed racial system had been shattered. The two races could not possibly coexist peacefully in the South, Stephens said, much less cooperate politically. He never wanted to take part in public affairs again under such conditions. "We are fast abandoning the teutonic systems on which our institutions are based and are rushing fast into the Asiatic system of Empire." Linton and many others remon-

51. AHS to LS, March 2, 1867, in Stephens Papers, MC; AHS to Brown, March 8, May 9, 1867, both in McLeod Collection, UG.
52. "Notes" in Hill, *Hill*, 730–813.
53. AHS to Walter F. Staples, March 8, 1867, in Stephens Papers, LC.

strated with him. Silence was not the wisest policy, his brother urged: "We will never get help until we raise an earnest cry for it." Aleck refused even to bleat. When in the mercy of God the time came for him to speak out and do some good, he told a friend, he would. But "I am not . . . looking to such a contingency." [54]

Stephens could not register to vote for the state constitutional convention. Like most white Georgians he believed it best simply to ignore the election. Oddly, though, he required every black on his property to register. Curiously, too, he finally broke his silence on the issue of black suffrage. He could not have held his peace for long anyway. "Bye and bye," he told a New York *Times* reporter, "they will come and ask me how to vote. What can I tell them but to go with their race?" [55]

Black Georgians hardly needed Stephens' advice to know where their interests lay. Although the two races were roughly equal in the number of registered voters, most whites boycotted the election, and the convention was overwhelmingly approved. About a week after it met in Atlanta on December 9, 1867, Stephens boarded a train for Philadelphia to go and check the proofs of the first volume of his book. So while the racially mixed Republican convention rewrote Georgia's constitution to comply with congressional mandates, Stephens applied his own outrageously meticulous standards to proofreading. [56]

While in the city Stephens stayed part of the time at the house of J. R. Jones, his publisher. He rarely ventured out of doors. The weather was foul and his health poor. On one of his walks, however, he slipped on an icy sidewalk and severely bruised the sciatic nerve in his hip. Although not a crippling injury, it would plague him for the rest of his life. Having endured Stephens for several months, Jones was no doubt relieved to see his shriveled little house guest depart on a tour of the Northeast. He made a special trip to Boston to see Mrs. A. W. Salter, his provident angel from Fort Warren days. The call betokened more than simple gratitude, however, for Linton had been most taken with

54. AHS to J. Barrett Cohen, May 25, 1867, in *ibid.*; LS to AHS, March 11, 1867, in Stephens Papers, MC; AHS to Hambleton, May 30, 1867, in Hambleton Collection, EU.

55. New York *Times*, July 22, 1867. In this election, Georgia's first under the Reconstruction acts, voters had to decide for or against a constitutional convention and at the same time elect delegates in case the convention were approved.

56. Elizabeth Studley Nathans, *Losing the Peace: Georgia Republicans and Reconstruction, 1865–1871* (Baton Rouge, 1968), 34, 54–55; AHS to LS, December 17, 1867, in Stephens Papers, MC.

Salter's daughter Mary during his brief stay in Boston two years before. And ever since then Little Aleck and the girl's mother had been furiously engaged in matchmaking. Such strategy conferences must have helped, because in June, 1867, Linton married Mary and took her back to Sparta.[57]

Prominent Yankees, including Oliver Wendell Holmes and Henry Ward Beecher, among others, made it a point to call on the famous former Confederate when he was in their city. Besides being a curiosity, Stephens always charmed visitors—and reporters too. He was good copy, although Cassandra herself could not have sounded more gloomy. Everything in Georgia was wretched, he told the Philadelphia *Inquirer* in February, 1868. "Incendiaries, the offscourings of the earth," had moved in to stir up strife. If blacks got control of the state, whites would abandon it, he predicted. He couldn't really blame the poor credulous blacks, though. They had been victimized by "political emissaries," "reckless partisans," "a class of insane politicians like Thad. Stevens." "Madness reigns," he said. "We are about to destroy freedom, to build up a party and a government that will devour us." The blacks had been completely demoralized by registration, he told another reporter. Most showed little interest in working to prepare the next season's crops. Under such conditions race warfare was inevitable.[58]

It appeared to Stephens that the Republicans meant to devour everything. The shocking spectacle of President Johnson's impeachment crowned the madness. Stephens stopped by to see Johnson on his way back to Georgia in mid-March, 1868, the third day of the impeachment trial in the Senate. With tears streaming down his face, Stephens urged Johnson to undertake his own defense. "Your safety demands it," he told him. Johnson wisely disregarded the distraught Georgian's counsel. His safety, in fact, depended on a few crucial swing votes in the Senate, enough of which he eventually secured to save himself the humiliation of being removed from office.[59]

White Georgians, meanwhile, witnessed the election of a Republi-

57. Von Abele, *Stephens*, 269–70.

58. Philadelphia *Inquirer* quoted in New York *Times*, February 23, 1868; New York *Herald*, March 17, 1868, clipping in Stephens Papers, LC.

59. St. George L. Sioussat, ed., "Notes of Col. W. G. Moore, Private Secretary to President Johnson, 1866–1868," *American Historical Review*, XIX (October, 1913), 125.

can governor, Rufus Bullock, an Augusta banker and railroad developer. And shortly after this mortification came another: ratification of the odious new state constitution. Georgia's Democrats had waged an ineffective, fuzzily focused campaign. Although their gubernatorial candidate, former Confederate general John B. Gordon, had run well, his popularity could not offset superior Republican organization and the masses of effectively mobilized black voters.[60]

Frustrated in their sporadic attempts to woo the blacks, Democrats turned to less refined tactics: organized terror under the aegis of the Ku Klux Klan. By the summer of 1868 the Klan had an effective grassroots organization throughout the state. From then until 1870, when the Democrats regained control, the Klan functioned as the military arm of the Democratic party—murdering, beating, and intimidating blacks and their white supporters. Federal troops, too sparse and widely scattered, could do little to counteract the violence.

Stephens first became acquainted with the Klan upon his return from the North. On the night of March 31, 1868, in Columbus, one George W. Ashburn, a local carpetbagger and organizer of black voters, had been shot and killed in his home. A week later the military arrested ten prominent young men of the town and charged them with the crime. Several people, including his old friend Martin Crawford, asked Stephens to defend the accused. Prosecuting for the government before the military tribunal was none other than Joseph E. Brown.[61]

The trial began in Atlanta in late June but never concluded. (The next month the General Assembly ratified the Fourteenth Amendment; Bullock took office; and on July 30, 1868, Georgia was readmitted to the Union. The Ashburn case, remanded to the civil authorities in Columbus, quietly dropped from sight.) Whether any of the accused were Klan members is not clear. It made no difference to Stephens. He defended them as ably as he knew how. The mob that had stormed Ashburn's door that night had intended only to tar and feather him, he argued. Ashburn had fired the first shot and had thus been killed in self-defense. Whether a panel of federal army officers would have been convinced by this argument is doubtful, but Robert Moses, who worked with Stephens on the case, says Little Aleck had evidence to

60. Nathans, Losing the Peace, 82–87.
61. Allen W. Trelease, White Terror: The Ku Klux Klan Conspiracy and Southern Reconstruction (New York, 1971), 76–77; Edward Stephens to AHS, June 8, 1868, Crawford to AHS, June 10, 1868, both in Stephens Papers, LC.

prove perjury from several prosecution witnesses: an unimpeachable alibi for at least one of the accused.[62]

"If there is in this world anything that I do hate and abhor, it is secret political bodies," Stephens told a northern newspaperman a few weeks after the trial. But, he quickly continued, there were no such societies in Georgia—that was "pure imagination." Some "excitable young men" in various parts of the South may have gathered into oath-bound societies in hopes of becoming part of the Klan—"which was said to have existed somewhere"—but the effort to prove this in the Ashburn trial had "utterly failed" in his opinion.[63]

Or so he said in October, 1868, when every good southern Democrat was laboring mightily to elect Horatio Seymour of New York president over his Republican opponent, Ulysses S. Grant. Obviously, admitting the existence of the Klan would not have been good politics for Stephens at this juncture. Besides, he wasn't personally convinced that the Klan existed anywhere except in Tennessee.

He naturally despised the idea of a secret society dedicated to violence. He revered the law too much to countenance the indiscriminate outrages masked thugs perpetrated on blacks and whites alike. Soon enough he realized he had been wrong about the Klan's existence in Georgia. Not only was it there, but in Crawfordville itself. Its "masked desperadoes" pistol-whipped Harry's "industrious thrifty, well balanced" Uncle Joshua for the crime of condemning the violence they had done to another man. One Saturday night shortly afterward a band of twenty masked riders shot up the town, terrified the citizens, and ransacked a shop for no apparent reason. Stephens had seen these things himself, he told Hidell; were he to mention other "atrocities" he had heard of, "it would require many pages." Barely over a month later he reported that the Klan had killed three more men near Crawfordville. Bad as the radicals were, he said, the Ku Kluxers were much worse. Such madness could only strengthen the radicals' hands, thus hastening the death of liberty forever.[64]

Despite his pledge to remain silent, Stephens could not stifle the impulse to advise his fellow Georgians. In late July, 1868, for example, several papers reported that Stephens had advised the Democrats in

62. Trelease, *White Terror*, 77–78; Robert Moses Autobiography, 81–82, in SHC/NC.
63. Augusta *Chronicle and Sentinel*, October 4, 1868.
64. AHS to Hidell, January 26, March 14, 1869, in Stephens Papers, HSP.

the assembly to vote for ratification of the Fourteenth Amendment. The report was false. Little Aleck had not lost his political acumen. With his eye to the November presidential election and not wanting to hurt Seymour's chances in any way, he had urged assembly Democrats to *allow* the radicals to pass the amendment—by abstaining from voting if necessary. Defeating the amendment could do Georgia no good, he reasoned. It had already gotten the requisite number of votes from other states. Georgia's defiance could only prolong radical rule in the state and might even force a worse constitution down her throat. Even Toombs (who in other forums was urging "the boys" to load up their weapons to kill carpetbaggers and blacks) had the good sense— or perhaps sobriety—to hold his peace on this issue. "You ought not to have given your enemies so fair a chance at you," he told Stephens.[65]

For the next few weeks Stephens gave his enemies no chance to criti- cize him. After penning a letter of explanation to the *Constitutionalist,* he took off for the mineral waters of White Sulphur Springs, West Vir- ginia. He spent almost two months in these pleasant surroundings. Stephens' health was not good and had not been for most of the year. Yet this trip to the springs had more than recuperatory objects. Many of the Confederacy's most prominent military and civilian leaders had gathered there to meet with General William S. Rosecrans, the head of the Democratic national campaign committee, to plot strategy for de- feating Grant in the coming election.[66]

The waters may have helped Stephens' health—he said they had— but they hardly brightened his political outlook. In an interview with the New York *Herald,* Stephens described the political situation as "ex- ceedingly deplorable." Despotism loomed: "If Grant is elected next No- vember I never expect to see another Presidential election." In his opin- ion, Grant was "entirely underrated by the country and the press . . . just the man for a *coup d'etat.*" The fight, he continued, was not so much against this man but against "the iniquity of the dominant party that has brought the country to the verge of ruin."[67]

65. Savannah *Morning News,* July 24, 1868; AHS to Johnston, August 3, 1868, in Johnston and Browne, *Stephens,* 494–95; Hidell to AHS, August 4, 1868, in Stephens Papers, LC; Toombs to AHS, August 9, 1868, in Phillips (ed.), *TSC Correspondence,* 702.

66. AHS to Johnson, August 7, 1868, in Johnson Papers, DU; Augusta *Constitu- tionalist,* August 27, 1868.

67. Augusta *Chronicle and Sentinel,* September 25, 1868; New York *Herald* quoted in *ibid.,* September 6, 1868.

As Stephens contemplated the horrors of four more years of Republican rule, the Georgia assembly infuriated both Governor Bullock and the national Republican party. In August it refused to elect either of Bullock's two choices for the U.S. Senate. Then in September, anti-Bullock forces in both houses expelled the black members of the assembly, replacing them with runner-up Democrats in each district. And if this arrogance were not enough, the state committed the unpardonable sin of going Democratic in the November canvass.[68]

Stephens took no part in the presidential campaign. Many other Democrats, however, threw themselves into the canvass with a vengeance. Assiduous efforts by the Klan and its rabble-rousing supporters on the stump contributed substantially to Grant's defeat. The Freedmen's Bureau reported thirty-one people killed between August and October and more than a hundred whipped, shot, beaten, or stabbed. The organized savagery had its desired effect. Blacks stayed home in droves in November. The Republicans carried only 32 percent of the vote; in eleven counties Grant got no votes at all.[69]

Georgia's vote notwithstanding, Grant carried the election easily. And Stephens escaped just as easily from his doomsday mood of the summer. He hoped the South would give the new president a fair trial, he told Brown: "Personally I like General Grant as you well know." Apparently Stephens had decided to make the best of a deplorable situation. A few days later he urged Brown to use his influence with the incoming administration to refrain from making wholesale changes among Democratic officeholders, "a matter of vast importance," he said, "in restoring harmony."[70]

It would have taken a far better magician than Joe Brown to prevent the Republicans from punishing Georgia. The state's many bloody sins screamed, if not to heaven, at least to Washington, for retribution. Bullock, shorn of his power base and laden with tales of atrocities in the state, repaired to the capital to lobby for a return to military government. Congress, however, moved ponderously on the Georgia question. Not until December, 1869—after the assembly rejected the proposed Fifteenth Amendment, which barred states from disqualifying

68. C. Mildred Thompson, *Reconstruction in Georgia: Economic, Social, Political, 1865–1872* (1915; rpr. New York, 1964), 210–14.

69. Trelease, *White Terror*, 117, 119.

70. AHS to Brown, November 20, 1868, in McLeod Collection, UG; AHS to Brown, November 24, 1868, in Brown-Hargrett Collection, UG.

voters because of race—did Congress pass the Georgia Reorganization Act and return the state to military control. Backed now by force, Bullock restored the blacks ousted by the assembly in 1868 and proceeded to purge the legislature of sundry "ineligible" Democrats. This new Bullock assembly promptly ratified the Fifteenth Amendment and elected the governor's two men for the Senate.

But Bullock's triumph quickly faded. By July, 1870, Congress had tired of the whole Georgia mess and passed a resolution declaring the state entitled to representation. Bullock's legislature tried to prolong its life but failed. In the December, 1870, elections the Democrats gained overwhelming control of the assembly, and Congress promptly seated the seven Democratic representatives elected at the same time. Unaccountably, the U.S. Senate chose to overlook Bullock's two stooges and seat Joshua Hill and H. V. M. Miller, the men elected by the 1868 legislature. Hill and Miller took their seats in early 1871. The governor tried to hold on, but his days were numbered. By October, 1871, with certain impeachment charges facing him, he fled the state. On January 12, 1872, Georgia inaugurated Democrat James M. Smith as governor. The state's "redemption" had come at last.[71]

Little was heard and even less seen of Alexander Stephens during this hubbub. His health, poor throughout 1868, worsened in 1869. In December, 1868, he had been elected to the chair of history and political science at the University of Georgia, a position he wanted but had to decline because of illness. Stephens had had trouble walking ever since his fall on the ice, but in February, 1869, he sustained another injury that crippled him for the rest of his life. While hobbling about the fields surrounding Liberty Hall, he tugged at a heavy iron gate, not realizing that it was off its hinges and merely leaning against the post. It toppled over onto him, straining his left ankle and further damaging the sciatic nerve in his left hip. Excruciating pain from the injury continued for months, and not until several weeks after the accident was he even able to sit up for a few hours.[72]

Throughout his suffering Stephens remained cheerful. Propped up on pillows and dictating to an amanuensis, he doggedly continued

71. The preceding paragraphs are based on Thompson, *Reconstruction in Georgia*, 255–72.

72. AHS to Johnson, January 5, 1869, in Johnston and Browne, *Stephens*, 496; AHS to Hidell, February 25, 1869, in Stephens Papers, HSP.

working on the second volume of his book. If it could not be finished before his death, he instructed, all but the part on the Hampton Roads conference should be destroyed. Some days he couldn't work at all. On others the never-ending stream of visitors nearly drove him to distraction. These annoyances aside, Stephens accepted the prospect of having to spend the rest of his life as an invalid, shut away in his home from public life, with perfect calm.[73]

The only hint of his former melancholy came to him—and then but rarely—in dreams. "Such a dream I have not had for years!" he told Linton after one of them. "It was all in relation to myself . . . I was miserable. Miserable beyond my power of description. I was deserted by all friends. You alone showed sympathy faith and pity for me." Perhaps, he mused, it had to do with his "lonely situation bad health and want of some genial spirit with whom in language of Bacon I could give the outflowing of the inner heart."[74]

The loneliness and terror Stephens had felt as a poor little orphaned boy stalked him for most of his life. But he wasn't lonely now, despite the conjurings of his nightmares. Sadness had become a stranger to him, a thing to be feared. He only dreamed of it—and awoke, glad to be alive, happy to be working, and even a bit shaken by the fragments of his past that flitted through his subconscious. The specter of death, once so morbidly fascinating to him, had by now become so familiar that he regarded it as almost part of his environment, no more to be remarked upon than his countless medicine bottles, the wallpaper in his rooms, or the graceful trees that shaded Liberty Hall from Georgia's scorching sun. "I fear I am beginning to grow old," he had written matter-of-factly to Linton before his accident. It wasn't a lament. Like Reconstruction, like Ulysses Grant, like his tiresome visitors and his pain, Stephens simply accepted the fact.[75]

With a resignation born of long experience, Stephens submitted himself to a fantastic array of medical treatments. Doctors from all over the country, each with a "cure" for one or another of his ailments, visited Crawfordville to demonstrate its efficacy. Pills, drugs, ointments, electric shock treatments, elixirs, even what seems to have been a primitive form of acupuncture—nothing worked. Stephens would never walk unassisted again. Crutches and his "roller chair" became

---

73. AHS to Johnston, March 12, 1869, in Johnston and Browne, *Stephens*, 497.
74. AHS to LS, October 26, 1868, in Stephens Papers, MC.
75. *Ibid.*, December 14, 1868.

part of the household scenery. But he got along, living on work mostly, and a few chicken wings and bowls of soup Eliza coaxed him to eat. Linton thought his brother's recurring spells of stomach and bowel trouble resulted from working too hard on his book, but even he had to admit that "Aleck's general health, his spirits, and his mental vigor were as good just before his late back-set as I ever saw them." [76]

Stephens finished the second volume of his *Constitutional View* in April, 1870, and then plunged immediately into a new project: preparing a textbook history of the United States. Although his income more than sufficed for his personal needs, his prodigious contributions to charity and the expense of keeping an open house for anyone who happened by Liberty Hall required him to work as much as possible. He also kept a careful eye on political events, continuing to correspond with hundreds of people across the country. Occasionally one of his articles or letters would find its way into the press. Generally, however, during these years the mass of Georgians were left to wonder what Stephens thought about anything. [77]

As always, Stephens stood for order. Much as he deplored the present situation, he strongly condemned violence or resistance outside of the law. His position on resistance, in fact, did not differ radically from the one Brown had taken in early 1867. So he had no trouble cooperating with Brown in matters of mutual interest. He pushed Brown's patronage candidates with the president, for example, and joined him in opposing Bullock's purge of the legislature in early 1870. The two men did not agree on the Fifteenth Amendment, though. Nothing could compel him ever to support it, Stephens said. "Still all that I would do in opposition would be quietly and sternly to enter my protest against it." [78]

Stephens considered both Reconstruction amendments void, unconstitutionally proposed and ratified. Nobody who accepted them deserved the name Democrat. It soon became clear, however, that most Georgians disagreed. Stephens took extraordinary interest in the state Democratic convention held during the summer of 1870 for just this reason. Since he couldn't go himself, he urged Herschel Johnson—

76. AHS to Hidell, February 25, April 15, 1869, in Stephens Papers, HSP; LS to Alfriend, January 14, 1870, in Stephens Papers, LC.

77. Von Abele, *Stephens*, 273.

78. Brown to AHS, December 31, 1869, in Stephens Papers, LC; AHS to Brown, January 3, 1870, in Brown-Hargrett Collection, UG.

fruitlessly, it turned out—to go to Atlanta and help organize the party "upon sound old Democratic principles and doctrines." What he really wanted was "men who bore their banner with Stephen A. Douglas in 1860" to lead the state party.[79]

The Democrats, Stephens believed, should stand on the national platform of 1868: opposed to Reconstruction and the Fourteenth and Fifteenth Amendments and against test oaths to determine eligibility for office. Thus argued Linton, in a fiery letter accepting chairmanship of the state Democratic executive committee. The immediate outcry from the national party chairman soon forced the younger Stephens to resign his post. Northern Democrats believed that to stand on such a platform would be fatal.[80]

Many southern Democrats now thought so too. C. P. Culver, a long-time Stephens correspondent, summed up most of Democratic Georgia's reaction. It seemed, he said, "quite superfluous to make these issues just now the *leading* ideas" of a local election. Personal sacrifices had to be made, Culver continued, for the sake of getting votes in Congress, "and none more so than in the yielding of opinions where there can be no sacrifice of *principles*."[81]

Stephens saw no distinction. To acquiesce, to accept the amendments and test oaths as irreversible results of the war, as many urged him to, were as unthinkable as repudiating secession and states' rights. Linton agreed. As always, the two brothers stood united—only this time they stood virtually alone.

Before too many more months passed, Linton's bullheadedness caused serious trouble with Georgia's Republican administration. On election day in Sparta in December, 1870, Linton let his zeal for the purity of the ballot box get the better of his prudence. He had the sheriff arrest thirteen black voters who had not paid their poll taxes. When the election managers—two blacks and a white—received the votes of these men anyway, Linton had them arrested too. At the ensuing trial, Linton served as prosecutor and, according to one witness, alternately "had the whole court house in tears" and then "half-wild with excitement, scarcely able to control the hate that seethed and boiled in their

79. AHS to Robert F. Dewar, July 20, 1870, in Stephens Papers, LC; AHS to Johnson, August 15, 1870, in Johnson Papers, DU.

80. Judson C. Ward, "Georgia Under the Bourbon Democrats, 1872–1890" (Ph.D. dissertation, University of Georgia, 1947), 42–43.

81. C. P. Culver to AHS, September 13, 1870, in Stephens Papers, LC.

hearts." In their fury the townspeople of Sparta almost lynched the sixteen hapless prisoners.[82]

Naturally Bullock could not ignore such an incident, so the following month he had a federal marshal arrest Linton on charges of hindering operation of the Enforcement Act. On January 23, 1871, the younger Stephens had to appear before a federal commissioner in Macon to answer these charges. Aleck helped as much as could with his brother's defense, worrying himself half to death in the process. Eventually, as Bullock's hold on the state grew more tenuous, the charges were quashed. But the episode had shaken the two brothers severely.[83]

Fretting over Linton's possible martyrdom for the cause of constitutional liberty wasn't the only problem bedeviling Stephens in early 1871. Carelessly he had gotten himself entangled in one of Joe Brown's financial schemes, and it cost him no small amount of embarrassment before he could extricate himself. Appalled by Governor Bullock's flagrant mismanagement of the Western and Atlantic Railroad—it was a fat chicken that various Bullock cronies plucked regularly—the Democrats in Georgia's assembly had passed a bill in October, 1870, requiring the state to lease the road to private interests. Soon after the bill passed, rumor had it that Brown was organizing a company to bid for the lease. Stephens read about this in the papers, figured it would be a good investment, and wrote Brown asking if he could be admitted to the company. He could subscribe ten thousand dollars to the venture, he said. His old friend happily obliged. Stephens' name on the board of directors would lend an air of undoubted legitimacy to the undertaking. Brown's letter asking him to join the company had crossed Stephens' in the mail.[84]

Near the end of the year the newspapers announced that Brown's company had won the lease over a rival company headed by A. K. Seago, an Atlanta businessman, and Foster Blodgett, an erstwhile Bullock ally temporarily out of favor with the governor. At the same time the other members of Brown's company were announced. Next to Stephens' name, surprising enough in context, were, among others, the names of even more unlikely partners: H. I. Kimball, a notorious scala-

82. N. E. Harris to AHS, December 20, 1870, *ibid.*

83. Von Abele, *Stephens*, 277.

84. Brown to AHS, December 12, 16, 1870, all in Stephens Papers, LC; AHS to Brown, December 10, 15, 1870, in Brown-Hargrett Collection, UG.

wag compadre of Bullock's; Simon Cameron, senator from Pennsylvania; Thomas A. Scott, millionaire railroad baron from the same state; John S. Delano, the secretary of the interior's son; and none other than Ben Hill, who had just made the astonishing announcement that the time for resisting Reconstruction had ended and that Georgians should accept the results of the war as final.

To many Georgians the whole affair smelled fishy. Hill's financial association with the same group he had so recently been denouncing smacked of bargain. Moreover, the terms of the lease raised eyebrows everywhere. Brown's company had won the lease on a bid of $25,000 a month; the rival company had bid $37,500. Given Brown's close ties to the governor, it appeared that Bullock was grossly swindling the state yet again. The facts of the case were tangled, but it is clear that Bullock did profit from the lease; the October bill authorizing it had passed the assembly only with his cooperation. Later investigation also revealed that the Seago-Blodgett company lacked enough security for its bid. Nonetheless, at the time it looked as though the people of Georgia had been defrauded out of their state road.[85]

The Democratic newspapers raised a storm of protest, not a few of them wondering how Stephens could have ever become involved in such a despicable scheme. Toombs, for one, was amazed to find his friend's name listed with "a lot of the greatest rogues on the continent." Once the magnitude of his error became clear, Stephens lost no time leaving the company. Pleading poor health, he wrote to Brown in early January and declined to serve on the board of directors. In a public letter a few days later he announced that he had withdrawn from the company and donated his one-quarter of one share of stock to the educational fund of the state.[86]

Herschel Johnson thought it "funny" that Stephens could ever have dreamed of affiliating with "such a crew of harpies" and even more strange that "you did not sniff the stinking air . . . even before the passing of the bill to lease the Road." It had been common knowledge in Atlanta, he said, that the Bullock ring would get the lease no matter who else bid on the road. "Brown owes you much that you still endorse his integrity," he concluded acidly.[87]

85. The preceding paragraphs are based on Nathans, *Losing the Peace*, 207–12.
86. Toombs to AHS, December 30, 1870, in Phillips (ed.), *TSC Correspondence*, 711; AHS to Brown, January 4, 1871, in Brown-Hargrett Collection, UG; Augusta *Chronicle and Sentinel*, January 10, 1871.
87. Johnson to AHS, January 27, 1871, in Stephens Papers, LC.

Somewhat sheepishly Stephens admitted that he had been "a little green in putting in with such a crowd." He had trusted Brown and relied on his knowledge of the railroad business to do what was right. Moreover, "I knew nothing of what you say was generally known." Stephens had been terribly naive. Desperately ill for most of the time and shut away in Crawfordville, he had lost touch with state affairs. To his credit, he abandoned this irregular financial venture as soon as he realized what it was. His rectitude in money matters had always been impeccable.[88]

Many Georgians weren't nearly so virtuous, nor did they share Stephens' passion for pure constitutional principles. There was money to be made in Georgia—lots of it—by fair means or foul. And it didn't matter how one interpreted the Constitution. Association with the "enemy" could often prove profitable. People like Brown and Hill knew this, and many others were beginning to find it out.

To Stephens this was gross heresy. Give up the struggle for states' rights as protected by the Constitution? Admit that the Fourteenth and Fifteenth Amendments had been legally enacted? Accept the current "usurpations" as the unalterable law of the land? Never! Like many another Democrat in the land, he was thinking about the next year's election. And he already had his platform. "The sentiments of Genl. Jackson's farewell address against consolidation and the maintenance of all the reserved Sovereign Rights of the States in their full vigor must . . . be proclaimed as the Party Shibboleth," he said.[89]

But even at this early date it was becoming apparent that the national party was moving in a different direction. One Democratic congressman told Stephens that the party should avoid Reconstruction issues in 1872 and concentrate on taxation and finance. Another spoke even more bluntly: many northern Democrats had agreed that it would be "political suicide" for the platform to declare the Fourteenth and Fifteenth Amendments unconstitutional. Furthermore, most in Washington agreed "that the less the South had to do with the platform of the Party, the better the chances of success."[90]

Stephens scorned such pusillanimous compromising. The party had to be called back to the true gospel. For several months he had been

88. AHS to Johnson, January 31, 1871, in Johnson Papers, DU.
89. AHS to Montgomery Blair, January 31, 1871, in Blair Family Papers, LC.
90. George W. Booker to AHS, March 12, 1871, W. W. Paine to AHS, April 10, 1871, both in Stephens Papers, LC.

searching for a vehicle to do just that, and in January, 1871, he found one. Working through his old friend J. Henley Smith, then employed with the Atlanta *Constitution*, Stephens bought half interest in another city paper, the Atlanta *Sun*, from its owner J. M. Spreight. In May a three-way partnership was formed. Smith in Atlanta would function as the paper's business manager, while "political editor" Stephens would work from his bed or study in Crawfordville.[91]

Stephens hoped to make a living from journalism, but from the first the *Sun* lost money. At the end of 1871 Stephens bought Spreight out. The paper struggled on through 1872; finally in the spring of 1873 it merged with the Atlanta *Constitution*. But not before Stephens had filled its pages with reams of turgid polemic—his editorials sometimes ran for four or five columns. And not before he had driven poor Smith nearly crazy with his incessant and fussy demands for perfection in everything, from business reports to grammar to the layout of the paper. (At the end of 1872 Smith gave up trying to please his boss and resigned.) This foray into journalism had cost Stephens twenty thousand dollars, and at the end of it his promissory notes were scattered from one end of Atlanta to the other. Hearing of his friend's plight, Toombs went around the capital and bought up the notes. Then, with the kind of grandiose gesture that typified him, he delivered them to Crawfordville and dumped them ceremoniously in Stephens' lap.[92]

By mid-1871 the vast majority of northern Democrats had the smell of victory in their nostrils. Following the lead of Ohioan Clement Vallandigham, most had embraced the New Departure movement, which aimed to recapture the White House by opposing Grant and accepting the Reconstruction amendments. Grant had proven to be a weak and ineffectual president, poorly served by his advisers and surrounded for the most part by an entourage of venal opportunists. Hints of widespread scandal and corruption were already on the wind. Even among Republicans, Grant had aroused substantial opposition. Gathering under the lead of such men as Charles Francis Adams, Horace Greeley, Lyman Trumbull, and Carl Schurz, these so-called Liberal Republicans hoped to supplant Grant as the party's standard-bearer in 1872, or, failing that, to run a candidate of their own.[93]

91. AHS to Hidell, January 10, 1871, in Stephens Papers, HSP.
92. AHS to Brown, July 14, 1872, in McLeod Collection, UG; J. M. Spreight's bill of sale, December 7, 1871, in Stephens Papers, LC; numerous letters from Smith to AHS during 1872, in Stephens Papers, LC, attest to Stephens' fussiness about the details of the paper; Johnston, *Autobiography*, 132–33.
93. Randall and Donald, *Civil War and Reconstruction*, 658–59.

The Democrats could not have devised a situation more to their liking. Inevitable logic seemed to dictate cooperation with the dissident Republicans. Southern Democrats also found the logic compelling and could not understand it when Stephens persisted in assailing the New Departure through the pages of the *Sun*. Even most of his friends questioned the wisdom of his course. Herschel Johnson said he regretted his friend's determination not to support the Democratic nominee "unless he be on your platform." "Circumstances," he continued, might make it the duty of all patriotic southerners to support him. ("Circumstances," Johnson would later conclude, demanded that he side with Stephens.) Peterson Thweatt sympathized with Stephens but opined that a Democrat even on a "rascally platform" was better than continued radical rule: "I fear . . . you have taken upon yourself a thankless task."[94]

Lost causes had never daunted Stephens before, especially when matters of vital "principle" were involved. But this time he stood virtually alone. About the only prominent supporter he had was Toombs, and Toombs, fast degenerating into a chronic alcoholic, had become almost a parody. Another war would have been fine with him. Not until "you can tear the live thunder from its home in the burning ether" would he accept the situation, he told a northern reporter. In his own way Stephens was just as intransigent. His uncompromising war on the New Departure, said the Columbus *Enquirer*, "is a very strange freak for a Southern Democrat, to say the least of it."[95]

Freakish it may have been, but no more so than the ensuing campaign for the presidency. Convening in May, 1872, the Liberal Republicans nominated Horace Greeley for president on a platform calling for an end to the spoils system and universal amnesty for southerners, among other things. With little choice but to follow the Liberals' lead, the Democrats endorsed both the candidate and his platform shortly afterward.[96]

Greeley! A man who for more than thirty years had skewered the Democratic party with his acid pen was the epitome of everything Democrats professed to hate. He was a high-tariff man and at one time or another had embraced almost every controversial nineteenth-century "ism", from relatively harmless ones like vegetarianism, to the truly

94. Johnson to AHS, August 17, 1871; Thweatt to AHS, August 26, 1871, both in Stephens Papers, LC.
95. New York *Tribune*, June 10, 1871; Columbus *Enquirer*, October 10, 1871.
96. Randall and Donald, *Civil War and Reconstruction*, 659.

loathsome like utopian socialism and pacifism. For southerners he was an even more bitter pill. From his earliest days as an outspoken abolitionist he had been a violent and abusive opponent of the South. Only a few short years before, he had denounced southerners as rebels and traitors. Now he was their candidate for president of the United States. Stephens was beside himself with amazement. "Who could have believed that men who could not vote for Douglas in 1860 would be huzzaaing for Greely [sic] now—Did the world ever witness such a spectacle before?" As far as he was concerned, choosing between Grant and Greeley was like choosing between hemlock and strychnine.[97]

But he gladly would have drunk either to avoid what the fates dealt to him in mid-July. For on the fourteenth of that month Linton died at his home in Sparta from what was diagnosed as congestion of the bowels and lungs. He had been sick a little over a week. In many ways Linton Stephens was just as high-strung and prone to illness as his older brother. Like Aleck, he was a perfectionist, often driving himself relentlessly in his work. His health had been poor since 1868, but with his marriage to Mary Salter and the quick addition of three more young mouths to feed, he had rarely found time to relax. He had recently added another burden of his already extensive business interests: service as the state's counsel in its investigation of the Bullock ring's frauds. Perhaps the strain had become too much for him.

Stephens had seen Linton for the last time two weeks before when he had stopped over for a few days on his way back home from the capital. Dick Johnson had been there too, and the three of them had whiled away the time with games of whist and euchre and pleasant conversation on the back piazza. Johnson and Linton left for Sparta on the first of July.[98]

When they brought him the news, Stephens reacted like a man who had been shot. One long, piercing scream tore itself from the depths of his soul, and then he sat dumb. Half of his very being had been ripped away. He had endured the deaths of so many he loved—his father, his brothers Aaron and John, his sisters, countless friends—but none of these, not ten deaths, could ever equal this one. For Linton had been everything to him. Daily for more than forty years Stephens had thought of him, prayed for him, loved him with all the tenderness and

97. AHS to Cohen, July 2, 1872, in Stephens Papers, LC; Atlanta *Sun,* August 20, 1872.
98. Von Abele, *Stephens,* 285–86.

passion he could never give to any woman. There had been few secrets between them. And it had been the same with Linton. "My brother is the wisest and best man I ever knew in my life," he had once said. "I don't know, even in history, any person who exceeded him in wisdom and goodness. To think, and know, that I have the whole heart of such a person is my blessed privilege." And now it was over. What could anyone say?[99]

Nothing, of course, but Stephens' close friends tried. "My God," cried Toombs, "what can I do but mingle my tears with yours?" From all over Georgia, from Washington, from the North and South came condolences. Dick Johnston, who was reading all the brothers' letters while writing a biography of Stephens, knew better than most how much they had meant to each other. But he also knew the other trials Stephens had endured and the strength of his friend's faith in God.[100]

Too ill to attend the funeral, Stephens stayed at home and tried to make sense of it all. He couldn't. When Mary and the children came over from Sparta the following week, all he could do at first was weep and repeat Linton's name over and over. "I am now passing through one of the severest agonies of my life," Stephens told Herschel Johnson. "The light of my life is extinguished and everything . . . earthly . . . is gloomy cheerless and almost hopeless."[101]

He spent hours at his desk, pouring out his grief in letters. "The more I realize my situation, the deeper I am impressed with the sense of my utter isolation from anything that can bind me to this world. I can write nothing—I can do nothing." He spent other countless hours in aimless reverie, remembering Linton as a schoolboy, as a lawyer, as a father, as a person he could always count on to be there in moments of grief and pain and loneliness. But even as he wrote, Stephens knew life would go on, even without Linton. Already he was drawing strength from the deep reservoirs of a faith that had seen him through so much sorrow and pain. "To the decrees of the Most High we must all submit," he realized, "with whatever resignation He shall afford us grace through faith in His mercy to command."[102]

And already he was discovering that he was not alone, that the suf-

99. Richardson, *Little Aleck*, 314.
100. Toombs to AHS, July 15, 1872, Johnston to AHS, July 16, 1872, both in Stephens Papers, LC.
101. AHS to Johnson, July 20, 1872, in Johnson Papers, DU.
102. AHS to Johnston, July 16, 1872, in Johnston and Browne, *Stephens*, 513.

fering of others still bound him to the earth as securely as if he had been shackled with a chain. Only five days after Linton's death he was telling Dick Johnston about his concern for "old Uncle Ben," the black servant who had nursed Linton in childhood. Seventy-two years old now and bedridden with rheumatism, the poor man had been greatly afflicted by Linton's death. Stephens sent a doctor to him and promised to go down and see him himself as soon as he was able. It would be a "relief," Stephens thought, to weep together with one who had loved Linton "as well as I." "I am grieved that he is suffering so much," Stephens concluded. "May God have mercy on us all!" [103]

Life would never be the same for Stephens again. Linton's passing had left a rent in his heart no other person could ever fill. But as he had proven so many times in the past sixty years, he was a resilient man. Within five weeks of Linton's death, he resumed his crusade against both national parties. Sometimes, though, in the stillness of the night, the ageless questions of all grief-striken survivors still rose up to haunt him. "Why am I permitted to live?" he would wonder. "What is it for?" [104]

But the night remained silent.

103. *Ibid.*, July 19, 1872, 515.
104. *Ibid.*, December 14, 1872, 517.

XXII

An Old Man from Another Time

By mid-August of 1872 Stephens had thrown himself back into the presidential fray so furiously that his erstwhile friend Peterson Thweatt accused the *Sun* of doing more harm to Greeley and the Democrats than ten Grant papers. Stephens ignored such criticism. He had heard it for months and would hear worse before the campaign ended.[1]

Thweatt's concern was understandable. Georgia's Democrats had officially endorsed the New Departure in June, but a small splinter group of people who agreed with Stephens prepared to repudiate the party line and select delegates for a convention of "straight out" Democrats in Louisville to nominate another man for the presidency. Even Herschel Johnson doubted the wisdom of this course. "Louisville will elect Grant," he said. Johnson greatly overestimated the Straights' chances. Only 23 of Georgia's 136 counties bothered to send delegates to the state convention in Atlanta. The Louisville convention was even more farcical. It nominated Charles O'Conor of New York for president—who promptly declined to run—but adjourned without withdrawing his name.[2]

---

1. Thweatt to AHS, August 18, 1872, in Stephens Papers, LC.
2. Johnson to AHS, August 16, 1872, *ibid.*

Stephens had expected as much. All he had wanted from the convention was "a sound Democratic platform for the future" and repudiation of Greeley. Few others in Georgia could make much sense of what Stephens was saying in the *Sun*, however. One irate reader complained that he was a "Grant Scalywag" who told "every bad thing Mr Greely ever done & more two, you tell no bad things on Grant." "The editor of the *Sun* clings to the past and looks behind him as he rows," echoed the Columbus *Enquirer*.[3]

Grant won a larger victory than he had in 1868, carrying every northern state plus many in the South. Greeley managed to carry only five states, including Georgia. O'Conor took less than 3 percent of the vote there; most Georgia Democrats had simply ignored Stephens' counsel.

They could not ignore the man himself, however. To many thousands of Georgians Little Aleck was a near-legendary figure who embodied all the best they believed possible of themselves—"the greatest statesman & . . . the purest patriot we have," as one admirer put it. So when word got out in late 1872 that Stephens might be a candidate for the Senate seat being vacated by Joshua Hill, many Democrats promptly forgot his late apostasy. One admirer assured Stephens that the people "are *with you* again and would prefer to see you in that *once august* body to any other *man* in the *state*."[4]

Although not averse to the possibility, Stephens would have preferred Herschel Johnson for the office. Far from repenting of his attacks on the New Departure, he was now even more determined to stamp it out. "Greeleyism . . . my dear sir," Stephens told his friend, "must be fought." Under no circumstances should both of their names be presented to the legislature. If his own were put up, Stephens continued, "it will be for the restoration of principle. I have no personal objects to attain. Personally I should a thousand times rather see you in the Senate than to be there myself."[5]

Johnson refused to run but agreed, much to Stephens' delight, to go up to Atlanta for the beginning of the legislative session and lobby for his friend. He thought it would do little good though. He had heard

---

3. AHS to Hidell, August 25, 1872, in Stephens Papers, HSP; David D. Hisley to AHS, September 6, 1872, in Stephens Papers, LC; Columbus *Enquirer*, September 10, 1872.
4. Mark Johnston to [Malcolm?] Johnston, November 23, 1872, Zeno Fitzpatrick to AHS, November 25, 1872, both in Stephens Papers, LC.
5. AHS to Johnson, December 13, 1872, in Simon Gratz Collection, HSP.

that John B. Gordon had already secured pledges of support from many in the legislature. Besides, the new assembly was "overwhelmingly Greelyish" and would probably divide the offices among themselves. Although he had to admit that Johnson might be right, Little Aleck could have sooner called Linton back from the grave than abandon a crusade for pure principles. "Events incalculable will depend upon this senatorial election," he said. "I feel a firm conviction that at no former period of my life did duty so imperiously demand of me the exertions of my utmost power as now."[6]

The contest generated extraordinary interest in Georgia. Besides Stephens and Gordon, Ben Hill and two lesser candidates were also in the running. On the night of January 18, 1873, four days before the balloting, the three principal candidates addressed the legislature. Stephens spoke for two hours, defending both his Confederate record and his course in the presidential election. On the night of the election Hill's men held the balance of power, and after five ballots Gordon won the seat with 112 votes to Stephens' 86 and Hill's 7.[7]

Gordon's careful middle-of-the-road tactics had triumphed. As the *Chronicle*'s correspondent "P.W." explained, Stephens had been defeated because of "his violent and ceaseless opposition to the Liberal Republican movement." His election would have been construed as an endorsement of his own "Straight-out" views, "and the representatives of Georgia were not willing that this endorsement should go before the country."[8]

Stephens' friends, however, refused to let this defeat daunt them. Immediately after the election Toombs called a meeting of all the Eighth District assemblymen in his rooms at the Kimball House. There they agreed that Stephens should be the district's candidate for congressman in a special election to fill a vacancy left by the death of the incumbent. Accordingly, all the other prospective candidates withdrew in his favor. Even this compliment, according to "P.W.," was not an endorsement of Stephens' views. The people of the district remained "overwhelmingly against him" on the issues. They would send him to Congress "not to rake up the dead issues of the past" but to lead the Democracy on the "vital, living, practical issues of the present."[9]

6. Johnson to AHS, December 9, 1872, in Stephens Papers, LC; AHS to Johnson, December 29, 1872, in Johnson Papers, DU.
7. Augusta *Chronicle and Sentinel*, January 20, 23, 1872.
8. "P.W." to Augusta *Chronicle and Sentinel*, January 23, 1873, in Augusta *Chronicle and Sentinel*, January 25, 1873.
9. *Ibid.*

This talk bothered Stephens enough to ask a constituent about the "*real general* sentiment & feelings of the people" in the district, but it hardly deterred him from announcing in his acceptance letter that he was "a Democrat of the 'straitest sect'—of the Jeffersonian school of politics." What exactly this meant, no one seemed to know—or care. One Mississippi editor confidently predicted that Stephens would not "re-open the flood-gates of anarchy by agitating questions irrevocably settled." [10]

In his happiness at returning to the House Stephens chose to ignore the truth: the voters had merely thrown him a sop. He was still immensely popular and almost universally respected. But his influence was gone. People simply were no longer interested in arguing about the Constitution. Economic issues dominated American politics at every level. The country was rushing headlong into industrialization. Giant corporations, headed by men of immense wealth, began forming to exploit the nation's seemingly inexhaustible natural resources in coal, oil, timber, and ore. Immigrants by the hundreds of thousands flooded into the country to provide sweat labor for the steel mills, textile plants, railroads, packing houses, and canneries. Politics took on a cynical hue, its practitioners often becoming commodities as easily bought and sold as the cattle roaming the Great Plains or the bogus stock issues ruining investors on Wall Street. William Marcy "Boss" Tweed, who bilked New York City of hundreds of thousands of dollars, was only the most notorious of his type: a new and ruthless local political power that could mobilize votes in the teeming cities of the Northeast or buy a local judge with equal ease.

Where amid this clamorous scramble for the main chance was there a place for a feeble old man from another time? Stephens saw his life as a tapestry with all its many strands—his love for Linton, for Georgia and its common people, for the South, for his black folk, for the law and the majesty of the Constitution—woven into a single bolt of sturdy beauty. He saw the history of the country the same way, as a single fabric. But the war had rent that fabric, leaving only a few connecting strands between ugly, ragged edges. Those strands were all that mattered to Stephens. Much of the ugliness he saw around him he either ignored or didn't understand. What he did understand he fought

10. AHS to F. M. Stovall, January 28, 1873, in E. P. Alexander Papers, SHC/NC; AHS to Augusta *Chronicle and Sentinel*, February 5, 1873, in Augusta *Chronicle and Sentinel*, February 8, 1873; Jackson *Weekly Clarion*, February 20, 1873.

against with all the fire of outraged righteousness he could muster. But when he did, no one listened any more.

This was a truth he would have found impossible to live with. So he invented fictions to delude himself into believing that what he thought still mattered. His election to the House, he told a friend, had been "evidence of the continued confidence not only of my old constituents but of the true Democracy of Georgia." As for the Senate race, he had made it only to vindicate principles and "to save the State from going off after the New Departure heresy." In this he had been "entirely successful. Georgia is all right I think in the future." [11]

Stephens would have been appalled to know how little he had stirred the hearts of people who heard him speak at the Methodist church in Thomson during the campaign. The audience, observed young Tom Watson, was small and unenthusiastic. Rarely gesticulating, Stephens had clung to the pulpit rail regaling his listeners with parts of the speech he had made on the Oregon statehood issue years before. Overall the speech made "no marked impression." Moreover, a few old-line Whigs and Know Nothings had never forgotten Stephens' past sins and his supporters had to work hard "to poll a creditable vote for the hero." [12]

Throughout the spring and summer of 1873 Stephens stayed as busy as he ever had been in his life. Until Eliza got sick and could no longer look after the kitchen, he had five law students boarding with him. And until he finally disposed of the *Sun* he wrote three or four articles a week for it. Answering letters and dispensing legal advice, most of it gratuitously, occupied much of his time. Toward the end of the summer he was named an associate editor of *Johnson's Encyclopedia*, a position that kept him busy writing articles on American history and the South for several years. And every so often he would read manuscripts for some aspiring author. [13]

One he doubtless scanned with special care was the text of a long biography of himself by Dick Johnston and William Hand Browne of the *Southern Messenger*. Originally Stephens had objected to the book

11. AHS to Cohen, March 2, 1873, in Stephens Papers, LC.
12. Thomas E. Watson, *Sketches: Historical, Literary, Biographical, Economic, Etc.* (Thomson, Ga., 1916), 6–7.
13. AHS to Hidell, June 7, 1871, in Stephens Papers, HSP; Johnston and Browne, *Stephens*, 520; Lanman, *Haphazard Personalities*, 350; AHS to John A. Stephens, April 16, 1873, in Stephens Papers, EU.

appearing in his lifetime. It might be construed as "some political manoeuvre" or "a desire to bring [himself] more prominently before the public," he thought. Finally, in 1878, the "many misrepresentations of [his] motives, objects, and acts on several occasions" prompted him to consent to its publication.[14]

In September he was invited to New York to make a speech in behalf of a coordinated plan for the nation's centennial. Stephens thought the idea an excellent way to promote harmony and instill national pride, and he looked forward to going. Unfortunately he got so sick later in the fall that couldn't make the trip. By December, though, he was well enough to travel to Washington and the opening of Congress.

Although he may have felt well enough himself, to most observers he looked like a refugee from a graveyard. Describing Stephens taxed the imaginative powers of the best reporters, but one of them in 1876 left the following marvelous portrait:

> A little way up the aisle sits a queer-looking bundle. An immense cloak, a high hat, and peering somewhere out of the middle a thin, pale, sad little face. This brain and eyes enrolled in countless thicknesses of flannel and broadcloth wrappings belong to Hon. Alexander H. Stephens, of Georgia. How anything so small and sick and sorrowful could get here all the way from Georgia is a wonder. If he were to draw his last breath at any instant you would not be surprised. If he were laid out in his coffin he need not look any different, only then the fires would have gone out in those burning eyes. Set as they are in the white-wax face, they seem to burn and blaze. Still, on the countenance is stamped that pathos of long continued suffering which goes to the heart.

Incredibly, this poor suffering bundle would remain in Congress for the next nine years.[15]

As if to prove he had lost none of his old touch, Stephens spoke often at first. He delivered his first address on December 11, 1873, just a few days after the session opened. Unfortunately, he chose the wrong side of a volatile issue. Most of the country had been outraged by a law passed in the previous session that raised the salaries of congressmen. A serious recession had set in during the year, and this "salary grab," which had allowed each member of Congress to take home an extra

---

14. William Hand Browne to AHS, September 15, 1873, in Stephens Papers, LC; AHS to Johnston and Browne, May 28, 1878, in Johnston and Browne, *Stephens*, 3.
15. Richardson, *Little Aleck*, 324.

five thousand dollars in retroactive pay increases, unleashed a storm of criticism and a spate of bills to repeal the raise.

Stephens, who had not received a cent of the bonus himself, told a House packed to the rafters that he saw nothing wrong with the law. Congressmen had to maintain a certain style and they were expected to entertain. How could they do so on what they were being paid? Without adequate pay they might easily become prey to the ever-present and well-heeled lobbyists. Not only this, but the pay for the "brains" of the government—the president, his cabinet, and the Supreme Court—was also ridiculously low: the chief executive ought to be paid at least $100,000 a year and the chief justice $50,000.[16]

Judging by the South's reaction, Stephens might have done better to endorse sodomy. Stephens, said the *Chronicle*, was sent to Washington to defend the "suffering South," not the "mammon of unrighteousness." A South Carolina editor charged him with being more interested in pleasing the White House than the "Georgians whom he misrepresents." It was "humiliating," wrote another Carolinian, "to see you murder the splendid reputation you were once entitled to." Several of Stephens' friends—Toombs, Herschel Johnson, Martin Crawford—who knew his high-mindedness in money matters, defended the speech. But his constituents didn't understand. As Johnson admitted, "The public mind is frensied on the subject & it will require time to bring 'the sober second thought.'"[17]

Stephens' next address pleased Georgians much better: it was a long and bitter attack on the so-called Supplemental Civil Rights Bill. This bill, pushed strongly by Charles Sumner, sought to strengthen the civil rights law of 1866 by barring racial discrimination in cemeteries, schools, public inns, conveyances, and places of amusement. Stephens rarely wrote his speeches out. This one he did; he considered it that important. He began by denying that he bore any prejudice against blacks. He believed that all people under federal jurisdiction should be afforded equal protection and redress under the law and had asserted this doctrine shortly after the war. But the bill under consideration was patently unconstitutional. Under the Fourteenth and the Fifteenth Amendments (which supporters of the bill cited) blacks had been ex-

16. *Congressional Record*, 43rd Cong., 1st Sess., II, 152–54.

17. Augusta *Chronicle and Sentinel*, December 19, 1873; Charleston *News and Courier*, December 15, 1873; George L. Aiken to AHS, December 20, 1873, Toombs to AHS, December 22, 1873, Johnson to AHS, January 1, 1874, all in Stephens Papers, LC.

tended the same constitutional protections as other citizens, no more, no less. Not only was the bill unconstitutional, he continued, it was also inexpedient. Blacks, at least in Georgia, didn't want to mix with whites, and this "voluntary separation" promoted harmony between the races far more than unnatural mixing would do.

All this was prelude to the main point Stephens wanted to make: that this bill struck yet another crippling blow "against the very genius and entire spirit of our whole system . . . the absolute, unrestricted right of State self-government in all purely internal municipal affairs." Now that the war had settled for all time the "*status* of the African race in the Southern States" and the passions engendered by the conflict were fast disappearing, the time had come to "return to the original principles of [the] fathers." If this were not done, dire consequences—perhaps even future violence—might follow.[18]

This was the last speech of any consequence Stephens would make in Congress. He had asserted his creed once again, as if his colleagues didn't already know it and as if it really meant anything anymore. Congress passed a slightly modified version of the civil rights bill during its next session.

The only other major address Stephens made in Congress was one on Lincoln's birthday in 1878 at the presentation to Congress of F. B. Carpenter's painting of Lincoln signing the Emancipation Proclamation. It was a singular honor because both houses requested him to speak. From his wheelchair he delivered a moving tribute to his old "warm-hearted," "generous," and "magnanimous" friend. Unfortunately he let himself ramble into some unnecessary remarks about the benefits blacks had enjoyed under slavery. In the main, however, the speech pleaded for sectional reconciliation, as Lincoln would have had it, and except for die-hard rebels like Jubal Early, it impressed almost everyone.[19]

Stephens went home to Georgia in April, 1874. He had been sick for the past ten weeks, and for the following months he suffered even more from neuralgia. Had it not been for the grim satisfaction he got from a protracted newspaper controversy with Ben Hill, he might have spent an awful summer. The argument arose from an address Hill had made to the Southern Historical Society in February, which, according

18. Speech in *Congressional Record*, 43rd Cong., 1st Sess., II, 378–82.
19. *Ibid.*, 45th Cong., 2nd Sess., VII, 971–72.

to Stephens, distorted the truth about the Hampton Roads conference. Sensitive about his Confederate record, especially since his political opponents used it freely against him, and utterly contemptuous of Hill, Stephens immediately attacked Hill's "unblushing arrogance, impudent insolence and brazen audacity in the perversion of facts."[20]

The acrimonious exchange lasted from April 11 to the end of June, and before it was over Stephens had written six long, bitter letters and Hill four. What the *Chronicle* originally called "The Battle of Intellectual Giants" swiftly turned into a sordid cat fight in which each man freely besmirched the integrity and veracity of the other. Stephens, prepared to carry on the controversy indefinitely, had already written two more articles when Hill brought the matter to an end. To Stephens' astonishment, his hated opponent moved that the board of trustees at the University of Georgia adopt the *Constitutional View* as a textbook. Once he recovered from the shock Stphens smugly concluded that this was "the completest answer that could have been made to all his charges."[21]

Controversy evidently helped keep Stephens healthy. Once the tiff with Hill ended, he got sick again, and by July was "barely able to sit up." Seeing little prospect of ever returning to Congress, he announced his intention to resign. In August, however, he changed his mind and allowed his name to be put in nomination at the Eighth District convention. Stephens led handily on the first ballot, but it took twelve hours and another 111 ballots before he secured the nomination. According to Toombs, the Greeley element accounted for the "obstinacy" against his friend, but some of the delegates must have wondered if Stephens could live another day.[22]

Compared to Little Aleck, a scarecrow would have looked robust. And yet there he was out on the stump, campaigning and bragging that he had gained seven pounds in the last seven weeks—all the way up to seventy-eight pounds! Not only did he look exceedingly odd, he sounded that way: more like a Republican, some thought, than a Democrat. Not only had he endorsed the infamous salary grab, but the idea of a third term for Grant didn't seem to bother him either. Even

20. AHS to editor of the Augusta *Constitutionalist*, April 11, 1874, in Augusta *Chronicle and Sentinel*, April 23, 1874.

21. AHS to Forbes L. Brown, September 2, 1874, in Stephens Papers, LC.

22. AHS to Philip Phillips, July 7, 1874, in Philip Phillips Family Papers, LC; Toombs to AHS, September 4, 1874, in Stephens Papers, LC.

worse, he refused to condemn Grant for his use of federal troops in Louisiana to restore Republican governor William P. Kellogg to office after he had been deposed by violence.[23]

Usurpation! stormed the Democratic press. Not so, said Stephens. "When thousands assemble, with arms in their hands, to subvert an existing government, even though oppressive in its character . . . I am far from saying the movement was right," he told a reporter for the New York *Herald*. As always, he stood for law and order. Grant had done nothing, he told the editor of the *Chronicle*, but uphold a government "recognized and upheld by the Courts of the State."[24]

Disregarding such heresies, Stephens' constituents returned him to Congress by an overwhelming majority over his Republican opponent. The people, asserted the *Chronicle*, still trusted him despite rather than because of his "peculiar views." They simply disagreed with Stephens about Grant. "Just as a man might possess an abnormal taste for broiled buzzard" without losing his friends, so it was with Stephens and the voters, so long as he didn't "insist upon making them partake of the delicacy."[25]

Although his health prevented him from performing anything more than routine duties, Stephens looked after the needs of his district and missed only a single day of the 1874–1875 session. And not until near its end did he serve up any more broiled buzzard for the folks back home. He was the only Democrat in the House to vote for allowing the report of the Committee on Louisiana Affairs to reach the floor, thereby allowing passage of a resolution recognizing the Kellogg government in Louisiana. Vainly did Stephens try to explain that his act also allowed formal condemnation of the corrupt Republican returning board in that state. The frauds on both sides, he told a friend privately, were "unequalled in the annals of Representative Government." Nonetheless, he spent weeks after his return home defending himself in the newspapers.[26]

Feeling better than he had for years, he spent part of the summer of

23. Augusta *Chronicle and Sentinel*, September 20, 1874.
24. New York *Herald*, September 21, 1874; AHS to the editors, October 28, 1874, in Augusta *Chronicle and Sentinel*, October 28, 1874.
25. Augusta *Chronicle and Sentinel*, October 3, 1874.
26. AHS to Hidell, March 14, 1875, in Stephens Papers, HSP; AHS to Savannah *News*, March 31, 1875, in Augusta *Chronicle and Sentinel*, April 8, 1875; AHS to Mrs. A. R. Lawton, March 15, 1875, in Stephens Papers, LC.

1874 in the Cherokee counties giving a round of speeches. This immediately fueled speculation that Stephens might be politicking early for the gubernatorial nomination. He was not, though many of his north Georgia friends would have been delighted if he were. The speeches were just part of a hectic summer.[27]

He planned to be just as busy in the fall, having arranged to deliver a series of lectures (for two hundred dollars apiece) in several midwestern cities. Unfortunately, he had to cancel the tour because of another excruciating attack of kidney stones. People from all over the country wrote him with cures or sent bottles of their favorite elixir: Eureka Liver Medicine, South Poland Mineral Spring Waters, Buffalo Lithia Waters. None seemed to do much good; he did not reach Washington until after the session began and almost immediately was afflicted again. He stayed sick and bedridden most of the year. Having lost his youthful distrust of doctors, he now allowed himself to be dosed regularly with a fantastic array of medicines. Not content with filling Stephens full of morphine, muriate of ammonia, bromides, quinine, tinctures of digitalis and gentian, Dr. H. H. Steiner also prescribed a frequent "interrupted current of electricity" to improve Stephens' heart action.[28]

It's difficult to say how dependent Stephens became on drugs, but evidently he came to rely on them heavily. According to Rebecca Felton, who spent months with him in Washington, Stephens "constantly stimulated himself with whiskey,"—his bottle of "Jeffersonian Democracy," as he jocularly called it. And when he was sick or in pain, "hypodermics," administered by a black servant, "were frequent." Dr. Steiner heartily disliked this practice, but he couldn't stop it. Stephens needed morphine to sleep. Sometimes his pain was so severe that he would scream out, unaware later that he had made a sound. Obviously his mind was affected by this freelance doctoring. "Mr. Stephens might have been unduly doped at times," Mrs. Felton thought, "[especially] when the size of the hypodermics were not known." Neverthe-

27. Augusta *Chronicle and Sentinel*, August 6, 7, 1875.

28. Carpenter and Sheldon to AHS, September 10, October 11, 1875, E. C. Hood to AHS, October 15, 1875, Thomas F. Good to AHS, October 13, 1875, all in Stephens Papers, LC; H. H. Steiner to AHS, August 3, 1876, in Stephens Papers, DU. Steiner was Stephens' physician. Stephens Papers, DU, contain many of his letters giving details of Stephens' medical treatment.

less, Stephens relied on opiates to relieve his suffering for the rest of his life, even though he didn't like to. They made him "quite sick the morning after," he said.[29]

The Democrats of the Eighth District nominated Stephens for Congress again by acclamation, although he was so ill that many of his friends thought he might never recover. The Republicans refused to run a candidate against him. Somehow Stephens managed to make it back to Washington for the fateful session of 1876–1877, but just as his health kept him out of the campaign in Georgia it now prevented him from participating in the Byzantine bargaining that put Republican Rutherford B. Hayes in the White House after it appeared that his opponent, Samuel J. Tilden, had won the election.[30]

Stephens had caught pneumonia. During most of the time his southern congressional colleagues schemed and parlayed to strike the best deal they could with the Republicans, the representative from Georgia lay in his rooms at the National Hotel fighting for his life. Had he not been so sick, Stephens no doubt would have been up to his eyeballs in the negotiations. When he was able, he conferred with colleagues in his room at the hotel. Early in the crisis Stephens sent a telegram from his sickbed denying that he advised "a friendly acceptance" by southerners of Hayes's inauguration. On the other hand, he disapproved of "forcible resistance," favoring "the peaceful instrumentalities of the Constitution" for redress of grievances. By the end of January, however, as the House discussed the electoral bill to appoint a commission to decide the disputed election, Stephens chaffed to be in his seat. Had he been able to, he said, he would have spoken and voted for the bill.[31]

At this point Stephens was lucky to be able to speak at all. He was hemorrhaging, and doctors watched him round the clock. On February 4, President Grant came to see him, and Stephens averred that he was sinking and would not live much longer. It must have appeared that way to many, for several newspapers reported his death. As one of those rare individuals who gets to read his own obituaries, Stephens was as good-humored as Mark Twain was in similar circumstances.

29. AHS to John A. Stephens, April 15, 1877, in Stephens Papers, EU; Felton, *Georgia Politics*, 345–46; AHS to Rebecca Felton, September 14, 1880, in Felton Papers, UG.

30. Augusta *Chronicle and Sentinel*, September 7, 15, 1876.

31. AHS to L. Q. C. Lamar, December 11, 1876, in L. Q. C. Lamar Papers, MDAH; Augusta *Constitutionalist*, December 17, 1876; Augusta *Chronicle and Sentinel*, January 30, 1877.

"Well," he remarked, after hearing one read to him, "they have written worse than that about me when I was living." Miraculously, he survived. On February 13, 1877, the *Chronicle* reported that even Stephens admitted he was better.[32]

The new administration suited Stephens well enough. Shortly after the inauguration, he let Hayes know through Assistant Secretary of State Frederick W. Seward that while recanting none of his opinions as a southerner and Democrat, "I expect and desire to die a union man." He would, of course, oppose partisan legislation but vote for all measures in the "true interests of the country." The true interests of the country meant the return to home rule in the South. And for this it didn't matter who occupied the White House. "What do the people care who governs?" Stephens was asking rhetorically two months later. "All they care for is a good government." Prompted by the massive labor strikes of 1877, Hayes had removed most of the federal troops from the South, so he more than met Stephens' standard of "good government." Little Aleck may not have always agreed with his Democratic colleagues, but he was in perfect accord with them about what home rule meant. There were no more Republicans in the South "except a few carpet-baggers and scalawags who want offices." And the blacks could be discounted completely. "[The Negro] is nothing but a machine," Stephens said matter-of-factly, "an instrument in the hands of the politicians to vote as they want. . . . He is not to be taken into account in making up the estimate."[33]

Home rule had been a fact in Georgia since 1872. But almost as soon as Georgians had rid themselves of the Republicans, the Democrats divided into factions and turned on each other. Throughout the 1870s and 1880s control of the party machinery in the state lay in the hands of a small ring of powerful, rich, and shrewd men: the Bourbons, all of whom preached the gospel of the New South—economic progress through industrial capitalism. The Bourbon leaders, the so-called Georgia Triumvirate, were Joe Brown, who with the fall of Bullock had ingratiated himself back into the Democratic fold; Alfred H. Colquitt, son of the antebellum senator, former major general in the

32. Augusta *Chronicle and Sentinel*, February 3, 13, 1877.
33. Frederick W. Seward, *Reminiscences of a War-Time Statesman and Diplomat, 1830–1915* (New York, 1916), 433–34; interview with Cincinnati *Enquirer*, quoted in Augusta *Chronicle and Constitutionalist*, May 27, 1877.

Confederate army, and a teetotaler of legendary Christian piety; and John B. Gordon, another Confederate hero and U.S. senator.

But centralized party control of Georgia was shaky. Some areas resented the intrusion of the state machine into local affairs. During Governor James Smith's administration, which began in 1872, murmurings of protest from Georgia's Seventh District, the Piedmont counties, got progressively louder. They exploded into a roar in 1874 when the Democratic executive committee tried to foist its own hand-picked candidate for Congress onto the voters.

The leader of the protest movement in the Seventh was a remarkably energetic physician—Methodist preacher named William H. Felton, who was equaled, if not surpassed, in political skills by his wife Rebecca. Together they turned Democratic politics in north Georgia on its head. Refusing to accept the ring candidate for Congress, Felton declared himself an Independent and captured the seat in 1874 without difficulty. He won just as handily in 1876 and 1878. By then the Independent virus had infected large parts of Georgia. In the congressional races in 1878 the Independents captured congressional seats in three districts and ran strongly in the other six.

Actually, the Independents might have claimed four districts that year, for in the Eighth Aleck Stephens sounded like Felton. Stephens had not been in particularly good odor with the Democratic oligarchy ever since 1874 when he had upheld Grant's actions in Louisiana. So when the regulars attempted to contest Stephens' renomination to Congress, he charged that he was being opposed by a "ring" and dared the Democrats of his district to depose him. He plainly implied that if spurned he would run as an Independent. This course did not become necessary, but Stephens added insult to injury by endorsing Felton in the Seventh District contest.[34]

This was only natural; the tall handsome doctor and the little crippled invalid had become good friends. And like many other women, Becky Felton was drawn to Stephens. While she was in Washington she spent hours with him in his rooms at the National Hotel, playing whist, reading to him, or simply talking politics, a subject in which they shared a passionate interest. During his critical illness of 1876—

34. The preceding paragraphs are based on Von Abele, *Stephens*, 301–304, and John E. Talmadge, *Rebecca Latimer Felton: Nine Stormy Decades* (Athens, Ga., 1960), 32–33, and Ward, "Georgia Under the Bourbons," 100–104.

1877, Mrs. Felton, along with Mary Butler Coleman, John J. Crittenden's daughter, constantly attended Stephens and saw to his needs. As
the years went by, the friendship between Stephens and the Feltons
deepened. At home they exchanged visits to one another's homes, and
by the early 1880s they were exchanging Christmas gifts as well.[35]

Stephens' sympathy for the Independents did not rest entirely on his
friendship with the Feltons. Aside from Joe Brown, Stephens disliked
most of the prominent Democratic leaders in Georgia. The Feltons'
passionate protest against the party line perhaps reminded Stephens of
all the times past when he too had stood against the tide. Moreover, he
had always respected the common people. Felton's people, the Piedmont farmers, were much like his own plain folk in the Eighth District. Throughout the years these people had been the backbone of his
political support. They had stood with him both for the Union and for
individual liberties under the Constitution. He could hardly remain
aloof from their protest. Besides, he sympathized with the Independents' social philosophy, an agrarian discontent with the changes industrialization was bringing to their simple way of life. Like them, Stephens distrusted change, especially when it seemed to put too much
power into the hands of too few people. "If ever there is another war in
this republic," he said, "it will not be sectional, but social. . . . If ever
the masses of the people can be made to understand our system of
class-legislation, taxes and finance, there will be trenchant reform or
frightful revolution."[36]

The gubernatorial campaign of 1880, pitting Colquitt against Independent candidate Thomas M. Norwood of Savannah, was one of the
bitterest in Georgia's history. But through it all, Stephens stayed at
home, uncharacteristically silent. He suffered greatly this summer, as
much in spirit as in body. In quick succession four of his close friends,
including Herschel Johnson, had died. The deaths of Johnson and another intimate friend, Miles W. Lewis, were "crushing," he said. The
truth was that he didn't care much about the election. His own seat in
Congress was secure; no one opposed him for reelection. As for the
governor's race, he thought neither man fit. He despised Norwood,

35. Talmadge, *Felton*, 50; AHS to Rebecca Felton, December 26, 1881, in Felton
Papers, UG.
36. Von Abele, *Stephens*, 304.

"the fee'd lobbyist of Huntington," only slightly more than Colquitt, whom he thought "utterly hollow-hearted, deceitful, unprincipled and dishonorable."[37]

Despite his friendship with the Feltons, Stephens dreaded the possibility of yet another rancorous split in the Democrats. For peace and harmony in the party, he thought Colquitt should have been allowed to serve as governor for another term. Fighting him would simply ensure his reelection. Stephens was right. Colquitt won the governorship easily, and Felton went down to defeat in the Seventh District. The Independents' passion could not offset the Bourbons' more tangible advantages: support of the blacks, possession of office, and a well-oiled statewide machine backed by most of the state press.[38]

The only election that interested Stephens in 1880—he virtually ignored the national presidential campaign—was the upcoming one for U.S. senator by the assembly. Clearly the triumverate would have no trouble electing Brown for a full term, a prospect that bothered Stephens not at all. Well before the election he informed his old friend that he would "in no event antagonize [him] in the Senatorial contest," and a few days later he advised Brown's chief opponent not to run. Brown would be too strong to beat.[39]

Again Stephens proved to be an accurate prophet. With Brown's election to the Senate in November of 1880, the Georgia Triumvirate fixed its control on the state for the next dozen years. But the Feltons and their allies continued to dream and scheme. Under the provisions of Georgia's 1877 constitution the governor's term ran for two years. Thus the Independents would have another try at gaining control of the state in the gubernatorial election of 1882.

To do this they were willing to affiliate with any disgruntled element in the state, even the Republicans. A coaliton of white Republicans and Independent Democrats had recently wrested control from the Bourbons in Virginia, and late in 1881 Felton suggested in an interview that Georgia Independents would follow a similar strategy. On December 29, 1881, therefore, Independent and Republican representatives met

37. AHS to Charles C. Jones, September 1, 1880, in Stephens Papers, DU; AHS to Mary Butler Coleman, August 29, 1880, in Crittenden Papers, DU; AHS to Rebecca Felton, September 14, 1880, in Felton Papers, UG.
38. AHS to Mrs. A. R. Lawton, September 20, 1880, in A. R. Lawton Papers, SHC/NC.
39. Brown to AHS, October 15, 1880, in Stephens Papers, LC; AHS to A. R. Lawton, October 18, 1880, in A. R. Lawton Papers, SHC/NC.

at Atlanta's Markham House Hotel to formulate a common platform for the coming election. In early January they issued a manifesto, which condemned binding party caucus decisions and the convict lease system and called for a free ballot and a fair count, a liberal system of federally financed internal improvements, and state guarantee of a "common English education" for every child.[40]

Felton's interview caused a sensation in "Georgia circles" in Washington, according to Stephens. Senator Ben Hill, up until then a firm friend of the Feltons, immediately branded the new movement "a second attempt to Africanize the state for the benefit of the Republican party." All federal patronage in Georgia, he predicted, would be put in Independent hands "for the purpose of buying Democrats." Doubtless the deal struck at the Markham House conference included provisions for the division of patronage, but the exact terms were not clear. What is clear is that Stephens understood it much as Hill did. If the fundamental principle of the new movement, he told Mrs. Felton in February, was that "a few specified irresponsible [Republicans]" would have "absolute control of all the Federal patronage in Georgia," he could never approve of it.[41]

If Stephens had unequivocally disapproved Felton's strategy, he might have spared himself embarrassment. But he did not. Confronted with a choice of declaring where his true sympathies lay, he instead muddled the issue with long, involved explanations that could be read, if one were so inclined, as qualified approval of the so-called "new movement." He genuinely liked and respected the Feltons, and he couldn't bring himself to tell them straight out that he disapproved dallying with Republicans under any circumstances. In a newspaper interview shortly after the Markham House conference, he was quoted as saying he believed in the organized Democracy and was satisfied with the party as it was. This news troubled his friends in Georgia, reported Judge James Hook, an Independent who had been at the conference. Mrs. Felton refused to believe the story. "I did not think you were pleased with the present status of the organization," she told Stephens,"—nor did I think you preferred the corrupt men in the organization to your honest friends outside." The Feltons were furious with

40. Talmadge, *Felton*, 69–70; Independents' manifesto in Felton, *Georgia Politics*, 340–41.
41. AHS to Rebecca Felton, January 10, February 21, 1882, both in Stephens Papers, LC; Hill quoted in Ward, "Georgia Under the Bourbons," 126.

Hill. One might as well "expect the green coated pond to send out healing vapors—or the mind of Satan to reflect virtue or goodness" as look for honesty or generosity in friendship from Hill, Mrs. Felton exclaimed.[42]

Stephens, for his part, did nothing to calm their rage. Hill's interview, he said, "had done a great deal towards advancing & strengthening the movement." His remarks about Africanizing the state had been "exceedingly impolitic & indiscreet, [and also] unjust." But, Stephens went on, he wanted his remarks kept from the public. "I am now really out of politics. I do not expect to be a candidate for office ever again. I am getting too old and feeble, and to tell the truth too much disgusted with the manner in which public affairs are administered. I am too far advanced in life to become a Reformer, or even to attempt it." All he wanted to do was finish revising the proofs of his history of the United States—a project that had occupied most of his time during 1881— and leave the shaping of the country's destinies to the present generation. Maybe so, but Stephens would never be too old to offer advice. Reformers should never forget "the fundamental organic principles upon which alone our free institutions were founded," he warned. "Those principles . . . are wholly inconsistent with the policies & objects of the Radical party North."[43]

The Feltons failed to discern the full import of what Stephens was saying. For more than anything else, they needed to capture him as their candidate for governor. To succeed, the Independents would have to avoid their mistake of 1880 and nominate a man popular and pure enough to win the election. Stephens more than filled the bill. Mrs. Felton had mentioned the possibility to him as early as October, but Stephens had been noncommittal.[44]

During the terrible falling-out with Hill, he had been silent. When he finally wrote again several weeks later, he seemed to shut the door on all the Independents' hopes. As a matter of "policy," he explained, he had stayed out of the Felton-Hill imbroglio. His mind had been made up "sometime ago never to take any active part in politics again. Friendships, with me, far outweigh any principle at present involved in parties & scrambles." He still seemed to sympathize with the Indepen-

42. James L. Hook to AHS, January 7, 1882, in Stephens Papers, DU; Rebecca Felton to AHS, January 1, 1882, in Stephens Papers, LC.

43. AHS to Rebecca Felton, January 10, 1882, in Stephens Papers, LC.

44. Talmadge, *Felton*, 60–61.

dents, however. "Bare party organization" had always been secondary to principles with him. "I never acknowledged, and never will acknowledge, allegiance to any political party organization of whatever name. . . . I am, always was, and always will be as independent of any one party organization as of another." [45]

Had the events of the next few months not shown Stephens so nearly senile or perhaps addled by morphine, they would have been comical. If the Independents wanted him for governor, so did the regular Democrats—only more so. The regular Democrats had precious few men untainted by the scandals of the 1870s. Stephens, although a heretic on occasion, could be forgiven, for he was honest and popular. Accordingly, when he was in Washington in March, Governor Colquitt offered the party nomination to him. Quite likely Colquitt also promised no one would oppose him. Stephens politely declined. He had decided to retire from public life at the end of his term, he said. His mind was made up. [46]

Well, almost. When news of this announcement hit the papers, however, it opened the final act in Stephens' political drama. Colquitt wrote again in April saying how much he would like to see Stephens governor. Meanwhile, in the capital Joe Brown began spending hours with his old friend, dining and taking him out for rides in the pleasant spring air in his fine carriage. Mrs. Felton, who watched the pages of the *Constitution* like a hawk for evidence of Stephens' intentions, began seeing disturbing reports that he was wavering in his resolve to retire. "People are much perplexed here as to what you are really going to do," one Independent told Little Aleck, warning him that "the Atlanta people would run you to death, and their 'true Democracy' . . . would kill an alligator." [47]

Nobody in Georgia was more anxious to find out exactly where Stephens stood than the Feltons. On May 6, Stephens told a newspaper correspondent that he was not a candidate for governor. The next day he told another reporter a different story. "I have simply given my assent to serve the people of Georgia as Governor if they should by unmistakable [d]emonstr[a]tions show me that it is their desire for me to do so," he explained to Mrs. Felton. He had no aspirations for the

45. AHS to Rebecca Felton, February 21, 1882, in Stephens Papers, LC.
46. Augusta *Chronicle and Constitutionalist*, March 8, 1882.
47. Atlanta *Constitution*, April 22, 1882; Jos. R. Randall to AHS, May 2, 1882, in Stephens Papers, LC.

office; only because of his desire to "produce harmony" and "save us from the horrible effects of division" had he consented at all.[48]

At this stage of the game the Feltons needed something more from Stephens than vague platitudes. A mass meeting of Independent Democrats had been scheduled to meet in Atlanta on June 1, but Felton would be in Atlanta on the following Monday, May 15. If Stephens desired it, Mrs. Felton wrote on May 12, "Dr. Felton and Independents will recommend you next Monday." If Stephens wanted this, he should telegraph Felton at the Markham House. "There is no intention to compel your candidacy," the letter continued. The Independents did not want to embarrass him, "but will endeavor to carry out your wishes."[49]

Stephens had already stated his wishes. He wanted to be a peacemaker. He had apparently concluded that he alone, of all the people in Georgia, could unite the party. The reality of the situation was quite different. Both of the Democratic factions wanted to use him for their own purposes. Even the Republicans would have made him *their* candidate if they could have.

Felton's letter reached Stephens on Sunday, May 14, a bad time for the old man. Five days before he had slipped on the Capitol steps and sprained his ankle. Now he lay propped up in bed, taking morphine to ward off the pain. One of his many visitors that day was Emory Speer, Independent congressman from the Ninth District. Somehow during their conversation, Speer learned about Mrs. Felton's letter. After discussing it with Stephens, he picked up a pen and wrote out a telegram, which Stephens approved after making a couple of minor corrections. The next morning Speer sent it to Felton in Atlanta: "I hope the committee of Independent Democrats, who meet today, will recommend Mr. Stephens as the people's candidate for governor. I know positively that he will not reject such recommendation and that if elected, that he will be governor of all the people, without regard to party. He will be controlled by no ring."[50]

An elated Independent steering committee in Atlanta immediately released this text to the papers and issued an address placing Stephens in the field as its candidate. Having apparently captured Stephens, it

48. Augusta *Chronicle and Constitutionalist*, May 9, 1882; AHS to Rebecca Felton, May 7, 1882, in Stephens Papers, LC.

49. Rebecca Felton to AHS, May 12, 1882, in Felton, *Georgia Politics*, 365–66.

50. AHS to Paul Hayne, May 15, 1882, in Stephens Papers, DU; Emory Speer to William Felton, May 15, 1882, in Felton, *Georgia Politics*, 367.

then canceled the mass meeting scheduled for June 1. Three days later Stephens wrote Felton: "I think you managed matters at Atlanta last Monday admirably looking . . . to the best interest of the State." His future course toward the governorship, he continued, "will depend on the voice of the people. The greatest objection that some people have to my being Governor seems to be that certain other people are willing to vote for me. Such is the weakness of human nature."[51]

Unfortunately, the Feltons barely had time to savor the news before Stephens himself reminded them of the vagaries of human nature. For at about the same time they received it, papers all over Georgia and the country ran a public notice from Little Aleck in Washington. He had seen a telegram from Atlanta, Stephens said, stating that he had telegraphed the Georgia Independents that he would accept their nomination for governor. "It is utterly untrue that I ever sent such telegram or authorized its being sent by anybody."[52]

In all his long life Stephens had never so blatantly betrayed a trust. The Independents were furious. Felton, kinder by far than his wife, thought that Stephens' mind had been so clouded with whiskey and drugs that he couldn't remember what he had done. Becky Felton believed for the rest of her life that Stephens' ambition had gotten the better of him in his old age. He had sold himself to the highest bidders and gone over "bag and baggage" to the Bourbons. She never wrote or spoke to Stephens again. Even Toombs disapproved. Stephens "must be in his dotage," he said, and he didn't see how any Democrat could vote for him.[53]

To a certain extent, all three were right. No one will ever know fully what the effects of Stephens' prolonged drug-taking had on him. The only certainty is that morphine and whiskey alter thought processes, and Stephens took enough of both to be affected. And the man was old, old beyond his seventy years—so frail, so sick, for so long. Was it not possible that the ravages of a lifetime finally were taking their toll on his mind? Did he really comprehend the terms of the political understanding he had come to with the Independents?[54]

51. Independents' address in Felton, *Georgia Politics*, 367–68; AHS to William Felton, May 18, 1882, in Stephens Papers, LC.

52. AHS public notice in Felton, *Georgia Politics*, 369–70.

53. *Ibid.*, 370–72.

54. At this time Stephens was taking one-eighth of a grain (seven milligrams) of morphine by injection three times a day (AHS to Hayne, May 15, 1882, in Stephens Papers, DU).

His own explanation of his action was at least consistent but so strained and attenuated that none but his most credulous partisans found it convincing. Stephens told Speer that he had denied only the telegram allegedly sent by himself, not the one that Speer actually sent. His other justifications involved complicated arguments about technicalities: his "authorization" to Speer and the difference between a "nomination" and a "recommendation."[55]

Actually Stephens had been playing a dangerous political game, and he had lost. About the only thing more appealing to him than retirement was a final vote of confidence from Georgia. Here at the end of his life was the chance to do something he had never before accomplished: unite all the people under his leadership, have them acknowledge by their votes what he had known about himself for years: that he was virtuous and upright and that he lived his life solely in service of the truth. Becky Felton was right. Stephens had never lost his ambition.

But political acumen eluded him. Unable to believe that he had simply become a pawn to be manipulated on Georgia's chessboard by the political grandmasters with real power, he chose instead to picture himself as he always had—as truth's prophet. And so he succumbed to the flattery from both sides. He listened to promises from Bourbon leaders about his sure election to "any vacancy that may occur in the Senate," after his election as governor. He allowed himself to be used, all the while maintaining the comforting fiction that his pure principles transcended the grubby political reality: without the Democratic party, he was nothing—and he knew it.[56]

The Feltons had let wishful thinking get in the way of plain common sense. Stephens would never have made outright war on the Democratic party, much less in league with Republicans. Stephens was surely aware of what he was doing when Speer sent that telegram. He wanted to be governor, and he wanted the "recommendation" of the Independents—"I could not reject or disregard . . . the recommendation of any respectable body of citizens," he later explained—not the embarrassment of a formal nomination. That, he knew, could come only from the party. And that was exactly what the Independents tried to forestall.[57]

---

55. Speer to Rebecca Felton, May 27, 1882, in Felton Papers, UG; AHS to Hidell, August 2, 1882, in Stephens Papers, HSP; Ward, "Georgia Under the Bourbons," 134.
56. E. P. Howell to AHS, May 19, 1882, in Stephens Papers, LC.
57. AHS to Hidell, June 11, 1882, in Stephens Papers, HSP.

Now they too had lost. Not only would it be "impossible" to defeat Stephens, wrote a prominent Independent, but also "undesirable." Judge Hook spoke for many of his Independent colleagues when he told Stephens that he was the choice of the "whole people" and would be "a perfectly non partisan Governor." [58]

The regular Democratic machine swung right into line. By the end of May, Governor Colquitt reeled off to Stephens the names of over two dozen papers in Georgia supporting him for the nomination. "Your 'call' to the Executive chair," he gloated, "will be attended with such unanimity as shall give it an eclat rarely if ever occurring in our party history." [59]

Back in Washington, Stephens sounded pitifully unsure. He was worried. "You who got me into the present position," he told a Bourbon leader, "must see to it that your objects shall not be thwarted." Perhaps his betrayal of the Feltons had begun to bother him. If the regular Democrats did not deliver the nomination, his embarrassment would have been unbearable. [60]

The Independents had not given up, despite the odds against them. Before the regular Democrats met in July, they nominated a candidate of their own for governor, former general Lucius Gartrell, whom the Republicans also agreed to support. As might have been expected, Felton published Stephens' letter of May 18, an act Stephens found "exceedingly unkind" and "intended to injure me deeply." From that point on, Stephens considered Felton "one of the bitterest enemies" he had. By June he was denying in the papers that he ever had any understanding with the Feltons. By August, after Felton had blasted him on the stump, Stephens was privately branding him a "vile, unprincipled knave, with neither honor nor truth in him." [61]

Stephens still had business to finish in Washington, but he took time out to come home for the Democratic convention in mid-July. He would not have missed this: the greatest testament to his personal popularity in his life. His only rival for the nomination was Augustus O. Bacon, put up by a group of Macon Democrats still unsure of Stephens because of his dalliance with the Independents. The machine,

58. Hook to AHS, June 10, 1882, in Stephens Papers, LC.
59. Alfred H. Colquitt to AHS, May 30, 1882, *ibid.*
60. AHS to L. N. Trammell, June 1, 1882, in Trammell Letters, EU.
61. AHS to Hidell, June 11, August 4, 1882, in Stephens Papers, HSP.

however, made good its promises. Every mention of Stephens' name caused wild cheering; delegates almost fought with each other for the privilege of nominating him by acclamation. The nomination was made unanimous when Bacon withdrew on July 21. "The democratic party of Georgia was never more harmonious, never more united," crowed the *Constitution* two days later, a questionable assertion on the face of it because the convention found it necessary to pass no less than five resolutions on party unity.[62]

Stephens returned to Washington and prepared to take his leave of the city that had been his second home for so long. On his last day there he asked Dick Johnston to come over from his nearby Maryland home to see him off and take him for a last carriage ride about the city. Much as he would have hated to admit it, he was saddened to leave this place. His sorrow showed on his face as he rode about, gazing at the hustle and bustle on the streets. Somehow he knew this was the last time he would ever see Washington. "I ought not to have accepted this nomination," Little Aleck sighed at one point. "I tell you I'm worn out. I sometimes feel like I wish, and . . . ought to pray, that Gartrell . . . would beat me." Johnston nodded, but he knew better. This nomination had meant more to Stephens than any other in his whole life. To be defeated now would be crushing.[63]

Back at the National Hotel callers flocked to say good-bye. At least twenty who came up and shook his hand were black servants in the hotel, and for each Stephens had a little parting memento. Then the ride to the station . . . and home.

The 1882 campaign in Georgia raged with its customary sound and fury. The only real dangers confronting the regulars were overconfidence and possible apathy—and a doubtful black vote. Stephens had not been too reassuring in his acceptance letter about the Independents, but he rectified this omission in his opening campaign speech in Atlanta by attacking Felton. The good doctor from Cartersville did not treat Stephens kindly on the stump either, reading excerpts from his letters to show how Little Aleck had "always been a disorganizer." At one point Stephens considered writing a review of Felton's course toward him, but he gave up the idea because he had too much "self respect to engage in a mud throwing controversy with anybody much

62. Atlanta *Constitution*, July 19–21, 23, 1882.
63. Johnston, *Autobiography*, 189.

less a parson & a woman." It was probably just as well. His letters to the Feltons over the past few years would have supplied them with more mud than he could sling himself.[64]

In line with his strategy of attracting votes from everybody, Stephens avoided attacking the Independents directly, and he discreetly stayed out of the Seventh and Ninth districts. From the first, Stephens meant to win this election by the force of his own personality and his popularity. Hence he refused to discuss issues. Aside from defending his war record—and blaming the loss of his legs on the rheumatism he had contracted in a damp Yankee prison cell—on the stump Stephens stuck to what he had said in his acceptance letter: his loyalty to the Jeffersonian Democratic tradition. Some Democrats, like William E. Simmons of Laurenceville, complained that the voters needed more than "glittering generalities," that "issues of vital importance have risen since the time of Jefferson." That was exactly the problem, Stephens scoffed. Too many people failed to appreciate the "great fundamental truths and principles" that underlay the magnificent American system of government.[65]

To his shock Stephens discovered that many of his former black supporters had deserted him. Republican money from Washington lured some away, but his being the white man's candidate was not lost on them either. To counteract administration money, Stephens urged L. N. Trammell to have the executive committee set aside a small sum for "*missionary*" work among the negro voters. Curiously, the race issue cut both ways. Because of his near-legendary kindness to blacks, Stephens found it necessary to reassure the whites that he would "stand by my race" if blacks tried to achieve "social or political advancement above the white race."[66]

For all his fretting about the strength of the opponents, Stephens need not have worried. On October 4, 1882, he was elected governor

64. Ward, "Georgia Under the Bourbons," 145–46; Wm. T. Wofford to AHS, September 23, 1882, in Stephens Papers, LC; AHS to Hidell, October 12, 1882, in Stephens Papers, HSP.

65. AHS to Trammell, August 19, 1882, in Trammell Papers, EU; [Virginia] *Index-Appeal*, September 27, 1882, clipping in Stephens Papers, LC; W. E. Simmons to AHS, August 19, 1882, in Stephens Papers, EU; AHS to Simmons, August 22, 1882, in Stephens Papers, LC.

66. J. M. Howell to AHS, September 18, 1882, in Stephens Papers, LC; AHS to Trammell, August 19, 1882, in Trammell Papers, EU; AHS to Thomas Harderman, August 2, 1882, in Stephens Papers, LC.

of Georgia by a handsome majority of over 60,000 votes, 107,253 to Gartrell's 44,896. Out of 137 counties, he lost only 7, all Independent strongholds. If nothing else, the vote proved that Stephens had not underestimated his popularity, among whites or blacks. Even so, the vote for governor had been surprisingly small; Stephens' totals ran about 12,000 votes behind the rest of the ticket. Clearly his defection had been the kiss of death to the Independents. Felton lost his bid for the Seventh District congressional seat, and Speer fell in the Ninth.[67]

After a magnificent inaugural at the DeRives Opera House in Atlanta on November 5, Stephens, along with numerous dogs, relatives, and black servants, moved into the executive mansion. He would not stay long. Some who had seen him during the campaign doubted he could survive that excitement, much less the burdens of the governorship. He should never have taken the job, but he could not have refused it, even if he knew it would take his life.

Stephens served as Georgia's governor for 119 days, during which time he labored much too zealously at the hundreds of tasks governors were expected to do. During his term of office he made 256 appointments, read and approved almost a hundred acts and resolutions of the legislature, and prepared fifty messages for the assembly. Hundreds of papers had to be signed; reports had to be read; letters had to be written. Even with a bevy of eager young assistants around to help, the governor did not shirk routine duties.[68]

Nor did he change his style of living. He kept the mansion open for anyone who needed something to eat or a place to stay. As governor he saw to the needs of his guests and callers just as he always had in Crawfordville. Only now there were a lot more of them, at all hours of the day and night. Nephew John, whom Uncle Aleck had appointed adjutant general and superintendent of public buildings, groused about "every grand rascal in Georgia" hanging around, but it did no good.[69]

Even in only four months Stephens managed to generate criticism.

67. Von Abele, *Stephens*, 311–12.
68. Official acts, appointments, pardons, correspondence, and so forth of the Stephens administration are listed in Warren Lee Jones, "Alexander Hamilton Stephens: Governor of Georgia 1882–1883" (M.A. thesis, University of Georgia, 1942), Appendixes A and B, 104–45.
69. Richardson, *Little Aleck*, 335–36.

Only five days after taking office, he began issuing pardons. Over the next forty-three days, he pardoned thirty-nine convicted criminals, men and women, black and white, including six murderers. One of the latter was Edward Cox, who had been convicted of killing a prominent citizen in a dispute over the convict lease system. Since Cox served as John B. Gordon's lessee, the case had attracted some notoriety. The pardon caused a considerable storm in Georgia's papers, and it even elicited hostile comment in some northern journals.[70]

The criticism annoyed Stephens, but not nearly so much as a long article in the New Orleans *Times-Democrat* that he suspected had been written by Jefferson Davis. Even with his busy schedule, Stephens found time to send people, including General Beauregard, reams of justification on his course during the war. He wrote a voluminous letter defending his suggestions for Confederate cotton policy, and he was gratified to hear that Beauregard intended to take "best advantage" of it in his forthcoming book.[71]

At first Stephens had "strong misgivings" about accepting an invitation to speak in Savannah on February 12, 1883. But it was to be a grand celebration, the city's sesquicentennial. The governor simply had to be there. And so he went, riding all night on the railroad, arriving at Savannah at seven-thirty in the morning. At the station he boarded a carriage for the ride to the Screven House, through streets festooned with flags and bunting, already alive with people who smiled and waved as they caught sight of the pallid little face under the dressy top hat. The air was cold and damp, not the sort of weather a frail old man should have been exposed to, even if he were accustomed to wearing tons of wraps. Unfortunately, Stephens' carriage had a broken windowpane. It was as cold inside as out.[72]

The speech passed off well enough, and Stephens returned to Atlanta. For a few days everything was normal. The governor returned to his frenetic pace and the lights burned late in the mansion's lower floor room at the end of the hall. But then he fell ill, the old familiar pains in

70. Jones, "Stephens," 80; Brown to AHS, December 22, 1882, in Stephens Papers, LC.
71. AHS to P. G. T. Beauregard, December 21, 1882, in Alfred Roman Papers, LC; Beauregard to AHS, December 23, 1882, in Stephens Papers, LC.
72. AHS to Hayne, January 3, 1883, in Hayne Papers, EU. The following account of Stephens' final days is from Avery, *In Memory*, 4–9.

the bowels. Opiates and astringents checked the attack, but he grew weaker. He began vomiting, couldn't take his food, slept fretfully, if at all.

He tried to keep on working. A single bed was moved down to the mansion's lower floor, with a cot in the corner for body servant Alex Kent. From there, on his bed, Stephens continued to receive visitors and sign papers. On February 28, as the fates would so weirdly have it, he signed a remission of a fifty-dollar fine for assault and battery for a man named John Stephens of Fulton County. It was his last official act.

His condition worsened again, and his doctors forbade work and visitors. Up to this point his mind had been clear, but now, because of the morphine, he began drifting in and out of reality. On the morning of March 3, he appeared to rally, taking some soft food and retaining it, but at noon he began to slip again. He was delirious now, drifting back in his mind to the campaign of long ago when, impelled by the best of his instincts, he took up arms against the Know Nothing bigotry. At one point he said clearly, "But I carried it individually by six hundred majority." And then he fell into a stupor again. At ten that night, Dr. Steiner said the words none of those there—John and Mary Stephens; I. W. Avery, the governor's aide; two other doctors; secretary C. W. Seidell—needed to hear: "The governor is dying."

Although there had been no announcement, word had spread through the town. The bottom floor of the mansion blazed with light. Scores of Georgia citizens, black and white, high and low, stood dumbly in the halls, waiting.

The dying man had one or two more lucid moments. He recognized John through eyes that no one for seventy years had ever seen so clouded. He complained once of pain. "Doctor, you hurt me," he said. It was almost a summary of his life.

The end came at 3:24 A.M. on Sunday, March 4, 1883. Mustard plasters at 2:00 had not brought blood. An hour later the feet were cold. "I'm afraid he is gone," Dr. Steiner muttered, looking into the wrinkled, peaceful face. And then louder: "He is dead." Outside in the hall, people were crying.

Bibliography

Primary Sources

Manuscript Collections

Duke University Library, Durham, North Carolina

Autograph Letters and Portraits of the Signers of the Constitution of the Confederate States.
Brown, Alexander. Papers.
Bryant, John Emory. Papers.
Campbell Family. Papers.
Clay, Henry. Papers.
Crittenden, John J. Papers.
Davis, Jefferson. Papers.
Giddings-Julian. Papers.
Harrison, J. Scott. Papers.
Johnson, Andrew. Papers.
Lanman, Charles. Papers.
Morrill, Justin S. Papers.
Phillips, Philip. Family Papers.
Roman, Alfred. Papers.
Sherman, William T. Papers.
Stephens, Alexander H. Manuscript Diary.

Thomas, Ella Gertrude. Diary.
Toombs, Robert. Papers.

Emory University Library, Atlanta, Georgia

Burke, Joseph F. Papers.
Davis, Jefferson. Papers.
Hambleton. Collection.
Jones, Joseph B. Papers.
Miscellaneous Collections. (Autograph Letters).
Stephens, Alexander H. Papers.
Thomas, James. Papers.
Trammell. Letters.
Wager, Ralph E. Papers.
Wilbur, Aaron. Papers.

Georgia Department of Archives and History, Atlanta

File II, Name File: A. R. Wright.
Johnston, Richard M. Papers.
Lamar, Charles A. L. Papers.
Miscellaneous File 434: Alexander H. Stephens Letter.
Smith, J. Henley. Papers.
Spullock, James Madison. Collection.

Historical Society of Pennsylvania, Philadelphia

Dreer, Ferdinand J. Collection of the Letters of American Statesmen.
Gratz, Simon. Collection of Administration Papers.
Stephens, Alexander H. Papers.

Library of Congress, Division of Manuscripts, Washington, D.C.

Bell, John. Papers.
Blair Family. Papers.
Brown, Joseph E. Collection.
Burwell, William C. Papers. (Personal Papers Miscellaneous).
Clayton, John. Papers.
Davis, Jefferson. Papers.
Giddings-Julian. Papers.
Harrison, J. Scott. Papers.
Johnson, Andrew. Papers.
Lanman, Charles. Papers.
Morrill, Justin S. Papers.
Phillips, Philip. Family Papers.

Roman, Alfred. Papers.
Sherman, William T. Papers.
Stephens, Alexander H. Manuscript Diary.
Stephens, Alexander H. Papers.
Toombs, Robert. Papers.
Trumbull, Lyman. Papers.
Wilson, Henry. Papers.
Wright-Shopshire Family. Papers.

Manhattanville College of the Sacred Heart, Purchase, New York

Stephens, Alexander H. Papers.

Mississippi Department of Archives and History, Jackson

Lamar, L. Q. C. Papers.

National Archives, Washington, D.C.

Amnesty Papers, Georgia, Stephens, Alexander H. Record Group 94, Folder 4190.
Letters Received by the Confederate Secretary of War, 1861–65. Record Group 109.
Union Provost Marshal's File of One-Name Papers Re Citizens. Record Group 109.

Southern Historical Collection, University of North Carolina Library, Chapel Hill

Alexander, E. P. Papers.
Berrien, John M. Papers.
Bragg, Thomas. Diary (typescript).
Graham, William Alexander. Papers.
Graves, Charles Iverson. Papers.
Hansell, Augustus H. Memoirs.
Hathaway, Leeland. Recollections.
King, Thomas Butler. Papers.
Lawton, A. R. Papers.
Moses, Robert. Autobiography (typescript).
Patterson-Orr. Papers.

Tulane University Library, New Orleans, Louisiana

Johnston, Albert Sidney, and William Preston. Papers.
Louisiana Historical Association Collection. Jefferson Davis Wartime Letters.

University of Georgia Library, Athens

Brown, Joseph E.–Hargrett, Felix. Collection.

Cobb-Erwin-Lamar. Collection.

Cobb, Howell. Papers.

Cobb, T. R. R. Letters.

Cuyler, Telamon. Collection.

Felton, Rebecca Latimer. Papers.

Jones, C. C. Collection.

Lumpkin, Joseph Henry. Papers.

McLeod. Collection. (Brown Family Papers).

Reid, Keith. Collection.

Spalding. Collection. (Joseph Emerson and Elizabeth Gresham Brown Collection).

Stephens, Alexander H. Letters.

Toombs, Robert. Papers.

Published Sources

"Alexander H. Stephens to Robert Sims Burch, 15 June 1854. *American Historical Review*, VIII (October, 1902), 91–97.

Alfriend, Edward Morrisson. "Social Life in Richmond During the War." *Southern Historical Society Papers*, XIX (1891).

Ambler, Charles Henry, ed. *The Correspondence of Robert M. T. Hunter, 1826–1876.* Vol. II of *Annual Report of the American Historical Association for the Year 1916.* Washington, D.C., 1918.

American Annual Cyclopedia and Register of Important Events of the Year 1861 Embracing Political, Civil, Military, and Social Affairs; Public Documents; Biography, Statistics, Commerce, Finance, Literature, Science, Agriculture and Mechanical Industry. New York, 1864.

American Annual Cyclopedia and Register of Important Events of the Year 1863 Embracing Political, Civil, Military, and Social Affairs; Public Documents; Biography, Statistics, Commerce, Finance, Literature, Science, Agriculture and Mechanical Industry. New York, 1866.

Armes, William Dallam, ed. *Autobiography of Joseph LeConte.* New York, 1903.

Avary, Myrta Lockett, ed. *Recollections of Alexander H. Stephens: His Diary Kept When a Prisoner at Fort Warren, Boston Harbor, 1865; Giving Incidents and Reflections of His Prison Life and Some Letters and Reminiscences.* New York, 1910.

Avery, I. W. *In Memory: The Last Sickness, Death, and Funeral Obsequies of Alexander H. Stephens, Governor of Georgia.* Atlanta, 1883.

Barnes, Thurlow Weed. *Memoir of Thurlow Weed*. Boston, 1884.

Basler, Roy P., ed. *The Collected Works of Abraham Lincoln*. 9 vols. New Brunswick, N.J., 1953–55.

Beale, Howard K., ed. *The Diary of Gideon Welles: Secretary of the Navy Under Lincoln and Johnson*. 3 vols. New York, 1960.

Boucher, Chauncey S., and Robert P. Brooks, eds. *Correspondence Addressed to John C. Calhoun, 1837–1849*. Vol. II of *Annual Report of the American Historical Association for the Year 1929*. Washington, D.C., 1930.

Brooks, Robert P., ed. "The Howell Cobb Papers." *Georgia Historical Quarterly*, V (March, 1921), 50–61, (June, 1921), 29–52, (September, 1921), 35–55, (December, 1921), 43–64; VI (1922), 35–84, 147–73, 233–64, 355–94.

Burnham, W. Dean. *Presidential Ballots, 1836–1892*. Baltimore, 1955.

Campbell, John A. "The Hampton Roads Conference." *Southern Magazine*, XV (November, 1874), 187–94.

Candler, Allen D., ed. *The Confederate Records of the State of Georgia*. 5 vols. Atlanta, 1909–11.

Chapman, Katherine Mood. "Some Benjamin Harvey Hill Letters." *Georgia Historical Quarterly*, XLVII (1963), 305–19, 436–52.

Congressional Globe. 111 vols. Washington, D.C., 1834–72.

Congressional Record. Washington, D.C., 1873–.

Cralle, Richard K., ed. *The Works of John C. Calhoun*. 6 vols. New York, 1854–55.

Davis, Varina Howell. *Jefferson Davis, Ex-President of the Confederate States of America: A Memoir by His Wife*. 2 vols. New York, 1890.

Dowdey, Clifford, ed. *The Wartime Papers of R. E. Lee*. New York, 1961.

Felton, Rebecca Latimer. *My Memories of Georgia Politics*. Atlanta, 1911.

Fielder, Herbert. *A Sketch of the Life and Times of Joseph E. Brown*. Springfield, Mass., 1883.

Flippin, Percy Scott, ed. "From the Autobiography of Herschel Johnson." *American Historical Review*, XXX (1925), 311–36.

Foote, Henry S. *Casket of Reminiscences*. Washington, D.C., 1874.

Grant, Ulysses S. *The Personal Memoirs of U. S. Grant*. 2 vols. New York, 1886.

Harris, Nathaniel E. *Autobiography: The Story of an Old Man's Life with Reminiscences of Seventy-Five Years*. Macon, Ga., 1925.

Herd, Don, ed. "Laurence M. Keitt's Letters from the Provisional Congress of the Confederacy, 1861." *South Carolina Historical Magazine*, LXI (1960), 19–25.

Hilliard, Henry W. *Politics and Pen Pictures at Home and Abroad*. New York, 1892.

Hull, A. L., ed. "The Making of the Confederate Constitution—Extracts from the Letters of Thos. R. R. Cobb." *Publications of the Southern Historical Society*, IX (September, 1905), 272–92.

Johannsen, Robert W., ed. *The Letters of Stephen A. Douglas*. Urbana, Ill., 1961.

Johnston, Richard Malcolm. *Autobiography of Col. Richard Malcolm Johnston*. Washington, D.C., 1900.

Jones, J. B. *A Rebel War Clerk's Diary at the Confederate States Capital*. 2 vols. Philadelphia, 1866.

Journal of the Congress of the Confederate States of America, 1861–1865. 7 vols. Washington, D.C., 1904.

Journal of the House of Representatives of the State of Georgia. [1836–1840.] 4 vols. Milledgeville, Ga., 1837–41.

Journal of the Senate of the State of Georgia. [1842.] Milledgeville, Ga., 1843.

Lanman, Charles. *Haphazard Personalities Chiefly of Noted Americans*. Boston, 1885.

Matthews, James M., ed. *The Statutes at Large of the Provisional Government of the Confederate States of America from the Institution of the Government, February 8, 1861 to Its Termination, February 18, 1862, Inclusive*. Richmond, 1864.

McClure, Alexander K. *Colonel Alexander K. McClure's Recollections of Half a Century*. Salem, Mass., 1902.

McCrary, Royce, ed. "The Authorship of the Georgia Platform of 1850: A Letter by Charles J. Jenkins." *Georgia Historical Quarterly*, LIV (1970), 585–90.

Meriwether, Colyer, ed. "The Correspondence of Thomas Read Rootes Cobb, 1860–1862." *Publications of the Southern History Association* XI (1907), 147–85, 233–66.

Nevins, Allan, and Milton Halsey Thomas, eds. *The Diary of George Templeton Strong*. 3 vols. New York, 1952.

"The Papers of John A. Campbell, 1861–1865." *Southern Historical Society Papers*, XLII (1917), 3–81.

Phillips, Ulrich B., ed. *The Correspondence of Robert Toombs, Alexander H. Stephens, and Howell Cobb*. 1913; rpt. New York, 1970.

Quaife, Milo Milton, ed. *The Diary of James K. Polk During His Presidency, 1845–1849*. 4 vols. Chicago, 1910.

Rabun, James Z., ed. "A Letter for Posterity: Alex Stephens to his Brother Linton, June 3, 1864." *Emory University Publications, Sources and Reprints*, Series VIII, No. 3 (1954).

Rawick, George P. *The American Slave: A Composite Autobiography*. 19 vols. 1972; rpt. Westport, Conn., 1977.

Rhett, R. Barnwell. "The Confederate Government at Montgomery." In

Robert U. Johnson and Clarence C. Buell, eds., *Battles and Leaders of the Civil War*. 4 vols., 1885–87; rpt. New York, 1956, I, 99–110.

Richardson, James D., comp. *A Compilation of the Messages and Papers of the Presidents, 1789–1902*. 10 vols. Washington, D.C., 1903.

———, ed. *The Messages and Papers of Jefferson Davis and the Confederacy Including Diplomatic Correspondence, 1861–1865*. 2 vols. 1906; rpt. New York, 1966.

A Richmond Lady. *Richmond During the War: Four Years of Personal Observation*. New York, 1867.

Rowland, Dunbar, ed. *Jefferson Davis, Constitutionalist: His Letters, Papers, and Speeches*. 10 vols., Jackson, Miss., 1923.

Russell, William Howard. *My Diary North and South*. Edited by Fletcher Pratt. 1863; rpt. Gloucester, Mass., 1969.

Seward, Frederick W. *Reminiscences of a War-Time Statesman and Diplomat, 1830–1915*. New York, 1916.

Sherwood, Adiel. *A Gazetteer of the State of Georgia, Containing a Particular Discription of the State, Its Resources, Counties, Towns, and Villages*. Washington, D.C., 1887.

Shryock, Richard Harrison, ed. *Letters of Richard D. Arnold, M.D., 1808–1876, Mayor of Savannah, Georgia, First Secretary of the American Medical Association*. Durham, N.C., 1929.

Sioussat, St. George L., ed. "Notes of Col. W. G. Moore, Private Secretary to President Johnson, 1866–1868." *American Historical Review*, XIX (October, 1913), 98–132.

Stephens, Alexander H. *A Constitutional View of the Late War Between the States: Its Causes, Character, Conduct and Results, Presented in a Series of Colloquies at Liberty Hall*. 2 vols. Philadelphia, 1868–70.

———. "Reminiscences of Alexander H. Stephens vs Those of General Richard Taylor." *International Review*, V (March, 1878), 145–54.

———. *The Reviewers Reviewed: A Supplement to the "War Between the States," Etc*. New York, 1872.

Stewart, J. A. *Conservative Views. The Government of the United States: What Is It? Comprising a Correspondence with Hon. Alexander H. Stephens, Eliciting Views Touching the Nature and Character of the Government of the United States, the Impolicy of Secession, the Evils of Disunion, and the Means of Restoration*. Atlanta, 1869.

U.S. House. "Kansas Affairs." *House Reports*, 34th Cong., 1st Sess., No. 200.

U.S. House. "Kansas Contested Election." *House Reports*, 34th Cong., 1st Sess., No. 3.

U.S. House. "Kansas Contested Election." *House Reports*, 34th Cong., 1st Sess., No. 275.

U.S. Senate. *Journal of the Congress of the Confederate States of America, 1861–1865. Senate Documents*, 58th Cong., 2nd Sess., No. 234.

U.S. War Department. *The War of the Rebellion: A Compilation of the Official Records of the Union and Confederate Armies*. 128 vols. Washington, D.C., 1881–1901.

White, Rev. George. *Historical Collections of Georgia: Containing the Most Interesting Facts, Traditions, Biographical Sketches, Anecdotes, Etc. Relating to Its History and Antiquities, from Its First Settlement to the Present Time*. New York, 1855.

——. *Statistics of the State of Georgia: Including an Account of Its Natural, Civil, and Ecclesiastical History Together with a Particular Description of Each County, Notices of the Manners and Customs of the Aboriginal Tribes and a Correct Map of the State*. Savannah, 1849.

Williams, Max R., ed. *The Papers of William Alexander Graham*. 5 vols. Raleigh, 1957–.

Woodward, C. Vann, ed. *Mary Chesnut's Civil War*. New Haven, 1981.

Newspapers

Atlanta *Constitution*, 1870–83.

Atlanta *Southern Confederacy*, 1860–65.

Atlanta *Sun*, 1872.

Augusta *Chronicle and Constitutionalist*, 1877–83.

Augusta *Chronicle and Sentinel*, 1836–76.

Augusta *Constitutionalist*, 1845–76.

Charleston *News and Courier*, 1873.

Columbus *Enquirer*, 1843–83.

Columbus *Times*, scattered.

Jackson *Weekly Clarion*, 1873.

Memphis *Morning Post*, 1866.

Milledgeville *Confederate Union*, 1862–65.

Milledgeville *Federal Union*, 1836–61, 1865–83.

Milledgeville *Southern Recorder*, 1836–83.

New York *Daily Tribune*, 1873.

New York *Herald*, 1874.

New York *Times*, 1851–83.

Richmond *Whig*, scattered.

Rome *Courier*, scattered.

Savannah *Morning News*, 1850–60.

Savannah *Republican*, 1850–60.

Washington *National Intelligencer*, 1843–60.

Secondary Sources

Books

Adams, Ephraim Douglass. *Great Britain and the American Civil War*. 2 vols. in one. New York, [1958?].

Amlund, Curtis Arthur. *Federalism in the Southern Confederacy*. Washington, D.C., 1966.

Andrews, J. Cutler. *The South Reports the Civil War*. Princeton, 1970.

Avery, I. W. *The History of the State of Georgia from 1850 to 1881 Embracing the Three Important Epochs: The Decade Before the War 1861–1865; The War; The Period of Reconstruction with Portraits of the Leading Public Men of This Era*. New York, 1881.

Banks, Enoch Marvin. *The Economics of Land Tenure in Georgia*. New York, 1905.

Barney, William L. *The Road to Secession: A New Perspective on the Old South*. New York, 1972.

Beales, Carleton. *War Within a War: The Confederacy Against Itself*. Philadelphia, 1965.

Bill, Alfred Hoyt. *The Beleagured City: Richmond, 1861–1865*. New York, 1946.

Billington, Ray Allen. *The Protestant Crusade, 1800–1860: A Study of the Origins of American Nativism*. New York, 1938.

———. *Westward Expansion: A History of the American Frontier*. 3d ed. New York, 1967.

Bradford, Gamaliel. *Confederate Portraits*. New York, 1914.

Brooks, Robert Preston. *The Agrarian Revolution in Georgia*. Madison, Wisc., 1914.

Bryan, T. Conn. *Confederate Georgia*. Athens, Ga. 1953.

Capers, Gerald M. *Stephen A. Douglas: Defender of the Union*. Boston, 1959.

Castel, Albert. *The Presidency of Andrew Johnson*. Lawrence, Kan., 1979.

Cleveland, Henry. *Alexander H. Stephens in Public and Private: With Letters and Speeches, Before, During, and Since the War*. Philadelphia, 1866.

Cole, Arthur C. *The Whig Party in the South*. Washington, D.C., 1914.

Coleman, Mrs. Chapman, ed. *The Life of John J. Crittenden with Selections from His Correspondence and Speeches*. 2 vols. Philadelphia, 1871.

Coleman, Kenneth, ed. *A History of Georgia*. Athens, Ga., 1977.

Conner, Seymour V., and Odie B. Faulk. *North America Divided: The Mexican War, 1846–1848*. New York, 1971.

Conway, Alan. *The Reconstruction of Georgia*. Minneapolis, 1966.

Cooper, William J., Jr. *The South and the Politics of Slavery, 1828–1856*. Baton Rouge, 1978.

Coulter, E. Merton. *The Confederate States of America, 1861–1865*. Baton Rouge, 1950.

———. *Georgia: A Short History*. Chapel Hill, 1947.

Craven, Avery. *The Coming of the Civil War*. Rev. ed. Chicago, 1957.

———. *The Growth of Southern Nationalism, 1848–1861*. Baton Rouge, 1953.

Crenshaw, Ollinger. *The Slave States in the Presidential Election of 1860*. Baltimore, 1945.

Cutting, Elisabeth. *Jefferson Davis, Political Soldier*. New York, 1930.

Dalzell, Robert F., Jr. *Daniel Webster and the Trial of American Nationalism, 1843–1852*. New York, 1975.

Dodd, William E. *Jefferson Davis*. Philadelphia, 1907.

Donald, David. *Charles Sumner and the Coming of the Civil War*. New York, 1960.

———, ed. *Why the North Won the Civil War*. Baton Rouge, 1960.

Dorris, Jonathan Truman. *Pardon and Amnesty Under Lincoln and Johnson: The Restoration of the Confederates to Their Rights and Privileges, 1861–1898*. Chapel Hill, 1953.

Dumond, Dwight Lowell. *The Secession Movement, 1860–1861*. New York, 1931.

Dyer, Brainherd. *Zachary Taylor*. Baton Rouge, 1946.

Eaton, Clement. *A History of the Southern Confederacy*. New York, 1954.

———. *Jefferson Davis*. New York, 1977.

———. *The Mind of the Old South*. Baton Rouge, 1967.

Escott, Paul D. *After Secession: Jefferson Davis and the Failure of Confederate Nationalism*. Baton Rouge, 1978.

Fehrenbacher, Don E. *The Dred Scott Case: Its Significance in American Law and Politics*. New York, 1978.

Flanders, Ralph Betts. *Plantation Slavery in Georgia*. Chapel Hill, 1933.

Flippin, Percy Scott. *Herschel V. Johnson of Georgia: State Rights Unionist*. Richmond, 1931.

Flood, Charles Bracelen. *Lee: The Last Years*. Boston, 1981.

Foner, Eric. *Free Soil, Free Labor, Free Men: The Ideology of the Republican Party Before the Civil War*. New York, 1970.

Foote, Shelby. *The Civil War, A Narrative*. 3 vols. New York, 1958–74.

Gillette, William. *Retreat from Reconstruction, 1869–1879*. Baton Rouge, 1979.

Goetzman, William H. *When the Eagle Screamed: The Romantic Horizon in American Diplomacy, 1800–1860*. New York, 1966.

Graebner, Norman A., ed. *Politics and the Crisis of 1860*. Urbana, Ill., 1961.

Griffith, Louis Turner, and John Erwin Talmadge. *Georgia Journalism, 1763–1950*. Athens, Ga., 1951.

Hain, Harry H. *History of Perry County, Pennsylvania, Including Descriptions of Indian and Pioneer Life from the Time of Earliest Settlement*. Harrisburg, 1922.

Hamilton, Holman. *Prologue to Conflict: The Crisis and Compromise of 1850*. New York, 1966.

————. *Zachary Taylor*. 2 vols. Indianapolis, 1941–51.

Hamlin, Charles E. *The Life and Times of Hannibal Hamlin*. Cambridge, Mass., 1899.

Hendrick, Burton J. *Statesmen of the Lost Cause: Jefferson Davis and His Cabinet*. New York, 1939.

Hesseltine, William B. *Civil War Prisons: A Study in War Pyschology*. Columbus, Ohio, 1930.

Hill, Benjamin H., Jr. *Senator Benjamin H. Hill of Georgia: His Life, Speeches and Writings*. Atlanta, 1893.

Hill, Louise Biles. *Joseph E. Brown and the Confederacy*. Chapel Hill, 1939.

Hopkins, Vincent C., S.J. *Dred Scott's Case*. New York, 1950.

Howe, Daniel Walker. *The Political Culture of American Whigs*. Chicago, 1979.

Hull, A. L. *A Historical Sketch of the University of Georgia*. Atlanta, 1894.

Jennings, Thelma. *The Nashville Convention: Southern Movement for Unity, 1848–1851*. Memphis, 1980.

Johannsen, Robert W. *Stephen A. Douglas*. New York, 1973.

Johnson, Michael P. *Toward a Patriarchal Republic: The Secession of Georgia*. Baton Rouge, 1977.

Johnston, Richard Malcolm, and William Hand Browne. *Life of Alexander H. Stephens*. Philadelphia, 1878.

Klein, Philip Shriver. *President James Buchanan: A Biography*. University Park, Pa., 1962.

Kirkland, Edward Chase. *The Peacemakers of 1864*. New York, 1927.

Kirwan, Albert D. *John J. Crittenden: The Struggle for the Union*. Lexington, Ky., 1962.

Knight, Lucian Lamar and Mrs. Horace M. Holden. *Alexander H. Stephens, The Sage of Liberty Hall, Georgia's Great Commoner*. [Athens, Ga., 1930].

Lee, Charles Robert, Jr. *The Confederate Constitutions*. Chapel Hill, 1963.

Malin, James C. *The Nebraska Question, 1852–1854*. Lawrence, Kan., 1953.

McCardell, John. *The Idea of a Southern Nation: Southern Nationalists and Southern Nationalism, 1830–1860*. New York, 1979.

McCormick, Richard P. *The Second American Party System: Party Formation in the Jacksonian Era*. New York, 1973.

McElroy, Robert. *Jefferson Davis: The Real and the Unreal*. 2 vols. New York, 1937.

McFeeley, William S. *Grant: A Biography*. New York, 1981.

McKitrick, Eric L. *Andrew Johnson and Reconstruction.* Chicago, 1960.

Merk, Frederick. *Slavery and the Annexation of Texas.* New York, 1972.

Milton, George Fort. *The Eve of Conflict: Stephen A. Douglas and the Needless War.* Boston, 1934.

Monaghan, Jay. *Civil War on the Western Border, 1854–1865.* New York, [1955].

Moore, Albert Burton. *Conscription and Conflict in the Confederacy.* New York, 1924.

Moore, Glover. *The Missouri Controversy, 1819–1821.* Lexington, Ky., 1953.

Montgomery, Horace. *Cracker Parties.* Baton Rouge, 1950.

———, ed. *Georgians in Profile: Essays in Honor of E. Merton Coulter.* Athens, Ga., 1958.

Murray, Paul K. *The Whig Party in Georgia.* Chapel Hill, 1948.

Nathans, Elizabeth Studley. *Losing the Peace: Georgia Republicans and Reconstruction, 1865–1871.* Baton Rouge, 1968.

Nelson, Larry E. *Bullets, Ballots, and Rhetoric: Confederate Policy for the United States Presidential Contest of 1864.* University, Ala., 1980

Nevins, Allan. *The Ordeal of the Union.* 2 vols. New York, 1947.

———. *The Emergence of Lincoln.* 2 vols. New York, 1950.

Nichols, Roy F. *Blueprints for Leviathan: American Style.* New York, 1963.

———. *The Democratic Machine, 1850–1854.* New York, 1923.

———. *The Disruption of American Democracy.* 1948; rpt. New York, 1967.

———. *Franklin Pierce: Young Hickory of the Granite Hills.* Philadelphia, 1931.

Norton, Frank H. *The Life of Alexander H. Stephens.* New York, 1883.

Norwood, Martha F. *Liberty Hall, Taliaferro County, Georgia: A History of the Structures Known as Liberty Hall and Their Owners from 1827 to the Present.* Atlanta, 1977.

Oates, Stephen B. *To Purge This Land with Blood: A Biography of John Brown.* New York, 1970.

Overdyke, W. Darrell. *The Know Nothing Party in the South.* Baton Rouge, 1950.

Owsley, Frank Lawrence. *State Rights in the Confederacy.* Chicago, 1925.

Parks, Joseph H. *Joseph E. Brown of Georgia.* Baton Rouge, 1977.

Parrington, Vernon L. *Main Currents in American Thought.* 2 vols. New York, 1927.

Patrick, Rembert W. *Jefferson Davis and His Cabinet.* Baton Rouge, 1944.

Pearce, Haywood J. *Benjamin H. Hill: Secession and Reconstruction.* Chicago, 1928.

Pendleton, Louis. *Alexander H. Stephens.* Philadelphia, 1907.

Perman, Michael. *Reunion Without Compromise: The South and Reconstruction, 1865–1868.* Cambridge, Eng., 1973.

Phillips, Ulrich B. *Georgia and State Rights: A Study of the Political History of Georgia from the Revolution to the Civil War, with Particular Regard to Federal Relations.* 1902, Rpt., Yellow Springs, Ohio, 1968.

————. *The Life of Robert Toombs.* New York, 1913.

Pletcher, David M. *The Diplomacy of Annexation: Texas, Oregon, and the Mexican War.* Columbia, Mo., 1973.

Poage, George Rawlings. *Henry Clay and the Whig Party.* Chapel Hill, 1936.

Potter, David M. *The Impending Crisis, 1848–1861.* Completed and edited by Donald E. Fehrenbacher. New York, 1976.

————. *Lincoln and His Party in the Secession Crisis.* New Haven, 1942.

Randall, James G., and David Herbert Donald. *The Civil War and Reconstruction.* 2nd ed. Lexington, Mass., 1969.

Rawley, James A. *Race and Politics: "Bleeding Kansas" and the Coming of the Civil War.* Philadelphia, 1969.

Rayback, Joseph G. *Free Soil: The Election of 1848.* Lexington, Ky., 1970.

Rayback, Robert J. *Millard Fillmore: Biography of a President.* Buffalo, 1959.

Richardson, E. Ramsey. *Little Aleck: A Life of Alexander H. Stephens, The Fighting Vice President of the Confederacy.* New York, 1937.

Roberts, Derrell C. *Joseph E. Brown and the Politics of Reconstruction.* University, Ala., 1973.

Rowland, Charles P. *The Confederacy.* Chicago, 1960.

Schwab, John Christopher. *The Confederate States of America, 1861–1865: A Financial and Industrial History of the South During the Civil War.* New York, 1901.

Sellers, Charles. *James K. Polk: Continentalist, 1843–1846.* Princeton, 1966.

Sewell, Richard H. *Ballots for Freedom: Antislavery Politics in the United States, 1837–1860.* New York, 1976.

Shryock, Richard Harrison. *Georgia and the Union in 1850.* Durham, N.C., 1926.

Simpson, John Eddins. *Howell Cobb: The Politics of Ambition.* Chicago, 1973.

Smith, Elbert B. *The Presidency of James Buchanan.* Lawrence, Kan., 1975.

Stovall, Pleasant A. *Robert Toombs: Statesman, Speaker, Soldier, Sage: His Career in Congress and on the Hustings—His Work in the Courts—His Record with the Army.* New York, 1892.

Strode, Hudson. *Jefferson Davis.* 3 vols. New York, 1955–64.

Sydnor, Charles S. *The Development of Southern Sectionalism, 1819–1848.* Baton Rouge, 1948.

Talmadge, John E. *Rebecca Latimer Felton: Nine Stormy Decades.* Athens, Ga., 1960.

Tatum, Georgia Lee. *Disloyalty in the Confederacy.* Chapel Hill, 1934.

Thomas, Emory. *The Confederacy as a Revolutionary Experience*. Englewood Cliffs, N.J., 1971.

———. *The Confederate Nation, 1861–1865*. New York, 1979.

———. *The Confederate State of Richmond: A Biography of the Capital*. Austin, 1971.

Thompson, C. Mildred. *Reconstruction in Georgia: Economic, Social, Political, 1865–1872*. 1915; rpt., New York, 1964.

Thompson, William Y. *Robert Toombs of Georgia*. Baton Rouge, 1966.

Todd, Richard Cecil. *Confederate Finance*. Athens, Ga., 1954.

Trelease, Allen W. *White Terror: The Ku Klux Klan Conspiracy and Southern Reconstruction*. New York, 1971.

Van Deusen, Glydon G. *The Jacksonian Era*. New York, 1959.

———. *The Life of Henry Clay*. Boston, 1937.

———. *William Henry Seward*. New York, 1967.

Von Abele, Rudolph. *Alexander H. Stephens: A Biography*. New York, 1946.

Waddell, James D., ed. *Biographical Sketch of Linton Stephens Containing a Selection of His Letters, Speeches, State Papers, Etc.* Atlanta, 1877.

Watson, Thomas E. *Sketches: Historical, Literary, Biographical, Economic, Etc.* Thomson, Ga., 1916.

Wilson, Edmund. *Patriotic Gore: Studies in the Literature of the American Civil War*. New York, 1962.

Wiltse, Charles M. *John C. Calhoun: Sectionalist, 1840–1850*. Indianapolis, 1951.

Wolff, Gerald. *The Kansas-Nebraska Bill: Party, Section, and the Origin of the Civil War*. Brooklyn, 1980.

Woodward, C. Vann. *Tom Watson: Agrarian Rebel*. Rev. ed. 1955; Rpt., New York, 1972.

Wooster, Ralph A. *The People in Power: Courthouse and Statehouse in the Lower South, 1850–1860*. Knoxville, 1969.

———. *The Secession Conventions of the South*. Princeton, 1962.

Wyatt-Brown, Bertram. *Southern Honor: Ethics and Behavior in the Old South*. New York, 1982.

Yearns, Wilfred Buck. *The Confederate Congress*. Athens, Ga., 1960.

Articles

Ambrose, Stephen E. "Yeoman Discontent in the Confederacy." *Civil War History*, VIII (September, 1962), 259–68.

Bass, James Horace. "The Attack upon the Confederate Administration in Georgia in the Spring of 1864." *Georgia Historical Quarterly*, XVIII (September, 1934), 228–47.

Bradford, Gamaliel. "Alexander H. Stephens: A Confederate Portrait." *Atlantic Monthly*, July, 1913, pp. 62–73.

Brumgardt, John A. "The Confederate Career of Alexander H. Stephens." *Civil War History*, XXVII (March, 1981), 64–81.

Coulter, E. Merton. "Alexander H. Stephens Challenges Benjamin H. Hill to a Duel." *Georgia Historical Quarterly*, LVI (Summer, 1972), 175–92.

———. "The Nullification Movement in Georgia." *Georgia Historical Quarterly*, V (March, 1921), 3–39.

Duncan, Kunigunde. "Preparation for Greatness." *Georgia Review*, I (Spring, 1947), 108–16.

Fitts, Albert N. "The Confederate Convention: The Provisional Constitution." *Alabama Review*, II (1949), 83–99.

Floyd, Josephine Boyd. "Rebecca Latimer Felton: Political Independent." *Georgia Historical Quarterly*, XXX (March, 1946), 14–24.

Govan, Thomas P. "Banking and the Credit System in Georgia, 1810–1860." *Journal of Southern History*, IV (May, 1938), 164–84.

Graebner, Norman A. "1848: Southern Politics at the Crossroads." *Historian*, XXV (November, 1962), 14–35.

Harrington, Fred H. "A Peace Mission of 1863." *American Historical Review*, XLVI (October, 1940), 76–86.

Johnson, Michael P. "A New Look at the Popular Vote for Delegates to the Georgia Secession Convention." *Georgia Historical Quarterly*, LVI (Fall, 1972), 259–75.

Malone, Henry T. "Atlanta Journalism During the Confederacy." *Georgia Historical Quarterly*, XXXVII (September, 1953), 210–19.

McCrary, Royce C. "Georgia Politics and the Mexican War." *Georgia Historical Quarterly*, LX (Fall, 1976), 211–27.

Mering, John V. "The Slave-State Constitutional Unionists and the Politics of Consensus." *Journal of Southern History*, XLIII (August, 1977), 395–410.

Montgomery, Horace. "Howell Cobb's Confederate Career." *In Confederate Centennial Studies*, No. 10. Tuscaloosa, Ala., 1959.

Murray, Paul. "Economic Sectionalism in Georgia Politics." *Journal of Southern History*, X (August, 1944), 293–307.

Parks, Joseph H. "State Rights in Crisis: Governor Joseph E. Brown versus President Jefferson Davis." *Journal of Southern History*, XXXII (February, 1966), 3–24.

Rabun, James Z. "Alexander Stephens and Jefferson Davis." *American Historical Review*, LVIII (January, 1953), 290–321.

———. "Alexander Stephens and the Confederacy." *Emory University Quarterly*, VI (October, 1950), 129–46.

Rayback, Joseph G. "Who Wrote the Allison Letters: A Study in Historical Detection." *Mississippi Valley Historical Review*, XXXVI (June, 1949), 51–72.

Richardson, Ralph. "The Choice of Jefferson Davis as Confederate President." *Journal of Mississippi History*, XVII (July, 1955), 161–76.

Robbins, John B. "The Confederacy and the Writ of Habeas Corpus." *Georgia Historical Quarterly*, LV (Summer, 1971), 83–101.

Russ, William A., Jr. "Radical Disfranchisement in Georgia." *Georgia Historical Quarterly*, XIX (September, 1935), 175–209.

Shadgett, Olive H. "James Johnson: Provisional Governor of Georgia." *Georgia Historical Quarterly*, XXXVI (March, 1952), 1–21.

Stephens, Robert Grier, Jr. "The Background and Boyhood of Alexander H. Stephens." *Georgia Review*, IX (Fall, 1953), 386–97.

[Summer, Mrs. John Osborne.] "Georgia and the Confederacy—1865." *American Historical Review*, I (October, 1895), 97–102.

Talmadge, John E. "The Death Blow to Independentism in Georgia." *Georgia Historical Quarterly*, XXXIX (March, 1955), 37–47.

———. "Peace-Movement Activities in Civil War Georgia." *Georgia Review*, VII (Summer, 1953), 190–203.

Trexler, Harrison A. "The Davis Administration and the Richmond Press, 1861–1865." *Journal of Southern History*, XVI (May, 1950), 177–95.

Twiggs, David Hamilton. "Presidency of the Confederacy Offered Stephens and Refused." *Southern Historical Society Papers*, XXXVI (1908), 141–45.

Ward, Judson C., Jr. "The Republican Party in Bourbon Georgia, 1872–1900." *Journal of Southern History*, IX (1943), 196–209.

Wooster, Ralph A. "The Georgia Secession Convention." *Georgia Historical Quarterly*, XL (March, 1956), 21–55.

Theses and Dissertations

Brumgardt, John Raymond. "Alexander H. Stephens and the Peace Issue in the Confederacy, 1863–1865." Ph.D. dissertation, University of California, Riverside, 1974.

Busbee, Westley Floyd. "Presidential Reconstruction in Georgia, 1865–1867." Ph.D. dissertation, University of Alabama, 1972.

Cashin, Edward Lawrence. "Alexander H. Stephens' Concept of the Confederacy." M.A. thesis, Fordham University, 1957.

Crutcher, Luke Fain III. "Disunity and Dissolution: The Georgia Parties and the Crisis of the Union, 1859–1861." Ph.D. dissertation, University of California at Los Angeles, 1974.

Harvey, Ray F. "The Political Theory of Alexander Hamilton Stephens." M.A. thesis, University of Oklahoma, 1930.

Irons, George V. "The Secession Movement in Georgia, 1850–1861." Ph.D. dissertation, Duke University, 1936.

Johnson, Michael P. "Secession and Conservatism in the Lower South: The So-

Index